S0-CAY-982

Principles of
Macroeconomics

Ninth Edition

JOHN E. SAYRE

Professor Emeritus
Capilano University

ALAN J. MORRIS

Associate Alumni
Capilano University

Mc
Graw
Hill
Education

PRINCIPLES OF MACROECONOMICS
Ninth Edition

Copyright © 2018, 2015, 2012, 2009, 2006, 2004, 2001, 1999, 1996 by McGraw-Hill Ryerson Limited. All rights reserved. No part of this publication may be reproduced or transmitted in any form or by any means, or stored in a database or retrieval system, without the prior written permission of McGraw-Hill Ryerson Limited, or in the case of photocopying or other reprographic copying, a license from The Canadian Copyright Licensing Agency (Access Copyright). For an Access Copyright license, visit www.accesscopyright.ca or call toll free to 1-800-893-5777.

Statistics Canada information is used with the permission of Statistics Canada. Users are forbidden to copy the data and redisseminate them, in an original or modified form, for commercial purposes, without permission from Statistics Canada. Information on the availability of the wide range of data from Statistics Canada can be obtained from Statistics Canada's Regional Offices, its World Wide Web site at www.statcan.gc.ca, and its toll-free access number 1-800-263-1136.

The Internet addresses listed in the text were accurate at the time of publication. The inclusion of a Web site does not indicate an endorsement by the authors or McGraw-Hill Ryerson, and McGraw-Hill Ryerson does not guarantee the accuracy of the information presented at these sites.

ISBN-13: 978-1-25-946084-5
ISBN-10: 1-25-946084-3

4 5 6 7 8 9 10 11 CTPS 22 21 20 19

Printed and bound in China.

Care has been taken to trace ownership of copyright material contained in this text; however, the publisher will welcome any information that enables them to rectify any reference or credit for subsequent editions.

PORTFOLIO DIRECTOR, BUSINESS AND ECONOMICS, INTERNATIONAL: Nicole Meehan
PORTFOLIO MANAGER: Kevin O'Hearn
DIRECTOR, PORTFOLIO MARKETING: Joy Armitage Taylor
CONTENT DEVELOPER: Melissa Hudson
SENIOR PORTFOLIO ASSOCIATE: Stephanie Giles
SUPERVISING EDITOR: Jessica Barnoski
PHOTO/PERMISSIONS EDITOR: Alison Lloyd Baker
COPY EDITOR: Rodney Rawlings
PLANT PRODUCTION COORDINATOR: Sarah Strynatka
MANUFACTURING PRODUCTION COORDINATOR: Emily Hickey
COVER DESIGN: Michelle Losier
COVER IMAGE: Yin Yang/Getty Images
INTERIOR DESIGN: Michelle Losier
COMPOSITION: Aptara®, Inc.
PRINTER: China Translation & Printing Services Ltd.

To my first
granddaughter:
Addy
(JES)

———————— A N D ————————

To the ones I love:
Brian, Trevor, and in memory of Jean
(AJM)

ABOUT THE AUTHORS

John E. Sayre earned a BSBA at the University of Denver and an MA from Boston University. He began teaching principles of economics while in the Peace Corps in Malawi. He came to Vancouver to do PhD studies at Simon Fraser University and ended up teaching at Capilano University for the next thirty-nine years. John was honoured with the designation of Professor Emeritus by Capilano University in June of 2014. Now retired from Capilano, John is an avid golfer who also enjoys walking with his dog, and listening to New Age and classical music.

Alan J. Morris, though loath to admit it, first worked as an accountant in England, where he became an Associate of the Chartered Institute of Secretaries and obtained his first degree in 1971 in Manchester, U.K. He subsequently obtained his Master's degree at Simon Fraser University, B.C., in 1973. He worked on his doctorate at Leicester University, U.K., and returned to work in business in Vancouver, B.C., until his appointment at Capilano University in 1988. Now retired, he currently lives in North Vancouver and is an avid devotee of classical music, birding, soccer, and beer. To his knowledge, he has never been an advisor to the Canadian government.

BRIEF CONTENTS

CONTENTS

PREFACE

To the Students

So, you may well ask, why take a course in economics? For many of you, the obvious answer to this question is, "Because it is a requirement for the program or educational goal that I have chosen." Fair enough. But there are other reasons. It is a simple truth that if you want to understand the world around you, then you have to understand some basic economics. Much of what goes on in the world today is driven by economic considerations, and those who know nothing of economics often simply cannot understand why things are the way they are. In this age of globalization, we are all citizens of the world and we need to function effectively in the midst of the enormous changes that are sweeping across almost every aspect of the social/political/economic landscape. You can either be part of this, and all the opportunities that come with it, or not be part of it because you cannot make any sense of it.

It is quite possible that you feel a little apprehensive because you have heard that economics is a difficult subject. Though there may be a grain of truth in this, we are convinced that almost any student can succeed in economics if he or she makes the effort.

Here are some tips on the general approach to this course that you might find helpful. First, read the **Economics Toolkit** that appears at the beginning of the book. The section "The Canadian Reality" offers basic information on Canada and its economic picture. "Graphing Reality" gives a quick lesson on graphs, which are an essential part of economics. These two sections will give you a solid foundation on which to build your knowledge of economics.

Second, before each lecture, quickly look over the chapter that will be covered. (In this preliminary survey, you do not need to worry about the glossary boxes, the Added Dimension boxes, the Test Your Understanding questions, or the integrated Study Guide.) Third, take notes as much as you can during the lecture, because the process of forcing yourself to express ideas *in your own words* is a crucial stage in the learning process. Fourth, re-read the chapter, again taking notes and using your own words (do not just copy everything word for word from the text). While doing this, refer to your classroom notes and try to integrate them into your reading notes. When you finish, you will be ready to take on the Study Guide.

As painful as it may be for you to hear, we want to say loud and clear that you should do *all* the questions and problems in the Study Guide. You may be slow at first, but you will be surprised at how much faster you become in later chapters. This is a natural aspect of the learning process. It might be helpful for you to form a study group with one or two other students and meet once or twice a week to do Study Guide questions. You may be amazed to find that explaining an answer to a fellow student is one of the most effective learning techniques.

If you ever come across a question you simply cannot understand, it is a sure sign that you need to approach your instructor (or teaching assistant) for help. Do not get discouraged when this happens; it will probably happen more at the beginning of your learning process than later on in the term.

We are convinced that if you follow this process consistently, beginning in the very *first* week of class, you will succeed in the course—and most likely do well. All it takes is effort, time management, and consistent organization.

Finally, an enormous part of becoming educated is gaining self-confidence and a sense of accomplishment. An A in a "tough" economics course can be a great boost. We wish you all the best.

To the Instructors

General Philosophy Over the years, we have become increasingly convinced that most economics textbooks are written to impress other economists rather than to enlighten beginning students. Such books tend to be encyclopedic in scope and intimidating in appearance. Small wonder, then, that students often emerge from an economics course feeling that the discipline really is daunting and unapproachable. We agree that the study of economics is challenging, but our experience is that students can also see it as intriguing and enjoyable if the right approach is taken. It starts with a really good textbook that is concise without sacrificing either clarity or accepted standards of rigour.

In preparing this book, we attempted to stay focused on four guiding principles. The first was to create a well-written text: to write as clearly as possible, to avoid unnecessary jargon, to speak directly to the student, and to avoid unnecessary abstraction and repetition.

Of equal importance was our second principle, a focused emphasis on student learning. Many years of teaching the principles courses have convinced us that students *learn* economics by *doing* it. To this end, Test Your Understanding questions are positioned throughout each chapter. This encourages students to apply what they have just read and gives them continuous feedback on their comprehension of the material being presented. Further, we feel that we offer the most comprehensive and carefully crafted Study Guide on the market, which has evolved over the years as a result of continued use in our own classes. In addition, all the chapter sections end with a Section Summary.

Our third principle has been to avoid an encyclopedic text. It seems that in an effort to please everyone, authors sometimes include bits and pieces of almost everything. The result is that students are often overwhelmed and find it difficult to distinguish the more important from the less important.

The fourth principle was to avoid problems of continuity that can occur when different groups of authors prepare separate parts of a total package. Accordingly, we are the sole authors of the text, the instructor's manual, and the integrated Study Guide. We have also carefully supervised the development of all supplementary materials. We have tried to ensure that as much care and attention went into the ancillary materials as into the main textbook.

Few things are more satisfying than witnessing a student's zest for learning. We hope that this textbook adds a little to this process.

Ninth Edition Changes There are eight additions or changes in all of the thirteen chapters. First, we have added a new feature, In a Nutshell, a half-page visual (humorous and/or thoughtful) that seeks to convey an important idea found within the chapter. Second, we have added a new feature at the beginning of each Study Guide Section entitled What's the Big Idea, in which we try to sum up the thrust of the chapter in a very simple, straightforward manner. Our third addition is a feature called It's News to Me, which consists of a short news item relating to material in the chapter along with two or more multiple-choice questions on the article.

Fourth, the end-of-chapter summaries are gone, replaced by Section Summaries throughout each chapter. Fifth, we have updated all data to the latest available (2016 or 2017). Sixth, we have moved the position of the Comprehensive Problem to the beginning of the Study Problems and provided answers and explanations alongside the question. Seventh, we are pleased to be able present the Study Guide sections in single columns, which makes them easier to read. Finally, the Study Tips section has been removed from the Study Guide and made available to students on the McGraw-Hill online resource.

- In **Chapter 1**, we reduced the number of Controversies in Section 1.1 from six to four and tried to give them a more topical slant. We reduced the size of the example of a student's choice of activities and more clearly brought out the point that opportunity cost involves lost benefits. A brief section on the five ways goods and services can be allocated was added. We divided Section 1.5 into two separate sections: Three Fundamental Questions and Four Types of Economies (while adding both ancient and modern examples of each type). A Great Economist box on Karl Marx was added, as was a new Added Dimension box titled "Just What Is an Economist?" Finally, we have added one more problem to Problems for Further Study.

- In **Chapter 2**, we changed the name of one of the determinants of supply from "business taxes" to "government taxes and subsidies." Glossary items for the terms "taxes" and "subsidies" were added. In the initial introduction to demand we now include a brief mention of all the other factors—in addition to price—that would also affect quantities demanded. We provided a new Added Dimension box titled "Just What Is a Product?" We added two new graphical Study Problems that require students to shift curves.

- In **Chapter 3**, we removed the Added Dimension boxes on Savings, the Asian Tigers, and Quesnay and added one on "Economic Growth and Productivity" and a second one titled: "Are Economic Growth and a Better Environment in Conflict?" We beefed up the discussion on consumption spending and gave a short explanation of why Canada's ranking in the HDI Index has fallen in recent years. We divided the previous Section 3.3 into two, one on measuring national income and one on the problems in doing so. Instructors who want to skip either of these topics can now do so more easily. We added one new problem in the Study Guide.

- In **Chapter 4**, we rewrote the Added Dimension boxes on "Economic Growth and Recessions" and "Galloping Inflation," and added two new Study Problems.

- In **Chapter 5**, we added a Great Economists box for Keynes and summarized the increase and decrease in aggregate demand and aggregate supply in table form. The Added Dimension box titled "Aggregate Demand and the Recession" was revised and we added a brief explanation for sticky prices.

- In **Chapter 6**, we sharpened the discussion around the three ways of viewing expenditures equilibrium and added a brief discussion of the savings/investment relationship. We added a paragraph showing how the three functions for taxation, savings, and consumption must add up to the level of income. We added one new Study Problem and also added additional questions to two of the Test Your Understanding problems.

- In **Chapter 7**, we added a table and explanation showing the circumstances under which a balanced budget can be countercyclical. We expanded the discussion about the ways that the affects of fiscal policy changes can be delayed. We made the discussion on cyclical and structural deficits graphical rather than algebraic. We replaced the Added Dimension box "Is There a World Financial Crisis?" with one titled "What Are Austerity Policies and Do They Work?" We added one Test Your Understanding question, a Study Problem, and a new Problem for Further Study. There is an Added Dimension box on the "Types of Taxes." We added the crowding out effect to the section "Shortcomings of Countercyclical Fiscal Policy." We added a discussion of the structural deficit to Section 7.4. We added an algebraic example to illustrate the difference between a structural and a cyclical deficit. We inserted a new Added Dimension box on provincial debt. We rewrote the Added Dimension box titled "Is There a World Financial Crisis?" Finally, we changed our example of a flat rate tax from a poll tax to that of bridge and highway tolls.

- In **Chapter 8**, we rewrote the Added Dimension box on electronic money and updated the other two Added Dimension boxes. We expanded the discussion of the different characteristics of money and added a section on how banks can use their reserves to leverage a multiple expansion of their loans and deposits. We added a new Test Your Understanding question and a new question in Problems for Further Study.

- In **Chapter 9**, we rewrote and simplified the section on calculating the rate of return on bonds. We added a graph in Section 9.1 illustrating the two causes of an increase in the interest rate: an increase in money demand or a decrease in money supply. We updated the Added Dimension box on the Governor of the Bank of Canada and simplified the box on bills and bonds. We also added a new box titled "Why Are Interest Rates So Low?" We reduced the discussion of quantitative easing and moved its placement. We added a Test Your Understanding question and added a question in Study Problem.

- In **Chapter 10**, we expanded the discussion on the various types of factor endowments and on the discussion of trade protection. We revised the Added Dimension boxes on Canada as the Great Trader and on NAFTA, and added a new box titled "Star Wars Vision of Future Trade." Study Problem 4 was simplified, and we added a new Test Your Understanding question and a new Study Problem question.

- In **Chapter 11**, we moved the material in the Added Dimension box on strong currencies into the text itself and rewrote the Added Dimension box on real exchange rates. In Section 11.2 we more clearly pointed out the benefits and costs of an appreciation and depreciation of the dollar. In Section 11.5 we added an explanation of how the figure for the balance-of-payments surplus is derived. We added a photo on the subject of the drop in oil prices.

- In **Chapter 12**, we rewrote and simplified the end of Section 12.1, explaining the effect of fiscal policy on exchange rates and therefore on exports. We rewrote the material on how supply-siders explained the effects of the OPEC oil crisis. We added two new graphs: one illustrating changes in the Canadian dollars over the past twenty-five years and one illustrating Japan's experience with deflation since 1995. This latter graph launches a new discussion on the causes and effects of deflation using Japanese examples. We added a Great Economists box on A.W. Phillips and an

Added Dimension box titled "Bold Policy in Both Monetary and Fiscal Policy." We added a question in Problems for Further Study.

- In **Chapter 13**, we rewrote Section 13.1 and revised the graphs of the three markets to more clearly illustrate the impact of the Great Depression. We improved the discussion of the horizontal aggregate supply curve and added a Great Economists box on Paul Samuelson. There is a new Added Dimension box titled "The Flawed Structure of the European Union." We beefed up the discussion on the growth of globalization. The material on the 2008 financial crisis was reduced and the discussion of events since then has been revised and updated using a new table and graph.

Textbook Features

As an initial review, and an ongoing resource, the book opens with the **Economics Toolkit**. The first section, The Canadian Reality, offers basic information on Canada and its economy. The second section, Graphing Reality, provides the student with a primer on how to interpret and create tables and graphs. We have provided a number of features to help the student come to grips with the subject matter.

Learning Objectives, listed at the beginning of each chapter, form a learning framework throughout the text, with each learning objective repeated in the margin at the appropriate place in the main body of the chapter. Each chapter opens with a vignette that provides context and an overview.

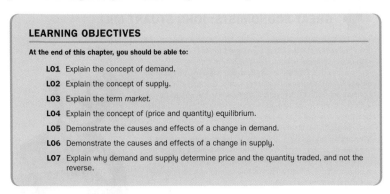

LEARNING OBJECTIVES

At the end of this chapter, you should be able to:

LO1 Explain the concept of demand.

LO2 Explain the concept of supply.

LO3 Explain the term *market*.

LO4 Explain the concept of (price and quantity) equilibrium.

LO5 Demonstrate the causes and effects of a change in demand.

LO6 Demonstrate the causes and effects of a change in supply.

LO7 Explain why demand and supply determine price and the quantity traded, and not the reverse.

Glossary terms indicate the first use of any term that is part of the language of economics. The term itself is in bold print. A complete glossary of terms appears at the end of the book.

Test Your Understanding question boxes appear at important points throughout the main body of each chapter. They give students immediate feedback on how well they understand the more abstract concept(s) discussed. In doing this, we have tried to establish what we believe to be a minimum standard of comprehension that all students should strive to achieve. Students can check their own progress by comparing their answers with those in the Student Answer Key, which is available on the McGraw-Hill online resource.

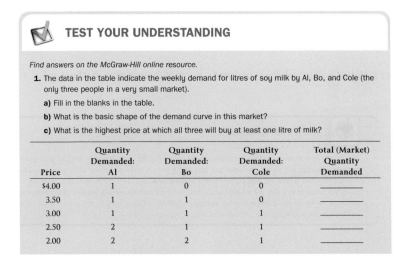

TEST YOUR UNDERSTANDING

Find answers on the McGraw-Hill online resource.

1. The data in the table indicate the weekly demand for litres of soy milk by Al, Bo, and Cole (the only three people in a very small market).

a) Fill in the blanks in the table.

b) What is the basic shape of the demand curve in this market?

c) What is the highest price at which all three will buy at least one litre of milk?

Price	Quantity Demanded: Al	Quantity Demanded: Bo	Quantity Demanded: Cole	Total (Market) Quantity Demanded
$4.00	1	0	0	_____
3.50	1	1	0	_____
3.00	1	1	1	_____
2.50	2	1	1	_____
2.00	2	2	1	_____

Added Dimension boxes identify material that is either general information or supplementary material that we hope adds a little colour to the students' reading.

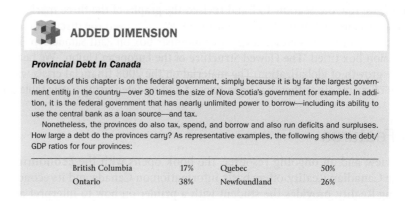

ADDED DIMENSION

Provincial Debt In Canada

The focus of this chapter is on the federal government, simply because it is by far the largest government entity in the country—over 30 times the size of Nova Scotia's government for example. In addition, it is the federal government that has nearly unlimited power to borrow—including its ability to use the central bank as a loan source—and tax.

Nonetheless, the provinces do also tax, spend, and borrow and also run deficits and surpluses. How large a debt do the provinces carry? As representative examples, the following shows the debt/GDP ratios for four provinces:

British Columbia	17%	Quebec	50%
Ontario	38%	Newfoundland	26%

Great Economist boxes include short biographies of some of the major economists, past and present, so that students can have an insight into the lives of the creators of the ideas that are the cornerstones of our discipline.

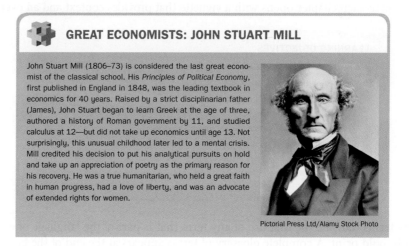

GREAT ECONOMISTS: JOHN STUART MILL

John Stuart Mill (1806–73) is considered the last great economist of the classical school. His *Principles of Political Economy*, first published in England in 1848, was the leading textbook in economics for 40 years. Raised by a strict disciplinarian father (James), John Stuart began to learn Greek at the age of three, authored a history of Roman government by 11, and studied calculus at 12—but did not take up economics until age 13. Not surprisingly, this unusual childhood later led to a mental crisis. Mill credited his decision to put his analytical pursuits on hold and take up an appreciation of poetry as the primary reason for his recovery. He was a true humanitarian, who held a great faith in human progress, had a love of liberty, and was an advocate of extended rights for women.

Pictorial Press Ltd/Alamy Stock Photo

A Question of Relevance boxes relate the material of the chapter to the lifetime experience of the reader.

A QUESTION OF RELEVANCE ...

Have you ever wondered why the prices of some products, such as computers or HDTVs, tend to fall over time, while the prices of other products, such as cars or auto insurance, tend to rise? Or perhaps you wonder how the price of a house can fluctuate tens of thousands of dollars from year to year. Why does a poor orange harvest in Florida cause the price of apple juice made in Ontario to rise? And why do sales of fax machines continue to fall despite their

Each chapter's **What's Ahead** box presents a brief summary of the topics to be covered in the chapter.

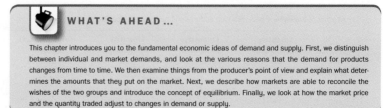

WHAT'S AHEAD ...

This chapter introduces you to the fundamental economic ideas of demand and supply. First, we distinguish between individual and market demands, and look at the various reasons that the demand for products changes from time to time. We then examine things from the producer's point of view and explain what determines the amounts that they put on the market. Next, we describe how markets are able to reconcile the wishes of the two groups and introduce the concept of equilibrium. Finally, we look at how the market price and the quantity traded adjust to changes in demand or supply.

Each **Section Summary** presents a brief review of the main topics of each section.

> **SECTION SUMMARY**
>
> a) Demand is the price–quantity relationship of a product that consumers are willing and able to buy per period of time.
>
> b) The demand curve is downward sloping because of
> - the substitution effect
> - income effect
>
> c) Products can be related as
> - complements
> - substitutes
>
> d) Market demand is the conceptual summation of each individual's demand within a given market.

The **It's News to Me** feature consists of a short news item relating to material in the chapter along with two or more multiple-choice questions on the article.

> **IT'S NEWS TO ME ...**
>
> Starbucks Corporation recently announced its plan to raise prices for packaged coffee and over-the-counter cups. They cited an increase in the price of Arabica coffee beans, caused by a severe harvest, as the reason for this action. A spokesperson for Starbucks said that, for both its package coffee and retail business, the overall cost structure was a major determining factor in its pricing policies.
>
> The increased price for the consumer translate into about 10 to 25 cents per over-the-counter cup and $1 a bag for packaged coffee.

The **In a Nutshell** feature is a half-page visual (humorous and/or thoughtful) that seeks to convey an important idea found within the chapter.

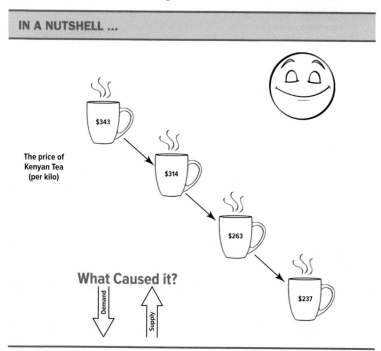

Highlighted concepts are important ideas pulled out and presented in a separate box—signalling to students that this material is particularly relevant and crucial to their understanding.

> An increase in price will lead to an increase in the quantity supplied and is illustrated as a movement up the supply curve.

> A decrease in price will cause a decrease in the quantity supplied and is illustrated as a movement down the supply curve.

Simple, clear, and uncomplicated **visuals** are found throughout the text. These are supported by captions that thoroughly explain the concepts involved.

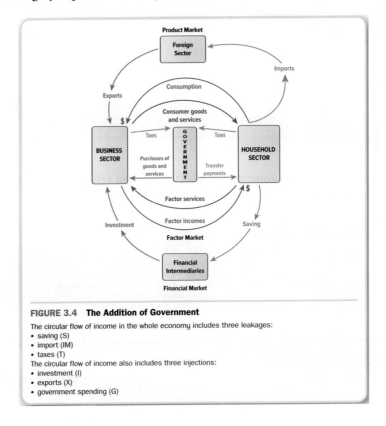

FIGURE 3.4   The Addition of Government

The circular flow of income in the whole economy includes three leakages:
- saving (S)
- import (IM)
- taxes (T)

The circular flow of income also includes three injections:
- investment (I)
- exports (X)
- government spending (G)

Integrated Study Guide Features

As mentioned earlier, we believe that answering questions and doing problems should be an *active part of the students' learning process*. For this reason, we have chosen to integrate a complete study guide within the covers of this text. The **Study Guide**, with pages screened in colour, immediately follows each chapter. We have been careful to write the questions in the Guide to cover all the material, but only the material found in the text itself. We hope the Guide's colourful, user-friendly design will encourage significant student participation.

The Study Guide is divided into two sections: a Review and a set of problems. These include a *Comprehensive Problem, Study Problems,* and *Problems for Further Study.*

The Review section contains a feature called *What's the Big Idea?* that sums up the main idea of the chapter in a student-friendly manner. There is also a section that lists *New Glossary Terms and Key Equations. Study Tips* (now on the McGraw-Hill online resource) are organized by learning objective and provide suggestions to help students manage the material in the chapter.

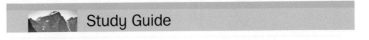

Review

WHAT'S THE BIG IDEA?

One of the important things to remember from this chapter is that the terms "demand" and "supply" do not refer to specific quantities. For instance, you cannot say that the demand for iPhones increased from 10 million units to 12 million units or that the supply of apples has fallen by 20 percent this year. As confusing as it might seem at first, you have to remember that economics defines them a little differently from everyday language. Both demand and supply refer to whole lists of prices and corresponding quantities. Think of these two concepts as tables of numbers, or better still, as lines on a graph. If you are able to do this, you will find that demand and supply analysis is a really powerful tool in understanding the world around us. The other important thing to remember is that the price of a product does not determine demand and supply. It's the other way around: demand and supply determines the price of most products.

NEW GLOSSARY TERMS AND KEY EQUATIONS

aggregate expenditures
consumption
disposable income
economic growth
equilibrium
exports
factor market
financial intermediaries

The **Comprehensive Problem** addresses several key chapter learning objectives and is complete with answers and explanations.

Comprehensive Problem

Questions

(LO 1, 2, 4, 5, 6) Table 2.11 shows the market for wool in the economy of Odessa (the quantities are in tonnes per year).

TABLE 2.11

Price ($)	100	200	300	400	500	600	700
Quantity Demanded	130	110	90	70	50	30	10
Quantity Demanded 2	—	—	—	—	—	—	—
Quantity Supplied	10	20	30	40	50	60	70
Quantity Supplied 2	—	—	—	—	—	—	—

a) Plot the demand and supply curves on Figure 2.15, and label them D_1 and S_1. Mark the equilibrium as e_1 on the graph.

The **Study Problems** have been grouped into three learning levels: basic, intermediate, and advanced. Students can judge their progress by working through these problems, and checking their answers against those in the Student Answer Key available on the McGraw-Hill online resource.

Study Problems

Find answers on the McGraw-Hill online resource.

Basic (Problems 1–11)

1. **(LO 3)** In Table 3.7, you are given data for the country of Sequoia.
   a) What is the value of GDP at market prices? _____
   b) What is the value of NDP at basic prices? _____
   c) What is the value of net national product at basic prices (national income)? _____

TABLE 3.7

Exports	130	Government spending	198
Consumption	430	Imports	118
Gross investment	126	Net foreign factor income	−22
Depreciation	64	Indirect taxes	80

Finally, there is a set of **Problems for Further Study** (with answers for instructors found on the McGraw-Hill online resource).

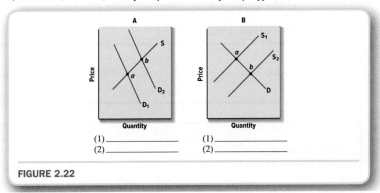

Problems for Further Study

Basic (Problems 1–6)

1. **(LO 5)** Circle which of the following factors will lead to an increase in the demand for cranberry juice (which is a normal good).
   a) a decrease in the price of cranberry juice
   b) a decrease in the price of cranberries
   c) the expectation by consumers that the price of cranberry juice is likely to increase
   d) an increase in the price of apple juice
   e) an increase in consumers' average income
   f) an improvement in the juicing process that lowers the cost of producing cranberry juice

2. **(LO 1, 2, 5, 6)** In each of the two graphs in Figure 2.22, explain the change in equilibrium from a to b in terms of
   1) an increase (or decrease) in demand (or supply)
   2) an increase (or decrease) in the quantity demanded (or quantity supplied)

(1)_____ (1)_____
(2)_____ (2)_____

FIGURE 2.22

connect 2

Connect2 Targets Course Management Pain Points

We listened to educators from around the world describe how effective course design and implementation is key to achieving success. We also heard educators describe the many key challenges and pain points associated with current course design and management solutions.

The Connect2 Solution

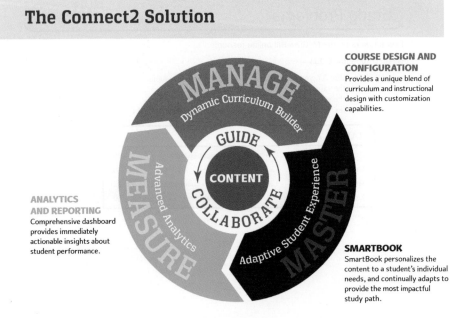

COURSE DESIGN AND CONFIGURATION
Provides a unique blend of curriculum and instructional design with customization capabilities.

ANALYTICS AND REPORTING
Comprehensive dashboard provides immediately actionable insights about student performance.

SMARTBOOK
SmartBook personalizes the content to a student's individual needs, and continually adapts to provide the most impactful study path.

Connect2 is a Collaborative Teaching and Learning Environment

Our unique approach offers a complete course framework that educators can customize with their own content. Every course is developed by a curriculum design expert to ensure content is aligned with instructional strategies and learning objectives for optimal student learning. Connect2 includes a proven adaptive learning system that drives learning mastery with measurable results. Educators receive onboarding support and in-program guidelines for a smooth implementation. The benefit is that educators save time and resources while improving student outcomes.

Complete Course Framework

You Can Easily Customize Every Connect2 course is informed by a deep understanding of curriculum design principles and data analytics from over a thousand adaptive products spanning hundreds of course areas. Our authors and instructional design teams apply the data to identify content elements that optimize learning with pinpoint precision.

The result is a tested and proven complete course framework that educators can customize with their own content—time savings with all the control and flexibility faculty expect and need.

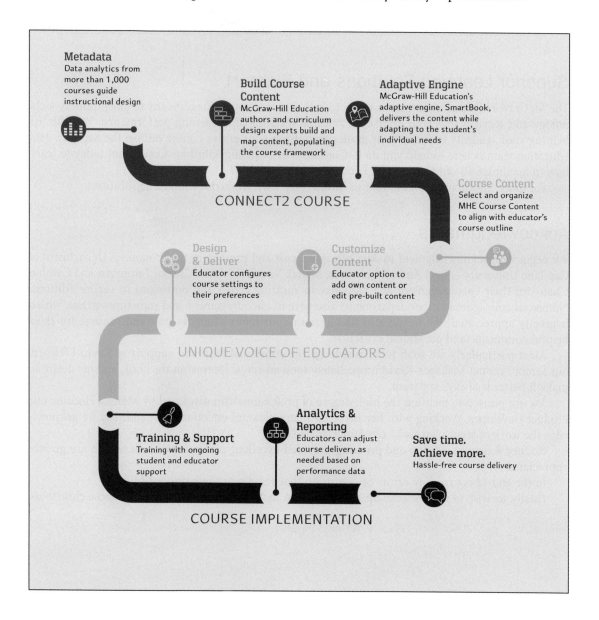

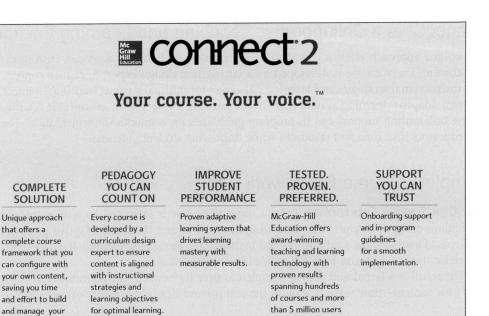

Superior Learning Solutions and Support

The McGraw-Hill Education team is ready to help you assess and integrate any of our products, technology, and services into your course for optimal teaching and learning performance. Whether it's helping your students improve their grades or putting your entire course online, the McGraw-Hill Education team is here to help you do it. Contact your Learning Solutions Consultant today to learn how to maximize all of McGraw-Hill Education's resources!

For more information, please visit us online: http://www.mheducation.ca/he/solutions

Acknowledgments

We begin with acknowledgment to our colleagues, past and present, in the Economics Department of Capilano University—Nigel Amon, Ken Moak, Mahak Yaseri, C.S. Lum, Chieko Tanimura, and Camlon Chau—for their encouragement and vigilance in spotting errors and omissions in earlier editions. Numerous colleagues in other departments also gave us encouragement, and sometimes praise, which is greatly appreciated. We would also like to thank our many students, past and present, for their helpful comments (and occasional criticism).

Most particularly, we wish to acknowledge the continued help and support of Kevin O'Hearn, our Senior Product Manager. Kevin immediately took an active interest in the book, and his desire to make it better is always apparent.

We are pleased to mention the high degree of professionalism displayed by Melissa Hudson, our Product Developer. Working with her involved many pleasant encounters. In addition we acknowledge the work of Jessica Barnoski, our Supervising Editor.

Rodney Rawlings' editing and proofing provided excellent professional skills, which are greatly appreciated.

In the end, of course, any errors or confusion that remain are our responsibility.

Finally, we wish to acknowledge the continued love and support of our families and those close to us.

ECONOMICS TOOLKIT

Some students take economics because it is a requirement for a program they have chosen or degree they are working toward. Some are interested in a career in business, and taking economics seems like a natural choice. Some even take it because they think that they might like it. Whatever your reasons for taking economics, we are glad you did and hope you will not be disappointed. Economics is a challenging discipline to learn, but it is also one of the most rewarding courses you will ever take. The logic and analysis used in economics is very powerful, and successfully working your way through the principles of economics over the next term will do for your mind what a serious jogging program will do for your body. Bon voyage!

The Canadian Reality

The Land

Canada is a huge country—in fact, the second-largest country on this planet. It contains 7 percent of the world's land mass. It stretches 5600 kilometres from the Atlantic to the Pacific Ocean and encompasses six time zones. Ontario alone, which is the second-largest province (after Quebec), is larger than Pakistan, Turkey, Chile, France, or the United Kingdom. Canada's ten provinces range in size from tiny Prince Edward Island to Quebec, which is nearly 240 times as large. In addition, its three territories—the Northwest Territories, Yukon, and Nunavut—demand that we describe this country's reach as being from sea to sea *to sea*.

Within Canada, there are at least six major mountain ranges: the Torngats, Appalachians, and Laurentians in the east, and the Mackenzie, Rocky, and Coast ranges in the west. Any one of these rivals the European Alps in size and grandeur. In addition, Canada has vast quantities of fresh water—9 percent of the world's total—in tens of thousands of lakes and numerous rivers, of which the St. Lawrence and the Mackenzie are the largest.

Canada is richly endowed with natural resources, including gas, oil, gold, silver, copper, iron, nickel, potash, uranium, zinc, fish, timber, and, as mentioned above, water—lots of fresh water. The conclusion is inescapable: Canada is a big, beautiful, and rich country.

The People

The word *Canada* comes from a Huron–Iroquois word meaning *village*. In a sense this is very appropriate, because, big as the nation is geographically, it is small in terms of population. Its over 35 million people make up only 0.5 percent of the world's population. In fact, there are more people in California or in greater Tokyo than there are in the whole of Canada. Interestingly, Canada's annual population growth rate, at 1 percent, is the highest among G8 countries, primarily because of Canada's high rate of immigration. Thirty-eight percent of Canadians live in the province of Ontario and 24 percent in Quebec. On the other hand, Prince Edward Island has a population of only 140 000, less than that of the cities of Sherbrooke, in Quebec, or North Vancouver, in British Columbia.

Despite the popular images of small Maritime fishing villages, lonely Prairie grain farmers, or remote B.C. loggers, Canada is, in fact, an urban nation. Over 80 percent of Canadians live in what Statistics Canada calls "urban" areas. There are six Canadian metropolitan areas with populations of over 1 million: Toronto, with 5.6 million; Montreal, with 3.8 million; Vancouver, with 2.3 million; Calgary and Edmonton, each with 1.2 million, and Ottawa–Gatineau, with 1.2 million. It is also true that the vast majority of the nearly 36 million Canadians live in a narrow band stretching along the border with the United States, which, incidentally, is the longest unguarded border in the world.

Approximately half of the Canadian population is active in the labour force. The labour-force participation rate in 2015 was 71 percent for males and 61 percent for females.

Multiculturalism

Within this vast, thinly populated country there is a truly diverse, multicultural mix of people. This reality was officially recognized in 1988 when Parliament passed the *Multiculturalism Act*.

There are two official languages in Canada, yet 18 percent of Canadians speak a language other than English or French. In fact, at least 60 languages are spoken in this country. In each year of the 2000s, more than 200 000 new immigrants arrived in Canada. Over 18 percent of the entire population are first-generation Canadians. In both Toronto and Vancouver, over half the students in the public school system are from non-English-speaking homes. There are over 100 minority language publications in Toronto, and Vancouver has three daily Chinese-language newspapers.

Canada's First Nations people number 1.1 million (3.8 percent of the total population), and a quarter of them live in Ontario.

Government

Canada is a constitutional monarchy with a democratic parliament made up of the House of Commons, with 308 elected members, and the Senate, with 105 appointed members. In addition to Parliament, the other two decision-making divisions of the federal government are the Cabinet, composed of the prime minister and 25 (or so) ministers and their departments, and the judiciary, which includes the Supreme Court as well as the federal and tax courts.

Just as there are two official languages in this country, Canada has two systems of civil law—one uncodified and based on common law in English Canada, and the other a codified civil law in Quebec. Canada's current constitution, the first part of which is the *Canadian Charter of Rights and Freedoms*, came into being in 1982, a full 115 years after Confederation created the country in 1867.

The fact that Canada is a confederation means the federal government shares responsibilities with the provinces. For example, while the federal government has jurisdiction in national defence, international trade, immigration, banking, criminal law, fisheries, transportation, and communications, the provinces have responsibility for education, property rights, health, and natural resources. Inevitably, issues arise from time to time that do not fit neatly into any one of these categories, with the result that federal–provincial disputes are a continuous part of the Canadian reality.

Canada the Good

Most Canadians are well aware that they live in a good country. But perhaps many do not realize just how good. The average family after-tax income is currently over $74 000, which puts the Canadian living standard among the highest in the world.

The United Nations maintains a Human Development Index that considers factors in addition to average income levels, including lifespans and years of schooling. In 2014, this index ranked Canada as the number nine nation in the world in which to live. One reason for this high ranking is that Canadian governments spend over 10 percent of the country's gross domestic product (GDP) on health care.

More than 70 percent of Canadians own their homes, well over 90 percent are literate, and over 80 percent of all Canadians have access to the Internet. All three of these statistics are among the highest in the world.

Canada the Odd

Canada is a good country in which to live; however, it does have its oddities. In 1965—98 years after Confederation—it was decided that Canada really should have a national flag. A parliamentary selection committee was set up to choose one, and received no less than two thousand designs. The flag debate was acrimonious, to say the least, although today most Canadians seem quite comfortable with the Maple Leaf. The English-language lyrics of Canada's national anthem, "O Canada," were formally approved only in 1975. Canada adopted the metric system of measurement in the 1970s. But the imperial system is still in wide use; for example, Statistics Canada still reports the breadth of this country in miles, we sell sizes of wood in inches (such as 2 × 4s), and football fields are 110 yards long.

In this bilingual country, it is odd to note that there are more Manitobans who speak Cree than British Columbians who speak French. In this affluent country of ours, it is also interesting to note that 4 percent of Canadian homes are heated exclusively by burning wood. Canada's official animal is—the beaver.

On a more serious note, it is a sad fact that the trade of many goods, and even some services, between any one province and the United States is freer than trade between provinces. There is an interesting history concerning trade patterns in North America. At the time of Confederation, trade patterns on this continent were mostly north–south. The Maritimes traded with the New England states, Quebec with New York, Ontario with the Great Lakes states to its south, and the West Coast with California. Canada's first prime minister, John A. Macdonald, was also elected as its third. During his second administration, he implemented his party's National Policy, which resulted in (1) the building of a railway to the west coast, which encouraged British Columbia to join Canada; (2) an offer of free land to new immigrants on the prairies in order to settle this area; and (3) the forcing of trade patterns into an east–west mode by erection of a tariff wall against American imports. British Columbia did join Confederation; people were enticed to settle in Manitoba, Saskatchewan, and Alberta; and the pattern of trade did become more east–west.

So was the National Policy a success? Some would argue yes, pointing out that it built a nation and that Canada as we know it might not exist today without it. Others are not so sure, and would argue that it set back Canada's development by encouraging and protecting new, less efficient industries through the creation of a branch-plant economy. This occurred because American firms that had previously exported to Canada simply jumped over the tariff walls and established Canadian branch plants. Some believe that the National Policy also promoted Canadian regionalism and aggravated relations between regions because both the West and the Maritimes felt that most of its economic benefits favoured central Canada.

In any case, as a result of the North American Free Trade Agreement (NAFTA) of 1992, trade with the United States (and Mexico) is now mostly without tariffs and north–south trade patterns are re-emerging. Historically, Canadian policy has come full circle. However, the trade barriers between provinces, which were built piece by piece over a century, remain.

The Economy

Canada is among the ten largest economies in the world, despite its small population. In 2015, Canada's GDP was $1983 billion. This figure can be broken down as illustrated in Table T.1.

TABLE T.1

Category	Amount ($billions)	% of GDP
Personal expenditures	1140	57.5
Investment spending	389	19.6
Government spending	500	25.2
Exports	547	31.5
Less imports	583	33.8
Net exports	<46>	<2.3>
Total GDP	1983	

Source: Adapted by the authors from the Statistics Canada CANSIM database, http://cansim2.statcan.ca, Table 380-0064, July 5, 2016.

The provincial breakdown of the 2015 GDP figure of $1983 billion is shown in Table T.2.

TABLE T.2

Province	Population (millions)	GDP ($billions)	GDP per Capita ($thousands)
Newfoundland (and Labrador)	0.53	30.1	56.8
Prince Edward Island	0.15	6.2	41.3
Nova Scotia	0.94	40.2	42.8
New Brunswick	0.75	33.1	44.1
Quebec	8.26	381.0	46.1
Ontario	13.80	763.3	55.3
Manitoba	1.30	65.9	50.7
Saskatchewan	1.13	79.4	70.3
Alberta	4.18	326.4	78.1
British Columbia	4.69	250.0	53.3
Yukon	0.04	2.7	72.5
Northwest Territories (pre-Nunavut)	0.04	4.8	109.1
Nunavut	0.04	2.5	67.0

Source: Adapted by the authors from the Statistics Canada CANSIM database, http://cansim2.statcan.ca, Tables 384-0038 and 051-0001, May 11, 2017.

This table illustrates the wide disparity in GDP per capita between provinces, from a low of $41 300 per person in Prince Edward Island to a high of $78 100 in Alberta.

In most years the economy grows and the GDP figure rises. To accurately compare growth in GDP, however, we need to use a common set of prices so that a simple rise in prices is not confused with an actual increase in the output of goods and services. Using *real* GDP figures, which correct for inflation, accomplishes this. Table T.3 looks at some recent real GDP figures, using 2007 prices.

TABLE T.3

Year	Real GDP ($billions)	Increase/Decrease ($billions)	% Increase
2011	1640	+47	+3.0
2012	1669	+29	+1.8
2013	1706	+37	+2.2
2014	1748	+42	+2.5
2015	1767	+19	+1.1

Source: Adapted by the authors from the Statistics Canada CANSIM database, http://cansim2.statcan.ca, Table 380-0064, July 5, 2016.

Next, let us look at a breakdown of Canada's GDP by industry in Table T.4, presented in order of importance.

TABLE T.4

Industry	Percentage of GDP
Real estate	12.9
Trade (wholesale and retail)	11.1
Manufacturing	10.6
Professional and technical	8.7
Mining/oil	8.1
Construction	7.2
Finance and insurance	7.0
Health	6.8
Public administration	6.5
Education	5.2
Transportation	4.3
Information and cultural	3.1
Utilities	2.3
Accomodation and food	2.1
Other services	2.0
Agriculture, fishing, and forestry	1.6
Arts and entertainment	0.7

Source: Adapted from the Statistics Canada CANSIM database, http://cansim2.statcan.ca, Table 379-0031, July 5, 2016.

This information is helpful in many ways. For example, it is certainly time to put to rest the idea that Canada is a resource-based economy and that Canadians are simply "hewers of wood and drawers of water," as many of us were taught in school. In fact, agriculture/fishing/forestry and mining/oil make up less than 10 percent of our economy's GDP. Only 4 percent of working Canadians are employed in primary industries, down dramatically from 13 percent a quarter of a century ago.

In contrast, one can marshal the argument that Canada is quite a sophisticated and technologically advanced economy. For example, it is not generally recognized that Canada was the world's third nation to go into space, with the *Alouette I* satellite in 1962. Canadian industries pioneered long-distance pipeline technology, and Canada is a world leader in several areas of aviation, including turboprop, turbofan, and firefighting aircraft, not to mention the well-known Canadarm used on space shuttles. Canada is also a world leader in commercial submarine technology, and routinely maintains one of the world's longest and most efficient railway systems.

One can also point to many outstanding Canadian companies that are truly world leaders in technology and performance, including Bombardier in transportation equipment, Ballard Power in fuel cell technology, SNC Lavalin in aluminum plant design, Rio Tinto in mining, Trizec Hahn in real estate development, and Magna International in automobile parts manufacturing.

Exports: The Engine That Drives the Economy

Exports are a fundamental part of the Canadian economy. Over 30 percent of its GDP is exported, which makes Canada one of the world's greatest trading nations. Exports to the United States alone directly support over 1.5 million Canadian jobs, and a $1 billion increase in exports translates into 11 000 new jobs. Again, contrary to historical wisdom, only 25 percent of Canadian exports are resources—the figure was 40 percent a quarter of a century ago.

Table T.5 breaks down the $625 billion worth of goods and services Canada exported in 2015 into nine categories in order of size.

TABLE T.5

Export Category	Percentage of Total Exports
Industrial goods	18.0
Services	16.0
Automotive products	14.0
Machinery and equipment	13.7
Energy products	13.4
Consumer goods	11.2
Forestry products	6.4
Agricultural and fishing products	5.1
Others	2.3

Source: Adapted from the Statistics Canada CANSIM database, http://cansim2.statcan.ca, Tables 228-0059, July 5, 2016.

A Mixed Economy

At the start of the twenty-first century, the market system dominates most of the world's economies, and Canada is no exception. Yet government also plays a big role in our economy. For example, in 2009 the three levels of government collected $586 billion in tax revenue, which represented over 38 percent of Canada's 2009 GDP. Table T.6 shows the sources and the uses of this revenue.

TABLE T.6

Government Revenues	% of Total	Government Expenditures	% of Total
Personal income taxes	32.3	Social services	25.6
Consumption taxes	18.3	Health	20.5
Property taxes	9.4	Education	16.1
Investment income	9.2	Protection of persons and property	8.5
Sales of goods and services	9.2	Debt charges	7.6
Corporate incomes taxes	8.5	Environment	6.3
Social security premiums	6.0	Transportation	5.4
Other taxes	5.3	Government services	3.8

Source: Adapted by the authors from the Statistics Canada CANSIM database, http://cansim2.statcan.ca, Table 385-0001, January 12, 2011.

The largest single source of the government's tax revenue, 32 percent, was personal income taxes. Consumption taxes include, most significantly, the GST (goods and services tax) and the PST (provincial sales tax) as well as gasoline, alcohol, and tobacco taxes, customs taxes, and gaming income. These indirect (consumption) taxes accounted for 18 percent of total revenue. Thus, we can see that the majority of the government's tax revenue comes from individual Canadians in the form of direct income taxes or consumption taxes.

And how does government spend these billions of dollars of tax revenue? The right column of Table T.6 shows us.

Here, we see that government's largest single category of spending, 26 percent, was on social service payments to individuals. The lion's share of this expenditure (approximately two-thirds) was social services (pensions, unemployment benefits, and welfare) payments. Thus, we see that a large percentage of spending by government is an attempt to direct income to poorer Canadians. Since all

Canadians pay for most of these expenditures, we can see that government is actively involved in *transferring* income from higher-income to lower-income families and individuals. This income distribution role is seen by many Canadians as an important function of government.

On the other hand, some Canadians take the view that government has gone too far in its interventionist role and yearn for less governmental involvement in the economy. They often point to the United States as an example of an economy in which welfare, unemployment, and pension payments to individuals and direct government aid to poor regions of the country are lower. The difference in the general approach of the two governments may well lie in historical differences in the attitudes of Canadians and Americans toward government. Over the years, Canadians, by and large, have trusted governments to act in their best interests and have been more tolerant of government attempts at income redistribution. Americans, on the other hand, have a history of being suspicious of big government and have repeatedly rejected attempts to expand its role. The recent controversy in the United States over attempts to implement a national health care (Obamacare) policy is an example. Another is the Canadian government's direct aid to cultural endeavours, including the funding of national television and radio networks, while no such efforts exist in the United States.

The next two largest categories of spending are on two essentials, health and education. In 2009, the Canadian government allocated 21 and 16 percent of spending in these two areas. The fourth category, protection of persons and property, includes expenditures on the military, police, fire departments, court system, and prisons. Interest on the national debt was the fifth-biggest item of spending at just under 8 percent. The amount spent in this area has steadily declined in the last few years as Canada has started to get government budget deficits under control. (As recently as 1998, servicing the national debt amounted to as much as 30 percent of total spending.) The other categories include a host of such items as culture (the Canada Council), housing, foreign affairs, immigration, labour, and research.

This completes our brief look at the Canadian economic reality. We hope that it has helped fill in some gaps in your knowledge of the country. We are confident that you will come to know your country much better after a thorough grounding in the principles of economics, for, in a very real sense, economics is about understanding and improving on what we already know.

Graphing Reality

Let's face it, a lot of students hate graphs. For them a picture is not worth a thousand words. It may even be true that they seem to understand some economic concepts just fine until the instructor draws a graph on the board. All of a sudden, they lose confidence and start to question what they previously thought they knew. For these students, graphs are not the solution but the problem. This section is designed to help those students overcome this difficulty. For those other, more fortunate students who can handle graphs and know that they are used to illustrate concepts, a quick reading of this section will reinforce their understanding.

It is probably true that if an idea can be expressed clearly and precisely with words, then graphs become an unnecessary luxury. The trouble is that, from time to time, economists find themselves at a loss for words and see no way of getting a certain point across except with the use of a graph. On the other hand, by themselves graphs cannot explain everything; they need to be accompanied by a verbal explanation. In other words, they are not a substitute for words but a complement. The words accompanied by a picture can often give us a much richer understanding of economic concepts and happenings.

Graphing a Single Variable

The graphing of a single variable is reasonably straightforward. Often, economists want to concentrate on a single economic variable, such as Canada's exports, or consumers' incomes, or the production of wine in Canada. In some cases, they want to look at the composition of that variable, say different categories of exports. In other cases, they are interested in seeing how one variable changed over a period of time, such as total exports for each of the years 2005 through 2009. In the first instance, we would be looking at a cross-section; in the second instance, we are looking at a time series.

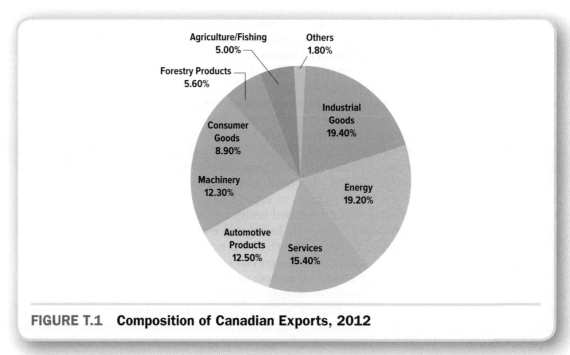

FIGURE T.1   Composition of Canadian Exports, 2012

Source: Adapted from the Statistics Canada CANSIM database, http://cansim2.statcan.ca, Tables 228-0059, January 9, 2014.

Cross-Sectional Graphs

One popular way of showing cross-sectional data is in the form of a pie chart. Figure T.1, for instance, shows the composition of Canada's exports for 2012 in terms of the type of goods or services that Canada sells abroad. (This is the same data as presented in Table T.5. Which presentation format—table or graph—do you prefer? Which do you find easier to read and understand?)

The size of each slice indicates the relative size of each category of exports. But the picture by itself is not always enough. We have added the percentage of total exports that each type represents. Note, however, that there are no dollar amounts for the categories.

Alternatively, the same information could be presented in the form of a bar graph, as in Figure T.2. Unlike the pie chart, the bar graph allows us to more easily compare the relative sizes of each category since they are now placed side by side.

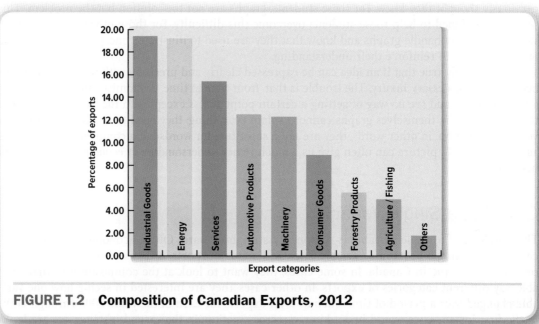

FIGURE T.2   Composition of Canadian Exports, 2012

Source: Adapted from the Statistics Canada CANSIM database, http://cansim2.statcan.ca, Tables 228-0059, January 11, 2011.

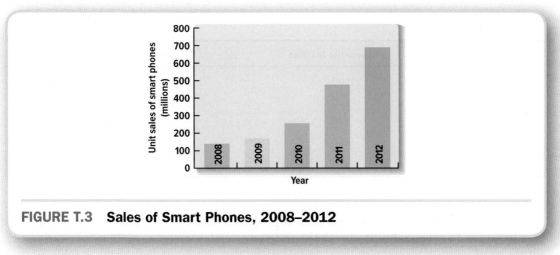

FIGURE T.3   Sales of Smart Phones, 2008–2012

Source: Adapted from Gartner.com, retrieved January 10, 2014.

Time-Series Graphs

Time-series data can also be presented in the form of a bar graph. **Figure T.3** is a bar graph showing the rapid growth in the worldwide sales of smart phones over the past five years.

The same information can be presented in a line graph, as is done in **Figure T.4**. Note that in both cases, the years (time) are shown on the horizontal axis; early years are on the left and later years on the right. This is because graphs are always read from left to right.

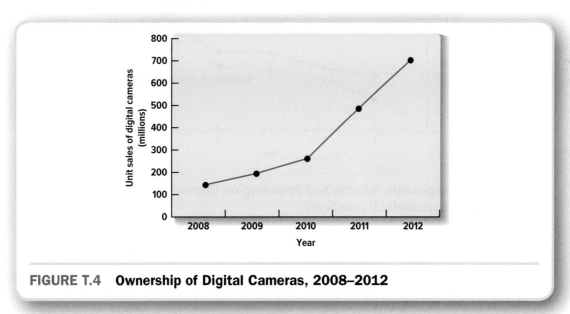

FIGURE T.4   Ownership of Digital Cameras, 2008–2012

Source: Adapted from Gartner.com, retrieved January 10, 2014.

Graphing Two Variables

Things get a little trickier when we want to deal with two variables at the same time. For instance, suppose we want to relate Canada's disposable income, which is the total take-home pay of all Canadians, and the amount spent on consumer goods (these numbers are in billions and are hypothetical). One obvious way to do this is with a table, as is done in **Table T.7**.

TABLE T.7		
Year	Disposable Income	Spending on Consumer Goods
1	$100	$ 80
2	120	98
3	150	125
4	160	134
5	200	170

A time-series graph, using the same data, is presented in **Figure T.5**. You can see that the two lines in **Figure T.5** seem to be closely related, and that is useful information. To more clearly bring out the relationship, we could plot them against each other. But if you look again at **Table T.7**, you will see that there are really three different variables involved: the time (five years), the values of disposable income, and the values of spending. However, it is very difficult to plot three variables, all three against each other, on a two-dimensional sheet of paper.

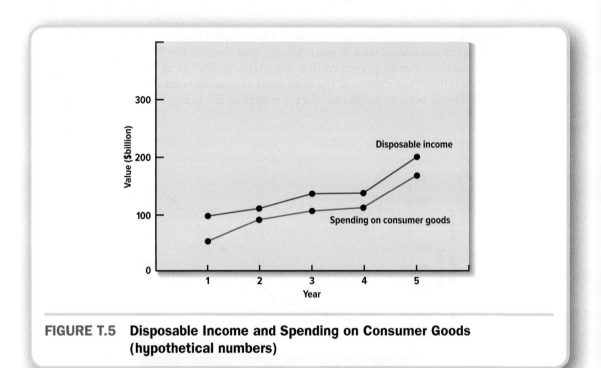

FIGURE T.5   Disposable Income and Spending on Consumer Goods (hypothetical numbers)

Instead, in **Figure T.6**, we will put disposable income on the horizontal axis (also called the *x-axis*) and consumer spending on the vertical axis (also called the *y-axis*) and indicate time with written notation. There is a rule about which variable goes on which axis, but we will leave that for later in this book.

Next, we need to decide on a scale for each of the two axes. There is no particular rule about doing this, but just a little experience will enable you to develop good judgment about selecting these values. We have chosen to give each square on the axes the value of $20. This can be seen in **Figure T.6**.

We started plotting our line using year 1 data. In that year, disposable income was $100 and consumer spending was $80. Starting at the origin (where the vertical and horizontal axes meet), which has an assigned value of zero, we move five squares to the right. Now, from this income of $100, we move up vertically four squares, arriving at a value of $80 for consumer spending. This is our first plot (or point). We do the same for year 2. First, we find a value of $120 on the horizontal (disposable income) axis and a value of $98 (just less than five squares) on the vertical axis. The place where these two meet gives us our

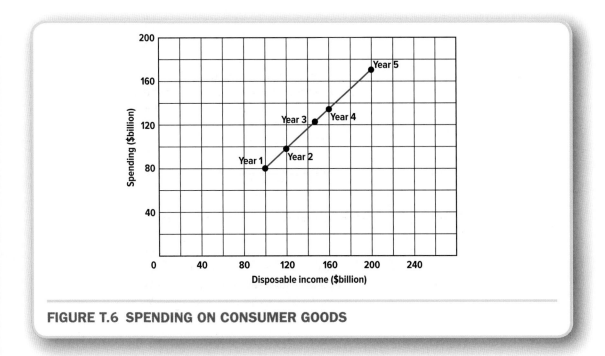

FIGURE T.6 SPENDING ON CONSUMER GOODS

second point to plot. We do the same for the three next years, and join up the five points with a line. Note that the relationship between income levels and consumer spending plots as a straight line.

Direct and Inverse Relationships

Next, if you look back at **Table T.7**, you will see that disposable income and consumer spending rise together over time. When two variables move together in this way, we say that there is a *direct* relationship between them. Such a direct relationship appears as an upward-sloping line. On the other hand, when two variables move in opposite directions so that one variable increases as the other variable decreases, we say there is an *inverse* relationship between them. In that case, plotting the two variables together would result in a downward-sloping line. (When we say "upward-sloping" and "downward-sloping," remember we are reading the graphs left to right.)

One last point: the income–consumer spending line in **Figure T.6** is straight. This is not always the case. Some data might plot as a straight line, and other data might be nonlinear when plotted (as in **Figure T.5**). Either, of course, could still be downward or upward sloping.

Measuring the Slope of a Straight Line

As you proceed with this course, you will find that you need to go a bit further than merely being able to plot a curve. (In economics, by the way, all lines are described as curves whether they are linear or nonlinear.) You will also need to know just how steep or how shallow the line is that you have plotted. In other words, you will need to measure the slope of the curve. What the slope shows, in effect, is how much one variable changes in relation to the other variable as we move along a curve. In graphic terms, this means measuring the change in the variable shown on the vertical axis (known as the *rise*), divided by the change in the variable shown on the horizontal axis (known as the *run*). The rise and the run are illustrated, using our disposable income/consumer-spending example, in **Figure T.7**.

Note that as we move from point *a* to point *b*, consumer spending increases by 80 (from 80 to 160). This is the amount of the rise. Looking along the horizontal axis, we see that disposable income increases by 100 (from 100 to 200). This is the amount of the run. In general, we can say

$$\text{Slope} = \frac{\text{rise}}{\text{run}} = \frac{\text{change in the value on the vertical axis}}{\text{change in the value on the horizontal axis}}$$

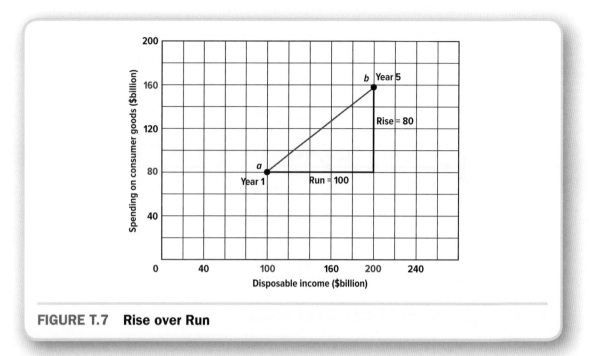

FIGURE T.7   Rise over Run

Specifically, the slope of our line is therefore equal to

$$\frac{+80}{+100} = +0.8$$

Figure T.8 shows four other curves, two upward sloping and two downward sloping, with an indication for each as to how to calculate the various slopes. In each case, we measure the slope by moving from point *a* to point *b*.

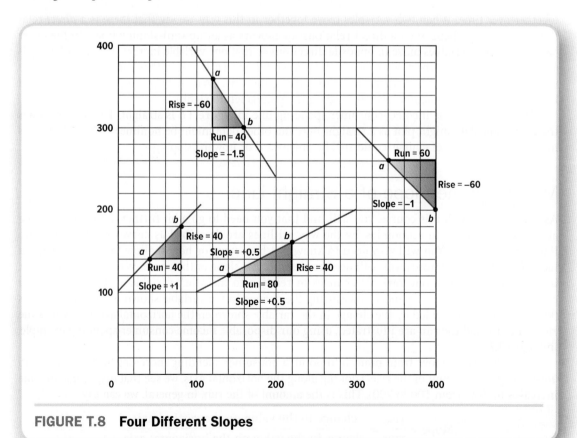

FIGURE T.8   Four Different Slopes

The Slopes of Curves

If a line is straight, it does not matter where on it we choose to measure the slope; the slope is constant throughout its length. But this is not true of a curve. The slope of a curve will have different values at every point. However, it is possible to measure the slope at any point by drawing a straight line that touches the curve at that point. Such a line is called a *tangent to the curve*. **Figure T.9**, for instance, shows a curve that, at various points, has a positive slope (the upward-sloping portion), a zero slope (the top of the curve), and a negative slope (the downward-sloping portion). We have drawn in three tangents at different positions along the curve. From these straight-line tangents we can calculate the value of the slope at each of these points.

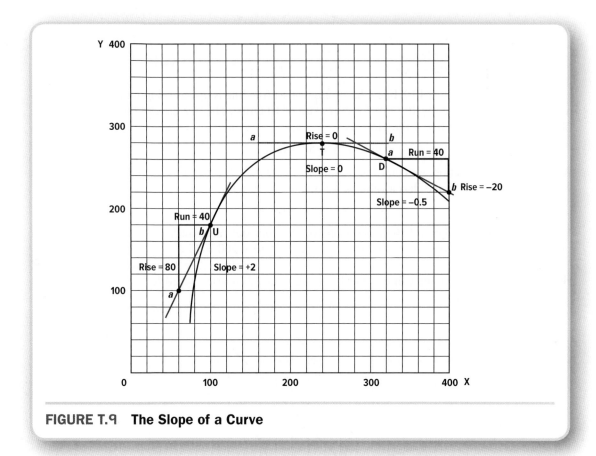

FIGURE T.9   The Slope of a Curve

At point U, for example, the curve rises quite steeply. So what is its slope? Well, its slope at this point is the same as the value of the slope of the straight-line tangent. As we already know the slope of a straight line is

$$\frac{\text{Rise}}{\text{Run}}$$

At point U, this is equal to

$$\frac{+80}{+40} = +2$$

This is also the value of the slope of the curve at point U.

    At point T, the tangent is a horizontal line, which, by definition, does not rise or fall. The rise/run at this point, therefore, is equal to zero. Finally, at point D, both the curve and the tangent are downward sloping, indicating a negative slope. Its value is calculated, as before, as rise/run, which equals −20/40 or −0.5.

Equations for a Straight Line

In economics, graphs are a very important and useful way to present information. Thus, you will find the pages of most economics books liberally sprinkled with them. But there are other, equally useful ways of presenting the same data. One of these is an algebraic equation. You will often find it very useful to be able to translate a graph into algebra. In this short section, we will show you how to do this. To keep things simple, we will restrict our attention to straight-line graphs.

In order to find the equation for any straight line, you need only two pieces of information: the slope of the line and the value of the Y-intercept. You already know how to calculate the value of the slope. The value of the Y-intercept is simply the value at which the line crosses the vertical axis. In general, the algebraic expression for a straight line is given as

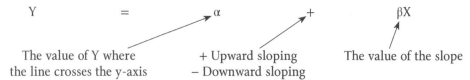

$$Y \qquad = \qquad \alpha \qquad + \qquad \beta X$$

The value of Y where the line crosses the y-axis   + Upward sloping − Downward sloping   The value of the slope

For instance, in **Figure T.10**, line 1 has a slope of +1 (the line is upward sloping and therefore has a positive slope and rises by 10 units for every run of 10 units). The line crosses the y-axis at a value of 50. The equation for line 1, therefore, is

$$Y = 50 + (1)X$$

Armed with this equation, we could figure out the value of Y for any value of X. For example, when X (along the horizontal axis) has a value of 40, Y must be equal to

$$Y = 50 + 40 = 90$$

You can verify this in **Figure T.10**. In addition, we can work out values of X and Y that are not shown on the graph. For example, when X equals 200, Y equals 50 + 200 = 250.

Let us work out the equations for the other lines shown in **Figure T.10**. Line 2 is also upward sloping, but it is steeper than line 1 and has a slope of +2 (it rises by 20 for every run of 10). Its

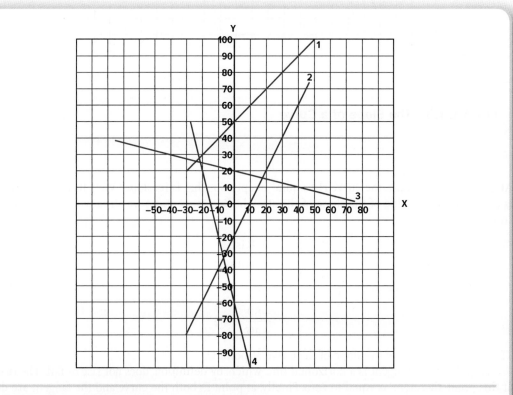

FIGURE T.10   Equations for Straight Lines

intercept, however, is in the negative area of the y-axis and crosses at the value of -20. The equation for line 2, then, is

$$Y = -20 + 2X$$

Again, you can check that this is correct by putting in a value for X, finding the corresponding value of Y, and looking on the graph to see if it is correct. For instance, when X has a value of 40, the equation tells us that

$$Y = -20 + 2(40) = 60$$

You can confirm in **Figure T.10** that this is indeed the case.

In contrast, line 3 has a negative slope of 0.25 and a Y-intercept at 20. Its equation, therefore, is

$$Y = 20 - 0.25X$$

Finally, line 4 has the equation

$$Y = -60 - 4X$$

Finding the Intersection Between Two Curves

A good deal of economics is concerned with investigating two variables that are related to a common factor. As we shall see in Chapter 2, the quantities of a product that consumers want to buy and the amount that producers wish to sell (demand and supply) are both related to the price of that product. Similarly, the number of employees who are willing to work and the number of people employers are willing to hire are both related to the wage offered. You will therefore often need to be able to graph two sets of data and find where they coincide.

Let us illustrate with a non-economics example. Suppose one early morning Jo is sitting at the bottom of a 2500 metre mountain, and Ed is sitting at the top. Assuming they start off at the same time (say 8 a.m.) with Jo climbing up at a rate of 400 metres per hour and Ed climbing down at 600 metres per hour, let us see if we can work out where on the mountain and at what time they will meet.

First, we need to transfer this data into a table showing where each individual climber will be at what time. This information is shown in **Table T.8**.

TABLE T.8

Jo's Ascent		Ed's Descent	
Elapsed/Time	Elevation (metres)	Elapsed/Time	Elevation (metres)
0 (8 a.m.)	0	0 (8 a.m.)	2500
1 (9 a.m.)	400	1 (9 a.m.)	1900
2 (10 a.m.)	800	2 (10 a.m.)	1300
3 (11 a.m.)	1200	3 (11 a.m.)	700
4 (12 noon)	1600	4 (12 noon)	100
5 (1 p.m.)	2000	4:10 (12:10 p.m.)	0
6 (2 p.m.)	2400		
6:15 (2:15 p.m.)	2500		

We can also show their ascent and descent graphically. In **Figure T.11**, we will use the vertical axis to show the elevation and the horizontal axis to show the time elapsed.

According to the graph, it seems that they will meet after exactly 2½ hours, that is, at 10:30 a.m. at an elevation of 1000 metres. We can confirm this result if we translate these data into an algebraic expression. Let us look at Jo's ascent. Her elevation depends on how fast she climbs and how long she climbs. We know she starts at the bottom of the mountain (elevation zero) and climbs at a rate of 400 metres per hour. If we let the elevation equal Y and the time elapsed equal X, then her ascent can be shown as

Jo's elevation: $Y = 0 + 400X$

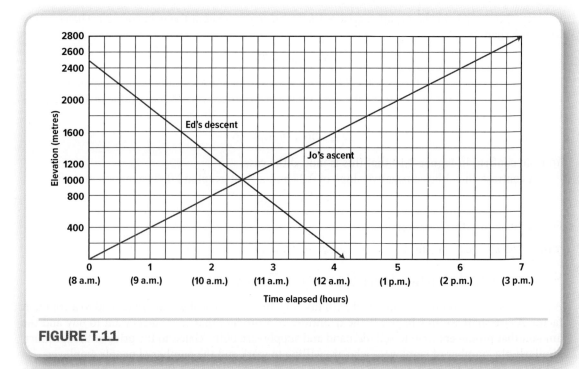

FIGURE T.11

In contrast, Ed starts at an elevation of 2500 metres and his elevation falls as he climbs down. His descent can therefore be shown as

Ed's elevation: $Y = 2500 - 600X$

To find out when and where they will meet is to recognize that whatever this point is, it occurs on the mountain at the same point for the two of them. In other words, Jo and Ed's elevation will be the same. Algebraically, we make the two equations equal and solve. Thus

$$400X = 2500 - 600X$$

$$1000X = 2500$$

$$X = 2.5$$

So they will meet after 2.5 hours (2 hours and 30 minutes), or at 10:30 a.m. To find out where they will meet, simply replace X with 2.5 in Jo's and/or Ed's elevation equation.

Jo: $400(2.5) = 1000$ (metres)

Ed: $2400 - 600(2.5) = 1000$

Graphs and Logic

Now let us look at some potential problems in illustrating data with graphs. For example, the relationship between income and consumer spending in **Table T.7** is hypothetical, since we created it so that it would plot well on a graph. However, any real-world relationship between two variables may not be as neat and simple as this. Data does not always plot into a nice straight line.

Even more seriously, we can never be totally certain of the nature of the relationship between the variables being graphed. There is a great danger of implying something that is not there. You therefore need to be on guard against logical fallacies. Suppose you were doing a survey of women's clothing stores across the country. In the data you have collected, you notice what seems to be a close relationship between two sets of numbers: the rent paid by the owners of the store and the average price of wool jackets sold. These data are shown in **Table T.9**.

The higher the monthly rent, the higher the price of jackets charged in that store. It seems clear, therefore, that the higher rent is the cause of the higher price, and the higher price is the effect of the higher rent. After all, the store owner must recoup these higher rent costs by charging her customers a higher price. If you think this, then you are guilty of the logical fallacy of *reverse causality*. As you will learn in economics, although rent and product prices are indeed related, the causality is in fact

TABLE T.9

Monthly Rent (per 100 m²)	Average Jacket Price
$1500	$ 80
1600	90
1700	100
1800	110
1900	120
2000	130

the other way around. This is because stores in certain areas can charge higher product prices because of their trendy location, and landlords charge those stores higher rents for the same reason—it is a desirable location. Higher prices, therefore, are the cause and high rents the effect. This is not obvious and illustrates how using raw economic data without sound economic theory can lead to serious error.

A second logical fallacy is that of the *omitted variable*, which can also lead to confusion over cause and effect. Table T.10 highlights this error. Here, we see hypothetical data on rates of alcoholism and the annual income levels of individuals.

TABLE T.10

Average Income Levels ($)	Alcoholism (per thousand of population)
5 000	40
15 000	35
25 000	30
35 000	25
45 000	20
55 000	15

There certainly seems to be a very close relationship between these two variables. Presented in this form, without any commentary, one is left to wonder if low income causes alcoholism or alcoholism is the cause of low income. Perhaps some people with low incomes drink in order to try to escape the effects of poverty. Or perhaps it implies that people who drink to excess have great difficulty in finding or keeping a good job. In truth, it is possible that neither of these views is true. Simply because two sets of data seem closely related does not necessarily mean that one is the cause of the other. In fact, it may well be that both are caused by an omitted variable. In the above example, it is possible, for instance, that both high alcoholism and low income levels are the result of low educational attainment.

A third fallacy can occur when people see a cause-and-effect relationship that does not really exist. This is known as the fallacy of *post hoc, ergo propter hoc*, which literally means "after this, therefore because of this." That is to say, it is a fallacy to believe that, just because one thing follows another, one is the result of the other. For example, just because my favourite soccer team always loses whenever I go to see them, that does not mean I am the cause of their losing!

There is a final fallacy you should guard against, a fallacy, unfortunately, that even the best economists commit from time to time. This is the *fallacy of composition*, which is the belief that because something is true for a part, it is true for the whole. You may have noticed, for instance, that fights occasionally break out in hockey games. These fights often occur in the corners of the rink, which makes them difficult to see. The best way for individuals to get a better view is by standing, and, of course, when everybody stands, then most people cannot see. Thus, what is true for a single fan—standing up to see better—is not true for the whole crowd. Similarly, a teacher who suggests that in order to get good grades students should sit at the front of the class is guilty of the same kind of logical fallacy!

We hope that this little primer on Canada and on graphing has been helpful. It is now time to move on to the study of economics.

Study Guide

Problems for Further Study

Indicate whether the following statements are true or false:

1. **T or F**   Canada is the world's largest country in area and has 1 percent of the world's population.

2. **T or F**   Ontario has the largest provincial economy and the largest provincial population, and it is Canada's largest province in area.

3. **T or F**   Over 50 percent of Canada's exports are resources.

4. **T or F**   The largest single source of government tax revenue is personal income taxes.

5. **T or F**   Spending on social services is the largest category of spending by (all) governments in Canada.

6. **T or F**   Three popular types of graphs are pie charts, bar graphs, and line graphs.

7. **T or F**   Since disposable income and consumer spending both rise together over time, there is a direct relationship between the two.

8. **T or F**   The slope of a straight line is measured by dividing the run by the rise.

9. **T or F**   If the equation $Y = 5 + 2X$ were plotted, the slope of the line would be equal to 1/2.

10. **T or F**   The logical fallacy *post hoc, ergo propter hoc* means "after this, therefore because of this."

Simple Calculations

11. Table T.11 shows the dollar value of commercial sea fishing in Canada for 2002.
    a) From these data, construct a bar chart.
    b) Construct a pie chart showing the percentage of the total that each species represents.

TABLE T.11

	$millions
Groundfish (including cod, halibut, etc.)	288
Pelagic fish (including salmon and herring)	185
Lobster	594
Crab	505
Shrimp	294
Other shellfish	254
Total value	**2 120**

12. Complete the following schedules, and plot the following equations:
    a) $Y = -200 + 2X$

Y	X
	0
	100
	200
	300
	400

b) $Y = 500 - 4X$

Y	X
	0
	100
	200
	300
	400

13. Given the lines shown in **Figure T.12**, complete the following tables, and calculate the equations for the lines:

a)

Y	X
	0
	20
	40
	60
	80
	100

b)

Y	X
	0
	20
	40
	60
	80
	100

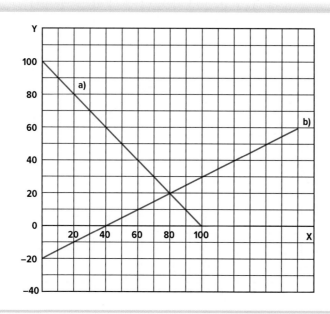

FIGURE T.12

14. The data in **Table T.12** show the results of market research done on the latest Guns 'n' Butter album. The numbers indicate the total quantity of albums that fans would purchase at the various prices.

TABLE T.12	
Price per CD	**Quantity (hundreds of thousands)**
$20	20
19	30
18	40
17	50
16	60
15	70
14	80

a) Graph the table with the price on the vertical (*y*) axis and the quantity on the horizontal (*x*) axis.
b) What is the slope of the line?
c) What is the value of the Y-intercept?
d) What is the equation for this line?

15. What are the values of the slopes of the four lines shown in **Figure T.13**?

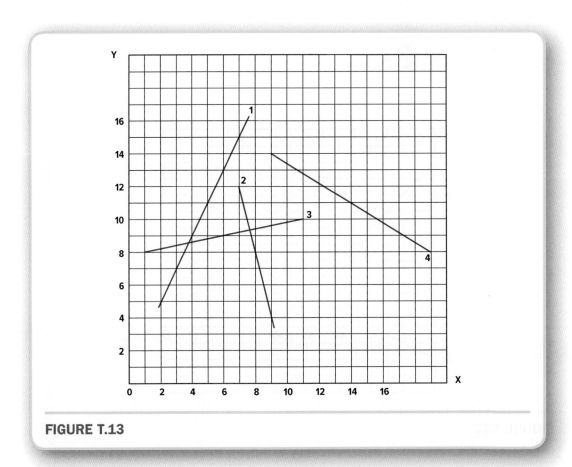

FIGURE T.13

16. What are the equations that correspond to the four lines shown in **Figure T.14**?

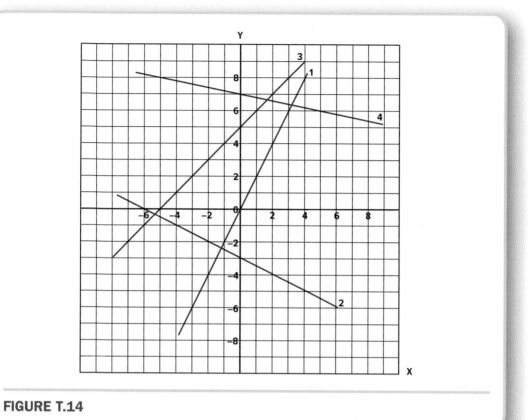

FIGURE T.14

17. Graph the following equations on a single graph, using the same scale for each axis, with the horizontal axis to 120 and the vertical axis to 200, both in squares of 10.
    a) Y = ½X
    b) Y = 40 + X
    c) Y = 160 − ½X
    d) Y = −10 + 2X

CHAPTER 1
The Economic Problem

LEARNING OBJECTIVES

At the end of this chapter, you should be able to:

LO1 Describe why economics is a very relevant discipline by demonstrating that many of the controversies in our society have a distinct economic flavour.

LO2 Define economics and then make a distinction between microeconomics and macro-economics.

LO3 Demonstrate that because scarcity, choice, and opportunity cost are at the heart of economics, efficiency—both productive and allocative—provides a major cornerstone.

LO4 Explain why greater trade results in more productive economies.

LO5 Explain the three fundamental questions that all societies must address.

LO6 Explain the four different ways that economic societies can be organized.

LO7 Use the production possibilities model to illustrate choice and opportunity cost, as well as efficiency and unemployment.

LO8 List the economic goals of society and explain why they are often difficult to achieve.

WHAT'S AHEAD...

In this first chapter, we introduce you to the study of economics and hope to arouse your curiosity about this fascinating discipline. First, we present four controversial statements to illustrate how relevant economics really is. Next, we discuss the nature of the discipline. From this, we derive a formal definition of economics. Then, we examine what efficiency means and why it is so important. The next step is to look at three of the fundamental questions that all societies face and see how four different types of economies address them. Following that, we introduce the production possibilities model, which enables us to illustrate many of these concepts. Finally, we discuss seven important macroeconomic goals and briefly look at the policy tools used to achieve them.

A QUESTION OF RELEVANCE ...

Jon and Ashok are both avid soccer fans and play for local teams. They both like old movies and chess and use Twitter. They are both seventeen years of age, neither has a steady girlfriend, and both are vegetarians. The other thing they have in common is that their fathers are in banking. Jon's father is the executive vice-president of customer relations for the Royal Bank of Canada in Toronto. Ashok's father is a night janitor at a branch of the Bank of India in the dock area of Bombay. All of these points are relevant in forming a mental picture of a person, but you will probably agree that a person's economic circumstances have an enormous impact. In truth, economics is one of the most relevant subjects you will study.

What might you expect from a course in economics? Well, it will probably not help you balance your chequebook and may not be directly helpful in your choice of the right stocks or bonds to buy. But the study of economics will give you a broad understanding of how a modern market economy operates and what relationships are important within it. If you see yourself as a budding businessperson, the study of economics can offer general insights that will be helpful; however, you will not find specific tools or instructions here. Economics is an academic discipline, not a self-help or how-to course.

The common perception that economics is about money is only partly true. Economists do study money, but their goal is to better understand how it works and the effects of different central-bank money policies rather than how to make it. The study of economics may or may not help you function better in the world, but it will certainly help you to better understand how the world functions.

1.1   The Relevance of Economics

> **LO1**   Describe why economics is a very relevant discipline by demonstrating that many of the controversies in our society have a distinct economic flavour.

Both of your authors believe that an introductory course in economics will be one of the most important and useful courses that you will take in your college/university career. Unfortunately, economics has acquired a reputation for being both dull and overly theoretical. Nothing could be further from the truth. In fact, economics is at the centre of many vital controversies that engage us all. One of the most effective ways to demonstrate this is to look at four important issues that are provoking public opinion and creating debate within the discipline.

Controversy One

- Economic growth is something that we should applaud and always strive to achieve.

PRO: In real terms—that is, after removing the effects of inflation—the economic well-being of the average Canadian has more than doubled in the last two generations. This has meant a huge improvement in people's lives and has come about not because the world has become fairer but because of economic growth. As a result of this growth, the individual choices available to Canadians—ranging from education and career choices to lifestyle choices—have increased significantly. In addition, economic growth contributes a great deal to social and political stability simply because finding ways to divide up a growing pie is much easier than trying to divide one that is shrinking, or even one that is stable. Over just the last few generations, economic growth has accompanied a falling birth rate, which has meant lower population growth rates. This provides welcome relief from threats to the environment.

CON: There is no question that economic growth has the benefits mentioned above but to embrace growth for growth's sake ignores the reality that there are substantial costs associated with growth as well. The threat of global warming is a classic example. If the pattern of growth we have been experiencing continues in the next couple of decades this threat will intensify—perhaps with catastrophic results. We need to shift our attitudes about economic growth by recognizing that it is the *type of growth* that really counts. If consumers become more conscious about the environmental effects of their purchases (electric cars, solar-powered houses, etc.); if large corporations accept the idea that more environmentally sound investment spending is worth the additional price tag; and if governments provide a judicious mix of incentives and tax policies that encourage more output but lower carbon emissions—then we could make a step toward embracing continued growth while addressing the more negative spinoffs of a serious problem that is clearly on humankind's horizon.

Controversy Two

- Government should use its policy tools—Employment Insurance, welfare coverage, and pension plans—to channel more income from the rich to the poor and encourage firms to pay a living wage to their employees.

PRO: There is too much poverty in this country, and the gap between the rich and poor is growing. In Canada, the average after-tax income disparity has increased dramatically in the last twenty years. While it is true that during this period those in both the lowest and the middle income quintile experienced a percentage rise in average income, those in the highest quintile saw their incomes rise by much higher percentage. Consequently, the difference between the top and the bottom income group increased by over 40 percent. This is a significant rise in income disparity, and a first move to reversing this trend would be an increase in government benefits and in pressure put on firms to pay a living wage.

CON: The solution to the problem of poverty is not to pay higher taxes for more unemployment coverage, welfare, and public pensions nor is it to impel firms to pay what some consider is a "living wage." Higher taxes, and higher wages, are a disincentive to the job creators who work hard and are willing to take on the risks of expanding more investment in the private economy. In contrast, polices that stimulate more growth will ultimately benefit all Canadians. This means lower, not higher, taxes. The ultimate answer to the issue of poverty is to grow the economy and enlarge the size of the income pie.

Controversy Three

- The time has come to introduce road pricing in congested Canadian cities to reduce traffic during peak "rush hours."

PRO: Economists know that people respond to financial incentives, and charging drivers for using highways and bridges (more during rush hours and less for off-peak times) will spread out road usage and thereby reduce congestion. This would also raise needed revenue for more road construction—highways and bridge are very expensive to build—and save lives through reduced accident rates.

CON: Our system of unrestricted and free road usage has worked for generations, and road pricing would simply be another government tax grab and an unfair burden on Canadian drivers. It would also mean that those with low income would pay proportionately more of their incomes for road fees than those with high-incomes. This is true for both drivers and non-drivers, since the bulk of all our purchases are transported by road.

Controversy Four

- Globalization only benefits large multinational corporations, not ordinary people.

PRO: Globalization leads to large corporations moving jobs from rich countries to poor countries. This creates a race to the bottom among the poor countries that are willing to maintain weak environmental- and labour-standards regulations to appease the corporations and thus attract new foreign investment. While this lowers the cost of production for the corporation, it comes at the expense of the people whose middle-level (and relatively well paid) jobs have been displaced.

CON: Globalization means increased world trade, and economic theory clearly demonstrates that more trade means more benefits to those who trade. In fact, UN statistics demonstrate that, within the last twenty years, a billion people in the world have been pulled up out of "abject poverty" (less than $1 a day income) into higher-income categories. Much of this is the direct result of the increased trade associated with globalization.

We could have examined many other controversies in addition to the four above. For example: Should we introduce private-market elements into our public health care system? Is a carbon-trading system better that a carbon tax to fight climate change? Are economic incentives better than government regulations for addressing environmental issues? But the point is made: Our complex society with its diverse interests and political views is rife with controversy.

We have put these four sample debates up front not because economists have the right answers to any of them but to demonstrate that almost any issue that faces us today as a society—and thus also as individuals—has an economic dimension. In short, economics is one of the most relevant courses you will ever take.

1.2   What Is Economics?

LO2   Define economics and then make a distinction between microeconomics and macroeconomics.

From our discussion of controversies, are we to conclude that any person's position on these issues is just a matter of opinion? No, we do not believe that. Economics, as you will discover, provides a unique way of approaching various controversies, helping us reach reasoned positions on these and other vital issues. You will, we hope, discover the importance of economic theories in doing this.

We all ask questions to make sense of our existence. The answers to What? When? and Where? are reasonably straightforward, because they involve questions of fact. But the most important question of all, and often the most difficult to answer, Why?, always involves cause and effect and addresses the relationship between facts. Few believe that things occur randomly in our world; we recognize that actions are related. A road is covered in ice and a car crashes; a person smokes heavily for forty years and dies of lung cancer; an army of beetles bores into a tree trunk and the tree falls. Explaining why these things happen is a matter of uncovering the links between phenomena. That is what theory is all about: explaining *why* things happen.

But in order to begin an explanation, we first need to know *what* happened. Theory is *not* just a matter of opinion; it is built on the solid foundation of facts, or what are termed **positive statements**. Positive statements are assertions about the world that can be verified using empirical data. "Sidney Crosby scored thirty goals last year" and "The unemployment rate in Canada is presently 6.2 percent" are both positive statements, because their truth can be verified by finding the appropriate data. But "Sidney Crosby should score more goals" or "The unemployment rate in Canada is far too high" are both what are termed **normative statements** because they are based on a person's beliefs or value systems and, as such, cannot be verified by appealing to facts. Note also that positive statements may not always be easily or readily verified. For instance, the statement "It will rain tomorrow" is a positive statement despite the fact that it cannot be verified until tomorrow.

Economic theory uses what we call the **scientific method** to find a relationship between positive statements. Consider the statement *If the price of apples decreases then people will buy more apples.* In order to build a theory about apple prices and apple purchases, we need to set up a simple *hypothesis.* For example, the lower the price of a product, the greater the quantity that will be bought. But along with the hypothesis, we need to define the terms involved. What types of apples are we talking about—Granny Smiths, Galas, or all types? And what price are we considering? Wholesale? Retail? Vancouver prices? Ottawa prices? Besides this, we need to spell out the assumptions (conditions) under which the hypothesis is true: People will buy more apples when the price falls, *as long as peoples' incomes do not fall* or *as long as the prices of other fruits remain the same,* and so on. The hypothesis is now ready for testing by gathering actual data and then accepting, rejecting, or possibly modifying the relationship under consideration.

The scientific method implies, among other things, that the results the theory predicts should be valid regardless of who does the testing and that different people should be able to repeat the tests and obtain the same results.

However, some say there is no way economics can ever be considered a true science, even though the discipline does use the scientific method. In some senses, this is true. Economics can never approach the pure sciences in terms of universality. It can never predict how every (or even one particular) consumer will react to a drop in the price of apples. But it can predict how the average consumer will react; that is, it deals in *generalities.* It is also true that the time lag between the cause and the effect is often far longer in the social sciences than it is in the pure sciences, which makes theorizing a lot more difficult. But to criticize economics because it is too abstract and unrealistic is not really fair. In fact, it might be suggested that the more realistic economic theory becomes, the less valuable it is. No one expects a map to be "realistic"; if it were, every tree, house, and road would have to be drawn to scale, and the scale would have to be 1:1! So, while a map can capture a great deal of reality, trying to make it even more realistic can also make it less useful.

The scientific method can be used to explain the apple market.

Kentoh/Dreamstime.com

You may have heard jokes about economists, such as, "What do you get when you put five economists in the same room? Answer: Six opinions." Economists do often disagree with one another, as is easily seen in the popular media. This is a natural by-product of a discipline that is part science and part art. An important reason for such disagreement is that, like everyone else, economists have particular sets of values accumulated over a lifetime, and these values vary, sometimes radically, from person to person. Nonetheless, if each of us uses the scientific method in developing our arguments, lively debate can be fruitful despite the different value systems with which we started.

It is also true, however, that there is wide agreement among economists on many questions—which is remarkable given that they ask a wide variety of questions many of which are not asked in other disciplines. For example, why do firms produce some goods internally and buy others in the market? Why do nations sometimes both export and import similar goods? Why does society provide some things to children without charge (education) but not other things (food)?

Trying to understand economic theory can be challenging and certainly does not come easily, but the rewards, in terms of a better understanding of the world we live in, are great. Economics is the study of ideas, and in a very real way this is the most important thing you can study. One of the most famous of twentieth-century economists, John Maynard Keynes, said: "The ideas of economists, both when they are right and when they are wrong, are more powerful than is commonly understood. . . . But soon or late, it is ideas, not vested interests, which are dangerous for good or evil."[1]

There are any number of definitions of economics but most agree that it is about how best to use the resources we have available. For instance:

> Economics studies the ways that humans and societies organize themselves to make choices about the use of scarce resources, which are used to produce the goods and services necessary to satisfy human wants and needs.

This gives us the essence of the discipline. We need, then, to understand how societies attempt to satisfy seemingly unlimited human wants in the face of limited resources. As we shall see in the next section, it means that we humans are faced with some very difficult choices.

 ADDED DIMENSION

Just What Is an Economist?

When a person says "I am an economist" he/she might actually be doing one of a variety of jobs. Broadly speaking these work types fall into four categories.

You are familiar with the first type: *academic economists* who are found teaching in educational institutions. In addition to their teaching duties, these economists also engage in research activities and sometimes are seconded to governments and other organizations for specific projects or advisory duties.

The second type might be called *financial economists*. These work in the many wealth-management firms and often engaged directly with members of the general public to help them plan their retirement or establish a safe, steady flow of income from the money they have acquired through their work or from an inheritance. These economists might also be employed at banks engaging in similar work.

Next, we have what might be called *corporate economists* who, as the name implies, are employed by large corporations (banks would be included here as well) and are engaged in relevant research, and sometimes branch out into broad management roles of many types, such as vice-president of domestic operations.

Finally, we have what might be called *governmental or organizational economists*. These work directly for provincial or federal governments in virtually every ministry collecting and analyzing data and are often engaged in research. Others work for any one of over 500 non-governmental organizations such as the World Bank, the International Monetary Fund, Oxfam, or the World Wide Fund for Nature.

If you are still wondering what you might major in, you might well consider economics. This is a major that closes no doors (for example, many students of law majored in economics as undergraduates) and will likely sharpen your ability to think logically and engage in the process of sound decision making—in work as well as in life.

Finally, we need to make the distinction between macroeconomics and microeconomics. **Macroeconomics** is the study of how the major components of the economy—such as consumer spending, investment spending, government policies, and exports—interact. It includes most of the topics a beginning student would expect to find in an economics course: unemployment, inflation, interest rates, taxation and spending policies of governments, and national income determination.

Microeconomics studies the outcomes of decisions made by individual people and firms, and includes such topics as supply and demand, the study of the costs of production, and the nature of market structures—competitive or monopolistic. This distinction can be described metaphorically as a comparison between the use of the wide-angle lens and the telephoto lens of a camera. In the first

---

[1] John Maynard Keynes, *The General Theory of Employment, Interest and Money* (1936).

instance (macroeconomics) we see the big picture. In the second instance (microeconomics) a very small part of that big picture appears in much more detail. Most colleges and universities offer a separate course for each of these fields of study.

The following table will help you understand the distinction between macro- and microeconomics.

Topic	Micro View	Macro View
Prices	Of particular products, such as gasoline or real estate	Of a composite of all prices, such as the Consumer Price Index, and the inflation associated with prices rising
Production	Of particular firms, such as Ford or Apple, or industries such as wheat or oil	Of the whole economy, such as Canada's gross domestic product and its influence on economic growth
Incomes	Wages by profession or factor incomes such as the amount going to wages and profits	Total (national) income, regardless of the source, and how this relates to the economic well-being of the population
Employment	By firm, industry, or occupation	Overall national employment (and unemployment)
Taxes	As they affect individual take-home pay or the profits of a particular firm	As they affect total consumption spending and government revenue

 TEST YOUR UNDERSTANDING

Find answers on the McGraw-Hill online resource.

1. Identify each of the following statements as either positive (P) or normative (N).

   a) The federal government's budget this year is the largest in history.

   b) The national debt is at a manageable level and therefore is nothing to worry about.

   c) The price of gasoline is higher than it needs to be.

   d) Rising Canadian exports are creating many new jobs in the country.

2. Identify which of the following topics would likely appear in a microeconomics course (Mi) and which in a macroeconomics course (Ma).

   a) The price of iPods

   b) Unemployment rates

   c) The presence of monopolies

   d) The rate of economic growth

SECTION SUMMARY

a) Economics is a social science that uses the *scientific method* in order to construct theories which explain the world about us. In doing so, it attempts to explain the relationship between events looking at actual data. It needs to be careful to distinguish between facts (positive statements) and personal beliefs (normative statements).

b) The discipline of economics is subdivided into microeconomics, which studies the decisions made by people and firms, and macroeconomics, which studies the results of those decisions, how the major components of the whole economy interact, and how well an economy achieves economic goals such as full employment and economic growth.

1.3   Efficiency and Allocation

> **LO3** Demonstrate that because scarcity, choice, and opportunity cost are at the heart of economics, efficiency—both productive and allocative—provides a major cornerstone.

Economists put a great deal of emphasis on scarcity and the need to economize. Individual households face income limitations and therefore must allocate income among alternative uses. Most individuals also face a scarcity of time and must somehow decide where to spend time and where to conserve it. In the same sense, an economy as a whole has limited resources and must allocate those resources among competing uses.

Thus, economists see **resources** (or **factors of production** or **inputs**) as *scarce* in the sense that no economy has sufficient resources to be able to produce all the goods and services everyone wants. Even though there may be some people who say they have all they want, there are millions of people who possess a seemingly endless list of wants, with millions more like them waiting to be born. Since the economy cannot produce all that everyone wants, the resources available for production are scarce.

And exactly what constitutes a resource? Well, of the myriad different resources that are or have been used to produce goods and services, economists are generally agreed that there are, in fact, four categories: labour, capital, land, and enterprise. **Labour** refers to a broad spectrum of human effort, ranging from the work of a skilled physician to that of a construction worker. **Capital** is made up of the tools, equipment, factories, and buildings used in the production process, and is not to be confused with financial capital, such as money, stocks, or bonds. **Land** is defined as any natural resource, such as fertile soil, forests, fishing grounds, or minerals in the ground. Finally, **enterprise** (some economists prefer the term *entrepreneurship*) is that very special human talent that is able to apply abstract ideas in a practical way. Entrepreneurs are innovators who invent new products or devise new forms of organization and are willing to take the risks to see such projects through to successful completion.

In a market economy, incomes are earned through the payment of wages, interest, rent, and profits to the private owners of the factors of production: labour, capital, land, and enterprise. The general term **wages** includes all forms of payment to the various kinds of labour services such as salaries, stock bonuses, gratuities, commissions, and various employee benefits. **Interest** means payments to the factor of real capital. **Rent** is the income received for the use of the factor of land, such as royalty payments for a stand of timber. Finally, **profit** is the return on entrepreneurial effort.

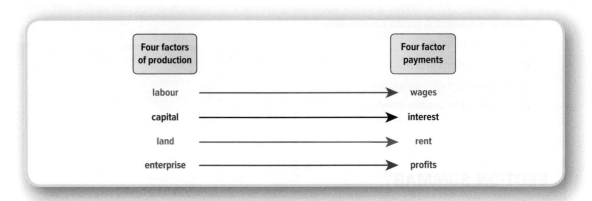

Now, the way these four factors of production are combined is what economists mean by a **technology**. A technology does not necessarily imply the use of things like machines or computers; it simply means a method of production. However, whatever technology we use to produce goods and services, the fact remains that we are simply not capable of producing everything people want.

Therefore, some kind of mechanism must be put in place for choosing what will be produced and, by implication, what will not be. This is why economics is sometimes called the *science of choice*.

In short:

> In the face of people's unlimited wants and society's limited productive resources, choice becomes a necessity. Because of these choices, the decision to produce one thing means that some other thing will not be produced.

This last point is so fundamental that economists have coined a special term to identify it: **opportunity cost**. For instance, suppose that government is considering the purchase of new military aircraft with a price tag of $5 billion. In the conventional sense, that is their cost. However, economists would argue that it is more revealing to measure the cost of the helicopters in terms of, say, ten hospitals that will not be built because a budget constraint does not allow the purchase of both. Opportunity costs can thus be defined as what must be given up as a result of making a particular choice: in this case, the hospitals are given up for the aircraft.

Let us continue to look at the concept of opportunity cost by shifting to a microeconomic context. Suppose it is lunchtime on Saturday and you have just returned home from your morning job at a local convenience store. You have the whole afternoon ahead of you and are wondering what best to do. One alternative would be to have a nice sleep on the sofa. You deserve it. Alternatively, you might hang out with friends at the mall. But then, you are going to see them all at tomorrow's game. Perhaps a nice bike ride? After all, it's a pleasant afternoon and you could do with some good exercise. But at the back of your mind you realize you need to study because two exams are coming up next week. What to do? Since you obviously can't do everything, you have to make a choice, and it really comes down to either studying or cycling. And what are the costs of each?

Well, economists look at costs in terms of benefits forgone. If you were to study for the rest of the afternoon, you will be sacrificing the benefits of cycling—better health, feeling good, and being fitter. And what if you were to go cycling instead? Well, this would mean that the benefit of a better grade in the upcoming exams is compromised. Notice that we have not viewed the costs in this situation in terms of money, which is the normal way, because many sacrifices in life do not involve money. But they are costly, nevertheless.

Recognizing that there are opportunity costs involved in making any decision forces us to rethink our idea of what we mean by "free." Simply because money does not change hands does not mean that a product is free. For the individual, the constraint is either a limited amount of time, as we just saw, or a limited amount of income. For example, you might think of the cost of going to two movies on the weekend as the sacrifice of a haircut. If you want to think of both these choices (two movies or one haircut) as each costing about $20, that is fine. But thinking of the one as costing the other is often more effective. In general, your income will not allow you to have everything you may want, and so you are forced to make choices about what you buy. And the cost of these choices can be measured in terms of what must be given up as a result of making the choice.

A classic example of this trade-off in economics is sacrificing consumer goods to produce more capital goods. As we shall see later in the chapter, nations that wish to grow more quickly can achieve this if they produce more factories, tools, and equipment—more capital goods—that are used to make other goods. But, of course, an increase in capital goods production necessarily means a reduction in the output of **consumer goods and services**, which are defined as products used to satisfy human wants and needs. Note that only consumers buy consumer goods and only firms (or governments) buy capital goods.

Our next example of opportunity cost is one that faces many students who have to choose between taking more courses at college or university and continuing to work in a part-time job. If a student is presently taking three courses and working twenty hours a week, and feels that this is a full-time load, then taking five courses next semester may well mean giving up the job. Thus, the opportunity cost of the two extra courses is the income sacrificed as a result of no longer working

IN A NUTSHELL ...

It's Saturday night and Alex has $12 left in his entertainment budget. Which to choose ... ?

The concept of opportunity cost reminds Alex that **you can't have both.**

at the part-time job. We should also point out that there must be some benefit to be gained from the alternative you do choose. For instance, returning to our example above, if you chose the two movies, the benefit from that choice, in your view, exceeds (or at least equals) the opportunity cost of the haircut.

A society faces a similar set of choices, imposed not by limited income but by a constraint on the quantity and quality of the available factors of production.

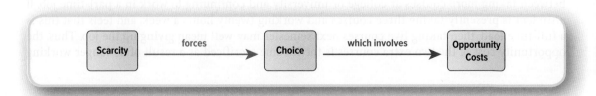

TEST YOUR UNDERSTANDING

3. Below is a list of economic goods. Decide whether each is a consumer good (C), a capital good (K), or possibly both (B), depending on the context in which it is used.

a) a jackhammer

b) a carton of cigarettes

c) an office building

d) a toothbrush

e) a hammer

f) a farm tractor

4. Below is a list of resources. Indicate whether the resource in question is labour (L), capital (K), land (N), or enterprise (E):

a) a bar-code scanner in a supermarket

b) fresh drinking water

c) copper deposits in a mine

d) the work of a systems analyst

e) the first application of e-technology to an economics textbook

f) an office building

IT'S NEWS TO ME …

The U.S. federal government has been subsidizing public school breakfast programmes in various designated poverty-area school districts for a long time. In a recent year over $3.3 billion flowed through this effort reaching 16 million schoolchildren in 89,000 schools. Children from households designated as "in poverty" received these meals free of charge.

Canada does not have such a federal programme but some provinces and a few large cities do have a limited version of free school-breakfasts in some schools.

Recently, we see an example of the private sector stepping up in this effort when the Vancouver Sun newspaper sponsored an "Adopt-a-School Breakfast Club" at the local Douglas Road Elementary School in Burnaby. The SFU Beedie School of Business then agreed to do a follow-up study of this experiment and reports a "significant positive impact on student performance and a reduction in the incidence of late attendance."

Source: *Star Power Reporting,* Summer 2016.

I. Is there such a thing as a "free meal"?

   a) Yes, if the money comes from private donors.

   b) Yes, if the money is provided by the government.

   c) Yes, if it is just a transfer of resources from one sector to another.

   d) No, if it involves the use of resources which have alternative uses.

II. In economics, what does "free" mean?

   a) It does not involve a cost to taxpayers.

   b) It does not involve a cost for consumers.

   c) It does not lead to the reduction of depletable resources.

   d) It does not require a payment by anyone.

III. How would an economist measure the cost of these school meals?

   a) The dollar costs of the labour and materials involved in their production

   b) The value of other activities that the funds could have been spent on

   c) The total cost to taxpayers or the corporate donors of providing for these meals

   d) The costs that parents would otherwise have incurred in providing these meals

The Importance of Efficiency

Perhaps not surprisingly, economists, like any other group of people, do not agree on the most important economic goals that an economy should pursue. Nor are they necessarily in agreement on the best methods to achieve those goals. However, they are generally in agreement on the importance of *efficiency*. In fact, this term crops up with great regularity in economic literature. As a result, it is important to have some initial understanding of what the term means and why economists attach so much importance to it.

One of the simplest ways of expressing efficiency is to suggest that it implies getting the most for the least. For example, a technology that requires the use of 10 units of inputs in order to produce an output of 100 units of goods and services would be preferable to one that uses 20 units of inputs to produce those same 100 units of output. Similarly, the same technology that uses 10 inputs to produce 100 units of output would be considered inferior to another technology that uses those same inputs but could produce an output of 150 units. In other words, economists define **productive efficiency** in terms of the ratio of outputs produced to inputs used. Those technologies that produce at a lower ratio will result in lower costs of production.

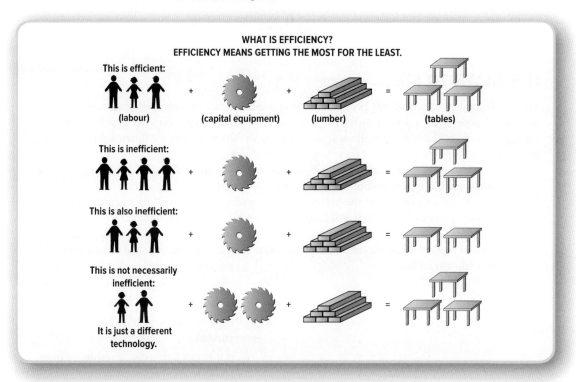

When you hear the term *productivity* used in the popular press it is usually referring to productive efficiency and is often measured in terms of the amount of output per hour of labour (or machine) input. If we want to be careful in our use of resources, it is of great importance that every one of us tries to be efficient. However, productive efficiency does not take us far enough. It is all right to produce things at low cost, but it is of little use if people are simply not interested in buying them. For instance, what would be the point of producing big-screen TVs at $50 each if they could only play programs in black and white? In other words, it is just as important to be efficient in what we produce as in how we produce it. Societies therefore need to ensure that the right type of products are produced, those that match the demands of the public. This is what economists mean by **allocative efficiency**.

Allocative efficiency puts the emphasis on the production of the right type of products. However, since all of us have different tastes, the right products for you might not be the right ones for someone else. So it is important that products be allocated efficiently among people. In *Filthy Lucre*, Joseph Heath gives an amusing example illustrating this idea. Imagine you have been given the task of allocating candies to a group of children at a birthday party. Trying to be fair, you count out the different types of candies so that each child gets an equal number of each. But you discover that some of the kids are not too happy. One is most upset because he has been given peanut brittle, and the poor boy is allergic to peanuts! One girl positively detests raisins. Some kids hate dark chocolate, others milk chocolate. You can see that without increasing the overall quantity of candies, you could increase the general happiness of these children just by redistributing the candies. The kids might easily handle this allocation themselves by trading, something that children tend to do quite naturally.

So what is the best method of allocating goods and resources? How do we decide who gets what? In general, there are five different ways:

1. *First come, first served.* This is the time-honoured way of distributing things in high demand. It means that products are given according to the order in which people apply whether that's done by lining up, by phoning in, or by registering on a website.
2. *Lottery.* Everyone is entered into a draw and has an equal chance of obtaining the product.
3. *Sellers' preference.* This means that the seller of the product makes the decision on who gets what and what criteria will be used.
4. *Government decree.* Here, the ruling authority decides on the allocation.
5. *The market.* This is where the forces of demand and supply determine how much each buyer obtains. To a large extent, this is based upon how much people are willing to pay and how much they can afford. It is this method of allocation that gets the most attention from economists and our next chapter will try to explain in some detail.

SECTION SUMMARY

a) Scarcity forces choice (for society, government, and the individual), and choice involves an opportunity cost which is the sacrificed benefit of the next best alternative.

b) Efficiency implies that economies make the best use of their resources and technology. There are two major types of efficiency: productive efficiency and allocative efficiency, and both are important.

c) There are five different allocative methods: first come, first served; lottery; sellers' preference; government decree; and the market.

1.4 The Power of Trade

LO4 Explain why greater trade results in more productive economies.

In the last quarter-century we have been witnessing something very significant: economies that put an emphasis on the market system and international trade—Canada, South Korea, and China, for example—continued to enjoy economic growth and a rising standard of living for their citizens, while economies that rely more on centrally controlled systems and self-sufficiency—the former USSR or today's Cuba and North Korea, for example—faltered.

Adam Smith, the father of economics, gave us a simple but elegant idea that goes a long way toward explaining why, throughout history, some economies have prospered, while others have not. This is the recognition that *voluntary trade* always benefits both parties to the trade. If two peasants voluntarily trade a sack of rice for two bags of carrots, then we can assume that they both must feel that they have benefited, as otherwise they would not have done it. If you buy a slice of pizza and a pop for lunch for $3.50, then we must assume that you feel you have gained by giving up the money and receiving the lunch—otherwise, why did you do it? Likewise, the owner of the business that sold you the lunch must feel that she gained, or she would not have been willing to offer the lunch for sale. There is a gain to both parties engaged in voluntary trade.

It follows that *the more trade there is, the greater are the overall benefits that accrue to those engaged in the trade.* It comes as a surprise to many people that the same principle that applies to individuals in this regard also applies to nations. We can demonstrate that this is true by using the concept of opportunity costs to construct a simple example of two hypothetical countries—Athens and Sparta—each of which produces only two goods: bread (a consumer good) and plows (a capital good).

Suppose that the maximum quantities that can be produced of each product are (in thousands of units):

Athens	20 bread	or	10 plows
Sparta	10 bread	or	20 plows

If each country is self-sufficient (no trade between them) and each devotes half its resources to producing the two products, the output in each country would be:

Athens   10 bread   and   5 plows
Sparta   5 bread   and   10 plows

Clearly, the combined output of the two economies is 15 units of bread and 15 plows. It is also clear that Athens is far better at producing bread and Sparta is much better at producing plows. Thus, if the two countries could overcome their sense of rivalry, and if Athens concentrated on producing bread and Sparta on producing plows, then the total combined production of the two countries would be:

Athens   20 bread   (no plows)
Sparta   20 plows   (no bread)

With specialization, the two countries can produce a combined total that is five more of each product (20 units of bread and 20 plows) than when each was self-sufficient. This illustrates why specialization is so important—countries enjoy more output when they do what they do best (produce only the products with the lowest opportunity cost) rather than trying to produce both products. For Athens, the opportunity cost of producing plows is a large sacrifice in bread production, while in Sparta the opportunity cost of producing bread is a large sacrifice in plow production. However, when they both specialize in what they do best, big benefits can be gained. But to reap the benefits of specialization, trade becomes imperative—unless, of course, the countries are happy just consuming one product (which is most unlikely). In our example, if Athens were to trade 10 bread for 10 plows from Sparta, both countries would finish up with 10 units of bread and 10 plows—an improvement for both.

Returning to our original point about market economies versus planned economies, we know that specialization and trade are maximized when markets are used extensively. This simple illustration helps us understand that every economy faces important choices about what to produce. Let us expand on this point by turning to the three fundamental economic questions faced by every economy.

SECTION SUMMARY

Greater specialization and trade can make economies more productive.

1.5   The Three Fundamental Questions

LO5   Explain the three fundamental questions that all societies must address.

A broad perspective on the discipline of economics can be obtained by focusing on the three fundamental questions of economics: *What? How?* and *For whom?* That is, economics is about what and how much gets produced, how it is produced, and who gets it.

What to Produce?

As we have just seen, underlying the question of *what* should be produced is the reality of scarcity. Any society has only a fixed amount of resources at its disposal. Therefore, it must have a system in place to make an endless number of decisions about production, from big decisions such as whether the government should buy more military aircraft or build more hospitals down to more mundane ones such as how many brands of breakfast cereal should be produced.

If we decide to produce hospitals, should we produce ten without research facilities for the study of genetics or eight without and one with such facilities? Should society exploit natural resources faster to create more jobs and more tax revenue, or slower to conserve these resources for the future? Should our resources be directed toward more preschool day-care facilities so that parents are not so tied to the home? Or should those same resources be directed toward increasing the number of graduate students studying science and technology so that the Canadian economy can win the competitive international race in the twenty-first century?

Let us once again emphasize that no economist would claim to have the *right* answer to any of these questions. That is no more the role of an economist than it is of any other member of society. What the economist can do, however, is identify and measure both the benefits and the costs of any one answer—of any one choice.

How to Produce?

Let us move on to the second fundamental economic question that every society must somehow answer: *What is the most appropriate technology to employ?* We could reword this question by asking *how* we should produce what we choose to produce.

For example, there are many ways to produce ten kilometres of highway. At one extreme, a labour-intensive method of production could be used involving rock crushed with hammers, roadbed carved from the landscape with shovels, and material moved in wheelbarrows. The capital equipment used in this method is minimal. The labour used is enormous, and the time it will take is considerable. At the other extreme, a capital-intensive method could be used involving large earthmoving and tarmac-laying machines, surveying equipment, and relatively little—but more highly skilled—labour. In between these two extremes is a large variety of capital–labour mixes that could also produce the new highway.

The answer to the question of how best to build the highway involves, among other things, knowing the costs of the various resources that might be used. Remember that technology means the way the various factors of production are combined to obtain output. The most appropriate technology for a society to use (the best way to combine resources) depends, in general, on the opportunity costs of these resources. Thus, in the example above, the best way to build a highway depends on the opportunity costs of labour and of capital as well as the productivity of each factor.

Capital-intensive technologies using heavy equipment are the most appropriate methods in many countries because they are relatively cheap.

Steve Allen/Getty Images

For Whom?

Now, let's move to the third fundamental economic question that every society must somehow answer: *For whom?* Here, we are asking how the total output of a society should be shared among its citizens. In the end, we are really asking how the total income in a society should be distributed. Should it involve an equal share for all, or should it, perhaps, be based on people's needs? Alternatively, should it be based on the contribution of each member of society? If so, how should this contribution be measured—in numbers of hours, in skill level, or in some combination of the two? Further, how should we define what constitutes an important skill and which ones are less important?

Wrapped up in all this is the question of the ownership of resources and whether it is better for certain resources (such as land and capital) be owned by society as a whole or by private individuals. In short, the *for whom* question cannot be adequately addressed unless we look at society's attitude toward the private ownership of resources and the question of who has the power to make crucial decisions.

You can see that in addressing the *for whom* question, other questions about the fairness of income distribution, the role of incentives, and the ownership of resources all come into play. John Stuart Mill pointed out, nearly 150 years ago, that once an economy's goods are produced and the initial market distribution of income has occurred, society can intervene in any fashion it wishes in order to redistribute such income; that is, there are no laws of distribution other than the ones that society wants to impose. Whether this observation by Mill gives enough consideration to the incentive for productive effort remains an open question to this day.

GREAT ECONOMISTS: JOHN STUART MILL

John Stuart Mill (1806–73) is considered the last great econo-mist of the classical school. His *Principles of Political Economy*, first published in England in 1848, was the leading textbook in economics for 40 years. Raised by a strict disciplinarian father (James), John Stuart began to learn Greek at the age of three, authored a history of Roman government by 11, and studied calculus at 12—but did not take up economics until age 13. Not surprisingly, this unusual childhood later led to a mental crisis. Mill credited his decision to put his analytical pursuits on hold and take up an appreciation of poetry as the primary reason for his recovery. He was a true humanitarian, who held a great faith in human progress, had a love of liberty, and was an advocate of extended rights for women.

Pictorial Press Ltd/Alamy Stock Photo

How these three fundamental questions actually get answered depends, to a large extent, on the way that different societies organize themselves. Let us now look at the four types of economic organization.

SECTION SUMMARY

The three fundamental questions that all societies must somehow answer are:

- What is the right combination of consumer goods to produce, and what is the right balance between consumer goods and capital goods?
- How should these various goods be produced?
- Who is to receive what share of these goods once they are produced?

1.6   Four Types of Economies: The Four Cs

LO6 Explain the four different ways that economic societies can be organized.

Societies have, throughout history, developed systems to coordinate their economies in order to answer the fundamental questions of what to produce, how, and for whom. Each of the numerous possible systems has used some blend of the four Cs: cooperation, command, custom, and competition. Whatever blend was used, it was a reflection of who owns and who controls the important resources of that economy.

Co-operative Economies

In the foraging societies of prehistory, the few tools, weapons, and cooking items the people possessed were commonly owned, belonging to the band as a whole and not to any one individual. Since these bands were nomadic, they did not preserve or store food, because carrying it around was difficult and seemed unnecessary. They lived very much a day-to-day existence. This meant that these societies did not produce a surplus above subsistence that could be used to support non-producers. Consequently, since all were producers of the necessaries of life, they had no armies, no leaders, no priests, and no ruling hierarchy. The result was a society where decision making was democratic and egalitarian. In short, the members of foraging bands relied primarily on *cooperation* with one another in order to survive the dual threats of starvation and predators.

It is difficult, if not impossible, to find an example of a country in the modern age in which the economic decisions are made cooperatively by all the citizens. However, we can find many examples of small, self-contained communes in which there is an emphasis on common ownership and consensus decision making. Included would be the kibbutzim of Israel or religious communities such as the Hutterites in the Canadian Prairies or (historically) the Doukhobors of British Columbia. Even the internal decision-making process in today's large corporations, one that stresses the use of team play and group consensus, is a form of cooperative behaviour. This same point can be made in reference to most family units within our society. Further, what, if not cooperation, would one call the fact that nearly half of all adults in our society engage (at some point in their lives) in voluntary unpaid activities such as coaching soccer or helping out at a local hospital or community centre?

Command Economies

There are many examples of command economies in the ancient world. In the empires of ancient Egypt and Rome, we see that the most important resource was slaves, and whoever owned slaves was, almost by definition, rich and powerful. An elite group headed by a pharaoh or emperor made decisions and dictates that were ruthlessly enforced. The fundamental questions of what to produce, how to produce, and who reap the rewards of production were answered by this elite, whose decisions were unopposed.

To find examples of command economies in the modern world, we need look no further than the brutal totalitarian regimes of the twentieth century: fascism in Italy, Nazism in Germany, and communism in the Soviet Union. In all three examples the state, which was totally controlled by the very few, had significant influences on the *what, how,* and *for whom* questions and also controlled many aspects of routine life.

Communism, as seen in the twentieth century, owes a great deal to the writings of Karl Marx, who was outraged at the cruel injustices of early capitalism. He felt that what he termed the "internal contradictions of capitalism" would eventually lead to its self-destruction. What he meant by this is that while production, as a result of the industrial revolution, was becoming increasingly "socialized" in that it needed a great deal of planning and coordination in order to mass-produce products, the ownership was still based upon the private ownership of resources. Marx argued that this "dichotomy" would eventually lead to its collapse. While this, of course, never happened, many subsequent critics of capitalism (the market system) were concerned at what they considered to be the chaotic and unpredictable nature of the system. In the twentieth century a number of countries, including France and Sweden (and in an extreme form the USSR), all introduced state planning into their economies to prevent then from suffering oversupply, bottlenecks, and shortages so that state investment behaviour could be modified in a timely fashion to reduce the incidence of market disequilibrium.

 GREAT ECONOMISTS: KARL MARX

Karl Marx (1818–1883) was a social philosopher and founder of scientific socialism. He is the author of the *Manifesto of the Communist Party* and of the seminal work *Das Kapital* (1869).

He was born in Trier, Prussia (Germany) to a Jewish family who converted to Protestantism. After studying in Germany, he spent most of his adult life in England.

His very name has called forth huge doses of vitriol, disgust, and hatred, and in almost equal measure he has been admired, revered, and worshipped; but what is undeniable is that he is difficult to ignore and has proven to be one of the most influential figures in history. The number of people who hate Marx without actually having read him is probably equal to those who venerate him also without bothering to do much reading.

© Ingram Publishing

Customary Economies

In the age of feudalism in Europe, which filled the vacuum left by the fall of the Roman Empire, we see power centred on the ownership of land. The landowners—royalty, the aristocracy, and the Church—were very powerful, and everyone else knew his or her place within this rigidly hierarchical system. It was the age of *custom* (or *tradition*), which dictated who performed which task—sons followed the work of their fathers and daughters followed the roles of their mothers—and traditional technology was superior to new ways of doing things, since it had been tried and tested and could therefore be trusted. Above all, custom required that serfs turn over a portion of their produce to the feudal lords.

Even very traditional societies can have a small role for the market.

Marion Bull/GetStock.com

In the modern age, custom is very much alive in a number of Islamic republics such as Iran, where traditional values, enforced by religion, dominate most aspects of people's lives. But we also see that custom has a part to play in our own society. For instance, movie theatres provide expensive washrooms free of charge while charging exorbitant prices for popcorn and soft drinks, rather than providing free drinks and charging a fee to enter the washrooms. A much more significant example is the custom in our market economy of allowing people to pass wealth on to their children in the form of inheritance, so that the income of the future generation is often based less on what they contribute to the economy and more on who their parents were.

Competitive Economies

The Industrial Revolution effectively brought feudalism to an end and ushered in the machine age. It is here that capital, in the form of factories, machines, and railroads, became the economy's most important resource, and the industrial capitalists became very rich and powerful, while the ordinary people, the land-less, capital-less working class, were left with nothing but their labour to sell. This marks the birth of the market system with its emphasis on *competition* as the coordinating mechanism and the private ownership of resources as a main characteristic. Many people are surprised to learn how modern an invention this form of economic organization really is. What today we call the *market economy* did not begin to emerge until approximately 250 years ago, although, of course, specific *markets* have existed for thousands of years.

Competition is the primary feature of today's capitalistic, or market, economies. Here, the forces of demand and supply determine most of what is produced, as well as what technology is used and how much people earn. In a pure market economy, government plays no role whatsoever. This means, for instance, that corporations would be totally unregulated, schools and hospitals would all charge fees, and those unable to work would simply receive no income and no support from government at all.

Mixed Economies

In today's world, there are probably no examples of countries using only a single one of the Four Cs. Instead, all modern economies use a combination of all four, with competition and command being the dominant ones. Perhaps this is due to the rise in the importance of knowledge as the most important resource in today's fast-changing world; it is difficult to monopolize ownership of this particular resource. At the same time, today we see only a single example of a purely command economy: North Korea. Even "communist" China and Cuba have opened up their economies to some private ownership and enterprise.

This blend of competition and command includes the large role played by governments through the provision of, for example, health care and education, leaving the private sector to provide the majority of consumer goods for personal use. The role of government in our economy represents the command function in the sense that the taxes needed to finance government activities are not voluntary, and in the same sense, the various laws governing human conduct and behaviour must be adhered to. This recognition of the roles of both market and government in our society is what we mean by the term *mixed economy*. On the one hand, few of us would wish to live in a pure market economy where, for example, young children from dysfunctional families with no income would be left to starve, and where there was no standardization of weights and measures and no "rules of the game" concerning the way business is conducted—think of meat inspection by government as an example. On the other hand, few of us would want to live in a society where every decision about our lives was made by government. Some blend of the market, and the efficiencies achieved from its use, combined with the order and fairness imposed by government, does seem to be the way to go. However, exactly what constitutes the right amount of government intervention imposed upon the market is, of course, an issue of endless debate.

You have no doubt heard the terms *capitalism* and *socialism* used in the media and in conversation. Just what do these terms mean to an economist? Basically, they distinguish different degrees in the competition–command mix used by society to organize its economic affairs and answer the three fundamental questions. In socialist Sweden, for example, the state (government) plays a much larger role in the economy than it does in the capitalist United States. While Sweden does not have central planning, as found in the former Soviet Union, and does have private property, it also has high taxes and high levels of social spending. Eighty percent of the work force is unionized; everyone receives a generous number of paid vacation days per year and generous sick leave benefits at nearly full pay. Sweden has a wide-ranging unemployment insurance plan, which also includes mandatory retraining for those laid off from their jobs. The Danish government mandates an investment fund requiring that corporations give a percentage of their profits to the central bank, which would then release these funds back to the companies in times of recession, with stipulations on how they were to be spent. By contrast, the United States has almost none of this and relies on a policy of *laissez-faire*, which minimizes the role of government and emphasizes the role of the market in the economy. Canada, France, and the United Kingdom lie somewhere in the middle of these examples.

SECTION SUMMARY

There are four fundamental ways to organize society:

- Cooperation (foraging societies)
- Command (totalitarian states)
- Custom (traditional, religious societies)
- Competition (market economies)

1.7   Production Possibilities

LO7   Use the production possibilities model to illustrate choice and opportunity cost, as well as efficiency and unemployment.

Economists often use economic models when trying to explain the world in which we live. Let us explain what we mean by a *model* and look at one example. Imagine walking into the sales office of a condominium project under construction. Part of the sales presentation is a model of the entire project sitting on a table. You would have no trouble recognizing the model as an abstraction, a representation of what the building will eventually look like. This is true despite the fact that many of the details such as the elevators, interior walls, and appliances are absent from the model.

So, too, in making their models, do economists abstract from reality only the features that are relevant, ignoring extraneous material. Clearly, economists cannot construct a physical model of the economic world. Instead, the level of abstraction is greater because the model is all on paper and often in the form of numbers, equations, and graphs. But for all that, the aim is not to make the simple and straightforward seem unnecessarily complicated. Just the opposite: the goal is to make the complexities of reality as clear and simple as possible.

Let us now construct a very basic model of a country's production possibilities. This allows us to return to a point that we made earlier: every economy is faced with the constraint of limited resources. Imagine a society that produces only two products—cars and wheat. Let us then figure out what this economy is capable of producing if it works at maximum potential. This would mean that the society is making use of all of its resources: the labour force is fully employed, and all of its factories, machines, and farms are fully operational. But it means more than this. It also means that the society is making use of the best technology and, as a result, overall efficiency is being achieved. Given all of this, and since it can produce either cars or wheat, the exact output of each depends on how much of its resources it devotes to the production of cars or how much to wheat. Table 1.1 shows six possible output combinations, as well as the percentage of the economy's resources used in producing each combination. There may well be hundreds of possible combinations, but six is enough to make our model effective. In the table they are labelled A through F.

TABLE 1.1
Production of Cars and Tonnes of Wheat (millions of units)

Possible Output Combination	CARS % of Resources Used	Output	WHEAT % of Resources Used	Output
A	0	0	100	100
B	20	50	80	95
C	40	90	60	85
D	60	120	40	65
E	80	140	20	40
F	100	150	0	0

The finite resources available to this economy allow it to produce up to a maximum of 100 tonnes of wheat per year if 100 percent of its resources are used in wheat production. Note that this can be done only if no cars are produced (combination A). At the other extreme, a maximum of 150 cars per year can be produced if all available resources are used in car production. This, of course, would mean that no wheat is produced (combination F). There are many other possible combinations in between these two extremes, and Table 1.1 identifies four (B, C, D, and E).

Since we want to focus on what is produced (the outputs) rather than on what resources are used to produce them (the inputs), we can present Table 1.1 in the form of a production possibilities table, as is shown in Table 1.2:

TABLE 1.2
Production Possibilities for Cars and Wheat

	A	B	C	D	E	F
Cars	0	50	90	120	140	150
Wheat	100	95	85	65	40	0

Further, we can take the data from Table 1.2 and use it to graph what is called a **production possibilities curve**, which is a visual representation of the various outputs that can be produced. What appears in **Figure 1.1** is simply another way of presenting the data in Table 1.2.

Now, recall that:

> The three assumptions that lie behind the production possibilities curve are full employment, the use of the best technology, and productive efficiency.

On the one hand, if any one of these three assumptions does not hold, then the economy will be operating somewhere inside the production possibilities curve, as illustrated by point *u*, which is 90 cars and 65 tonnes of wheat. On the other hand, point *x* represents an output of 120 cars and 95 tonnes of wheat, which, given this economy's current resources and technology, is unattainable.

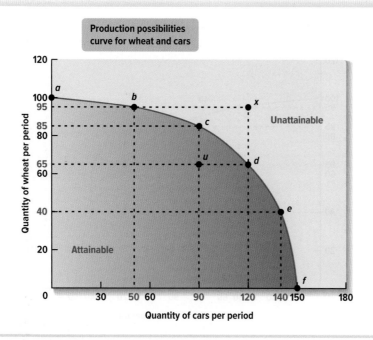

FIGURE 1.1   Production Possibilities Curve I

This society's limited resources allow for the production of a maximum of 100 tonnes of wheat if no cars are produced, as represented by point *a*. Moving down the curve from point *a*, we find other combinations of fewer tonnes of wheat and more cars until we reach point *f*, where 150 cars and no wheat are produced. Point *u* indicates either the underemployment of resources, inefficiency in resource use, or the use of inappropriate technology. Point *x* is unattainable.

The Law of Increasing Costs

Next, let us consider the actual shape of the curve. Why is it bowed out this way? We need to understand the implication of this particular shape. **Figure 1.2** will help.

Assume that our hypothetical economy is currently producing 95 tonnes of wheat and 50 cars, as illustrated by point *b* on the production possibilities curve. Then, assume that production decisions are made to reallocate 20 percent of the productive resources (labour, machines, materials) from wheat production to car production. This new output is illustrated by point *c*. Note that the opportunity cost of producing the additional 40 cars is *not* the additional 20 percent of resources that must be allocated to their production *but* the decreased output of wheat that these resources could have produced. That is to say, the additional 40 cars could only be obtained by reducing the output of wheat from 95 tonnes to 85 tonnes. Thus, 40 more cars cost 10 tonnes of wheat. This can be restated as *1 more car costs 0.25 tonnes of wheat* (10 divided by 40). This seems clear enough, but we are not done.

Next, assume that society, still at point *c*, decides to produce even more cars, as illustrated by moving to point *d* (120 cars and 65 tonnes of wheat). This time, an additional 20 percent of the resources produces only 30 more cars (90 to 120) at a cost of 20 units of wheat (85 to 65). This can be restated as *0.67 tonnes of wheat for every additional car.* This is considerably more than the previous cost of 0.25 units of wheat per car. Another shift of 20 percent of resources would move the economy from point *d* to *e*, which adds only 20 more cars at a cost of 25 tonnes of wheat. Now each additional car costs 1.25 (20 divided by 25) units of wheat. **Table 1.3** summarizes all the figures above.

We have just identified what economists call the **law of increasing costs**. This law states that as the economy's total production of any single item increases, the per-unit cost of producing additional units of that item will rise. Note that this law is developed in the context of a whole economy and, as we will see in later chapters, need not apply to the situation of an individual firm.

As the total production of cars increases, the rising per-unit cost of cars gives the production possibilities curve its bowed-out shape.

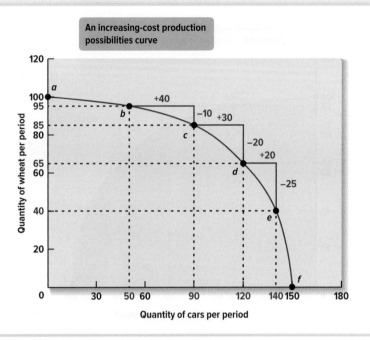

FIGURE 1.2   Production Possibilities Curve II

At point *b*, 95 tonnes of wheat and 50 cars are being produced. If this society decided that it wanted 40 more cars (point *c*), then 10 tonnes of wheat would have to be sacrificed. Thus, 1 more car would cost 0.25 tonnes of wheat. Moving from point *c* to *d* would increase car production by 30 (90 to 120) at a sacrifice of 20 tonnes of wheat (from 85 to 65). In this instance, 1 more car costs 0.67 tonnes of wheat. Moving from point *d* to *e* would increase car production by only 20 (from 120 to 140), while wheat production would drop by 25 (from 65 to 40). Thus, the cost of 1 more car rises to 1.25 tonnes of wheat.

TABLE 1.3
Opportunity Cost per Car

Graphical Movement	Gain in Cars	Opportunity Costs in Wheat	Opportunity Cost per Car
a to *b*	50	5	0.10
b to *c*	40	10	0.25
c to *d*	30	20	0.67
d to *e*	20	25	1.25
e to *f*	10	40	4.00

But why does the per-unit cost of cars increase—what is the reason behind the law of increasing costs? The answer is that not all resources are equally suitable for the production of different products. Our hypothetical society has a fixed amount of resources that are used to produce different combinations of both wheat and cars. However, some of these resources would be better suited to producing cars, whereas others would be better suited to producing wheat. An increase in the production of cars requires that some of the resources currently producing wheat would need to be reallocated to the production of cars. It is only reasonable to assume that the resources that are reallocated first are the ones that are relatively well suited to the production of cars and are perhaps not so well suited to farming. (Perhaps some of the farm workers are immigrants with manufacturing experience, or maybe some of them are allergic to the dust present in the harvesting of wheat.) After all this has taken place, if even *more* cars are to be produced, the only resources left to reallocate will be ones that are not very well suited for the production of cars. Therefore a larger quantity of less well suited resources will have to be reallocated to obtain the desired increase in car production. This will increase the per-unit cost of cars, because a larger sacrifice of wheat production will be required.

 TEST YOUR UNDERSTANDING

5. Given the accompanying figure:

   a) If society produces 1000 units of butter, what is the maximum number of guns it can produce?

   b) Suppose that society produces the combination shown as point *b* on the production possibilities curve. What is the cost of 1000 additional units of butter?

   c) Would the opportunity cost of 1000 additional units of butter be greater, the same, or smaller as society moves from point *c* to *d*, compared with a move from point *b* to *c*?

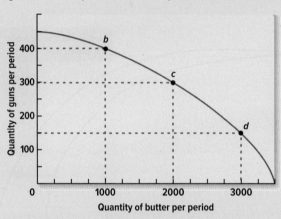

Shifts in the Production Possibilities Curve: The Causes of Economic Growth

A production possibilities curve is like a snapshot of an economy: it shows in one quick diagram what our hypothetical economy is capable of producing at a particular moment. But economies change from year to year—usually, although not always, for the better. The sources of economic growth have been debated for centuries, but our simple model is able to explain some of the important aspects of growth. **Figure 1.3**, for instance, illustrates three ways growth can be shown diagrammatically. In **Figure 1.3A** we see that maximum car production has increased; the PP (production possibilities) curve has shifted out along the horizontal axis. Previously, the maximum amount of cars the country could produce was 150 but this has now increased to 180. In **Figure 1.3B** we see a shift up the vertical axis showing that the maximum production of wheat has increased from 100 tonnes to 120 tonnes. Then in **Figure 1.3C** we see a shift out in the curve indicating that the output of both products increases.

We have to be careful about how we interpret these shifts. Remember that a production possibilities curve shows us what an economy is *capable* of producing; it does not show us what it is *actually* producing. The rightward shift from PP1 to PP2, then, does *not* say that this is economy is now producing more goods and services. It simply shows that it is capable of producing more products; in other words, its potential has now improved. And what could have brought about this change? The conditions under which we constructed the curve provide a clue.

We have assumed that the economy is operating at maximum efficiency: that is to say, it is fully employing its resources and using the best technology. An improvement in either the quantity or quality of resources, or a change in technology, will therefore shift the curve in one of the three ways just illustrated. An increase in quantity of resources could mean things such as increased population, the discovery of new oil fields, or perhaps improved infrastructure. An increase in quality of resources could be the result of a better educated work force, smarter machines, or perhaps whole new ways of organizing production (remember the legendary story of the importance of assembly line production introduced by Henry Ford).

Looking back at **Figure** 1.3A we see what might have been better machines in car production, while in **Figure** 1.3B it might have been better fertilizers used in the production of wheat, and in **Figure** 1.3C perhaps it was the computer revolution that improved the production possibilities of both products.

Now let us use **Figure** 1.4 to explain a phenomenon that students often find, at first, hard to believe. Start with the economy operating efficiently on the production possibilities curve PP1 at point *a*. Now let us assume that a new technology becomes available that has application *only* in car production. This is illustrated by a shift outward in the curve along the horizontal axis as seen in the new curve PP2. Next we recognize that there are three possible results. First, as one would expect, the same quantity of wheat production but more consumer car production can be produced as represented by *b*. Second, more of *both* goods can also be produced, as represented by point *c*. And third, this economy could now increase the production of wheat if the same number of cars were produced (point *d*) *despite* the fact that this new technology could only be applied to car production. As pointed out above, these last two points are obtained by shifting some resources from car production to wheat production. Thus, we see that even when

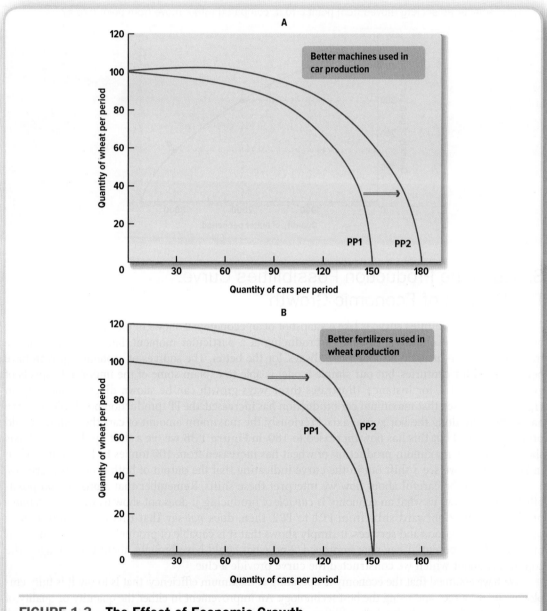

FIGURE 1.3   The Effect of Economic Growth

In graph A, the production possibilities curve has shifted from PP1 to PP2, which shows that this economy is now capable of producing more cars but not more wheat. In B, the shift from PP1 to PP2 shows that the economy is now capable of producing more wheat but not more cars. In C we note that more of both goods can be produced.

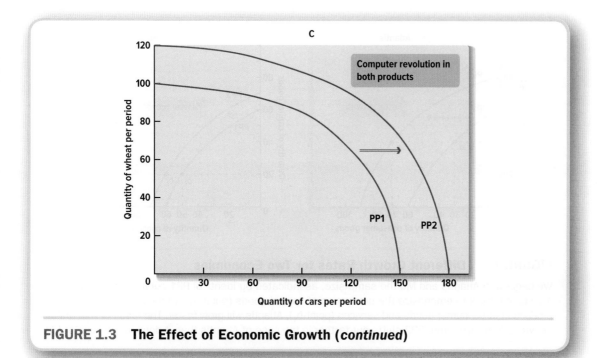

FIGURE 1.3   The Effect of Economic Growth (*continued*)

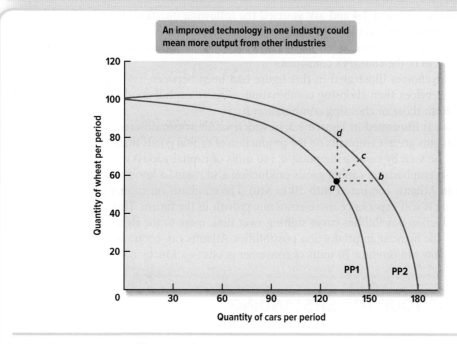

FIGURE 1.4   The Effect of Technological Change on the Production Possibilities Curve

Start at point *a*, which is a point of efficient production on PP1. An improvement in technology in the car industry shifts the production possibilities curve to PP2. This creates three possible results. First, the same quantity of wheat and more cars can now be produced, as represented by point *b*. Alternatively, more wheat as well as cars could be produced, as represented by point *c*. Point *d* represents the third possible result, which is more wheat along with the same quantity of cars, despite the fact that the technological change was in the consumer goods and services industry.

technological change is restricted to one particular industry, the benefit can be transferred to the other industry as well—technological change in car production can raise wheat production.

This emphasizes the important role of technological change. It widens the choices (that word again!) available to society and is often seen in a positive light. Alas, technological change also has costs, and this is a subject that will receive our attention later.

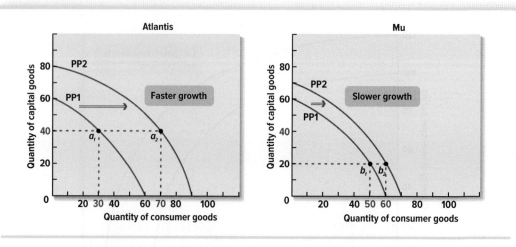

FIGURE 1.5   Different Growth Rates for Two Economies

We begin with Atlantis and Mu the same size, as indicated by identical PP1 curves. However, since Atlantis chooses to emphasize the production of capital goods (point a_1), while Mu emphasizes the production of consumer goods and services (point b_1), Atlantis will grow faster. The result of this faster growth is that, over time, PP2 shifts out farther in the case of Atlantis than it does in the case of Mu.

Now, look again at **Figure 1.4** and ask yourself the following question: Which of the three new possible combinations is preferable? Since the choice had been between two consumer goods, such as wheat and cars, we cannot give a definitive answer to this question without knowing something about the preferences of the country's consumers.

However, if the choices illustrated in this figure had been between, say, capital goods and consumer goods and services, then choosing combination *d*—more capital goods—leads to significantly different effects from those of choosing combination *b*.

This difference is illustrated in **Figure 1.5**, in which we show two different economies. Let us assume that Atlantis puts greater emphasis on the production of capital goods than does Mu (which chose point *b*). This can be seen by comparing point b_1 (40 units of capital goods) with point b_1 (20 units of capital goods). This emphasis on capital goods production also means a lower production of consumer goods (30 units in Atlantis compared with 50 in Mu). The emphasis on capital goods production in Atlantis means that it will experience more economic growth in the future. This faster growth is illustrated by the production possibilities curve shifting, over time, more to the right in the case of Atlantis than in Mu. After the increase in production possibilities, Atlantis can continue producing 40 units of capital goods but now can produce 70 units of consumer goods (a_2). Mu, by contrast, can produce only

 TEST YOUR UNDERSTANDING

6. Assume that the economy of Finhorn faces the following production possibilities:

		QUANTITIES PER YEAR		
	A	B	C	D
Grain	0	25	40	50
Tools	12	8	4	0

a) Draw a production possibilities curve (PP1). Label the horizontal axis Tools and the vertical axis Grain. Now assume the development of a new technology that can be used only in the tool industry, and that it increases tool output by 50 percent.

b) Draw a new production possibilities curve (PP2) that reflects this new technology.

c) If Finhorn produced 12 units of tools per year, how many units of grain could be produced after the introduction of the new technology?

60 units of consumer goods and services while maintaining capital goods production at the original 20 units (b_2). All of this is a result of a different emphasis on the output choices by the two economies.

A sage of some bygone age once said, "There is no such thing as a free lunch." We can now make some sense out of this idea. Producing more of anything—a lunch, for example, which involves the use of scarce resources—necessarily means producing less of something else. The lunch might be provided free to the people who eat it, but from the point of view of society as a whole, it took scarce resources to produce it, and therefore the lunch is *not* free.

SECTION SUMMARY

The production possibilities model is an abstraction and simplification that helps illustrate

- the necessity of choice in deciding what to produce (movement along the PP curve)
- the opportunity cost involved in making a choice (movement along the PP curve)
- inefficient production and the consequences of unemployed resources (inside the PP curve)
- economic growth (outward shift in the PP curve)

1.8   Macroeconomic Goals

> **LO8**   List the economic goals of society and explain why they are often difficult to achieve.

The production possibilities model highlights important economic issues, including the costs of unemployment and the benefits of growth. But, more importantly, it graphically illustrates the important concepts of choice and cost. The dilemma facing policy makers in all governments is the same one that faces all of us daily: how to satisfy conflicting goals. We know we cannot have everything in life and so we have to make choices. You have six hours available. You want to go for a walk. You want to visit friends. You want to study economics. What do you do? You could abandon two of your goals and decide to study for the whole six hours. More probably you will decide to divide your time among the three activities. But do you allocate two hours to each activity or rank them in importance and spend more time on things you consider of greater importance? These same considerations also face policy makers who have to decide among a number of competing goals.

This raises the important question:

> What are the typical economic goals of a modern market economy such as Canada's?

Goal 1: Improved Standard of Living

An important goal for most of us is achieving and maintaining a decent standard of living. Each generation wants to improve on what the previous generation had and to leave the next generation even better off. Our standard of living is mostly determined by our income levels, and Canada has been successful in producing comparatively high incomes for its citizens, as **Figure 1.6** illustrates.

In Canada, each decade has seen an improvement in real incomes (after the effects of inflation are removed), from an average of just over $7000 in the 1930s to almost $48 000 per person in recent years. It is important to realize that higher incomes do not simply translate into bigger houses or more cars. A richer country has the power to enrich the lives of its people with better health care and education. It can also allow citizens to enjoy a clean environment, open parklands, and access to cultural pursuits. It is in this broad sense that people define the standard of living, rather than simply in terms of the quantity of goods produced. **Table 1.4** confirms what most Canadians realize: that they live in one of the richest countries in the world. (The incomes are shown in U.S. dollars in terms of purchasing power. We have omitted a few smaller countries such as the Bahamas and Cayman Islands from the rankings.) Of the G8 countries (the world's biggest and most economically advanced nations), Canada is third, behind Norway and the United States, and has an average income over four times the world average.

If a country has a high national income, it does not guarantee that all of its citizens will enjoy a high standard of living. And it is equally true that not all citizens of poor countries are doomed to low standards of living. A high and growing national income, though, is a necessary condition for a high standard of living for most citizens. This brings us to the second goal: achieving economic growth.

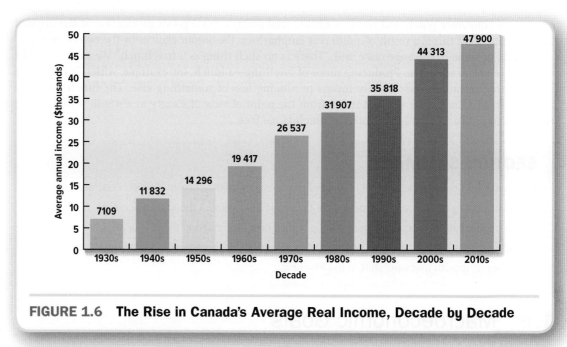

FIGURE 1.6   The Rise in Canada's Average Real Income, Decade by Decade

Source: Adapted by the authors from the Statistics Canada publication "Historical Statistics of Canada," 1983, Catalogue 11-516, July 29, 1999, and from Statistics Canada CANSIM database, http://cansim2.statcan.ca, Tables 380-0002, 380-0016, and 051-0001, July 7, 2016.

TABLE 1.4
Average Incomes for G8 and Selected Countries in 2015

	Average (Mean) Income (in US$)	World Rank	G8 Rank
Norway	93 820	1	
U.S.	54 960	5	1
Canada	**47 500**	11	2
Germany	45 790	15	3
U.K.	43 170	17	4
France	40 580	22	5
Japan	36 680	24	6
Italy	32 790	26	7
Russia	11 400	59	8
China	7 820	71	
Average of 172 countries	10 437		

Source: International Bank for Reconstruction and Development/The World Bank: *World Development Indicators*, 2016. Creative Commons Attribution CC BY.

Goal 2: Economic Growth

Canada's present high standard of living is as much the result of actions in the past as it is the result of actions in the present. Past actions have provided a social and economic climate that encourages productivity and inventiveness. The growth of production (or *real GDP*, as it is termed) is necessary in order to improve our standard of living and is essential in order to keep pace with the growth in Canada's population. As **Figure 1.7** shows, just a small change in growth rates can have a big impact on incomes and the standard of living.

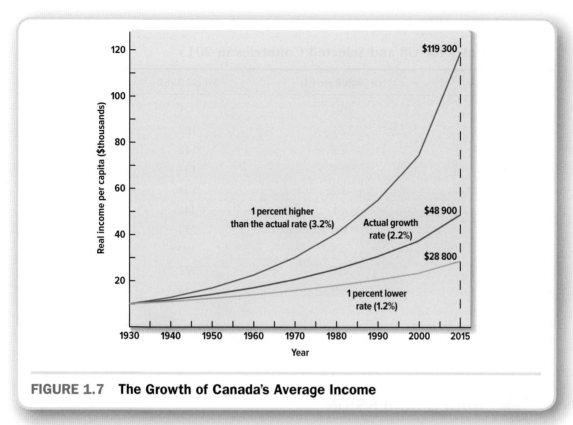

FIGURE 1.7   The Growth of Canada's Average Income

Source: Adapted by the authors from the Statistics Canada publication "Historical Statistics of Canada," 1983, Catalogue 11-516, July 29, 1999, and from Statistics Canada CANSIM database, http://cansim2.statcan.ca, Tables 380-0017 and 051-0001, July 7, 2016.

Over the past 80 years or so, the average income of Canadians has grown at a rate of 2.2 percent per year. While this may not sound impressive, it resulted in a quadrupling of incomes over this period. And an improvement of just 1 percent on our actual performance would have created an average income per person of over $119 000, more than double our present average. (By the same token, a slightly lower rate of 1.2 percent per year would have left the average Canadian with an income today of just under $29 000.)

High growth rates do indeed increase our prosperity, but keep in mind that economic growth can be a two-edged sword. It can improve our standard of living, but unless the growth is handled sensibly, it can also have exactly the opposite result. This is because economic growth can often cause high rates of pollution, traffic congestion, noise, and stress. It can also lead to resource depletion and pressure on our natural environment, all of which can lower our quality of life despite leaving us with higher incomes. Table 1.5 gives data on Canada's growth rate performance compared with the rest of the world. It should be noted that developed nations seldom have annual growth rates above 4 percent. High growth rates are often associated with developing nations who are starting from a very low level of GDP.

Goal 3: Full Employment

Ensuring that all citizens who want to work have jobs appears to be a straightforward goal. Since most people's incomes are derived from employment, few of us could survive for long without working. However, when we look at the question closely, we discover that the goal of full employment may be difficult to achieve. For instance, does it mean that everyone should have a job (whether they want one or not), or does it apply only to those who are willing and able to work? If we believe that it means the latter, should our goal be to ensure that such people have jobs, any jobs, or that they have jobs that are satisfying or stimulating, jobs they have been trained or educated for, or jobs that are highly paid? If we grant that the goal of absolute full employment for all citizens all the time may be an impossibility, then what level of unemployment is acceptable? Two percent? Five percent? Ten

TABLE 1.5
Growth Rates for G8 and Selected Countries in 2015

	Growth Rate (%)	World Rank	G8 Rank
Ethiopia	10.2	1	
U.S.	2.4	107	1
U.K.	2.2	112	2
Germany	1.5	134	3
Canada	**1.2**	**138**	**4**
France	1.1	141	5
Italy	0.8	153	6
Japan	0.5	157	7
Russia	−3.7	172	8
China	6.9	14	
(182 countries)			

Source: *World Economic Outlook*, IMF, April 2016. Creative Commons Attribution CC BY.

 ADDED DIMENSION

Technology, Growth, and Personal Fortunes

The idea that new technology leads to increased economic growth is not new—think of the steam engine, steel, railroads, and electricity in the nineteenth century and mass-produced automobiles, the airplane, television, antibiotics, and the Internet in the twentieth. Each of these innovations stimulated whole new industries and generated significant economic growth. As well, various individuals certainly became very rich.

As we shift our focus to the current century, we see a continuation of new technology in the production of physical things such as Apple's iPhone/iPad and Tesla Motors' electric car.

However, a whole new set of technologies has emerged: Microsoft's operating system for the personal computer, Amazon's giant Internet department store, Facebook's and Twitter's amazingly successful social networks, YouTube's vast viewership, and Google with its one billion search requests a day.

Not only have these twenty-first century technologies stimulated growth, but they have also created enormous fortunes for the innovators and each of the above-listed companies trace back to identifiable individuals who started with little more than an idea. Most of us have heard their names: Steve Jobs (Apple), Elon Musk (Tesla), Bill Gates (Microsoft), Jeff Bezos (Amazon), Mark Zuckerberg (Facebook), Chad Hurley (YouTube), Jack Dorsey (Twitter), and Larry Page and Sergey Brin (Google). These individuals are all now multibillionaires.

percent? As **Figure 1.8A** demonstrates, Canada's record on employment is a bit mixed. Although unemployment dropped steadily during the 1990s, it has barely gone below 6 percent in the last thirty years. Canada's unemployment record might be regarded as average at best. **Table 1.6** shows that in 2015 Canada was sixth among the G8 countries and eightieth in the world.

Goal 4: Stable Prices

High rates of inflation can cause a great deal of damage to an economy and its people. But before we jump to the conclusion that a zero rate of inflation (no change in the overall price level) is desirable,

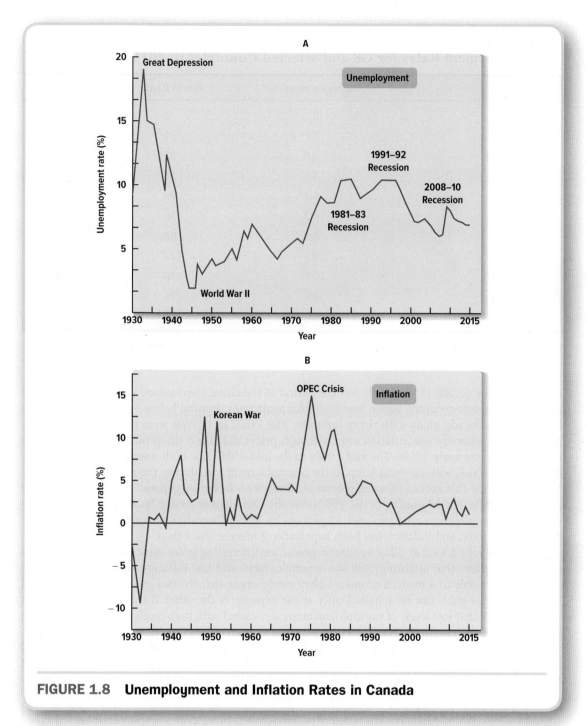

FIGURE 1.8   Unemployment and Inflation Rates in Canada

Adapted from the Statistics Canada publication "Historical Statistics of Canada," 1983, Catalogue 11-516, July 29, 1999, and from Statistics Canada CANSIM database, http://cansim2.statcan.ca, Tables 109-5304, 282-0002, and 326-0021, July 7, 2016.

remember that we are looking at things from a macroeconomic perspective. Thus, while higher prices may be viewed with alarm by consumers, they may be greatly welcomed by sellers. Perhaps some increase in prices is desirable. But how much—1, 3, or 5 percent per year? Furthermore, is inflation such a bad thing if wages, pensions, and welfare rates can be increased by the same amount? As we shall see in Chapter 4, the major problem is not so much inflation itself—though it does cause a great deal of suffering for a number of groups in society—but the fact that its unpredictability can cause uncertainty and thus adversely affect economic growth.

Figure 1.8B shows Canada's experience with inflation since the 1930s. Looked at in combination with the unemployment rates, some interesting features become apparent. We can see that the 1930s was a period of high unemployment and low inflation (in fact, a period of falling prices, or deflation,

TABLE 1.6
Unemployment Rates for G8 and Selected Countries in 2015

	Unemployment (%)	World Rank	G8 Rank
Qatar	0.3	1	
Japan	3.7	31	1
Germany	5.0	55	2
Russia	5.1	58	3
U.S.	6.2	75	4
U.K.	6.3	76	5
Canada	**6.9**	**86**	**6**
France	9.9	123	7
Italy	12.5	140	8
Mauritania	31.0	174	
Average of 174 countries	8.6		

Source: International Bank for Reconstruction and Development/The World Bank: *World Development Indicators 2016*. Creative Commons Attribution CC BY.

until 1933). The decade of the 1930s was the period of the Great Depression. World War II brought about an economic recovery, which saw unemployment rates dipping below 5 percent for the first time in over a decade, along with rising inflation. The 1950s and 1960s were periods of low unemployment and generally low inflation rates, although prices did take a sharp turn upward during the Korean War in the early 1950s. The mid-1960s to the mid-1980s saw both unemployment and inflation starting to rise, with an extra jump in the unemployment rate during the recession of the early 1980s. Following this recession, unemployment, along with inflation, generally fell throughout the rest of the 1980s. The beginning of the 1990s saw the Canadian economy head into another recession, with unemployment rising to over 11 percent by 1992. Thereafter, unemployment fell consistently in the 1990s, and inflation has been kept under 2 percent since then.

Before we take a look at other economic goals, one interesting point must be mentioned. Many economists believe that attaining *both* low unemployment and low inflation rates concurrently is virtually impossible in a modern economy. They would argue that the two goals are in conflict and that one of these goals can be achieved only at the expense of the other. If this is true, Figure 1.8 should indicate that low levels of unemployment are associated with high levels of inflation and high unemployment with low inflation. A cursory glance at the two curves does not show an obvious relationship of this nature, although until the mid-1960s there were a few periods when the two did seem to move in opposite directions. However, since 1967, the two curves have, if anything, moved together more or less in tandem. In other words, when inflation rates were high, so, too, were unemployment rates. All of this raises interesting questions that we will try to answer in later chapters.

Canada has performed well in controlling inflation in recent years and has, along with most of the G8 countries, one of the lowest rates in the world, as Table 1.7 demonstrates. Another feature that Table 1.7 shows is that for many countries—especially the industrialized ones—the possibility of *deflation* is as likely as that of inflation.

Goal 5: Viable Balance of International Trade

Canada is truly one of the world's greatest trading nations, and many would suggest that our high standard of living is a result of this. Economists would tend to agree that international trade is beneficial for all nations, since it encourages specialization and promotes competition. As we saw in the section "The Power of Trade," it is better for a nation to concentrate its resources on producing the goods and services that it can produce more efficiently and cheaply than can others. Then, with the proceeds, it is able to buy those things that others can produce more cheaply. The difference between what a nation exports and what it imports is known as the *balance of trade*. It may not be possible to

TABLE 1.7
Inflation Rates for G8 and Selected Countries in 2015

	Inflation Rate	World Rank	G8 Rank
Lebanon	−3.7	1	
France	0.0	36	1
Italy	0.0	37	2
U.K.	0.1	38	3
U.S.	0.1	40	4
Germany	0.2	46	5
Japan	0.8	59	6
Canada	1.1	69	7
Russia	15.5	150	8
Venezuala	121.7	155	
Average of 155 countries	3.9		

Source: International Bank for Reconstruction and Development/The World Bank: *World Development Indicators*, 2016. Creative Commons Attribution CC BY.

have a trade surplus (when a country exports more than it imports) every year, but a country will also experience a number of economic problems if it consistently has trade deficits. **Figure 1.9** shows the Canadian experience for the last four decades.

As the figure illustrates, the 1990s saw a dramatic upswing in international trade for Canada, mainly as a result of the North American Free Trade Agreement (NAFTA). In the past decade, Canada has exported and imported as much as 45 percent of its national income, though in recent years that figure has declined to just over 30 percent. But we should add a note of caution: it is not enough for a country to sell abroad as much or more than it buys. The types of things a country sells can make a difference to its long-term welfare. For example, is a country selling manufactured and processed goods or selling off its raw materials? Is it selling goods and services or selling off its assets? These are important questions.

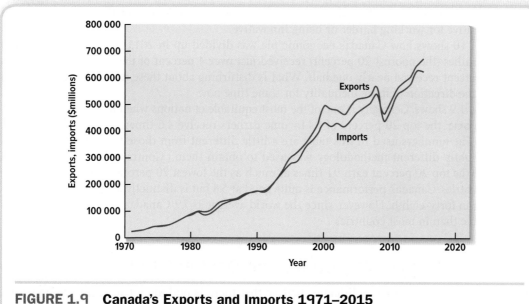

FIGURE 1.9   Canada's Exports and Imports 1971–2015

Source: Adapted from Statistics Canada CANSIM database, http://cansim2.statcan.ca, Table 380-0027, January 23, 2014.

Interestingly, we could add that, except Russia and China, the world's top seven trading nations are also among the world's top-ranked GDP nations (Table 1.8).

TABLE 1.8
Exports for G8 and Selected Countries 2015

	Exports ($billions)	World Rank	G8 Rank
China	2524	1	
U.S.	2343	2	1
Germany	1771	3	2
Japan	863	4	3
France	861	5	4
U.K.	845	6	5
Italy	632	9	6
Canada	565	12	7
Russia	564	13	8
Netherlands	730	7	
Average of 146 countries	154		

Source: International Bank for Reconstruction and Development/The World Bank: *World Development Indicators*, 2016. Creative Commons Attribution CC BY.

Goal 6: An Equitable Distribution of Income

Someone once said that the true test of a civilized country is how it treats its poorest members. After all, from a social and moral point of view, an increase in a nation's prosperity could prove rather hollow if just a select few are able to enjoy and share in it. Large and growing disparities in incomes can lead to social unrest in the form of an angry population acting out of a sense of unfairness. Increased social apathy and cynicism, and polarized politics can easily follow. Thus, it is important that a country have a system in place to ensure that its democracy remains healthy. But just how equal incomes should be distributed is a vexing question. If everyone were guaranteed the same income regardless of their efforts, this would conflict with our desire to promote economic growth, since there would be little incentive for working harder or being innovative.

Figure 1.10 shows how Canada's economic pie was divided up in 2011. The lowest quintile of Canadian families (the poorest 20 percent) received just over 4 percent of the national pie, whereas the top 20 percent received nearly one half. What is disturbing about these figures is that the trend has been in the direction of more inequality for some time now.

As Table 1.9 shows, Germany is one of the most equitable of nations when it comes to the distribution of income: the top 20 percent of its income earners receive 4.6 times as much as the lowest 20 percent. (The numbers used in this table are a little different from those from Statistics Canada because a slightly different methodology was used to obtain them.) Contrast this with the United States, where the top 20 percent earn 9.1 times as much as the lowest 20 percent. Compared with the other G8 countries, Canada's performance is quite good at 5.8 but is distinctly average in world rankings, coming in forty-eighth. However, since the world average is 7.9, Canada's income distribution is more equitable than in most countries.

Goal 7: A Manageable Government Debt and Deficit

Most economists (unlike some politicians) believe that there is nothing intrinsically wrong with a government spending more than it earns in any one year—in other words, with running a budget deficit. It really depends on the state of the economy at any given time. But if a government runs deficits regardless of the state of the economy or runs deficits year in and year out, it is certainly

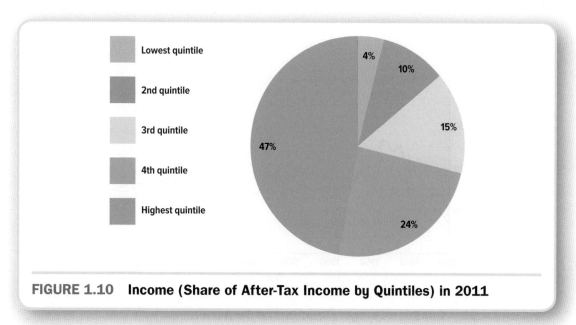

FIGURE 1.10   Income (Share of After-Tax Income by Quintiles) in 2011

Source: Adapted by the authors from Statistics Canada CANSIM database, http://cansim2.statcan.ca, Table 202-0405, January 13, 2014.

TABLE 1.9
Income Distribution for G8 and Selected Countries in 2015

	Income Distribution (top 20% vs. bottom 20%)	World Rank	G8 Rank
Germany	4.6	24	1
France	5.3	36	2
U.K.	5.3	37	3
Japan	5.4	42	4
Canada	**5.8**	**48**	**5**
Italy	6.7	60	6
Russia	8.2	74	7
U.S.	9.1	79	8
Haiti	32.5	106	
Average of 106 countries	7.9		

Source: International Bank for Reconstruction and Development/The World Bank: *World Development Indicators*, 2016. Creative Commons Attribution CC BY.

going to cause grief for the nation and create a higher public debt. It is prudent, then, for a government to exercise a certain degree of fiscal responsibility. A look at **Figure 1.11** shows how the Canadian government has performed in the fiscal stakes over the past 75 years. As we shall see in later chapters, it is perhaps unavoidable that a government might overspend in a depression (because of falling tax revenues) or during wartime (with rising expenditures), but it would be difficult to justify the high deficits that Canada experienced in the 1980s and early 1990s. It is only in recent years that the Canadian government seems to have corrected this trend.

   Table 1.10 points out two important ideas. First, it shows that countries suffering a recession tend to run up budget deficits as government tax revenues drop. The recession of 2008–12 resulted in a drop in national income for most countries, as well as an increase in budget deficits though these have grown smaller in recent years. Second, the table shows that Canada has outperformed most countries in managing its deficits. In fact, until the recession hit Canada, it had produced

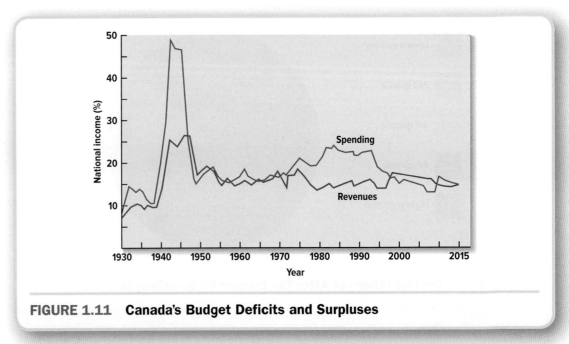

FIGURE 1.11   Canada's Budget Deficits and Surpluses

Source: Adapted from the Statistics Canada publication "Historical Statistics of Canada," 1983, Catalogue 11-516, Series H18 and H19-34, July 29, 1999; data regarding budget expenses and revenues from the Department of Finance Canada, Fiscal Reference Tables, July 2016. Reproduced with the permission of the Minister of Public Works and Government Services, 2014.

TABLE 1.10
General Government Surpluses/Deficits as % of GDP for G8 and Selected Countries in 2015

	Surplus/Deficit (% of GDP)	G8 Rank
Norway	+5.7	
Germany	+0.7	1
Russia (2013)	+0.3	2
Canada	−1.3	3
Italy	−2.6	4
France	−3.5	5
U.K.	−4.4	6
U.S. (2014)	−4.9	7
Japan (2014)	−6.2	8
Spain	−10.6	

Source: Based on data from *Economic Outlook No 87—June 2010* under OECD Economic Outlook under *Economic Projections* from OECD Stat Extracts, http://stats.oecd.org, accessed on January 22, 2014.

budget surpluses every year since the mid-1990s. Canada has ranked among the top G8 countries in managing its budget over the past ten years. (The figures are depicted in terms of the country's budget surplus or deficit as a percentage of its national income.)

We will discuss some theories about recessions and budget deficits in Chapter 7 and the realities in Chapter 13.

Finally, few people would disagree with the economic goals that we have briefly described, though they might argue about their order of importance. It is also clear that trying to achieve all seven goals simultaneously and consistently might be impossible. While some of these goals such as economic growth and full employment are complementary, others are likely to be in conflict.

We have already mentioned how trying to achieve full employment and stable prices at the same time may be very difficult. The same may also be true if we try to stimulate economic growth by providing tax incentives for corporations and high-income groups. While this may increase growth, it may also lead to an increase in the government's budget deficit and also adversely affect equitable distribution of income.

One of the major tasks of government then, is to try to balance these goals in a way that secures the long-term well-being of all of its citizens. To accomplish this difficult task, government has a number of tools at its disposal.

Tools for Achieving Macroeconomic Goals

Governments around the world pursue what economists call *fiscal* and *monetary policies* in an attempt to achieve the macroeconomic goals that they have decided are most important, particularly full employment, stable prices, and economic growth. The term *fiscal policy* refers to government's taxation and spending policies, which we will study in detail in Chapter 7. Decreases in taxes or increases in spending will stimulate the economy toward more growth and lower unemployment.

Conversely, increased taxes and lower spending tends to reduce growth and increase unemployment—but may well reduce inflation. *Monetary policy*, however, refers to the policies of the country's central bank regarding interest rates and the money supply. We will look at this in detail in Chapter 9. Lower interest rates have a stimulative effect on the economy, while higher rates are often used to control inflation.

There is also a category of policies that we call *direct controls*, which run the gamut from tariffs and quotas on imports, to minimum-wage laws, to antipollution regulations. These are used to address more specific macroeconomic goals.

We have discussed a number of issues in this chapter and have introduced a number of terms, some of which may be unfamiliar to you. It is not vital for you to understand everything all at once, and for that reason, we have avoided giving too many precise definitions. The topics discussed here, after all, are the subject matter of the whole book, and we will be returning to them throughout. It is hoped, however, that you can now at least taste the flavour of the various issues and debates.

SECTION SUMMARY

a) The overall performance of an economy is measured by how well it achieves these seven economic goals:

- improving the standard of living
- maintaining economic growth
- full employment
- stable prices
- a viable balance of payments
- an equitable distribution of income
- maintaining a manageable government debt and budget deficit

b) The three tools that policy makers use to achieve economic goals are

- fiscal policy
- monetary policy
- direct controls

 Study Guide

Review

WHAT'S THE BIG IDEA?

The production possibilities model is a good way to look at some of the important aspects of economics. Although it is used mostly to describe what happens in an economy, it is equally useful in adding insights to business or everyday life.

Imagine yourself as the CEO of production facility that has a maximum capacity to produce either 1000 trucks or 20/00 SUVs per week and you have decided to produce one-half each kind of vehicle—500 trucks and 1000 SUVs. Things are humming along fine for a while, but this begins to change. You notice that while you continue to sell all of the 1000 SUVs the demand for trucks must have increased, as your orders for more trucks begin to exceed the output of 500 per week. Since your *resources are scarce* (the plant is running at capacity) this apparent increase in the demand for trucks forces you to make a *choice*—sit tight and disappoint some of your potential truck customers or shift some production from SUVs to trucks. At this point, the visualization of the production possibilities curve pops into your head—SUVs on the vertical axis, trucks on the horizontal axis. More trucks carries an opportunity cost of fewer SUVs as you move along the downward-sloping curve. While this cost is currently 1 truck for 2 SUVs, you also remember that the *law of increasing cost* will mean that this cost will escalate, since the capital and labour resources used in production are not equally good at producing both trucks and SUVs—that is, the PP curve gets steeper as more trucks are produced.

Is there another way out of this "satisfy customer demand but absorb higher production costs" dilemma? Yes. You could expand you plant capacity (graphically, shift the PP curve out to the right) so that you could produce more trucks and keep production of SUVs at its current level. But this takes time and money and is thus a risk—one that may well pay off in the long run if truck demand reminds high, but still a risk.

Then you remember, way back in your Econ 101 course, the instructor saying, "Welcome to the real world of economics."

NEW GLOSSARY TERMS

allocative efficiency	land	productive efficiency
capital	law of increasing costs	profit
consumer goods and services	macroeconomics	rent
enterprise	microeconomics	resources
factors of production	normative statement	scientific method
inputs	opportunity cost	technology
interest	positive statement	wages
labour	production possibilities curve	

Comprehensive Problem

Questions

(LO 7)   **Table 1.11** contains the production possibilities data for capital goods and consumer goods in the economy of New Harmony.

TABLE 1.11

	A	B	C	D	E
Capital goods	0	8	14	18	20
Consumer goods	30	27	21	12	0

a) Use the grid in **Figure** 1.12 to draw the production possibilities curve for New Harmony, and label it PP1. Label each of the five output combinations with the letters *a* through *e*.

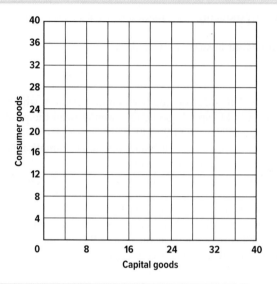

FIGURE 1.12

b) Assume that the people of New Harmony have decided to produce 12 units of consumer goods. How many units of capital goods could be produced?

c) Assume that the people of New Harmony have decided to produce 11 units of capital goods. Approximately how many units of consumer goods could be produced?

Answers

a) See the following figure:

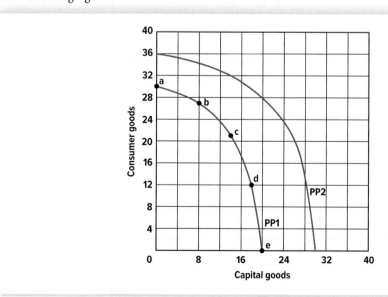

FIGURE 1.12   (COMPLETED)

b) 18 units of capital goods. This is combination D in Table 1.4.
c) 24 units of consumer goods. This is halfway between combinations B and C. Halfway between 21 and 27 consumer goods is 24 units.

Questions

d) What is the total cost of the first 14 capital goods produced?
e) Assuming the economy is producing combination C, what is the total cost of 6 additional consumer goods?
f) Assuming the economy is producing combination B, what is the approximate per-unit cost of an additional capital good?
g) Assuming the economy is producing combination C, what is the approximate per-unit cost of an additional capital good?
h) What law is illustrated in your answers to (f) and (g)?

Answers

d) 9 units of consumer goods. This means going from combination A, which entails 0 capital goods, to combination C, which entails 14 capital goods. This would mean the production of consumer goods would drop from 30 to 21, a difference of 9 units.
e) 6 capital goods. This means going from combination C to combination B. This would cause a drop in capital goods from 14 to 8, a difference of 6 units.
f) 1 consumer good. An additional capital good means moving from combination B to C. This would mean an additional 6 capital goods at the cost of 6 consumer goods, a drop from 27 to 21. If 6 capital goods cost 6 consumer goods, 1 capital good would cost 1 consumer good.
g) 2¼ (2.25) consumer goods. An additional capital good means moving from combination C to D. This would mean an additional 4 capital goods at the cost of 9 consumer goods, a drop from 21 to 12. If 4 capital goods costs 9 consumer goods, 1 capital good would cost 9/4 consumer goods.
h) The Law of Increasing Costs: The cost per unit of capital goods increases as we try to produce more capital goods.

Questions

i) Fill in Table 1.12 assuming that, 10 years later, the output potential of capital goods has increased by 50 percent while the output potential for consumer goods has risen by 6 units for each combination A through D in Table 1.12.

TABLE 1.12

	V	W	X	Y	Z
Capital goods	—	—	—	—	—
Consumer goods and services	—	—	—	—	—

j) Using the data from this table, draw PP2 on Figure 1.12.
k) As a result of the economic growth, can New Harmony now produce 24 capital goods and 26 consumer goods?
l) What are three possible reasons that would explain the shift from PP1 to PP2?

Answers

i) See Table 1.12 (Completed).

TABLE 1.12 (COMPLETED)

	V	W	X	Y	Z
Capital goods	0	12	21	27	30
Consumer goods	36	33	27	18	0

j) See **Figure 1.12 (Completed)** above.
k) No, it would be impossible to produce this combination.
l) Improved technology; an increase in its resources (such as a larger capital stock); or an improvement in its resources (such as a better-trained labour force or increased efficiency).

Study Problems

Find answers on the McGraw-Hill online resource.

Basic (Problems 1–3)

1. **(LO 7)** Answer the questions below based on **Figure 1.13**, which is for the country of Quantz.

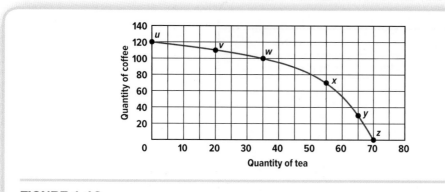

FIGURE 1.13

How much tea is gained and what is the cost in coffee?
a) In moving from u to v _____ tea is gained at the cost of _____.
b) In moving from w to x _____ tea is gained at the cost of _____.
c) In moving from y to z _____ tea is gained at the cost of _____.

2. **(LO 7)** Table 1.13 shows the production possibilities for the country of Emilon.

TABLE 1.13

	A	B	C	D	E
Rice	0	50	90	120	140
Beef	50	45	35	20	0

Complete the following (approximate) possibilities for Emilon:
a) 130 rice and _____ beef
b) _____ rice and 40 beef
Which of the following possibilities is Emilon capable of producing?
c) 100 rice and 40 beef _____
d) 70 rice and 35 beef _____

3. **(LO 7)** Table 1.14 shows the production possibilities for the country of Emilon.

TABLE 1.14

	A	B	C	D	E
Rice	0	50	90	120	140
Beef	50	45	35	20	0

a) What is the total cost of producing 90 rice?
   Answer: _____ (rice/beef)
b) What is the total cost of going from possibility C to possibility D?
   Answer: _____ (rice/beef)
c) What is the approximate per-unit cost of going from possibility C to possibility D?
   Answer: _____ (rice/beef)
d) What is the total cost of going from possibility D to possibility C?
   Answer: _____ (rice/beef)

Intermediate (Problems 4–7)

4. **(LO 7)** Utopia produces only two products: cheese and wine. The production levels are shown in Table 1.15.

TABLE 1.15

CHEESE		WINE	
% Inputs	**Output**	**% Inputs**	**Output**
0	0	0	0
20	30	20	40
40	50	40	70
60	65	60	95
80	75	80	105
100	80	100	110

a) From these data, calculate Utopia's production possibilities to complete Table 1.16.

TABLE 1.16

	A	B	C	D	E	F
Cheese	0	___	___	___	___	___
Wine	___	___	___	___	___	0

b) Can Utopia produce 65 cheese and 95 wine?
   Answer: _____
c) If Utopia is at D, what is the total cost of 10 more cheese?
   Answer: _____
d) If Utopia is at D, what is the total cost of 25 more wine?
   Answer: _____

5. **(LO 7)** Table 1.17 shows Lanark's production possibilities:

TABLE 1.17

	A	B	C	D	E	F
Wheat	0	20	35	45	50	52
Cars	21	20	18	14	8	0

a) If Lanark is producing 16 cars, approximately how much wheat can it produce?
Answer: _____
b) If Lanark is currently producing combination C, what is the cost of 10 more wheat?
Answer: _____
c) If Lanark is currently producing combination D, what is the approximate unit cost of an additional car?
Answer: _____

6. **(LO 7)** Shangri-La produces only two goods: bats and balls. Each worker comes with a fixed quantity of material and capital, and the economy's labour force is fixed at 50 workers. Table 1.18 indicates the amounts of bats and balls that can be produced daily with various quantities of labour.

TABLE 1.18

Number of Workers	Daily Production of Balls	Number of Workers	Daily Production of Bats
0	0	0	0
10	150	10	20
20	250	20	36
30	325	30	46
40	375	40	52
50	400	50	55

a) Complete the production possibilities in Table 1.19.

TABLE 1.19

	A	B	C	D	E	F
Balls	0	___	___	___	___	___
Bats	___	___	___	___	___	0
Bats 2	___	___	___	___	___	0

b) What is the opportunity cost of increasing the output of bats from 46 to 52 units per day? _____

c) Suppose that a central planning office dictates an output of 250 balls and 61 bats per day. Is this output combination possible? _____
d) Now, assume that a new technology is introduced in the production of bats so that each worker can produce half a bat more per day. Complete the Bats 2 row in Table 1.19.
e) Can the planning office's goal of 250 balls and 61 bats now be met? _____

7. **(LO 6)** The data below show the total production (in millions) of the only two goods produced in Kitchener and Waterloo, two small planets in deep space:

Kitchener: 16 kiwis or 12 trucks; **Waterloo:** 8 kiwis or 14 trucks
a) What is the opportunity cost of a kiwi in Kitchener? _____
b) What is the opportunity cost of a kiwi in Waterloo? _____
c) What is the opportunity cost of a truck in Kitchener? _____
d) What is the opportunity cost of a truck in Waterloo? _____
e) If, before trade, each planet was devoting half its resources to producing each product, what is the total amount produced by both? _____
f) If the two planets were to specialize in producing the product they do best, what would be the total amount they could produce? _____
g) What are the total gains as a result of specialization? _____

Advanced (Problems 8–10)

8. **(LO 7)** The data in Table 1.20 are for the small country of Xanadu. Assume that the economy is originally producing combination C, but technological change occurs that enables it to produce 60 percent more units of capital goods (for outputs B through F).

TABLE 1.20

	A	B	C	D	E	F
Capital goods	0	25	40	50	55	58
Capital goods 2	___	___	___	___	___	___
Consumer goods	50	40	30	20	10	0

a) Complete the Capital goods 2 row in Table 1.20.
b) If the economy wants to continue with the same quantity of consumer goods, how many more capital goods can it now have as a result of the technological improvement? _____
c) If the economy wants to continue with the same quantity of capital goods, how many more consumer goods can it now have as a result of the technological improvement? _____
d) Before the technological change, what was the opportunity cost of the first 40 consumer goods? _____
e) After the technological change, what was the opportunity cost of the first 40 consumer goods? _____

9. **(LO 7)** Jennifer is planning how to spend a particularly rainy Sunday, and the choice is between watching video movies (each lasting two hours) or studying her economics textbook. She has 10 hours available to her. If she decides to study, she could read the following number of pages at the rate as shown in Table 1.21.

TABLE 1.21

Hours	Pages
2	80
4	130
6	160
8	175
10	180

a) From this information, complete the production possibilities in Table 1.22.

TABLE 1.22

	A	B	C	D	E	F
Movies watched	0	___	___	___	___	___
Pages studied	___	___	___	___	___	0

b) From Table 1.22, draw Jennifer's production possibilities curve between movies watched and pages studied on the grid in Figure 1.14.

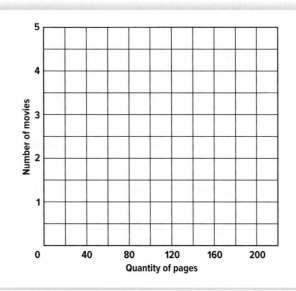

FIGURE 1.14

c) What is the opportunity cost of watching 2 movies? _____

d) Could Jennifer watch 3 movies and study 150 pages of her textbook? _____

e) If Jennifer has already watched 4 movies, what is the opportunity cost of watching the fifth movie? _____

10. **(LO 5)** Below are the data for the maximum production of the only two products for the countries of Oz and Zas.

Oz: 40 food units OR 20 equipment units
Zas: 20 food units OR 30 equipment units

a) If each country is self-sufficient, with no trade between them, and each uses one-half of its resources to produce each of the two products, what is the output in each country?
Oz: _____ food units and _____ equipment units _____
Zas: _____ food units and _____ equipment units _____

b) What is the total production of each product? _____ food units and _____ equipment units

c) If, instead, each country specializes and produces only the product that it can produce best, what will be the output in each country?
Oz: _____ food units and _____ equipment units _____
Zas: _____ food units and _____ equipment units _____

d) Now what is the total production of each product? _____ food units and _____ equipment units

e) What is the term economists use to explain your answers when comparing answers (b) and (d)? It is the _____.

Problems for Further Study

Basic (Problems 1–6)

1. **(LO 8)** Match the letters on the left with the numbers on the right. Place the correct letter in the blank. (Data refer to Canada.)

a) over $40 000 per person   1. inflation   _____

b) 2.2 percent per year   2. unemployment   _____

c) above 6 percent for last 20 years   3. economic growth   _____

d) below 3 percent for last 20 years   4. standard of living   _____

2. **(LO 3)** Identify each of the following statements as positive or normative:
   a) Canada is the best country in the world to live in. _____
   b) Canada's national income has risen for the last five years. _____
   c) If the world price of wheat rises, Canada will export less wheat. _____
   d) Unemployment is a more serious problem than inflation. _____

3. **(LO 4)** Below is a list of resources. Indicate whether each is labour (L), capital (K), land (N), or enterprise (E).
   a) an irrigation ditch in Manitoba _____
   b) the work done by Jim Plum, a labourer who helped dig the irrigation ditch _____
   c) a lake _____
   d) the air we breathe _____
   e) the efforts of the founder and primary innovator of a successful new software company _____

4. **(LO 4)** Below is a list of economic goods. You are to decide whether each is a consumer good (C), a capital good (K), or possibly both (B), depending on the context in which it is used.
   a) a pair of socks _____
   b) a golf course _____
   c) a Big Mac hamburger _____
   d) a wheelbarrow _____

5. **(LO 3)** Explain why the discipline of economics is sometimes called the *science of choice*.

6. **(LO 6)** Identify and explain the four factors of production and the names given to payments received by each.

Intermediate (Problems 7–9)

7. **(LO 3, 6)** Write down a normative statement that relates to economics. Next, change your statement to make it a positive one.

8. **(LO 7)** Illustrate economic growth using a production possibilities curve (remember to label the axes). What are two possible causes of economic growth?

9. **(LO 7)** Suppose the country of Catalona produces leather shirts and leather moccasins, and the production of each requires the same amount of leather and the same tools. Workers in Catalona are equally capable of producing either product. Draw a production possibilities curve for Catalona, and comment on its shape.

Advanced (Problems 10–15)

10. **(LO 3)** Explain the analogy between the use of theory and the use of a map.

11. **(LO 6)** To what extent is the organization of a family based on the four Cs? Give examples of how each of the four Cs is used to assign household chores to its members. What blend of the four Cs do you think is preferable, and why?

12. **(LO 4)** Kant Skatte is a professional player in the National Hockey League. Because he loved the game so much, Kant dropped out of high school and worked very hard to develop his physical strength and overcome his limitations. Eventually, he made it to the NHL. What data are needed to estimate Kant's annual opportunity costs, in dollars, of continuing to play in the NHL?

13. **(LO 7)** Assume that an economy can produce either 300 tonnes of coffee and no rubber or 100 tonnes of rubber and no coffee. You may further assume that this 3:1 coffee/rubber ratio is constant. Draw a production possibilities curve for this economy with coffee on the vertical axis. Next, indicate with the letters *a* and *b* an increase in rubber production. Finally, illustrate with a triangle the cost of this additional rubber.

14. **(LO 8)** Does a high income level mean a higher standard of living? Why, or why not?

15. **(LO 8)** Can an economy grow too fast? What might be some of the problems of high growth?

16. **(LO 3)** What are the *five* methods of allocation? Explain each briefly.

CHAPTER 2
Demand and Supply: An Introduction

LEARNING OBJECTIVES

At the end of this chapter, you should be able to:

LO1 Explain the concept of demand.

LO2 Explain the concept of supply.

LO3 Explain the term *market*.

LO4 Explain the concept of (price and quantity) equilibrium.

LO5 Demonstrate the causes and effects of a change in demand.

LO6 Demonstrate the causes and effects of a change in supply.

LO7 Explain why demand and supply determine price and the quantity traded, and not the reverse.

WHAT'S AHEAD ...

This chapter introduces you to the fundamental economic ideas of demand and supply. First, we distinguish between individual and market demands, and look at the various reasons that the demand for products changes from time to time. We then examine things from the producer's point of view and explain what determines the amounts that they put on the market. Next, we describe how markets are able to reconcile the wishes of the two groups and introduce the concept of equilibrium. Finally, we look at how the market price and the quantity traded adjust to changes in demand or supply.

A QUESTION OF RELEVANCE ...

Have you ever wondered why the prices of some products, such as computers or HDTVs, tend to fall over time, while the prices of other products, such as cars or auto insurance, tend to rise? Or perhaps you wonder how the price of a house can fluctuate tens of thousands of dollars from year to year. Why does a poor orange harvest in Florida cause the price of apple juice made in Ontario to rise? And why do sales of fax machines continue to fall despite their lower prices? This chapter will give you insights into questions such as these.

If the average person were to think about the subject matter of economics, it is unlikely that she would immediately think of choice or opportunity costs, which were principal topics of Chapter 1. More likely, she would think in terms of money or interest rates and almost certainly demand and supply. Most people realize, without studying the topic, that demand and supply are central to economics. In our own ways, and as a result of our experiences in life, most of us feel that we know quite a lot about the subject. After all, who knows more about the reaction of consumers to changes in the market than consumers themselves? However, as we will see shortly, the way economists define and use the terms *demand* and *supply* differs from the everyday usage. To make matters worse, there does not seem to be a consensus among non-economists about the meaning of either of these two words: there is a range of meanings. This is often the case with language, but it does lead to a great deal of confusion, which can be illustrated in the following exchange between two observers of the consumer electronic goods market:

Justine: "Have you noticed that the price of HDTVs has dropped quite a bit recently?"

Eric: "Well, yes, but that is just supply and demand."

Justine: Are you saying that the supply has gone up?"

Eric: "Sure, must have."

Justine: "But why would supply go up if the price is going down?"

Eric: "Well, I don't know—maybe it is because demand has gone up, as well."

There is much confusion here. While Eric's belief that the price has fallen because supply went up is probably correct in this context, we see that price will also fall if demand decreases. Justine's second question about why supply would go up if the price goes down reveals a common confusion over cause and effect. And Eric's final response is confused because he is not aware that demand and supply factors are separate and not interrelated.

We hope to soon clarify all of this type of confusion. It is probably clear to you already that economists are very fussy about defining and using economic terms correctly, and this is particularly true in a discussion about demand and supply. As we shall see in this chapter, demand does not simply mean *what people want to buy*, and supply is not just *the amount being produced*.

Another source of confusion in the above discussion is a misunderstanding of cause and effect. Is the change in TV prices the effect of changing demand, or is it the cause? This chapter will clear up some of the confusion and give us a basis upon which to analyze and clarify some real, practical problems. First, let us take a look at the concept of demand.

2.1 Demand

> **L01**   Explain the concept of demand.

Individual Demand

There are several dimensions to **demand**. First, economists use the word in the sense of wanting something, not in the sense of commanding or ordering. However, this "want" also involves the ability to buy. In other words, demand refers to both the *desire* and the *ability* to purchase a good or service.

This means that although I may well have a desire for a new top-of-the-line BMW, I unfortunately do not have the ability to buy one at current prices and therefore my quantity demanded is zero. Similarly, I might have the income to buy only expensive, upmarket wines but no desire to do so.

Second, there are many factors which might affect an individual's demand for a product. Certainly, how much you and I have to pay for the product is an important factor. But there are many others too. For instance, how much a person earns certainly affects their ability to purchase. (Surprise, rich people buy more than poor people!) As well, if you are going to buy a used Honda, for example, you will probably want to check out the prices of other comparable cars before you make a deal. Similarly, you might hold off buying altogether if you hear that the car company is going to have a sale next month. So in addition to the price of the product, people are obviously affected by how much they earn, the price of comparable products and their expectations of the future. We will look at each of these factors and others later in the chapter. For now, we will concentrate on what many consider to be the most important factor when deciding whether to purchase: the price of the product.

When we look at the concept of demand then, we are investigating the relationship between the price of the product and the quantities people are willing and able to purchase assuming all these other factors remain the same. The Latin phrase for this perspective is *ceteris paribus*. Literally the phrase means "other things being equal"; however, it is usually interpreted by economists to mean "other things remaining the same." Demand is the relationship between the price of a product and the quantities demanded, *other things remaining the same.*

Third, demand is a hypothetical construct that expresses this desire and ability to purchase, not at a single price, but over a *range of* hypothetical prices. Finally, demand is also a flow concept in that it measures quantities over a period of time. In summary, demand

- involves both the desire and the ability of consumers to purchase
- assumes that other things are held constant
- refers to a range of prices
- measures quantities over time

All of these aspects of demand are captured in Table 2.1, which shows the **demand schedule** for energy bars for Tomiko, who is an energy bar enthusiast and buys her bars by the case once a month.

TABLE 2.1
Individual Demand

Price per Case	Quantity Demanded (number of cases per month)
$18	6
19	5
20	4
21	3
22	2

Once again, what we mean by demand is the entire relationship between the various prices and the quantities that people are willing and able to purchase. This relationship can be laid out in the form of a demand schedule. The above schedule shows the amounts per month that Tomiko is willing and able to purchase at the various prices shown. Note that there is an inverse relationship between price and quantity. This simply means that at higher prices, Tomiko would not be willing to buy as much as at lower prices. In other words:

The higher the price, the lower will be the quantity demanded, and the lower the price, the higher will be the quantity demanded.

Another less obvious statement of this law of demand is to say that in order to induce Tomiko to buy a greater quantity of energy bars, the price must be lower. Tomiko's demand schedule is graphed in **Figure 2.1**.

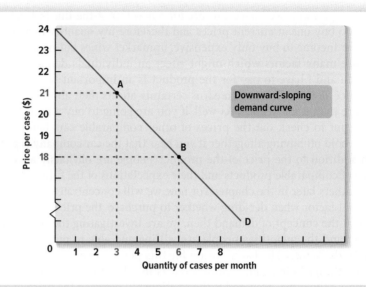

FIGURE 2.1   Individual Demand Curve

At a price of $18 per case, Tomiko is willing and able to buy 6 cases per month (point B). At a higher price, $21 per case, the amount she is willing and able to buy falls to 3 cases (point A). The higher the price, then, the lower is the quantity demanded. (Note that the vertical axis contains a "broken" portion. In general, an axis is often broken in this manner whenever the information about, say, low prices, is unavailable or unimportant.)

In **Figure 2.1**, at a price of $21 per case, the quantity demanded by Tomiko is 3 cases per month, while at a lower price of $18 per case, she would be willing to buy 6 cases. The demand is therefore plotted as a downward-sloping curve by connecting these two price/quantity coordinates and then extending a straight line. (To economists, curves include straight lines!) Once again, note that when we say *demand, demand schedule,* or *demand curve,* we are referring to a whole array of different prices and quantities.

It is very important for you to note that since the price of any product is part of what we call the "demand" for that product, a change in the price cannot change the demand. It can, however, affect the amounts we are willing to purchase, and we express this by saying that:

A change in the price of a product results in a **change in the quantity demanded** for that product.

In other words, point A in **Figure 2.1** represents a price of $21 and a quantity demanded of 3 cases. Point B shows another possible combination: at a price of $18, the quantity demanded is 6 cases. The *quantity demanded*, then, is a single point on the demand curve, whereas the *demand* is the entire collection of points.

This is illustrated in **Figure 2.2**. Graphically, as we move the demand curve from $19 to $18, the quantity demanded increases from 5 to 6 cases; as we move up from $21 to $22, the quantity demanded decreases from 3 to 2 cases.

Why Is the Demand Curve Downward Sloping?

People tend to buy more at lower prices than at higher prices. Most of us can confirm from experience that a lower price will induce us to buy more of a product or to buy something that we would or could not purchase before. Witness the big crowds attracted to

A SALE sign is often all it takes to attract consumers.

PhotoLink/Getty Images

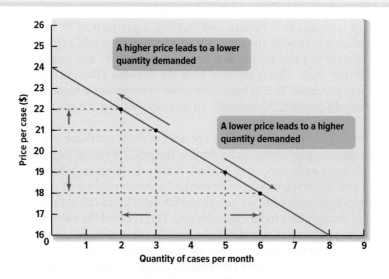

FIGURE 2.2 Changes in the Quantity Demanded

Whenever the price changes, there is a movement along the demand curve. A decrease in the price from $19 to $18 leads to an increase in the quantity demanded from 5 to 6. An increase in the price from, say $21 to $22, causes a decrease in the quantity demanded from 3 to 2. Neither the demand nor the demand curve changes, however.

 ADDED DIMENSION

Just What Is a Product?

Economist speak a great deal about the supply of, and demand for "products" such as cars, computers, cell phones, and houses. This is done so that we are able to focus on the *concept* of demand—people want to buy these things—and supply—firms want to make a profit providing these things. This process is what the current chapter is all about.

But you do need to realize that "car" is also a bit of an abstraction. It might mean a current-model Honda Civic, Ford Fiesta, or Chevy Cruze, costing around $20 000; or an Audi A3 or Hyundai Genesis with a price tag around twice as much.

A "car" might also mean a meticulously reconstructed 1957 Chevy Impala with vintage licence plates that some enthusiast spent countless hours and $100 000 working on.

Economics is full of abstractions, but that is the only way we can develop and construct concepts that help us better understand the world in which we live. So how do we chose to define "a product" in this text? A product is simply any item offered for sale. It can be a service or an item. It can be physical or in virtual or cyber form.

nothing more than a sign saying "SALE." In addition, most microeconomic research done over the years tends to confirm this law of demand, and theories of consumer behaviour (such as the marginal utility theory, which we will study in Chapter 5) lend additional support to the idea. But is it that simple? Let us explore the question of why people tend to buy more at lower prices.

Remember that our demand for products is a combination of our desire to purchase and our ability to purchase. A lower price affects both of these. The lower the price of a product, the more income a person has left to purchase additional products. Assume, for instance, that the price of energy bars in Table 2.1 was $20 and Tomiko was buying 4 cases per month for a total expenditure of

$80 per month. If the price decreases to $18, Tomiko could buy the same quantity for an outlay of $72, saving a total of $8. It is almost as if Tomiko had received a pay raise of $8. In fact, in terms of its effect on Tomiko's wallet, it is exactly the same. Or, as economists would express it, her **real income** has increased. A decrease in price means that people can afford to buy more of a product (or more of other products) if they wish. This is referred to as the **income effect** of a price change, and it affects people's *ability* to purchase. This is because a lower price means a higher real income, so people will tend to buy more of a product. (Conversely, an increase in the price effectively reduces a person's real income.)

In addition to this, a price change also affects people's *desire* to purchase. We are naturally driven to buy the cheaper of competing products, and a drop in the price of one of them increases our desire to substitute it for a relatively more expensive product. If the price of granola bars were to drop (or if the price of energy bars were to increase), then some energy-bar lovers might well switch to what they regard as a cheaper substitute. In general, there are substitutes for most products, and people will tend to substitute a relatively cheap product for a more expensive one. This is called the **substitution effect**. A higher price tends to make the product less attractive to us than its substitutes, and so we buy less of it.

When the price of a product drops, we buy more of it because we are *more able* (the income effect) and because we are *more willing* (the substitution effect). Conversely, a price increase means we are less able and less willing to buy the product, and therefore we buy less.

The close relationship that exists between price and the quantity demanded is so pervasive that it is often referred to as the *law of demand*.

Market Demand

Up to this point, we have focused on individual demand. Now, we want to move to **market demand** (or total demand). Conceptually, this is easy enough to do. By summing every individual's demand for a product, we are able to obtain the market demand. Table 2.2 provides a simple example.

TABLE 2.2
Deriving the Market Demand

	NUMBER OF CASES PER MONTH				
Price per Case	Tomiko's Quantity Demanded	Meridith's Quantity Demanded	Abdi's Quantity Demanded	Jan's Quantity Demanded	Market Quantity Demanded
$18	6	3	4	9	22
19	5	2	4	7	18
20	4	2	4	6	16
21	3	0	3	3	9
22	2	0	3	1	6

Let us say we know not only Tomiko's demand but also the demands of three of her friends in a small, four-person economy. The market demand, then, is the horizontal summation of individual demands, so to find the quantities demanded at $18, we add the quantities demanded by each individual: 6 + 3 + 4 + 9 = 22. The same would be done for each price level. This particular market demand is graphed in Figure 2.3. Note that this demand curve, which is the summation of the specific numbers of the four people in Table 2.2, is not a straight line. Yet it is still downward sloping and so conforms to the law of demand. (For the most part, we will work with straight-line demand curves, although there is no reason to assume that all real-life demand curves plot as straight lines.)

Note that, as with the individual demand curve, the market demand curve also slopes downward. This is because people buy more as the price drops—and more people buy. In our example, Meridith is not willing to buy any energy bars at a price of $22. Only if the price is $20 or lower will all four people buy energy bars.

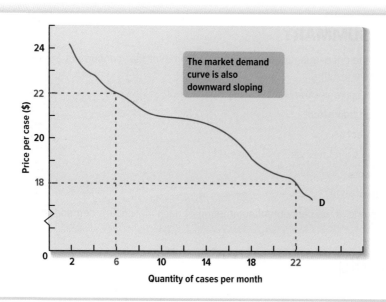

FIGURE 2.3   The Market Demand Curve

At a price of $18, the total or market quantity demanded equals 22 cases. As with individual demand, when the price increases to $22, the quantity demanded will drop, in this case to 6. This is because at a higher price each individual buys less, and there are fewer people who can afford or are willing to buy any at all. (Meridith has dropped out of the market.)

Finally, before we look at the supply side of the market, note again that our demand schedule tells us only what people *might* buy; it tells us nothing about what they are actually buying. To know this, we need to know the actual price. And to find out what the price of energy bars should be, we need to know ... yes, the supply.

   TEST YOUR UNDERSTANDING

Find answers on the McGraw-Hill online resource.

1. The data in the table indicate the weekly demand for litres of soy milk by Al, Bo, and Cole (the only three people in a very small market).

a) Fill in the blanks in the table.

b) What is the basic shape of the demand curve in this market?

c) What is the highest price at which all three will buy at least one litre of milk?

Price	Quantity Demanded: Al	Quantity Demanded: Bo	Quantity Demanded: Cole	Total (Market) Quantity Demanded
$4.00	1	0	0	_____
3.50	1	1	0	_____
3.00	1	1	1	_____
2.50	2	1	1	_____
2.00	2	2	1	_____

SECTION SUMMARY

a) Demand is the price–quantity relationship of a product that consumers are willing and able to buy per period of time.

b) The demand curve is downward sloping because of

- the substitution effect

- income effect

c) Products can be related as

- complements

- substitutes

d) Market demand is the conceptual summation of each individual's demand within a given market.

2.2 Supply

LO2 Explain the concept of supply.

Individual Supply

In many ways, the formulation of supply is very similar to that of demand. Both measure hypothetical quantities at various prices, and both are flow concepts. However, we now need to look at things through the eyes of the producer rather than the eyes of the consumer. We will assume for the time being that the prime motive for the producer is to maximize profits, although we will examine this assumption in more detail in a later chapter. For now, we can certainly agree with Adam Smith who, in *The Wealth of Nations*, noted that few producers are in business to please consumers. Neither, of course, do consumers buy products to please producers. Both are motivated by self-interest.

The term **supply** refers to the quantities that suppliers are *willing* and *able* to make available to the market at various prices. Table 2.3 shows a hypothetical **supply schedule** for Flic, the owner of an energy bar manufacturing firm.

TABLE 2.3
The Supply Schedule for Flic, the Energy Bar Manufacturer

Price per Case	Quantity Supplied (number of cases per month)
$18	2
19	3
20	4
21	5
22	6

Note that there is a *direct* relationship between price and the quantity supplied, which means that a higher price will induce Flic to produce more. Remember that Flic's reason for being in business is to make as much profit as possible. How much would Flic, hypothetically, be prepared to supply if the energy bars could be sold at $18 per case? Knowing what her costs are likely to be, she figures that she could make the most profit if she produces two cases. At a higher price, there is a likelihood of greater profits, and therefore she is willing to produce more. Also, as we shall see in Chapter 6, when firms produce more, the cost per unit tends to rise. Therefore, a producer needs the incentive of a higher price *in order to* increase production. For the time being, however, we can rely on the proposition that a higher price means higher profits and therefore will lead to higher quantities produced. This is illustrated in **Figure 2.4**.

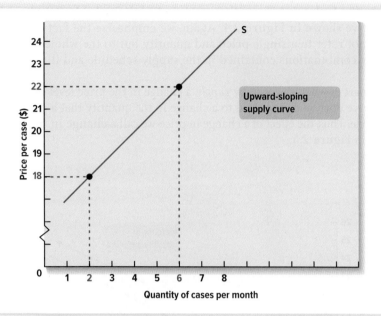

FIGURE 2.4   Individual Supply Curve

At a low price of $18, the most profitable output for Flic is 2 cases. If the price increased, she would be willing and able to produce more, since she would be able to make greater profits. At $22, for instance, the quantity she would produce increases to 6 cases.

 ## GREAT ECONOMISTS: ADAM SMITH

Adam Smith (1723–90) is generally regarded as the founding father of economics. In his brilliant work *The Wealth of Nations*, Smith posed so many interesting questions and provided such illuminating answers that later economists often felt that they were merely picking at the scraps he left behind. Smith was born and brought up in Scotland and educated in Glasgow and Oxford. He held the Chair of Moral Philosophy at Glasgow College for many years. He was a lifelong bachelor and had a kind but absent-minded disposition.

Smith was the first scholar to analyze the business of "getting and spending" in a detailed and systematic manner. In doing this, he gave useful social dignity to the professions of business and trading. Besides introducing the important idea of the *invisible hand*, which was his way of describing the coordinating mechanism of capitalism, he examined the division of labour, the role of government, the function of money, the advantages and disadvantages of free trade, what constitutes good and bad taxation, and a host of other ideas. For Smith, economic life was not merely a peripheral adventure for people but their central motivating force.

Library of Congress Prints and Photographs Division

Joining the individual points from the supply schedule in **Table** 2.3 gives us the upward-sloping supply curve shown in **Figure** 2.4. Again, we emphasize the fact that, like *demand*, the term *supply* does not refer to a single price and quantity but to the whole array of hypothetical price and quantity combinations contained in the supply schedule and illustrated by the supply curve.

Since price is part of what we mean by *supply*, a change in the price level cannot change the supply. A change in price does, of course, lead to a change in the quantity that a producer is willing and able to make available. Thus, the effect of a change in price we call a **change in the quantity supplied**. This is illustrated in **Figure** 2.5.

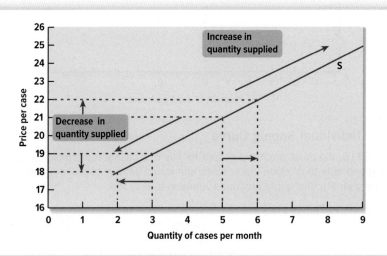

FIGURE 2.5   **Changes in the Quantity Supplied**

A price change will lead to a movement along the supply curve. An increase in the price from, say, $21 to $22 will cause an increase in the quantity supplied from 5 to 6. A decrease in the price from $19 to $18 will lead to a decrease in the quantity supplied from 3 to 2. The supply curve itself, however, does not change.

To summarize:

An increase in price will lead to an increase in the quantity supplied and is illustrated as a movement up the supply curve.

A decrease in price will cause a decrease in the quantity supplied and is illustrated as a movement down the supply curve.

Market Supply

As we did with the market demand, we can derive the **market supply** of a product by summing the supply of every individual supplier. A word of caution, however. We must make the assumption that producers are all producing a similar product and that consumers have no preference as to which supplier or product they use. Given this, it is possible to add together the individual supplies to derive the market supply. In our example, suppose that the manufacturer Flic is competing with three other manufacturers of similar size and with similar costs. The market supply of energy bars in this market would be as shown in **Table 2.4.**

TABLE 2.4
Deriving the Market Supply

NUMBER OF CASES PER MONTH			
Price per Case	Flic Quantity Supplied	Quantity Supplied of Other Manufacturers	Market Quantity Supplied
$18	2	6	8
19	3	9	12
20	4	12	16
21	5	15	20
22	6	18	24

The total quantities supplied by the three other manufacturers are equal to the quantities that Flic would supply at each price, multiplied by three. The fourth column, market supply, is the addition of every energy bar manufacturer's supply—the second column plus the third column.

The market supply is illustrated in **Figure** 2.6.

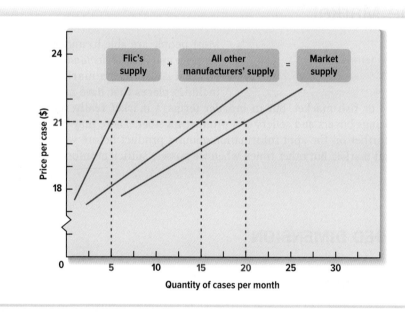

FIGURE 2.6   The Market Supply

The market supply is the horizontal summation of each individual producer's supply curve. For instance, at a price of $21, Flic would supply 5 cases; the other manufacturers combined would supply 15 cases. The market quantity supplied, therefore, is the total quantity supplied of 20 cases. In short, to derive the market supply curve, we add the totals of each supplier at each price level.

The *market* supply curve is upward sloping primarily for the same reason the *individual* supply curve is upward sloping: because higher prices imply higher profits and will therefore induce a greater quantity supplied. But there is an additional reason. In our example, we assumed, for simplicity's sake, that the suppliers are of similar size and have similar costs. In reality, that is unlikely; costs and size probably differ, so a price that generates a profit for one firm may mean a loss for another.

In summary, a higher price, which deters consumers from buying more, is an incentive for suppliers to produce more. Conversely, a lower price induces consumers to buy more but is a reason for suppliers to cut back their output.

The motives of consumers and producers are very different: consumers wish to obtain the lowest price possible, and producers want to sell at the highest. How can their wishes converge? How is trade possible at all in these circumstances? Certainly, it is not possible for *all* prospective consumers and suppliers to be satisfied. But it is almost always possible for *some* of these people to be satisfied. Of course, this will require that they be able, in some sense, to meet and get together. A market enables them to do just that.

SECTION SUMMARY

a) Supply is the price–quantity relationship of a product that producers are willing and able to sell per period of time.

b) The supply curve is upward sloping because higher prices imply higher profits and therefore increased production.

c) Market supply is the conceptual summation of each firm's supply within a given market.

2.3   The Market

LO3 Explain the term *market*.

Most people are able to understand the terms *market price* and *market demand*, but many are not clear on what constitutes a **market**. Certainly, the term includes places that have a physical location such as a local produce or fish market. But in broader terms, a market really refers to any exchange mechanism that brings buyers and sellers of a product together. There may be times when we need to inspect or get further on-the-spot information about a product before we buy it, and this is the purpose of the retail market. But other times, when we possess sufficient information about a product

 ADDED DIMENSION

Reinventing the Market

The modern market system first emerged and began to spread about 250 years ago, as commerce moved out of the village markets of Europe into the age of factory-centred manufacturing, which was later combined with widespread systems of wholesaling and retailing. However, this transformation also introduced a less predictable chain of supply and demand. While the seller in the village market was in direct contact with the buyer, the evolution of mass markets and mass production techniques gave rise to vast gulfs in time and space between buyer and seller. Producers became much less sure of what the demand for their product was, and buyers were never sure there wasn't a better deal somewhere else. In response to this, sellers used the blunt tool of a fixed price list and adjusted output in response to fluctuations in demand, while buyers just did the best they could. The invention of the Internet is also reinventing commerce; as the seller's market horizon expands, buyers have more information, real-time sales become routine, and the need to stockpile inventory diminishes. In short, supply-chain bottlenecks are being eradicated. What is emerging is far *more efficient markets* and the rise of dynamic pricing based on constantly fluctuating demand and supply.

or a producer, it is not necessary to actually see either of them before we purchase. This applies, for instance, if you wish to buy stocks and bonds or make a purchase on the Internet. Increasingly, in these days of higher costs of personal service and greater availability of electronic communication, markets are becoming both wider and more accessible. The market for commodities such as copper, gold, and rubber, for instance, is both worldwide and anonymous in that the buyers and sellers seldom meet in person.

By a market, then, we mean any relatively open environment in which buyers and sellers can communicate and that operates without preference. So when we speak of the market price, we mean the price available to *all* buyers and sellers of a product. By market demand we mean the total quantities demanded, and market supply we mean the quantity made available by all suppliers at each possible price.

Later, you will encounter several different types of markets, some of which work very well and others that work poorly if at all. The analysis in this chapter assumes that the market we are looking at is very (economists call it "perfectly") competitive. We will devote all of Chapter 8 to examining this type of market in more detail. For now, we need to mention that a perfectly competitive market is, among other things, one in which there are many small producers, each selling an identical product. With this caution in mind, let us see how such a market works.

SECTION SUMMARY

A market is a mechanism that brings buyers and sellers together.

2.4 Market Equilibrium

LO4 Explain the concept of (price and quantity) equilibrium.

We now examine the point at which the wishes of buyers and sellers coincide by combining the market demand and supply for energy bars in Table 2.5.

TABLE 2.5
Market Supply and Demand

	NUMBER OF CASES PER MONTH		
Price per Case	Market Quantity Demanded	Market Quantity Supplied	Surplus (+)/ Shortage (−)
$18	22	8	−14
19	18	12	−6
20	16	16	0
21	9	20	+11
22	6	24	+18

You can see from this table that there is only one price, $20, at which the wishes of consumers and producers coincide. Only if the price is $20 will the quantity demanded and the quantity supplied be equal. This price level is referred to as the **equilibrium price**. Equilibrium, in general, means that there is balance between opposing forces; here, those opposing forces are demand and supply. The word *equilibrium* also implies a condition of stability. If this stability is disturbed, there will be a tendency to automatically find a new equilibrium.

To understand this point, refer to **Table** 2.5 and note that if the price were, say, $18, then the amount being demanded, 22, would exceed the amount being supplied, which is 8. At this price, there is an excess demand, or more simply, a shortage of energy bars, to the tune of 14 cases. This amount is shown in the last column and marked with a minus sign. In this situation, there would be a lot of unhappy energy-bar eaters. Faced with the prospect of going without their bars, many of them will be prepared to pay a higher price and will therefore bid the price up. As the price of energy bars starts to rise, the reaction of consumers and producers will differ. Some energy-bar eaters will not be able to afford the higher prices, so the quantity demanded will drop. On the supply side, producers will be delighted with the higher price and will start to produce more—and the quantity supplied will increase. Both these tendencies will combine to reduce the shortage as the price goes up. Eventually, when the price has reached the equilibrium price of $20, the shortage will have disappeared and the price will no longer increase. Part of the law of demand suggests, then, that:

Shortages cause prices to rise.

This is illustrated in **Figure** 2.7.

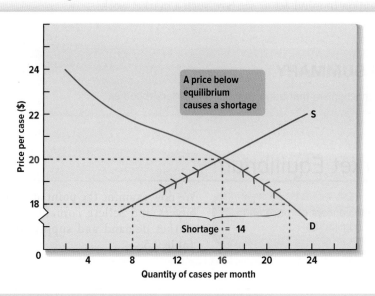

FIGURE 2.7   How the Market Reacts to a Shortage

At a price of $18, the quantity supplied of 8 is far below the quantity demanded of 22. The horizontal distance between the two shows the amount of the shortage, which is 14. As a result of the shortage, price bidding between consumers will force up the price. As the price increases, the quantity demanded will drop, but the quantity supplied will rise until these two are equal at a quantity of 16.

Now, again using **Table** 2.5, let us see what will happen if the price happens to be above equilibrium, at $22 a case. At this price, the quantity demanded is 6 cases, and the quantity supplied is 24 cases. There is insufficient demand from the producers' point of view, or more simply, there is a surplus (or excess supply) of 18 cases. This is shown in the last column of **Table** 2.5 as +18. This is not a stable situation because firms cannot continue producing a product that they cannot sell. They will be forced to lower the price in an attempt to sell more. As the price starts to drop, two things happen concurrently. Consumers will be happy to consume more, or to use economic terms, there will be an increase in the quantity demanded.

In **Figure** 2.8, note that as the price falls the quantity demanded increases, and this increase is depicted as a movement down the demand curve. At the same time, faced with a falling price, producers will be forced to cut back production—decreasing the quantity supplied. In the same figure, this is shown as a movement along (down) the supply curve. The net result of this will be the eventual elimination of the surplus as the price moves toward equilibrium. In other words:

Surpluses cause prices to fall.

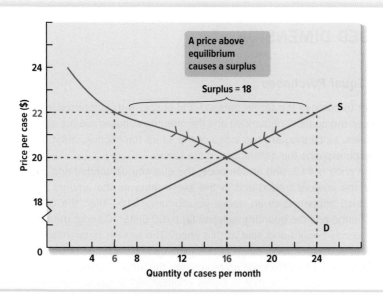

FIGURE 2.8 How the Market Reacts to a Surplus

A price above equilibrium will produce a surplus. At $22, the quantity supplied of 24 exceeds the quantity demanded of 6. The horizontal distance of 18 represents the amount of the surplus. The surplus will result in producers dropping the price in an attempt to increase sales. As the price drops, the quantity demanded increases, while the quantity supplied falls. The equilibrium quantity is 16.

Only if the price is $20 will there be no surplus or shortage, and the quantity produced will be equal to the quantity demanded. This is the equilibrium price. The quantity prevailing at the equilibrium price is known as the **equilibrium quantity**, in this case 16 cases. This equilibrium quantity is the quantity both demanded and supplied (since they are equal).

 TEST YOUR UNDERSTANDING

2. What effect does a surplus have on the price of a product? What about a shortage?

3. The following table shows the demand and supply of eggs (in hundreds of thousands per day).

  a) What are the equilibrium price and the equilibrium quantity?

  b) Complete the surplus/shortage column. Using this column, explain why your answer to question (a) must be correct.

  c) What would be the surplus/shortage at a price of $2.50? What would happen to the price and the quantity traded?

  d) What would be the surplus/shortage at a price of $4? What would happen to the price and the quantity traded?

Price	Quantity Demanded	Quantity Supplied	Surplus/ Shortage
$2.00	60	30	_____
2.50	56	36	_____
3.00	52	42	_____
3.50	48	48	_____
4.00	44	54	_____

ADDED DIMENSION

Sales Always Equal Purchases

It is important not to confuse the terms *demand* and *supply* with *purchases* and *sales*. As we have seen in this chapter, the quantity demanded and the quantity supplied are not always equal. However, purchases and sales, since they are two sides of the same transaction, must always be equal. The accompanying graph explains the differences in the terms.

The equilibrium price is $12, and at this price, the quantity demanded and supplied are equal at 40 units—this is the amount traded and is the same thing as the amount sold and purchased. However, if the price happened to be above equilibrium—$16—then the quantity demanded is denoted by *a* (30 units) and the quantity supplied by *b* (60 units). Clearly, the two quantities are not equal. But how much is bought and sold at this price? The answer is quantity *a*. It really does not matter how much is being produced, since at this price quantity *a* is the maximum amount that consumers are willing to buy. The difference *ab* represents the amount unsold, or a surplus of 30.

But what is the effect of a price that is below equilibrium? Suppose the price is $8, where the quantity supplied of 20 units (*c*) is less than the quantity demanded of 50 units (*d*)? This time, how much is being bought and sold? The answer must be quantity *c*. It does not matter how much of this product consumers want to buy if producers are only making quantity *c* available. In general, the amount bought and sold is always equal to the smaller of the quantity demanded or the quantity supplied.

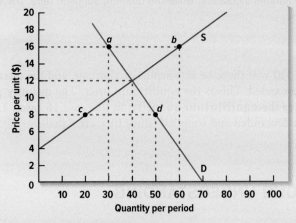

SECTION SUMMARY

a) Shortages cause prices to rise; surpluses cause prices to fall.

b) Market equilibrium occurs when the quantity demanded and the quantity supplied are equal at a particular price.

2.5   Change in Demand

> **L05**   Demonstrate the causes and effects of a change in demand.

Recall from the definition of demand that the concept refers to the *relationship* between various prices and quantities. In other words, both price and quantity make up what is known as demand. Thus, a change in price cannot cause a change in demand but does cause a change in the quantity demanded. That said, we must now ask: What are the other determinants, besides price, that influence how much of any particular product consumers will buy? Or once equilibrium price and quantity have been established, what might disturb that equilibrium? One general answer to this question is a **change in demand**. Table 2.6 shows such a change in the demand for energy bars.

TABLE 2.6
An Increase in Demand

	NUMBER OF CASES PER MONTH	
Price per Case of Energy Bars	Quantity Demanded 1	Quantity Demanded 2
$18	16	22
19	15	21
20	14	20
21	13	19
22	12	18

Here, we will introduce new figures for demand in order to revert to straight-line demand curves. Let us say that D_1 is the demand for energy bars that existed last month and D_2 is the demand this month. Demand has increased by 6 cases per month at each price, so whatever the price, consumers are willing and able to consume an additional 6 cases. Thus, there has been an increase in demand. **Figure 2.9** graphically illustrates an increase in demand.

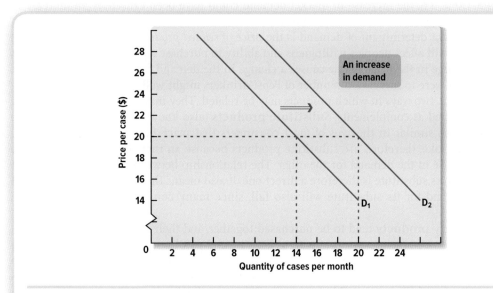

FIGURE 2.9   An Increase in Demand

At each price, the quantities demanded have increased. In this example, the increase is by a constant amount of 6, thus producing a parallel shift in the demand curve. For example, at $20 the quantity demanded has increased from 14 to 20.

An increase in demand, then, means an increase in the quantities demanded *at each price*, that is, a total increase in the demand schedule, which is illustrated by a rightward shift in the demand curve. Similarly, a decrease in demand means a reduction in the quantities demanded at each price—a decrease in the demand schedule—and this is illustrated by a leftward shift in the demand curve.

Determinants of a Change in Demand

Now that we know what an increase in demand looks like, we need to look at the factors that could bring about such a change. Some of these determinants of demand affect people's willingness to purchase, others affect their ability to purchase, and still others affect both.

The first factor that affects our willingness to purchase a product is our own *preference*. An increase in demand as shown in Table 2.6 could simply have been caused by a change in consumer preferences: consumers now prefer more energy bars.

But many things could affect our preferences. Tastes change over time and are influenced by the weather, advertising, articles and reports in books and magazines, opinions of friends, special events, and much more. Specific examples would include decreased demand for steak as the summer barbecue season passes, increased demand for a book after it wins a prestigious literary award, or increased demand for hotel rooms in the host city of the Olympics.

The second factor affecting the demand for a product is the *income* of consumers. This affects their ability to consume. Generally speaking, you would expect that an increase in income leads most people to increase their purchases of most products and that a decrease in income generally causes a drop in demand—that is, there is a direct relationship between income and demand. This is true for most products that we buy. These products are called **normal products** and they include items such as sushi, soft drinks, cars, and movies.

But it is certainly not true for all people and all products. For instance, as the incomes of most people increase, these consumers tend to buy less of such things as low-quality meats, boxes of macaroni and cheese, cheap toilet paper, and so on. Instead, they start to substitute higher-quality and higher-priced articles that they could not previously afford. When income is low, we buy lower-quality staple products that economists call **inferior products**. There is an inverse relationship between income and the demand for inferior products: as income levels go up, the demand goes down. It also means that as incomes fall, demand for these inferior products will rise. In our energy bars example from Table 2.6, the increase in market demand could have been caused by an increase in incomes because energy bars are normal products.

A third important determinant of demand is the *price of related products*. A change in the price of related products will affect people's willingness and ability to purchase a particular good. Products are related if a change in the price of one causes a change in the demand for the other. For instance, if the price of Pepsi were to increase, a number of Pepsi drinkers might well switch over to Coke.

There are, in fact, two ways in which products may be related. They may be related as substitutes, or they may be related as complements. **Substitute products** (also known as *competitive products*) are those that are so similar in the eyes of most consumers that price is the main distinguishing feature. Pepsi and Coke, therefore, are substitute products because an increase in the price of one will cause an increase in the demand for the other. The relationship between the price of a product and the demand for its substitute is therefore a direct one. It also means that if the price of a product falls, then the demand for its substitute will also fall, since many consumers are now buying a cheaper product.

Complementary products tend to be purchased together, and their demands are interrelated. Skis and ski boots are complementary products, as are cars and gasoline or beer and pretzels. If the price of one product increases, causing a decrease in the quantity demanded, then people will also purchase less of the complement. If the price of greens fees were to increase so that people were buying fewer rounds of golf, then we would also expect a decrease in the demand for complementary products such as golf balls and golf tees.

There is, in this case, an inverse relationship between the price of a product and the demand for its complement: an increase in price of one product leads to a decline in the demand for the complementary product. Similarly, a decrease in the price of a product will lead to an increase in the demand for a complement.

A fourth determinant of demand is consumers' *expectations of the future*. There are many ways that our feelings about the future influence our present behaviour. Future expected prices and incomes can affect our present demand for a product, as can the prospect of a shortage. If consumers think that the price of their favourite beverage is likely to increase in the near future, they may well stock up, just in case. The present demand for the product will therefore increase. Conversely, expected future price declines cause people to hold off their current purchases while awaiting the hoped-for lower prices.

An anticipated pay increase may cause some people to spend more immediately as they adjust to their expected higher standard of living. People who fear a layoff or some other loss of income may cut down spending in advance of the fateful date. Finally, the possibility of future shortages, such as those caused by an impending strike, may cause a frantic rush to the stores by anxious customers trying to stock up in advance.

These four determinants of demand—preferences, income, prices of related products, and future expectations—affect individual demand to varying degrees. If we shift our attention to market demand, these four factors still apply. In addition, a few other factors need to be mentioned. The *size of the market population* will affect the demand for all products. An increase in the size of the population, for example, leads to an increase in the demand for everything from houses and cars to sports equipment and credit cards. In addition, a *change in the distribution of incomes* leads to an increase in the demand for some products and a decrease in the demand for others. For example, if the percentage of total income earned by those over 65 years of age rises, while the percentage going to those under the age of 24 falls, then we would expect to see an increase in the demand for holiday cruises and a decrease in the demand for entry into popular night clubs.

The same will also be true for the *age composition of the population*. An aging population increases the demand for products that largely appeal to older people (Bruce Springsteen albums) and decrease the demand for those that appeal only to the young (Justin Bieber recordings).

Note that one factor is *not* included on this list of determinants of demand: supply. Economists are scrupulous in their attempts to separate the forces of demand and supply. Remember that the demand formulation is a hypothetical construct based on the quantities that consumers are willing and able to purchase at various prices. There is an implied assumption that the consumer will be able to obtain these quantities, otherwise the demand schedule itself would not be relevant. In other words, when specifying demand, we assume that the supply will be available, just as when formulating supply, we make the assumption that there will be sufficient demand.

In summary, the determinants of demand are as follows:

- consumer preferences
- consumer incomes
- prices of related goods
- expectations of future prices, incomes, or availability
- population size, or income and age distribution

Increasingly busy lifestyles and more demands in the workplace have increased the sales of energy bars in Canada.
McGraw-Hill Education Mark Dierker Photographer

 TEST YOUR UNDERSTANDING

4. The accompanying table shows the initial weekly demand (D_1) and the new demand (D_2) for packets of pretzels (a bar snack).

To explain the change in demand from D_1 to D_2, what might have happened to the price of a complementary product such as beer? Alternatively, what might have happened to the price of a substitute product such as nuts?

Price	Quantity Demanded (D_1)	Quantity Demanded (D_2)
$2.00	10 000	11 000
3.00	9 600	10 600
4.00	9 200	10 200

The Effects of an Increase in Demand

We have just seen that the demand for any product is affected by many different factors. A change in any of these factors will cause a change in demand, which, as we shall see, leads to a change in price and production levels. Let us first consider the effects of an *increase* in the demand for a product. Any one of the following could cause such an increase in the market demand:

- a change in preferences toward the product
- an increase in incomes if the product is a normal product or a decrease in incomes if the product is an inferior product
- an increase in the price of a substitute product
- a decrease in the price of a complementary product
- the expectation that future prices or incomes will be higher or that there will be a future shortage of the product
- an increase in the population or a change in its income or age distribution

Any of these changes could cause people to buy more of a product, regardless of its price. As an example, let us combine supply and demand data in Table 2.7.

TABLE 2.7
The Effects of an Increase in Demand on the Market

	NUMBER OF CASES PER MONTH		
Price per Case	Quantity Supplied	Quantity Demanded 1	Quantity Demanded 2
$18	10	16	22
19	12	15	21
20	14	14	20
21	16	13	19
22	18	12	18

You can see that at the old demand (Demand 1) and supply, the equilibrium price was $20 and the quantity traded was 14 cases. Assume now that the demand for energy bars increases (Demand 2). Since consumers do not usually signal their intentions to producers in advance, producers are not aware that the demand has changed until they have evidence. The evidence will probably take the form of unsatisfied customers. At a price of $20 a case, the producers in total have produced 14 cases. At this price, the new quantity demanded is 20 cases. There is a **shortage** of 6 cases, and some customers will go home disappointed because there are not enough energy bars, at a price of $20, to satisfy all customers. Will these manufacturers now increase production to satisfy the higher demand? The surprising answer is no—at least, not at the present price. Manufacturers are not in the business of satisfying customers, they are in the business of making profits. As Adam Smith wrote over 200 years ago:

> It is not from the benevolence of the butcher, the brewer, or the baker that we expect our dinner but from regard to their own self-interest.[1]

You may say that unless firms are responsive to the demands of customers, they will soon go out of business. And you are right. But a firm that is *solely* responsive to its customers will go out of business even faster. Look again at the supply schedule in Table 2.7. At a price of $20, the manufacturers are prepared to produce 14 cases. They are not prepared to produce 20 cases, the amount that consumers now want. Why is that? It may be because they can make more profits from producing 14 cases than from producing 20 cases; otherwise, they would have produced 20 in the first place. In fact, it may well be that if they produced 20 cases at the current price of $20, they would end up incurring

---

[1] Adam Smith, *The Wealth of Nations* (Edwin Cannan edition, 1877), pp. 26–27.

a loss. Does this mean that the shortage of energy bars will persist? No. As we saw earlier, *shortages drive prices up* until the shortage disappears and the new quantity demanded is equal to the quantity supplied. This will occur at a price of $22, where the quantity demanded and the quantity supplied are equal at the equilibrium quantity of 18. This adjustment process can be seen in **Figure 2.10**.

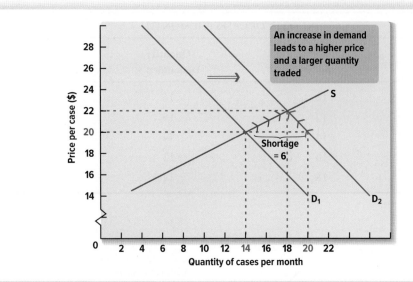

FIGURE 2.10 Adjustment to an Increase in Demand

The increase in demand from D_1 to D_2 creates an immediate shortage of 6. This will cause an increase in the price of energy bars. The increase affects both producers, who will now increase the quantity supplied, and consumers, who will reduce the quantity demanded. Eventually, the price will reach a new equilibrium at $22, where the equilibrium quantity is 18 and there is no longer a shortage.

You can see in the graph that at the old price of $20, the new quantity demanded exceeds the quantity supplied. This shortage causes the price to rise. As it does so, the quantity of energy bars that producers make also rises; that is, there will be an increase *in the quantity supplied*. Producers will produce more, not because there is a shortage but because the shortage causes a rise in price. Note also that the increase in price causes some customers to reduce their purchases of energy bars that is, there is a decrease *in the quantity demanded*. The price of these bars will continue to increase as long as there is a shortage and will stop as soon as the shortage disappears. This occurs when the price has increased to $22. At the new equilibrium price, the quantity demanded will again equal the quantity supplied but at a higher quantity traded of 18 cases.

> An increase in demand causes an increase in both price and the quantity traded.

The Effects of a Decrease in Demand

Now, let us see what happens when there is a decrease in demand. Remember that a decrease in demand cannot be caused by an increase in price but is caused by a change in any of the nonprice determinants, including

- a decrease in preferences for the product
- a decrease in incomes if the product is a normal product, or an increase in incomes if the product is an inferior product
- a decrease in the price of a substitute product
- an increase in the price of a complementary product
- the expectation that future prices or incomes will be lower
- a decrease in the population or a change in its income or age distribution

A decrease in demand is shown in Table 2.8 and illustrated in Figure 2.11.

TABLE 2.8
The Effects on the Market of a Decrease in Demand

NUMBER OF CASES PER MONTH			
Price per Case	Quantity Supplied	Quantity Demanded 1	Quantity Demanded 3
$18	10	16	10
19	12	15	9
20	14	14	8
21	16	13	7
22	18	12	6

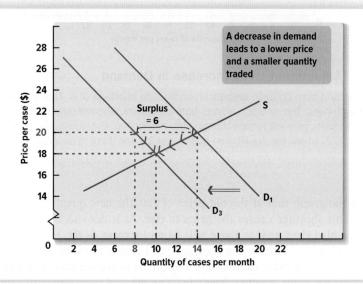

FIGURE 2.11   Adjustment to a Decrease in Demand

The drop in demand from D_1 to D_3 will cause an immediate surplus of 6, since the quantity supplied remains at 14 but the quantity demanded drops to 8. This surplus will cause the price to fall, and as it does, the quantity demanded will increase while the quantity supplied will fall. This process will continue until the surplus is eliminated. This occurs at a new equilibrium price of $18 and an equilibrium quantity of 10.

The initial equilibrium price is $20, and the quantity traded is 14. Assume that the demand now decreases to Demand 3 in the table and D3 in Figure 2.11. At a price of $14, producers will continue to produce 14 cases, yet consumers now wish to purchase only 8 cases. A **surplus** is immediately created in the market. The growth of unsold inventories and more intensive competition between suppliers will eventually push down the price. Note in Figure 2.11 that as the price decreases, the quantity supplied also starts to decrease, and the quantity demanded begins to increase. Both these factors will cause the surplus to disappear. The price will eventually drop to a new equilibrium of $18, where the quantity demanded and the quantity supplied are equal at 10 cases. In short:

A decrease in demand will cause both price and the quantity traded to fall.

TEST YOUR UNDERSTANDING

5. What effect will the following changes have on (i) the demand for, (ii) the price of, and (iii) the quantity traded of commercially brewed beer?

   a) a new medical report affirming the beneficial health effects of drinking beer (in moderation, of course)

   b) a big decrease in the price of home-brewing kits

   c) a rapid increase in population

   d) talk of a strike by brewery workers

   e) a possible future recession

SECTION SUMMARY

a) All products are either normal products or inferior products. With normal products, demand *increases* when incomes increase; with inferior products demand *decreases* when incomes increase.

b) Market demand changes if there is a change in

- consumers' preferences
- consumers' incomes
- the price of related products
- expectations of future prices, incomes, or availability
- the size of the market, or income and age distribution

c) An increase in demand will cause a shortage and cause both price and the quantity traded to rise.

d) A decrease in demand will cause a surplus and cause both price and the quantity traded to fall.

2.6 Change in Supply

> **LO6** Demonstrate the causes and effects of a change in supply.

Let us reiterate what we mean by supply: it is the relationship between the price of the product and the quantities producers are willing and able to supply. Price is *part* of what economists call supply. In other words, supply does not mean a single quantity. We now need to address what could cause a **change in supply**. What factors will cause producers to offer a different quantity on the market, even though the price has not changed—what will cause a change in supply? We begin with **Table 2.9**, where an increase in supply is illustrated. For reasons we will soon investigate, suppliers are now willing to supply an extra 6 cases of energy bars at every possible price. This is illustrated in **Figure 2.12**.

TABLE 2.9
An Increase in Supply

	NUMBER OF CASES PER MONTH	
Price per Case of Energy Bars	Quantity Supplied 1	Quantity Supplied 2
$18	10	16
19	12	18
20	14	20
21	16	22
22	18	24

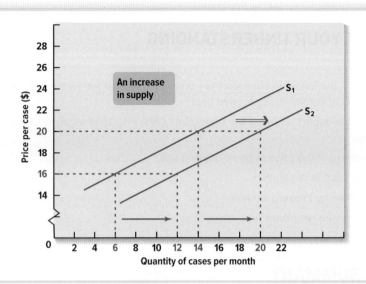

FIGURE 2.12   An Increase in Supply

At each price, the quantities supplied have now increased; that is, the supply curve has shifted right, from S_1 to S_2. For example, at a price of $20, the original quantity of 14 has now increased to 20. Similarly, at a price of $16, the quantity supplied has increased from 6 to 12. In this example, the quantities supplied have increased by 6 units at every price level, thus causing a parallel shift in the supply curve.

An increase in supply causes the whole supply curve to shift right. (Do not be tempted to describe it as a downward shift, because then you would be saying that as the supply goes up, the supply curve goes down, which could make things very confusing! It would be better to talk about a rightward shift.) This means that at each and every price, producers are now willing to produce more.

Determinants of a Change in Supply

What could have happened in the manufacturers' world to make them wish to produce more, even though the price is unchanged? Since we are assuming that the prime motivation for the supplier is profit, then something must have happened to make the manufacture of energy bars more profitable, which is inducing a higher supply. Profit is the difference between revenue and cost, and since the price (and therefore revenue) is unchanged, then something must have affected the cost of producing energy bars.

First, we will look at the *price of resources*. For energy-bar makers, this includes the price of wheat, granola honey, and other ingredients, as well as the cost of baking ovens, and so on. If any of these should drop in price, then the cost for the makers will fall, and profits will rise. Under these circumstances, since they are now making a bigger profit on each case of energy bars, they will be very willing to produce more. A fall in the price of resources will lead to an increase in supply. Conversely, an increase in the price of resources will cause a decrease in supply.

Another way of looking at the increase in supply, as shown in Figure 2.12, is to say that rather than firms being willing to produce more at a given price, they are willing to accept lower prices to produce any given quantity. For instance, previously, in order to induce the manufacturers to supply a total of 20 cases per week, the price needed to be $17. Now that the costs of production have dropped, these same manufacturers are able to make the same profits by producing the 20 cases at a lower price of $14: the manufacturers are now willing to produce the same quantities as before at lower prices. Again, this would produce a rightward shift in the supply curve.

It is often suggested that the availability of resources is a major determinant of the supply of a product. A poor grape harvest—grapes being the key input in the making of wine—will obviously have an impact on the supply of wine. However, it is not really the difficulty in obtaining grapes that causes a decrease in the wine supply, since most things can be obtained *at a price*. But there's the rub. A poor grape harvest will cause the price of grapes to increase, and this increase will reduce the profitability and production of wine producers.

A poor grape harvest is likely to cause the price of grapes to rise.

sonsam/Shutterstock

A second major determinant of supply is *government taxes and subsidies*. The major type of taxes imposed on suppliers are sales taxes such as the GST (general sales tax) and, in some provinces, the HST (harmonized sales tax). In addition, there are **excise taxes** which are special sales taxes imposed on products like alcohol, cigarettes, and gasoline. For suppliers, these taxes are similar to the other costs of doing business, and an increase in them will lead to a decrease in the firm's profits and thus cause a decrease in supply. A reduction in these taxes, on the other hand, will encourage firms to increase supply. In contrast, a **subsidy** is the reverse of a tax and is a payment made by the government to suppliers. The Canadian government, for instance, provides subsidies to the farmers of certain types of agricultural products and other specific products like solar panels. A subsidy will encourage greater production and therefore an increase in supply. A reduction or elimination of a subsidy will decrease supply.

A third determinant of supply is the *technology* used in production. An improvement in technology means nothing more than an improvement in the method of production. This will enable a firm to produce more with the same quantity of resources (or to produce the same output with fewer resources). An improvement in technology will not affect the actual price of the resources, but because more can now be done with less, it will lead to a fall in the per-unit cost of production. This means that an improvement in technology will lead to an increase in supply.

The price of related products also affects supply, just as it affected demand. But we must be careful, since we are looking at things from a producer's point of view and not a consumer's. What a producer regards as related will usually differ from what a consumer regards as related. A fourth determinant of supply, then, is the *price of substitutes in production*. To a wheat farmer, the price of other grains such as rye and barley will be of great interest because the production of all grain crops are related in terms of production methods and equipment. A significant increase in the price of rye may well tempt the wheat farmer to grow rye in the future instead of wheat. In other words, an increase in the price of one product will cause a drop in the supply of products that are substitutes in production. A decrease will have the opposite effect.

A fifth determinant of supply is the *future expectations of producers*. This is also analogous to the demand side of the market, but with a difference. While consumers eagerly look forward to a drop in the price of products, producers view the same prospect with great anxiety. Producers who feel that the market is going to be depressed in the future and that prices are likely to be lower may be inclined to change production now, before the anticipated collapse. Lower expected future prices therefore tend to increase the present supply of a product. Anticipating higher prices has the opposite effect; producers hold off selling all of their present production hoping to make greater profits from the future higher prices, assuming the product is something like oil, which is not perishable.

Finally, market supply will also be affected by the *number of suppliers*. An increase in the number of suppliers will cause an increase in market supply, whereas a decrease in the number of suppliers will reduce overall market supply.

Again, note that one thing omitted from this list of supply determinants is any mention of demand. At the risk of repetition, firms are not in business to satisfy demand but to make profits. Increased demand for a product does not mean that producers will immediately increase production to satisfy the higher demand. However, the higher demand will cause the price to increase, and this increase induces firms to supply more. But this is an increase in the quantity supplied and *does not* imply an increase in supply—the supply curve remains unchanged.

In summary, the determinants of market supply are

- prices of resources
- business taxes
- technology
- prices of substitutes in production
- future expectations of suppliers
- number of suppliers

The Effects of an Increase in Supply

We have just discussed six different factors that might affect the supply of a product. Let us be more specific and look at what can cause an *increase* in supply:

- a decrease in the price of resources
- a decrease in business taxes (or increase in subsidies)
- an improvement in technology
- a decrease in the price of a productively related product
- the expectation of a decline in the future price of the product
- an increase in the number of suppliers

Let us see the effects of an increase in supply using the original demand for energy bars and the increase in supply in Table 2.10.

TABLE 2.10
The Effect of an Increase in Supply on the Market

	NUMBER OF CASES PER MONTH		
Price per Case of Energy Bars	Quantity Demanded 1	Quantity Supplied 1	Quantity Supplied 2
$18	16	10	16
19	15	12	18
20	14	14	20
21	13	16	22
22	12	18	24

At the original demand (Quantity Demanded 1) and supply (Quantity Supplied 1), the equilibrium price was $20 per case, and the quantity traded was 14 cases. Assume that the supply now increases to Quantity Supplied 2. At the present price of $20, there will be an immediate surplus of 6 cases.

Before we look at the implications of this surplus, we ought to address a couple of possible qualms that some students might have. The first is this: Won't customers take up this excess of energy bars? It is easy to see that at this price, consumers have already given their response. They want to buy 14 cases, not 20 cases, or any other number. In other words, consumers are buying energy bars to satisfy their own tastes, not to satisfy the manufacturers. A second question is this: Why would producers produce 20 cases, knowing that the demand at this price is only 14 cases? The answer is that they do not know. Producers know the circumstances in their own companies and know that, until now, they have been able to sell everything they have produced. With the prospect of higher profits coming from, say, a decrease in costs, a manufacturer wants to produce more. If all producers do the same, there will be a surplus of energy bars. Figure 2.13 shows what happens as a result of this surplus.

Faced with a surplus of energy bars, market price will be forced down. As price falls, the quantity demanded increases and the quantity supplied falls. Production increased initially but is now dropping slightly because of the resulting drop in price. The price will continue to drop until it reaches $18. Table 2.10 shows that at this price the quantity demanded and the quantity supplied are now equal at 16 cases. The effect of the increase in supply, then, is a lower price and a higher quantity traded.

We leave it to you to verify that a decrease in supply will cause a shortage that will eventually raise the price of the product. (The factors that cause such a decrease in supply are exactly the same as those mentioned above that cause an increase—except they move in the opposite direction.) The net result will be a higher price but a lower quantity traded.

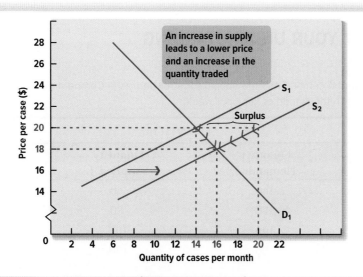

FIGURE 2.13   Adjustment to an Increase in Supply

The increase in the supply has the immediate effect of causing a surplus because the demand has remained unchanged. In this figure, at a price of $20, the quantity supplied has increased from 14 to 20, causing a surplus of 6. This will cause the price to drop, and as it does, the quantity demanded increases and the quantity supplied decreases until a new equilibrium is reached at a new equilibrium price of $18 and quantity of 16.

IN A NUTSHELL ...

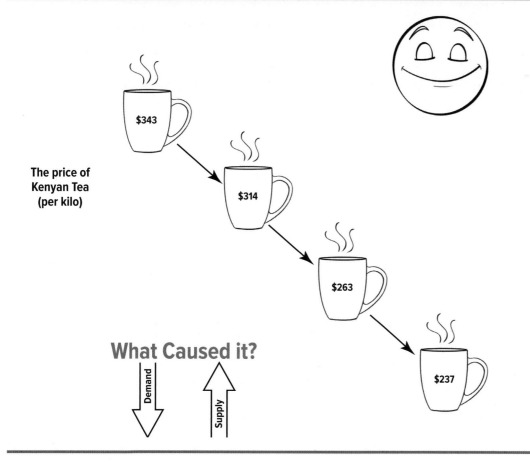

TEST YOUR UNDERSTANDING

6. Suppose that the demand and the supply for strawberries in Corona are as follows (the quantities are in thousands of kilos per week):

	QUANTITY		
Price	Quantity Demanded	Quantity Supplied 1	Quantity Supplied 2
$4.00	140	60	_____
4.50	120	80	_____
5.00	100	100	_____
5.50	80	120	_____

    a) What are the present equilibrium price and equilibrium quantity? Graph the demand and supply curves, labelling them D_1 and S_1, and indicate equilibrium.

    b) Suppose that the supply of strawberries were to increase by 50 percent. Show the new quantities in the Quantity Supplied 2 column. What will be the new equilibrium price and quantity? Draw in S_2 on your graph, and indicate the new equilibrium.

7. What effect will the following changes have on the supply, price, and quantity traded of wine?

    a) A poor harvest in the grape industry results in a big decrease in the supply of grapes.

    b) The number of wineries increases.

    c) The sales tax on wine increases.

    d) The introduction of a new fermentation method reduces the time needed for the wine to ferment.

    e) Government introduces a subsidy for each bottle of wine produced domestically.

    f) Government introduces a quota limiting the amount of foreign-made wine entering Canada.

    g) There is a big increase in wages for the workers in the wine industry.

    h) A big increase occurs in the prices of wine coolers (an industry that is similar in technology to the wine industry).

SECTION SUMMARY

a) Market supply changes if there is a change in

- the price of resources
- government taxes and subsidies
- technology
- prices of substitutes in production
- future expectations of suppliers
- the number of suppliers

b) An increase in supply causes a surplus and results in price falling and the quantity traded rising.

c) A decrease in supply causes a shortage and results in the price rising and the quantity traded falling.

2.7   Final Words

| LO7 | Explain why demand and supply determine price and the quantity traded, and not the reverse. |

To complete this introduction to demand and supply, let us use the following chart as a summary:

↑ Demand	→	shortage	→	↑ P	and	↑ Q traded
↓ Supply	→	shortage	→	↑ P	and	↓ Q traded
↓ Demand	→	surplus	→	↓ P	and	↓ Q traded
↑ Supply	→	surplus	→	↓ P	and	↑ Q traded

Note that when demand changes, both price and the quantity traded move in the same direction; when supply changes, the quantity traded moves in the same direction, but price moves in the opposite direction.

From this table, you should confirm in your own mind that it is the supply of and demand for a product that determine its price and not price that determines supply and demand. A change in any of the factors that affect demand or supply will therefore lead to a change in price. The price of a product *cannot* change *unless* there is a change in either demand or supply. It follows therefore that you cannot really analyze any problem that starts: "What happens if the price increases (decreases). . . ?" The reason for this, as the above chart makes clear, is that an increase in the price of a product might be caused by either increasing demand or decreasing supply. But in the case of an increase in demand, the quantity traded also increases, whereas in the case of a decrease in supply, the quantity traded falls. In the first case, we are talking about an expanding industry; in the second, we are looking at a contracting industry.

Finally, make sure you understand clearly the distinction between changes in the quantities demanded and supplied and changes in demand and supply as illustrated in Figure 2.14.

 ADDED DIMENSION

The Famous Scissors Analogy

Since the time of Adam Smith, economists have emphasized the importance of understanding the role of price determination. Toward the end of the nineteenth century, there were two schools of thought about what determined price. The first was made up of those who believed that the cost of production was the main determinant—the supply-side view. The second was made up of those, including the famous economist Alfred Marshall, who believed that consumer demand was the main determinant—the demand-side view.

Marshall, writing at the end of that century, was the first to present a lucid synthesis of the two views and suggest that neither demand nor supply alone can provide the answer to the determination of price. His famous analogy of the scissors states, "We might as reasonably dispute whether it is the upper or the under blade of scissors that cuts a piece of paper as whether value [price] is governed by utility or cost of production. It is true that when one blade is held still, and the cutting is effected by moving the other, we may say with careless brevity that the cutting is done by the second; but the statement is not strictly accurate and is to be excused only so long as it claims to be merely a popular and not a strictly scientific account of what happens."[2]

---

[2] Alfred Marshall, *Principles of Economics*, 8th edition, Macmillan (1920). Reproduced with permission of Palgrave Macmillan.

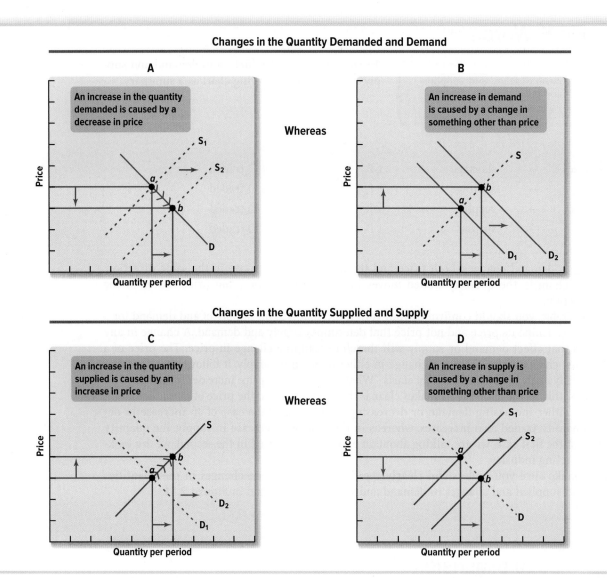

FIGURE 2.14   Distinction Between Changes in the Quantities Demanded and Supplied and Changes in Demand and Supply

Finally, let us look back at the discussion that started this chapter and see if we can make sense of it. Justine made an observation about the price of HDTVs falling, and Eric responded rather flippantly, "But that is just supply and demand." We now know that price can fall because either supply increased or demand decreased. Justine asked if Eric thought that the price fall was due to an increase in supply and Eric said, "Sure." Then came the really hard question: Why would supply go up if price was falling? Eric once again responded that this was just supply and demand. Of course, we now know that Eric should have said that the supply had gone up—perhaps because of increased technology—and that increased supply caused the price to fall. That is, changes in supply cause changes in price, not the other way around.

All of this is summarized in **Figure 2.14**. In graph A, we see a movement from point *a* to *b*, which is an increase in the quantity demanded resulting from the fall in price caused by an increase in supply (S_1 to S_2). Graph B shows an increase in demand, which causes an increase in price and in the quantity supplied (*a* to *b*). Graph C shows an increase in the quantity supplied (*a* to *b*), which follows an increase in price caused by an increase in demand (D_1 to D_2). Finally, in graph D, we see an increase in supply (S_1 to S_2) resulting in a fall in price and an increase in the quantity demanded (*a* to *b*). This allows us to conclude that:

An increase in the quantity demanded results when an increase in supply pushes price down (A). An increase in demand increases price, and thus the quantity supplied increases (B).

An increase in the quantity supplied results when an increase in demand pushes price up (C). An increase in supply decreases the price and thus the quantity demanded increases (D).

You now know what an important and versatile tool supply-and-demand analysis can be—but, like all tools, you must handle it properly and clean it after every use!

 TEST YOUR UNDERSTANDING

8. The following are changes that occur in different markets. Explain what will happen to either demand or supply and to the equilibrium price and quantity traded.

a) an increase in income on the market for an *inferior product*

b) a decrease in the price of steel on the *automobile industry*

c) a government subsidy given to operators of *day-care centres*

d) a government subsidy given to parents who want their children to attend *day-care centres*

e) a medical report suggesting that *wine* is very fattening

f) a big decrease in the amount of Middle East oil exports on the *refined-oil market*

g) an increase in the popularity of *antique furniture*

h) an increase in the price of coffee on the *tea market*

IT'S NEWS TO ME ...

Starbucks Corporation recently announced its plan to raise prices for packaged coffee and over-the-counter cups. They cited an increase in the price of Arabica coffee beans, caused by a severe harvest, as the reason for this action. A spokesperson for Starbucks said that, for both its package coffee and retail business, the overall cost structure was a major determining factor in its pricing policies.

The increased price for the consumer translate into about 10 to 25 cents per over-the-counter cup and $1 a bag for packaged coffee.

Source: *Star Power Reporting.* Summer 2016.

I. The increase in price of coffee was the result of

  a) an increase in demand
  b) a decrease in demand
  c) an increase in supply
  d) a decrease in supply

II. The increase in price of coffee beans was the result of

  a) an increase in demand
  b) a decrease in demand
  c) an increase in supply
  d) a decrease in supply

SECTION SUMMARY

The demand for and supply of a product determine the price; price does not determine demand and supply.

Study Guide

Review

WHAT'S THE BIG IDEA?

One of the important things to remember from this chapter is that the terms "demand" and "supply" do not refer to specific quantities. For instance, you cannot say that the demand for iPhones increased from 10 million units to 12 million units or that the supply of apples has fallen by 20 percent this year. As confusing as it might seem at first, you have to remember that economics defines them a little differently from everyday language. Both demand and supply refer to whole lists of prices and corresponding quantities. Think of these two concepts as tables of numbers, or better still, as lines on a graph. If you are able to do this, you will find that demand and supply analysis is a really powerful tool in understanding the world around us. The other important thing to remember is that the price of a product does not determine demand and supply. It's the other way around: demand and supply determines the price of most products.

Now suppose that you are thinking of starting up your own small company offering lawn cutting and garden services to households in your neighbourhood. One of the reasons for this is that it seems like easy money! You've figured out that many of the other companies now charge $50 a cut for the average lawn whereas only two years ago the price was $35. But before you start investing your money and energy, it will pay you to find out why the price has increased. In general, this can only be caused by an increase in the demand or a decrease in supply. If it is because of a higher demand, find out why. More homes have been built, perhaps? Or more lawns laid? Higher income people moving into the area? Or perhaps, people in the neighbourhood getting older? Or could the cause be that the supply has dropped? Perhaps other firms have had difficulty hiring workers and have to increase wages significantly? Or have a number of firms gone out of business because of conditions in that industry?

So whenever you hear of prices going up or down, try to work out whether it is demand or supply that has changed. If it is demand, think of the 5 factors that might cause this; if it is supply, remember there are 6 major causes.

NEW GLOSSARY TERMS

ceteris paribus
change in demand
change in supply
change in the quantity demanded
change in the quantity supplied
complementary products
demand

demand schedule
equilibrium price
equilibrium quantity
excise taxes
income effect
inferior products
market
market demand
market supply

normal products
real income
shortage
subsidy
substitute products
substitution effect
supply
supply schedule
surplus

Comprehensive Problem

Questions

(LO 1, 2, 4, 5, 6)   Table 2.11 shows the market for wool in the economy of Odessa (the quantities are in tonnes per year).

TABLE 2.11

Price ($)	100	200	300	400	500	600	700
Quantity Demanded	130	110	90	70	50	30	10
Quantity Demanded 2	—	—	—	—	—	—	—
Quantity Supplied	10	20	30	40	50	60	70
Quantity Supplied 2	—	—	—	—	—	—	—

a) Plot the demand and supply curves on **Figure** 2.15, and label them D_1 and S_1. Mark the equilibrium as e_1 on the graph.

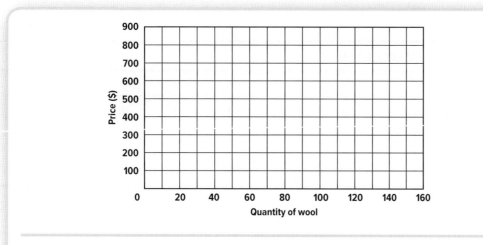

FIGURE 2.15

b) What are the values of equilibrium price and quantity?
c) If the price of wool were $600, would there be a surplus or shortage? How much? Indicate the amount of the surplus or shortage on the graph.

Answers

a) See the following figure:

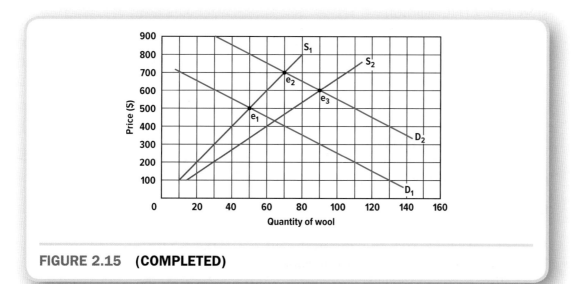

FIGURE 2.15   (COMPLETED)

The plotting of the curves is straightforward. For the demand curve, plotting just the first point (price $100 and quantity demanded 130) and the last point (price $700, quantity demanded 10) is sufficient. Similarly with the supply curve.
b) Equilibrium price: $500; equilibrium quantity: 50.
c) Surplus of 30. A price of $600 is above the equilibrium price of $500. Any price above equilibrium will produce a surplus because the quantity supplied will exceed the quantity demanded. The amount of the shortage is the distance between the curves. In this case it is 3 squares or 30 units.

Questions

d) Suppose that the demand were to increase by 60. Show the new Quantity Demanded 2 in Table 2.11.
e) Draw and label the new demand curve as D_2. Mark the new equilibrium as e_2 on the graph.
f) What are the new values of equilibrium price and quantity?

Answers

d) See the following table:

TABLE 2.11 (COMPLETED)

Price ($)	100	200	300	400	500	600	700
Quantity demanded	130	110	90	70	50	30	10
Quantity demanded 2	190	170	150	130	110	90	70
Quantity supplied	10	20	30	40	50	60	70
Quantity supplied 2	15	30	45	60	75	90	105

e) An increase in the demand of 60 means that the demand curve shifts parallel to the right by 6 squares to D_2 in **Figure 2.15 (Completed)**. D_2 intersects with S_1, at e_2.
f) Equilibrium price: $700; equilibrium quantity: 70 (where the quantity demanded 2 equals the quantity supplied).

Questions

g) Following the change in (d), suppose that the supply were to increase by 50 percent. Show the new Quantity Supplied 2 in **Table 2.11**.
h) Draw and label the new supply curve as S_2. Mark the new equilibrium as e_3.
i) What are the new values of equilibrium price and quantity?

Answers

g) See **Table 2.11 (Completed)**:
h) An increase in supply of 50 percent means that the supply curve shifts right to reflect a quantity that is 50 percent higher at each price level (for example, at price $300 it is now 45 rather than 30). This is plotted above as S_2 in **Figure 2.15 (Completed)**. The intersection with the D_2 curve is marked as e_3.
i) Equilibrium price: $600; and equilibrium quantity: 90 (where the quantity demanded 2 equals the quantity supplied 2).

Study Problems

Find answers on the McGraw-Hill online resource.

Basic (Problems 1–5)

1. **(LO 4)**
   a) Given the data in **Table 2.12**, draw the demand curve in **Figure 2.16**.
   b) What is the equilibrium price and quantity?
       Price: _____ Quantity: _____

TABLE 2.12

Price	Quantity Demanded
1	80
2	70
3	60
4	50
5	40
6	30

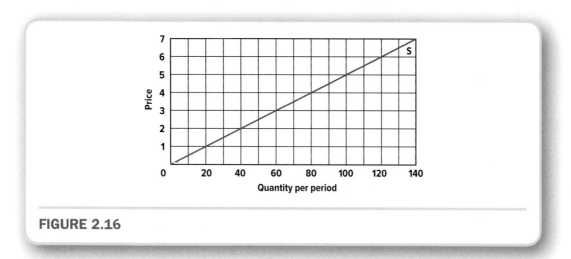

FIGURE 2.16

2. **(LO 3)** Figure 2.17 shows the market for large bags of potato chips.

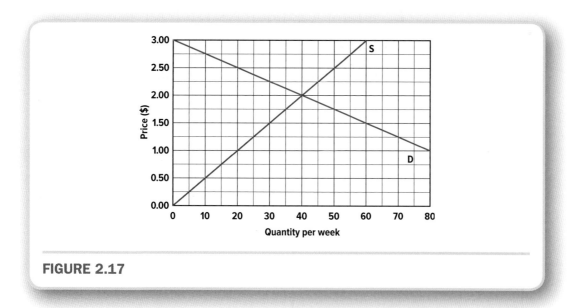

FIGURE 2.17

a) What is the equilibrium price and quantity?
   Price: _____ Quantity: _____
b) If the price is $2.25, is there a surplus or shortage of potato chips?
   Surplus/shortage _____ of _____ units
c) If the price is $1.50, is there a surplus or a shortage of potato chips?
   Surplus/shortage _____ of _____ units

3. **(LO 4, 5, 6)** Table 2.13 shows the market demand and supply for Fuji apples in Peterborough.

TABLE 2.13

Price	Quantity Demanded	Quantity Supplied 1	Quantity Supplied 2
0	180	90	_____
2	170	110	_____
4	160	130	_____
6	150	150	_____
8	140	170	_____
10	130	190	_____

a) What is the equilibrium price and quantity traded?
   Price: _____ Quantity: _____
b) Suppose that supply increases by 30. Complete the column in Table 2.13.
c) What would be the price and quantity traded at the new equilibrium?
   Price: _____ Quantity: _____
d) After the increase in supply, what would be the surplus/shortage at a price of $8?
   Surplus/shortage of _____

4. **(LO 3)** Figure 2.18 shows the market for halibut fillets.

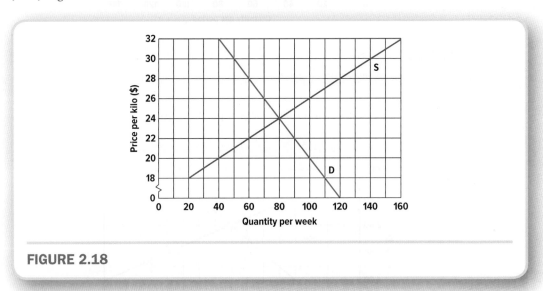

FIGURE 2.18

For the halibut market, fill in Table 2.14 showing the amount of surplus (+) or shortage (-) at each price.

TABLE 2.14

Price per Kilo $	+/−
18	_____
20	_____
22	_____
24	_____
26	_____
28	_____
30	_____

5. **(LO 5)** Figure 2.19 shows the market for pizzas.

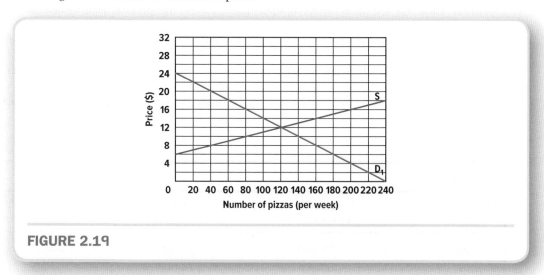

FIGURE 2.19

a) Suppose that the demand for pizzas were to increase by 60 pizzas per day. Show the new demand, labelled D_2, in Figure 2.19.

b) If the price stays at the old equilibrium, there would be a _____ (surplus/shortage) of _____ pizzas.

c) What would be the new equilibrium price and quantity?
   Equilibrium price: $ _____
   Equilibrium quantity: _____

Intermediate (Problems 6–8)

6. **(LO 4, 5, 6)** Table 2.15 shows the demand for new townhouses for 2011, 2012, and 2013.

Price $	2011 Quantity Demanded	2012 Quantity Demanded	2013 Quantity Demanded
TABLE 2.15			
320 000	5 200	5 500	5 300
340 000	5 100	5 400	5 200
360 000	5 000	5 300	5 100
380 000	4 900	5 200	5 000
400 000	4 800	5 100	4 900
420 000	4 700	5 000	4 800
440 000	4 600	4 900	4 700

a) When the price in 2011 changed from $400 000 to $420 000, what happened in the market for townhouses?
   Answer: There was a(n) (increase/decrease) of _____ in the (demand/quantity demanded) _____.

b) What happened between 2011 and 2012?
   Answer: There was a(n) (increase/decrease) of _____ in the (demand/quantity demanded) _____.

c) What happened between 2012 and 2013?
Answer: There was a(n) (increase/decrease) of _____ in the (demand/quantity demanded) _____.

d) When the price in 2013 changed from $400 000 to $380 000, what happened in the market for townhouses?
Answer: There was a(n) (increase/decrease) of _____ in the (demand/quantity demanded) _____.

7. **(LO 4, 5, 6)** Table 2.16 shows the demand and supply for the World Cup Final game in the Maracana Stadium in Rio.

TABLE 2.16

Price $ per Ticket	Quantity Demanded 1	Quantity Supplied	Quantity Demanded 2
150	119 000	79 000	_____
200	109 000	79 000	_____
250	99 000	79 000	_____
300	89 000	79 000	_____
350	79 000	79 000	_____
400	69 000	79 000	_____
450	59 000	79 000	_____

a) If the organizers wish to ensure a sellout for the final game, what is the highest price per ticket they should charge?
Price of: _____
b) What would happen if the organizers decided to charge a price of $200 per ticket?
Answer: There would be a (surplus/shortage) _____ of _____ tickets.
c) Suppose that the demand for each game in the qualifying rounds is 20 000 less than for the final game. Show the new demand in Table 2.16.
d) If the organizers wish to ensure a sellout for each game, what is the highest price per ticket they can charge for a qualifying round game?
Price of: _____

8. **(LO 5)** Figure 2.20 shows the market for soya beans:

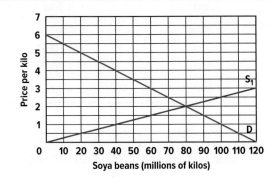

FIGURE 2.20

a) Suppose that due to a bad harvest the supply of soya beans is reduced by 50 percent. (The quantities at every price are one-half of what they are at present.) Draw the new supply curve, labelled S_2.

b) As a result of the drop in supply, what are the new equilibrium price and quantity?

Equilibrium price: $ _____

Equilibrium quantity: _____

Advanced (Problems 9–12)

9. **(LO 1, 4)** In Kirin, at a market price of $1 per kilo, there is a shortage of 60 kilos of avocados. For each 50-cent increase in the price, the quantity demanded drops by 5 kilos while the quantity supplied increases by 10 kilos.

a) Complete Table 2.17.

TABLE 2.17

Price	1.00	___	___	___	___	___	___	___	___
Quantity Supplied	100	___	___	___	___	___	___	___	___
Quantity Demanded	___	___	___	___	___	___	___	___	___
Surplus/ Shortage	−60	___	___	___	___	___	___	___	___

b) What will be the equilibrium price?

Price: _____

c) What will be the surplus/shortage at a price of $4.50?

Surplus/shortage of kilos: _____

10. **(LO 4)** **Figure 2.21** shows the market for the new Guns and Butter album, *Live at Saskatoon*.

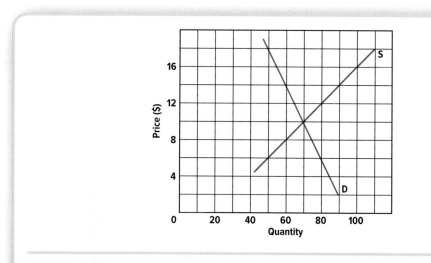

FIGURE 2.21

a) Suppose that the album producers put it on sale for $8 each. How much will be the surplus or shortage? How many will be sold?
Surplus/shortage of: _____
Quantity sold: _____
b) What is the maximum price at which the quantity actually sold in (a) could have been sold?
Maximum price: _____
c) If the album producers had actually put the album on the market at the price mentioned in (b), what would have been the resulting surplus/shortage?
Surplus/shortage of: _____

11. **(LO 4)** Figure 2.21 shows the market for the new Guns and Butter album, *Live at Saskatoon*.
a) Suppose that the album producers put it on sale for $14 each. How much will be the surplus or shortage? How many will be sold?
Surplus/shortage of: _____
Quantity sold: _____
b) What is the minimum price that suppliers would accept in order to produce the quantity actually sold in (a)?
Minimum price: _____
c) If the album producers had actually put the album on the market at the price mentioned in (b), what would have been the resulting surplus/shortage?
Surplus/shortage of: _____

12. **(LO 4, 5, 6)** Table 2.18 shows the market for probiotic yogurt in Canada.

TABLE 2.18

1	2	3	4	5	6
Price per Carton	Quantity Demanded (1)	Quantity Supplied (1)	Quantity Demanded (2)	Quantity Demanded (3)	Quantity Supplied (2)
2.00	120	60	_____	_____	_____
2.25	115	70	_____	_____	_____
2.50	110	80	_____	_____	_____
2.75	105	90	_____	_____	_____
3.00	100	100	_____	_____	_____
3.25	95	110	_____	_____	_____
3.50	90	120	_____	_____	_____

a) Suppose the price of a complementary product were to increase in price causing the demand to change by 30. Show the new demand in column 4 in Table 2.18.
b) What will be the new equilibrium price and quantity?
Price: _____ Quantity: _____
c) Suppose that *instead* the average income were to increase (and probiotic yogurt is a normal product), causing the demand to change by 15. Show the new demand in column 5 in Table 2.18.
d) What will be the new equilibrium price and quantity?
Price: _____ Quantity: _____
e) Suppose that *instead* the price of factors of production were to decrease causing the supply to change by 45. Show the new supply in column 6 in Table 2.18.
f) What will be the new equilibrium price and quantity assuming the original quantity demanded in column 2?
Price: _____ Quantity: _____

Problems for Further Study

Basic (Problems 1–6)

1. **(LO 5)** Circle which of the following factors will lead to an increase in the demand for cranberry juice (which is a normal good).
   a) a decrease in the price of cranberry juice
   b) a decrease in the price of cranberries
   c) the expectation by consumers that the price of cranberry juice is likely to increase
   d) an increase in the price of apple juice
   e) an increase in consumers' average income
   f) an improvement in the juicing process that lowers the cost of producing cranberry juice

2. **(LO 1, 2, 5, 6)** In each of the two graphs in **Figure 2.22**, explain the change in equilibrium from *a* to *b* in terms of
   1) an increase (or decrease) in demand (or supply)
   2) an increase (or decrease) in the quantity demanded (or quantity supplied)

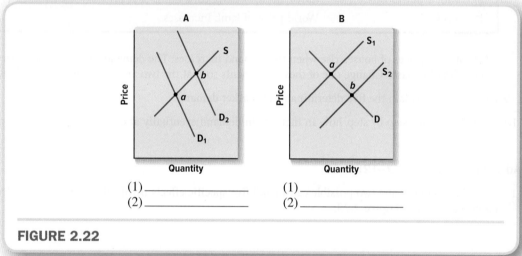

(1) _____   (1) _____
(2) _____   (2) _____

FIGURE 2.22

3. **(LO 4, 5, 6)** Suppose that new medical research strongly indicates that the consumption of coffee can cause cancer of the colon. What effect will this news have on the equilibrium price and quantity traded of the following products?
   a) coffee beans
      Price: _____ Quantity traded: _____
   b) tea, a substitute for coffee
      Price: _____ Quantity traded: _____
   c) Danish pastries, a complement to coffee
      Price: _____ Quantity traded: _____
   d) teapots, a complement to tea
      Price: _____ Quantity traded: _____

4. **(LO 5, 6)** What must have happened to demand or supply to cause the following changes?
   a) The price of guitars falls, but the quantity traded increases.
      Demand/supply must have _____.
   b) The price and quantity traded of saxophones decrease.
      Demand/supply must have _____.
   c) The price of trombones increases, while the quantity traded falls.
      Demand/supply must have _____.
   d) The price and quantity traded of clarinets increases.
      Demand/supply must have _____.

5. **(LO 1, 5)** What is the distinction between demand and quantity demanded?

6. **(LO 1, 4)** Explain the effect of a shortage on prices.

88   CHAPTER **2**   DEMAND AND SUPPLY: AN INTRODUCTION

Intermediate (Problems 7–10)

7. **(LO 4, 5, 6)** Consider the effects of each of the events outlined in Table 2.19 on the market indicated. Put a (↑), (↓) or (−) under the appropriate heading to indicate whether there will be an increase, a decrease, or no change in demand (D), supply (S), equilibrium price (P), and the quantity traded (Q).

TABLE 2.19

	Market	Event	D	S	P	Q
a)	Printer inks	A technological improvement reduces the cost of producing printers.				
b)	Butter	New medical evidence suggests that margarine causes migraines.				
c)	Newspapers	Because of worldwide shortages, the prices of pulp and paper increase dramatically.				
d)	Low-quality toilet paper	Consumer incomes rise significantly.				
e)	Movie downloads	Movie theatres halve their admission prices.				
f)	Beef	World price of lamb increases.				

8. **(LO 1, 5)** "The prices of houses rise when the demand increases. The demand for houses decreases when prices increase." Change one of these statements so that the two are consistent with each other.

9. **(LO 5)** Briefly explain the five determinants of market demand.

10. **(LO 4, 5)** Explain, step by step, how an increase in demand eventually affects both price and quantity traded.

Advanced (Problems 11–12)

11. **(LO 4, 5, 6)** Identify any two possible causes and five specific effects involved in the movement from point *a* to *b* to *c* in Figure 2.23.

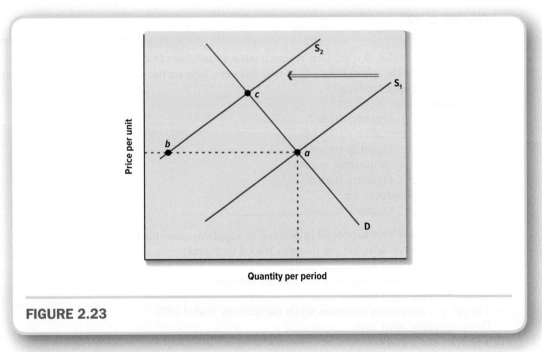

FIGURE 2.23

12. **(LO 6)** Suppose that in response to the high rent and low supply of affordable rental accommodation in the Toronto market, the city constructed 5000 additional rental units and put them on the market at below-equilibrium rents. Draw a supply-and-demand graph showing the effects on the rental market.

Appendix to CHAPTER 2
The Algebra of Demand and Supply

THE ALGEBRA OF THE MARKET

We have described the marketplace in both tables and graphs. This appendix explains how we can also analyze demand and supply algebraically. Suppose that **Figure A1** shows the demand for soya milk in Canada.

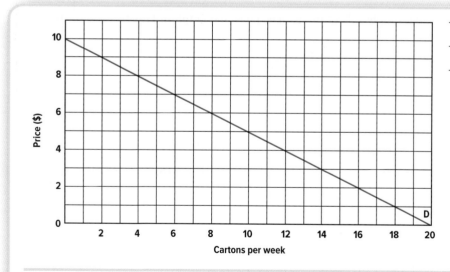

Number of Cartons per Week	
Price ($)	Quantity
0	20
1	18
2	16
3	14
4	12
5	10
6	8
7	6
8	4
9	2
10	0

FIGURE A1

You will remember from the Toolkit that, in general, the algebraic expression for a straight line is

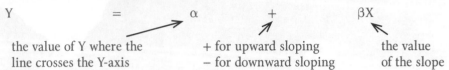

Y	=	α	+	βX
	the value of Y where the line crosses the Y-axis		+ for upward sloping − for downward sloping	the value of the slope

On our graph, price is shown on the vertical (Y) axis and the quantity demanded on the horizontal (X) axis. Therefore, the general expression for the demand curve is given as

$$P = \alpha + \beta Q^d$$

Here, the value of α is equal to ($)10. This is where the demand curve crosses the price axis; that is, it is the highest price payable. The value of the slope is the ratio of change, or *rise over run*. In terms of the demand curve, the slope shows by how much the quantity changes as the price changes.

$$\text{The slope} = \frac{\Delta \text{ (change in) P}}{\Delta \text{ (change in) Q}}$$

For our demand curve, that value equals

$$\frac{1}{-2}$$

This means that each time the price changes by $1, quantity changes (in the opposite direction) by 2 units. The equation for this demand curve, then, is

$$P = 10 - \frac{1}{-2} \, Q^d \quad \text{or} \quad P = 10 - \frac{1}{2} \, Q^d$$

Though this is graphically the correct way to express it, in terms of economic logic the quantity demanded is dependent on price rather than the other way around, so let us rearrange the terms, as follows:

$$Q^d = 20 - 2P$$

Now, let us look at the supply side of things. The table and graph in **Figure A2** show the supply of soya milk in the market.

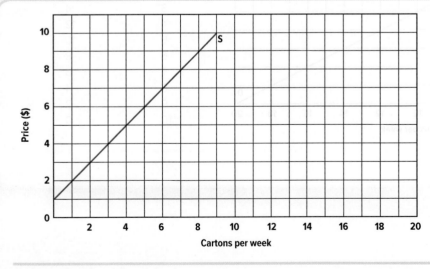

Number of Cartons per Week	
Price ($)	Quantity
0	—
1	0
2	1
3	2
4	3
5	4
6	5
7	6
8	7
9	8
10	9

FIGURE A2

The general equation for the supply curve is

$$P = \alpha + \beta Q^s$$

As with the demand curve, α shows the value where the curve crosses the vertical (price) axis. This happens at a price of $1. The value of the slope is, again, the same as for the demand curve.

$$\frac{\Delta \ (\text{change in}) \ P}{\Delta \ (\text{change in}) \ Q}$$

For this supply curve, it equals

$$\frac{1}{+1}$$

A $1 change in price causes a change of 1 unit in the quantity supplied. The equation for this supply curve, then, is

$$P = 1 + Q^s$$

As we did with the demand curve, let us rearrange this equation in terms of Q^s. Thus

$$Q^s = -1 + P$$

Bringing demand and supply together, in **Figure A3**, allows us to find the equilibrium values. From either the table or the graph, it is easy to see that the equilibrium price is equal to $7. At this price, the quantity demanded and the quantity supplied are both 6 units. Finding equilibrium algebraically is also straightforward. We want to find the price at which the quantity demanded equals the quantity supplied. We know the equations for each, and so we simply set them equal.

$$Q^d = Q^s$$

$$20 - 2P = -1 + P$$

That gives us

$$3P = 21$$

Therefore,

$$P = 7$$

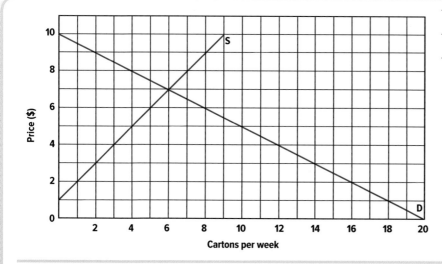

Number of Cartons per Week		
Price ($)	Q^d	Q^s
0	20	—
1	18	0
2	16	1
3	14	2
4	12	3
5	10	4
6	8	5
7	6	6
8	4	7
9	2	8
10	0	9

FIGURE A3

Substituting in either equation (and it is best to do both to make sure you are correct) gives us

$$Q^d = 20 - 2(7) = 6$$
$$Q^s = -1 + (7) = 6$$

Doing things algebraically sometimes makes things easier. For instance, suppose market demand increased by 3 units; that is, the quantities demanded increased by 3 units at every price. What effect would this have on the equilibrium price and quantity? Algebraically, this is quite straightforward to calculate. The increase in demand means that the value of the (quantity) intercept increases by 3 and gives us a new demand equation:

$$Q_2^d = 23 - 2P$$

The supply has not changed, and so we can calculate the new equilibrium as

$$(Q_2^d = Q^s)\ 23 - 2P = -1 + P$$

This gives us

$$3P = 24$$

Therefore,

$$P = 8$$

The new equilibrium quantity becomes 7. We can obtain this quantity by inserting the price of $8 into both equations. Thus

$$Q_2^d = 23 - 2(8) = 7 \text{ and } Q^s - 1 + (8) = 7$$

 Study Guide

Problems for Further Study

1. If $Q^d = 40 - 2P$ and $Q^s = 10 + 3P$, what are the equilibrium values of price and quantity?

2. a) If $Q^d = 100 - 5P$ and $Q^s = 10 + P$, what are the equilibrium values of price and quantity?
   b) If demand increases by 12 and price remains the same as in (a), will there be a surplus or a shortage? How much?
   c) If demand increases by 12, what will be the new equilibrium price and quantity?

3. a) If $P = 61 - 0.25Q^d$, what is the algebraic expression for Q^d?
   b) If $P = 16 + 2Q^s$, what is the algebraic expression for Q^s?
   c) What are the equilibrium values of price and quantity?

4. The following table shows the demand and supply of kiwi fruit in Montreal.
   a) What is the algebraic expression for the demand curve?
   b) What is the algebraic expression for the supply curve?
   c) Find algebraically the values of equilibrium price and quantity.

Price per Kilo	Quantity Demanded	Quantity Supplied
$0	675	0
1	575	50
2	475	100
3	375	150
4	275	200
5	175	250

5. Suppose that the demand equation is $Q^d = 230 - 3P$ and the supply equation is $Q^s = -10 + 9P$.
   a) If the price is 15, will there be a surplus or a shortage? How much?
   b) If the price is 22, will there be a surplus or a shortage? How much?

6. Suppose that the demand equation is $Q^d = 520 - 3P$ and the supply equation is $Q^s = 100 + 4P$.
   a) If the quantity presently supplied is 380, what is the price?
   b) At the price in (a), what is the quantity demanded?
   c) At the price in (a), is there a surplus or a shortage?

CHAPTER 3
Measuring the Economy 1: GDP and Economic Growth

LEARNING OBJECTIVES

At the end of this chapter, you should be able to:

LO1 Describe the circular flow of national income.

LO2 Explain the concept of equilibrium and why national income can rise and fall.

LO3 Describe the components of GDP accounting.

LO4 Understand some of the problems in determining official statistics.

LO5 Measure and describe the benefits of economic growth.

LO6 Explain the importance of productivity in encouraging growth and some of the problems of unchecked growth.

 WHAT'S AHEAD...

What determines the level of an economy's national income and how that income relates to real output are at the heart of macroeconomics. In this chapter, we begin the explanation of this determination by introducing the circular flow of income approach. We then look at the methods for measuring national income. Next, we look at the immense importance of economic growth and explain how it is measured, which takes us to an examination of the sources of growth. Lastly, we look at some of the problems often associated with economic growth.

A QUESTION OF RELEVANCE ...

Most young people these days are aware that they may not be able to rely on a state pension to provide them with enough money when they retire and that they should start saving from an early age. What they may not realize is the importance of compounding. If they were to put aside $200 each month, earning annual interest of 2 percent for the next forty years, they would accumulate a nest egg of nearly $150 000. However, the same amount invested at 5 percent annually would pay them more than $300 000 over the same period. The growth of savings is of great interest (pun intended) to each person. Even more important for us all is the growth of the economy. If the economy were to grow by just 2 percent each year, the average Canadian's income would rise from $48 000 to $106 000 over the next forty years. Just 1 percentage point more would increase that income to over $157 000.

In 2015, Canada's national income was $1983 billion. What are the major determinants of a country's income? How is national income measured? And what causes it to grow? More importantly, how can we ensure that growth is sustainable? Further, if economic growth is good for a nation, is more growth better than less? Finally, can an economy grow too fast? All these questions need reasonably-well-thought-out answers. The first step in the process of finding these answers is to understand how income flows within an economy. To do this, we will construct a simplified model of the economy.

3.1   Circular Flow of Income

LO1   Describe the circular flow of national income.

Flow of Factor Services

Imagine a simple economy with only two sectors: the household sector and the business sector. Clusters of individuals make up the household sector, whereas businesses of various types and sizes, from small family-run proprietorships to large corporations, make up the business sector. Next, recall from Chapter 1 that the factors of production (think of them as production inputs, if that is helpful) are divided into four categories: land, labour, capital, and enterprise.

   You may also recall that economists consider *land* to be anything that is natural, such as minerals, all natural vegetation, natural harbours, supplies of water, and so on. The term *labour* is used in the broadest sense to describe a wide range of human endeavour, including that of a skilled surgeon, a construction worker, or a symphony musician. *Capital* is defined as the physical plant, tools, and equipment used to produce other goods or services. In everyday language, capital is often used as an alternative term for money or funds needed to start up a business. In economics, however, capital refers to the tools, equipment, and machines that are used to produce other goods. Money can be used to purchase capital goods, but it is not, in itself, a factor of production. Finally, *enterprise* is the specialized human effort that organizes the other factors of production, innovates, and accepts the risks of doing so.

   These four factors of production combine to produce the goods and services that individuals consume on a daily basis. In our private enterprise or market economy, the factors of production are, ultimately, owned by individuals. Individuals control the sale of their own labour, individuals own land and mineral rights, and individuals own the shares of a corporation's assets or (for our purposes) their capital.

   We can now begin to build our model with a series of diagrams. The lower blue loop in **Figure 3.1** represents the provision of factor services from the household sector to the business sector. Businesses use these factor services, which are provided by the household sector, in order to produce

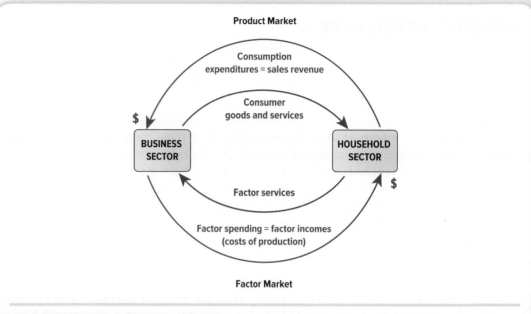

Product Market

Consumption
expenditures = sales revenue

Consumer
goods and services

$

BUSINESS
SECTOR

HOUSEHOLD
SECTOR

$

Factor services

Factor spending = factor incomes
(costs of production)

Factor Market

FIGURE 3.1   The Financial Flows

The inner blue circle represents the flow of factor services from households to business and the flow of consumer goods from business to households. The outer red circle shows the corresponding financial flows with a flow of factor spending going from business to households (to which it is an income) and consumption spending flowing from households to business (to which it represents sales revenue).

goods and services. This production flow is illustrated by the upper blue loop flowing from the business sector to the household sector, which represents the provision of consumer goods and services from firms to households.

The Flow of Incomes

Next, let us turn to the financial flows that move in the opposite direction. The business sector must pay for the factor services they receive. This payment is income to the household sector, becomes income, and is divided into the specific categories of wages, interest, rent, and profits. Remember that many of these terms differ from their conventional everyday usage. *Rent*, for instance, is the income received from the use of the factor land—that is, the payment for the use of a natural resource, such as royalty payments for a stand of timber—and is not the payment for the use of an apartment or other building. *Wages* means the income received for the use of labour services and includes commissions, tips, and all employee benefits. *Interest* means the income received for the use of the factor capital, which again differs from conventional usage. Finally, by *profits* economists mean income that is left over after the three factors of production have been paid, and it can be thought of as a reward for the fourth factor: enterprise. Thus, the lower red loop in **Figure 3.1** represents the financial flow of factor incomes (costs of production to the firm), wages, interest, rent, and profits from the business sector to the household sector.

Individuals in the household sector earn income by receiving payment for the factors they sell or rent. And what do these same individuals do with their incomes? Primarily, they engage in **consumption**—paying for the consumer goods and services received from the business sector. This flow represents an expenditure for households but is an income (in the way of sales revenue) for the firms. This financial flow is the upper red loop. So now we have two financial flows, as shown by the red circle in **Figure 3.1**.

Households sell factor services to the business sector and earn income. With this income, they pay for the goods and services received from the business sector.

A number of additions are on the way, but each can be handled easily if you keep this basic circular flow clear in your mind.

We have now identified what economists call the **product market**, which is the buying and selling of goods and services (the upper loops), and the **factor market**, which is the buying and selling of the factors of production (the lower loops).

It is important to keep in mind that every buy/sell transaction in either market is income to one sector and spending to the other. Thus:

> Income is the *sum of all earnings* from economic transactions or the *sum of all spending*.

The Flow of Income Versus the Stock of Money

Before going any further, there is a straightforward but very fundamental point that must be understood. We are building a circular flow of **income** model, and it is important that we distinguish between the flow of income and the stock of **money**. This crucial distinction was a focus of Francois Quesnay, an eighteenth-century French physician/economist, who founded a group of scholars called the Physiocrats. This group is credited with the idea that the interaction of nature and human activity produces wealth and income that then flows from one group in society to another.

Using this idea, let us imagine a simple economy made up of only three businesses: Bill owns and operates a bakery, Ani is the proprietor of a natural soap-making business, and Tammy has a tailor's shop. Within this economy, there is only a single $10 bill, which is currently in the possession of Bill, the baker. So we begin our story with three businesses (and three households), a stock of money equal to $10, and no income (yet). Let us assume that Ani has just produced some natural soap and that Bill, the baker, notices that he is out of soap. He goes to Ani and buys $10 worth of soap and pays cash. Ani, in receipt of $10, decides she needs to purchase a new pair of jeans produced by Tammy, the tailor, which just happen to cost $10. Tammy has spent all day producing these jeans and for her efforts receives $10 from Ani. After all this work, Tammy requires sustenance and makes her way to Bill, the baker, to buy some freshly baked bread, which has a price of $10. Bill, the baker, receives the $10 bill for his efforts. Let us summarize today's activities in this mini-economy:

- Total production came to a value of $30.
- Total spending came to $30 and total income is $30.
- All of this activity was financed by a single $10 bill.

Clearly, the stock of money and the flow of income are not the same thing! To cement this simple point, think of a retired couple with a lot of money—$200 000 in a bank account—but relatively little income—$16 000 a year in interest. Compare this with the young double-income professional couple just starting out, with an annual household income of $90 000 but almost no money in the bank because all the income is going to mortgage and car payments and the expenses of a fast-lane lifestyle. Again, the fundamental point—distinguishing between the flow of income and the stock of money—is important. In 2012, Canada's stock of money was approximately $300 billion. The flow of income during the same year was approximately $1820 billion. These figures tell us that the **velocity of money** in Canada for that year was 6.1. In other words,

$$\text{Velocity of money} = \frac{\text{total income (or GDP)}}{\text{money supply}} = 1820/300 = 6.1 \qquad [3.1]$$

This means that each unit of currency in Canada was used (changed hands) approximately six times during that year.

Closed Private Model

The simple economy described above seems to demonstrate that the value of (1) total production ($10 each worth of soap, bread, and jeans); (2) total expenditure (the purchase of each of these three items); and (3) total income (what Bill, Ani, and Tammy each receive) are equal. Does this always hold true, or is it merely a coincidence? We will answer this question soon, but for now you should realize that a good part of macroeconomics is concerned with the link between these three aggregates: production, expenditure, and income.

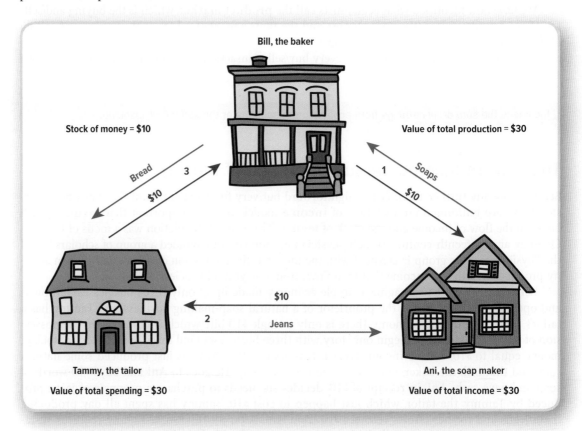

Keeping all this in mind, let us now return to the circular flow and introduce the first complication by asking: What else do individuals in the household sector do with their income besides spend on consumption? They save. **Saving** (S) can be defined as income (Y) received but not spent on consumption (C).

$$S = Y - C \qquad\qquad [3.2]$$

Saving thus becomes a **leakage** from the circular flow of income. A leakage, then, is a flow of income that is diverted out of the circular flow and doesn't flow directly back. This is shown in **Figure 3.2**.

The reasons that people want to save can be quite varied: for retirement; for a major purchase in the future, such as a house, car, or a holiday trip; for a child's future education; or, quite simply, for a rainy day. In this model, the primary determinant of how much people are able to save is their level of income.

It should be noted as well that while a business can also save by not paying out all of its after-tax profits in dividends, we will ignore this and focus on saving by households. Savings make up the portion of wealth that is held in the form of financial instruments, such as bonds, term deposits, savings accounts, and chequing accounts. Normally, these savings are deposited with various **financial intermediaries**, such as banks, credit unions, and trust companies, and are available for loan as shown in **Figure 3.2**.

Next, we want to add the concept of an **injection**, which is any expenditure received by firms in the business sector that does not come from the household sector in the form of consumption and thus does not depend on the level of income.

One form of injection is **investment** spending. Investment is defined as spending that results in a physical increase in plant or equipment. Another way of thinking of investment is spending that increases the economy's stock of capital goods.

Why would a firm invest in new machinery or equipment, thereby expanding its production capacity? Quite simply, to grow and increase potential profit in the future.

You will note that this definition of investment again differs from the conventional use of the term. If you overheard a fellow student say, "I invested in some General Corporation shares today," you

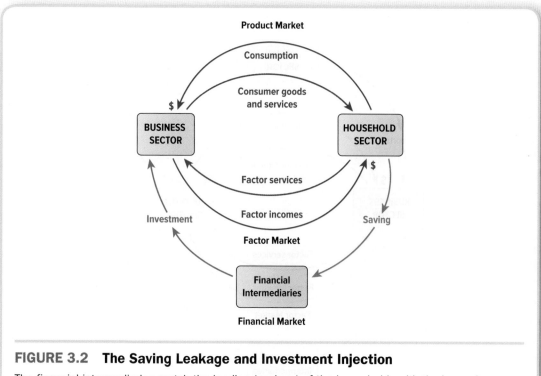

FIGURE 3.2   The Saving Leakage and Investment Injection

The financial intermediaries match the lending (savings) of the households with the borrowing (investment) of the business sector.

would correctly understand him to mean that he had bought some shares of General Corporation. Yet he has technically misused the term "investment," at least from the economist's point of view!

Let us get this sorted out. The person in our example was able to buy the shares through his broker only because someone else wanted to sell General Corporation shares. Someone sold the shares, someone bought them, brokers arranged the transaction and took a commission. From the point of view of the overall economy, what has changed? Very little. The portfolios of the two people in our example have changed, but the economy has not experienced any new investment.

In economics, investment is an increase in the economy's capacity to produce goods and services, and is done by business for profit.

To re-emphasize:

> The reasons individuals save (for retirement, future purchases, and so on) differ from the reasons businesses invest. Saving (a leakage) and investment (an injection) are quite distinct actions.

Does this imply that there is no connection between saving and investment? Not at all. Most of the time, investment by business is financed with borrowed funds, and it is the savings in the economy that provide the pool of funds: the savings available in the economy enable business investment to occur.

In other words, without savings there would be no investment. However this does not mean that all savings will necessarily be invested, and this leads us to a fundamental truth:

> Saving is a *necessary but not sufficient* condition for investment.

Open Private Model

Putting saving and investment aside for now, let us turn to a second pair of leakages/injections: imports and exports. First, the leakage. Some of the goods and services that households buy, as well as some of the investment goods purchased by business, are goods and services imported from

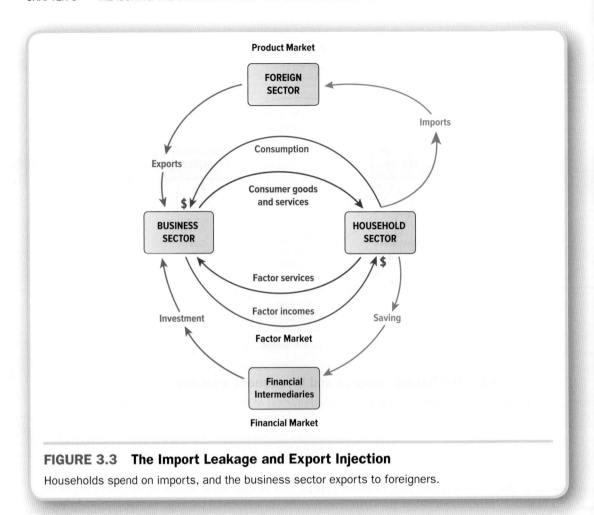

Product Market

FOREIGN SECTOR

Imports

Consumption

Exports

Consumer goods and services

$

BUSINESS SECTOR

HOUSEHOLD SECTOR

$

Factor services

Investment

Factor incomes

Saving

Factor Market

Financial Intermediaries

Financial Market

FIGURE 3.3   The Import Leakage and Export Injection

Households spend on imports, and the business sector exports to foreigners.

outside the domestic economy. Such expenditure does not flow back into the domestic economy, but instead leaks out. We refer to this import spending in the model as plain **imports** (IM). Although it is usually business that does the actual importing of goods, we will illustrate this leakage as coming from the household sector, reflecting the fact that the ultimate consumers of most imports are individuals.

Conversely, the business sector receives payment for goods and services exported, and this payment is in addition to the consumption expenditure from (domestic) households. **Exports** (X) are therefore an injection into the circular flow of income. (The flows shown here are the financial flows; we have ignored the flow of goods and services.) Note, then, that the value of exports does not depend on the level of income in this country but on the level of income in the rest of the world. The foreign sector, which is made up of the import leakages and the export injections, is illustrated in **Figure 3.3**.

Open Private Model with the Public Sector

The third pair of leakages/injections that we will consider is not so simply handled. First, we must add another sector to our analysis: government. The government sector taxes both the household sector and the business sector, and so taxes (T) are the third leakage. At the same time, the government sector purchases goods and services from the business sector, and so **government spending** (G) on goods and services is the third injection. In addition, government also disburses what are called **transfer payments** (TP). These are defined as payments made for which no goods or services are given in exchange (at the time of the payment). Examples of transfer payments would be Employment Insurance payments, Canada Pension Plan payments, and subsidies to businesses. For simplicity's sake, we will treat all transfer payments as a flow from the government sector directly to

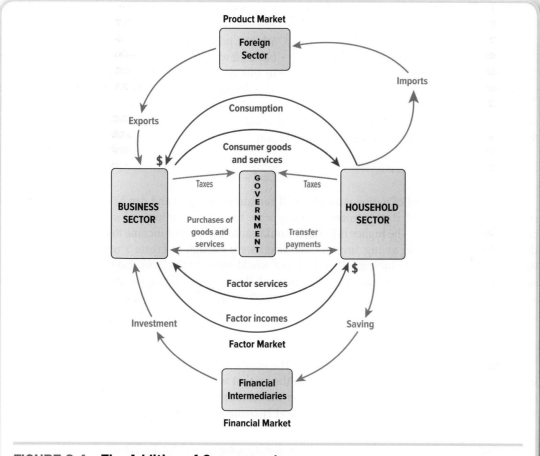

FIGURE 3.4   The Addition of Government

The circular flow of income in the whole economy includes three leakages:
- saving (S)
- import (IM)
- taxes (T)

The circular flow of income also includes three injections:
- investment (I)
- exports (X)
- government spending (G)

individuals in the household sector. Since households pay taxes and receive transfer payments we could use the term **net tax revenue** (taxes minus transfer payments) to denote the leakage. However, for simplicity's sake, we will continue to use the term *taxes*. The addition of the government sector is illustrated in **Figure** 3.4.

SECTION SUMMARY

a) The circular flow model illustrates both the financial and the real flows among the three sectors of the economy: business, household, and government.

b) Within this model, we find

- three leakages: savings, imports, and taxes

- three injections: investment, exports, and government spending on goods and services

- the idea that if injections are greater than leakages national income will rise, and if leakages exceed injections national income will fall

3.2 Equilibrium and the Level of National Income

> **LO2** Explain the concept of equilibrium and why national income can rise and fall.

We are now ready to take on the first of two very basic views of **equilibrium** that we will encounter in our development of macroeconomic principles. The dictionary definition of this term is "a state of balance or equality between opposing forces." The opposing forces here are leakages on the one hand and injections on the other. If these two opposing forces are in balance, the economy is in equilibrium.

Thus, in equilibrium,

$$S + IM + T = I + X + G \qquad\qquad [3.3]$$

In this case, the level of national income will remain unchanged and can be said to be in equilibrium. On the other hand, if investment spending were to rise, then injections would exceed leakages, creating disequilibrium. The higher injections would cause the level of income to continue to rise until the resulting increases in saving, imports, and taxes were enough to create a new equilibrium. Conversely, if tax rates were to increase, then leakages would exceed injections and this would cause consumption spending to fall and income to continue to fall until the resulting decreases in saving, imports, and (total) taxes were sufficient to bring injections and leakages back into equilibrium. In summary, if

$$I + G + X > S + T + IM \quad \text{then GDP rises} \quad \text{(economic growth)}$$
$$I + G + X < S + T + IM \quad \text{then GDP falls} \quad \text{(recession)}$$

A decrease in taxes would, of course, have the same effect as the increase in investment spending mentioned above. This gives an insight into a theme that we will be developing in subsequent chapters: changes in spending have a big impact on the level of income.

Thus, our first formal definition of **national income equilibrium** is:

> That level of income where the total of all three leakages equals the total of all three injections.

There is a second view of equilibrium, which introduces the concept of the **value of production** (or the value of total output). We measure the value of production by adding up what producers get as revenue when they sell their output, that is, by summing the total sales revenue of producers. The amount that producers receive for their products is equal to the amount paid by those who buy the output, and in turn, this total spending by buyers is called **aggregate expenditures**. Thus, the aggregate expenditures of buyers and the total sales revenue of the business sector are the same thing. But we can also measure the value of production in terms of how much it costs to produce that output. Since the costs of production (including profits) represent income to those who provide factor services, total costs of production must be equal to total income.

$$\text{Value of production} = \text{sales revenue} = \text{aggregate expenditures} \qquad\qquad [3.4]$$

and

$$\text{Value of production} = \text{cost of production (including profits)} = \text{total income} \qquad\qquad [3.5]$$

To emphasize, when an economy is in equilibrium, aggregate expenditures are equal to total incomes, and both are equal to the value of production.

Let us use a simple example here. If, in a given period, aggregate expenditures (consumption spending, investment spending, government spending, and net exports) equal $100, then sales revenue will, of course, also be $100. If we assume that inventories remain the same in this period, then it is also true that the value of production must have been $100, since this is the amount of goods that were bought. And how much income was generated in producing these goods? Exactly $100 worth—in the form of wages, interest, rents, and profits.

Once again, the fundamental point is:

> Equilibrium implies not only that total leakages equal total injections but also that aggregate expenditures equal total income.

Now that this second definition of equilibrium is well in hand, we are ready to move on to the measurement of national income.

IN A NUTSHELL ...

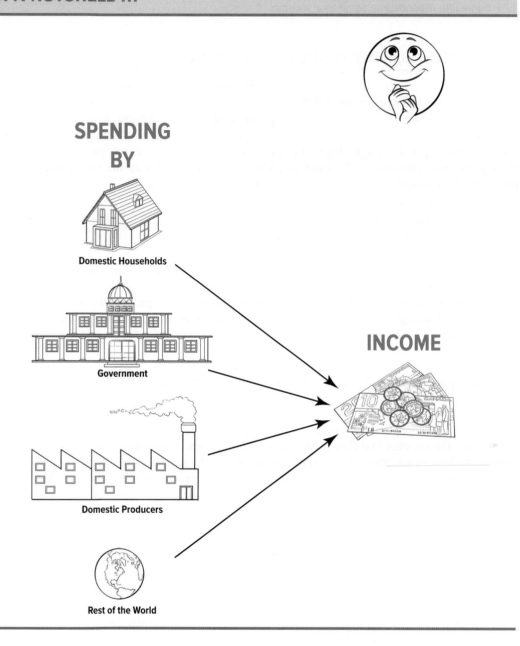

SPENDING
BY

Domestic Households

Government

Domestic Producers

Rest of the World

INCOME

TEST YOUR UNDERSTANDING

Find answers on the McGraw-Hill online resource.

1. If the economy is in disequilibrium because total income exceeds aggregate expenditure, what must be happening to inventories?

2. Does the term *consumption* refer to spending by households on domestically produced goods and services only? Does the term *investment* include the purchase of stocks and bonds?

SECTION SUMMARY

National income equilibrium occurs when

- total leakages equal total injections
- aggregate expenditures equal total income

3.3   Measuring National Income

LO3   Describe the components of GDP accounting.

The development of the circular flow of income model is complete. We now turn to the measurement of national income. Just as the circular flow diagram is helpful in conceptualizing equilibrium, it can also be helpful in recognizing that there are two different ways to measure income. The first is the *expenditures approach.* As the name implies, this approach adds up the four forms of expenditures, which, once again, are

- C = consumption
- I = investment spending
- G = government spending on goods and services
- X = exports

and then subtracts spending on imports (IM) because what we are after is total spending on Canadian-produced goods and services.

In short, the basic expenditure—consumption of domestically produced goods—plus the three injections give us aggregate expenditures (AE). This gives us an equation you will become quite familiar with:

$$AE = C + I + G + (X - IM) \qquad [3.6]$$

Defining **net exports** (X_N) as $X - IM$, we could rewrite this as

$$AE = C + I + G + X_N$$

The second conceptual approach to measuring national income—called the *incomes approach*—simply adds the incomes that flow to the three major sectors: households, business, and government. Adding the total expenditures in the economy or adding the total incomes in the economy are both valid measurements of the value of production. When the economy is in equilibrium, these two sums will equal each other (after three technical adjustments, which we will soon explain).

Measuring National Income: The Mechanics

This section contains many terms and may come to seem a little tedious, but every student of economics needs to have some understanding of how production is accounted for.

The most-used economic statistic is **gross domestic product** (GDP), which is defined as the money value of all final goods and services produced in the whole economy within a given year.

For our purposes, the other significant statistic is **gross domestic income** (Y). (Government agencies use the symbol GDI for gross domestic income, but we will use Y to be consistent with later chapters.) National income is defined as the total income received by the three main sectors in the economy in a given period.

There are two different ways to look at the value of any particular thing produced. The first and most straightforward is in terms of the price it finally sells for, for example, $3 for a tube of toothpaste off the retailer's shelf. Thus, one view is that $3 is its price and thus will equal the amount spent on acquiring it. The other view, equally valid, is that there is $3 worth of income to distribute to all those factors that went into the activity of getting that tube of toothpaste to the retailer's shelf. So the value of the toothpaste is the $3 of total income generated, which is paid to the various factors of production. In short:

The value of output is determined by the income generated in getting something into the hands of the consumer and is equal to the amount that consumers have paid for it.

Conceptually, then, at *equilibrium* GDP, the value of output must equal AE, which must equal Y.

$$GDP = AE = Y \qquad [3.7]$$

Measuring GDP by the Expenditure Method

Let us next explain exactly what Statistics Canada includes in each item of expenditure. The actual figures (in $billions) for Canada in 2015 were as follows:

C	I_g	G	$X_N (= X - IM)$
1140	389	500	−46 (= 625 − 671)

Summing these four figures gives us a GDP of $1983 billion.

First, consumption includes spending on consumer goods and services, which represents 57 percent of GDP and is subdivided into various components, such as:

Component	% of Total Consumption
Consumer durables (e.g., cars and household appliances)	13%
Semi-durables (e.g., clothes)	7%
Non-durables (e.g., food and beverages)	24%
Consumer services (e.g., educational, financial, health care, legal, and so forth)	56%

It's worth noting that while the amounts spent on consumer goods (durables, semi-durables, and non-durables) has increased decade by decade, the actual proportion spent on them has consistently fallen from 60 percent in 1961 to the present 44 percent. This is probably the result of them becoming relatively cheaper. Conversely, the proportion spent on consumer services has risen considerably as more people hire professionals to perform many services—child care, decorating, gardening, etc.—that in the past were done by householders themselves.

The next item, investment (20 percent of GDP), is composed of spending on machinery and equipment, changes in the value of inventories, and spending on all construction, including residential construction. (The change in business inventory from one period to the next is regarded by Statistics Canada as a form of investment and is what economists term *unplanned investment*.) The term I_g used below refers to **gross investment**—that is, before any depreciation is taken into account. Gross investment minus depreciation is **net investment**. The distinction between the two terms can be illustrated in terms of stocks and flows as follows:

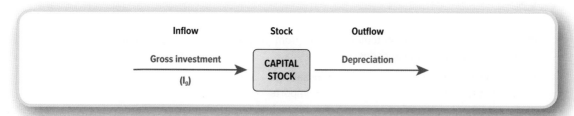

The capital stock of a country will grow as long as gross investment is greater than depreciation. The growth of the capital stock is what we mean by net investment, that is,

$$I_N = I_g - \text{depreciation} \qquad [3.8]$$

In many countries during the Great Depression of the 1930s depreciation exceeded gross investment so that these countries were not even able to replace worn-out capital; therefore, net investment was negative and the size of the capital stock was decreasing, but this is not the normal situation. What this means is that there are two types of investment: depreciation (replacement capital) and net investment (additions to the capital stock), so

$$I_g = I_N + \text{depreciation} \qquad [3.9]$$

The next category of spending, government spending, is the total spending on goods and services at all levels of government (including investment spending by government) and in 2015 represented

25 percent of GDP. Of course, governments spend on a huge variety of things: health services; education; military spending; security services, including the police, emergency services, courts, and prisons; pensions, including both Canadian Pension and Old Age pension; subsidies to firms; highway construction; salaries to bureaucrats and government administrators; and welfare payments and unemployment benefits. As we mentioned earlier, we must make a distinction between the two types of government spending: transfer payments, such as pensions, welfare, and unemployment benefits, which do not represent the payment for a good or service provided to government; and government spending on health, education, and so forth, which does represent payment for a good or service rendered. In short, transfer payments are not included as part of government expenditures.

Finally, net exports is the total value of all exports (whether of consumer goods, capital goods, or government services) less the total value of all imports. It is a positive number when exports exceed imports and negative when imports exceed exports.

Although Statistics Canada refers to this particular number as the gross domestic product, it could also be called aggregate expenditures since it represents the total amount of spending (including sales taxes) on Canadian products. As we shall see, it also represents the amount of income received by producers (including the government).

Next, let's determine how much revenue producers have remaining to pay their bills. To do this, we need to make certain adjustments. Firstly, firms are required to set up a fund for the replacement of worn-out capital. This is termed *depreciation* (or *consumption* of fixed capital, as StatsCan calls it) and is not available for distribution to either employees or shareholders. The second adjustment is for sales taxes (known as *indirect taxes* such as the HST) that firms are required to collect on behalf of the government. This figure is given net of any subsidies that the government has given to firms. (StatsCan calls this item *taxes less subsidies on products and imports.*) Subtracting these two items, we get

Gross domestic product (GDP) at market prices	1983
Less depreciation	338
Less indirect taxes (net of subsidies)	132
Net domestic product (NDP) at basic prices	1513

The term *net* in "net domestic product" means after depreciation, *basic prices* means prices excluding taxes, and *domestic* refers to the amount produced in Canada.

Next, we want to know how much of this total was actually produced by Canadian producers. To do this, we need to make one last adjustment. Most of the revenue that was produced in Canada stayed in the country and went to pay for wages, rent, and all the other business expenses. However,

TEST YOUR UNDERSTANDING

3. Identify the items in the statements below (from the point of view of the Canadian economy) according to the following codes:

C = consumption	S = savings
I = investment	IM = imports
G = government spending on goods and services	T = taxes
	X = exports
N = not applicable	

a) A student gets her haircut from a self-employed hairdresser.

b) The hairdresser buys a pair of scissors from the Ace Beauty Supply Company.

c) Out of each day's revenue, the hairdresser puts $5 in her piggybank.

d) Every time she has enough set aside, the hairdresser buys a GM share.

e) GM expands its computer facilities in its head office.

f) American tourists go skiing in the Canadian Rockies.

g) Two Canadians go to Tokyo and stay at the Hilton Hotel.

h) Russia buys beef from Alberta cattle ranchers.

i) The province of Saskatchewan pays for the building of a new highway.

in the case of foreign corporations operating in this country, a portion of that income in the form of interest and dividends was paid to owners abroad. Similarly, some Canadians earn income from their investment in other countries. Furthermore, we subtract the income of foreigners working in Canada and add in the salaries of Canadians working abroad. The term *net foreign factor income*, then, refers to the total amount of income coming into Canada less the amount that was paid abroad. (The figure might be a plus or a minus. In most years, more of this income leaves the country than enters it, so generally it has been a minus.) Thus,

Net domestic product (NDP) at basic prices	1513
+/− Net foreign factor income	−28
Net national product (NNP) at basic prices	1485

This last statistic, net national product, is the total amount of production that Canadians and Canadian firms are responsible for, regardless of where they are operating.

Measuring GDP by the Income Method

When measuring GDP by the income method, Statistics Canada lists the various incomes received by the three major sectors in the economy—households, business, and government—and shows five separate categories.

The first of these, *compensation of employees*, includes all wages and salaries (before any payroll deductions) as well as the value of other benefits received (including things like tips, commissions, and bonuses). In addition, it includes the employers' portion of CPP and EI. Next is *gross operating surplus*, which represents the gross profits of corporations before any deductions for depreciation or for profit taxes. The third category is *gross mixed income*, which includes the gross profits of nonincorporated businesses, like partnerships and self-proprietorships (again, before depreciation and taxes). It is referred to by this title because it is difficult to assess how much of this income represents the wages of the owners and how much represents profits.

The next two items are incomes for the government. This does not constitute their total revenue since they also receive income tax from both employees and corporations. *Taxes (net of) subsidies on production* are mostly made up of property taxes (paid to municipal governments). Finally, *indirect taxes (net of subsidies)* are sales taxes like the HST that we mentioned earlier. The amounts for these categories in 2015 (again in $billions) were as follows:

Compensation of employees	1024
Gross operating surplus	510
Gross mixed income	232
Taxes (net of subsidies) on production	85
Indirect taxes (net of) subsidies	132

Therefore gross domestic income (GDI) equals $1983 billion.

This represents the total gross income in all forms received in Canada and, as you can see, is the same as GDP as measured by the expenditure method. The other income statistics are analogous to the expenditure statistics.

Table 3.1 illustrates that the flow of expenditures and income are conceptually the same thing.

In summary, gross domestic product (GDP) is the same amount as gross domestic income (GDI), net domestic product (NDP) at basic prices equals **net domestic income (NDI)** at basic prices, and net national product (NNP) is the same as net national income (NNI); the latter is usually referred to simply as **national income** (Y).

Our next focus is on the term **personal income**, which can be thought of as people's gross income, that is, income before payroll deductions. National income can be thought of as earned income, whereas personal income is received income (before income tax). This means that we have to deduct from national income any items that people have earned but do not receive, and add in items that have been received but not earned. To do this, we need to make four adjustments (again we show the figures for 2015):

National income (or NNP at basic prices)	1486
Plus government transfer payments	269
Less undistributed corporate profits	71
Less corporate profit taxes	63
Less other income not paid out	101
= Personal income	1520

TABLE 3.1

Expenditures			Incomes	
Consumption	1140		Compensation of employees	1024
Gross investment	389		Gross operating surplus	510
Government	500		Gross mixed income	232
Net exports	−46		Taxes (net of subsidies) on production	85
			Indirect taxes (net of subsidies)	132
GDP @ market prices	1983	=	**GDI @ market prices**	1983
Less depreciation	−338		Less depreciation	−338
Less indirect taxes (net of subsidies)	−132		Less indirect taxes (net of subsidies)	−132
NDP @ basic prices	1513	=	**NDI @ basic prices**	1513
+/− Net foreign factor income	−27		+/− Net foreign factor income	−27
NNP @ basic prices	1486		**NNI @ basic prices**	1486

The first adjustment is for income that some people receive but have not earned for their services (at least in the current year). These are the transfer payments (for pensions, unemployment, and welfare) that we talked about in the circular flow discussion earlier in this chapter. These are added because they do become part of people's personal income but are not part of national income.

Since we are trying to determine the amount of income that households actually receive, we must make a couple of adjustments for the income that some of these households received as shareholders. From the gross profits that corporations earn, a portion is paid to the government in the way of corporate profit taxes and another portion is retained (saved) by those corporations. The remainder is paid to shareholders in the way of dividends.

Obviously, only the portion paid in dividends actually goes to individuals and thus becomes part of personal income. Therefore, the portion that goes to taxes and the portion that is saved are not part of personal income and must be subtracted from national income to get personal income.

The last adjustment, *other income not paid out*, includes quite technical items such as transfers from nonresidents and government investment income not paid out.

To complete our national income accounting framework, we need one final adjustment:

Personal income	1520
Less personal income taxes	−331
= Disposable income	1189

Disposable income can be thought of as people's take-home, or net, income and is the amount received after deduction of income tax (and other payroll deductions). This is what is at the disposal of the household. From the point of view of national income accounting, however, households really have only two choices about what to do with their disposable income—they can spend it or they can save it. Since we know how much they spent (consumption was $1140 in 2015), personal saving must have been $49 ($1189 disposable income less $1140 spent on consumption):

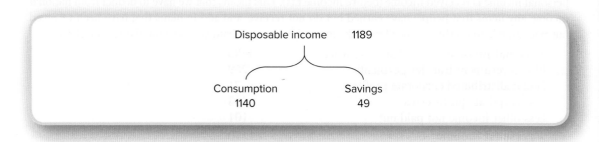

TEST YOUR UNDERSTANDING

4. If personal income is $986, personal income taxes are $227, and consumption is $686, what is the value of savings?

5. Given the following data for the country of Hemlock, determine the value of X_N.

Net foreign factor income	−10
National income	600
Government spending on goods and services	175
Indirect taxes (net of subsidies)	50
Gross investment	60
Consumption	420
Depreciation	20

6. Given the following data for the country of Seymour, determine the value of national income.

Personal income	589
Undistributed corporate profits	42
Corporate profit taxes	41
Other income not paid out	52
Government transfer payments	172

SECTION SUMMARY

a) The expenditures approach to measuring gross domestic product (GDP) involves adding up the four components of spending:

- *consumption* spending by households
- *investment* spending by businesses
- spending by foreigners on *net exports*
- *government spending* on goods and services

b) The incomes approach to measuring gross domestic product (GDP) involves adding up the five types of income:

- compensation of employees
- gross operating surplus
- gross mixed income
- taxes less subsidies on production
- indirect taxes (net of subsidies) on products

c) The other important statistics are

- net domestic product (income), or NDP at basic prices, which equals GDP after the deduction of depreciation and indirect taxes
- net national product (national income), which equals NDP minus an adjustment for foreign factor income
- personal income, which is national income plus transfer payments and minus undistributed profits, corporate profit tax and other income items
- disposable income, which is personal income after the deduction of personal income taxes

3.4 Problems in Measuring GDP

> **LO4** Understand some of the problems in determining official statistics.

Since many policy decisions are based on the level and growth of GDP, it is important for you to understand that there are some limitations in collecting and measuring the various statistics.

The real problem is in deciding what should and should not be measured. Let us spell out exactly what it is that we are trying to measure: the value of all final goods and services produced in an economy in a year. By and large, this will mean the market value of all items produced, plus government-provided services (which are included at cost). However, we do not want to include the market value of everything that has been produced. For instance, we do not want to include both the value of tires produced and the finished value of the car they are a part of; the inclusion of these intermediate goods would represent double-counting. As the definition suggests, we want to include the value of final goods only.

Perhaps an example will make this clear. In Table 3.2 we examine the sale of bread at each stage of its production.

TABLE 3.2
Stages in the Production of Bread

Producer	Purchases	Value Added	Value of Final Sale
Mrs. Farmer	$ 0	$ 1200	$ 1 200
Mr. Miller	1200	800	2 000
Mrs. Baker	2000	1000	3 000
Mr. Safeway	3000	2000	5 000
Totals	**$6200**	**$5000**	**$11 200**

Let us initially suppose that Mrs. Farmer uses her own seeds to produce the wheat. The value added by her and by the other producers is the total of their expenses and includes a profit. The wheat is sold to Mr. Miller for $1200 and after his value of $800 is added, the flour is sold to Mrs. Baker for $2000. The bread is then sold to Mr. Safeway for $3000, and he, after adding his services and profit, sells the bread to the final customers for $5000.

If we add the final sales of each producer, the total comes to $11 200, but this would be double-counting (more like quadruple-counting), since each producer's sales are included in the next producer's sales. To get the true value of productive activity, we can either take the value of the final product—Mr. Safeway's sales to consumers—of $5000 or we could add up the total of the value-added column. You can see from Table 3.2 that the total of the value added, $5000, is the same as the value of Mr. Safeway's final sales. Statistics Canada uses both approaches: it takes the value of the final sales ($5000), and it also calculates the amount of the value added. To get this figure, it adds up the sales by all companies (in our example, $11 200) and then subtracts their purchases from other companies (that is, the inter-company sales) of $6200.

Other obvious exclusions from measured GDP are the sale and purchase of financial instruments, such as shares. Although these are market activities, they do not represent real production but rather the transfer of asset ownership between people. (The value of the services of the stockbroker who made this transfer would be included in GDP.) For a similar reason, public transfer payments (CPP, EI, and so on)

Squeegee labour would be considered part of the "underground economy." Although not illegal, the income is not reported to tax collectors and is therefore not part of GDP measurement.

Macleans/The Canadian Press (Phill Snel)

and private transfers (such as gifts and donations) are also excluded. Also, because GDP is trying to measure current production only, second-hand sales would also be excluded, since their value was included when they were first produced. In summary, economic transactions that are not included in the measurement of GDP are

- the sale of intermediate goods
- sales that merely transfer ownership of assets
- both public and private transfer payments
- the sale of second-hand goods

Finally, we should mention a number of items that are excluded from the measurement of GDP even though they often do represent real productive effort. Some of these are excluded because Statistics Canada simply has no record of them. This includes all illegal activities such as drug dealing, selling illegal weapons, and so on, and other activities that, though not illegal, are not reported to the tax collector (perhaps in-home hairdressing and child care). The existence of this "underground economy" means that the GDP may be seriously understated. Also excluded are productive services, such as the value of the activities of a homemaker, do-it-yourself work, and volunteer work. They are excluded because, again, they are non-market activities. A non-market activity is, quite simply, any economic activity that does not involve a payment (or for which the payment received is not reported to Revenue Canada). If the work were paid for, it would be included. This means, of course, that if one-half of the population were to do the housework of the other half and vice versa and each paid the other, the GDP would increase dramatically!

It means also that one must be very careful when making comparisons of GDP over a period and between countries. It is certainly true that the GDP of Canada has grown substantially over the years. But a part of the reason is that many of the services now provided commercially were once provided on a non-market voluntary basis. We now have commercial homemakers, day-care centres,

 ADDED DIMENSION

How Well Is Canada Doing?

In terms of real GDP per capita, Canada ranks well below many countries in the world. (Its ranking is something like 11th or 19th, depending on what exchange rate is used in the calculations.) Yet, when the United Nations Human Development Index (HDI) is used as a measure of the well-being of a country's citizens, Canada's ranking is very high—until recently it has been consistently in the top five. The UN's HDI is an attempt to measure people's choices as indicated by the view that "the most critical of these wide-ranging choices are to live a long and healthy life, to be educated, and to have access to resources needed for a decent standard of living." It therefore includes not only real GDP per capita but also life expectancy rates and (until recently) levels of literacy. The UN recognizes that additional choices could include political freedom, guaranteed human rights, and personal self-respect, but that "a quantitative measure of these aspects has yet to be designed." One might also argue that any attempt at constructing this type of composite index of well-being should include a measure of religious freedom, crime rates, levels of taxation, and an environmental index. (Since 2010, the UN is using years of schooling rather than literacy rates as its educational component. As a result, Canada slipped from fourth to ninth place, as the following table shows.)

UN List of the Top Countries in 2015 (based on HDI)	
1. Norway	6. Germany
2. Australia	7. Ireland
3. Switzerland	8. United States
4. Denmark	9. Canada
5. Netherlands	10. New Zealand

Source: United Nations Development Programme, *Human Development Report 2015*, published 2015. Reproduced with permission of Palgrave Macmillan.

interior decorators, gardeners, aerobics instructors, and so on, whereas in the past these services were mostly non-market activities. In summary, productive activities that are excluded from the measurement of GDP are

- underground activities
  - illegal activities
  - unreported (but legal) activities
- non-market activities
  - services of homemakers
  - do-it-yourself production
  - volunteer services

 TEST YOUR UNDERSTANDING

7. Forty years ago, few households employed a housekeeper and almost no one had a nanny. Today, more and more households employ part-time housekeepers and nannies are not uncommon. What has this change in employment pattern done to GDP? Is more produced as a result of this change?

8. How could reported GDP remain constant while real production rose?

SECTION SUMMARY

a) For various reasons, national income statistics exclude

- intermediate goods

- transfers (both private and public)

- second-hand sales

- sales taxes

- the value of productive non-market activities and illegal activity

b) The following items are excluded from official statistics even though they involve the production of goods and services:

- underground activities (both illegal and unreported (but legal activities)

- non-market activities such as the services of homemakers, do-it-yourself production, and volunteer services.

3.5   Economic Growth

LO5 Measure and describe the benefits of economic growth.

The discussion in Chapter 1 about growth as an economic goal established that growth has both positive and negative aspects. Before we discuss this in more depth, we need to define **economic growth**. Although the media often refer to any increase in GDP as economic growth, economists prefer to define it as an increase in an economy's *real* GDP (we explain the term "real" below). Often, this is further refined to include an increase in real GDP per capita, which is real GDP divided by total population. This recognizes the fact that the population as a whole will not experience the benefits of growth unless real GDP grows faster than the population.

Let us first look at how modern economies measure economic growth; later, we will see exactly why growth presents difficult challenges that all economies have to face. Economic growth undoubtedly improves the welfare of people today and also gives society opportunities to address social needs to an extent that was undreamed of by previous generations. But we need to recognize that growth is a two-edged sword that can also inflict costs on society.

Measuring Growth

We have seen that Statistics Canada measures the GDP of Canada by taking the market value of all final goods and services produced in the country in a year. It is possible, then, for GDP to increase from one year to the next simply because market prices rise. In fact, the economy may not have produced more. Thus, we need to make the important distinction between **nominal GDP** and real GDP. To see if an economy is growing, we need to know if it did actually produce more goods and services. In other words, we need to eliminate the effect of rising prices. Statistics Canada does this by measuring each year's output in terms of constant prices. This distinction between nominal and real GDP is so important that we need to go through a detailed example to really nail it down.

In Table 3.3A, we assume a simple economy that produces four different goods—machines (a capital good), kilometres of road construction (a government good), bread, and cars (consumer goods). The value of production (nominal GDP) is simply the market value of those goods measured at current (year) prices. The total GDP, which is $42 000, is the sum of the four products.

TABLE 3.3A GDP Year 1			
	Quantity of Output	Prices Year 1	Nominal GDP
Machines	100	$100	$10 000
Kilometres of road	50	300	15 000
Bread	500	2	1 000
Cars	20	800	16 000
Total			$42 000

Now let us look at Table 3.3B and see how production changed in year 2. You will note that the quantities of output of machines, bread, and cars all increased compared with year 1, but the output of roads declined. You can also see that the prices of all four products increased in year 2 compared with year 1.

TABLE 3.3B GDP Year 2					
	Quantity of Output	Prices Year 2	Nominal GDP	Prices Year 1	Real GDP
Machines	120	$120	$14 400	$100	$12 000
Kilometres of road	40	320	12 800	300	12 000
Bread	600	2.50	1 500	2	1 200
Cars	25	820	20 500	800	20 000
Total			$49 200		$45 200

So nominal GDP increased from $42 000 to $49 200. However, this increase is partly due to the increase in production and partly to the increase in prices. In order to eliminate the effect of higher prices, the last two columns in Table 3.3B show the value of production if prices had remained constant at year 1's values. Using year 1 prices, we see that the value of **real GDP** is, in fact, only $45 200. In other words, what we mean by real GDP is the value of GDP assuming that prices do not change.

So how much did this economy grow between year 1 and year 2? Well, in terms of nominal GDP, it increased by $7200, from $42 000 to $49 200, or by 17.14 percent. This is calculated using the following formula:

$$\text{Growth of nominal GDP} = \frac{(\text{GDP in current year} - \text{GDP in previous year})}{\text{GDP in previous year}} \times 100 \quad [3.10]$$

However, if we measure the growth rate of *real* GDP, we find that it is only 7.6 percent ($3200 ÷ $42 000) × 100). (Note that in year 1, nominal and real GDP are the same thing.)

In summary, the annual economic growth rate is best measured in terms of the percentage change in real GDP from one year to the next, where real GDP is calculated by working out the value of production assuming that prices remain the same.

To cement these ideas, let us see what happened to this economy in year 3 as shown in Table 3.3C.

TABLE 3.3C
GDP Year 3

	Quantity of Output	Prices Year 3	Nominal GDP	Prices Year 1	Real GDP
Machines	130	$125	$16 250	$100	$13 000
Kilometres of road	50	350	17 500	300	15 000
Bread	650	3	1 950	2	1 300
Cars	26	840	21 840	800	20 800
Total			$57 540		$50 100

Here, we see the outputs of each item increased over year 2, as did all the prices. As a result, the value of nominal GDP increased to $57 540, which is an increase of $8340 or 16.95 percent ($8340 ÷ $49 200 × 100). But what about real GDP? Remember that to calculate real GDP, we need to assume that prices remain the same. But which prices do we use? We use the prices that were in effect in the base year. The choice of the *base year* is, in many ways, arbitrary. Statistics Canada usually uses a census year (1971, 1981, and so forth) as the base year, but this is not always the case. In our example, we will make year 1 our base year. The last two columns of Table 3.3C show the value of year 3's production using base year (year 1) prices. Real GDP in year 3, then, comes to $50 100, an increase of $4900 or 10.8 percent ($4900 ÷ $45 200 × 100) over year 2.

So calculating real GDP means that we have made allowance for the fact that inflation increases the GDP figures. However, as mentioned above, we may also want to consider the fact that while real GDP may have risen, the population may have increased as well. If that were the case, then the average person might not be any better off. To calculate real GDP per capita, we simply divide real GDP by the population.

$$\text{Real GDP per capita} = \frac{\text{real GDP}}{\text{population}} \quad [3.11]$$

Suppose, for example, that the population of our hypothetical economy in year 1 was 1.1 million and it increased to 1.2 million in year 2 and 1.3 million in year 3. Assuming that our GDP data were all in millions of dollars, we can easily calculate real GDP per capita for all three years as shown in Table 3.4.

TABLE 3.4
Nominal GDP, Real GDP, and GDP per Capita

	Year 1	Year 2	Year 3
Nominal GDP ($millions)	42 000	49 200	57 540
Real GDP ($millions)	42 000	45 200	50 100
Population ($millions)	1.1	1.2	1.3
Real GDP per capita	38 182	37 667	38 538

We can now see that the average person was actually worse off in year 2 compared with year 1 and was only slightly better off in year 3.

Our final piece of calculation is to show the change in real GDP per capita in percentage terms. The growth of real GDP per capita is by far the best and most important measure of how the average person's standard of living has changed.

$$\text{(Economic) growth rate} = \frac{(\text{real GDP per capita in current year} - \text{real GDP in previous year})}{\text{real GDP in previous year}} \times 100 \quad [3.12]$$

In year 2, the economy suffered negative growth:

$$\frac{(\$37\ 667 - \$38\ 182)}{\$38\ 182} \times 100 = \frac{-\$515}{\$38\ 182} \times 100 = -1.3\%$$

And year 3's growth rate (over year 2) was

$$\frac{(\$37\ 538 - \$37\ 667)}{\$37\ 667} \times 100 = \frac{+\$872}{\$37\ 667} \times 100 = +2.3\%$$

It is interesting to see how Canada has performed in recent years. Table 3.5 presents the data.

TABLE 3.5
Canada's Real GDP per Capita, 2007–2015

Year	Nominal GDP	Real GDP ($billions) (2007 = 100)	Population (millions)	Real GDP per Capita	Annual Growth Rate (%)
2007	1566	1566	32.9	47 599	1.1
2008	1646	1584	33.2	47 710	0.0
2009	1567	1541	33.6	45 863	−3.9
2010	1663	1593	34.0	46 853	2.2
2011	1760	1634	34.3	47 638	1.7
2012	1820	1662	34.8	47 759	0.0
2013	1892	1690	35.2	48 011	0.5
2014	1973	1734	35.5	48 845	1.7
2015	1983	1752	35.9	48 802	0.0

Source: Adapted by the authors from Statistics Canada CANSIM database, http://cansim2.statcan.ca, Tables 380-0064 and 051-0001, July 11, 2016.

Note that over the whole nine-year period, Canada's real GDP per capita rose by $2304—an increase of 3.6 percent, or approximately 0.5 percent per year, as Canada and other countries experienced a fairly large recession in the early part. However, during that recession, and unlike many countries, Canada experienced only one year of negative growth.

 TEST YOUR UNDERSTANDING

9. The economy of Rustica produces only two products, carrots and tractors. In 2016, it produced 5 million kilos of carrots and 2000 tractors. In 2017, production of carrots increased to 6 million and tractors to 2200. Calculate the value of nominal and real GDP in the two years, if the price of carrots increased from $2 to $2.50 per kilo and the price of tractors increased from $50 000 to $52 000.

Despite all of this, students are often bemused by the concern that economists show over growth rates. What difference does it make, many wonder, if the annual growth rate of an economy is only 3 percent rather than 4 percent? Well, considering that in 2015 Canada's nominal GDP was $1983 billion (in current prices), a 1 percent difference in growth translates into $19.8 billion. Dividing that by the approximately 10 million families in Canada, we get $1980. Could your family use an extra $1980 per year *every year* from now on? As you can see, even small differences in the growth rate can be significant over time.

Table 3.6 illustrates a fact that seems to come as a surprise to many Canadians: the country's growth in real GDP has been quite good compared to that of most countries over the past few years. For example, it was the highest of all the G7 nations (the G8 minus Russia) following the recession of 2008–10 and has been performing reasonably well in recent years.

TABLE 3.6
Growth Rates of Real GDP for G7 Countries

Country	Average Growth of Real GDP 2007–2012 (%)	Average Growth of Real GDP 2013–2017 (%)
Canada	1.3	1.9
Germany	1.2	1.4
U.S.	0.8	2.1
France	0.6	1.1
U.K.	0.4	2.2
Japan	0.3	0.6
Italy	–1.0	0.2

Source: Based on data from OECD (2016), *Economic Outlook No. 99 June 2016 OECD.*

The Benefits of Economic Growth

For many of us, the benefits of high economic growth are easily observed and enjoyed. High growth equates to a higher standard of living, which, in turn, translates into more exotic vacations, big-screen HD televisions, fancy smart phones, and bigger and better-equipped homes. But high economic growth can do so much more than merely providing us with more things; it can transform our lives immeasurably. To see this, we need only look back a few pages in history to the time before the biggest transformation that has occurred on our planet: the Industrial Revolution. Prior to that revolution, economic growth was so small as to be immeasurable. The life of the average peasant living in, say, southern Italy in the 1600s was little different from that of his father or his grandfather. In fact, in many ways, his life was probably little changed from that of peasants living 200, 400, or even 800 years earlier. In contrast, the life of the average person in Canada today is vastly different from that of a Canadian growing up 50 years ago, let alone back in the nineteenth century. And it is economic growth that has brought this about.

Economic growth does not just mean that we have more of everything; that is a truism. It also brings about a much more fundamental change in our social landscape. A rich country not only ensures that its people are free from poverty and hunger, it also enables them to be far healthier and live longer. In the past 150 years, for instance, we have seen the almost total eradication of communicable diseases such as diphtheria, typhoid fever, polio, and tuberculosis, which previously killed millions of people. The result is that life expectancy, especially in the richer countries, has increased dramatically in the past century or so. In Canada, life expectancy at birth in 1900 was less than fifty years; today it is over eighty-one years.

Not only is a rich country able to provide better and more accessible health services, it can also offer its citizens more education; grade 12 graduation has replaced grade 8 as a standard measure. Many poor countries cannot provide such a standard, and we know well that they have insufficient funds to provide the facilities. Nor can the parents in such countries afford to leave their children in school when they need them to help support their families. In most rich countries, including Canada,

ADDED DIMENSION

Are Economic Growth and a Better Environment in Conflict?

The activities of both production and consumption relate to the environment in two fundamental ways. We draw resources from the environment to produce goods and services and we emit wastes into the environment in the process of consuming them.

We think of economic growth as beneficial because it means a higher GDP. On the other hand, we think that protecting the environment represents spending that could otherwise have been spent on consumption or investment spending and therefore lowering GDP. This is the perceived conflict.

Economic growth is often seen as an indicator of the health of our economy. However, it is *not* a particularly good yardstick. A simple example will illustrate the point. If people learned the importance of taking good care of our constructed assets—homes, vehicles, industrial equipment, etc.— we would spend less on their replacement. This would reduce our GDP, but it would not reduce our ability to produce; in fact, it would do the opposite.

Furthermore, the thinking that market prices cover the true costs of products—is sadly off base. For instance, the cost of automobile use, today enormously subsidized, is a classic example. We build and maintain roads with revenues from general taxes, giving drivers the false sense that driving on them is "free." Similarly, the cost of parking space (think of your garage) is hidden in the mortgage payments on the house or provided by the employer at the plants or in the office buildings where goods or services are being produced, and the costs are hidden in the prices of that production. If individual car users actually paid all these true costs, the price of using the autos would increase dramatically. The result would be a powerful signal for us all to avoid unnecessary trips, shorten trip lengths (move closer to work), shift some our movements to transit, and maybe even walk and bike more.

In addition, and this is a crucial point, if auto registration fees and gasoline taxes were increased to pay for the true costs while being offset by reductions in general taxes and prices of other products, much more accurate price signals would be sent even though we would not be paying any more overall. As a result automobile use would decline and the environment would benefit.

Better indicators of our well-being and a more accurate pricing system would lead to the realization that pitting the economy against the environment is foolish and instead would help us recognize the reality that what we want is both prosperity and a sustainable planet Earth.

education is regarded as a right and not a privilege, and the number of people enrolled in postsecondary education increases every year. In Canada, in 2014, almost 60 percent of 25-to-34-year-olds were, or had been, enrolled in higher education—one of the highest rates in the world.

Besides the immensely important areas of health and education, economic growth provides other important benefits. It can enable a government to provide a good, well-maintained highway system, clean and plentiful parks and open spaces, funds to promote the arts and culture, and protection for the environment. A rich country offers its citizens the opportunity to work less and retire early without making a huge income sacrifice.

Finally, economic growth can enable a country to embrace social diversity. Through universal public education, it can also help countries eliminate discrimination against women and minorities, promote democracy, and uphold basic human rights. It comes as no surprise to most of us that those countries with the poorest records on human rights tend to be those that are economically the poorest and least developed. Economic growth, then, provides nations and people with the chance to achieve their greatest potential and can enable individuals to fulfill their aspirations. That does not necessarily mean they *will*, but the opportunity to do so is enhanced. To put a different twist on Oscar Wilde, it is difficult to look at the stars when your head is in the gutter. Economic growth can help lift us out of that gutter and make life a little less harsh and a little less cruel.

The benefits of economic growth include

- better health services
- improved quality and length of education
- better transport, more support for the arts and culture, and better protection of the environment
- protection of human rights with increased democratic involvement

SECTION SUMMARY

a) Nominal GDP is calculated by finding the value of production using current year market prices; real GDP is calculated by finding the value of production at base year prices.

b) Real GDP per capita is computed by dividing real GDP by the size of the population.

c) The benefits of economic growth include

- better health care services
- improved quality and length of education
- better transport, more support for the arts and culture, and better protection of the environment
- protection of human rights with increased democratic involvement

3.6   Sources of Economic Growth

LO6 Explain the importance of productivity in encouraging growth and some of the problems of unchecked growth.

Let us start this discussion by pointing out that the most obvious sources of economic growth are people themselves. Since labour is the most important economic resource, an increase in the size of the labour force, caused by either population growth or a higher participation rate (a greater percentage of people in the labour force), will enable a country to produce more. But we must not get carried away. An increase in the working population will not, by itself, guarantee economic growth. If it did, the world's most populous countries, China and India, would also be the most economically developed.

In reality, there is a growing consensus among economists that the *quality of an economy's labour resources* is the prime source of economic growth. A highly educated population results in a labour force that is mobile, adaptable, and highly motivated. As the world moves farther into the twenty-first century, these traits of mobility and adaptability are likely to become more and more important. We are witnessing a shift in the paradigm (the fundamental pattern) of what makes an economy successful.

Between 100 and 200 years ago, what would become today's successful economies shifted from an emphasis on agriculture to one on manufacturing. Tomorrow's successful economies are already in the process of a shift from a manufacturing base to an information/communications base, in which the whole world is the market. The areas in which new jobs are being created are changing—in fact, the definition and nature of work is also experiencing a paradigm shift. Gone are the days when a high-school graduate could step into a job at the local mill and earn, for a lifetime, an above-average income. Young people today will probably change careers three or four times in their working lives; training and education, both formal and self-taught, will be essential. Thus, the need to educate, and not just train, young people becomes increasingly important. And what of older workers who have been laid off from factories, which are now moving to other parts of the world? Here, we see the need for some form of retraining and encouragement to relocate. The old words used to describe a high-quality labour force might have been "hard-working and dedicated." The new words are likely to be "smart, mobile, and adaptable."

What we are driving at in this discussion is a very important concept that economists call *productivity*. **Labour productivity** is the output per unit of labour input during a specific period.

$$\text{Labour productivity} = \frac{\text{output per period}}{\text{units of labour}} \qquad [3.13]$$

As an example, assume that 100 workers produce 6000 tonnes of paper in a week. Here, labour productivity would be 60 tonnes per unit of labour or per worker. If, in three years, that figure rises from 60 to 70 tonnes per worker, there has been an increase in labour productivity. To a large extent, economic growth is about just such increases in productivity. But as the nature of work changes, ideas about what is productive and what is not also change. In the industrialized countries of the world, the output per unit of a factory worker is becoming less important than the creativity of computer programmers, product designers, and organizational managers. All this brings a whole new meaning to the term *labour quality*. This last point emphasizes the importance of what economists call **human capital**, which is defined as the accumulated skills and knowledge of human beings. An economy with a government that encourages human capital investment with well-funded and innovative education and training efforts, combined with a population that embraces the desire to improve its accumulated skills and knowledge, will be an economy with bright growth prospects.

A second fundamental source of economic growth is the amount of physical capital available within the economy. A worker with a mechanical backhoe will move more earth in a day than a worker with a hand shovel could in a week. Thus, an economy with a *higher capital/labour ratio* will be an economy with higher labour productivity.

Increasing the amount of capital stock in an economy is a direct result of more investment spending, which can be defined as a physical increase in the economy's plant and equipment. Canada has one of the highest capital/labour ratios in the world, and this, along with our rich supply of natural resources, has resulted in relatively high labour productivity in past years. However, things are now changing so fast that we cannot continue to rely on huge machines or natural resources to provide us with continued economic growth.

The third source of economic growth is *technological change.* Here, we are referring to not just more machines (capital) but better machines, not just finding more natural resources but finding and extracting them more efficiently. Technological change often involves better machines and equipment and always involves better methods of production, better ways of organizing work, and better ways of solving problems—in short, becoming more productive. A society that fosters and embraces technological change will soon be far ahead of one that does not. To some extent, this involves the attitudes of people as much as it does the brainpower that a society has at its disposal. Technological change can also be stimulated by spending, in both the public and the private sectors, on research and development—something that the Japanese have done more than any other society.

The assembly line method of production is a traditional source of high productivity and growth. But is it still a major source?

John A. Rizzo/Getty Images

Finally, it is important to mention that the amount and quality of an economy's natural resources can be a source of growth. Canada is generously endowed in this area, but that does make growth easier. This was particularly true in the early development of this country, in which beaver, fish, lumber, grain, and minerals played a significant role in growth. But we should not assume that plentiful natural resources alone can ensure economic growth. Think of Brazil with its rich endowment and poor growth record. Nor should we assume that a scarcity of natural resources means no growth. Witness Japan, which has practically no natural resources but an above-average growth record.

In summary, the sources of economic growth for an economy are as follows:

- the quantity and quality of labour resources (the level of human capital)
- the amount of physical capital available
- the rate of technological change
- the amount and quality of natural resources

 TEST YOUR UNDERSTANDING

10. Use the following information to calculate labour productivity (to one decimal place) per unit in both years. Approximately what percentage increase in labour productivity has occurred?

Year	Output	Labour Input
2016	12 400 tonnes	80 units
2017	14 400 tonnes	90 units

Growth and Economic Welfare

Despite the benefits that flow from economic growth as discussed above, we do need to add a significant word of caution to the general discussion of continued long-term economic growth. First, we should recognize that GDP figures are not designed to measure welfare in the sense of people's well-being; instead, they simply measure the market activity related to the production of goods and services. In this context, we cannot always simply assume that a higher GDP necessarily means a better life. A clear example of this point is that, as mentioned earlier, there are services—such as child care, housework, and changing the oil in the family car—that are now paid for that were previously provided by family, friends, and oneself and thus were not measured in GDP. The conclusion is that it is possible for measured GDP to grow even though the society as a whole is not actually producing more. In short, our world does not improve if we all do each other's laundry (for pay) even through our GDP would rise.

Second, GDP figures give no indication of the quality of goods produced. Neither do they tell us what types of goods are being produced: a gun and an economics textbook are rated equally if they are priced the same. Third, there is the point that if people begin to value leisure time more and *choose* to work less, then GDP would grow more slowly (in the extreme may even decline) but people would presumably consider themselves better off as a result.

There is another factor that we need to consider. Just because a country's national income is increasing does not mean that everyone is better off. It does not even mean that the average person is better off. In fact, the higher income may well be going to just the top-income earners in a country leaving the vast majority with the same or even a lower income. In other words, national income figures do not give us any indication of how fairly that income is distributed. Here, we need to make a distinction between average (or mean) income and median income. Average income is calculated simply by dividing a nation's total income by its population whereas the median income of a country is the income of the average (or middle) person. For instance in 2011 in Canada, the average family income was $66 200; the median income however was only $48 300.

All of the above pales in comparison to the point that the planet could be approaching the tipping point where the environmental costs of continued economic growth may well exceed its economic benefits. It is not difficult to find examples of these costs. The wonders of, and possible environmental damage caused by, hydraulic fracturing (fracking) in pursuit of more oil and natural gas are continually in the news today. So too is the ongoing debate over building more pipelines to move oil from Alberta to the west coast of British Columbia for export to Asia, or to eastern Canada, or to Texas to feed the giant to the south. Canada's Atlantic fisheries have been permanently crippled, Beijing's air quality is a health hazard, Russia's Aral Sea, once the world's fourth-largest, is a puddle, and the world's rain forests are being depleted. Holes in the atmosphere's ozone layer are still expanding in parts of the world. Heavy metals are accumulating in food chains, synthetic poisons are used more and more widely in agriculture around the globe, nuclear wastes from power plants continue to accumulate, and climate change is now obvious to all but a small group of deniers.

What underlies this entire litany of troubling and serious problems is the fact that the world's production of the things that define the way we live is growing at a rate never before seen in history. This growth takes more energy, and when a power plant or factory or car uses energy from oil, coal, or electricity the second law of physics (entropy) tells us that degraded energy is created as a result. Expressed as simply as possible, the fundamental problem is that human economic activity is generating far more degraded energy than the biosphere can handle without becoming dysfunctional. If this impairment continues much longer, the biosphere will lose its ability to support human life as we know it.

Many have suggested that we need to find ways of living together that require the use of less energy. This would mean that our attention must be turned from a focus on economic growth for its own sake to one that allows us to live in a way that at least has a chance of being sustainable.

In summary, economic growth does not necessarily mean that citizens are better off because

- a higher GDP may be the result of including the value of some services that were previously excluded
- the quality or desirability of the goods produced is ignored
- increased leisure, since it means less growth, is regarded as a bad rather than good thing
- GDP figures do not indicate how fairly a country's income is distributed
- the social and environmental costs of higher GDP are ignored

At times the cost of economic growth may exceed its benefits.
Costa007/Dreamstime.com

Because of these five factors, it has been recognized for some time by most economists that using the single statistic of real GDP per capita as a measure of a country's overall well-being is simplistic. Consequently, many attempts have been made to develop a better index of people's welfare. As we saw in an earlier Added Dimension box, the most significant of these attempts is the United Nations' Human Development Index (HDI), which produced its twenty-fifth annual report in 2015. In it, life expectancy rates, along with the mean and expected years of schooling plus the standard measurement of real GDP per capita, are blended to achieve a measure of human well-being. Canada has consistently ranked high on this index and in 2015 was ranked ninth in the world, but prior to 2010 it had ranked as high as third. The drop has resulted from the change in the education component, which previously included adult literacy rates (in which Canada ranked very high) but now measures years of schooling (in which Canada does less well).

IT'S NEWS TO ME ...

Recently, Kinder Morgan amended their application for approval of the 5.4 billion expansion of the Trans-Mountain Pipeline from Edmonton to Vancouver's harbour. They submitted a report which suggested that its risk assessment and 60-year history operating the existing pipeline show "the probability of a large pipeline spill is low." Kinder Morgan's submission doesn't ignore the negatives: it points out that oil spills are devastating to fishing and tourism industries, and notes the negative impacts on human health, damage to property and harm done to "cultural resources." However, the report also suggests that there are economic benefits that result from oil spills—the major one being that "Pipeline spills can have both positive and negative effects on local and regional economies, both in the short- and long-term," and that "Spill response and cleanup creates business and employment opportunities for affected communities, regions, and cleanup service providers."

Source: *Star Power Reporting*, Summer 2016.

I. What are the economic effects of an oil spill?

   a) The economic benefits always exceed the costs.
   b) The costs can never be accurately measured.
   c) The cost of the cleanup can be measured by what the money could otherwise have been spent on.
   d) The risks of a spill are so small that there is very little cost involved.

II. When Kinder Morgan says "spill response and cleanup creates business and employment opportunities . . ." what economic concept is being ignored?

   a) the circular flow of income
   b) supply
   c) demand
   d) opportunity cost

SECTION SUMMARY

a) Long-term economic growth is dependent on improvements in labour productivity, which is defined as *output per period/units of labour*.

b) The major sources of long-term growth are
  • the quantity and quality of labour resources (the level of human capital)
  • the amount of physical capital available
  • the rate of technological change
  • the amount and quality of natural resources

c) Economic growth does not always mean that people are better off.
  • A higher GDP may include the value of some services that were previously excluded.
  • The quality or desirability of the goods produced is ignored.
  • Increased leisure, since it means less growth, is regarded as a bad rather than good thing.
  • GDP figures do not indicate how fairly a country's income is distributed.
  • The social and environmental costs of higher GDP are ignored.

Study Guide

Review

WHAT'S THE BIG IDEA?

The two key concepts in this chapter are the circular flow and real GDP. If we want to measure how well an economy is doing, probably the best measure is the value of production. However, it is impossible to add together lumber and cars, computers, and fish, so what we need to do is find out the value of these various goods.

What's a new house worth, for instance? We might add up all the costs that went into producing it, but its real value is what somebody is prepared to pay for it. And that is true for all products. That payment represents an expenditure for the buyer, and income for the seller. "One person's spending is another person's income." We might therefore measure GDP (production) either in terms of spending or in terms of income. The two measures should be equal, and Statistics Canada calculates both.

However, we encounter a problem when looking at GDP over a period of time, simply because it is measured in terms of the value of products at the prices paid for them in those years. But we know that prices vary—and usually increase—for most products, so GDP might be rising simply because of higher prices and not because production went up. In fact, production might easily have fallen. To overcome this problem, economists, instead of looking at *nominal* GDP (the actual value of production each year), prefer to use *real* GDP, which simply asks what the value of GDP is assuming prices had remained the same every year.

NEW GLOSSARY TERMS AND KEY EQUATIONS

aggregate expenditures	human capital	net national product (NNP)
consumption	imports	net exports
disposable income	income	net investment
economic growth	injection	net tax revenue
equilibrium	investment	nominal GDP
exports	labour productivity	personal income
factor market	leakage	product market
financial intermediaries	money	real GDP
government spending	national income equilibrium	saving
gross domestic income (Y)	national income	transfer payments
gross domestic product (GDP)	net domestic income (NDI)	value of production
gross investment	net domestic product (NDP)	velocity of money

Equations:

[3.1] $\text{Velocity of money} = \dfrac{\text{total income (or GDP)}}{\text{money supply}} = 182/300 = 6.1$

[3.2] $S = Y - C$

[3.3] $S + IM + T = I + X + G$

[3.4]   Value of production = sales revenue = aggregate expenditures

[3.5]   Value of production = cost of production (including profits) = total income

[3.6] $AE = C + I + G + (X - IM)$

[3.7]   At equilibrium : $GDP = AE = Y$

[3.8] $I_N = I_g - \text{depreciation}$

[3.9] $I_g = I_N + \text{depreciation}$

[3.10] $\text{Growth of nominal GDP} = \dfrac{(\text{GDP in current year} - \text{GDP in previous year})}{\text{GDP in previous year}} \times 100$

[3.11] Real GDP per capita $= \dfrac{\text{real GDP}}{\text{population}}$

[3.12] (Economic) growth rate $= \dfrac{(\text{real GDP per capita in current year} - \text{real GDP in previous year})}{\text{real GDP in previous year}} \times 100$

[3.13] Labour productivity $= \dfrac{\text{output per period}}{\text{units of labour}}$

Comprehensive Problem

(LO 1, 2, 3) **Figure 3.5** is the circular flow diagram for the economy of Argos.

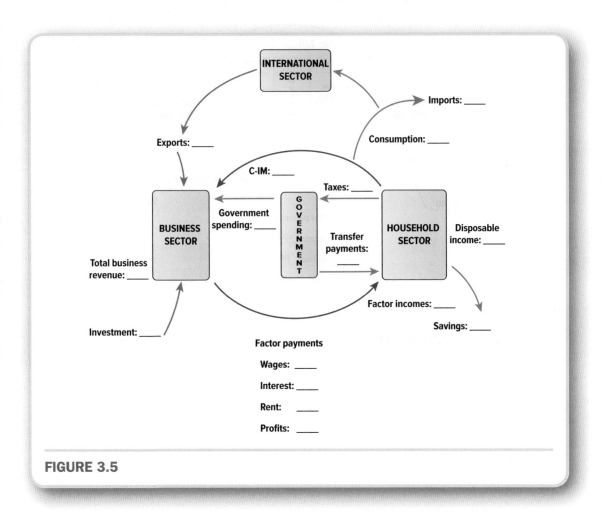

FIGURE 3.5

Questions

a) Place the numbers below in the appropriate blanks on the diagram in **Figure** 3.5.

Rent	$100	Savings	$100
Wages	400	Government spending	280
Profits	60	Exports	100
Interest	80	Imports	80
Taxes (households only)	360	Investment	40
Transfer payments	120		

What are the values of each of the following?

b) costs of production

c) total factor payments

d) disposable income
e) aggregate expenditures
f) total revenue of all businesses

Answers

a) See the following figure:

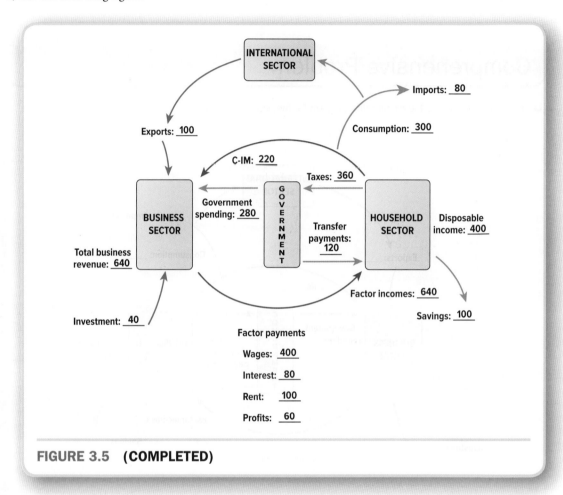

FIGURE 3.5   (COMPLETED)

b) Costs of production: $640. This is the total of: wages ($400), interest ($80), rent ($100), and profits ($60).
c) Total factor payments: $640.
d) Disposable income: $400. This is equal to $640 in factor payments less $360 paid in taxes plus $120 in transfer payments.
e) Aggregate expenditures: $640. This is made up of: consumption ($300) less imports ($80) plus government spending ($280), investment ($40), and exports ($100).
f) Total receipts: $640. Total receipts of all businesses are the same as aggregate expenditures because what is spent by households, the government, other businesses, and foreigners is received by the business sector.

Questions

g) total injections and leakages (*Hint:* Use net tax revenue, that is, taxes less transfer payments.)
h) balance of trade (net exports)
i) government's budget surplus/deficit (*Hint:* Use net tax revenue.)

Answers

g) Total injections: $420; total leakages: $420. Total injections consist of: investment ($40) plus exports ($100) and government spending ($280). Total leakages are: savings ($100) plus imports ($80) plus *net* taxes of $240 ($360 − $120).
h) The balance of trade (net exports): +$20. Net exports equals exports ($100) less imports ($80).
i) Government's budget: deficit of $40. The budget is net taxes ($240) minus government spending ($280).

Study Problems

Find answers on the McGraw-Hill online resource.

Basic (Problems 1–11)

1. **(LO 3)** In Table 3.7, you are given data for the country of Sequoia.
   a) What is the value of GDP at market prices? _____
   b) What is the value of NDP at basic prices? _____
   c) What is the value of net national product at basic prices (national income)? _____

TABLE 3.7

Exports	130	Government spending	198
Consumption	430	Imports	118
Gross investment	126	Net foreign factor income	−22
Depreciation	64	Indirect taxes	80

2. **(LO 3)** In Table 3.8, you are given data for the country of Hemlock.
   a) What is the value of personal income? _____
   b) What is the value of disposable income? _____

TABLE 3.8

National income	600
Personal income taxes	140
Other income not paid out	40
Corporate profit taxes	45
Undistributed profits	28
Transfer payments	90

3. **(LO 3)** In Table 3.9, you are given data for the country of Spruce.
   a) What is the value of GDI (at market prices)? _____
   b) What is the value of NDI (at basic prices)? _____
   c) What is the value of (net) national income? _____

TABLE 3.9

Net foreign factor income	−17
Gross mixed income	123
Depreciation	152
Compensation of employees	425
Indirect taxes (net of subsidies)	97
Gross operating surplus	261
Taxes less subsidies on production	41

4. **(LO 5)** In 2016 the country of Vertigo had a real GDP of $500 billion and a population of 20 million. In 2017, real GDP rose by 5 percent while its population grew by 2 percent. What are the values of GDP per capita in 2016 and 2017 (to the nearest dollar)? 2016 $_____ 2017 $_____

5. **(LO 5)** The economy of Turista produces only two products, protein bars and snowboards. In 2016 it produced 20 million protein bars and 100 000 snowboards. In 2017, production of protein bars rose to 24 million, and snowboards to 105 000. The price of protein bars rose from $2.50 to $2.80 over this period, while the price of snowboards rose from $280 to $300.

a) Complete Table 3.10.

b) What are the values of nominal GDP for Turista in 2013, and its nominal and real GDP in 2017?

    2016 Nominal GDP: _____ 2017 nominal GDP: _____ 2017 real GDP: _____

TABLE 3.10

	2016			2017				
	Quantity	Price	Nominal GDP	Quantity	Price	Nominal GDP	Price 2016	Real GDP
Protein bars	____	____	____	____	____	____	____	____
Snowboards	____	____	____	____	____	____	____	____
Total			____			____		____

6. **(LO 6)** Table 3.11 shows labour data for Eturia.

    a) Calculate the productivity rates for each year. _____, _____, and _____

    b) In which year was labour productivity highest? _____

TABLE 3.11

Year	Output per Week (millions of cases)	Labour Input (millions of workers)
2015	120	8.00
2016	126	8.07
2017	130	8.55

7. **(LO 3)** In Table 3.12, fill in the missing data for the country of Birchwood.

TABLE 3.12

Expenditures		Incomes	
Consumption	400	Compensation of employees	550
Gross investment	140	Gross operating surplus	____
Government spending	210	Gross mixed income	90
Net exports	100	Taxes less subsidies on production	50
		Indirect taxes (net of subsidies)	60
Gross domestic product @ market prices	____	**Gross domestic income @ market prices**	____
Less depreciation	40	Less depreciation	40
Less indirect taxes (net of subsidies)	60	Less indirect taxes (net of subsidies)	60
Net domestic product at basic prices		**Net domestic income at basic prices**	____
+/− Net foreign factor income	−50	+/− Net foreign factor income	−50
Net national product at basic prices	____	**(Net) national income**	____
		Add transfer payments	120
		Less undistributed profit	35
		Less corporate profit tax	50
		Less other income items	25
		Personal income	____
		Less personal income taxes	210
		Disposable income	____
		Savings =	____
		Consumption =	400

Intermediate (Problems 8–9)

8. **(LO 3)** Table 3.13 shows actual 2010 data for Canada. Using these data, fill in the blanks.

TABLE 3.13

Expenditures		Incomes	
Consumption	939	Compensation of employees	839
Gross investment	309	Gross operating surplus	____
Government spending	449	Gross mixed income	193
Net exports	____	Taxes less subsidies on production	75
		Indirect taxes (net of subsidies)	____
Gross domestic product @ market prices	1665	**Gross domestic income @ market prices**	____
Less depreciation	____	Less depreciation	276
Less indirect taxes (net of subsidies)	98	Less indirect taxes (net of subsidies)	____
Net domestic product at basic prices	____	**Net domestic income at basic prices**	1291
+/− Net foreign factor income	−32	+/− Net foreign factor income	____
Net national product at basic prices	____	**(Net) national income**	____
		Add transfer payments	____
		Less undistributed profit	66
		Less corporate profit tax	55
		Less other income items	105
		Personal income	1268
		Less personal income taxes	____
		Disposable income	____
		Savings =	74
		Consumption =	____

9. **(LO 5)** The data in Table 3.14 show the total output (a mixture of consumer, capital, and government services) and the prices of each product for the distant country of Vindaloo. All figures are in billions of dollars, and the base year is 2016.
   a) Complete the table, and answer the questions that follow (to one decimal place).
   b) What is the value of nominal GDP? 2017: $____ 2018: $____
   c) What is the value of real GDP? 2017: $____ 2018: $____
   d) What is the annual growth rate of nominal GDP? 2017: ____ 2018: ____
   e) What is the annual growth rate of real GDP? 2017: ____ 2018: ____

TABLE 3.14

1	2	3	4	5	6	7	8	9	10	11	12	13	14
		2016			2017					2018			
Item	Quantity	Prices Year 2016	Nominal GDP	Quantity	Prices Year 2017	Nominal GDP	Prices Year 2016	Real GDP	Quantity	Prices Year 2018	Nominal GDP	Prices Year 2016	Real GDP
Hot dogs	50	2	100	55	2.40				58	2.50			
DVDs	10	12	120	12	13				14	13.50			
Farm tractors	3	100	300	4	95				4	110			
Parking meters	4	50	200	4	60				5	70			
Totals			720										

Suppose that the population in Vindaloo is as shown in Table 3.15.
f) What is the real GDP per capita? 2016: $____ 2017: $____ 2018: $____
g) What is the growth rate in real GDP per capita? 2017: ____% 2018: ____%

TABLE 3.15

2016	2017	2018
23 million	24 million	25 million

Advanced (Problems 10–11)

10. **(LO 3)** Table 3.16 shows the data for the country of Magnolia. Complete the national income accounting framework by filling in the missing data.

TABLE 3.16

Expenditures		Incomes	
Consumption	____	Compensation of employees	860
Gross investment	370	Gross operating surplus	370
Government spending	400	Gross mixed income	____
Net exports	−40	Taxes less subsidies on production	90
		Indirect taxes (net of subsidies)	160
Gross domestic product @ market prices	____	**Gross domestic income @ market prices**	____
Less depreciation	____	Less depreciation	120
Less indirect taxes (net of subsidies)	____	Less indirect taxes (net of subsidies)	____
Net domestic product at basic prices	____	**Net domestic income at basic prices**	____
+/− Net foreign factor income	____	+/− Net foreign factor income	−20
Net national product at basic prices	____	**(Net) national income**	____
		Add transfer payments	240
		Less undistributed profit	60
		Less corporate profit tax	160
		Less other income items	70
		Personal income	1300
		Less personal income taxes	260
		Disposable income	____
		Savings =	120
		Consumption =	____

11. **(LO 3)** Table 3.17 shows some of the national income accounts for the economy of Elmwood (all figures are in billions of dollars).
From this information, calculate the value of
a) consumption _____
b) net exports _____
c) gross investment _____
d) GDP at market prices _____

e) gross mixed income _____

f) NDP at basic prices _____

g) national income _____

h) personal income _____

TABLE 3.17

Personal income taxes	160
Indirect taxes (net of subsidies)	130
Corporate profit taxes	40
Exports	45
Government spending on goods and services	240
Disposable income	820
Personal savings	100
Imports	85
Compensation of employees	620
Investment (net)	90
Net foreign factor incomes	+20
Gross operating surplus	190
Transfer payments	170
Depreciation	80
Taxes less subsidies on production	90
Other income not paid out	20

Problems for Further Study

Basic (Problems 1–5)

1. **(LO 3)** Identify the items in the statements below (from the point of view of the Canadian economy) according to the following code:

   C = consumption   S = savings
   G = government spending   T = taxes
   X = exports   IM = imports
   I = investment   N = not applicable

   a) A Canadian tourist visits Athens. _____

   b) A shipment of Canadian hothouse cucumbers is sent to the United States. _____

   c) A medical doctor in Alberta buys a new car that was built in Ontario. _____

   d) An accountant makes a regular monthly contribution to her RRSP fund. _____

   e) The federal government buys new equipment for the military. _____

2. **(LO 3)** Indicate which of the following are productive activities (P) and which are nonproductive (N). Then indicate which of them are included (I) in national income statistics and which are excluded (Ex).

   a) the sale of 100 shares of EA Sports _____

   b) child care at home _____

   c) a person employed by the Tumbleweed Day Care Centre _____

   d) the time spent by a person volunteering time at a local hospital _____

   e) the money spent to renovate a storefront for a new retail business _____

   f) the time spent by a householder to renovate a garden shed _____

3. **(LO 1)** In Figure 3.6, replace each "*" with the appropriate term(s).

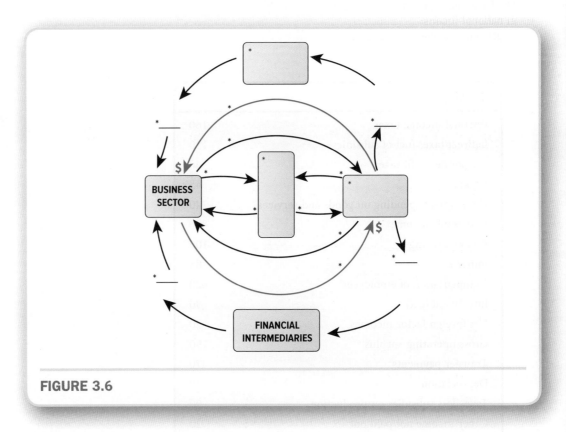

FIGURE 3.6

4. **(LO 1)** Distinguish between savings and investment.
5. **(LO 5)** Define *economic growth*.

Intermediate (Problems 6–10)

6. **(LO 3)** Compare the expenditures approach to GDP measurement to the incomes approach.
7. **(LO 1)** Explain the difference between the stock of money and the flow of income.
8. **(LO 2)** What two things are true when an economy is in equilibrium?
9. **(LO 4)** Are all productive activities that are not included in the measurement of GDP illegal?
10. **(LO 3)** Why has the proportion of income spent on consumer goods in Canada decreased over the past 50 years?

Advanced (Problems 11–13)

11. **(LO 3)** Suppose that new automobile purchases were treated like new housing purchases in national income accounts. How would that affect savings, consumption, investment, GDP, and DI? (*Hint:* This question is about reclassification, not about cause and effect.)
12. **(LO 4)** Explain why transfer payments are excluded from the measurement of GDP.
13. **(LO 6)** Explain why a high economic growth rate does not necessarily mean an improvement in economic welfare.

CHAPTER 4
Measuring the Economy 2: Unemployment and Inflation

LEARNING OBJECTIVES

At the end of this chapter, you should be able to:

LO1 Describe what unemployment is and how it is measured.

LO2 Explain the different types of unemployment and the costs of unemployment.

LO3 Explain what inflation is and how it is measured.

LO4 Explain the two types of inflation and describe the costs of inflation.

WHAT'S AHEAD...

In this chapter, our general introduction to macroeconomics extends to a focus on unemployment and inflation—two eternal issues that tend to dominate the economic news. First, we describe how unemployment is measured and look at the different types of unemployment and how the cost of unemployment can be measured. Next, we look at how inflation is defined and two ways it is measured. Finally, we investigate the causes and costs of inflation.

A QUESTION OF RELEVANCE ...

Canada came out of the financial crisis of 2009–11 rather well as growth in GDP rose about 2 percent per year, and unemployment fell in 2012–14. But the collapse in the price of oil in 2015 hit the economy hard with growth rates dropping and unemployment increasing. Will you be able to avoid being an unemployment statistic during your working life? Is inflation, the other "twin evil," really a big problem, and how does it affect you personally? These questions begin to take on more urgency as you approach the transition from student to active participant in the labour force with career aspirations. This chapter will help you think more deeply about these issues.

We look first at unemployment: exactly what it is, what causes it, and its real costs to individuals and society. The second issue is inflation—what are the costs of containing it, and are those costs too high? It is necessary to add that in this chapter we are not attempting to provide complete answers to the causes of unemployment or inflation. (We will do this in the next chapter by constructing a model of the macroeconomy.) For now, we will focus on how we go about measuring unemployment and inflation and see some of the problems that are involved in doing so. This will give us a much better sense of what these terms mean.

4.1   Unemployment

LO1   Describe what unemployment is and how it is measured.

In the purest sense, unemployment as a concept can apply to any of the three factor markets—labour, land, or capital. If the economy is not producing at full capacity, then some of the factors of production must be idle—or unemployed (assuming efficient methods of production). However, for our purposes we will focus only on the labour market. **Unemployment** can be defined as the number of persons fifteen years of age and older who are not in gainful employment but who are actively seeking employment.

Measuring Unemployment

To get us started on the actual measurement of Canada's **unemployment rate**—the percentage of the labour force actually unemployed—we turn to Table 4.1 for some 2015 data.

TABLE 4.1
Population and Employment in Canada, 2015 (millions)

Total population	35.85
Working-age population	29.28
Labour force	19.28
Employed	17.95
Unemployed	1.33

Source: Adapted from Statistics Canada, CANSIM database, http://cansim2.statcan.ca, Tables 282-0002 and 051-0001, July 13, 2016.

The term **working-age population** is defined as the country's total population, *excluding*

- those under 15 years of age
- those living on aboriginal reserves
- full-time residents of mental and penal institutions or hospitals
- those in the armed forces

(National labour statistics do not include data for the territories, which are published separately.)

As can be seen in Table 4.1, 6.57 million (35.85–29.28) people fell into one of these three excluded categories. Next, Statistics Canada takes all those in the working-age population and subtracts those considered to be "not in the labour force." The result gives us the **labour force**. Those not in the labour force include retired people, those who are financially independent, those who have become discouraged and ceased looking for work, and those who choose not to participate in the labour market for reasons such as devoting full attention to child rearing. As the table shows, those in the labour force category totalled 19.28 million, while those not in the labour force totalled 10 million (29.28–19.28).

The information from Table 4.1 can be represented visually.

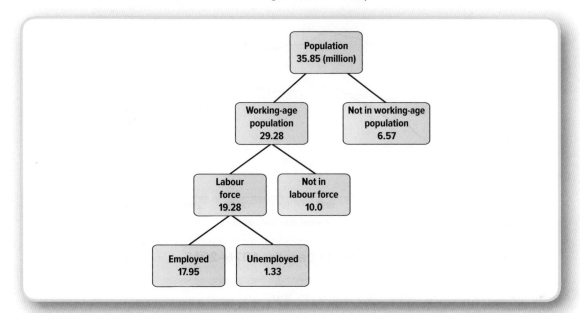

The actual mechanics of computing these data involve a random survey of 56 000 Canadian households done each month. Questions are asked of each household member fifteen years of age and older. The questions used to determine if an individual is in the labour force are:

1. Is he or she currently gainfully employed for at least one hour per week or self-employed?
2. Is he or she employed but not on the job due to illness, vacation, or industrial dispute?
3. Is he or she laid off (within the past twenty-six weeks) but expecting to be recalled?
4. Is he or she not employed but starting a new job within thirty days?
5. Is he or she not employed or laid off, but actively seeking employment?

If none of the above five categories applies, then that person is categorized as "not in the labour force." Having identified those who are in the labour force (employed and unemployed), the next distinction is between those who have gainful employment of at least one hour per week—those who are **employed** (categories 1 and 2 above)—and those who are **unemployed** (categories 3, 4, and 5), since they do not currently hold paid employment. It is important to note that just because a person does not have a job does not mean he or she is unemployed. To be considered unemployed, the person must be available for work *and* actively seeking employment.

Out of these various categories come two important rates. First is the **participation rate**, which is the percentage of the working-age population who are in the labour force.

$$\text{Labour force participation rate} = \frac{\text{labour force}}{\text{working-age population}} \times 100 \qquad [4.1]$$

In Canada, for 2015, this rate was

$$\text{Labour force participation rate} = \frac{19.28}{29.28} \times 100 = 65.8\%$$

Figure 4.1 shows this rate as a total and for both genders over a forty-year period. Over these years, the female participation rate in Canada rose from 45.7 to 61.2 percent, while the male participation rate fell from 77.7 to 70.6 percent. This shows dramatically the trend of rising female labour force participation over the past half-century and represents a major change in the social reality of our nation. In addition, the size of Canada's overall labour force also grew.

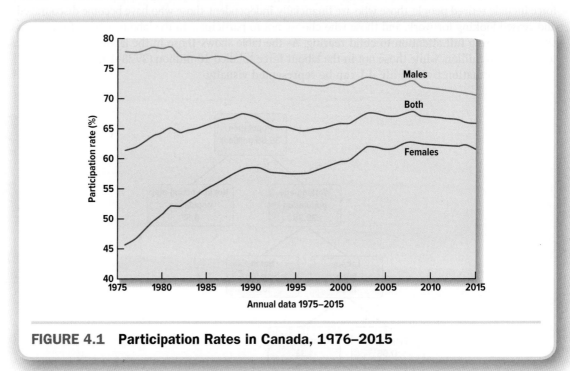

FIGURE 4.1   Participation Rates in Canada, 1976–2015

Source: Statistics Canada, Table 282-0002. Accessed July 13, 2016.

The second important employment statistic is the unemployment rate, the percentage of the labour force actually unemployed. The equation for the this rate is

$$\text{Unemployment rate} = \frac{\text{number of unemployed}}{\text{labour force}} \times 100 \qquad\qquad [4.2]$$

We can use the 2015 data to illustrate:

$$\text{Unemployment rate} = \frac{1.33}{19.28} \times 100 = 6.9\%$$

Figure 4.2 shows Canada's unemployment rates since 1990 and illustrates an important feature of the economy. Unemployment rates have generally declined, from a high of 11.4 percent as the country emerged from the recession of 1990–93 to a low of 6.0 in 2007; rose again as a result of the recession that began in 2009; then fell again in recent years. It is interesting to note also that the unemployment rate for women is consistently lower than that for men.

Since Canada is such a diverse nation, there are significant differences in unemployment rates across the country, as **Figure** 4.3 illustrates.

As a final note on the measurement of unemployment, we should point out that the figures in **Table** 4.1 and those often reported in the media are actually what Statistics Canada calls "seasonally adjusted" rates. That is, increases and decreases that are *purely* the result of seasonal influences are removed. The rationale for this is that the seasonally adjusted rate is a better indicator of the economy's current performance than an unadjusted rate, which would always rise in the winter and fall in the summer.

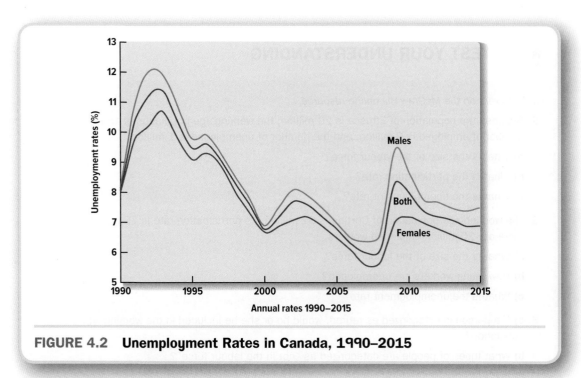

FIGURE 4.2   Unemployment Rates in Canada, 1990–2015

Source: Statistics Canada, Table 282-0002. Accessed July 13, 2016.

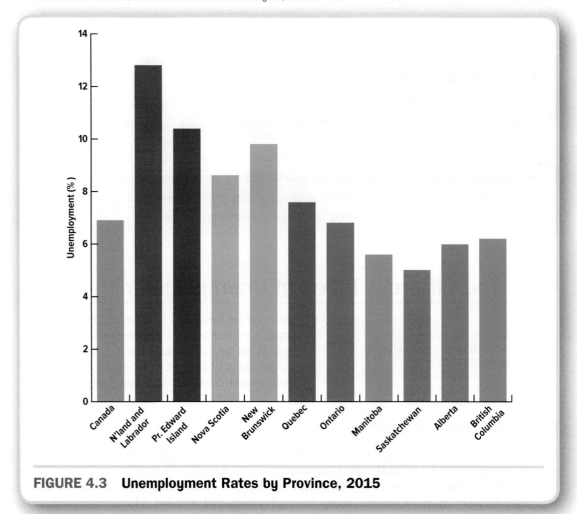

FIGURE 4.3   Unemployment Rates by Province, 2015

Source: Adapted from Statistics Canada, CANSIM database, http://cansim2.statcan.ca, Table 282-0002. Accessed July 13, 2016.

TEST YOUR UNDERSTANDING

Find answers on the McGraw-Hill online resource.

1. Suppose the population of Etrusca is 20 million, the working-age population is 15 million, the number of employed is 9 million, and the number of unemployed is 1 million.

   a) What is the size of the labour force?

   b) What is the participation rate?

   c) What is the unemployment rate?

2. The working-age population of Cortina is 32 million, its participation rate is 75 percent, and there are 20 million employed workers.

   a) What is the size of the labour force?

   b) How many workers are unemployed?

   c) What is the unemployment rate?

3. a) If a person is categorized as retired, would he or she be included in the working-age population?

   b) What types of people are categorized as "not in the labour force"?

   c) Is it possible for the total number of people employed and the total number of people unemployed to rise at the same time?

SECTION SUMMARY

Important definitions for this section are as follows:

- working-age population (excludes young people, those in the armed forces, and people who live on aboriginal reserves or are full-time residents of institutions)
- employed (people who hold paid employment for more than one hour per week)
- unemployed (people who do not hold paid employment but are actively seeking work)
- participation rate (the percentage of the working-age population who are in the labour force)
- unemployment rate (the percentage of the labour force that is unemployed)

4.2 The Different Types of Unemployment

LO2 Explain the different types of unemployment and the costs of unemployment.

Now that we have seen how unemployment is measured, we must address a more fundamental question: What actually causes unemployment? In this section, we will look at three distinct types of unemployment: frictional, structural, and cyclical.

Frictional Unemployment

In a free society, where employees have the right to quit a job and employers have the right to dismiss their employees, **frictional unemployment** is inevitable. This is simply a reflection of the fact that few people who leave or are dismissed from a job on, say, Friday, start a new job on the following Monday. In more general terms, unemployment and unfilled job vacancies can exist simultaneously because it takes time for a match to be found between available jobs and people seeking employment.

In addition to this matching process, there are other aspects to frictional unemployment. The first is the growing number of people searching for the *right* job rather than for just any job. These days, an increasing percentage of households has more than one wage earner. Thus, if one partner earns a good income, the unemployed partner can take more time to find a satisfying job. There is a benefit to society when more people have jobs closely matching their interests and skills. However, prolonging the job search increases frictional unemployment.

Unemployment can affect all ages.
Royalty-Free/CORBIS

Another factor that can result in more frictional unemployment is the result of employment insurance benefits that allow people, in some circumstances, to accept periodic layoffs without actually searching energetically for other work.

Examples of the frictionally unemployed include students who complete school and begin looking for a job, as well as homemakers who enter (or re-enter) the labour market. These people often do not find work immediately and are therefore frictionally unemployed until they do.

Frictional unemployment is a part of a modern market economy. It will never be eliminated—and we do not want to eliminate it. It takes time to match people and jobs, and some people take extra time to search for the right job. In addition, there are some on layoff who are not actively searching for alternative employment. We can therefore conclude that frictional unemployment in Canada is a significant portion of the official unemployment rate reported monthly in the popular press.

Structural Unemployment

Next, we want to examine **structural unemployment**. Some call this "long-term frictional unemployment" but such a description does not capture the major shifts continuously taking place in the economy that result in structural unemployment. A natural spinoff of a dynamic, growing economy is the fact that new industries constantly emerge and enter the expansionary stage—think of computer software, communications technology, and cardboard packaging for the fast-food industry.

Other spinoffs include "sunset" industries, which have experienced declining employment for years—the East Coast fishery and paper manufacturing, for example. The root cause of structural unemployment, then, is changing tastes and technology. Over the years, people's preferences change, and their demand for certain products and services increases (winter vacations, soccer uniforms), while the demand for other things (newspapers, cigarettes) decreases. Similarly, new products are invented (iPods, laptops, smart phones) causing others (CD players, typewriters, fax machines) to become obsolete. These changes cause the rise and fall of firms and industries and, along with them, jobs and occupations.

People working in sunset industries may require both a geographical and an occupational move in order to transfer into a new job in a growth industry. Think of a forty-something Nova Scotia coal miner who has worked all his adult life in a mine that has just closed. What options are now open to him? One possibility is for him to retrain in a new trade, assuming that his local community college has suitable programs available. But who is going to pay for this—the unemployed miner or the government? Alternatively, if he decides to relocate to another part of the country, forcing him to sell his home and uproot his family, will the government provide assistance or should he be left to his own resources? And should that miner be given any choice in the matter if there are jobs available elsewhere? Can he be "required" to relocate and retrain? It's clear that whether retraining or relocating is required or not, it is a painful adjustment and may take some time to accomplish.

In short, continuous structural changes within the economy always lead to a certain amount of structural unemployment. In addition, some economic observers argue that the forces of globalization in the world today have increased the rate at which businesses, and even whole industries, leave Canada in order to set up in a lower-wage country. This has been true of the textile industry in Quebec, which has seen business decline rapidly, while at the same time high-tech industries in the Ottawa Valley have grown appreciably. Measured across the country, structural unemployment becomes a significant problem.

Some economists consider seasonal unemployment to be a type of structural unemployment because the skills of those people who are laid off for parts of the year are no longer needed. This applies to a number of occupations in farming, construction, and tourism. Examples include a ski instructor, a racetrack employee who is unemployed in the winter, and a contract college instructor who has no work in the summer.

Cyclical Unemployment

In the next chapter, we will look at fluctuations in the economy called *business cycles*. These fluctuations are reflected in changes in the level of employment and unemployment. A complete cycle consists of an expansion phase followed by a contractionary phase. This sequence of expansion and contraction change is recurrent but is not regular in either length or duration.

When the business cycle is at its expansionary peak, the economy will likely be at, or near, what is called **full employment**. Another way of looking at this is to realize that *full employment* refers to the situation in which any unemployment in the economy is a result of purely frictional and structural causes. **Cyclical unemployment** occurs in recessionary phases of the business cycle, so full employment only exists when there is no cyclical unemployment.

It is from the concept of zero cyclical unemployment that economists get the **natural rate of unemployment**. This exists when there is frictional and structural unemployment but no cyclical unemployment. When an economy is in a recession, cyclical unemployment exists because the total amount of unemployment is greater than the sum of frictional and structural unemployment, and is therefore above the natural rate.

Thus, we can say that full employment exists when the economy is experiencing only the natural rate of unemployment. This natural rate is considered to be the lowest unemployment rate an economy can achieve without accelerating inflation. In other words, it is possible to achieve a lower rate of unemployment, but only at the cost of higher prices. In addition, the natural rate of unemployment can vary from country to country, and from time to time within the same country, as social and economic conditions change. For example, Japan, where the practice of changing jobs frequently is thought to show a lack of loyalty (a highly regarded virtue), is likely to have a much lower natural rate of unemployment than, say, North America, where people do frequently change jobs. As another example, some economists argue that Canada's natural rate of unemployment has increased over the years because of the increased coverage and benefits of employment insurance as well as an increase in two-income families. Today, it appears that Canada's natural rate of unemployment is in the range of 5 to 7 percent, although it should be noted that there is no official rate generally recognized or accepted by everyone, nor is it measured by Statistics Canada.

We should re-emphasize that, regardless of the phase of the business cycle, there is always unemployment in the economy and there are always job vacancies. The labour market is dynamic; the type and place of the vacancies are constantly in flux, and the people who are unemployed may or may not have the particular skills or experience to fill those vacancies. Many economists would argue that this points up the need for government-sponsored job placement and retraining services.

Thus, whatever the level of performance in the economy, there will always be thousands of existing job vacancies. In fact, the number of vacancies might well equal the number of unemployed people. This phenomenon serves to emphasize the notion that the natural rate of unemployment is the result of unavoidable mismatching in the labour market. When an economy is suffering from cyclical unemployment it has this mismatching problem combined with the fact that there are simply not enough jobs to go around; the number of unemployed people often greatly exceeds the number of available jobs.

ADDED DIMENSION

Economic Growth and Recessions

A recession is defined by Statistics Canada as a decline in real GDP in two consecutive quarters. We know that a drop in real GDP will lead to layoffs in the economy and thus a rise in unemployment. Therefore the average person is more likely to define a recession as an increase in the unemployment rate rather than a decrease in the growth rate. Are these two perspectives one and the same?

Although it is true that a negative or low positive growth rate is usually associated with high unemployment and that a high growth rate implies a low unemployment rate, this relationship is not exact. For example, in the early years of the Great Depression of the 1930s, the Canadian economy experienced negative growth rates and high unemployment. Then, from 1934 onward, the economy actually experienced positive growth in real GDP at an average annual rate of 7.1 percent, yet the unemployment rate remained at an annual average rate of 12.3 percent.

In addition, if we look at growth rates today, we find that the highest growth rates are often recorded in very poorly developed countries (in 2015, Ethiopia, Palau, and Papua New Guinea topped the list). Conversely, developed nations often have much lower growth rates (Japan was the highest-ranked country among the G8 but came in only twenty-seventh in the world growth-wise). It should be noted that developed nations also tend to have very low unemployment rates, so it would be a mistake to associate low growth with high unemployment and high growth with low unemployment.

TEST YOUR UNDERSTANDING

4. Categorize each of the following sets of circumstances as frictional, structural, or cyclical unemployment.

a) Sanjit, a pulp mill worker, is laid off because the mill's inventories are at an all-time high.

b) Five weeks ago, Alison left a job she did not like and is still looking for another job.

c) Ian was a fisher on the East Coast but sold his boat after years of hard work with little return. He has been unemployed for almost a year.

If the natural unemployment rate in Canada today is 5 to 7 percent, it is surely higher than it was just 25 or 30 years ago. There are three possible explanations for this increase in the natural rate of unemployment. First, as we mentioned above, changes in employment insurance (EI) over the past decades significantly increased benefits. Second, more time is being taken by job seekers, who are more affluent than they used to be and therefore can afford to extend the time spent looking for a satisfying job. Third, an increase in the female participation rate has contributed to an increase in the number of people looking for employment. If these explanations are valid, then any future reductions in EI coverage and benefits, and the expected levelling of the female participation rate, may well result in a decrease in the natural rate of unemployment in Canada in the coming decades. In summary, the natural rate of unemployment could change if

- employment insurance benefits change
- the average job search time changes
- labour-force participation rates change

The following diagram helps us get a good overview of the dynamics of the labour market.

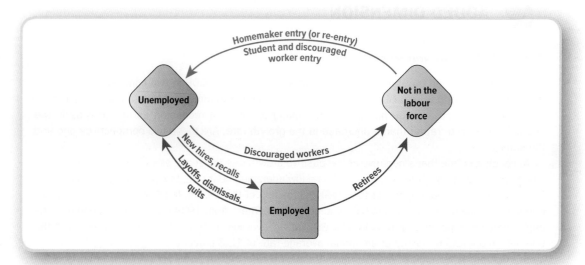

Criticism of the Official Rate

There are four grounds on which one could criticize the official unemployment rate, despite the fact that the interview and statistical techniques used by Statistics Canada to measure it are statistically valid and recognized around the world as among the best. The first two criticisms that we look at to cause the official rate to be *understated*.

To begin, we must realize that people who say that they worked only part time (and it may be as little as one hour a week) in the previous week will be classified as employed. However, many of these people would likely prefer to work more hours and, in some cases, full time. If this is true, then some real unemployment is being missed in the reported statistics.

Second, we must consider what critics refer to as the **discouraged worker** phenomenon. According to the official definitions used by Statistics Canada, a person who is *not* actively seeking work is not in the labour force and thus would not be counted as unemployed. Yet some argue that many individuals have become so discouraged in their job search that they have stopped looking. To exclude these discouraged workers is to understate the magnitude of the unemployment. It also means, ironically, that a rise in the unemployment rate could actually be proclaimed as a good sign by the labour minister because it shows that the economy is on an upswing and that many previously discouraged workers have now become encouraged to start looking for work (and have become temporarily unemployed) since their prospects are now so much brighter.

The third common criticism of unemployment statistics is one that may cause the official rate to be *overstated*. When people collecting EI or welfare payments are asked if they are actively seeking work, the response is very likely to be yes. Yet at least some of these individuals are not involuntarily unemployed but are, instead, simply waiting for benefits to expire (or their claim to be challenged) before returning to active participation in the job market.

The fourth cause of unreliability is the fact that there is a whole group in the underground economy who are working in illegal occupations and, for obvious reasons, are going to declare themselves unemployed. The same may well be true for people with legal jobs who are not declaring their incomes (to avoid paying income tax). They, too, would probably declare themselves unemployed.

We will make no attempt to judge whether reasons one and two, which tip the scale one way, outweigh reasons three and four, which tip it the other way. What is probably more important to note is that measuring the unemployment rate *consistently* is crucial if we are to make sense out of comparisons over time. Measured consistently, the official rate allows valid conclusions to be drawn about the economy's performance in one year compared with another, and that is useful. In summary, the reported unemployment rates can be

- understated because part-timers are included as full-timers
- understated because they exclude discouraged workers
- overstated because of false information from some EI recipients
- overstated because of false information from those working in the underground economy

Costs of Unemployment

How serious a problem is unemployment? Should we really be concerned with it? Certainly, there are some obvious personal economic costs associated with unemployment. In addition, there are serious social costs that can affect all of us. Therefore the true costs of unemployment cannot be measured simply in terms of EI or welfare payments going to those not working. In a sense, you might regard them as costs for the taxpayer, but obviously, from the recipient's point of view, they definitely represent a benefit. Overall, to an economist, they are not true economic costs at all but merely transfer payments. The true economic costs come from the fact that unemployment in an economy means that the quantity of goods and services being produced is less than it could be. (Like time, this lost production is gone forever.) This means that a country is producing below its potential, or in terms of Chapter 1's model, the economy is operating inside its production possibilities boundary. The amount of lost goods and services that were not produced because the economy was operating at less than full employment is what economists refer to as the **GDP gap**, which in the form of an equation is shown as

$$\text{GDP gap} = \text{potential GDP} - \text{actual GDP (real or nominal)} \qquad [4.3]$$

An American economist, Arthur Okun, established a relationship between the amount of cyclical unemployment in the economy and the size of the GDP gap. **Okun's law** observes that for every 1 percent of cyclical unemployment, the economy's level of GDP falls 2.5 percent short of its potential. This gap can be calculated by using the following equation:

$$\text{GDP gap} = 2.5 \times \text{cyclical unemployment (\%)} \times \text{actual GDP (real or nominal)} \qquad [4.4]$$

For example, in 2010, near the beginning of the last recession, the unemployment rate in Canada was 8 percent. If one assumes 6 percent as the natural rate of unemployment, then Canada was experiencing a cyclical unemployment rate of 2 percent. In that year, its nominal GDP was $1662 billion. Given this information, we are able to calculate the size of its GDP gap.

$$\text{GDP gap} = 2.5 \times 2\% \times \$1662 = \$83.1 \text{ billion}$$

This is a measurement of the economic cost of unemployment and is a significant figure. If Canada had been able to eliminate this cyclical unemployment, its potential GDP would have been $83 billion higher at $1745 billion, and each person in Canada would have earned on average an additional $2434 in that year ($83 billion/34.1 million).

As important as these dollar amounts are, the social costs to the individual and to society can represent an even greater waste. Cyclical unemployment of 2 percent, given Canada's labour force of 18.5 million, translates into approximately 371 000 people being involuntarily unemployed. In those 371 000 stories, one would find a lot of bitterness, disappointment, anger, loss of self-esteem, and a sense of failure. In addition, people who are unemployed for a significant period often lose some of their job skills. Such feelings are not a recipe for social harmony. Alcoholism, accidents, claims on the health care system, violence, and crime all rise as a result. Furthermore, these social costs do not exist evenly across society. Young people and those with less education are hit the hardest, as are those who live in the Maritime provinces and Quebec.

Whether we try to categorize these costs as social, psychological, economic, or political, the fact remains that unemployment is expensive by any measure.

TEST YOUR UNDERSTANDING

5. What would happen to the size of the labour force if 100 000 unemployed people became discouraged workers? What effect, if any, would this have on the unemployment rate?

6. Given a natural rate of unemployment of 8 percent, an actual rate of 10 percent, and real GDP of $800 billion, calculate potential GDP.

IT'S NEWS TO ME ...

A new report by Statistics Canada shows that the labour force participation rate, the percentage of the population 15 and over that is either working or actively looking for work, now sits at 65.5 percent the lowest it has been since December 1999. The rate has been in a long-run downward trend since hitting a pre-recession peak of 67.8% in April 2008. Economists suggest there are a number of explanations for this. One major contributor is the growth in the number of *discouraged workers* who have given up searching for a job. When a discouraged worker stops actively looking for work, they are no longer counted as "in the labour force" which causes the participation rate to fall. Since they are no longer in the labour force, these workers also no longer meet the definition of "unemployed" and thus would not be included in the unemployment rate either.

Another reason for the declining participation rate is thought to be the increase in the number of baby boomers who are taking early retirements.

Source: *Star Power Reporting,* Summer 2016.

I. If the number of discouraged workers increases dramatically, then:

a) Both the unemployment rate and the participation rate will fall.
b) The unemployment rate will fall but the participation rate will rise.
c) The unemployment rate will rise but the participation rate will fall.
d) Both the unemployment rate and the participation rate will rise.

II. If the number of retirees increases dramatically, then:

a) Both the unemployment rate and the participation rate will fall.
b) The unemployment rate will fall but the participation rate will rise.
c) The unemployment rate will rise but the participation rate will fall.
d) Both the unemployment rate and the participation rate will rise.

SECTION SUMMARY

a) The three types of unemployment are
  • frictional (results when people move between jobs)
  • structural (resulting from structural changes in the economy's major industries)
  • cyclical (caused by fluctuations in the economy's growth rate)
b) Criticisms of the official unemployment rates are that
  • part-time employees are regarded as fully employed
  • discouraged workers are excluded
  • some employment insurance recipients give false information
  • those working in the underground economy are not counted
c) One way to measure the costs of unemployment is Okun's law, which relates cyclical unemployment to the GDP gap.

4.3 Inflation

> **LO3** Explain what inflation is and how it is measured.

Let us now turn to inflation. Public-opinion polls consistently show that people consider inflation, or the threat of inflation, to be a major problem facing society. In fact, people's concern about inflation usually ranks above their concern about unemployment. The reason is probably the simple fact that while unemployment in the economy directly touches only the unemployed and others close to them, inflation touches everyone daily. For our purposes, **inflation** can be defined as an increase in the general level of prices sustained over a period in an economy.

Price Indexes

Although inflation measures the amount that prices increase from one year to the next, this does not mean that the prices of all products increase. In fact, the price of some products may well decrease. As the definition suggests, inflation measures the change in the general, or average, level of prices. However Statistics Canada does not actually measure average prices—it uses an index of prices. Like any index, this is nothing more than converting the value of something in a particular year (called *the base year*) into the number 100 and then tracking the change in this value in subsequent years. The value of an index then is always equal to 100 in the base year. For example, if the value of the index increased by 8 percent in the following year, then the new index would have a value of 108.

When measuring price changes, Statistics Canada constructs many different price indexes that are of use to different groups: producers' price index, house construction price index, farmers' price index, and so on. The two most well-known and widely used indexes are the consumer price index and the GDP deflator. Let us look first at the consumer price index.

Measuring Inflation Using the Consumer Price Index

Statistics Canada derives the **consumer price index (CPI)** by first defining a representative bundle of goods and services and then collecting prices on each item every month. The basket reflects the spending habits of a family of four, and the prices are weighted to reflect a typical consumption pattern.

Suppose that we construct our own price index for a representative Canadian student using some simple, and very hypothetical, data. In the first year, we discover that an average student pays $600 per month for accommodation, lives on 30 pizzas a month (costing $8 each), and goes to the movies 8 times each month at a cost of $10 per ticket. Her spending is summarized in Table 4.2A.

TABLE 4.2A
Monthly Spending by an Average Student, January 2015

Item	Quantity	Price	Cost
Accommodation rental	1	$600	$600
Pizzas	30	8	240
Movie tickets	8	10	80
Total cost			$920

In January of the following year, we revisit this student to see how much she is now paying for these items. Perhaps not surprisingly, we find the prices of all three items have increased, as shown in Table 4.2B.

TABLE 4.2B
Monthly Spending by an Average Student, January 2016

Item	Quantity	Price	Cost
Accommodation rental	1	$620	$620
Pizzas	30	8.60	258
Movie tickets	8	11	88
Total cost			$966

We can now convert this data into our own Student Price Index by simply assigning our basket of goods a value of 100 in the base year (2015), which enables us to find the value of the index in the next year, 2016.

$$\text{CPI} = \frac{\text{cost of basket in a given year}}{\text{cost of basket in base year}} \times 100 \qquad [4.5]$$

Using the above data gives us the value of the basket in 2016.

$$\text{CPI} = \frac{\$966}{920} \times 100 = 105$$

That is all there is to it. To find out the inflation rate, we simply calculate the percentage change in the value of the price index.

$$\text{Inflation rate} = \frac{(\text{price index this year} - \text{price index last year})}{\text{price index last year}} \times 100 \qquad [4.6]$$

Thus, for 2016

$$\text{Inflation rate} = \frac{(105 - 100)}{100} \times 100 = 5\%$$

To reinforce these ideas, let us calculate the inflation rate in 2017, supposing that the value of our student's bundle of goods rose to $995. If that is the case, then using formula 4.5, the price index for 2017 would be

$$\text{CPI} = \frac{\$995}{920} \times 100 = 108.15$$

And, using formula 4.6, the inflation rate for 2017 would be

$$\text{Inflation rate} = \frac{(108.15 - 105)}{105} \times 100 = \frac{3.15}{105} \times 100 = 3\%$$

So, now that we know how to calculate inflation rates, let us look at Table 4.3 for the actual CPI and inflation rates for Canada in recent years. These rates are low compared with those experienced in the 1970s and 1980s, when Canada's inflation went as high as 12.4 percent. (See Figure 1.8B for data since 1930.) In fact, the annual rate of inflation has not risen above 3.0 percent since 1991.

In addition to the CPI, Statistics Canada also publishes a *core CPI* which excludes items whose prices can fluctuate wildly from period to period. These items include fruits and vegetables, gas, fuel oil, mortgage interest, and tobacco. The core CPI then gives a better indication of long-term underlying inflation rates.

TABLE 4.3

Consumer Price Index and Inflation Rates in Canada, 2008–2015
(2002 = 100)

	CPI	Inflation Rate (%)
2008	114.1	2.2
2009	114.4	0.3
2010	116.5	1.8
2011	119.9	2.9
2012	121.7	1.5
2013	122.8	0.9
2014	125.2	2.0
2015	126.6	1.1

Source: Adapted from Statistics Canada, CANSIM database, http://cansim2.statcan.ca, Table 326-0021, July 31, 2016.

IN A NUTSHELL ...

Measuring Inflation Using the GDP Deflator

Although the CPI is the most publicized price index and generally the one used to measure inflation, it is not the only one, and therefore it is not the only way of measuring inflation. In fact, many suggest it is better to use the **GDP deflator** to measure the inflation rate of an economy because the bundle of goods it uses does not consist of consumer goods only. As its name suggests, it is a price index that includes the other goods included in GDP in addition to consumer goods—capital goods, exported goods, and government services. Also, because the GDP measures goods and services produced domestically, it excludes imports—the CPI is a reflection of consumer spending, and many of those products are made abroad. In other words, the CPI includes the prices of imported goods. Obviously, since the two indexes measure different things, their values may differ. For instance, if the prices of capital goods are rising much faster than those of consumer goods, the GDP deflator will be higher than the CPI. Conversely, if the prices of imported goods are rising sharply, the CPI will have the higher value.

The two indexes also differ significantly in how they are constructed. As we have seen, the CPI is derived from the expenditures of a representative consumer and tracks the value of a bundle of goods over time, assuming that the bundle of goods remains the same. It is referred to as an *explicit index*. By comparison, the GDP deflator is known as an *implicit index*, and as we shall see, the bundle of goods does, in fact, change from period to period.

So what bundle of goods does Statistics Canada use? It uses the actual goods and services currently produced, that is, the current GDP of the country. Let us work out the value of this deflator using the data that we used for a hypothetical economy in Table 3.4 of Chapter 3 (partly reproduced in Table 4.4).

TABLE 4.4
Nominal and Real GDP

	Year 1	Year 2	Year 3
Nominal GDP ($millions)	42 000	49 200	57 540
Real GDP ($millions)	42 000	45 200	50 100

The value of nominal GDP in year 1 for this particular country was $42 000 (in millions of dollars). The following year, its GDP rose to $49 200. However, when we calculated its real GDP (its GDP using constant, year 1, prices), we found that it had only risen to $45 200. In other words, with no price change, its GDP was $45 200; including inflation it rose to $49 200. The relative difference between these figures must therefore represent the inflation rate. In other words, while nominal GDP rose by approximately 17 percent, real GDP rose only 8 percent. So inflation must have been the difference, approximately 9 percent. To calculate the value of the GDP deflator, we measure the ratio of the two.

$$\text{GDP deflator} = \frac{\text{nominal GDP}}{\text{real GDP}} \times 100 \qquad [4.7]$$

We can therefore calculate the value of the GDP deflator for year 2.

$$\text{GDP deflator} = \frac{\$49\ 200}{45\ 200} \times 100 = 109$$

Again, looking at Table 4.4, we can calculate the value of the GDP deflator for year 3.

$$\text{GDP deflator} = \frac{\$57\ 540}{50\ 100} \times 100 = 114.9$$

To summarize, the value of the GDP deflator in year 1 was 100, rising in year 2 to 109, and in year 3 to 114.9. To calculate the inflation rates, using formula 4.6 is straightforward. In year 2, it came to 9 percent. (You could probably do that in your head!) The inflation rate in year 3 came to $(114.9 - 109)/109 \times 100 = 5.4$ percent.

Having seen how we calculate inflation using each of the indexes, let us summarize their differences.

- The CPI is an explicit index using a constructed bundle of goods; the GDP deflator is an implicit index measuring the ratio of nominal to real GDP.
- The bundle of goods remains constant with the CPI; the bundle of goods in the GDP deflator changes each year.
- The CPI does not include capital or government goods and services; the GDP deflator includes them.
- The CPI includes imported goods; the GDP deflator excludes imported goods.

Finally, it is important to clearly understand the relationship among nominal GDP, real GDP, and the GDP deflator. For instance, if we know that nominal GDP in Canada in 2015 was $1983 billion, and the value of its GDP deflator was 112.2 (2002 was the base year), it is a fairly simple matter to figure out the value of real GDP for that year by just rearranging formula 4.7.

$$\text{Real GDP} = \frac{\text{nominal GDP}}{\text{GDP deflator}} \times 100 \tag{4.8}$$

$$\text{Real GDP} = \frac{1983}{112.2} \times 100 = \$1767$$

Similarly, if we know the value of real GDP and the GDP deflator, it is straightforward to figure out the value of nominal GDP by rearranging this basic formula.

$$\text{Nominal GDP} = \text{real GDP} \times \frac{\text{GDP deflator}}{100} \tag{4.9}$$

For instance, knowing that the real GDP in Canada in 2010 was $1593 and its GDP deflator was 104.4, we can calculate the nominal GDP.

$$\text{Nominal GDP} = \$1593 \times \frac{104.4}{100} = \$1663$$

TEST YOUR UNDERSTANDING

7. Fill in the blanks (to one decimal place) in the table of Etruria's GDP statistics.

	2015	2016	2017
Nominal GDP ($billion)	443	____	507
Real GDP ($billion)	374	389	____
GDP deflator (2010 = 100)	____	121.9	126.1
Population (millions)	26.1	26.4	27
Real GDP per capita	____	____	____

Measuring the Past

As we saw with the GDP deflator, one of the main purposes of a price index is to enable us to look at values from the past and compare them with the present. For instance, it would be difficult these days to get by on an annual salary of $10 000. However, a $10 000 salary thirty years ago could enable a person to live a fairly comfortable lifestyle. That is because one dollar 30 years ago went a lot farther than it does today. Using a price index will allow us to compare past incomes (or other money values) with present incomes. We can do this by expressing all values, past and present, in terms of the same year's prices. Generally, the common year will be the base year. The following equation will help us to make this calculation:

$$\text{Real value (in year B\$)} = \frac{\text{nominal value in year A}}{\text{price index in year A}} \times \text{price index in year B (or base year)} \quad [4.10]$$

For instance, in Table 4.5, let us compare a $10 000 income earned in 1955, 1975, 1995, and 2015. (The base year is 2002.)

TABLE 4.5
Nominal and Real Income

Year	Nominal Income	Price Index	Real Income
1955	$10 000	14.1	$70 922
1975	10 000	29.0	34 483
1995	10 000	87.6	11 416
2015	10 000	126.6	7 899

To find real income we simply divide **nominal income** (or current income) by the price index and multiply the result by 100 (the price index in the base year of 2002). For example, the real income in 1955 was equal to

$$\frac{\$10\ 000}{14.1} \times 100 = \$70\ 922$$

This table shows us how the real value of income has been eroded by inflation over the years. A $10 000 income in 2015 was worth only 11 percent of its value in 1955.

To cement this idea a little, let us look at some actual data for Canada over the past few years. Table 4.6 presents information on average (after-tax) family incomes in Canada from 2004 to 2011 (2011 = 100).

TABLE 4.6
Average After-Tax Family Income

Year	Nominal Average Income	Δ Nominal Income (%)	Price Index	Δ Price Index (Inflation Rate %)	Real Average Income	Δ Real Income (%)
2004	50 796	+3.4	88.3	1.6	57 500	+1.8
2005	52 256	+2.9	89.8	1.6	58 200	+1.2
2006	54 619	+4.5	91.5	1.9	59 700	+2.6
2007	57 844	+5.9	93.4	2.1	61 900	+3.7
2008	59 605	+3.0	95.1	1.7	62 700	+1.3
2009	60 812	+2.0	96.7	1.7	62 900	+0.3
2010	61 981	+1.9	98.4	1.8	63 000	+0.2
2011	63 000	+1.6	100	1.6	63 000	0.0

Source: Adapted by the authors from Statistics Canada, CANSIM database, http://cansim2.statcan.ca, Tables 326-0021 and 202-0603, January 31, 2014.

Average nominal income rose by $12 204 over this seven-year period, which is a rise of 24 percent. However, much of this increase was eroded by inflation. The price index over this period rose from 88.3 to 100. This is an increase of 11.7 percentage points (100 − 88.3), which translates into an inflation rate of 13.2 percent ($11.7/88.3 \times 100$). The net result was that real income increased by a much more modest $5500—or less than $800 a year.

We can extend our understanding a little further by calculating how real income changed year by year. We can do this by working out the change in real income and expressing it as a percentage. For instance, real income in 2006 increased $1500 (from $58 200 to $59 700). As a percentage, this works out to

$$\frac{\$1500}{\$58\ 200} \times 100 = +2.6\%$$

The rest of the last column is worked out in a similar fashion. However, an alternative method would be to use the following formula which enables us to work out the change directly.

% change in real income = % change in nominal income − inflation rate   [4.11]

For example, Table 4.6 shows us that nominal income changed by +4.5 percent in 2006, while the inflation rate for that year was 1.9 percent. Subtracting the inflation rate from the change in nominal income gives us a change in real income of 2.6 percent, which confirms our previous calculation.

What this means then is that a 10 percent pay increase, for example, in a year in which the inflation rate is only 1 percent means that real income has risen by 9 percent. However, if the inflation rate was 8 percent, real take-home pay went up by only 2 percent.

One interesting use of the CPI is that it allows us to compare the actual price of a product in the past in terms of today's prices. For example, the actual price of a movie in 1958 was (about) $1, while today it is, say, $12 (it varies from city to city). On the other hand, we know that people's wages and incomes are also much higher in 2015 than they were in 1958. So did the real price of a movie increase or not? We can answer this question using equation 4.10.

$$\text{Real value (in year B\$)} = \frac{\text{nominal value in year A}}{\text{price index in year A}} \times \text{price index in year B (or base year)}$$

Using this equation, and knowing the price indexes in 1958 and 2015, gives us

$$\text{Real value in 2015} = \frac{\$1}{15.2} \times 122.8 = \$8.08$$

So $12 is pretty expensive! If, alternatively, we want to know 1958 ticket prices in terms of 2002 (base year) prices, we would have

$$\text{Real value in 2002} = \frac{\$1}{15.2} \times 100 = \$6.58$$

Along the same lines, which movie do you think is Hollywood's biggest box office hit? Well, the top-grossing movies worldwide (as of July 2016) will probably not come as a big surprise to most of you. They are (in millions of dollars) as follows:

	Domestic Sales ($millions)	Overseas Sales ($millions)	Worldwide Sales ($millions)
1. Avatar (2009)	761	2028	2788
2. Titanic (1997)	659	1528	2187
3. Star Wars: The Force Awakens (2015)	937	1131	2068
4. Jurassic World (2015)	652	1018	1670
5. Marvel's The Avengers (2012)	623	895	1519
6. Furious 7 (2015)	353	1163	1516

One thing that they all share is the fact that they are recent movies—released within the last fifteen years or so. However, we know that ticket prices are much higher today than they were in the past. If we allow for inflation, by adjusting the revenues of all movies to present-day prices, the results (for domestic sales) are more than a little surprising.

	Ranking by Actual $'s	Adjusted Sales ($millions)
1. Gone with the Wind (1939)	171	1773
2. Star Wars: A New Hope (1977)	8	1528
3. The Sound of Music (1965)	272	1222
4. E.T.: The Extra-Terrestrial (1982)	12	1217
5. Titanic (1997)	2	1162
6. The Ten Commandments (1956)	1109	1124
11. Star Wars: The Force Awakens (2015)	3	928
15. Avatar (2009)	1	834

So, in terms of revenue adjusted for inflation, it turns out that number one is *Gone with the Wind* (1939), number two is *Star Wars: A New Hope* (1977), number three is *The Sound of Music* (and even *Snow White and the Seven Dwarfs* made $855 in 1937): all movies made 40 years ago and more. In fact, only one movie in the top ten (*Titanic*) was made within the last 35 years. Astonishingly, *The Ten Commandments*, made sixty years ago, comes in at number 6 on the adjusted list but is not even in the top *one thousand* in actual dollars! All this points up a significant change in movie audiences: in the days when going to a movie was a family event—mom, dad, brothers, and sisters—the top-grossing films were historical dramas (*Gone with the Wind*), animated fantasies (*Snow White*) and light musicals (*The Sound of Music*). Today's audiences want action (*Jurassic World*), fantasy adventures (*Avatar*), or hero fantasy (*Superman*). This is dramatic shift in preferences that reflects the economic punch of the young who wouldn't be caught dead in a movie with their parents!

Finally, you must have heard stories from your parents or grandparents about "the good old days" and how it was possible then for a guy to take his girlfriend to the movies, have a meal afterward, and still have enough change left over from a $5 bill to take the bus home. Right! We know of course that comparing prices of yesteryear with those of today means nothing unless we can compare them with today's prices in *real* terms. So was everything really cheaper in bygone days? Well, it turns out that some things really were cheaper, but many other things were far more expensive. Here, for instance, are some items that have not changed very much in real terms in more than 50 years.

	Canadian Price in 1958 ($)	Real Value in 2015 ($)	Actual Price in 2015 ($)
Coffee (pound)	0.85	7.08	6.30
Bacon (pound)	0.63	5.25	6.40
T-bone steak	0.89	7.41	6.00–10.00
Chevrolet Impala	2600	21 650	26 000

But the following items are definitely more expensive now than they were 50 years ago.

	Canadian Price in 1958 ($)	Real Value in 2015 ($)	Actual Price in 2015 ($)
Movie ticket	1.00	8.30	12.00
Newspaper	0.07	0.58	1.50
Gasoline (litre)	0.08	0.67	1.10–1.30
Cigarettes (pack)	0.25	2.08	10.00–13.00

But then again, many other things are actually cheaper now than in the past.

	Canadian Price in 1958 ($)	Real Value in 2015 ($)	Actual Price in 2015 ($)
Electric toaster	13	108	25
AM/FM radio	80	665	50
Flight Vancouver–London	623	5189	1000–1500
TV 24-inch	309	2574	200

So, although the CPI tells us how average prices change over the years, we need to understand that not all prices change by the same rate. As our example shows, some prices rise far more than others.

The Rule of 70—A Helpful Tool

We have all heard how a few years of rapid inflation can ravage an economy or how compound interest can dramatically increase a given sum of money over time. The "rule of 70" (actually the number is closer to 72, but most people approximate it) is useful in estimating the time it will take for a figure to double in value given a certain percentage growth rate. The formula is

$$\text{Number of years to double} = \frac{70}{\%\ \text{growth rate}} \qquad [4.12]$$

For example, if inflation is 5 percent per year, the CPI will double in

$$\frac{70}{5} = 14 \text{ years}$$

Or $1000 in a savings account earning 10 percent will double in

$$\frac{70}{10} = 7 \text{ years}$$

Another example would be an economy that is growing by 3.5 percent per year. It would experience a doubling of GDP in

$$\frac{70}{3.5} = 20 \text{ years}$$

A final example has great import for us all. By 1960, the growth rate of the world's population reached 1.75 percent (it attained its maximum of over 2 percent by the mid-sixties). Although 1.75 percent does not sound like a very big figure, it meant that the population was due to double in only 40 years (70 ÷ 1.75). And that is exactly what happened. In 1960, the world population had reached three billion. By 2000, it stood at six billion. Fortunately, this growth rate has slowed down in recent years: as of 2010, it was 1.3 percent. Even so, at this rate, the population will again double from its present 6.5 billion to 13 billion by the year 2064.

TEST YOUR UNDERSTANDING

8. Etruria's nominal GDP rose from $42 billion in 2016 to $45 billion in 2017. During the same period, its inflation rate was 5 percent (calculate answers to one decimal place).

    a) By what percentage did nominal GDP increase between 2016 and 2017?

    b) By what percentage did real GDP increase between 2016 and 2017?

9. If Kerri's nominal income increased during the year from $40 000 to $42 800, and the inflation rate for the year was 4 percent, by what percentage has her real income increased?

10. a) If the inflation rate is 7 percent, how long will it take for prices to double?

    b) If a sum of money invested in the bank doubles in seven years, what rate of interest is it earning?

SECTION SUMMARY

a) Inflation is measured by the percentage change in a price index from one period to the next.

b) There are two ways of measuring inflation:

- using the consumer price index (CPI), which tracks the value of a bundle of goods from period to period
- using the GDP deflator, which is calculated by dividing nominal GDP by real GDP and multiplying by 100

c) There are some important differences between the CPI and the GDP deflator.

- The CPI is an explicit index using a constructed bundle of goods; the GDP deflator is an implicit index measuring the ratio of nominal to real GDP.
- The bundle of goods remains constant with the CPI; the bundle of goods in the GDP deflator changes every year.
- The CPI does not include capital or government goods and services; the GDP deflator includes them.
- The CPI includes imported goods; the GDP deflator excludes imported goods.

d) Real income is derived by dividing nominal income by the price index. The percentage change in real income can be calculated by dividing the change in real income by the original real income and multiplying by 10. It can also be calculated by subtracting the inflation rate from the percentage change in nominal income.

4.4   The Costs of Inflation

> **LO4** Explain the two types of inflation and describe the costs of inflation.

Like unemployment, inflation involves some very heavy costs. However, inflationary effects on the real income of different groups are quite uneven. The classic contrast is between an elderly couple living primarily on a private pension and a yuppie couple who both work in sales and receive, as income, a percentage of total sales volume. The real income of the elderly couple is eroded annually by inflation—in fact, during the high inflation years between 1972 and 1981 it was cut in half! Meanwhile, it is quite possible that the yuppie couple gained from inflation because their sales volume grew faster than the overall rate of inflation. When a society's real income is redistributed in undesirable ways by inflation itself, we refer to this as **redistributive costs**. Inflation can be unfair in that at times it hurts the economically weak and often leaves the strong unaffected or perhaps even benefits them. In general, those whose nominal income increases less than the rate of inflation will suffer because their real income decreases.

A second example of the effect of inflation is the experience of employees who have weak bargaining power in the marketplace—they might be non-unionized or working in a declining industry.

In contrast, employees who are members of a powerful trade union or are working in a growing industry may well be able to keep up with inflation.

Inflation can also redistribute wealth, particularly if the inflation rate takes an unexpected jump. The easiest way to see this is to imagine yourself borrowing $1000 today, assuming a current inflation rate of 5 percent. This means that what costs you $1000 today will cost you $1050 a year from now. Anyone lending you $1000 now will definitely want to ensure they get the equivalent amount back. But, in addition, they will want to earn a return on the money they lend. Let us say that they want to earn a real return of 7 percent. In other words, the lender wants to earn 7 percent irrespective of the inflation rate. This is what is meant by the **real interest rate**: the rate of interest when inflation is zero, or put another way, the rate of interest assuming the value of the dollar remains constant. The lender would therefore charge you 5 percent to cover anticipated inflation + 7 percent = 12 percent.

$$\text{Nominal interest rate} = \text{real interest rate} + \text{inflation rate} \qquad [4.13]$$

So let us say that you agree to the nominal rate of 12 percent and therefore to the repayment of $1120 in a year's time. If the actual inflation rate turns out to be 5 percent, then your friend will receive in real terms exactly what he expected to receive. But what would happen if the actual inflation rate turned out to be 10 percent? You will still pay back $1120 to your friend. But how much is this worth to him in purchasing power compared with the $1000 he lent to you a year ago? The answer is only approximately $1020, because of the increase in prices. Therefore, he earned, in real terms, only $20 on $1000, or 2 percent. In other words, rearranging formula 4.13 we have

$$\text{Real interest rate} = \text{nominal rate} - \text{the inflation rate} \qquad [4.14]$$

Inserting the appropriate figures gives us

$$\text{Real interest rate} = 12\% - 10\% = 2\%$$

This clearly hurts the lender of the $1000, while you are not hurt. If your real income rises because of the higher inflation, then you, the borrower, will actually gain. In general, an unexpected rise in inflation hurts lenders and can benefit borrowers, with the result being an unpredictable redistribution of wealth. On the other hand, an unexpected drop in the inflation rate will hurt borrowers and help lenders.

While these redistribution costs hurt some people, they help others. But inflation can have another cost that really does hurt everyone. These are what are termed the **output costs**.

Let us start this discussion by pointing out that long-term investment is an uncertain business at the best of times. Consider the example of a company that will have to spend $10 million to produce and market a new product. The financial viability of such a decision depends on many variables, from expected sales to production costs. If estimating these unknowns also requires that uncertain inflation rates—which will affect both revenue and production costs—must be factored in, then the risks may become too large to accept. As a result, the company may shelve the launching of the new product. All the investment spending and new hiring that would have resulted is forgone.

The key phrase in the above paragraph is "uncertain inflation rate." Any inflation rate—0, 10, or 20 percent—is not a problem, in terms of this discussion, as long as it remains unchanged and therefore predictable. It is the *uncertainty* associated with inflation that generates concern about investment decisions. If such hesitancy reduces the amount of investment in the economy, then the rate of economic growth slows and total output will be lower than it would have been.

There are other examples of the output costs of inflation. Consider what are termed the *menu costs of inflation*. This refers to the business costs involved in changing prices, which is something that must be done more often in times of higher inflation. Let us take the case of Colonial Music, a small wholesaler of musical instruments that are imported from Asia and sold to school boards across North America. Colonial Music produces three separate printed catalogues that it mails out— one for English Canada, one for French Canada, and one for the United States—as well as a website that has the same three categories. Since the company offers hundreds of instruments, the production of the catalogues and the updating of the website costs tens of thousands of dollars every year. Any increase in the inflation rate may necessitate the production of new catalogues sooner than the regularly scheduled time, and this clearly adds to the costs of doing business.

Our final example of the output cost of inflation is the negative effect it has on Canadian exports. Higher inflation pushes up the prices of Canadian goods and so makes us less competitive in world markets thus reducing Canadian exports. Furthermore, Canadian consumers will begin to substitute imports for the now higher-priced Canadian products. The result is less production in Canada, and this means less national income and fewer jobs. In summary, the output costs of inflation include

- lower level of investment
- menu costs
- lower level of net exports

Before leaving this discussion of the costs of inflation, it is worth taking a minute to look at the problems of the opposite situation—falling prices—which is called *deflation*. Japan, for example, has been facing just this situation for nearly two decades. One of the effects of deflation is a reduction in both consumer and investment spending, because when prices are falling people put off purchases until the future in order to take advantage of the lower prices. In addition, investment spending is likely to be further affected because of the effects of deflation on the real interest rate. A number of studies have concluded that over the last 300 years or so the real rate of interest has hovered around the 4 percent level. Table 4.7 shows what the nominal rate needs to be in order to achieve a real rate of 4 percent.

TABLE 4.7
Hypothetical Real Rates of Inflation

Real Rate of Interest	Inflation Rate	(Needed) Nominal Interest Rate
4%	2%	6%
4%	12%	16%
4%	−4%	0%

For instance, if the inflation rate is 2 percent, a nominal rate of 6 percent is needed to ensure a real rate of 4 percent, which will satisfy both lenders and borrowers. However, if the inflation rate rises to 12 percent, a nominal interest rate of 16 percent is needed to yield a real rate of 4 percent. Now, consider the effects of deflation. If the *deflation* rate is 4 percent, those who have money to lend can gain a real rate of interest of 4 percent by doing nothing except holding on to their money. Therefore they will not be willing to lend, and since nominal interest rates cannot become negative (except for a very short time) nothing will change to correct this situation. In short, deflation freezes credit markets, and this also reduces output.

Two Types of Inflation

In a very real sense, the entire catalogue of macroeconomic principles is necessary to understand what causes inflation. Nevertheless, it is useful to briefly identify two categories of causes at this point.

The first is referred to by economists as **demand-pull inflation**, which occurs when the total demand for goods and services in the whole economy exceeds its capacity to produce those goods. That is to say, people are trying to buy more goods and services than the economy is capable of producing, even at full employment. This excessive demand will pull up prices and cause demand-pull inflation.

But don't we also experience inflation at times when unemployment is high and, thus, when there is no demand-pull inflation? Yes, we do, and this is the second classification of inflation, called **cost-push inflation**. This occurs on the supply side of the economy, whereas demand-pull inflation is a demand-side phenomenon. Cost-push inflation has three variations.

The first of these is *wage-push inflation*. For example, if a union succeeds in pushing the nominal wage rate up more than any recent increase in labour productivity would justify, the employer's real cost will rise. If we assume that this increase was not simply a catch-up in response to inflation from some other cause, we have the makings of inflation. If the employer who agreed to the increased nominal wage did so thinking that by increasing the price of the products she sells she can recoup the increased costs, and if the employer has sufficient market power, we have a completed picture of wage-push inflation: increased wages pushing up costs, which push up prices. While the impact of one union and one employer probably is not noticeable, if the above scenario is typical of a general pattern, the impact will become very apparent.

The second variation of cost-push inflation, called *profit-push inflation*, can occur if firms have enough market power to enhance profits by simply increasing the prices of what they sell. This is more likely to occur in industries in which competition is weak and aggregate demand is strong.

The name of the third variation, *import-push inflation*, is almost self-explanatory. The classic example is the OPEC oil price increases of the 1970s, which affected every economy in the world, particularly those that imported significant quantities of oil. Here, the cost of imported oil triggered price increases in all industries that were heavily dependent on oil. This had a snowball effect throughout the economy.

 ADDED DIMENSION

Galloping Inflation

In the twentieth century, some unfortunate countries have been ravaged by extreme rates of inflation that economists term *galloping inflation* or *hyperinflation*. The experience of Germany following World War I is both instructive and well documented. As a result of the Versailles Peace Treaty at the end of that war, Germany was presented, by the victorious nations, with a staggering reparations bill of 132 billion gold marks, which was an estimate of the war damage "caused" by Germany. Although the German government was allowed to pay this reparation in annual installments, the amount was far in excess of what it could reasonably raise through taxation or by borrowing. Germany, therefore, resorted to a method used by despotic kings, emperors, and corrupt governments throughout history—it simply printed more money in order to pay its bills. The result of too much money chasing too few goods was that prices rose by 5470 percent in 1922 alone. In 1923, things got even worse, and prices rose an astonishing 1 300 000 000 000 times!

Prices rose so rapidly at one point that waiters changed the amount charged for menu items throughout the meal. Workers demanded to be paid daily, and then, later, twice a day. Immediately upon being paid, people would rush to buy almost anything that was available for sale—especially nonperishable goods. Eventually, money was literally not worth the paper it was printed on. It was used by people to light the fire in stoves or by children to make building blocks. At this point, the economy collapsed, and unemployment and violence rose quickly. All of this contributed to one of the darkest chapters in human history—the rise of Hitler and the Nazi Party.

A more recent example of hyperinflation occurred in Zimbabwe, where inflation, which had been growing over the past decade, peaked in November 2008 at a monthly rate of 7.96×10^{10}. This translates into a 98 percent daily rate, which means that prices were doubling every 25 hours!

This brief glimpse emphasizes that the cause of inflation can be either a demand-side or a supply-side phenomenon. We will explore this more thoroughly in a later chapter.

In summary, cost-push inflation can take three forms:

- wage-push
- profit-push
- import-push

A final note, as we complete our investigation of the "twin evils." As we shall see in Chapter 12, there is a great deal of evidence suggesting that many economies suffering from a recession with high unemployment generally have low inflation rates. Conversely, the good news for those economies suffering high inflation rates is that they seldom suffer high unemployment. The bad news is that efforts to reduce unemployment tend to push up inflation rates, and attempts to bring down inflation tend to increase unemployment. In other words, there seems to be a trade-off between the two (the famous Phillips Curve). In a way, it is a bit like a teeter-totter: as you push down on one side (unemployment), the other side (inflation) will rise.

TEST YOUR UNDERSTANDING

11. a) If you borrowed a sum of money for one year at a nominal rate of interest of 11 percent, and during that same year the inflation rate was 4 percent, what real rate of interest did you pay?

   b) Assume that you retire with a pension fixed at $12 000 per year, and that in each of the two years following retirement, the inflation rate is 5 percent. At the end of those two years, what will be the amount of your real income?

SECTION SUMMARY

a) The costs of inflation are subdivided into redistributive costs and output costs. Redistributive costs include

- shifting income from the economically weak to the economically strong

- shifting income from lenders to borrowers

b) Because of increased uncertainty, output costs

- reduce the level of investment and economic growth

- increase menu costs (such as the cost of revising catalogues, websites, and so forth)

- reduce exports and increase imports

c) The two causes of inflation are demand-pull and cost-push. Cost-push is subdivided into

- wage-push

- profit-push

- import-push

 Study Guide

Review

WHAT'S THE BIG IDEA?

An important thing to remember about unemployment is that it does not mean the same thing as not having a job. In fact, there are three groups of people who are not counted as working: children and people in institutions; those, like homemakers and retired people, who chose not to work; and people actively looking for work. It is only this last group who are considered unemployed. If you don't have a job but you are not actively searching for one you are not considered unemployed.

Another important concept to grasp is that of the *natural rate of unemployment*, which simply means the lowest unemployment an economy (and its government) is likely to achieve given present conditions. This will never be zero, because there will always be some people leaving or starting new jobs (a situation called *frictional unemployment*) or those forced to find other work when firms and whole industries are in decline (*structural unemployment*). It's estimated that these days this natural rate in Canada is in the range of 5 to 7 percent. Any unemployment above this is called *cyclical unemployment* and is both avoidable and costly. The best measure of this cost is called *Okun's law*, which suggests that every 1 percent of this type of unemployment costs the Canadian economy 2½ percent in GDP.

Inflation is measured using a price index, and this index is a necessity when we come to look at the idea of *real income*. This latter is a bit misnamed: it certainly doesn't measure anything "real"; rather it asks what income would be if there had been no inflation.

The best way of understanding the concept of real income is to look at the income of your grandfather in 1957, your father in 1987, and your sister in 2017. Suppose they all had good jobs earning respectively $7 000, $32 000 and $60 000. Who was better off? Well, one thing they had in common was their love of Oka cheese which they would buy in whole wheels. The costs of those wheels has changed considerably: back in 1957 you could buy one for $12, by 1987 the price had increased to $50, and today it would cost you $100. A few calculations quickly show us that your grandfather could afford to buy 583 cheeses on his salary, your father 640, and your sister 600. Your father, then, had the highest real income. If we were to express their salaries in terms of the 2016 cheese price of $100 (that is, the price index = 100 in that year), their real incomes come to $58 300, $64 000, and $60 000 respectively.

NEW GLOSSARY TERMS AND KEY EQUATIONS

consumer price index (CPI)
cost-push inflation
cyclical unemployment
demand-pull inflation
discouraged worker
employed
frictional unemployment
full employment

GDP deflator
GDP gap
inflation
labour force
natural rate of unemployment
nominal income
Okun's law
output costs

participation rate
real interest rate
redistributive costs
structural unemployment
unemployed
unemployment
unemployment rate
working-age population

Equations:

[4.1]   Labour force participation rate $= \dfrac{\text{labour force}}{\text{working-age population}} \times 100$

[4.2]   Unemployment rate $= \dfrac{\text{number of unemployed}}{\text{labour force}} \times 100$

[4.3]   GDP gap = potential GDP − actual GDP (real or nominal)

[4.4]   GDP gap = 2.5 × cyclical unemployment (%) × actual GDP (real or nominal)

[4.5] $\text{CPI} = \dfrac{\text{cost of basket in a given year}}{\text{cost of basket in base year}} \times 100$

[4.6] $\text{Inflation rate} = \dfrac{(\text{price index this year} - \text{price index last year})}{\text{price index last year}} \times 100$

[4.7] $\text{GDP deflator} = \dfrac{\text{nominal GDP}}{\text{real GDP}} \times 100$

[4.8] $\text{Real GDP} = \dfrac{\text{nominal GDP}}{\text{GDP deflator}} \times 100$

[4.9] $\text{Nominal GDP} = \text{real GDP} \times \dfrac{\text{GDP deflator}}{100}$

[4.10] $\text{Real value (in year B\$)} = \dfrac{\text{nominal value in year A}}{\text{price index in year A}} \times \text{price index in year B (or base year)}$

[4.11]   % change in real income = % change in nominal income − inflation rate

[4.12] $\text{Number of years to double} = \dfrac{70}{\text{\% growth rate}}$

[4.13]   Nominal interest rate = real interest rate + inflation rate

[4.14]   Real interest rate = nominal rate − the inflation rate

Comprehensive Problem

(LO 3) The data in **Table 4.8** shows the total output (a mixture of consumer, capital, and government services) and the prices of each product for the distant country of Vindaloo. (All figures are in billions of dollars, and the base year is 2015.)

TABLE 4.8

1	2	3	4	5	6	7	8	9	10	11	12	13	14
		2015			2016					2017			
Item	Quantity	Prices Year 2015	Nominal GDP	Quantity	Prices Year 2016	Nominal GDP	Year 2015	Real GDP	Quantity	Prices Year 2017	Nominal GDP	Year 2015	Real GDP
Pizzas	30	12	—	35	13	—	—	—	40	14	—	—	—
Movie tickets	20	10	—	22	11	—	—	—	24	12	—	—	—
Farm tractors	3	100	—	4	95	—	—	—	4	110	—	—	—
Parking meters	4	50	—	4	60	—	—	—	5	70	—	—	—
Totals			—			—		—			—		—

Questions

a) Complete the table.

Answer the following questions (to one decimal place).

b) What is the value of nominal GDP in 2015? 2016? 2017?

c) What is the value of real GDP in 2015? 2016? 2017?

d) What is the value of the GDP deflator in 2015? 2016? 2017?

e) What is the inflation rate (using the GDP deflator) in 2016? 2017?

Answers

a) See the following table:

TABLE 4.8 (COMPLETED)

1	2	3	4	5	6	7	8	9	10	11	12	13	14
		2015			2016					2017			
Item	Quantity	Prices Year 2015	Nominal GDP	Quantity	Prices Year 2016	Nominal GDP	Prices Year 2015	Real GDP	Quantity	Prices Year 2017	Nominal GDP	Prices Year 2015	Real GDP
Pizzas	30	12	360	35	13	455	12	420	40	14	560	12	480
Movie tickets	20	10	200	22	11	242	10	220	24	12	288	10	240
Farm tractors	3	100	300	4	95	380	100	400	4	110	440	100	400
Parking meters	4	50	200	4	60	240	50	200	5	70	350	50	250
Totals			1060			1317		1240			1638		1370

Column 7 is completed by multiplying columns 5 and 6 together. Columns 8 and 13 are simply a repeat of column 3. Column 9 is completed by multiplying columns 5 and 8 together. Column 12 is determined by multiplying columns 10 and 11 together. Column 14 is determined by multiplying columns 10 and 13 together.

b) From columns 4, 7, and 12:

2015: $1060;   2016: $1317;   2017: $1638

c) From columns 4, 9, and 14:

2015: $1060;   2016: $1240;   2017: $1370

d) Nominal GDP/real GDP × 100 for each year:

2015: 100;   2016:106.2;   2017:119.6

e) Inflation rate = (price index this year − price index last year)/price index last year × 100

2016 = 6.2% (6.2/100 × 100); 2017 = 12.6% (13.4/106.2 × 100)

Questions

f) Suppose that the representative consumer in Vindaloo buys five units of each consumer good. What is the cost of each bundle in 2015? 2016? 2017?

g) Converting the cost of each bundle into a consumer price index, what is the value of the index in each year using 2015 as the base year? 2015? 2016? 2017?

h) What is the inflation rate using this price index? 2016? 2017?

Answers

f) 5 pizzas + 5 movie tickets would cost each year:

2015: $110;   2016: $120;   2017: $130

g) Price index = (value of bundle in current year/value of bundle in base year) × 100

Price indexes: 2015 = 100 (110/110 × 100); 2016 = 109.1 (120/110 × 100); 2017 = 118.2 (130/110 × 100)

h) Inflation rate = (price index this year − price index last year)/price index last year × 100

2016 = 9.1% (9.1/100 × 100); 2017 = 8.3% (9.1/109.1 × 100)

Study Problems

Find answers on the McGraw-Hill online resource.

Basic (Problems 1–5)

1. **(LO 3)** The data in Table 4.9 are for the country of Eturia. Answer questions (a) and (c) to one decimal place.

TABLE 4.9

	2015	2016	2017
Nominal GDP ($billions)	420	456	500
Real GDP ($billions)	400	422	447
Population (millions)	16	16.56	17.14

a) Calculate the GDP deflator.
   2015: _____ 2016: _____ 2017: _____
b) Calculate real GDP per capita.
   2015: _____ 2016: _____ 2017: _____
c) Calculate the growth rate of real GDP per capita.
   2016: _____ 2017: _____

2. **(LO 1)** The labour force data for Eturia (in millions) are shown in Table 4.10.

TABLE 4.10

	2015	2016	2017
Population	20	21	22.05
Working-age population	12	12.5	12.8
Labour force	8.4	9	9.2
Unemployed	0.7	0.8	0.85
CPI (2002 = 100)	108.2	109	110.3

a) What are the (labour force) participation rates in each year?
   2015: _____ 2016: _____ 2017: _____
b) What are the unemployment rates in each year?
   2015: _____ 2016: _____ 2017: _____
c) Calculate the annual inflation rate.
   2016: _____ 2017: _____
d) Calculate the percentage increase in population.
   2016: _____ 2017: _____
e) If the population continues to increase at this rate, how long will it take for the population to double? Number of years: _____

3. **(LO 3)** The average nominal incomes earned in Eturia and the CPI are shown in Table 4.11.

TABLE 4.11

	2015	2016	2017
Nominal income ($)	28 000	29 600	32 000
CPI (2002 = 100)	116	121	128

a) Calculate real incomes.
   2015: _____ 2016: _____ 2017: _____
b) Calculate the percentage that real incomes rose.
   2016: _____ 2017: _____

4. **(LO 3)** The data for three countries (all with the same base year, with figures converted to Canadian dollars) are shown in Table 4.12.

TABLE 4.12

	Population (millions)	Nominal GDP ($billions)	Price Index 2009 = 100
Altria	35	$ 715	140
Bergan	75	2200	120
Casper	150	2875	180

Calculate the real GDPs per capita for each country and rank them in size.

Country	Real GDP per Capita
1. _____	$_____
2. _____	$_____
3. _____	$_____

5. **(LO 3)** Terana's nominal GDP rose from $200 billion in 2016 to $224 billion in 2017. During the same period, the inflation rate was 7 percent. (Calculate answers to one decimal place.)
   a) By what percentage did nominal GDP increase between 2016 and 2017? _____
   b) By what percentage did real GDP increase between 2016 and 2017? _____

Intermediate (Problems 6–8)

6. **(LO 1)** The information in Table 4.13 is for the economy of Mensk.

TABLE 4.13

Working-age population	20.0
Number of people in full-time employment	11.5
Number of people in part-time employment	2.0
Number of people unemployed	1.5
Number of discouraged workers	1.5

a) What is the unemployment rate? _____
b) What is the participation rate? _____

7. **(LO 1, 2)** Table 4.14 shows national data (in billions of dollars) for the economy of Westfall. Answer the questions to one decimal point.

TABLE 4.14

	2015	2016	2017
Nominal GDP ($)	850	958	____
GDP deflator (2010 = 100)	109	____	118
Real GDP	____	833	____
Population (millions)	30	____	31
Real GDP per capita	____	27 311	28 390

a) Fill in the blanks in the table.
b) What is the inflation rate in 2016? _____
c) What is the growth rate of real GDP per capita in 2017? _____

8. **(LO 2)** The data in Table 4.15 are for the economy of Merton, which has a natural rate of unemployment of 5 percent.

TABLE 4.15

	2015	2016	2017
Real GDP ($)	600	600	630
Unemployment rate	8%	6%	6%

Calculate the size of the GDP gap.
2015: _____
2016: _____
2017: _____

Advanced (Problems 9–12)

9. **(LO 2)** Suppose that the labour force is currently 5 million and the unemployment rate is 11 percent. On August 1, government announces that it will create 40 000 new jobs to be filled over the next three months. Only people who were unemployed on August 1 will be hired. As a result, 120 000 people immediately apply for the jobs; half of these people had previously not been actively seeking work.
a) Has the labour force changed as a result of this announcement? Explain. _____
b) What will be the unemployment rate before the jobs are filled? _____
c) Once all the jobs are filled, what will the unemployment rate be? _____

10. **(LO 3)** Suppose that James's income in year 1 is $36 000. Over the next four years, his income increases by 3 percent per year. At the same time, the economy experiences an inflation rate of 1.5 percent per year.
a) Complete Table 4.16.

TABLE 4.16

Year	Nominal Income	Price Index	Real Income
1	$36 000	100.0	___
2	___	___	___
3	___	___	___
4	___	___	___
5	___	___	___

b) What will be James's real income in year 5? $_____

11. **(LO 2)** Suppose the actual real GDP in Merryland is $400 billion and its potential GDP is $450 billion. If the natural rate of unemployment is 6 percent, what is its present unemployment rate? _____

12. **(LO 3)** The economy of Sumer produces only three products: rice, pajamas, and beer. The base year is 2015. The quantities and prices of these products in 2015 and 2016 are shown in Table 4.17.

TABLE 4.17

	2015			2016			2016		
Item	Quantity	Price	Nominal GDP	Quantity	Price	Nominal GDP	Quantity	2015 Price	Real GDP
Rice	400	$ 5	___	430	$ 5.20	___	430	___	___
Pajamas	220	15	___	250	16	___	250	___	___
Beer	125	20	___	130	24	___	130	___	___
Totals			___			___			___

a) Complete Table 4.17.
b) What is the value of the GDP deflator in 2016?

c) Suppose the average inhabitant of Sumer consumes 10 units each of beer and rice and 2 units of pajamas each year. Complete Table 4.18.

TABLE 4.18

Item	Quantity	Prices 2015	Basket Cost	Prices 2016	Basket Cost
Rice	——	——	——	——	——
Beer	——	——	——	——	——
Pajamas	——	——	——	——	——
Total	——		——		——

d) What is the value of the CPI for 2016? _____

13. **(LO 2)** Table 4.19 shows the labour force data for the country of Parsha in 2016 (figures in millions):

TABLE 4.19

	2016	2017		2016	2017
Population	42	42			
Working-age population	35	——	Not in working-age population	7	——
Labour force	25	——	Not in labour force	10	——
Employed	23.5	——	Unemployed	1.5	——
Labour force participation %	71.4	——	Unemployment %	6.0	——

Suppose the only change that occurs in 2017 is that the number of discouraged workers increases by 0.3 (million). Complete Table 4.19.

14. **(LO 2)** Table 4.20 shows the labour force data for the country of Parsha in 2016 (figures in millions):

TABLE 4.20

	2016	2017		2016	2017
Population	42	42			
Working-age population	35	——	Not in working-age population	7	——
Labour force	25	——	Not in labour force	10	——
Employed	23.5	——	Unemployed	1.5	——
Labour force participation %	71.4	——	Unemployment %	6.0	——

Suppose that the only change that occurs in 2017 is that the number of retired workers increases by 1.0 (million). Complete Table 4.20.

Problems for Further Study

Basic (Problems 1–5)

1. **(LO 3)** The CPI in Eturia is as shown in Table 4.21. What are the annual inflation rates?
2016: _____ 2017: _____

TABLE 4.21

	2015	2016	2017
CPI (2010 = 100)	116	121	128

2. **(LO 3)** The population growth of Eturia is shown in Table 4.22.

TABLE 4.22

	2015	2016	2017
Population (millions)	16	16.56	17.14

a) Calculate the percentage growth in population.
   2016: _____ 2017: _____
b) If the population continues to increase at this rate, how many years will it take for the population of Eturia to double? _____

3. **(LO 3)** Interest rates in Eturia are shown in Table 4.23. Calculate the real interest rate in each year.
   2015: _____ 2016: _____ 2017: _____

TABLE 4.23

	2015	2016	2017
Nominal interest rate	8%	6%	5.2%
Inflation rate	6.8%	4.3%	5.9%

4. **(LO 3)** What is the GDP deflator? How is it measured, and what is it used for?

5. **(LO 2)** Distinguish between frictional and cyclical unemployment.

Intermediate (Problems 6–8)

6. **(LO 3)** If the inflation rate unexpectedly rises from 2 to 5 percent, would each of the following individuals gain or lose as a result?
   a) Nigel, who borrowed $20 000 last year, repayable over three years, to buy a new boat _____
   b) Lars, an elderly man living on a fixed company pension _____
   c) Yoko, who keeps her savings in a credit union that pays a fixed 4 percent on customers' deposits _____
   d) Joan, an assembly-line worker whose employment is covered by a two-year union contract that calls for an annual wage increase of 5 percent _____
   e) Robert, who owns shares in the company where Joan works _____

7. **(LO 1)** How are the participation rate and the unemployment rate measured?

8. **(LO 4)** Give two examples of the output costs of inflation.

Advanced (Problems 9–10)

9. **(LO 4)** In times of deflation, is it better to buy now or in the future? Why? Is it better to lend or to borrow? Why?

10. **(LO 2)** Explain how an increase in the rate of unemployment might suggest an improvement in economic conditions.

CHAPTER 5
Aggregate Demand and Supply

LEARNING OBJECTIVES

At the end of this chapter, you should be able to:

LO1 Explain the concepts of potential GDP, the business cycle, and the source of economic growth.

LO2 Explain the concepts of aggregate supply, aggregate demand, and macroeconomic equilibrium.

LO3 Describe the factors that can affect aggregate demand and aggregate supply.

LO4 List the causes of recessions and inflationary booms.

LO5 Explain the main points of disagreement between neoclassical and Keynesian economics.

LO6 Explain the modern view of aggregate demand and aggregate supply.

 WHAT'S AHEAD ...

This is the first of two chapters on what economists call the *product market*, the market in which consumer goods and services are bought and sold. In this chapter, we use an economic model that examines the interaction of aggregate demand and aggregate supply to determine the level of GDP, or national income, and the price level. We will use this same model in later chapters when we discuss various economic policies. The chapter concludes by looking at a fundamental question—whether a macroeconomy is capable of self-adjustment.

A QUESTION OF RELEVANCE ...

Which of the following acts do you think will improve economic conditions more: buying a new tablet for $600 or increasing your work productivity effort by 20 percent? Besides your obvious objection that neither action will have much impact on the whole economy, you would probably opt for the second one, since it seems to involve real production. After all, if we each became 20 percent more productive at our work, the economy would surely be wealthier than if people simply bought more things. Surprisingly, in the short run, the two actions will have about the same effect on the economy. In the longer run, however, a sustained productivity increase will make for a healthier economy.

In the last two chapters, we looked at how economic growth, unemployment, and inflation are measured and briefly discussed some of the problems related to these issues. In this chapter, we want to be more analytical and develop a model that will help us understand the causes of these problems. As we shall see, economic growth, inflation, and unemployment are all interrelated, and in order to understand one we need to understand all three. Our model of aggregate demand and aggregate supply will do that for us.

As we are all aware, the level of production and real GDP in Canada has risen over time. The reasons for this are not complicated. The size of the labour force grows, the amount of capital stock in the economy grows, and most importantly, there are continuous advances in the level of technological knowledge. All of this leads to increases in productivity. However, it would be a mistake to assume that production and real GDP rise at a steady rate or even that they rise each and every year. In fact, in some years, firms find that their sales fall off and they need to cut their level of production. This leads to layoffs, rising rates of unemployment, and falling levels of income. When this happens, we say that the economy is in a recession. In other years, firms might well experience exactly the opposite set of circumstances with rising levels of sales, increased production, and additional hiring. These lead to falling rates of unemployment and rising levels of income. We can recognize that there is an underlying trend that is pushing up production and income, but at the same time there are short-term fluctuations that sometimes push the economy beyond this trend (an economic boom) and sometimes below this trend (an economic recession). We begin developing our model by looking at this long-term upward trend.

5.1   Potential GDP

> **LO1**   Explain the concepts of potential GDP, the business cycle, and the source of economic growth.

In Chapter 3, we defined economic growth as an increase in an economy's real GDP per capita. Although this is the standard definition used by most economists, Statistics Canada prefers to measure economic growth in terms of the growth in real GDP, ignoring the effects of a growing population. However, an increasing number of economists prefer to define economic growth as an increase in the economy's capacity to produce, rather than as a simple increase in actual production. The economy's *capacity* refers to the maximum level at which the country is able to produce, assuming that it is at full employment. In other words, it is the amount of GDP that would be produced if all of its labour and all other resources were fully employed (at normal levels of utilization). This is what is meant by **potential GDP**. It could also be called *full-employment GDP* or *economic capacity*. Some economists refer to it as the **long-run aggregate supply**, or LAS, and this is how we will depict it in our graphs. But economies do not always reach their potential, either in the short run or the long run. In other words, the idea that an economy reaches its potential in the long-run is a possibility rather than an inevitability, as we shall see in the last section of this chapter. In this sense, potential GDP can be looked at as the amount of GDP when the economy is at its natural rate of unemployment (when there is no cyclical unemployment).

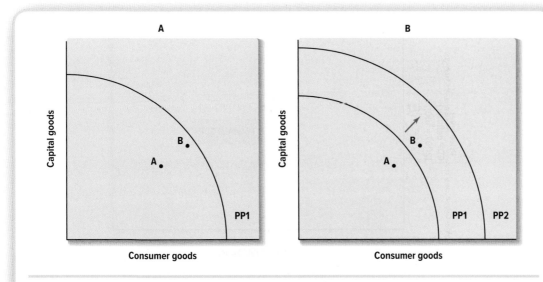

FIGURE 5.1   Economic Growth and Production Possibilities

Figure A shows the economy growing from point A to point B. But this growth may not be sustained, since its potential level (the PP curve) has not changed. Figure B shows similar economic growth from point A to point B. But in this case, the growth is more likely to be sustained, since its potential has similarly increased (from PP1 to PP2).

In emphasizing potential rather than actual GDP, economists are making the point that without increases in potential GDP, the prospects for sustained growth in the future are limited. There is an important difference between actual growth in the present and sustainable growth in the future. This distinction can be illustrated using the production possibilities diagram in **Figure 5.1A**, where the production possibilities curve, PP1, shows the maximum quantities of capital and consumer goods that this economy is presently capable of producing.

You will recall that the curve itself does not show what the economy is actually producing or what it would like to produce (there is no indication of demand), it merely shows what it is capable of producing, that is, its potential levels of production. Let us assume that initially this economy is producing at point A in **Figure 5.1A**, and since this is inside the curve, it is producing less than it is capable of. In the following year, let us suppose that the economy increases its output of both capital and consumer goods, as depicted in the movement to point B. The economy has experienced economic growth and is now close to its potential output. Since an economy cannot (permanently) go beyond its production possibilities boundary, the amount by which it can increase production past point B is limited.

Now contrast this to the situation in **Figure 5.1B**. Here, point A is the same starting point shown in **Figure 5.1A**, and the movement to point B is also the same. However, we also see that the production possibilities curve has shifted from PP1 to PP2, which indicates an increase in the economy's potential GDP. Obviously, the prospects for future growth in this case are much brighter. Economists would be more impressed by the growth depicted in **Figure 5.1B**, since not only is the economy producing more, it is also capable of sustaining this level of production in the future.

The ideas we have just presented can easily be shown in terms of a demand–supply diagram. On the vertical axis of **Figure 5.2**, we show the price level for the economy in terms of a GDP deflator. The horizontal axis shows the total output of all finished goods and services in the economy—its real GDP. The figures shown here are the approximate numbers for the Canadian economy in 2015.

To calculate potential GDP is reasonably straightforward making use of Okun's law, which we looked at in Chapter 4. The unemployment rate in Canada in 2015 was 6.9 percent, and the real GDP was $1752 billion. If we assume that the natural rate of unemployment is 5 percent, then its GDP gap is 1.9 percent (cyclical unemployment) × 2.5 × $1752, which comes to $83 billion. Potential GDP, therefore, was $1752 + $83, or $1835 billion. This figure is not affected by the price level. The vertical nature of the potential GDP curve illustrates the fact that while a higher price level would raise *nominal* GDP, it would leave potential *real* GDP unaffected. Put another way, what an economy is

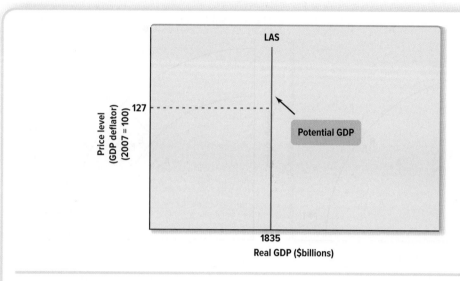

FIGURE 5.2   Potential GDP

Potential GDP is a straight vertical line showing the amount of GDP at full employment. In 2012, it equaled $1835 billion.

physically capable of producing is not affected by the prices those goods and services happen to be sold at. Think of it like this: An economy has a certain size of labour force, a certain quantity of raw materials, and a certain amount of capital goods. If it were to perform at maximum efficiency using its best technology, the potential GDP tells us the maximum output that could be produced *regardless of the price level*. In fact, as far as its potential GDP is concerned, the price level is irrelevant. Bear in mind that potential GDP is merely a benchmark—albeit an important one—and does not tell us what the economy is actually producing or even what policy makers might want it to produce. We will look at actual production a little later.

 TEST YOUR UNDERSTANDING

Find answers on the McGraw-Hill online resource.

1. Suppose the unemployment rate in Concordia is 8 percent and real GDP equals $600 billion. If the natural rate of unemployment is 5 percent, what is the amount of the GDP gap, and what is the value of potential GDP?

Next, we want to address the question of what makes an economy grow. What will cause an increase in an economy's potential real GDP? Graphically, this is a rightward shift in the LAS curve and is, in many ways, analogous to asking: What factors will graphically shift the production possibilities curve to the right?

Sources of Economic Growth

We saw in Chapter 3 that the most important factor affecting a country's long-term economic growth is the level of its labour productivity. We also saw that this productivity itself depends upon a number of important determinants. Let us review them briefly. First, the quality of a country's human capital has a major impact on productivity and economic growth. By *human capital* we mean the accumulated knowledge, skills, and education of the labour force. But it depends on the imagination and ingenuity of its people as well as their motivation and the incentives that the country provides for them. Needless to say, the labour force participation rate also determines the amount of people who are actively engaged in production.

The second major factor that can improve labour productivity is the amount of physical capital that a country possesses. The quality of that capital is also significant. Is the country's physical plant and equipment modern and well maintained, or is the country handicapped by having capital that is worn out and out of date?

The third productivity factor is the extent to which a country embraces and encourages technological change. One of the major indicators of the extent to which a country is willing to adopt new technology is the amount of its resources that it devotes to research and development. It comes as no surprise to learn that countries such as the United States, Germany, Japan, Canada, and more recently China are at the forefront in terms of both research and development and labour productivity.

Finally, the presence and accessibility of natural resources can help a long way in raising a country's growth rate. In fact, for many countries—Brazil comes to mind—it may well be the most important factor.

 ADDED DIMENSION

Economic Capacity

To economists, the idea of capacity is best understood with reference to costs. Capacity does not literally mean the absolute maximum that can be produced in the short run. Firms can and do produce at full physical capacity from time to time, but it is a very expensive proposition in terms of overtime pay, high maintenance costs, and so on. Such high costs could not be sustained in the long run. Capacity, then, means the output level at which the firm can produce at the lowest per-unit cost, and this level may well be only 70, 80, or 90 percent of the physical capacity of the plant.

In summary, the sources of economic growth for an economy are

- the quantity and quality of its labour resources (the level of human capital)
- the amount of physical capital available
- the rate of technological change
- the amount and quality of its natural resources

The result of a change in any one of the factors just discussed would increase the economy's potential to produce. In **Figure** 5.3, potential GDP has increased by 3 percent each year shifting the

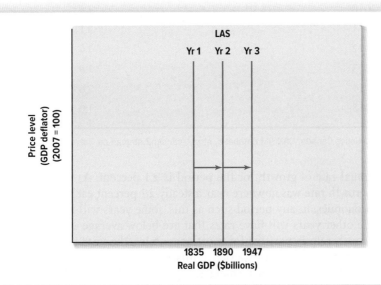

FIGURE 5.3 Economic Growth and Potential GDP

A positive change in any of the determinants of economic growth will result in a rightward shift of the potential GDP curve.

LAS from $1835 billion in year 1 to $1890 billion in year 2 to $1947 billion in year 3. This is illustrated by a rightward shift in the LAS (potential GDP) line.

Economic Growth and the Business Cycle

Although Statistics Canada does not publish estimates of potential GDP on a regular basis, evidence suggests that it tends to increase by small, regular amounts each year. Research indicates that for Canada, potential GDP has grown, on average, by about 3 percent per year since the beginning of the 1990s.

However, actual economic growth is seldom so smooth and steady. Table 5.1 shows the annual growth in actual real GDP for Canada for 1997 to 2015.

TABLE 5.1
Canada's Rate of Growth in Real GDP 1997–2015

Year	% Growth Rate of Real GDP
1997	4.5
1998	4.1
1999	5.4
2000	5.4
2001	1.4
2002	2.7
2003	2.0
2004	3.1
2005	3.2
2006	2.4
2007	2.2
2008	1.0
2009	−3.2
2010	2.9
2011	3.1
2012	1.6
2013	1.9
2014	2.6
2015	1.0

Source: Adapted from Statistics Canada, CANSIM database, http://cansim2.statcan.ca, Table 380-0106, July 21, 2016.

The average annual rate of growth for the period is 2.1 percent. As you can see from the data, however, the actual growth rate was nowhere near a steady 2.1 percent each year. This is true for most periods and most economies. In any period such as this, some years will have high growth rates, say, 4 or 5 percent, while other years will have rates that are below average or even negative. While the *average* long-run growth rate is positive for most economies, the year-to-year fluctuations can be quite unstable. In short, all economies experience **business cycles**—expansionary and contractionary phases in the rate at which real GDP changes. Figure 5.4 illustrates this point using Canadian data. On the horizontal axis, we have time, starting with 1997, while on the vertical axis we have the growth rate (in real GDP).

You can see that the growth rate generally rose between 1997 and 2000 (an expansionary phase) and then experienced a contractionary phase leading to a trough in 2001. After a minor peak and trough, the economy then entered another contractionary phase, leading to a major trough in 2009,

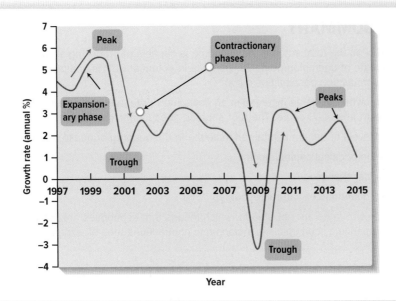

FIGURE 5.4 **The Business Cycle**

The rate of growth in real GDP reflects two major contractionary phases (in red) and two expansionary phases (in blue). The average annual growth rate for the period is 2.1 percent.

before recovering in 2010. These expansionary and contractionary phases in the growth of real GDP form the business cycle—what goes up comes down and vice versa.

In order to better understand the business cycle and explain why there are periodic fluctuations in the economy—in all economies, not just the Canadian economy—we need to look at the forces of supply and demand that lie behind patterns of growth which we will do in the next section.

 ADDED DIMENSION

Robinson Crusoe and Economic Growth

Let us assume that Robinson Crusoe, the celebrated fictional castaway, is troubled by the prospects of making it on his own for an indefinite period on his uninhabited island. He obviously needs to catch a lot of fish to do more than just survive. He has a crude fishing pole and has been catching the odd fish recently, but he wonders if there is a better way to catch more and thus improve his standard of living. Perhaps there is another location on the island where the fish are more plentiful, bigger, and easier to catch. But spending time looking for another place would leave less time for his current fishing efforts. Alternatively, he could stay where he is and hope that his fishing skills improve with experience and persistence (he curses the day he chose a course in Chinese cooking rather than a fishing class at night school). Finally, there is the possibility of fashioning a crude net or even building a boat, but again, either of these activities would take time away from actual fishing. He has three choices in trying to improve his economic well-being:

- increase the resources available to him (find a better fishing spot)
- improve the level of his human capital (become a better fisher through experience)
- increase his physical capital (a net or a boat rather than just a pole)

Each of these choices requires that he sacrifice time plus the fish that would be caught during this time (consumption) but promises a richer harvest of fish in the future. In effect, every economy faces the same choices and sacrifices because economic growth involves more effort, less leisure, and less present consumption—but the rewards can be great and continue to pay off long into the future.

SECTION SUMMARY

a) Potential GDP is the total amount the economy is capable of producing at full employment (at the natural rate of unemployment). An increase in potential GDP is analogous to a rightward shift in the production possibilities curve.

b) Economic growth implies an increase in an economy's potential GDP and is illustrated by a rightward shift in its LAS curve. The four sources of economic growth are

- improved levels of human capital (an increase in the quantity or quality of labour employed)

- increases in physical capital stock

- technological change

- additional quantities of natural resources

c) Economic growth rates are not steady, which means that economies are subject to business cycles—the periodic economic expansions and contractions they all experience.

5.2   Aggregate Supply and Demand

> **LO2**   Explain the concepts of aggregate supply, aggregate demand, and macroeconomic equilibrium.

In this section, we will construct our first simple model of the economy using the tools of aggregate supply and demand. Some of you will recognize that the basic principles behind their construction are not greatly different from supply, demand, and equilibrium in microeconomics. Let us begin with a look at the idea behind aggregate supply.

Aggregate Supply

Aggregate supply refers to the total quantity of goods and services that firms in the economy would be willing and able to produce at various prices, assuming that the prices of factors of production remain constant. Essentially, this means that, in the short term, wages and the prices of raw materials and other resources are assumed to remain unchanged. This is not an unrealistic assumption. While most firms have little control over the market demand for their products, they can and do try to exercise as much control over their own supply as they can, and this certainly includes their own costs, both present and future. They can address future costs by entering into contracts with their suppliers and with their employees (or their unions) to achieve some certainty of future resource prices and wage rates. Because of these contracts, a firm is able to increase production and employ more factor services without experiencing an increase in the costs of those resources.

This implies that if demand increases and firms can sell their products at a higher price, they will be only too willing to produce more (and employ more resources) because when resource costs remain constant (at least for a while), their total profits will rise. On the other hand, lower prices represent lower profits and will cause the firm to reduce production (and employment). In other words:

> The higher the price levels, the greater the aggregate quantity supplied; the lower the price level, the smaller the aggregate quantity supplied.

The aggregate supply curve therefore is upward sloping. However, it is unlikely to be a straight line. The reason for this, as we shall discuss in detail later in the chapter, is that, at some point, as production increases in the economy, productivity is likely to fall as firms are forced to use less suitable and less efficient resources. This will cause the unit cost of production to rise (even though the prices of resources remain the same) so that firms will only produce more at a higher price.

Figure 5.5 illustrates this idea: an increase in the price level from P_1 to P_2 will increase the aggregate quantity of goods and services that firms are willing to produce and thus real GDP from Y_1 to Y_2.

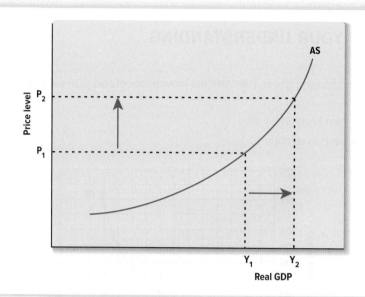

FIGURE 5.5   The Shape of the AS Curve

An increase in the price level from P_1 to P_2 will increase the profits of firms and lead to an increase in the quantity of goods and services supplied, and therefore to an increase in GDP from Y_1 to Y_2.

Another, more instructive way of explaining the slope of the AS curve is in terms of the **real wage**. As we said at the outset, the AS curve is drawn on the (realistic) assumption that in the short run, factor prices—including wage rates—remain constant. Now, let us look at things from an employee's point of view. Given that her wages are constant, it is clear that if the price level in the economy were to rise, she will be worse off as she will not be able to afford to buy the same quantity of products as before. Put another way, her real wage will decline. The real wage then refers to the amount of goods and services that a worker can obtain for a given amount of **nominal wage**.

$$\text{Real wage} = \frac{\text{nominal wage}}{\text{price level}} \qquad [5.1]$$

We can see from this equation that a person's real wage will decline if *either* her nominal wage falls *or* the price level increases. The result of this—looking at things graphically—is that as we move up the AS curve, the real wage level prevailing in the economy declines.

Now let us look at things from the employer's point of view. Since it is the employer that is paying these wages, a higher price level—with wages remaining constant—means that real wage costs are declining. (From the employer's point of view it does not matter whether the lower real wage is the result of a higher price level or a lower nominal wage rate. In either case, the employer would benefit from a drop in the real wage because a lower real wage means higher profits per unit produced and will cause her to increase production.)

To recap, a higher price level, with wages remaining constant, will increase profit for the average firm and will cause a higher level of output. Conversely, a lower price level implies lower profit and a lower level of output.

Aggregate Demand

Let us now turn our focus to **aggregate demand**, which is the total quantity of goods and services that people are willing to buy at different price levels. Its components are already familiar to you: consumption expenditures, investment spending, government purchases of goods and services, and net exports. In other words,

$$\text{Aggregate demand (AD)} = C + I + G + X_N$$

TEST YOUR UNDERSTANDING

2. Using the accompanying graph, calculate the growth rate of real GDP for a price increase of 10 percent

a) if the price level is currently 80

b) if the price level is currently 100

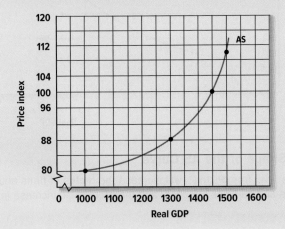

Figure 5.6 shows an aggregate demand curve illustrating the output of goods and services that people will buy at various price levels. We have labelled the horizontal axis Real GDP and indicated the particular level at different prices as Y_1, Y_2, and so on. This reflects the fact that the value of production (real GDP) and the level of real income are always equal, as you learned in Chapter 3. The vertical axis is labelled Price Level, and you can think of this as the value of the GDP deflator—the weighted composite of prices for all goods and services. At price level P_1, real GDP is Y_1. At a lower price level, P_2, real GDP is higher, as seen in Y_2. Similarly, at price level P_3, real GDP is Y_3.

Now we need to understand why aggregate spending is lower when the price level is higher, that is, why the AD curve is downward sloping. To most people, whether or not they have studied

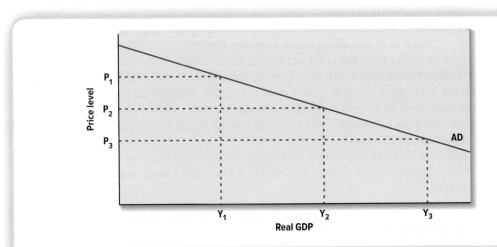

FIGURE 5.6   The Aggregate Demand Curve

As the price level drops from P_1 to P_2 and to P_3, the quantity of goods and services that buyers are willing and able to purchase increases from Y_1 to Y_2 and to Y_3.

economics, one possible explanation seems fairly straightforward: if the price level goes up, people will simply buy less. But we need to be very careful here, since microeconomics suggests that one of the reasons for this is that people would substitute other products for the now more expensive ones. However, here we are looking at the average price level of all goods and services, and there are no substitutes for all goods—at least when we speak of domestically supplied goods.

The other possible reason for the downward slope (as we remember from microeconomics) is that with higher prices, people simply cannot afford as much. However, this explanation is equally invalid; while higher prices mean that buyers cannot afford as much, it also means that the incomes of sellers must also be rising, since they are receiving the benefit of the higher prices.

Our focus then needs to be on the level of *real* GDP. If the price level goes up, then the measured value of nominal expenditures and nominal GDP increase proportionately, while the values of both real GDP and real consumption remain unchanged. Therefore, what we need to work out is the effect on spending if both the price level and nominal incomes rise by the same proportion so that real income remains the same. You might suggest that under these circumstances expenditures may well remain unchanged. And while the nominal value of your wealth (your house, your car and so on) has increased, you are really no better or worse off because should you sell your assets, the price of other things that you might buy with the money has also increased. However, one portion of wealth that is affected by a price change is the real value of savings, which will decline as the price level rises.

For instance, suppose that you have managed to save $10 000 (whether it is in a box under your bed or deposited in a savings account at a bank does not matter). What will happen to the value of those savings over the next year if the economy experiences inflation of 10 percent? With the average price of products rising, your money will certainly not go so far if you decide to use it to make a purchase. Although the nominal value remains $10 000 (or a little higher if you earned interest at the bank), its real value has dropped by 10 percent. You are definitely worse off as a result of the inflation; in fact, your real wealth has declined as a result.

This is what is referred to as the **real-balances effect**. Lower real wealth will cause people to cut down on spending, so a higher price level leads to lower real wealth, lower consumption, and lower aggregate expenditures and will produce a lower level of real GDP. In Figure 5.6 we see that a higher price level, such as P_1, will lead to a lower real GDP, Y_1. A lower price level will produce the opposite result: it will cause the value of real balances and consumption spending to increase, as we can see in the combination of P_3 and Y_3.

We have now established that the aggregate demand curve is downward sloping because consumption expenditures are inversely related to the price level. There are two additional explanations for the downward-sloping aggregate demand curve. First, a higher price level tends to push up interest rates, which, in turn, causes a reduction in investment spending and therefore aggregate expenditures. This is known as the **interest-rate effect**. In addition, higher Canadian prices make our exports less attractive while making imports more appealing to Canadians. This is called the **foreign-trade effect**. We will examine both these effects in detail in later chapters. So, in addition to lower levels of consumption, higher prices cause a drop in investment spending and in net exports. Lower prices will, of course, have the opposite effect.

In summary, the aggregate demand curve is downward-sloping and a lower price level means:

- ↑ consumption (real-balances effect)
- ↑ investment (interest-rate effect)
- ↑ net exports (foreign-trade effect)

Conversely, a higher price level means lower consumption, investment and net exports.

 TEST YOUR UNDERSTANDING

3. Explain how a drop in the price level could affect consumption, investment, and net exports.

Macroeconomic Equilibrium

Macroeconomic equilibrium exists when the aggregate quantity demanded equals the aggregate quantity supplied. Only at one price level will the total that people want to buy equal the total that is produced. This is illustrated in **Figure** 5.7A, where P_ε and Y_ε are the equilibrium values for the price level and real GDP.

Only at price level P_ε are the quantity demanded and quantity supplied equal. It is possible that the price level, temporarily, may not be at equilibrium, but if so it is an unstable situation. This is illustrated in **Figure** 5.7B, where the price level is above equilibrium at P_2. At this higher price level, there is a surplus of goods and services because the quantity supplied exceeds the quantity demanded. To rid themselves of such surpluses, firms will be forced to cut prices and will continue to do so until the price level is back to equilibrium. In contrast, a lower price level of P_3, as seen in **Figure** 5.7C, would result in a shortage of goods and services, and prices would be pushed up until the economy is back at equilibrium, with neither surpluses nor shortages.

It is important to point out that there is no guarantee that equilibrium also means that the economy is operating at its potential (capacity) full-employment level of GDP. In fact, equilibrium could exist at any level of real GDP, as **Figure** 5.8 illustrates.

These figures show three possible positions for an economy. In **Figure** 5.8A, the economy is in equilibrium because the quantity of aggregate demand is equal to the quantity of aggregate supply.

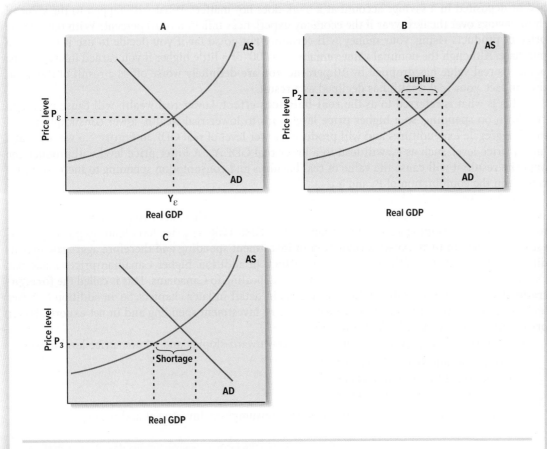

FIGURE 5.7   Macroeconomic Equilibrium

Equilibrium exists where the aggregate demand and the aggregate supply curves intersect. This determines the equilibrium price level P_ε and the equilibrium real GDP level Y_ε, as seen in Figure A. In Figure B, P_2 is a price level above equilibrium, and there is a surplus of goods and services. In this circumstance, firms will be forced to cut prices. At prices below equilibrium, as seen by P_3 in Figure C, there is a shortage, which will force the price level up.

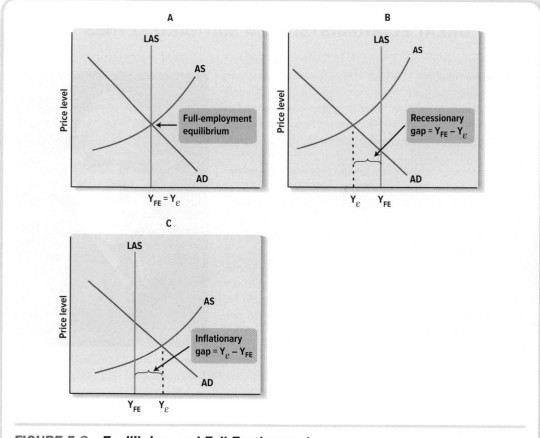

FIGURE 5.8   Equilibrium and Full Employment

Figure A shows an economy in equilibrium, and this equilibrium is also at full employment. In other words, the AD and AS curves intersect at potential GDP (LAS curve). Figure B shows equilibrium occurring below full employment; that is, there is a recessionary gap. In Figure C, equilibrium occurs above full employment; that is, there is an inflationary gap.

In addition, this economy is also at potential GDP. In **Figure 5.8B**, the economy is suffering a **recession** because, while it is also in equilibrium (the AD curve intersects the AS curve at the level of real GDP, Y_ε), this equilibrium is below potential GDP shown by the LAS curve. The difference between equilibrium GDP and potential full-employment GDP when the economy is in a recession is known as a **recessionary gap**. A recessionary gap implies that some of the factors of production are unemployed. That's why, in most people's minds, recession and unemployment are synonymous. It was, of course, John Maynard Keynes who thought this was the situation in which many economies found themselves in the 1930s during the Great Depression. It is also the situation many economies, particularly in Europe, found themselves in during the last recession starting in 2009. In these situations, unemployment is high and production is low, and there is often little incentive for firms to produce more because they are barely selling what they are presently producing. Despite this recessionary gap, such economies are stable because there is neither a tendency nor an incentive to change.

Figure 5.8C shows the opposite situation. Here, again, the economy is in equilibrium at a real GDP level of Y_ε, but the equilibrium occurs above the full-employment potential GDP, shown by the LAS curve. In this situation, unemployment is below its natural rate, which means that labour is scarce relative to the demand for it. This is the situation of an **inflationary gap**. People are trying to buy more goods and services than the economy can produce on a sustainable basis. The level of aggregate demand, indicated by Y_ε, exceeds the level of sustainable potential output. The result is a situation that could be termed "too much spending chasing too few goods" but is often erroneously

GREAT ECONOMISTS: JOHN MAYNARD KEYNES

John Maynard Keynes (1883–1946) is the most well-known and, arguably, the greatest economist of the twentieth century. He was truly "a man for all seasons": advisor to the British government at the 1919 Versailles Peace Conference (which he left in disgust over the matter of German reparation payments); author of a widely used mathematical textbook; successful (but also risk-taking) financial investor (for himself as well as for his university); bibliophile, patron of the arts and husband of Lydia Lopokova, the famous ballerina who later became mayor of Cambridge. He was also influential in setting up the World Bank and the International Monetary Fund at the end of World War II.

In his *General Theory of Employment, Interest and Money* (1935) he unlocked the confusion in economics about the causes and solutions for the Great Depression. In doing so, he revolutionized macroeconomic thinking leading to one high-profile (and initially critical) colleague to say "we are all Keynesians now."

World History Archive/Alamy Stock Photo

described as "too much money chasing too few goods." But we know that money is a stock and spending is a flow, and we must be careful how we state things. Certainly, in such a situation, prices and wages will start to increase, but it may not have anything to do with the amount of money in the economy.

 ADDED DIMENSION

Can an Economy Produce More Than It Is Capable Of?

On the surface, this seems to be a ridiculous question! And yet our diagram suggests that an economy may be capable of producing in excess of its potential, thus creating an inflationary gap. How could this be so? Well, the answer lies in how we define the terms "capacity" and "full employment." To an economist, capacity output (for a firm or an economy) does not mean the absolute maximum it is capable of producing. Rather, it implies the maximum production that can be sustained *in the long run* (alternatively, the output that produces the lowest average cost of production). Very few firms will want to produce at their maximum with the plant and all its available equipment working flat out 24/7. It usually prefers to have some spare capacity to prevent burnout. For most manufacturing firms in Canada, this is usually at around 75–80 percent of maximum capacity.

In a similar vein, full employment does not mean that employees are working every hour of every day. Instead, the idea of full employment is socially defined. In the nineteenth century, this could well have meant over 70 hours per week. Slowly over the past century, the number of weekly hours that constitute full employment has been reduced so that, for most people, it is probably around 34 to 38 hours a week.

In all likelihood, a firm and its employees could, and often do, work in excess of full employment and capacity output, so suggesting that an economy could be above its potential GDP is not so far-fetched. However, such a situation is not sustainable for the economy in the long run, since it tends to be very costly and therefore inflationary.

What is certainly true is that the amount of spending is in excess of the economy's present ability to produce goods. Such a situation is going to result in buyers bidding up prices in an effort to secure what they want and firms being forced to pay higher wages to attract labour, which is in high demand. Such price increases are, of course, inflationary, and the gap between Y_e and Y_{FE} is the inflationary gap. This situation is not stable, since the economy simply cannot continue to produce a level of real GDP above its full-employment level on a sustained basis. In summary, equilibrium in the macroeconomy might

- occur at full employment
- result in a recessionary gap
- result in an inflationary gap

What we need to do now is look at how these various situations come about and what will happen as a result. In other words, we need to look at the dynamics of the model.

 TEST YOUR UNDERSTANDING

4. Following are the aggregate demand and supply schedules for the economy of Tagara.

Price Index	Aggregate Quantity Demanded ($)	Aggregate Quantity Supplied ($)
90	1200	950
95	1150	1025
100	1100	1100
105	1050	1150
110	1000	1190
115	950	1220

    a) What is the equilibrium level of prices and real GDP?

    b) If the price level were 95, would there be a shortage or surplus? How much? What if the price level was 115?

5. Given the following graph and assuming that the economy is in equilibrium, calculate the inflationary or recessionary gap if

    a) potential GDP (LAS) is $600

    b) potential GDP (LAS) is $800

    c) potential GDP (LAS) is $900

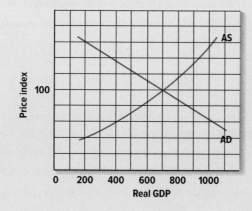

IN A NUTSHELL ...

It's a difficult balancing act!

Potential / (Long Run) GDP

SECTION SUMMARY

a) The aggregate quantity supplied varies directly with the price level because factor prices are constant and increases in the price level will raise profits, resulting in producers increasing output.

b) The aggregate quantity of goods and services demanded varies inversely with the price level because of the
   - real-balances effect
   - interest rate effect
   - foreign-trade effect

c) Equilibrium real GDP occurs when the aggregate quantity of goods and services demanded equals the aggregate quantity supplied (the AD curve intersects the AS curve).

d) Equilibrium real GDP at a level other than full employment will mean one of the following:
   - a recessionary gap, which means an output level below potential GDP (the LAS)
   - an inflationary gap, which means an output level greater than potential GDP (the LAS)

5.3   Determinants of Aggregate Demand and Supply

> **LO3**   Describe the factors that can affect aggregate demand and aggregate supply.

The main thrust of our analysis in this chapter is to discover what brings about change in an economy's price level and its real GDP. These two important concepts are known as determinant variables. That is to say, they are the result of changes in other things that affect aggregate demand and supply. They are the effect, and not the cause, of changes in the economy. So changes to the price level and real GDP are the result of anything that affects aggregate demand or aggregate supply. Let us look at aggregate demand first.

Determinants of Aggregate Demand

There are a number of factors that will cause aggregate demand to change and therefore cause the aggregate demand curve to shift. Remember that aggregate demand is simply the amount of total expenditure at various price levels. You will recall from Chapter 3 that the components of aggregate expenditures are consumption, investment, government spending on goods and services, and net exports. Anything that changes any one of these components will also change aggregate demand. We need to be very clear about the fact that we are talking about the aggregate demand curve *shifting*, so we need to isolate the factors *other than a change in the levels of prices or real GDP* that change aggregate demand. In other words, if either the price level or real GDP changes, it will cause a movement along the aggregate demand curve, not a shift in it.

Changes in Consumption

Let us start with consumption spending. How might you react if you suddenly discovered that you had won $2000 on Lotto 6/49? Would you immediately deposit it in the bank, or more likely, would you go out and buy yourself something special? If the latter, then your consumption level will go up despite the fact that your income and the price level have not changed. We have just isolated the first factor that can change consumption: *changes in wealth*. An increase in the nation's wealth will cause an increase in aggregate demand, reflected in a rightward shift of the AD curve. It is interesting to note that the stock market can have a significant impact on the wealth of a big segment of the population. A sudden and serious drop in stock prices can have a significant effect on the real wealth of investors, and as a result, might cause them to curtail some of their planned consumer spending.

The second factor is the age of consumer durables. For most of us, when the car gets older and begins to wear out, we somehow find the means to either spend more on car repairs or maybe even buy a new car. This means that the greater the *age of consumer durables* in the economy, the more likely it is that they will be replaced, causing an increase in consumer spending.

A third factor involves *consumer confidence*. As confidence in the economy's future improves, people tend to loosen the purse strings and increase their consumption.

Changes in Investment

Turning to investment spending, a primary determinant of a change in investment spending is the rate of interest. The reason for this is straightforward—most major investment projects are funded with borrowed money, and if the cost of borrowing falls because of a decrease in the interest rate then investment spending will increase. Once again, note that this is true even though the level of national income or the price level has not changed. Since most economists regard the interest rate as a crucial factor in determining the amount of investment spending in the economy, it is worth our while to explicitly spell out the relationship.

The Canadian Press/Ryan Remiorz

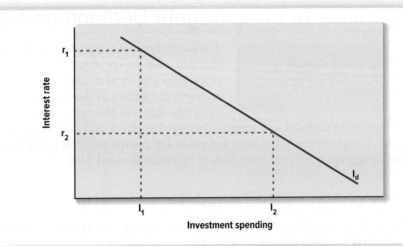

FIGURE 5.9   Investment Demand Curve

At a high rate of interest, r_1, investment spending will be small at I_1 because it will be costly to borrow. At a low interest rate of r_2, investment spending will be higher at I_2 because it will be cheap to borrow.

Figure 5.9 depicts an investment demand curve (I_d). It is downward sloping because if interest rates are high, say at r_1, then firms will not be inclined to spend very much on new capital goods because they will have to pay high interest costs to borrow funds to finance such spending. So the level of investment spending will be a low I_1. On the other hand, if the interest rate was very low, say r_2, then it would be very cheap to borrow and therefore firms will tend to invest more at I_2.

But what if firms do not need to borrow money in order to invest because they have sufficient funds themselves? Would the interest rate be irrelevant for such firms? No—it is still very relevant. For instance, suppose that a firm has an "idle" million dollars and is contemplating using these funds to purchase a new piece of equipment. In fact, these idle funds are unlikely to be that idle! In all likelihood, the firm has these funds deposited in a bank or other financial institution and is earning interest on them. The firm then needs to decide if it should continue to *save* money and earn X percent in the bank, or *invest* that money in the firm by buying new equipment and thus earn Y percent for itself? You can see that the lower the interest rate the firm is presently earning, the more it will be inclined to invest. Conversely, the higher the interest it is earning, the less likely will it be to invest.

To recap:

A high interest rate will lead to low investment spending; a low interest rate will lead to high investment spending.

The second determinant of investment spending is the *purchase price and the installation, operating, and maintenance costs of the capital asset.* These might well be determining factors for a firm trying to decide whether to go ahead with a particular investment. If there is a sudden decrease in the purchase price of a new piece of equipment, many firms will be encouraged to go out and buy, thus increasing the amount of investment spending. This is especially true if their present equipment is fairly old or has been in constant use. Thus, the third determinant of investment is the *age and amount of spare capacity of the present capital stock.* A firm with new machinery that often sits idle is unlikely to embark on any new investment any time soon. Additionally, a firm may well be encouraged to invest if the future of the industry or the economy as whole looks bright, and will be disinclined if the future looks gloomy. Since investment spending can be postponed—unlike much of consumer spending—*business confidence* have an important role to play in determining the level of investment. Finally, *government policies and regulations,* which sometimes increase red tape, can add considerably to the cost of doing business and might affect the potential profitability of investing.

An increase in investment as a result of a change in any of these factors will cause an increase in aggregate demand, reflecting a higher level of spending whatever the price level.

Changes in Net Exports

Three factors combine to determine the level of Canadian net exports. First is the *value of the exchange rate*. A lower Canadian dollar means that Canadian goods, in the eyes of foreigners, are cheaper and may result in more Canadian goods being sold abroad. In addition, a lower Canadian dollar will mean that Canadians will buy fewer imports because they are now more expensive. Higher exports and lower imports mean an increase in net exports and an increase in aggregate demand. Similarly, an *increase in the level of incomes abroad* will have the same positive effect on Canadian exports. If Americans are enjoying higher levels of income, they will spend more on consumption, including buying more Canadian goods. Third is the *price level of competitive (foreign) goods*. If the Brazilians raise the price of their short-range jet aircraft, Bombardier Corporation will sell more of its Canadian-made aircraft.

A low Canadian dollar makes for a lot of unhappy Canadian cross-border shoppers and more Americans in our malls.

Sampete/Dreamstime

The fourth determinant of net exports is the *tastes of foreigners*. For instance, if softwood lumber becomes a more popular building material around the world, the demand for Canadian exports would increase.

Changes in the Government Sector

The role of government in the economy is affected by a number of factors, ranging from the social and cultural standards of the people and their expectations to the political philosophy of the governing party and the amount of time left in its mandate. Its specific role in directing the economy will be reflected in changes in government's revenue (through taxation), in its spending, or both. As we shall see when we look at fiscal policy in Chapter 7, these changes are designed to have an impact on the amount of spending in the economy. Aggregate demand will increase as a result of a decrease in taxes (whether it is a decrease in sales taxes, income taxes, or corporate profit taxes) or an increase in spending by government (whether on government-provided services, such as health or education, or on transfer payments, such as pensions or welfare). In addition, as Chapter 9 will explore in detail, a change in the money supply can also affect aggregate demand. This is because an increase in the supply of money, for instance, tends to push interest rates down, and as we mentioned earlier, this will increase investment spending. A decrease in the money supply, on the other hand, will reduce aggregate demand because it causes interest rates to increase and investment to fall.

If any of the determinants of aggregate demand were to change, it would mean that at any given price level buyers would be willing to buy more or less goods and services than before. This is illustrated in Figure 5.10.

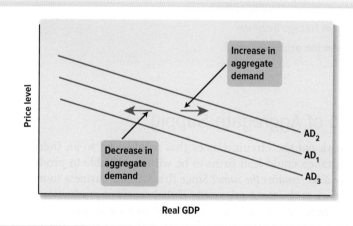

FIGURE 5.10 Shifts in the Aggregate Demand Curve

An increase in aggregate demand shifts the AD curve to the right, from AD_1 to AD_2. This means that at every price level, the quantity of goods and services demanded has increased. In contrast, a decrease in aggregate demand will shift the AD curve to the left, in this case from AD_1 to AD_3.

The causes of a change in aggregate demand are summarized in Table 5.2 and Table 5.3.

TABLE 5.2
Aggregate demand in Canada will increase as a result of:

Consumption	Investment	Net Exports	Government
↑ consumer wealth	↓ interest rates	↓ Canadian $	↑ government spending
↑ age of consumer durables	↓ price of capital goods	↑ foreign incomes	↓ tax rates
↑ consumer confidence	↑ age of capital goods	↑ foreign prices	↑ money supply
	↑ business confidence	↑ taste for Canadian products	
	↓ government regulations		

TABLE 5.3
Aggregate demand in Canada will decrease as a result of:

Consumption	Investment	Net Exports	Government
↓ consumer wealth	↑ interest rates	↑ Canadian $	↓ government spending
↓ age of consumer durables	↑ price of capital goods	↓ foreign incomes	↑ tax rates
↓ consumer confidence	↓ age of capital goods	↓ foreign prices	↓ money supply
	↓ business confidence	↓ taste for Canadian products	
	↑ government regulations		

 TEST YOUR UNDERSTANDING

6. Which of the following factors will lead to an increase or decrease in aggregate demand (and a shift in the AD curve)?

a) a decrease in the stock market index

b) an increase in interest rates

c) a decrease in government spending

d) an increase in foreign incomes

e) a decrease in the exchange rate

Determinants of Aggregate Supply

We now need to work out the circumstances that would lead to an increase in aggregate supply. What factors, for instance, could lead firms to be willing and able to produce more than at present, *even though the price level remains the same*? Since firms are in business to make profits, it is clear that they will produce more at the same price only if their costs of production fall, and this will happen only if productivity increases or factor prices fall. Let us look at productivity increases first.

At the beginning of the chapter, we investigated those factors that would result in economic growth and enhance a country's potential GDP. Each of these factors tends to increase an economy's productivity, which will increase its potential GDP and graphically shift the LAS curve. But, in addition, producers will now be able to produce at lower per-unit costs and thus make greater per-unit profits. Since profits are now higher, firms will be willing and able to produce more without the incentive of higher price, that is, it will also increase the economy's aggregate supply and shift the AS curve. Thus, there will be

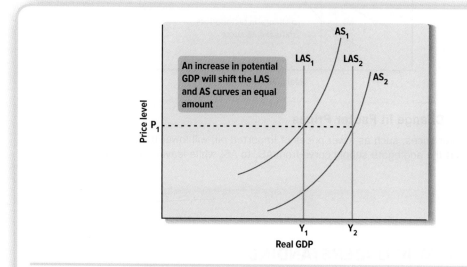

- An improvement in human capital
- An increase in the amount of capital
- Technological improvement
- An increase in natural resources

Increased productivity ⟶ LAS

Increased profitability ⟶ AS

In summary, then, if potential GDP increases then both the LAS and AS curves will shift right. This is illustrated in **Figure 5.11**.

An increase in potential GDP will shift the LAS and AS curves an equal amount

FIGURE 5.11   An Increase in Aggregate Supply

An increase in the size or the quality of the labour force, an increase in the amount of capital stock and natural resources, or an improvement in technology shifts the aggregate supply curve to the right. (It also equally shifts the LAS.)

Figure 5.11 shows how, for instance, a technological improvement will increase an economy's potential GDP, shifting it from LAS_1 to LAS_2. In addition, technological improvements will also cut production costs and increase profits. This will cause an increase in the aggregate supply from AS_1 to AS_2.

In addition to these productivity factors, there is one other thing that will affect the aggregate supply: a drop in wage rates or in the prices of factor services. Lower wage rates will increase a firm's profits and lead to an increase in aggregate supply. So too will a fall in the prices of resources, such as oil, steel, wood—raw materials in general. Note, however, that since productivity is not affected these drops do not impact potential GDP and therefore the LAS does not shift. Thus

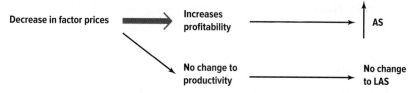

Decrease in factor prices ⟶ Increases profitability ⟶ AS

No change to productivity ⟶ No change to LAS

On the other hand, an increase in resource prices (including wage rates) will cause profits to fall and lead to a reduction in aggregate supply. But again, it does not affect an economy's potential GDP and therefore its LAS.

A change in factor prices is shown in **Figure 5.12**. This figure shows the effect of, say, a significant reduction in the prices of imported inputs, such as steel. This will cause a drop in production costs in

Canada and will encourage firms to produce more at the present price level. This implies a rightward shift in the aggregate supply curve from AS₁ to AS₂. Once again, since a change in factor costs has no effect on the productive capacity of the economy, there is no change in potential GDP and the LAS.

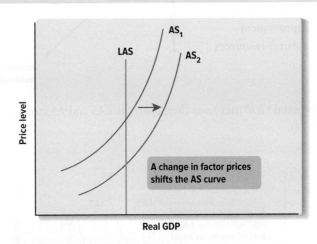

FIGURE 5.12   Change in Factor Prices

A decrease in factor prices, such as lower prices of imported oil, will lower the costs of production and therefore shift the aggregate supply curve from AS₁ to AS₂ while leaving potential GDP and the LAS unaffected.

 ## TEST YOUR UNDERSTANDING

7. What effect will the following changes have on aggregate supply and on potential GDP (LAS)?

a) an increase in the price of imported crude oil

b) an increase in the number of immigrants entering Canada

c) the discovery of extensive oil deposits in northern Canada

d) a substantial increase in wage settlements

e) the introduction of a microchip that reduces computer processing time by 80 percent

8. Suppose the LAS (potential GDP) for the country of Taymar is $1100 and the aggregate supply is as shown in the table.

a) Plot the aggregate supply curve, and draw in the LAS.

b) Assume that the aggregate supply changed by $100 as a result of increased productivity. Plot the new AS curve, and show the new LAS.

Price Index	Aggregate Quantity Supplied ($)
90	950
95	1025
100	1100
105	1150
110	1190
115	1220
120	1240

SECTION SUMMARY

a) Aggregate demand will change, causing the AD curve to shift, if the money supply changes or if there are changes in any of the four components of total spending.

- consumption spending as a result of changes in wealth, the age of consumer durables, or expectations
- investment spending as a result of changes in interest rate, purchase price, the age of capital goods, or expectations
- net exports as a result of changes in the exchange rate, income levels abroad, or the price of competitive (foreign) goods
- government spending on goods and services or taxes

b) A change in any of the four factors that cause economic growth will cause *both* potential GDP and aggregate supply to change, causing the LAS line *and* the AS curve to shift. If factor prices change, only aggregate supply and the AS curve are affected; the LAS remains the same.

5.4 Determinants of Real GDP and the Price Level

LO4 List the causes of recessions and inflationary booms.

It is now time to put this model to work and see how it explains various changes in the economy. It is clear that changes in the aggregate demand and aggregate supply can bring about changes in the price level and in real GDP, so let us take each one in turn.

A Change in Aggregate Demand

Suppose that firms become more optimistic about future economic conditions in Canada and, as a result, start to loosen their purse strings and spend more on investment. The effect of this will be an increase in aggregate demand. But the important question here is: How much will aggregate demand increase? Will an increase in investment spending of, say, $10 billion increase aggregate demand by the same $10 billion? Surprisingly, the answer is no, and the reason is what economists call the **multiplier**, or expenditures multiplier. Let us examine this important concept.

When firms spend this additional $10 billion, it means an increase in income for the contractors, suppliers, and their employees who provide the investment goods. And what will these people do with this increase in income? Well, some of it will be paid in taxes, some of it will be saved, and some of it will be spent on imports. However, a significant portion of it will be spent on domestically produced goods and services. Let us assume that 40 percent is paid in taxes, saved, or spent on imports, and that 60 percent, or $6 billion, is spent on the consumption of Canadian goods and services. When this $6 billion is spent, there is a further increase in income of the same $6 billion, which generates another round of tax payments, savings, import purchases, and the buying of more Canadian goods and services. This process continues and we get a series of income increases.

Using **Figure 5.13**, we can track the total increase in income that results from the initial increase in investment spending of $10 billion.

Initial round	$10.0 billion
Second round	6.0
Third round	3.6
Fourth round	2.2
Fifth round	1.3
All subsequent rounds	1.9
Total increase in income	25.0

In this example, an increase in investment spending of $10 billion will result in an increase in income of $25 billion, which means a multiplier of 2.5. If the portion spent on domestic production were higher, then the value of the multiplier would be larger. On the other hand, if taxes, savings, and

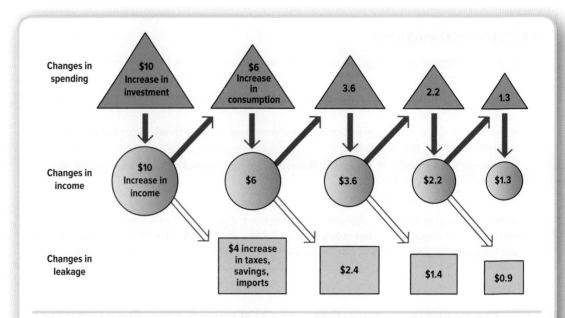

FIGURE 5.13   The Multiplier in Action

One person's spending becomes another person's income. However, in this example, at each round only 60 percent of income gets spent (the rest is leaked to taxes, savings, and spending on imports). The spending in each round, therefore, is only 60 percent of the previous round's spending. But the process continues indefinitely.

imports were higher, then the value of the multiplier would be smaller. Also, we should point out that while our example illustrates the effect of an increase in investment spending, increases in other types of spending, such as exports, government spending, or consumption, would have the same effect.

This multiplier effect is illustrated graphically in **Figure 5.14**. We see here that the aggregate demand curve shifts to the right, from AD_1 to AD_2, as a result of the $10 billion increase in investment spending. If the price level (and for that matter, interest rates) were to remain unchanged, at P_1,

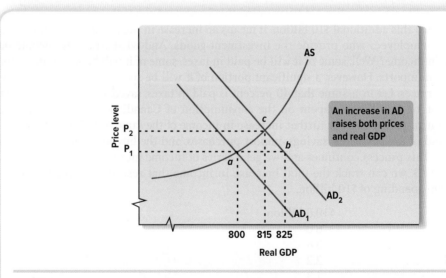

FIGURE 5.14   The Effect of an Increase in Aggregate Demand on Real GDP

The increase in investment of $10 will increase aggregate demand by $25 from AD_1 to AD_2, which would result in an increase in real GDP from $800 to $825 (point *a* to *b*) if the price level did not change from its original level of P_1. However, since the equilibrium price level does rise to P_2, the increase in real GDP is smaller as seen by point *a* to *c*.

then a multiplier of 2.5 would result in the level of real GDP increasing from $800 to $825, as seen by the movement from point *a* to *b*. However, since the AS curve is upward sloping, the increase in equilibrium real GDP will only be the movement of *a* to *c*, which is from $800 to, say, $815. What we are saying here is that the multiplier will have its full effect only if the AS curve is horizontal. Normally, some of the effect of the multiplier would be cancelled out by an increase in the price level associated with any increase in demand. We will have more to say about this important concept of the multiplier in the next chapter.

In summary, an increase in aggregate demand will lead to an increase in both the price level and the level of real GDP. In contrast, a decrease in aggregate demand will decrease both the price level and real GDP.

A Change in Aggregate Supply

As we have seen, a number of factors influence aggregate supply, but we want to focus on factor prices, since they do not affect the potential GDP. Assume, for instance, that the price of imported oil were to fall. **Figure** 5.15 illustrates the effect of such a change. When there is a decrease in factor costs, the aggregate supply curve will shift to the right, and the result is a decrease in the price level and an increase in real GDP. Other factors that might also cause an increase in aggregate supply include a decrease in the prices of raw materials or a decrease in money wage levels. If any of these factors move in the opposite direction, it produces a leftward shift and has the opposite result on the price level and the real GDP. The world witnessed such a shift in the 1970s as a result of the OPEC crisis, which caused a dramatic increase in the world price of oil and consequently on the costs of production of most products. The resulting drop in aggregate supply led to higher prices (inflation) and a reduction in GDP (a stagnant, recessionary world climate). The combination of these twin evils of inflation and unemployment caused the outbreak of a new economic "disease" given the term *stagflation*. We will be looking at this phenomenon in more detail in Chapter 12.

We can generalize this to say that:

Any decrease in the price of any of the factors of production will shift the aggregate supply curve to the right.

Any increase in the price of any of the factors of production will shift the aggregate supply curve to the left.

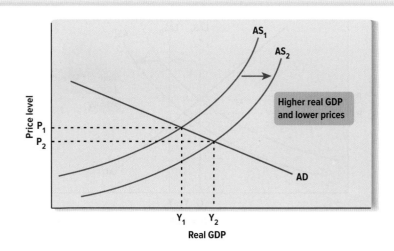

FIGURE 5.15   **An Increase in Aggregate Supply**

A decrease in the price of imported oil will improve profitability, causing the aggregate supply curve to shift to the right from AS_1 to AS_2. This change will cause the price level to drop from P_1 to P_2 and the level of real GDP to increase from Y_1 to Y_2.

What impact would a decrease in the price of imported oil have on the aggregate supply?
Royalty-Free/CORBIS

As we mentioned earlier, a change in productivity will also lead to a change in aggregate supply. In addition, it will cause a change in potential GDP and therefore the LAS. Assume, for instance, that the labour-force participation rate increases, which effectively means that the size of the labour force increases. Let us examine the effect of such a change on an economy. (We assume that the economy is initially at full-employment real GDP.) We know that in this case, both the aggregate supply and potential GDP will increase simultaneously, as illustrated in Figure 5.16.

As a result of the increase in the size of the labour force, the aggregate supply curve shifts to the right as does the LAS. The new equilibrium is where the AD and the AS_2 curves intersect, which is at real GDP level, Y_2. The result of the change is a lower price level, P_2, and a higher level of real GDP, Y_2. Note that a recessionary gap now exists, since the new level of equilibrium real GDP is below the new level of potential real GDP at LAS_2 (Y_3). As can be seen in Figure 5.16, the potential real GDP (LAS_2) is now greater than the new output level. Actual real GDP has grown, but potential real GDP has grown more, resulting in a recessionary gap.

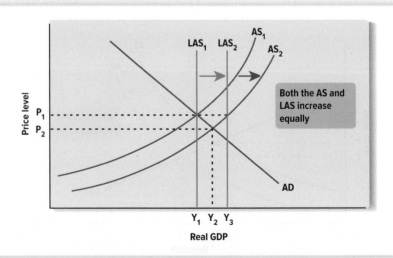

FIGURE 5.16   An Increase in Aggregate Supply and LAS

An increase in the size of the labour force will shift the aggregate supply curve to the right (from AS_1 to AS_2) and also increase potential GDP, shifting the LAS from LAS_1 to LAS_2. This change causes a reduction of the price level from P_1 to P_2 and an increase in real GDP from Y_1 to Y_2. The economy is now experiencing a recessionary gap; that is, the GDP is at Y_2, which is below the new potential GDP, LAS_2.

These changes in aggregate supply are summarized in Table 5.4 and Table 5.5:

TABLE 5.4
The following factors will increase aggregate supply:

Factor	Aggregate Supply	Potential GDP (long-run aggregate supply)
↓ wages	↑	/
↓ factor prices	↑	/
↑ quantity/quality of human capital	↑	↑
↑ quantity/quality of physical capital	↑	↑
↑ technology	↑	↑
↑ quantity/quality of natural resources	↑	↑

TABLE 5.5
The following factors will decrease aggregate supply:

Factor	Aggregate Supply	Potential GDP (long-run aggregate supply)
↑ wages	↓	/
↑ factor prices	↓	/
↓ quantity/quality of human capital	↓	↓
↓ quantity/quality of physical capital	↓	↓
↓ technology	↓	↓
↓ quantity/quality of natural resources	↓	↓

TEST YOUR UNDERSTANDING

9. The following table shows the aggregate demand and aggregate supply schedules for the economy of Zee.

Aggregate Quantity Demanded ($)	Price Index	Aggregate Quantity Supplied ($)
1950	90	1620
1900	95	1700
1850	100	1760
1800	105	1800
1750	110	1830
1700	115	1850

a) What are the equilibrium values of price and real GDP?

b) Assume that aggregate demand decreases by $200 at every price level. What will be the new equilibrium values of price and real GDP?

(Continued)

10. Potential GDP (LAS) for the economy of Ithica is $1500. The aggregate demand and aggregate supply schedules are shown in the following table.

Price Index	Aggregate Quantity Demanded ($)	Aggregate Quantity Supplied ($)
90	1700	$950
95	1650	1150
100	1600	1300
105	1550	1420
110	1500	1500
115	1450	1540

a) What are the equilibrium values of price and real GDP? What type of equilibrium is this?

b) Assume that an increase in productivity increases aggregate supply by $300. What will be the new equilibrium values of price and real GDP? Is there now a recessionary gap or an inflationary gap? How much is the gap?

SECTION SUMMARY

AD will increase more than the initial change in spending because of the multiplier.

- An increase in AD will increase both real GDP and the price level.

- An increase in AS only will increase real GDP but decrease the price level.

- An increase in potential GDP will also increase AS and will increase real GDP and decrease the price level but will leave the economy below full-employment GDP.

5.5 Keynesians Versus the Neoclassical School

LO5 Explain the main points of disagreement between neoclassical and Keynesian economics.

The way in which changes in aggregate demand and supply affect the economy, and indeed, what causes the changes, has been open to some dispute in economics over the last eighty years. There are two opposing camps: the long-established neoclassical school of thought and the Keynesian school, which represented a direct challenge to this orthodoxy. Although the heat has died down a little since the sometimes-acrimonious debates that raged between the two in the decades following the publication of Keynes's *General Theory of Employment, Interest and Money* in 1936, there are still occasional flareups.

The neoclassicists generally believed that markets are competitive and efficient and will adjust rapidly whenever there is a general shortage or surplus. By adjustment, they meant that prices and wages would move up or down quickly and easily to ensure full employment. In addition, the economy would always remain at its potential full-employment level. This is illustrated in **Figure 5.17**.

The neoclassical school believed that the aggregate supply curve is a vertical straight line at the full-employment level of real GDP, Y_{FE}; that is, it is the same as the LAS. In other words, the economy's natural position is to be at full-employment GDP, that is, at its potential. The position of the curve is determined by the real variables that we discussed in reference to economic growth. The neoclassicists saw the aggregate demand curve as the normal downward-sloping demand curve. This means that a change in aggregate demand will leave real GDP unaffected but will most definitely cause a change in the price level. Furthermore, wages would change by the same percentage as the price level, leaving the real wage unaffected. At full employment, then, the real wage is constant. Since a change in the money supply is the only thing that can affect aggregate demand, according to neoclassical economists, there could be only one type of inflation: demand-pull inflation. Moreover, they felt that the economy can only grow if there is a growth in the factors of production or in labour productivity. In their version of the model, a major depression or recession is impossible.

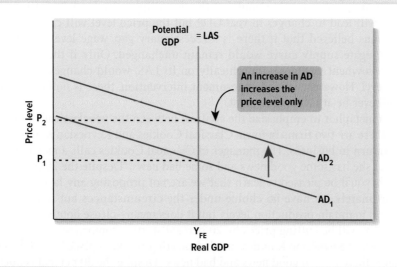

FIGURE 5.17   Neoclassical Aggregate Demand–Supply

The neoclassical AS is synonymous with potential GDP. This means that the price level has no effect on the quantity supplied. The aggregate supply curve will always be at the full-employment level of real GDP, labelled Y_{FE}. Changes in aggregate demand, therefore, have no effect upon real GDP and affect only the price level. An increase in aggregate demand from AD_1 to AD_2, for instance, will increase the price level from P_1 to P_2 but will leave real GDP unaffected at Y_{FE}.

In contrast, Keynesian economists believed that the market is not very competitive because of the existence of big corporations and unions. They felt that this made prices and wages inflexible or *sticky*. In general, they argued, employers and employees tend to prefer the certainty of stable wages rather than allow them to fluctuate, perhaps wildly, with changes in demand. As a result, an increase in aggregate demand for example, will have little impact on the price level. This is shown in **Figure** 5.18.

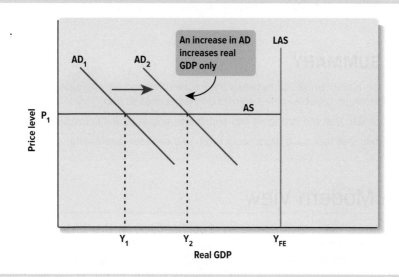

FIGURE 5.18   The Keynesian View of Aggregate Demand–Supply

The aggregate supply curve, according to Keynesians, is horizontal at the prevailing price level. Changes in aggregate demand therefore have no effect on the price level but do cause changes in real GDP. An increase in aggregate demand from AD_1 to AD_2 will cause an increase in real GDP from Y_1 to Y_2 but leave the price level unchanged at P_1.

The aggregate supply curve is horizontal at the prevailing price level, P_1. Shifts in the aggregate demand can and will lead to changes in real GDP, but the price level will change little, if at all. In addition, Keynesians believed that if there is a recessionary gap, wage levels would not drop and therefore the aggregate supply curve would remain unchanged. Only if the economy were at its potential full-employment GDP level (graphically on its LAS) would changes in aggregate demand affect the price level. However, without government intervention, there is nothing to guarantee that the economy will ever be at full employment.

We can use a metaphor to emphasize the contrast between the neoclassical and Keynesian viewpoints. Suppose there are two firms in town, Classical Cookies and Keynesian Kandies, both of which are facing a downturn in business. The manager of Classical Cookies calls a meeting of her staff and informs them that she has some good news and some bad news: "Despite the 20 percent reduction in orders this month, you'll be pleased to learn that we are not proposing any layoffs. You will all keep your jobs. Unfortunately, we have no choice under the circumstances but to reduce your pay by 20 percent. We will maintain production levels, but it does mean—please note, sales department—that in order to do so, we will be cutting prices by 20 percent starting tomorrow."

Meanwhile, over at Keynesian Kandies, another meeting is taking place between its manager and staff, and similarly, there is both good news and bad news: "Despite the 20 percent reduction in orders this month, you'll be pleased to learn that we are not proposing any pay cuts for our staff. Unfortunately, we have no choice under the circumstances but to lay off 20 percent of you, starting tomorrow. We will maintain present prices, but it does mean—please note, production department—that we will be cutting production levels by 20 percent."

There is another reason why prices tend to be sticky, and this is because of the menu costs of inflation we mentioned in Chapter 4. For many firms, it is simply too expensive to keep changing brochures, catalogues, and websites every time their prices change.

 TEST YOUR UNDERSTANDING

11. Explain what will happen to nominal GDP and real GDP if there is an increase in aggregate demand according to

a) Keynesians (if the economy is below full employment)

b) neoclassicists

SECTION SUMMARY

At the heart of the historical debate between the Keynesians and neoclassicists is the question of whether the economy is capable of self-adjusting to an economic gap.

- Neoclassicists say that the economy can adjust and any gaps will immediately disappear.
- Keynesians say that that such gaps occur often and can last indefinitely.

5.6   The Modern View

> **LO6**   Explain the modern view of aggregate demand and aggregate supply.

Looking back on this historical debate, what can we say now? Who won the battle? Perhaps understandably, neither side. The modern view of the aggregate supply curve, as we mentioned earlier, is that it is neither horizontal nor vertical but an amalgam of the neoclassical and Keynesian ideas. **Figure 5.19** shows the modern view of the aggregate supply curve.

At low levels of real GDP on the AS curve (the left portion), the curve is flat, illustrating the Keynesian belief that prices are inflexible. The right portion of the AS curve, where the GDP is higher,

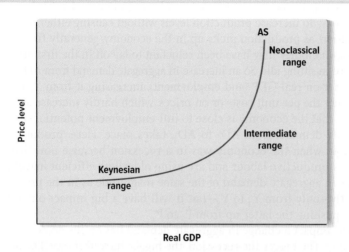

FIGURE 5.19 The Modern View of the Aggregate Supply Curve

The modern view of the AS curve is that at low GDP levels the curve is quite flat (the Keynesian range) but gets progressively steeper as real GDP approaches full-employment (potential) GDP, where the curve becomes almost vertical (the neoclassical range). In between the two extremes is the intermediate range.

is very steep, reflecting the neoclassical view that real GDP is not affected by price changes. In between the two extremes is the intermediate range.

The shape of the AS curve has big implications for the economy should aggregate demand change. The effect of such a change will vary considerably, depending on what the present level of GDP is. **Figure** 5.20, for example, illustrates what will happen if aggregate demand increases.

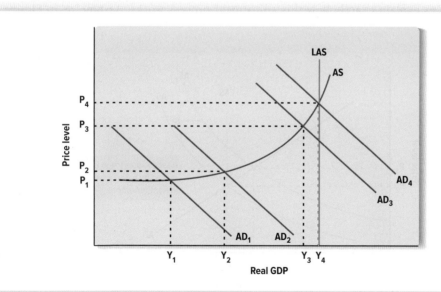

FIGURE 5.20 The Effect of an Increase in Aggregate Demand

Because the AS curve is flat at low levels of income and gets steeper as the economy approaches its potential level, an increase in AD will have different effects, depending on when it occurs. At low incomes, such as Y_1, most of the impact is on real GDP, increasing it to Y_2, while the price level only increase to P_2. At an income close to full employment, such as Y_3, the same increase in AD impacts mostly on the price level, increasing it to P_4, while GDP increases only a little to Y_4.

We have seen that, as Keynes suggested, in a modern economy prices and wages tend to be inflexible. Given this, it is easy to increase production levels without causing either wages or prices to change appreciably. In addition, as production picks up in the economy, generally firms will be able to rehire productive workers, whom they may have been reluctant to lay off in the first place, and to make use of machines that have been sitting idle. So an increase in aggregate demand from AD_1 to AD_2 in **Figure** 5.20 will have a big impact on real GDP (and employment), increasing it from Y_1 to Y_2 while not having much impact on either the per-unit costs or on prices, which hardly increase at all from P_1 to P_2.

But now assume that the economy is close to full-employment potential GDP at Y_3, and a similar increase in aggregate demand, from AD_3 to AD_4, takes place. Here, productivity per worker will probably be less than when the economy was in a recession because now firms have to hire less-experienced and less-productive labour and are using older, less-efficient machines. In these circumstances, an increase in aggregate demand of the same magnitude as in the previous example will not increase GDP greatly—only from Y_3 to Y_4—but it will have a big impact on both the per-unit costs and the price level, pushing the latter up from P_3 to P_4.

To conclude, the impact a change in aggregate demand has on the economy depends on the condition of the economy. The bigger the recession, the bigger the effect on GDP; in contrast, at or close to potential full-employment GDP, the effect of increased demand will be more inflationary.

Is the Economy Self-Adjusting?

Since modern macroeconomic theory is a synthesis of two contrasting—Keynesian and neoclassical—schools of thought, we might ask the modern view on the possibility of a sustained recession. Remember that neoclassical economists felt that any recession would be short-lived, since the market economy is very efficient and adjusts quickly to bring an economy back to full employment. (That's why they make no distinction between the short run and the long run.) Keynes argued that this was highly unlikely because the modern world is not as perfectly competitive as the neoclassical economists suggest. As a result, the economy could be doomed to remain in a recession unless it was bailed out by government.

Again, the modern view is something of a compromise between the two positions. The view of most economists these days is that neither extreme view is valid. Although prices and wages are often inflexible in the short run, eventually they do adjust to the changing conditions of the economy. Let us explain exactly how this adjustment process works. Assume, as in **Figure** 5.21,

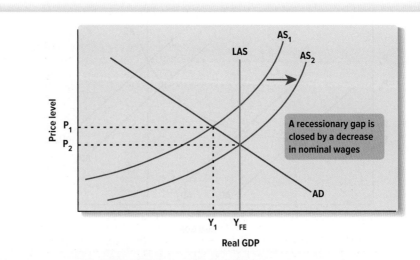

FIGURE 5.21   **Adjustment from a Recessionary Gap**

Initially, the economy is at price level P_1 and real GDP level Y_1, below the full-employment level, Y_{FE}. This situation will put downward pressure on wages. As nominal wages fall, the aggregate supply curve shifts to the right until it is at AS_2. The net result will be a lower price level, P_2, and a full-employment real GDP, Y_{FE}.

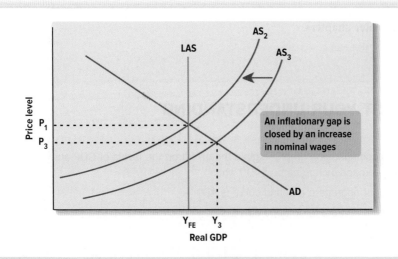

FIGURE 5.22   Adjustment from an Inflationary Gap

The economy is initially at equilibrium, with the AD curve intersecting AS₃ at the real GDP level, Y_3. With real GDP above its potential level, the unemployment rate is below the natural rate. The high demand for labour will push up nominal wage rates, causing aggregate supply to decrease and pushing the AS curve back to AS_2. The new equilibrium level of real GDP is now lower and the price level is higher than initially—price increases from P_3 to P_1.

that the economy finds itself in a recessionary-gap situation, with actual real GDP below potential real GDP, the LAS.

The economy is currently in equilibrium at real GDP level, Y_1, where the aggregate quantity demanded is equal to the aggregate quantity supplied. However, the LAS is at Y_{FE}. In this recessionary-gap situation, unemployment is above its natural rate. In other words, there is a certain amount of cyclical unemployment. That means firms find it easy to hire labour, and workers find it difficult to get jobs. Under these conditions, eventually nominal wage levels will be forced down. Remember that aggregate supply is based on a particular unchanging level of nominal wages; that is, the wage rate is constant along the AS curve. If the nominal wage level drops, this means that the aggregate supply curve will shift rightward. As this happens, firms hire more workers, production (real GDP) increases from Y_1 to Y_{FE}, and the price level falls from P_1 to P_2. As a result of this process, the economy finds equilibrium at Y_{FE}, where the new aggregate supply curve, AS_2, intersects the aggregate demand curve. This new equilibrium is at full employment.

Let us turn to the opposite situation and work out how the economy adjusts to an inflationary-gap situation. Assume that the economy finds itself in equilibrium at the real GDP level, Y_3 in **Figure 5.22.**

The economy is above full employment, which means that faced with a high demand, firms are producing more than they would consider their normal capacity output. Firms find it difficult to hire labour and workers find it easy to get jobs. In this situation, nominal wage rates will be pushed up. This will cause the aggregate supply curve to shift left, pushing the price level up and real GDP down until the economy is back at potential full-employment equilibrium, with the aggregate demand curve, AD, intersecting the new aggregate supply curve AS_2 and the LAS at Y_{FE}.

You might object that in the modern world, while price and wage levels do seem to increase year by year, they very seldom decrease. Yet this model suggests that this is exactly what happens when there is a surplus of production or labour. The problem here is not so much a defect of the model but the limitation of picturing changes in terms of a two-dimensional graph. In reality, all economies are in a perpetual state of flux, with both the aggregate demand and supply constantly changing. If we could, it would be better to depict rates of change rather than actual changes, but then the analysis becomes unnecessarily complicated. In actuality, rather than the nominal wage level dropping, it rises, but at a slower pace than the price level.

This completes our discussion of the aggregate demand–supply model. We will use it to look at various issues in later chapters.

TEST YOUR UNDERSTANDING

12. Using the accompanying graph, explain the effect on the levels of GDP and the price level if aggregate demand increases by $400 when

a) the present aggregate demand curve is AD_1

b) the present aggregate demand curve is AD_2

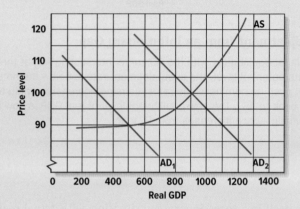

ADDED DIMENSION

Aggregate Demand in Canada Since 2010

The financial crisis that started on Wall Street in 2008 and then swept across much of the world led a serious two-year recession in Canada. However, strong *investment* spending, along with a modest 1.2 percent increase in federal *government* spending, fuelled a 3 percent surge in economic growth in 2011 and this resulted in strong job growth in 2012.

In 2013, Canadian *exports* were up and higher household *consumption* spending lead to another surge in economic growth. However, the level of investment spending did not continue its strong performance of the previous year.

In 2014 growth in Canada's GDP slowed (but remained positive) and, as a result, fell below that of the United States for first time in four years. The good news in this year was a drop in the unemployment rate due to a boom in *investment* spending in Alberta's oil sands. In the three years of 2012–14 *government* spending was flat.

Investment spending dropped in 2015 but noncommodity *exports* surged and *government* spending increased by 2 percent. However, a fall in average weekly earnings tarnished Canada's overall economic performance.

Throughout this 2010–15 period, inflation remained below 2 percent and growth in GDP per person averaged 1.5 percent per year—quite respectable numbers.

However, the same period also presented a rather chilling statistic: income levels of the top 10 percent of earners grew significantly while growth in the lower-income groups was nearly nonexistent.

IT'S NEWS TO ME ...

The Conference Board of Canada has just downgraded its forecast for growth in in the Canadian economy for 2016 to 1.4%. The Board's previous estimate, made three months earlier, was 1.6%.

The reasons cited for the downgrade were: continued weakness in business investment highlighted by a $19B drop in the oil and gas sector; a slowdown in the growth of Canadian non-commodity exports because of weakening US economic growth; the Fort McMurray wildfires which are now estimated to subtract 0.1% from the year's total growth.

Furthermore, global economic uncertainty, caused by the U.K.'s decision to leave the European Union and growing concern about the terrorist threat, will adversely affect consumer expectations and Canadian exports to Europe.

Source: *Star Power Reporting.* Summer 2016.

I. Which of the following determinants of demand is not referred to in the article above?

a) Investment spending
b) Export spending
c) Government spending
d) Consumer spending abroad

II. Which of the following factors would cause a slowdown in economic growth?

a) An increase in exports
b) A decrease in exports
c) A decrease in imports
d) An increase in net exports

SECTION SUMMARY

Modern economists say that

- Recessionary gaps are eliminated by factor prices eventually falling and the AS curve shifting to the right.
- Inflationary gaps are eliminated by factor prices eventually rising and the AS curve shifting to the left.

Study Guide

Review

WHAT'S THE BIG IDEA?

Many of the ideas you learned in Chapter 2 are equally applicable in this chapter. For instance, you will perhaps remember that demand is not a single quantity but a range of quantities that buyers are willing and able to buy at different prices: similarly, supply is not a single quantity but a range of quantities that sellers are willing and able to sell at different prices. The big difference in Chapter 5 is that here we are dealing with *aggregate* quantities: the total amounts of goods and services that consumers, firms, governments, and foreign buyers want to purchase and producers want to sell at different prices. Since we cannot literally add together these thousands of products, what we do is add together the amounts spent on these products, that is, aggregate expenditures, which is the same as real GDP and is the amount shown on the horizontal axes of our diagrams. Similarly, the price on the vertical axis is not the price of a particular product but the aggregate (or more particularly) the average price of all products, illustrated by a price index. All the other aspects: what is meant by equilibrium, what can cause surpluses and shortages, what is the effect of an increase or decrease in demand or supply, and so on, are very much the same as you learned in Chapter 2. There are, however, a few big differences. First, there are many more—and different—factors that affect aggregate demand than affect the demand for a single product: anything that affects consumption, investment, net exports, or government will impact aggregate demand (15 factors!). The other big difference is that there is an additional curve to consider: potential GDP (or the long-run aggregate supply) curve. Think of this curve as nothing more than a marker, a line showing the amount of real GDP that the economy is capable of producing. It doesn't show the amount that is being produced, nor the amount that policy makers would like the economy to produce—simply what the economy is able to produce if the economy were fully employed. This means that the equilibrium quantity, where aggregate demand and supply are the same, may not coincide with potential GDP. If it is less, the economy is in a recession (a recessionary gap); if it is more, the economy is booming (an inflationary gap). If the equilibrium occurs at the potential GDP, the economy is in full-employment equilibrium.

The last thing to remember is that any factor that affects potential GDP (such as improved human or physical capital, a better technology, or an increase in natural resources) will also affect aggregate supply. The two curves will move together in the same direction. However, a change in wage rates or in the prices of resources (such as steel, lumber, oil, etc.) will shift the aggregate supply curve only; the potential GDP is not affected.

NEW GLOSSARY TERMS AND KEY EQUATIONS

aggregate demand
aggregate supply
business cycles
foreign-trade effect
inflationary gap

interest-rate effect
long-run aggregate supply
macroeconomic equilibrium
multiplier
nominal wage

potential GDP
real-balances effect
real wage
recession
recessionary gap

Equations:

[5.1] $\text{Real wage} = \dfrac{\text{nominal wage}}{\text{price level}}$

Comprehensive Problem

(LO 1, 2, 3, 4, 5, 6)   Table 5.6 shows AD and AS for the economy of Everton. Potential GDP (LAS) is currently 200.

TABLE 5.6

Price Index	Aggregate Quantity Supplied 1 (AS₁) ($)	Aggregate Quantity Demanded 1 (AD₁) ($)	Aggregate Quantity Demanded 1 (AD₂) ($)	Aggregate Quantity Supplied 2 (AS₂) ($)
65*	0	260	——	100
70*	100	240	——	180
75	160	220	——	220
80	200	200	——	245
85	230	180	——	260
90	250	160	——	270
95	260	140	——	274
100	270	120	——	275

*The price level is inflexible downward at $70 for AS₁ and at $65 for AS₂.

Questions

a) On **Figure 5.23** draw in and label curves AS₁, AD₁, and LAS.

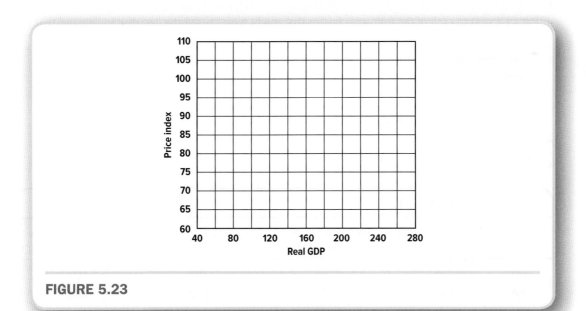

FIGURE 5.23

b) What are the equilibrium values for the price level and real GDP?

Answers

a) The plotting is fairly straightforward, though you will appreciate that the AS is not a straight line and therefore needs a little care in drawing it. The LAS (potential GDP) curve is a vertical straight line at

$200. Since Everton is in equilibrium and at full employment, the LAS is located at the intersection of the AD₁ and AS₁ curves. See the following figure:

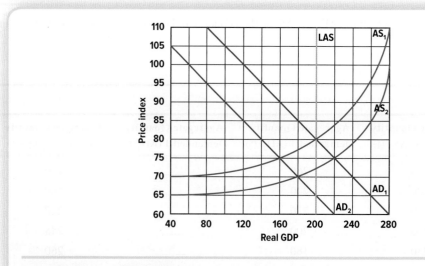

FIGURE 5.23   Completed

b) Price: 80; real GDP: $200. The equilibrium values can be read off the graph or by glancing at Table 5.3 and locating the price at which the quantity demanded is equal to the quantity supplied.

Questions

c) Suppose that aggregate demand in Everton decreased by 60. Complete Table 5.6 showing the new demand, demand 2.
d) Draw a new AD₂ curve on Figure 5.23 to show this change.
e) What are the new equilibrium values for the price level and real GDP?
f) Is there now a recessionary gap or an inflationary gap? What is the amount of this gap?
g) Put an X next to each of the following factors that might have caused the decrease in demand that you illustrated in (c):

- increased exports
- higher taxes
- higher interest rates
- lower government spending

Answers

c) See the following table:

TABLE 5.6 (COMPLETED)

Price Index	Aggregate Quantity Supplied 1 (AS₁) ($)	Aggregate Quantity Demanded 1 (AD₁) ($)	Aggregate Quantity Demanded 2 (AD₂) ($)	Aggregate Quantity Supplied 2 (AS₂) ($)
65*	0	260	200	100
70*	100	240	180	180
75	160	220	160	220
80	200	200	140	245
85	230	180	120	260
90	250	160	100	270
95	260	140	80	274
100	270	120	60	275

d) See **Figure** 5.23 (Completed): The new AD$_2$ curve is 3 squares to the left of AD$_1$.
e) Price: 75; real GDP: $160.
f) Recessionary gap of $40. (The difference between the new equilibrium GDP and the LAS (potential GDP).
g) Higher interest rates X; lower government spending X

Questions

h) Assuming the original AD$_1$, suppose that aggregate supply changed as a result of a dramatic decrease in the price of oil as shown by AS$_2$ in **Table** 5.6. Draw in the new AS$_2$ in **Figure** 5.23.
i) What are the equilibrium values for the price level and real GDP now?
j) Is there now a recessionary or inflationary gap? What is the amount of this gap?

Answers

h) See **Figure** 5.23 (Completed).
i) Price: 75; real GDP: $220.
j) Inflationary gap of $20. (The difference between the new equilibrium GDP and the LAS (potential GDP).

Study Problems

Find answers on the McGraw-Hill online resource.

Basic (Problems 1–5)

1. **(LO 1)** Suppose the real GDP of an economy is $480 billion dollars and its unemployment rate is 7 percent. If the natural rate of unemployment is estimated at 5 percent, what is the value of the country's potential GDP (LAS) in billions of dollars? $_____

2. **(LO 4)** Assume that the potential GDP (LAS) of the economy of Arion is $1000 and that the aggregate demand and the aggregate supply are as shown in **Table** 5.7.

TABLE 5.7

Aggregate Quantity Demanded ($)	Aggregate Quantity Demanded	Price Index	Aggregate Quantity Supplied ($)
1080	___	96	880
1060	___	97	940
1040	___	98	965
1020	___	99	985
1000	___	100	1000
980	___	101	1015
960	___	102	1025
940	___	103	1033
920	___	104	1040
900	___	105	1045

a) What is the value of equilibrium real GDP and the price level? Is there a recessionary gap or an inflationary gap?
Real GDP: _____ Price level: _____
(Recessionary/inflationary) _____
gap of $_____
b) If firms become more optimistic and aggregate demand increases by $65, complete the aggregate demand 2 column in **Table** 5.7.
c) What will be the new values of equilibrium real GDP and the price level?
Real GDP: _____ Price level: _____

d) Is there a recessionary gap or an inflationary gap? What is the size of the gap?
   (Recessionary/inflationary) _____
   gap of $_____

3. **(LO 2)** Assume that the nominal wage rate increases from $18 to $20.80 per hour, and at the same time the price index increases from 120 to 130. By how much has the real wage rate changed? _____

4. **(LO 2)** Assuming that the economy shown in **Figure** 5.24 is in equilibrium, calculate the recessionary or inflationary gap under the following conditions:
   a) Potential GDP (LAS) is $500.
   b) Potential GDP (LAS) is $700.
      (Recessionary/inflationary) _____
      gap of $_____
   c) Potential GDP (LAS) is $900.
      (Recessionary/inflationary) _____
      gap of $_____

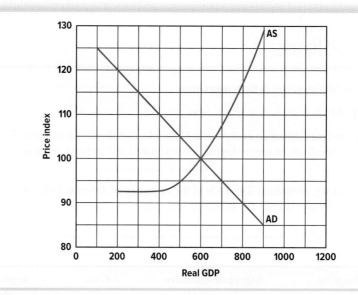

FIGURE 5.24

5. **(LO 6)** Use the graph in **Figure** 5.25 to calculate the growth rate of real GDP for a price increase of 20 percentage points under the following conditions.

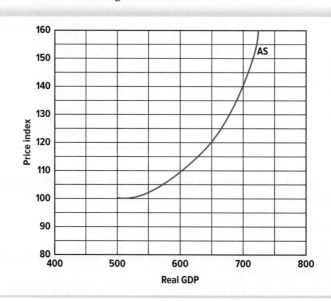

FIGURE 5.25

a) The present price index is 100.
   Growth rate: _____%
b) The present price level is 120.
   Growth rate: _____%

Intermediate (Problems 6–7)

6. **(LO 1)** Figure 5.26 depicts the economy of Altrua, which is presently in equilibrium.

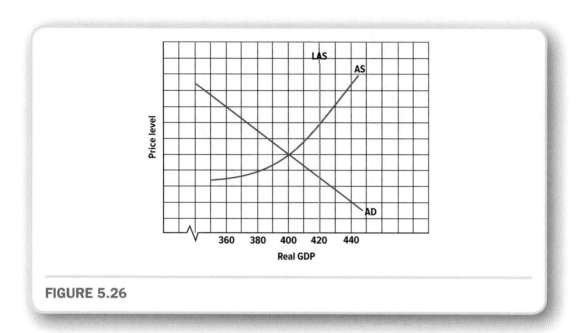

FIGURE 5.26

a) What is the size of its recessionary gap? $_____
b) What is the size of this gap as a percentage of its actual GDP? _____%
c) If the natural rate of unemployment is 6 percent, use Okun's law to calculate the amount of actual unemployment in Altrua. _____%

7. **(LO 4)** Table 5.8 shows the aggregate demand for the economy of Itera. Its potential GDP (LAS) is $800.

TABLE 5.8	
Price Index	**Aggregate Quantity Demanded ($)**
70	800
90	750
110	700
130	650

a) Draw the aggregate demand curve and the Potential GDP (LAS) curve on Figure 5.27.
b) What is the equilibrium level of GDP and the price index?
   GDP: $_____ Price index: _____
c) Is there a recessionary or inflationary gap in Itera? Of how much?
   (Recessionary/inflationary) _____
   gap of $_____
d) If aggregate demand in Itera were to increase by $150, draw in the new (AD₂) curve in Figure 5.27.

e) What is the new equilibrium level of GDP and the price index?
   GDP: $_____
   Price index: _____
f) Is there now a recessionary or inflationary gap in Itera? How much?
   (Recessionary/inflationary) _____
   gap of $_____

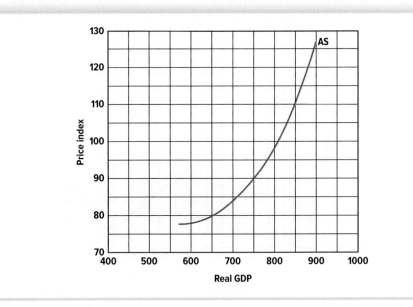

FIGURE 5.27

Advanced (Problems 8–10)

8. **(LO 1, 4)** Villareal's nominal GDP increased from $168 billion to $220 billion last year. During the year, its economy experienced inflation, with its price index increasing from 105 to 110, while the number of persons employed increased from 20 million to 23.5 million. By what percentage did its labour productivity increase during the year? _____ %

9. **(LO 5)** Table 5.9 shows the aggregate demand for the economy of Zandu. Table 5.10 shows two aggregate supplies for the same economy.

TABLE 5.9

Price Index	Aggregate Quantity Demanded ($)
75	850
80	800
85	750
90	700
95	650
100	600
105	550
110	500

TABLE 5.10

Price Index	Aggregate Quantity Supplied (1) ($)	Price Index	Aggregate Quantity Supplied (2) ($)
75	800	100	600
80	800	100	650
85	800	100	700
90	800	100	750
95	800	100	800
100	800	100	850
105	800	100	900
110	800	100	950

a) Which of the two aggregate supply schedules, (1) or (2), is the neoclassical aggregate supply? Which is the Keynesian aggregate supply?

Neoclassical supply: _____ Keynesian supply: _____

b) According to the neoclassical school, what would be the equilibrium levels of price and real GDP?

Price: _____ Real GDP: _____

c) According to the Keynesian school, what would be the equilibrium levels of price and real GDP?

Price: _____ Real GDP: _____

d) If aggregate demand increased by $150, what would be the equilibrium values of price and real GDP according to the neoclassical school?

Price: _____ Real GDP: _____

e) If aggregate demand increased by $150, what would be the equilibrium values of price and real GDP according to the Keynesian school?

Price: _____ Real GDP: _____

10. **(LO 6)** Suppose that the economy of Witland in **Figure** 5.28 is at full-employment equilibrium and the present nominal wage is $24 per hour.

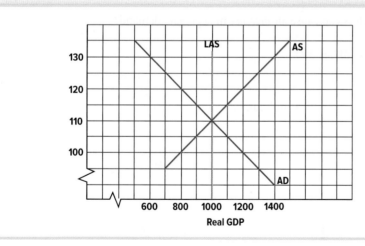

FIGURE 5.28

a) What is the real wage rate (in base year prices)? $_____

b) Suppose that the aggregate demand increases by $400. Draw in the new AD curve in **Figure** 5.28.

c) At the new equilibrium real GDP level, what will be the value of the real wage rate? _____

d) As a result of the change in prices in (b), suppose the nominal wage increases, causing aggregate supply to change by $400. Draw in the new AS curve in **Figure** 5.28.

e) At the new equilibrium, what will be the new real wage rate? _____

f) At the new equilibrium in (e), what is the value of the nominal wage rate? _____

Problems for Further Study

Basic (Problems 1–6)

1. **(LO 1)** What are the four sources of economic growth?

2. **(LO 3, 4)** Starting from full-employment equilibrium, indicate whether each of the following factors will affect aggregate demand (AD) or aggregate supply (AS) and whether the effect would be an increase or a decrease. Then, indicate what will happen to the price level and the level of real GDP and what type of equilibrium will result.
   a) A decrease in interest rates: _____
      Price level: _____ Real GDP: _____ Type of equilibrium: _____
   b) An improvement in technology: _____
      Price level: _____ Real GDP: _____ Type of equilibrium: _____
   c) An increase in the exchange rate: _____
      Price level: _____ Real GDP: _____ Type of equilibrium: _____
   d) A decrease in government spending: _____
      Price level: _____ Real GDP: _____ Type of equilibrium: _____
   e) An increase in the money supply: _____
      Price level: _____ Real GDP: _____ Type of equilibrium: _____
   f) An increase in the nominal wage rate: _____
      Price level: _____ Real GDP: _____ Type of equilibrium: _____

3. **(LO 4)** Starting from equilibrium, explain in terms of changes in either AD or in AS (not both) how each of the following results could have occurred.
   a) Real GDP increases, and the price level increases.
   b) Real GDP decreases, and the price level increases.
   c) Real GDP increases, and the price level decreases.
   d) Real GDP decreases, and the price level decreases.

4. **(LO 6)** Explain, in terms of a graph, how an increase in aggregate demand could have no effect on the price level.

5. **(LO 1)** What does the term *potential GDP* mean?

6. **(LO 3)** What factors can cause an *increase* in aggregate demand?

Intermediate (Problems 7–12)

7. **(LO 4)** Use the graph in Figure 5.29 to illustrate the effect of the Great Depression on the Canadian economy, when prices, production, and employment all decreased dramatically in the 1930s. (Assume the economy was originally at full-employment equilibrium.)

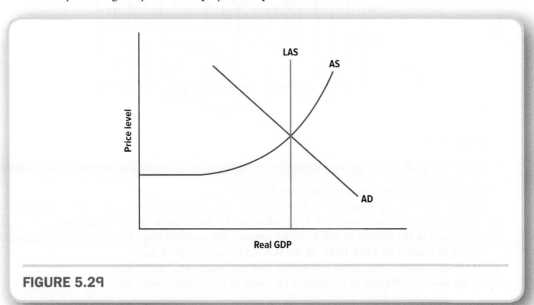

FIGURE 5.29

8. **(LO 4)** In **Figure** 5.30, show a new equilibrium on the graph illustrating demand-pull inflation, and then name three things that could have caused the change.

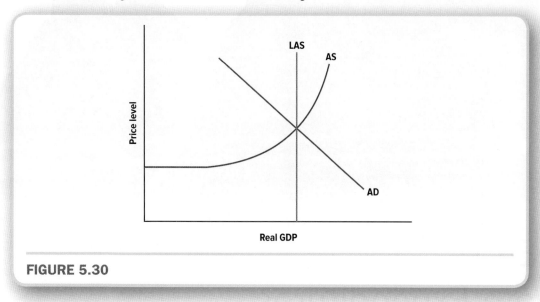

FIGURE 5.30

a) _____

b) _____

c) _____

9. **(LO 1)** Assume that the size of the labour force in the economy of Mersin remained unchanged in the year 2011 while labour productivity increased. If real GDP also remained unchanged, what change in the labour market must have occurred?

_____

_____

10. **(LO 2)** You are given the following options.
    1. ↑ aggregate demand
    2. ↓ aggregate demand
    3. ↑ aggregate supply
    4. ↓ aggregate supply
    5. ↑ aggregate supply and potential GDP
    6. ↓ aggregate supply and potential GDP
    Which of options 1–6 will occur as the result of the following changes?
    a) an increase in investment spending _____
    b) a decrease in imports _____
    c) an increase in factor prices _____
    d) a decrease in productivity _____
    e) a decrease in factor prices _____
    f) an increase in human capital _____

11. **(LO 2)** What are the three reasons for the downward slope of the aggregate demand curve?

12. **(LO 4)** Starting from full-employment equilibrium, explain what effect an increase in aggregate demand will have on price, real GDP, and equilibrium.

Advanced (Problems 13–15)

13. **(LO 4)** Why does an increase in potential GDP (LAS) leave the economy in a recessionary gap? _____

_____

_____

_____

14. **(LO 4)** Suppose that the economy of Bunderland is initially at full-employment equilibrium. Explain, in terms of shifts in AD or AS, how the following results could occur.
    a) Real GDP increases; the price level increases; the economy is experiencing an inflationary gap.
    b) Real GDP increases; the price level decreases; the economy is experiencing an inflationary gap.
    c) Real GDP decreases; the price level increases; the economy is experiencing an inflationary gap.

15. **(LO 6)** How does the economy adjust if there is a recessionary gap? If there is an inflationary gap?

CHAPTER 6
Aggregate Expenditures

LEARNING OBJECTIVES

At the end of this chapter, you should be able to:

LO1 Describe the marginal propensity to consume and how consumption, saving, and investment relate to national income.

LO2 Explain the concept of expenditures equilibrium.

LO3 Explain how the multiplier produces big changes in national income as a result of small changes in spending.

LO4 Describe how government's budget balance and the balance of trade both relate to national income.

LO5 Derive aggregate demand from aggregate expenditures.

WHAT'S AHEAD ...

Like Chapter 5, this chapter focuses on the product market. Here, we look in detail behind aggregate demand to see how the level of GDP or national income is determined. This model emphasizes how the various parts of the economy—from consumption spending and investment to government spending and exports—are interrelated. This expenditures model allows us to see clearly how a change in one of these variables affects the others.

A QUESTION OF RELEVANCE ...

You are probably aware that Canada is one of the best countries in the world in which to live. One reason is our relatively high level of national income, which, of course, means a high level of per capita income. But have you wondered what determines this level? Why does it grow quickly only sometimes? What role does consumer spending play in all this? And how is it influenced by business investment and exports? This chapter will help you answer these questions.

In Chapter 5, we studied the aggregate demand/aggregate supply (AD/AS) model and saw how changes in both aggregate demand and aggregate supply can produce changes in production (and therefore income and employment) and in the price level (and therefore inflation). While changes in aggregate supply can cause radical and long-term changes to an economy, their short-term effects can go unnoticed. As well, such changes are difficult for governments and policy makers to instigate. However, changes in spending (demand) are likely to have a more obvious short-term effect and are more easily effected by governments.

For this reason, changes in spending lay at the heart of Keynes's *General Theory of Employment, Interest and Money*, which was first published in 1936. Keynes realized that inadequate spending was the root cause of the Great Depression and that an increase in spending was necessary to cure it. In *General Theory*, Keynes downplayed the role of prices and inflation (though he certainly did not ignore it), since for him and many others, the major problems facing the economy at that time were low (and negative) growth and massive unemployment. As a result, the price level plays a very minor role in the model we will be looking at.

In this chapter, we are concerned with the level of aggregate expenditures—what affects it and how it affects the economy. Aggregate expenditures and aggregate demand mean very much the same thing, except that we ignore the price level when we talk about aggregate expenditures, whereas aggregate demand is the total amount of aggregate expenditures at various prices. Since both are the total of consumption, investment spending, government spending, and net exports, anything that affects aggregate demand will also affect aggregate expenditures. At the end of the chapter, we will look more closely at how the two are linked.

We will begin by looking at a simplified model of the economy that includes only consumption and investment spending, and bring out some of the important interrelationships. Later in the chapter we will include the government sector and finally derive a complete model by introducing the foreign sector. But let us begin gradually.

6.1   Consumption, Savings, and Investment Functions

> **LO1** Describe the marginal propensity to consume and how consumption, saving, and investment relate to national income.

It is clear that the amount households spend on consumer goods and services (consumption) is closely related to household income. Quite simply, it seems obvious that high-income earners spend more than low-income earners. The same is true for the whole economy: the higher the level of national income, the higher the level of consumption. We will begin building our model for the hypothetical economy of Karinia by assuming its economy is both private and closed. By this we mean that in Karinia there is no government intervention (no government spending or taxation) and the economy is closed to international trade so that there are neither exports nor imports. Table 6.1 shows how consumption spending is related to national income, and since there is no taxation, national income is the same as disposable income. (All the figures in this chapter are in billions of dollars.)

TABLE 6.1
Consumption and Savings Functions

National Income (Y)	Consumption (C)	Saving (S)
0	50	−50
100	125	−25
200	200	0
300	275	25
400	350	50
500	425	75
600	500	100
700	575	125
800	650	150

Since saving is that portion of income not spent on consumption, the savings column is derived by simply subtracting consumption from national income.

If you look closely at the consumption column, you can see that even at the zero level of income, there is still a certain level of consumption in Karinia (the people have to live, after all). This amount of spending—which is independent of the level of income—is referred to as **autonomous spending** or **expenditures**. Autonomous spending is the absolute minimum level of spending that occurs. However, most of our spending is the result of our earning an income; in other words, a good portion of consumption is induced by higher income levels. This is called **induced spending**. Thus

$$\begin{matrix} \text{Total spending} \\ \text{(aggregate expenditures)} \end{matrix} = \text{autonomous spending} + \text{induced spending} \qquad [6.1]$$

So we have both autonomous consumption and induced consumption. Table 6.1 shows that the amount of autonomous consumption is $50 (the level of consumption at zero income). The amount of induced consumption varies with the level of income. The extra proportion of consumer spending that results from higher incomes is referred to as the **marginal propensity to consume** (MPC). In the form of an equation, this is

$$\text{Marginal propensity to consume (MPC)} = \frac{\Delta \text{ consumption}}{\Delta \text{ income}} \qquad [6.2]$$

(Δ simply means "change in.")

You will note that Table 6.1 shows income increasing by $100 at each level. Every time it does, consumption increases by $75 (from $25 to $100, from $100 to $175, and so on). The value of the MPC in Karinia is therefore equal to $75/$100 or 0.75. Given this information, we can spell out the precise relationship between the level of consumption and the level of income in a **consumption function**.

$$C \quad = \quad 50 \quad + \quad 0.75Y$$
(Total consumption = autonomous consumption + induced consumption)

Presenting the consumption function algebraically allows us to calculate the values of consumption at levels of income not given in the table. For instance, when income is $360, we can easily calculate that consumption must equal 50 + 0.75 (360) = $320. And at an income level of $1000, consumption will equal 50 + 0.75 (1000) = $800.

Now, you might reasonably ask how householders in Karinia are able to spend anything at all if they are not receiving any income? The answer is that they will be forced to make use of their own past savings or borrow (make use of someone else's past savings). This is referred to as **dis-saving**. At an income of zero, Table 6.1 shows us that dis-saving equals $50. Note that as incomes increase not only do people spend more—consumption increases—they also save more. At incomes above $200, people are no longer dis-saving; there is now positive saving. The proportion of extra saving that results from higher incomes is referred to as the **marginal propensity to save** (MPS). In the form of an equation, it is

$$\text{Marginal propensity to save (MPS)} = \frac{\Delta \text{ saving}}{\Delta \text{ income}} \qquad [6.3]$$

In this economy, the value of the MPS equals 25/100 or 0.25. The equation for the **saving function** therefore is

$$S \quad = \quad -50 \quad + \quad 0.25Y$$
$$\text{(Total saving = autonomous dis-saving + induced saving)}$$

Since, by definition, the amount of income that is not spent must be saved (remember Y = C + S), it follows that

$$MPC + MPS = 1 \qquad [6.4]$$

We can see this equality if we add together the consumption and saving functions for Karinia.

$$
\begin{array}{rl}
C & = \quad 50 + 0.75Y \\
S & = \quad -50 + 0.25Y \\
\hline
C + S & = \qquad\qquad Y
\end{array}
$$

The consumption and saving functions are both graphed in **Figure 6.1**.

The value of the Y intercept (the point at which the consumption function crosses the vertical axis) is the amount of autonomous consumption (in this case, $50). Similarly, where the saving function crosses the vertical axis is the amount of autonomous dis-saving (−$50). The slope of the consumption function is the value of the MPC, in this case 0.75, and the slope of the saving function is the MPS and is equal to 0.25. The higher the value of the MPC, the steeper the slope of the consumption function. (It will also imply a smaller MPS and flatter saving function.)

For simplicity's sake, in this chapter we will assume that the MPC and MPS are constant. In reality, this may not be true, though a surprising amount of evidence suggests that in modern economies, it is not far from the truth. However, if we look at the long term, it does seem that the MPC tends to get smaller. In other words, as a country—and its people—grow richer, they tend to spend proportionately less and, consequently, save proportionately more of their income. Also, within most economies

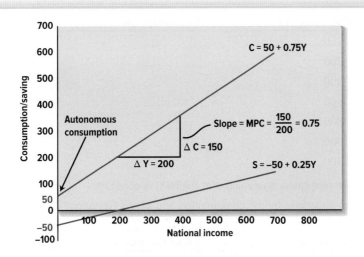

FIGURE 6.1   Consumption and Saving Functions

Both the consumption and saving functions are upward sloping, showing that both consumption and saving increase with incomes. The slope of the consumption function is equal to the MPC and the slope of the saving function is equal to the MPS. The points at which the curves cross the vertical axis show the amounts of autonomous consumption and autonomous dis-saving.

poorer members of society usually have a higher MPC than richer members. The implications of this are clear: a tax cut given to the poor will increase spending in the economy more than an identical tax cut given to the rich.

 TEST YOUR UNDERSTANDING

Find answers on the McGraw-Hill online resource.

1. The following graph shows the consumption function for the economy of Astrid.

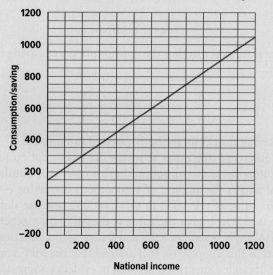

National income

a) Complete the table that follows.

b) What is the equation for the consumption function?

c) Draw the savings line in the graph.

d) What is the equation for the savings function?

National Income (Y)	Consumption (C)	Saving (S)
0	—	—
200	—	—
400	—	—
600	—	—
800	—	—
1000	—	—
1200	—	—

2. a) Complete the next table, assuming that the MPC is constant.

b) What are the equations for the consumption and saving functions?

National Income	Consumption	Saving
0	60	—
200	220	—
400	—	20
600	—	60
800	700	—

Investment

In any modern economy such as Karinia's, investment spending is far more volatile than consumption; it can fluctuate unpredictably from year to year. There are a number of reasons for this, but an important one is the fact that investment can be postponed, which is not the case with consumption. (People are not likely to put off eating or wearing clothes until the economy improves.) More especially, and again in contrast to consumption, investment is not as closely related to national income. For instance, there have been a number of years in Canada's history when both GDP and investment increased, but there have been many others in which the two went in opposite directions. For this reason, we will regard investment as autonomous from the level of income, as illustrated in Table 6.2.

TABLE 6.2
Investment Function

National Income (Y)	Investment (I)
0	75
100	75
200	75
300	75
400	75
500	75
600	75
700	75
800	75

The algebraic expression for the investment function therefore is straightforward:

$$I = 75$$

This graphs as a straight line, horizontal to the axis as illustrated in Figure 6.2.

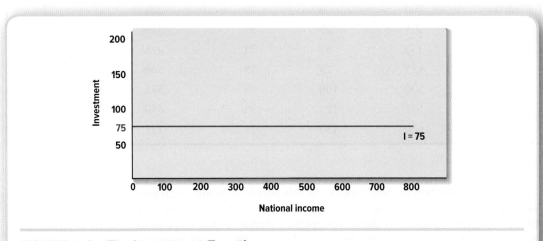

FIGURE 6.2   The Investment Function

Investment is autonomous, which means it remains constant whatever the level of income. It therefore plots as a horizontal straight line. In our example, the level of investment is a constant 75.

This graph shows that regardless of the level of national income, investment remains a constant $75.

SECTION SUMMARY

a) Production generates income that goes to households. Individuals use this income to
   - buy domestically produced goods and services and imports
   - save
   - pay taxes

b) Both consumption and saving have autonomous and induced portions. The marginal propensity to consume (MPC) relates the change in consumption to the change in income that induced it. Similarly, the marginal propensity to save (MPS) relates the change in saving to the change in income that induced it.

c) Investment is regarded as wholly autonomous with respect to national income.

6.2 Expenditures Equilibrium

LO2 Explain the concept of expenditures equilibrium.

Let us now combine the data we have on this economy's consumption and investment functions in Table 6.3.

TABLE 6.3
National Income and Aggregate Expenditures

National Income (Y)	Consumption (C)	Saving (S)	Investment (I)	Aggregate Expenditures (AE) (C + I)	Unplanned Investment [shortage (−)/ surplus (+)]
0	50	−50	75	125	−125
100	125	−25	75	200	−100
200	200	0	75	275	−75
300	275	25	75	350	−50
400	350	50	75	425	−25
500	425	75	75	500	0
600	500	100	75	575	+25
700	575	125	75	650	+50
800	650	150	75	725	+75

Since there are two spending sectors in this simple economy, aggregate expenditures (AE) equal the total of consumption and investment spending combined. You can see that the aggregate expenditures column is similar to the consumption column in that there is an amount of autonomous spending—50 in the case of consumption and 125 in the case of aggregate expenditures—and that both consumption and aggregate expenditures increase by the same 75 as income rises. In other words, as we mentioned at the outset,

$$\text{Total AE} = \text{autonomous AE} + \text{induced AE}$$

The relationship between the change in aggregate expenditures and income is referred to as the **marginal propensity to expend** (MPE). In the form of an equation, it is

$$\text{Marginal propensity to expend (MPE)} = \frac{\Delta \text{ aggregate expenditures}}{\Delta \text{ income}} \qquad [6.5]$$

The value of the MPE in Karinia is equal to 75/100 = 0.75. In fact, here it has the same value as the MPC, though this will not remain the case as we expand our model. The marginal propensity to expend tells us how much of each extra dollar earned is spent on purchasing domestically produced goods. In other words, it tells us what fraction remains in the circular flow of income that we developed in Chapter 3. The remainder is the amount that leaks out. The **marginal leakage rate** (MLR) is therefore the fraction of extra income that leaks out.

$$\text{Marginal leakage rate (MLR)} = \frac{\Delta \text{ total leakages}}{\Delta \text{ income}} \qquad [6.6]$$

And since, together, the MPE and MLR add up to one, it follows that

$$\text{Marginal leakage rate (MLR)} = (1 - \text{MPE}) \qquad [6.7]$$

In Karinia, the value of the marginal leakage rate is equal to (1 − 0.75) = 0.25 and has the same value as the marginal propensity to save (MPS), though this is true only in this simplified model.

The equation for the aggregate expenditure function, then, is

$$AE = 125 + 0.75Y$$

As we mentioned at the outset, conceptually we can regard gross domestic product (GDP, the value of production) as equal to national income. However, these two are not necessarily equal to aggregate expenditures. In fact, in **Table 6.3** we see that at an income level of zero in Karinia, aggregate expenditures are equal to $125. At this level of income, spending is far in excess of production. The result would be a shortage of goods and services to the tune of $125. This amount is shown in the final column of **Table 6.3**, Unplanned Investment, and can be calculated as the difference between national income and aggregate expenditures.

It is certainly pertinent to ask how, in an economy such as Karinia, people are able to physically buy $125 of goods and services if the country has, in fact, produced nothing—which must be the case since income is equal to zero. (We know that they are going to have to borrow in order to pay for them.) The answer is that buyers must be purchasing goods produced in previous years. In other words, they are buying up existing inventory. The last column of **Table 6.3** also shows us that the shortage of goods would be smaller at an income (and production) level of $100 and smaller still at an income level of $200. However, it is only at an income level of $500 that production is equal to aggregate expenditures. This is what is referred to as **expenditure equilibrium**. At income levels above $500, the opposite situation would prevail: production would exceed expenditures and the resulting surplus of goods would cause inventories to build up. Since a change in inventories is part of investment, it is for this reason referred to as **unplanned investment**.

> Equilibrium income is that level of income (and production) at which there is neither a surplus nor a shortage of goods.

Before we can fully grasp all the details of the expenditure model, we need to return to our discussion of what *equilibrium* means. Imagine throwing a stone into a pond and watching the concentric ripples fade as they widen. In response to the shock of the stone striking the surface, the surface immediately begins returning to normal or a smooth state—to equilibrium. Equilibrium can be thought of as a state of rest or normalcy that can from time to time be disrupted by various shocks. Similarly, the concept of equilibrium in economics contains not just the idea of equality between things but also a point of rest, or balance, toward which the economy will naturally move.

So expenditure equilibrium not only means that income and production are equal to aggregate expenditures but also that if they are not equal, there will be forces that help move them toward equality and equilibrium. And the motivating force is simply the desire by firms to make profits and avoid losses. All this means is that if, in total, firms were producing in excess of sales (a surplus of goods), they would face a buildup of unsold inventories and have little alternative but to cut output (and possibly prices) in the next period. Alternatively, a shortage of goods would imply a depletion of inventories and cause firms to produce more in subsequent periods.

The concept of equilibrium can also be seen from a different viewpoint by recognizing (from our circular flow model) that it occurs when injections equal leakages. If you look at the equilibrium row (bolded) in Table 6.3, you can see that only at the equilibrium level of $500 do injections (investment) equal leakages (saving) of $75 each.

We can see the that expenditures equilibrium implies three things:

- Income (Y) = aggregate expenditures (AE)
- No unplanned investment, that is, no surplus, no shortage of goods and services
- Total leakages = total injections

These three ideas are illustrated in Figure 6.3A.

Here, we introduce a 45° line, which enables us to easily locate expenditure equilibrium. Any point on the line indicates that what is being measured on the horizontal axis and what is being measured on the vertical axis are equal. (Of course, this assumes that the scales of the axes are the same.) We have labelled the 45° line Y = AE. Expenditure equilibrium occurs where aggregate expenditures equal income, and this is where the AE function crosses the line. This occurs in our model at the $500 level of income. Note that at incomes below $500, the AE function is above the line. This means aggregate expenditures exceed national income.

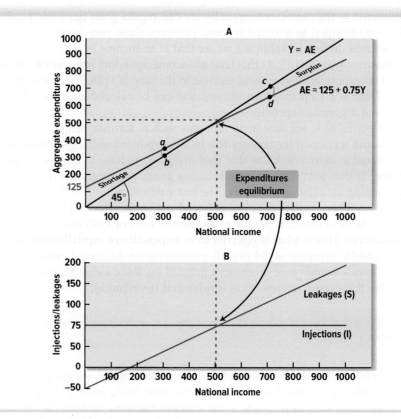

FIGURE 6.3   Expenditures Equilibrium

Autonomous aggregate expenditures are $125. The slope of the aggregate expenditures function is 0.75 so that expenditures increase by $75 for each increase of $100 in income. When income reaches $500, aggregate expenditures will have increased by $375 and will now equal income of $500. This is expenditure equilibrium and is graphically indicated by the AE function crossing the 45° line.

Total injections are an autonomous $75. Total leakages increase with income and are equal to injections at the equilibrium income of $500.

Any gap between the two curves, say the distance *ab*, represents the amount of shortage (unplanned dis-investment) that exists at that income level (the shortage equals $50 at the $300 income level in this case). At incomes greater than $500, the AE function is below the 45° line, which illustrates the fact that income (and production) exceeds aggregate expenditures, resulting in a surplus (unplanned increase in investment). For example, at an income level of $700, the distance *cd* (equal to $50) is the amount of the surplus.

Figure 6.3B shows the third way of looking at expenditures equilibrium. Here we see that at the equilibrium income of $500, total injections are equal to total leakages of $75.

Finally, let us see how we can derive expenditures equilibrium algebraically. Although we already know the algebraic expression for aggregate expenditures (AE = 125 + 0.75Y), it may be helpful to derive it formally:

$$
\begin{array}{rcl}
C & = & 50 + 0.75Y \\
I & = & 75 + \\
\hline
AE & = & 125 + 0.75Y
\end{array}
$$

By definition, expenditures equilibrium occurs where national income is equal to aggregate expenditures (Y = AE). So, if we substitute Y for AE in the above equation,

$$Y = 125 + 0.75Y$$

therefore,

$$0.25Y = 125$$

and

$$Y = 500$$

 TEST YOUR UNDERSTANDING

3. You are given the table that follows for a private, closed economy.

   a) Fill in the AE column.

   b) What are the equations for the consumption, investment, and aggregate expenditures functions?

   c) What is the value of expenditures equilibrium?

National Income	Consumption	Saving	Investment	Aggregate Expenditures
0	100	−100	200	—
200	280	−80	200	—
400	460	−60	200	—

4. Given that for a private, closed economy C = 80 + 0.6Y and I = 120, what is the algebraic expression for AE, and what is the value of expenditures equilibrium?

SECTION SUMMARY

a) Expenditures equilibrium occurs where

   • Y = AE

   • injections = leakages

   • there is no unplanned investment (neither a surplus nor a shortage)

b) Expenditures equilibrium can be shown graphically where the AE function intersects the 45° (Y = AE) line.

6.3   The Multiplier

LO3 Explain how the multiplier produces big changes in national income as a result of small changes in spending.

As we mentioned at the beginning of this chapter, spending—aggregate expenditures—lies at the heart of this Keynesian model of the economy, and therefore it is important that we get a handle on what determines the level of spending in a modern economy and what happens when it changes. Let us start by asking: What can cause a change in the level of spending? **Figure 6.4** illustrates two very different causes.

Figure 6.4A shows on the vertical axis how spending rises (from $900 to $1200) as a result of an increase in the level of national income on the horizontal axis (from $800 to $1200). This is what we mean by an increase in induced spending. **Figure 6.4B** is very different. Again, spending has increased from $900 to $1200, but in this case income has remained the same at $800. In other words, the change in spending was independent of the income level. This is what we mean by a change in autonomous aggregate expenditures.

In summary:
- a change in induced spending implies a movement along the AE curve;
- a change in autonomous spending implies a shift in the AE curve

Let us take look at some of the factors that affect autonomous spending.

Determinants of Consumption

First, what will change autonomous consumption? Economists know that the wealth held by people can influence consumption spending. This is called the **wealth effect**. To use a micro-level example, imagine a middle-aged professional computer programmer driving home from work, reflecting on how well her life seems to be unfolding—good job, kids well on their way to growing up, spouse working at something he likes, and a mortgage that is now quite manageable. She then hears the day's closing stock quotations, which prompts her to do quick calculations after dinner on the current value of the $5000 she put into shares a couple of years back. She is pleasantly surprised to realize that the shares are now worth over $8000—at least on paper. Her thought is to surprise the family

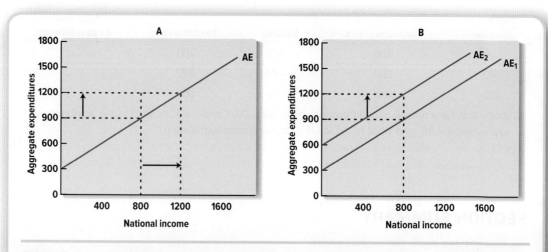

FIGURE 6.4   Change in Induced Spending and Change in Autonomous Spending

Figure A illustrates how an increase in income from $800 to $1200 increases aggregate expenditures from $900 to $1200 billion. This is an increase in induced expenditures, causing a movement along the AE curve. Figure B shows a similar increase in aggregate expenditures from $900 to $1200, though the income level remains at $800. This is caused by an increase in autonomous expenditures, causing a shift in the AE curve from AE_1 to AE_2.

with a proposal for a spontaneous holiday or perhaps announce that the hot tub they had been discussing will, indeed, be purchased. The point is that the rise in wealth might well lead to increased consumption, even though income is unchanged.

Stockholders' wealth changes daily.

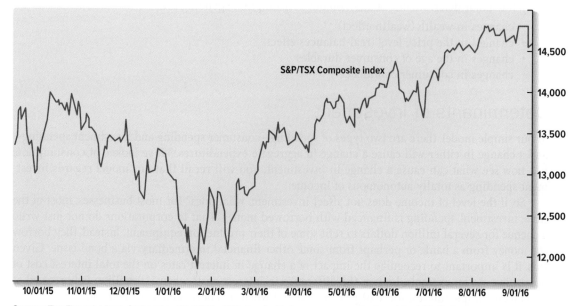

Source: *The Financial Post*, September 12, 2016. 160; Used with the express permission of Post Media Inc.

Next, let us recognize, as we did in Chapter 5, that the level of consumption also depends on the price level. A change in the price level will cause consumption spending to change. The reason for this may seem obvious. However, it is not simply a case of lower prices causing spending to rise because people can afford more, and of higher prices causing people to spend less because they cannot afford as much. The proper explanation has to do with the real value of assets. Suppose, for instance, that both prices *and* your own money income were to increase by 10 percent so that your real income remained constant. Would this change have any real effect on your consumption? On the surface, the answer is no—in real terms, your financial status has not changed. However, even though your real income is unchanged, one portion of your wealth is adversely affected by the price increase: the value of your financial assets. Your wealth now has a lower purchasing power and has, in fact, declined in value. Under these conditions, you may well cut your consumption and save more to replenish your real wealth. Similarly, a drop in prices will increase the real value of your wealth and lead to an increase in consumption. The effect of a change in the price level on the level of real wealth and therefore on consumption, as you will remember from Chapter 5, is the real-balances effect.

Changes in the stock market can have a big impact on investors' wealth and on their spending.

PhotoLink/Getty Images

A third factor that can affect the level of autonomous expenditures is the fact that most households today possess a number of durable goods, from kitchen appliances to iPhones, from cars to furniture. These things get replaced for two reasons. First, people get tired of them and can afford to replace them. Such action is obviously dependent on income. Second, durables get replaced simply because they wear out and must be replaced, regardless (within reason) of the current state of the householder's income flow. When the water heater quits, most of us just shrug, mumble that we will have to manage somehow, and arrange for a replacement. Thus, as the stock of consumer durables gets older, the likelihood of increased consumption spending grows as the need for replacement increases.

Finally, at any given time, there is a prevailing mood among an economy's consumers concerning the future state of the economy, particularly in the areas of job availability, trends in salary and wage rates, and expected changes in future prices. If this mood changes, say, from pessimistic to optimistic, then an autonomous increase in consumption spending is very likely to occur as well. In short, a change in consumer confidence can cause an autonomous change in consumption spending. In summary, the major determinants of autonomous consumption spending are

- changes in wealth (wealth effect)
- changes in the price level (real-balances effect)
- changes in the age of consumer durables
- changes in consumer confidence

Determinants of Investment

In our simple model, there are two types of spending—consumer spending and investment spending—and a change in either will cause a change in aggregate expenditures. We've looked at consumption; let's now see what can cause a change in investment. You will recall that our model regards investment spending as totally autonomous of income.

So, if the level of income does not affect investment, what does? For most businesses, most of the time, investment spending is financed with borrowed money. That is, corporations do not just write a cheque for several million dollars to refit some of their production equipment. Instead, they borrow the money from a bank, or perhaps from some other financial intermediary via a bond issue. Given this, it is important to recognize the impact of a change in interest rates on the total interest cost of borrowing. As an example, look at the difference in interest costs when $10 million is borrowed at 10 percent simple interest for a 20-year period and when it is borrowed at 12 percent:

$10 million @ 5% for 20 years = $10 million

$10 million @ 8% for 20 years = $16 million

It is clear that a particular investment possibility might be judged to be "worth it" at, say, 5 percent interest, but not at 8 percent because of the additional $6 million interest.

 ADDED DIMENSION

Are Interest Rates Important?

Some might argue that there is an important omission from this list of the major determinants of consumption: interest rates. It is certainly true that increases in interest rates may cause some people to think twice before taking out consumer loans or buying a new car. (Remember from Chapter 3 that new house purchases are regarded—at least by Statistics Canada—as a form of investment and will definitely be affected by changes in interest rates.) If that is the case, then, why are most economists reluctant to include interest rates as a determinant of consumption? The reason is that research on the topic is inconclusive.

It may well be that higher interest rates mean some people will cut down on consumer loans and save more because of the higher return they can now expect. But others may see the higher interest rates as a reason to cut back on their monthly saving, since they can put less aside yet still earn as much as they did before, given the higher interest rates.

Keynes himself felt that interest rates are not important determinants of consumption and saving. Most of us, he felt, are creatures of habit and it is a fairly painful exercise to readjust our spending patterns, which is what we would have to do if we changed our level of saving every time there was a change in interest rates. Income levels, as well as the other factors we have mentioned, are far more significant when it comes to figuring out our spending levels.

It should be noted that not everyone agrees with this. Some economists suggest that while low interest rates may indeed have little impact on consumer spending, very high interest rates may well choke off expenditures.

In short, whether an investment project looks profitable or not depends on the interest costs of the money that must be borrowed to finance it. Note also that even if the investment is self-financed by a company, the rate of interest is still a determining factor in deciding whether to invest, since the alternative to investing is simply to leave the money in some form of savings certificate, or in a savings account, and earn a guaranteed return.

Suppose, for example, that your firm has $20 million in surplus funds and you are wondering whether you should invest that in a new processing machine. You have calculated that this machine will increase your after-tax profits by $1.5 million, which amounts to a return of 7.5 percent ($1.5/20 × 100) per year. The question is: Should you save these funds (in a bank or other financial institution) or invest these funds in your firm? The answer is clear: if you can earn more than 7.5 percent in the bank, you should save the money; if, on the other hand, the bank is paying an interest rate less than 7.5 percent, you would be better off investing that money in your firm. From this we can conclude that, in general, when interest rates are low, firms tend to invest and when interest rates are high, they tend to save.

In all of this, it is important to realize, as we mentioned in Chapter 4, that the real, not the nominal, rate of interest is the important determinant of investment spending. A firm that must pay a nominal rate of interest of 10 percent per annum over the next three years will be less inclined to borrow if it believes the rate of inflation is going to be 2 percent per annum over that period (making the real rate of interest it has to pay equal to 8 percent) than if it believes inflation will be 7 percent (which would make the real rate equal to only 3 percent).

Besides the interest rate, the initial price that must be paid for equipment or construction has a clear impact on whether that purchase will be profitable. Similarly, the maintenance and operating costs involved over the life of the new machine, equipment, or building must also be considered in calculating potential profitability.

Sometimes, new investment must be undertaken simply because equipment has worn out or a building is in a serious state of disrepair. As the age of an economy's capital stock increases, this sort of thing occurs with greater frequency, and investment spending is higher than it would otherwise have been. But it's not just the age of capital goods that determines how much investment will be done. The amount of investment will also depend on the amount of spare (unused) capacity that exists, because machines do not always run twenty-four hours a day and at times they sit entirely idle. If there is a lot of spare capacity in the economy, it is unlikely that firms will want to invest any time soon. In addition, investment spending may well increase when businesspeople are optimistic about the future and decrease when pessimism sets in. These psychological factors have an important bearing on investment decisions.

Finally, bureaucracy or "red tape" requirements add to costs, impacting the potential profitability of any proposed investment project. If red tape were cut, one would also expect investment spending to increase.

In summary, the major determinants of investment spending are

- interest rates
- purchase price, installation, maintenance, and operating costs of capital goods
- the age of capital goods and the amount of spare capacity
- business confidence
- government regulations

The Multiplier Graphically

One of the important ideas Keynes popularized (though he did not invent it) was that of the multiplier. Simply put, the idea is that an increase in (autonomous) spending can have an impact on income well in excess of that spending. Perhaps it is easiest to see this graphically.

As we have seen, many factors influence the level of autonomous spending in a country, and we need to be able to work out the effect of these changes. Let us start with the assumption that businesses in Karinia become more optimistic about the future. As a result, they decide to increase spending on new investment projects. Instead of spending $75 billion on investment, as they did last year, let us suppose they increase investment spending to $125 billion. Karinian businesses place additional orders for new construction, equipment, computers, and other capital projects. This will, of course, increase production by $50 billion above that of the previous year and boost income by the

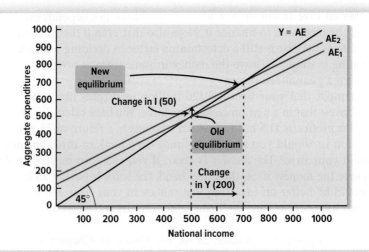

FIGURE 6.5   The Multiplier

The increase in autonomous spending of $50 has an immediate effect of increasing aggregate expenditures by $50. This results in a shortage. This will lead to an increase in production and, thus, income. The economy will eventually move to a new equilibrium, where the new AE function (AE$_2$) crosses the Y = AE curve. As a result, income here increases by a total of $200, four times as much as the initial increase in spending.

same amount. But is that the end of the story? Is it simply the case that an extra $50 billion in investment spending translates into $50 billion of extra income? The answer is, in fact, no. As we shall soon see, income will increase by more than $50 billion. **Figure 6.5** helps explain this.

The increase in investment spending increases aggregate expenditures by $50 at every level of income so that there is a parallel shift up in the AE function from AE$_1$ to AE$_2$. After the shift, there would be a shortage of goods and services of $50 *at the original level of income of $500*. The result of the shortage is that production will increase. Even if income rises by $50 (the same amount as the increase in spending) to $550, there would still be a shortage of goods and services, since at this income level AE$_2$ is still above the Y = AE line. The new equilibrium, in fact, occurs at the $700 level of income. In other words, income will increase by *four times* the amount of the increase in aggregate expenditures. The reason for this phenomenon is termed the *multiplier* (or *expenditures multiplier*), and it is one of the more intriguing aspects of macroeconomics.

The Multiplier Derived

Let us look at this decision to increase investment spending in more detail. **Table 6.4** illustrates the effect of an increase of $50 from $75 to $125 (let's make it millions of dollars). Suppose that initially this money is spent on a new meat-packing plant in Karinia. In one month, this money goes to build and outfit the plant and becomes income to the various suppliers—contractors, plumbers, electricians, machine manufacturers, and so on. And what will these firms and individuals do with this new money? The answer is that they will spend it—or at least a portion of it. Suppose that the marginal propensity to consume in Karinia is 0.75. This means that 75 percent, or $37.5 million (we have rounded it up to $38) will be spent and the remainder, $12 million, will be saved. And what will the money be spent on? In some cases, it might go to buy a new car or an HD TV or perhaps, more simply, on new clothes for the kids. So in month 2 this $38 million is spent on those items and, in turn, becomes incomes to the car dealerships, electronic stores, department stores, and so on. In month 3, the recipients of this will themselves spend some of the additional money (75 percent of $38 million, or approximately $28 million) and save the remaining $10 million. In the following month, the $28 million that was spent becomes other peoples' income and they, too, will spend a portion ($21 million) and save the rest ($7 million). This process of getting and spending will continue for months to come.

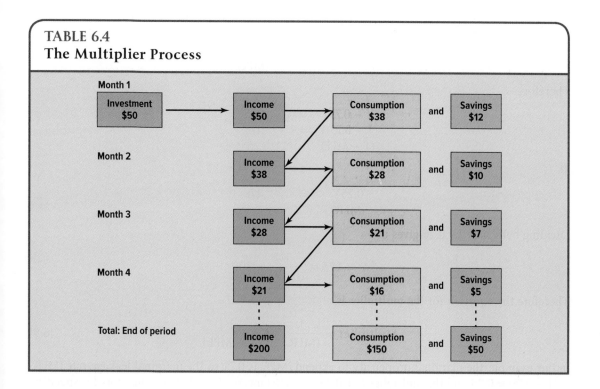

TABLE 6.4
The Multiplier Process

The basis of this process is the same concept that lies behind the circular flow model we developed in Chapter 3: one person's spending is another person's income. The result is that each time income increases, spending increases by 75 percent of it. When will this process come to an end? In our model, income and spending will continue to increase until the total new savings (the leakage) is equal to the original investment (injection). This occurs when income has risen by $200 and savings has increased by $50.

Let's return to our earlier analogy of throwing a stone into a pond. The initial impact causes a big wave that spreads out from the point of impact. But this disturbance also causes successive smaller waves, which spread out farther and farther across the pond until eventually the lake returns to its former placid equilibrium. The multiplier effect means that the initial impact is felt at the time and place in which it occurs. Think of the billions in new investment in the up coming Tokyo Olympics. Most of the money will be spent in the Tokyo city area during the construction phase. However, its effect will eventually be felt throughout Japan and for years into the future.

In summary, then, an initial increase in investment of $50 induced an increase of $200 in national income. On the surface, this seems to provide a dramatic solution to any recession and a simple formula for growth. We just need to encourage people to spend more! But as you probably suspect, there is a little more to it than that.

We have just seen the multiplier at work. This is the process by which changes in autonomous expenditures are translated into a multiplied change in national income.

$$\text{Multiplier} = \frac{\Delta \text{ income}}{\Delta \text{ autonomous expenditures}} \qquad [6.8]$$

In our model, the initial increase of $50 led to an increase in income of $200. In other words, the value of the multiplier was equal to 200/50 = 4.

To understand where this number came from, let us do a little algebra integrating the change in investment:

$$
\begin{array}{rl}
C & = \quad 50 + 0.75Y \\
I & = \quad 125 \qquad \text{(used to be 75)} \\
\hline
AE & = \quad 175 + 0.75Y
\end{array}
$$

The Japanese government is hopeful that the billions in investment in the upcoming 2020 Olympics will have a multiplier effect throughout Japan for years into the future.

© Letuve | Dreamstime.com

Equilibrium is where Y = AE, so

$$Y = 175 + 0.75Y$$
$$(MPE)$$

Therefore,

$$Y - 0.75Y = 175$$
$$(1 - 0.75)Y = 175$$
$$(1 - MPE)$$

So

$$0.25Y = 175$$
$$(MLR)$$

Dividing both sides by 0.25 gives us

$$Y = 175 \times \frac{1}{(0.25)} = 700$$

Therefore the equation for the multiplier is

$$\text{Multiplier} = \frac{1}{(MLR)} \text{ or } \frac{1}{(1 - MPE)} \qquad [6.9]$$

In our example, the marginal propensity to expend (MPE) is 0.75, so the marginal leakage rate (MLR) is (1 − 0.75) = 0.25, and the multiplier is 1/0.25 = 4. This means that whenever autonomous spending (in this case, investment) changes by any amount, income will change four times as much.

It follows then that:

The higher the value of the MPE (the smaller the MLR), the bigger the multiplier.

To illustrate the idea that a higher value of MPE implies a bigger multiplier, in **Figure** 6.6 we contrast two economies with different MPEs. The economy shown in **Figure** 6.6A has an MPE of 0.5, which is the value of the slope of its AE curve—every $200 increase in income is associated with a $100 increase in aggregate expenditures. At present, the economy is in equilibrium at an income of $1200 (all figures in billions of dollars). Suppose now that investment were to increase by $100. This

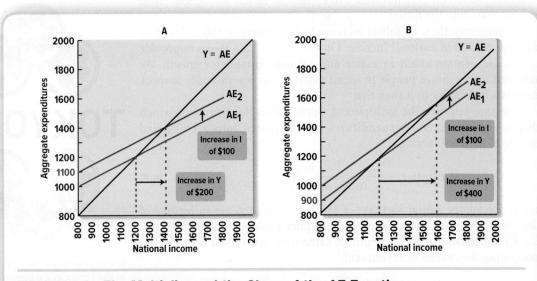

FIGURE 6.6   The Multiplier and the Slope of the AE Function

is shown graphically by a parallel shift upward of $100. The new equilibrium income as a result has risen by $200 to $1400. The value of the multiplier, then, is 2. We can verify its value easily by noting that if the MPE = 0.5, then the MLR = $(1 - 0.5) = 0.5$. The value of the multiplier is equal to 1/MLR or 1/0.5 = 2.

Now, let's see what happens in the economy shown in **Figure 6.6B**. Here, too, the initial income is $1200 and it also experiences an increase in investment of $100. However, the MPE in this second economy equals 0.75. (The curve is steeper than in graph A with aggregate expenditures increasing by $300 for every income rise of $400.) With an MPE of 0.75, its MLR is $(1 - 0.75) = 0.25$, and its multiplier then is 1/0.25 = 4. The rise in investment of $100 therefore has a bigger impact in this second economy and causes, as we see in the graph, an increase in income of $400 to $1600. This confirms our point then that the bigger the MPE (and the bigger the slope of the AE function), the greater the value of the multiplier.

TEST YOUR UNDERSTANDING

5. Given the following values for the MPE, calculate the values of the MLR and multipliers.

a) 0.9

b) 0.75

c) 0.6

d) 0.5

6. In the accompanying graph:

a) What is the algebraic expression for aggregate expenditures?

b) What is the value of the multiplier?

c) What is the value of expenditures equilibrium?

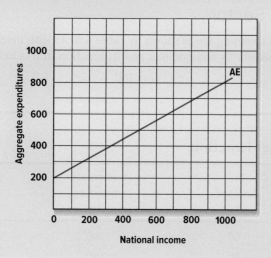

Now, before we get carried away with this idea, we shall see when we fully expand our model that the value of the multiplier will actually be much smaller than 4 (and in many countries it is considerably less than this). It should also be noted that the multiplier works in reverse: a drop in autonomous expenditures will produce a multiplied decline in income. In any case, perhaps you now better realize why market watchers pay a great deal of attention to the pattern of consumption spending in the economy.

SECTION SUMMARY

a) The multiplier refers to the fact that an increase in autonomous spending leads to a multiplied increase in income. Its formula is

$$\text{Multiplier} = \frac{1}{\text{MLR}} \text{ or } \frac{1}{1 - \text{MPE}}$$

b) Changes in *autonomous consumption* are a result of
- the wealth effect
- the real-balances effect
- changes in the age of consumer durables
- changes in consumer expectations

c) Changes in *autonomous investment* are a result of
- changes in the interest rate
- changes in the purchase price or maintenance costs of capital goods
- changes in the age of capital goods
- changes in business expectations
- changes in government regulations

6.4   The Complete Expenditure Model

LO4   Describe how government's budget balance and the balance of trade both relate to national income.

We now need to make our model more realistic by including the other spending sectors of the economy. First, let us add in government spending and taxation.

The Government Sector

Suppose that taxation and spending are as shown in **Table 6.5**. As with investment spending, government spending is treated as wholly autonomous, and its function in this example is

$$G = 160$$

TABLE 6.5
Government Budget Function

National Income (Y)	Tax Revenue (T)	Government Spending (G)	Budget Surplus (+)/ Deficit (−) (T − G)
0	60	160	−100
100	80	160	−80
200	100	160	−60
300	120	160	−40
400	140	160	−20
500	160	160	0
600	180	160	+20
700	200	160	+40
800	220	160	+60

Now, you might object to this, and you might believe that the amount government is able to spend is, in turn, determined by the amounts of tax and other revenues it receives. Since such revenue is dependent on income, wouldn't this mean that the amounts government spends are also dependent on the level of income? While there is some truth in this, it would be a gross simplification. In fact, governments can and do spend whatever they feel is necessary, irrespective of the tax revenues they receive. Therefore, we will regard government spending as autonomous. Making this assumption again offers the advantage of simplicity. We will return to this point later.

On the other hand, tax revenues, as is the case in most economies, definitely does depend on the level of incomes. However, note that in Karinia, taxes are $60, even when income is zero. This is the level of autonomous taxes. There are several examples of autonomous taxes, including highway tolls, user fees, property taxes, and so on. These taxes do not depend on the level of income. However, the majority of the Karinian government's tax revenue comes from induced taxes—taxes that depend directly on, or are related to, income levels. Examples would be personal income taxes, corporate taxes, and sales taxes.

Total taxes are made up of autonomous taxes and induced taxes:

$$\text{Total taxes} = \text{autonomous taxes} + \text{induced taxes} \qquad [6.10]$$

The rate at which tax revenues increase with national income is known as the **marginal tax rate** (MTR).

$$\text{Marginal tax rate (MTR)} = \frac{\Delta \text{ taxes}}{\Delta \text{ income}} \qquad [6.11]$$

We can see in **Table 6.5** that as national income increases by 100, tax revenues increase by 20. Put another way, for every additional $1 in income $0.20 goes to taxes. The marginal tax rate for this economy is therefore equal to $20/100 = 0.2$, and the tax function is

$$T = 60 + 0.2Y$$

The government budget balance is simply the difference between its tax revenue and its spending $(T - G)$. You can see in **Table 6.5** that as national income increases, government's budget deficit decreases and eventually becomes a surplus.

We illustrate these ideas in **Figure 6.7**. In graph A, since government spending is wholly autonomous, it plots (like investment spending) as a straight line horizontal to the axis. The tax function, however, varies directly with the level of income. It does not start at the origin, since there is $60 of autonomous taxes. The steepness of the tax function is determined by the value of the marginal tax rate. In Karinia, this has a value of 0.2, and this is the slope of its tax function. When government spending is above the tax function, the difference between them represents a budget deficit. When the tax function is above the government spending function, the difference is a budget surplus. There is a budget balance where the two lines intersect.

The condition of government's budget deficit is shown explicitly in the budget line in graph B. It starts at a deficit of $100 and is upward sloping; as the level of income increases (and along with it, the government's tax revenue) the size of the budget deficit gets smaller. It is balanced at an income of $500 and becomes a surplus at higher incomes. We can derive an equation for the budget line by noting that the budget balance is equal to $T - G$, or, in our example,

$$\text{Budget balance} = 60 + 0.2Y - 160 \text{ or} = -100 + 0.2Y$$

Now, let us integrate both government spending and taxation into our numerical model of equations, going back to the original data with $I = 75$. This is done in **Table 6.6**. Our third column, Disposable Income, is simply (national) income after taxes.

$$\begin{aligned}\text{Disposable income} &= \text{national income less tax} \\ Y_D \quad\quad &= \quad\quad (Y - T) \qquad [6.12]\end{aligned}$$

Understandably, the amount of consumption is now lower at every level of income. In fact we have a new consumption function. You can see this in the table where total consumption spending starts at a value of $5 and now increases by only $60 for each $100 increase in the level of national income. Our new consumption function is

$$C = 5 + 0.6Y$$

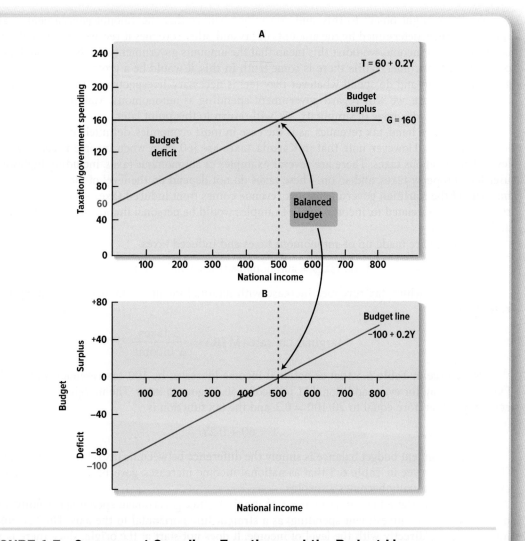

FIGURE 6.7   Government Spending, Taxation, and the Budget Line

This graph plots government spending as a horizontal line at $160. The tax function starts at an autonomous level of $60 and increases at a (marginal tax) rate of 0.2. The two curves intersect, and there is a balanced budget at an income level of $500. Below that level there are budget deficits, and above it there are budget surpluses.

This graph shows government's budget position in the form of the budget line. It starts at a deficit of $100 at zero income and is upward sloping, since deficits get smaller (and surpluses bigger) as income rises. The budget line crosses the axis at $500, where the budget balance is zero.

In addition, the level of savings has also dropped, and the new savings function is

$$S = -65 + 0.2Y$$

The concept of expenditures equilibrium remains unchanged and occurs where national income is equal to aggregate expenditures. However, we now have an additional expenditure sector: government spending. Aggregate expenditures are therefore equal to the total of consumption (C), investment (I), and government spending (G). Expenditures equilibrium occurs at a national income level of $600.

Besides adding another injection, we have also added another leakage: taxes (T). It remains true, however, that total injections are equal to total leakages at equilibrium.

$$
\begin{array}{ccccccc}
I & + & G & = & S & + & T \\
(75 & + & 160 & = & 55 & + & 180 & = & 235)
\end{array}
$$

Equilibrium for our expanded model is illustrated in **Figure** 6.8. The value of the Y intercept in graph A, $240, is the amount of autonomous aggregate expenditures. This constitutes autonomous

TABLE 6.6
Expenditures Equilibrium

National Income (Y)	Tax (T)	Disposable Income (Y_D)	Consumption (C)	Saving (S)	Investment (I)	Government Spending (G)	Aggregate Expenditures (AE) (C + I + G)
0	60	−60	5	−65	75	160	240
100	80	20	65	−45	75	160	300
200	100	100	125	−25	75	160	360
300	120	180	185	−5	75	160	420
400	140	260	245	+15	75	160	480
500	160	340	305	+35	75	160	540
600	180	420	365	+55	75	160	600
700	200	500	425	+75	75	160	660
800	220	580	485	+95	75	160	720

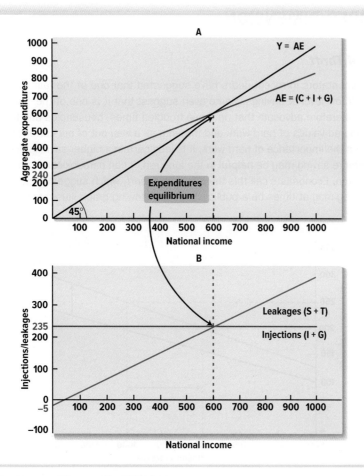

FIGURE 6.8   **Expenditures Equilibrium**

The autonomous aggregate expenditures are $240. The slope of the AE function is 0.6 so that expenditures increase by $60 for each $100 increase in national income. The expenditure equilibrium is where the AE function crosses the Y = AE (45°) line at an income of $600.

The total injections (I + G) are an autonomous $235. The total leakages increase with income and are equal to injections at the equilibrium income of $600.

consumption of 5, investment of 75, and government spending of 160. The slope of the aggregate expenditures is equal to marginal propensity to expend. However, it is now smaller than it was in our simplified model. Its value is now equal to 60/100, or 0.6. Our spending is lower than before, simply because some of our income is going to taxes.

Earlier, we saw how to calculate the value of equilibrium income algebraically. The equation for aggregate expenditure is

$$AE = 240 + 0.6Y$$

We might also derive its value, as we have seen, by summing the (now) three spending functions:

$$
\begin{aligned}
C &= 5 + 0.6Y \\
I &= 75 \\
G &= 160 \\
\hline
AE &= 240 + 0.6Y
\end{aligned}
$$

Setting this equal to Y,

$$Y = 240 + 0.6Y$$

Therefore

$$0.4Y = 240$$
$$Y = 600$$

ADDED DIMENSION

The Paradox of Thrift

A number of commentators in recent years have suggested that one of the failings of contemporary economies is their low level of savings. Some even suggest that it is one of the causes of struggling economies. They therefore advocate that, in these troubled times, households and firms should practise the time-honoured values of hard work and frugality as a way out of our current difficulties. While no one argues with the importance of hard work, it is less certain if higher savings are beneficial to an economy. While more saving may be helpful in the long run, it can paradoxically cause a great deal of harm in the short run. Economists call this the *paradox of thrift*, which suggests that while savings are a private virtue, they may at times be a public vice. The following graph illustrates this paradox.

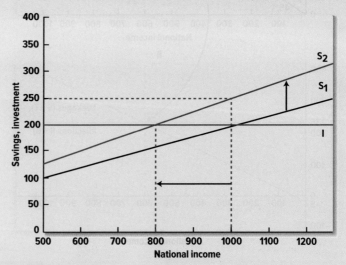

Suppose initially that the economy is in equilibrium with savings and investment equal to $200 billion at a national income of $1000. The savings rate is 20 percent. Now suppose that the government encourages the public to increase their savings rate to 25 percent. This implies that consumer spending will drop a similar amount with the result that—via the multiplier effect—national income will fall to $800. The economy returns to equilibrium where savings and investment are again equal. Unfortunately, the economy is now in a serious recession and savings did not in fact increase but returned to the previous level of $200 (20% × $1000 = 25% × $800 = $200).

Note that since the value of the MPE is now smaller (0.6 compared with 0.75), the value of the marginal leakage rate is bigger (0.4), and the value of the multiplier is smaller (1/0.4 or 2.5).

We can also find the value of the marginal leakage rate by simply adding together the marginal values of the two leakages we have looked at so far. Since the MTR is 0.2 and the MPS is also 0.2, the MLR must be 0.4. What this says is that of every extra dollar produced (and earned) in Karinia, 60 percent is spent on Karinian goods and services and the rest, 40 percent, goes to taxes and savings. As we soon shall see, this latter percent is going to get a lot smaller.

Note that there are now three uses for our income: some is taxed, some is saved and the rest is spent on consumption. If we add them together, we get

$$
\begin{aligned}
C &= 5 + 0.6Y \\
S &= -65 + 0.2Y \\
T &= 60 + 0.2Y \\
\hline
C + S + T &= Y
\end{aligned}
$$

Adding the Foreign Sector

As we saw earlier, an increase in the level of income leads to an increase in spending, whether this spending is on domestically produced or foreign-produced goods. This means that the amount that Canada imports is strongly related to our own national income. By the same token, our sale of goods abroad depends on foreign incomes and not on our own incomes, so exports are autonomous of national income. This is illustrated in Table 6.7.

TABLE 6.7
Net Exports Function

National Income (Y)	Exports (X)	Imports (IM)	Net Exports (XN) (X − IM)
0	100	40	+60
100	100	50	+50
200	100	60	+40
300	100	70	+30
400	100	80	+20
500	100	90	+10
600	100	100	0
700	100	110	−10
800	100	120	−20

However, the level of imports is directly related to the level of income. The relationship between imports and the level of income is known as the **marginal propensity to import** (MPM). Formally, this is

$$
\text{Marginal propensity to import (MPM)} = \frac{\Delta \text{ imports (IM)}}{\Delta \text{ income (Y)}} \qquad [6.13]
$$

For Karinia, the value of the MPM is 0.1, since Table 6.7 shows that for every $100 increase in national income, imports increase by 10, that is, 10/100 = 0.1.

Note that there is also an autonomous component to imports, since the level of imports is $40 when income is zero. Presumably, since Karinia does not possess certain products and resources, it will need to import them from abroad regardless of its income level. That is, import spending is both autonomous (the $40) and induced (the MPM × the level of income), just as we saw when we looked at the consumption function.

So the equation for the import function is

$$IM = 40 + 0.1Y$$

TEST YOUR UNDERSTANDING

7. What does it mean when we say that some amount of imports may be autonomous? Explain the phrase, and give examples to illustrate your answer.

Let us turn now to net exports, which is simply the difference between exports and imports. It is also referred to as the **balance of trade**, and this balance can be positive or negative. Note in Table 6.7 that net exports are positive and highest when income is lowest. This is because autonomous exports are a constant $100, whereas imports are mostly induced and thus rise as income rises. In fact, at income levels above $600, imports rise to exceed exports. As a result, net exports become negative. This means that as Karinia enjoys a higher income it starts to see a reduction in its trade surplus and subsequently an increase in its trade deficit. This is illustrated in Figure 6.9A.

We see in Figure 6.9A that since exports are an autonomous $100, the export function is a horizontal line at that level. Since imports are partly autonomous, the import function starts at $40. However, it is also related to incomes so that the import function rises from that point. The slope of the import function is equal to the value of the MPM, which, you recall, has a value of 0.1 in Karinia.

Figure 6.9B shows that the net export function begins at a surplus of $60, since this is the amount of the difference between autonomous exports and autonomous imports. As income rises, imports also rise. However, exports do not change with income level so that *net* exports (or the trade surplus, as it is usually called) decline. At an income level of $600, exports are equal to imports, which means that net exports are zero; that is, there is a zero balance of trade. This is indicated by the net export function crossing the horizontal line. In algebraic terms,

$$X_N = X - IM$$

Therefore, for our model, it is equal to

$$X_N = 100 - (40 + 0.1Y)$$

or

$$X_N = 60 - 0.1Y$$

Determinants of Net Exports

We have established that exports are wholly autonomous, whereas imports are partially autonomous and partly induced by income. There are four major factors affecting net exports.

First, net exports will be affected by the level of prices in a country compared with prices abroad. If the prices of goods and services were to fall in Karinia, foreigners would be more likely to buy Karinian exports and Karinians would be less likely to buy as many foreign imports.

Second, the value of a country's currency in relation to foreign currencies will also affect net exports. A decrease in the value of the Karinian dollar (with respect to foreign currencies) has the same effect as a decrease in the price of Karinian goods and services. This means that a fall in the Karinian dollar will increase net exports; a rise will decrease net exports.

Third, Karinian exports (but not imports) are affected by the level of income in the countries that import Karinian products.

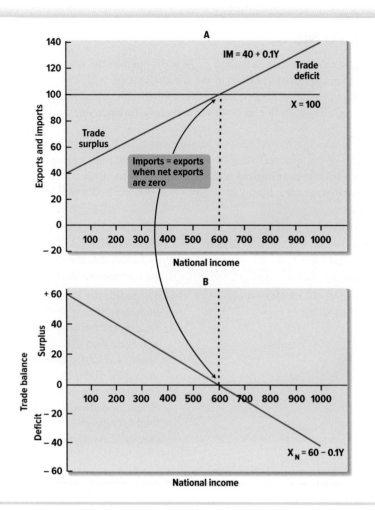

FIGURE 6.9   The Net Export Function

This graph shows that imports increase as income levels increase so that the import function is upward sloping. Exports are autonomous of income levels, and therefore its function is a horizontal line. At low income levels, exports exceed imports, which results in a trade surplus. At higher income levels, however, imports exceed exports, which implies a trade deficit. At an income level of $600, the trade balance is zero.

In this graph, the net export function starts at a surplus of 60 but decreases in value as income increases. It has a value of zero (exports = imports) where the line crosses the axis at an income of $600.

The fourth factor is foreign tastes. If Karinian products become more popular this will lead to an increase in Karinian exports. A change in any of these four factors will cause a change in net exports. In summary, the factors that determine net exports are

- comparative price levels
- the value of the exchange rate
- income levels abroad
- foreign tastes

Our final task is to integrate net exports into our model, which is done in Table 6.8. With international trade now included in our model, aggregate expenditures become the total of C, I, G, and net exports (X_N). However, the general principle continues to apply: expenditure equilibrium occurs where national income and aggregate expenditures are equal, and this occurs only at a national income of $600.

IT'S NEWS TO ME ...

The media has just reported that Canadian exports dropped in the second quarter of the year and this contributed to a 1.5% quarterly drop in the country's GDP.

While the drop in exports included declines in motor vehicles and some consumer products, the major factor as a significant decline in crude oil and crude bitumen due to the wild fires in Northern Alberta in May.

Looking deeper into the second quarter statistics, the Bank of Canada notes that the month of June (third month of the quarter) showed an uptick in GDP and a jump in bitumen exports as production moved back to near normal following the end of the fires.

Desjardins senior economist, Jimmy Jean, notes that this "... bodes well for the third quarter."

Source: *Star Power Reporting,* Summer 2016.

I. Which of the following is an accurate description of the effect of the wild fires in Northern Alberta?

   a) an induced decline in investment spending
   b) an autonomous decline in exports
   c) an induced decline in exports
   d) an autonomous decline in GDP

II. Why does the level of Canada's exports closely impact its GDP?

   a) The multiplier effect for exports is larger than any other type of spending.
   b) Exports are the largest component of aggregate demand.
   c) There is always a time lag between a change in exports and a change in GDP levels.
   d) Exports are one of the four components of total spending and the GDP level reflects total spending.

TABLE 6.8
Expenditures Equilibrium: Full Model

National Income (Y)	Tax (T)	Disposable Income (Y_D)	Consumption (C)	Saving (S)	Investment (I)	Government Spending (G)	Exports (X)	Imports (IM)	Net Exports (X_N)	Aggregate Expenditures (AE) ($C + I + G + X_N$)
0	60	−60	5	−65	75	160	100	40	+60	300
100	80	20	65	−45	75	160	100	50	+50	350
200	100	100	125	−25	75	160	100	60	+40	400
300	120	180	185	−5	75	160	100	70	+30	450
400	140	260	245	+15	75	160	100	80	+20	500
500	160	340	305	+35	75	160	100	90	+10	550
600	**180**	**420**	**365**	**+55**	**75**	**160**	**100**	**100**	**0**	**600**
700	200	500	425	+75	75	160	100	110	−10	650
800	220	580	485	+95	75	160	100	120	−20	700

The value of autonomous aggregate expenditure—the amount of aggregate expenditures when Y equals zero—now equals $300, and we can see in Table 6.8 that aggregate expenditures increase by 50 for every $100 increase in national income. Thus, the marginal propensity to expend is 50/100 or 0.5. The equation for the aggregate expenditure function is

$$AE = 300 + 0.5Y$$

To find equilibrium income algebraically, we simply equate AE to Y:

$$Y = 300 + 0.5Y$$

This gives us

$$0.5Y = 300$$
$$Y = 600$$

We also know that equilibrium implies that injections equal leakages, and this can be confirmed by inspecting their values at equilibrium income.

$$\begin{array}{cccccccccccc} I & + & G & + & X & = & S & + & T & + & IM \\ 75 & + & 160 & + & 100 & = & 55 & + & 180 & + & 100 & = & 335 \end{array}$$

Equilibrium is also shown in **Figure 6.10A**. The value of the Y intercept is equal to $300, which is the value of autonomous aggregate expenditures. The slope is 0.5 and is equal to the value of the MPE. Expenditures equilibrium occurs where income and aggregate expenditures are equal or where the Y = AE (45°) line crosses the AE function. In **Figure 6.10** the two cross at a value of $600.

Figure 6.10B indicates that the injections (I + G + X) are all wholly autonomous and have a value of $335. The leakages (S + T + IM), however, are all directly related to national income. Another

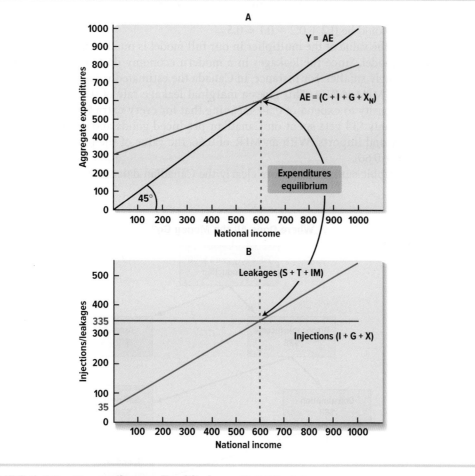

FIGURE 6.10   Expenditures Equilibrium: Full Model

The autonomous aggregate expenditures are $300. The slope of the AE function is 0.5 so that expenditures increase by $50 for each $100 increase in national income. The expenditure equilibrium is where the AE function crosses the 45° line at an income of $600.

The total injections (I + G + X) are an autonomous $335. The total leakages increase with income and are equal to the injections at the equilibrium income of $600.

way to determine equilibrium income, then, is to find the level of income that will induce leakages of $335. This occurs at an income level of $600.

We could also have derived an equation for aggregate expenditures by summing each separate equation:

$$
\begin{array}{rcl}
C &=& 5 + 0.6Y \\
I &=& 75 \\
G &=& 160 \\
X_N &=& 60 - 0.1Y \\
\hline
AE &=& 300 + 0.5Y
\end{array}
$$

Note that with the addition of another leakage, imports, the values of the MPE and, thus, the multiplier have decreased. The equation for the MPE in our open economy is now

$$\text{Marginal propensity to expend (MPE)} = \text{MPC} - \text{MPM} \qquad [6.14]$$

Since the MPC is 0.6 and the MPM is 0.1, the MPE has a value of 0.5 and the value of the MLR is $(1 - 0.5) = 0.5$. The value of the multiplier, then, is $1/0.5 = 2$.

Alternatively, the MLR can be found by simply summing the three marginal leakages (all out of income):

$$\text{MLR} = \text{MPS} + \text{MTR} + \text{MPM} \qquad [6.15]$$

In our example, that would be $0.2 + 0.2 + 0.1 = 0.5$.

You can see that the value of the multiplier in our full model is much smaller than it was in our original simplified model. Since the leakages in a modern economy do tend to be quite high, the multiplier is accordingly smaller. For instance, in Canada the estimated value of the MPS is 0.20, the MTR is 0.12, and the MPM is 0.34. This gives a marginal leakage rate of 0.66 ($0.20 + 0.12 + 0.34$) and a marginal propensity to expend of 0.34, meaning that for every extra $100 of production (and income) in Canada, only $34 gets spent on Canadian-produced goods and services. The other $66 goes to saving, taxes, and imports. With an MLR of 0.66, the value of the multiplier for Canada is estimated at 1.52 ($= 1/0.66$).

The following graphic summarizes more clearly the Canadian data from above:

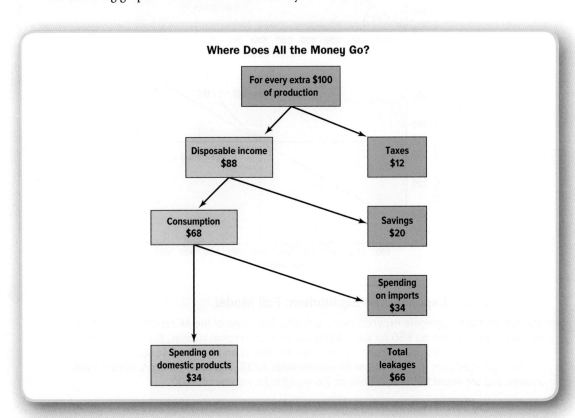

ADDED DIMENSION

Real-World Multipliers

In the modern world, the size of the expenditure multiplier is quite small. This is because savings, imports, and tax rates are quite high in most countries. The following table shows the estimated size of multipliers in the G8 countries (in size order) using average rather than marginal rates. (Tax data are for 2014; all other data are for 2015.)

VALUE OF THE MULTIPLIER FOR SELECTED COUNTRIES					
Country	**Savings/ GDP %**	**Imports/ GDP %**	**Taxes/ GDP %**	**Marginal Leakage Rate**	**Multiplier**
Germany	27.4	39.1	11.5	78.0	1.28
France	20.4	31.4	23.3	75.1	1.33
Italy	18.9	27.0	23.6	69.5	1.44
United Kingdom	12.4	29.4	25.0	69.5	1.44
Canada	20.4	33.8	11.8	66.0	1.52
Russian Federation	25.9	21.2	13.4	60.5	1.65
Japan	24.8	18.9	10.9	54.6	1.83
United States	17.6	15.5	10.9	44.0	2.27

Source: International Bank for Reconstruction and Development/The World Bank: World Development Indicators, 2016.

TEST YOUR UNDERSTANDING

8. If $T = 50 + 0.25Y$; $G = 200$; $IM = 30 + 0.1Y$; and $X = 120$, what are the budget balance $(T - G)$ and the trade balance $(X - IM)$ at the following income levels?

a) 400

b) 600

c) 900

d) 1200

9. You are given the following table for the economy of Narkia. Assume that the MPC, MTR, and MPM are constant and I, G, and X are all autonomous.

a) Fill in the table.

b) Calculate the value of the expenditures equilibrium.

Y	T	Y_D	C	S	I	G	X	IM	X_N	AE
0	20	—	30	—	50	—	—	10	—	___
100	—	60	102	—	—	70	—	—	−2	___
200	60	—	—	—	—	—	20	—	—	___
300	—	220	246	−26	—	—	—	—	−26	___

10. Find the value of MPE, MLR, and the multiplier if the MPS = 0.075, the MTR = 0.25, and the MPM = 0.075.

The Expenditures Model: A Summary

The level of national income is determined by the level of aggregate expenditures. An increase in any of the following will cause the level of income to increase.

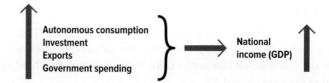

Of course, a decrease in any of the above items will cause a multiple decrease in income. Furthermore, an increase in either of the following will cause a decrease in national income.

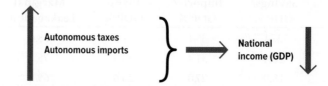

And a decrease in either of them will cause an increase in national income. The size of the increase or decrease is determined by the value of the multiplier. Finally, the value of the multiplier will *increase* if any of the following *decrease:*

- marginal propensity to save
- marginal tax rate
- marginal propensity to import

The above summary brings out the essence of the expenditures model. Income depends on the level of autonomous spending; if this spending changes, income will change by some multiplied amount. That is to say, small changes can have a larger effect on the level of income.

IN A NUTSHELL ...

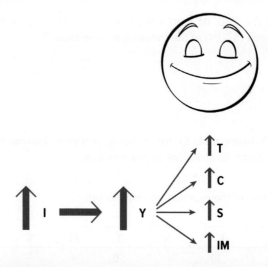

Also, we realize that the model demonstrates that the macroeconomy is always driving income to its equilibrium level. But we should add a cautionary note by asking: Is it a desirable level of income? Not necessarily. Simply because an economy is at an expenditure equilibrium tells us nothing about how well it is performing. As we saw in Chapter 5, an economy might be in equilibrium but perform well below its potential, that is, suffer a recessionary gap. Conversely, it might be above potential and suffering an inflationary gap. This is the message of Keynesian economics: though competitive markets naturally tend to move toward equilibrium, they do not necessarily move toward full employment. In fact, according to Keynes, the only way to move toward full employment is by achieving the *right level* of aggregate expenditures. This is a topic we will explore in detail in Chapters 7 and 9.

TEST YOUR UNDERSTANDING

11. a) Which of the following circumstances would lead to an increase in national income?

   i) an increase in the marginal propensity to import

   ii) an increase in autonomous consumption

   iii) a decrease in the marginal tax rate

   iv) a decrease in government spending

   v) an increase in the marginal propensity to consume

   vi) a decrease in investment

b) Which of them would result in an increase in the size of the multiplier?

SECTION SUMMARY

a) Government spending is regarded as wholly autonomous with respect to national income. Taxes, however, are partly autonomous and partly induced.

b) The marginal tax rate (MTR) is defined as ratio of change in taxes to a change in income.

c) Exports are regarded as wholly autonomous with respect to national income.

d) The marginal propensity to import (MPM) is defined as ratio of change in imports to a change in income.

e) The MPE for the full model is equal to MPC − MPM.

f) Changes in exports are a result of comparable price levels the value of the exchange rate income levels abroad.

g) National income will increase as a result of an increase in autonomous C, I, G, or X a decrease in autonomous T or IM.

h) The size of the multiplier will increase as a result of a decrease in the MPS, MPM, or MTR.

6.5 Deriving Aggregate Demand

> **LO5** Derive aggregate demand from aggregate expenditures.

To wrap up this chapter, let us show how aggregate demand, which we looked at in Chapter 5, is an extension of, and is derived from, aggregate expenditures.

We have already discussed three ways that a change in the price level can have an impact on total expenditures. We saw that an increase in the price level reduces the level of real consumption by affecting the real value of money balances. In addition, we know that a change in domestic prices affects net exports: a higher domestic price reduces exports and increases imports. Finally, we noted that higher prices will push up interest rates and reduce investment spending.

We now want to show explicitly how a price change affects aggregate demand. Since aggregate demand equals the amount of aggregate expenditures at various price levels, we want to find the quantity of aggregate expenditures at price levels P_1, P_2, P_3, and so on. **Figure 6.11** shows how we can derive an aggregate demand curve directly from the expenditures equilibrium diagram.

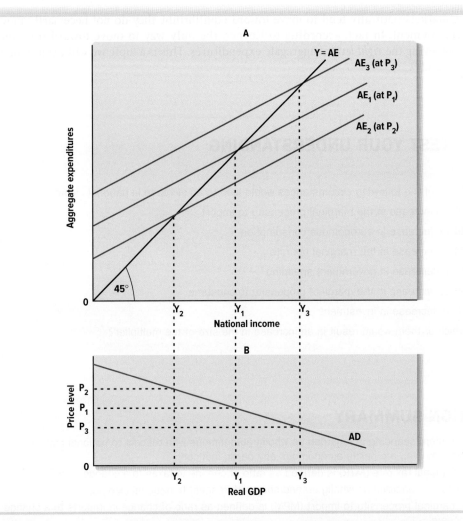

FIGURE 6.11   The Aggregate Expenditures and Aggregate Demand Curve

This graph shows that at price P_1, equilibrium GDP is Y_1. A higher price of P_2 lowers aggregate expenditures to AE_2 and leads to a lower income of Y_2. A lower price of P_3 increases aggregate expenditures to AE_3 and increases income to Y_3.

In this graph, we see that joining these points produces a downward-sloping aggregate demand curve.

In **Figure 6.11A**, the initial expenditure equilibrium is at Y_1, where AE_1 crosses the $Y = AE$ (45°) line. This spending is done at a particular price level. Let us call this level P_1 and show in **Figure 6.11B** that when the price level is P_1, equilibrium real GDP is at Y_1. (You should note that we have made a change in the way we label the horizontal axes. When we use aggregate expenditures on the Keynesian 45° graph, the horizontal axis is labelled National Income. When we use the aggregate demand graph, we label the horizontal axis Real GDP. Of course, real GDP and real income are conceptually the same, but this change will help you keep the two graphs distinct.)

Now, we want to figure out the effect on aggregate expenditures if the price level is higher. We just mentioned that a higher price reduces the real value of money balances (as well as other assets denominated in money). Earlier in the chapter, we called this the *real-balances effect* and suggested that the result of people holding assets with reduced values will be a reduction in their consumption spending. In addition, higher domestic prices also make our products less competitive in international markets so that the value of exports will fall and domestic consumers will be encouraged to buy comparatively cheaper foreign goods. It will also lower investment because interest rates will rise. As a result, net exports will decline.

Lower consumption, lower net exports, and lower investment will mean a lower level of aggregate expenditures at each level of income. This implies a downward shift in the aggregate expenditure curve, as shown in **Figure 6.11A**, from AE_1 to AE_2. This results in a lower level of real income, from Y_1 to Y_2. Therefore, we see in **Figure 6.11B** that a higher price level, P_2, is matched with a corresponding lower real GDP of Y_2. A lower price level will produce the opposite results: it will cause real balances, consumption spending, investment, and net exports to increase in value. A lower price level will therefore shift the AE curve up from the original AE_1 to AE_3. This leads to a higher equilibrium income level, Y_3. **Figure 6.11B** shows that a lower price level (P_3) means a higher level of real GDP (Y_3). As you can now see, every point on the aggregate demand curve is a point of equilibrium between aggregate expenditures and income. Simply put, the aggregate demand curve is downward sloping because consumption, net exports, and investment are inversely related to the price level.

TEST YOUR UNDERSTANDING

12. Which of the following will increase if prices fall, and why?

   a) exports

   b) investment

   c) government spending

   d) imports

   e) consumption

SECTION SUMMARY

We can derive the *aggregate demand curve* used in the previous chapter from the aggregate expenditures graph.

Study Guide

Review

WHAT'S THE BIG IDEA?

One of the main ideas in this chapter is that GDP (and income) are greatly affected by changes in spending. But the chapter also tries to show the interrelationship of things in the economy. For instance, a change in a country's GDP will also affect the government's tax revenues, the total amount of consumer spending, and the amount of savings and imports. But it is a two-way street: a change in spending—particularly a change in investment, government spending, or exports—will impact GDP. In a modern economy, it is often a change in those autonomous (independent-of-income) elements that bring about change. A rise in exports (over which we have little control) will cause an increase in GDP and income, which will in turn raise tax revenues, consumption, savings, and imports.

The other big idea in this chapter is that of the multiplier, whereby a small change in autonomous spending can lead to even bigger changes in income. The reason for this is that spending by one person becomes another person's income. But the story doesn't end there. The person who receives the additional income will mostly spend a good portion of it, which then becomes a third person's income, and so on. But the size of this multiplier will be reduced if people's spending "leaks" into taxes or savings, or goes to buy imported foreign products.

NEW GLOSSARY TERMS AND KEY EQUATIONS

autonomous spending (expenditures)   induced spending   marginal propensity to save
balance of trade   marginal leakage rate   marginal tax rate
consumption function   marginal propensity to consume   saving function
dis-saving   marginal propensity to expend   unplanned investment
expenditure equilibrium   marginal propensity to import   wealth effect

Equations:

[6.1]   Total spending (aggregate expenditures) = autonomous spending + induced spending

[6.2]   Marginal propensity to consume (MPC) = $\dfrac{\Delta \text{ consumption}}{\Delta \text{ income}}$

[6.3]   Marginal propensity to save (MPS) = $\dfrac{\Delta \text{ saving}}{\Delta \text{ income}}$

[6.4]   (In a closed, private economy) MPC + MPS = 1

[6.5]   Marginal propensity to expend (MPE) = $\dfrac{\Delta \text{ aggregate expenditures}}{\Delta \text{ income}}$

[6.6]   Marginal leakage rate (MLR) = $\dfrac{\Delta \text{ total leakages}}{\Delta \text{ income}}$

[6.7]   Marginal leakage rate (MLR) = (1 − MPE)

[6.8]   Multiplier = $\dfrac{\Delta \text{ income}}{\Delta \text{ autonomous expenditures}}$

[6.9]   Multiplier = $\dfrac{1}{(\text{MLR})}$ or $\dfrac{1}{(1 - \text{MPE})}$

[6.10]   Total taxes = autonomous taxes + induced taxes

[6.11]   Marginal tax rate (MTR) = $\dfrac{\Delta \text{ taxes}}{\Delta \text{ income}}$

[6.12] $Y_D = (Y - T)$

[6.13]   Marginal propensity to import (MPM) = $\dfrac{\Delta \text{ imports (IM)}}{\Delta \text{ income (Y)}}$

[6.14]   Marginal propensity to expend (MPE) = MPC − MPM

[6.15]   Marginal leakage rate (MLR) = MPS + MTR + MPM

Comprehensive Problem

Questions

(LO 4) Table 6.9 shows some of the expenditure amounts in the economy of Arkinia. The MPC, the MTR, and the MPM are all constant, as are the values of the three injections.

TABLE 6.9

Y	T	Y_D	C	S	I	G	X	IM	X_N	AE ($C + I + G + X_N$)
0	—	—	—	—	60	150	50	—	—	—
100	—	50	—	−10	—	—	—	—	30	—
200	75	—	120	5	—	—	—	—	—	—
300	100	—	180	—	—	—	—	40	—	—
400	125	—	—	35	—	—	—	50	—	—
500	—	—	300	—	—	—	—	60	—	—
600	—	425	—	—	—	—	—	—	—	—
700	—	—	420	—	—	—	—	—	—	—
800	—	575	—	95	—	—	—	—	−40	—

a) Complete **Table 6.9**, and in **Figure 6.12** graph a 45° line and the aggregate expenditure function, labelled AE_1. Identify expenditure equilibrium with the letter e_1.

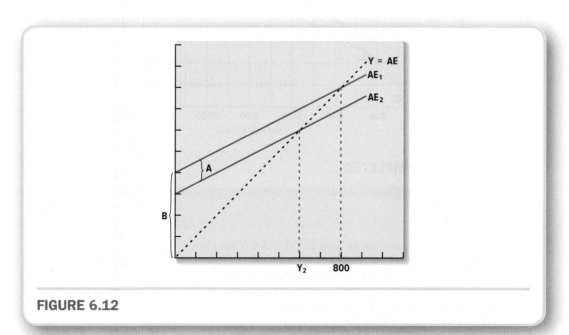

FIGURE 6.12

b) What is the value of equilibrium income?
c) What are the values of total injections and total leakages at equilibrium?
d) What is the value of the MPE in Arkinia?
e) What is the value of the multiplier in Arkinia?

Answers

a) See the following table and figure:

TABLE 6.9 (COMPLETED)

Y	T	Y_D	C	S	I	G	X	IM	X_N	AE $(C + I + G + X_N)$
0	25	−25	0	−25	60	150	50	10	40	250
100	50	50	60	−10	60	150	50	20	30	300
200	75	125	120	5	60	150	50	30	20	350
300	100	200	180	20	60	150	50	40	10	400
400	125	275	240	35	60	150	50	50	0	450
500	150	350	300	50	60	150	50	60	−10	500
600	175	425	360	65	60	150	50	70	−20	550
700	200	500	420	80	60	150	50	80	−30	600
800	225	575	480	95	60	150	50	90	−40	650

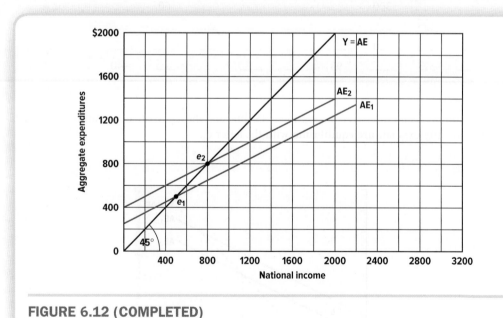

FIGURE 6.12 (COMPLETED)

b) Income: $500
   Equilibrium national income can be seen in Table 6.9 (Completed) where Y (national income) is equal to AE_1, which in this case is $500. In Figure 6.12 (Completed) this is at e_1, where the AE curve intersects the 45° line, which is also at an income level of $500.
c) Reading the values from Table 6.9 (Completed) for income level of $500 shows the following:
   Total injections: I (60) + G (150) + X (50) = $260
   Total leakages: S (50) + T (150) + IM (60) = $260

d) MPE: 0.5
   (Aggregate expenditures (AE) changes by 50 for every change of $100 in income (Y), which is 50/100 or 0.5.)
e) Multiplier: 2
   (The value of the MLR is $(1 - 0.5) = 0.5$, and therefore the value of the multiplier is $1/0.5 = 2$.)

Questions

f) Suppose that exports from Arkinia were to increase by $150. Draw the new aggregate expenditure function on **Figure** 6.12, and label it AE_2. Identify the new expenditure equilibrium as e_2.
g) What is the value of the new equilibrium income, and at equilibrium, what is the value of net exports?

Answers

f) See **Figure 6.12 (Completed)**.
g) Income: $800; net exports: + $110
   The new equilibrium income occurs where the new AE_2 curve intersects the 45° line, which is at an income of $800. (Since the multiplier is 2, an increase in exports of $150 will increase equilibrium income by $2 \times \$150$, or $300 to the new value of $800.) **Table 6.9 (Completed)** shows that imports increase by $10 for every $100 increase in the level of income (the marginal propensity to import is 0.1). Therefore, if income increases by $300, imports will increase by 300×0.1 or $30 to $90. Net exports will equal exports of $200 (an increase of 150 from 50) minus imports of $90.

Study Problems

Find answers on the McGraw-Hill online resource.

Basic (Problems 1–8)

1. **(LO 4)** The economy of Irinika has the following parameters:
   Autonomous exports = $400 million
   Autonomous imports = $100 million
   MPM = 0.25
   a) What is the balance of trade at an income of $800? _____
   b) What is the balance of trade at an income of $2000? _____
   c) At what income level is there a zero balance of trade? _____

2. **(LO 1)** Use the information in **Table** 6.10 to answer questions about the economy of Watis.

   TABLE 6.10

Y	C	S
0	40	____
50	70	____
100	____	____
150	____	20
200	____	40

   a) Complete the table assuming that the MPC is constant.
   b) What are the values of the MPC and MPS?
      MPC: _____
      MPS: _____
   c) What are the equations for the consumption function and the saving function?
      C = _____
      S = _____

3. **(LO 1)** Figure 6.13 shows the saving function for an economy.

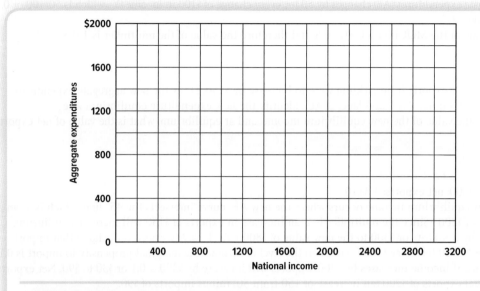

FIGURE 6.13

a) Complete Table 6.11.

TABLE 6.11

National Income	Consumption	Saving
0	——	——
100	——	——
200	——	——
300	——	——
400	——	——
500	——	——
600	——	——
700	——	——
800	——	——

b) Add the consumption function to Figure 6.12.

4. **(LO 3)** The simple economy of Altria shown in Table 6.12 has no government or taxes and no international trade. Its investment is autonomous and its MPC is constant.

TABLE 6.12

Y	C	S	I	AE
0	100	——	150	——
200	250	——	——	——
400	——	0	——	——
600	——	——	——	——
800	——	——	——	——
1000	——	100	——	——

a) Complete Table 6.12.
b) What is the value of expenditures equilibrium? _____
c) What is the value of the multiplier? _____

5. **(LO 3)** The following are the parameters for the simple economy of Minnerva, which has no government involvement and no international trade:

$$C = 240 + 0.68Y \qquad I = 440$$

a) What is the value of expenditures equilibrium?
b) What is the value of the multiplier?
c) If investment increases by 80, what will be the new value of expenditures equilibrium?

6. **(LO 2)** Suppose that a simple economy has the following parameters:

$$C = 100 + 0.5Y \qquad I = 300$$

a) Complete Table 6.13.

TABLE 6.13

Y	C	S	I	AE
0	——	——	——	——
100	——	——	——	——
200	——	——	——	——
300	——	——	——	——
400	——	——	——	——
500	——	——	——	——
600	——	——	——	——
700	——	——	——	——
800	——	——	——	——
900	——	——	——	——
1000	——	——	——	——

b) What is the value of expenditures equilibrium? _____
c) What are the values of injections and leakages at expenditures equilibrium? _____

7. **(LO 3)** Irkania's aggregate expenditures function is shown in Figure 6.14.

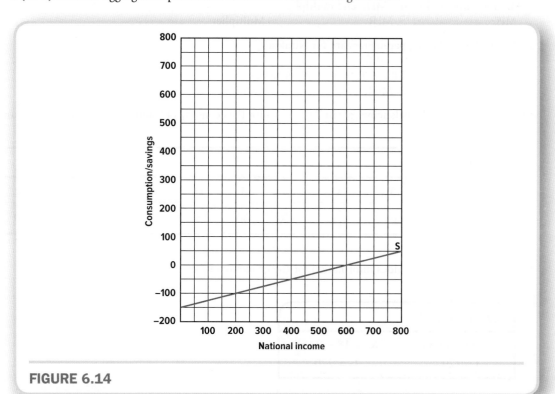

FIGURE 6.14

a) What is the value of equilibrium income? _____

b) What is the value of the multiplier in Irkania? _____

c) If investment were to increase by $2000, draw in the new AE curve labelled AE_2.

d) What is the new level of equilibrium income? _____

8. **(LO 4)** The partial data in Table 6.14 are for the economy of Arinaka. Planned investment, government spending, and *all* taxes are autonomous. Furthermore, you may assume that the MPC, MPS, and MPM are constant.

TABLE 6.14

Y	T	Y_D	C	S	I	G	X_N	AE	Unplanned Investment
$400	$40	____	$320	$40	$60	$50	+$10	____	____
450	____	____	____	45	____	____	−5	____	____
500	____	____	____	____	____	____	____	____	____
550	____	____	____	____	____	____	____	____	____

a) Fill in the blanks in Table 6.14.

b) What is the value of equilibrium income? _____

c) If planned investment decreases by 20, what is the new value of equilibrium income?

_____

Intermediate (Problems 9–13)

9. **(LO 4)** Suppose that $T = 120 + 0.2Y$; $G = 680$; $IM = 100 + 0.15Y$; and $X = 550$.

a) What is the trade balance (X − IM) when the government's budget is balanced? $_____

b) What is the government's budget balance (T − G) when the trade balance is zero?

$_____

10. **(LO 4)** In Arkania, income rose by $200 million over the past year. During the same period, tax revenue increased by $40 million, savings rose by $16 million, and imports rose by $24 million. What are the values of its MPE, MLR, and multiplier?

MPE: _____ MLR: _____ Multiplier: _____

11. **(LO 4)** The following parameters are for Nirakia:

MPC = 0.675 and MPM = 0.175

What are the values of its MPE, MLR, and multiplier?

MPE: _____ MLR: _____ Multiplier: _____

12. **(LO 4)** Complete the balancing row in Table 6.15 for the economy of Kaniria, which is in equilibrium.

TABLE 6.15

Y	T	Y_D	C	S	I	G	X	IM	X_N	AE
____	____	____	____	110	80	180	____	80	10	800

13. **(LO 4)** Table 6.16 provides information for the economy of Zawi.

TABLE 6.16

$C = 42 + 0.65Y$	$X_N = 18 − 0.15Y$
$I = 120$	$G = 220$

a) What is the value of equilibrium income? _____

b) Set up a balancing row to verify your calculations (the tax equation is T = 60 + 0.2Y and X = 200).

Y	AE
— — — — — — — — — — —	

c) If exports decrease by 50, what is the new equilibrium income? _____

Advanced (Problems 14–17)

14. **(LO 3)** Figure 6.15 shows the economy of Itassuna.

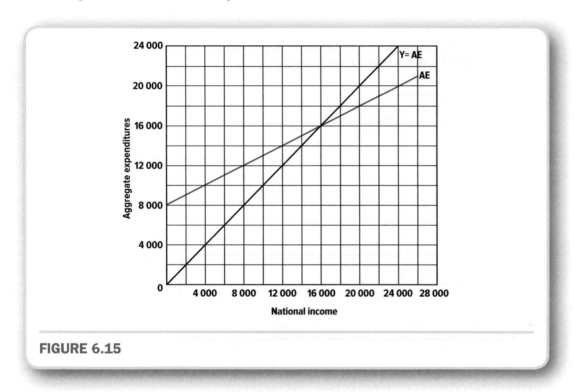

FIGURE 6.15

a) If the value of A is 50 and the multiplier is 4, what is the value of Y_2? _____

b) If the value of Y_2 is 700 and the value of A is 60, what is the value of the multiplier? _____

c) Given AE_1, if the value of the multiplier is 2, what is the value of B? _____

15. **(LO 4)** Table 6.17 shows the parameters for the economy of Hutu.

TABLE 6.17

C = 80 + 0.6Y	X_N = 140 − 0.1Y
I = 200	G = 300

a) What is the value of equilibrium income? _____

b) If exports were to increase by 30, what would be the new value of equilibrium income? _____

c) Given your answer in (b), what is the new value for X_N? _____

d) Given the equilibrium income in (a), if full-employment income is 1350, what change in government spending is necessary to move the economy to this level? _____

16. **(LO 4)** The data in Table 6.18 are for the economy of Nubia.

TABLE 6.18

Y	T	Y_D	C	S	I	G	X	IM	X_N	AE
0	50	−50	20	−70	60	70	100	50	+50	____
100	60	40	92	−52	60	70	100	62	+38	____
200	70	130	164	−34	60	70	100	74	+26	____
300	80	220	236	−16	60	70	100	86	+14	____
400	90	310	308	+2	60	70	100	98	+2	____

a) Complete the AE column.
b) Write out expressions for the tax function, the consumption function (related to national income [Y]), the net export function, and the AE function.
   T = _____
   C = _____
   X_N = _____ A_E = _____
c) Use algebra to find out the value of equilibrium income.
   Y = _____

17. **(LO 4)** In the economy of Akron, the tax and savings functions are as follows:
   T = 200 + 0.2Y   S = −170 + 0.3Y
   a) What is the equation for the consumption function?
      C = _____
   b) If Y = 1000, complete the following table:

TABLE 6.19

Y	T	Y_D	C	S
1000	____	____	____	____

Problems for Further Study

Basic (Problems 1–2)

1. **(LO 1)** What is meant by *autonomous expenditures*?

2. **(LO 4)** Explain *marginal propensity to import*. What is the formula for calculating it?

Intermediate (Problems 3–7)

3. **(LO 2)** What is meant by the term *expenditures equilibrium*? What are the three equivalent ways of expressing it?

4. **(LO 3)** What four factors will cause a change in autonomous consumption?

5. **(LO 3)** If the AE curve is relatively flat, what does this suggest about the size of the multiplier? Explain.

6. **(LO 4)** Which of the following would lead to a decrease in national income?
   a) an increase in imports
   b) a decrease in interest rates
   c) a decrease in the money supply
   d) an increase in the exchange rate
   e) a decrease in foreign incomes

7. **(LO 4)** Which of the following would increase the value of the multiplier?
   a) an increase in the marginal tax rate
   b) an increase in the marginal propensity to save
   c) an increase in the marginal propensity to consume
   d) a decrease in the marginal propensity to import

Advanced (Problems 8–10)

8. **(LO 4)** The following data provide information on Akinira's economy in a particular year:

Y = $500	Investment spending = $100
Savings = $120	Government spending = $200
Taxes = $180	Balance of trade = +$70

   a) Explain which variables depend on others.
   b) Is the economy in equilibrium, and what has happened to the country's level of inventories in this particular year?
   c) Comment on what implications this might have for the following year's GDP.

9. **(LO 4)** What is the difference between expenditures equilibrium and full-employment equilibrium?

10. **(LO 4)** "Any factor that shifts the AE function also shifts the AD function." True or false? Explain.

CHAPTER 7
Fiscal Policy

LEARNING OBJECTIVES

At the end of this chapter, you should be able to:

LO1 Describe why the federal government's budget depends on three factors: the rate of taxation, the size of the GDP, and its own spending levels.

LO2 Explain the pros and cons of a budget policy aimed at achieving full-employment equilibrium.

LO3 Explain the pros and cons of a budget policy aimed at achieving a balanced budget in each fiscal year.

LO4 Explain the pros and cons of a budget policy aimed at achieving both full employment and a balanced budget over the life of the business cycle.

LO5 Discuss the cause, size, and problems of the national debt.

 WHAT'S AHEAD...

We now turn to one of most important tasks of governments around the world—making economic policy. The focus here is on fiscal policy, which refers to the government's approach to spending and taxation: in short, government's annual budget. We begin by defining several important terms, including net tax revenue, budget deficits, surpluses, and national debt, and then go on to discuss what can cause each of these to change. We then examine two distinct approaches to the use of fiscal policy, including the shortcomings of each one. This leads to a discussion of a third, compromise policy. We end with a discussion of the national debt.

A QUESTION OF RELEVANCE ...

Do you remember what you were doing the evening the last federal budget was unveiled in Parliament? Probably not. Furthermore, you quite likely think "it has nothing to do with me." Yet the truth is that government's annual budget affects you more than almost any other regularly scheduled event in your life, other than such personal events as birthdays and anniversaries. It determines the taxes you pay, the chances of your getting a job next summer, the likelihood of getting a student loan, and even the size of your classes next year. This chapter will help you learn more about the budget.

It is a truism that governments have to spend, and therefore they have to tax. So what should the government's attitude be toward its own spending and taxation? How small or large should this spending and taxation be? Should the two be equal? Does the condition of the economy have anything to do with the answers to these questions? For example, when the economy is in the middle of a recession with high unemployment—as was the case just a few short years ago—what should the attitude of government be? Should government decrease its own spending, increase it, or change nothing? Alternatively, should we expect it to cut taxes, to increase taxes, or to change nothing? These are the types of questions we will be looking at in this chapter. But first, we need to define some terms.

 ADDED DIMENSION

How Much Does Your Government Spend? Canada Compared to the United States

There is much discussion today about the growing size of government spending, which often morphs into a political debate about whether this is a welcome result of growing affluence (we are richer now and can "buy" more government-provided services) or a threat to future prosperity (will this mean higher taxes that will stunt economic growth). Comparisons between Canada and the United States are also often mixed into this debate.

Let us make some comparisons. Before World War II, the size of government spending as a percentage of GDP was below 15 percent in both countries. Today, the percentages are around 35 percent in Canada and 32 percent in the United States Clearly, government spending has grown considerably. If we look at the major categories of spending we may get an insight into why.

In the years before World War II, income security (social assistance and public pensions) and public health expenditures were nearly nonexistent, while education expenses were much smaller than today. As short as this explanation is, it just about sums up the growth in government spending over the past hundred years. People have access to comprehensive health care, more kids are completing high school and going into higher education, and we now have a public pension program; thus government spending as a percentage of GDP has increased. And what are the major differences in public spending between the United States and Canada? In this country, we have more income security (11 percent of GDP compared to 7 percent) and less national defence (1.2 percent compared to 4 percent).

Category of Spending	Percentage of GDP: Canada	Percentage of GDP: U.S.
Income security	11	7
Education, health, and general public service	15	15
Housing, culture, and recreation	1.5	0.8
Public safety	2	2
National defence	1.2	4

Source: Data derived by authors from information found in Department of Finance Canada, Working Paper 2003–05. Department of Finance, The Minister of Public Works and Government Services, 2011.

7.1   Fiscal Policy and the Budget

> **LO1**   Describe why the federal government's budget depends on three factors: the rate of taxation, the size of the GDP, and its own spending.

Fiscal policy refers to a government's approach toward its own spending and taxation. When the minister of finance brings down the budget in Parliament each spring, this reveals government's fiscal policy for the coming year. The annual projected budget contains estimates of government revenues and expenditures. Budget day is headline news, and TV screens across the country are filled with political comments about how good or bad the new budget is.

Table 7.1 shows the federal government's budgeted expenses and revenues for the fiscal year ending March 31, 2016. All figures are actual revenues and expenditures in billions of dollars.

Revenues are government's total receipts, which were $291.2 billion for the fiscal year 2015–2016, which began on April 1, 2015. This figure represents approximately 14.9 percent of Canada's GDP in 2015. These revenues do not include the CPP payments that are made by Canadians, since this program is administered independently of the budget. By far the largest source of revenue is *personal income tax* which came to $142.7 billion, while *EI premiums* are $23.0 billion. *Corporate income and other taxes* are taxes on profits paid by companies and non-residents; they totalled $45.1 billion. GST and excise taxes of $49.8 billion include the federal sales tax as well as excise taxes on gasoline, alcohol, and cigarettes, plus tariff revenues on certain imports. *Nontax revenues*, at $30.6 billion, include income from government Crown corporations and other government investments, plus Bank of Canada earnings.

Total expenses were $296.6 billion. *Transfers to persons* totalled $83.1 billion and include payments toward Old Age Security, Guaranteed Annual Income Supplements, Spouse's

William Francis Morneau, Minister of Finance since November 2015.

The Canadian Press/Adrian Wyld

TABLE 7.1
Federal Government's Budget for Fiscal Year Ending March 2016 ($billions)

REVENUES	
Personal income taxes	142.7
Corporate and other income taxes	45.1
EI premiums	23.0
GST, excise, and energy taxes	49.8
Nontax revenues	30.6
Total Revenues	**291.2**
EXPENSES	
Transfers to persons	83.1
Spending grants to other levels of government	65.8
Public debt charges	25.7
Direct program spending	122.0
Total Expenses	**296.6**
Budget Deficit	**5.4**

Source: Department of Finance Canada, *Annual Financial Report 2015–16*. Reproduced with the permission of the Department of Finance, 2016.

Allowances, and the EI program. Once again, CPP payments are not included here. *Spending grants to other levels of government*, at $65.8 billion, was the amount of spending on postsecondary education, health, and social assistance, as well as equalization payments, which are aimed at six provinces (all but Alberta, B.C., Newfoundland, and Saskatchewan). Aid to the developing nations and dues to international organizations, such as the United Nations, are also included in this category. *Public debt charges*, at $25.7 billion, are the interest payments on government's national debt; these are also treated as a form of transfer payment in national income accounting. The last item, *direct program spending* of $112.0 billion, is part of the total spending on goods and services (G) that we first identified in the circular flow treatment in Chapter 3 and includes everything from computers for government offices to salaries of the civil servants working in those offices. The total budget deficit for the year is $5.4 billion, with total government expenses exceeding total revenues. This compares with a surplus of $1.9 billion for the previous year.

The distribution of revenues and expenses is shown in the following pie graph.

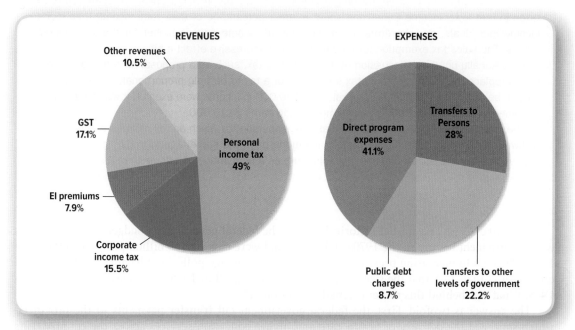

Source: Adapted from Public Accounts of Canada, Department of Finance 2015.

Let us now define some of the important terms we will be using. You may recall from Chapter 3 that net tax revenue is defined as the total tax revenue received by government less transfer payments.

$$NTR = \text{tax revenue} - \text{transfer payments} \qquad [7.1]$$

Government's budget balance is defined as the difference between net tax revenues and government spending:

$$\text{Budget balance} = NTR - G \qquad [7.2]$$

A positive balance means a **budget surplus**, since net tax revenue would be greater than spending on goods and services. Conversely, a negative balance means a **budget deficit**, since net tax revenues would be lower than government spending. It is important to note that government tax revenues, spending, and the deficit (or surplus) are all flows because they occur over a period of time. If we were to add up all the deficit flows over the years and then subtract the sum of all the surpluses over the same period, we would get the **national debt**. The national debt, or, as it is sometimes called, the *public debt*, is a stock concept because it is the total outstanding at any particular point in time and is the summation of the flows of all previous deficits and surpluses. We will return to this topic toward the end of the chapter.

ADDED DIMENSION

Types of Taxes

A quick glance at **Table 7.1** shows that by far the largest source of tax revenue individual Canadians pay, and the federal government collects, is the personal income tax. It is what economists call a *progressive* tax, which means the higher one's income, the higher the percentage of income paid in tax. Those who have incomes of $100 000 obviously pay more total taxes than those whose incomes are $40 000. But because the Canadian income tax is progressive, they also pay a higher percentage of their income. The rationale is that the level of sacrifice of paying the tax is thereby made more equal. The more tax loopholes available to higher-income taxpayers in the income tax code (RSP contributions, for example), the less progressive the income tax.

Canada's GST and the excise tax on gasoline (as well as the provincial sales taxes) are *regressive* taxes in that lower-income Canadians spent a larger percentage of their total income than higher-income individuals, and therefore the percentage of income paid is higher for the lower-income groups. The sales tax exemption for food reduces this regressive effect a bit.

Occasionally you hear discussion of a *proportional* tax, such as a proposal for a flat-rate income tax, to replace the existing income tax structure. For a tax to be truly proportional, all income would have to be taxed at a flat rate—if the first, say, $20 000 in income were exempt, it would mean more to someone earning $25 000 than to someone who earns $125 000.

The most regressive of all taxes is a flat-rate-per-person tax, such as toll charges on bridges and highways or parking ticket fines, whereby everyone pays the same amount regardless of income. With such a tax, the poorer pay considerably more as a percentage of income than the wealthier.

In **Figure 7.1** we take a brief historical look at the federal government's budget balance. Deficits were a permanent feature in the 1970s and 1980s, and were close to $40 billion per year in the early 1990s. This led to increasing pressure on government to change policy and balance the budget. You can see in **Figure 7.1A** that the size of the deficit started to fall in 1995 and turned into a surplus in 1998. What was behind this rather dramatic turnaround?

The answer is twofold. First, the federal government cut transfer payments to the provinces, which squeezed the delivery of health care and higher education services across the country. This resulted in growing waiting lists for surgery and a reduction in the number of hospital beds, while college and university classes grew in size and professors' salaries were frozen. Second, despite the cut in government spending, the rate of economic growth, fuelled by increased exports to the United States, accelerated and raised government revenues, since more people were working and paying income tax and total spending was up, which meant more consumption tax (GST/HST) revenue.

As the twenty-first century began, government faced a new issue: debate over what to do with the budget surpluses. In 2008, after eleven consecutive years of budget surpluses, the country, along with all other industrialized nations, entered a severe recession with the result that the government started to run up deficits as tax revenues fell and spending on income support programs rose. In addition to this, the government embarked on the Canada Action Plan, which was designed to stimulate the economy by pumping in over $60 billion (over two years) of extra government spending. The result was Canada's highest budget deficit ever, in 2009–10. However, as the Canadian economy recovered, so too did its budget position and the deficits reduced; by 2015 a budget surplus had been produced.

However, why Canada's national debt has grown so much in the last thirty years, as shown in **Figure 7.1B**, is the topic of a deeper discussion at the end of this chapter.

Changes in the Economy and Government Revenues

It is important to emphasize that changes in the economy can have an impact on government revenues. A prime example of this occurred between the budget years of 1996 and 1997. In those two

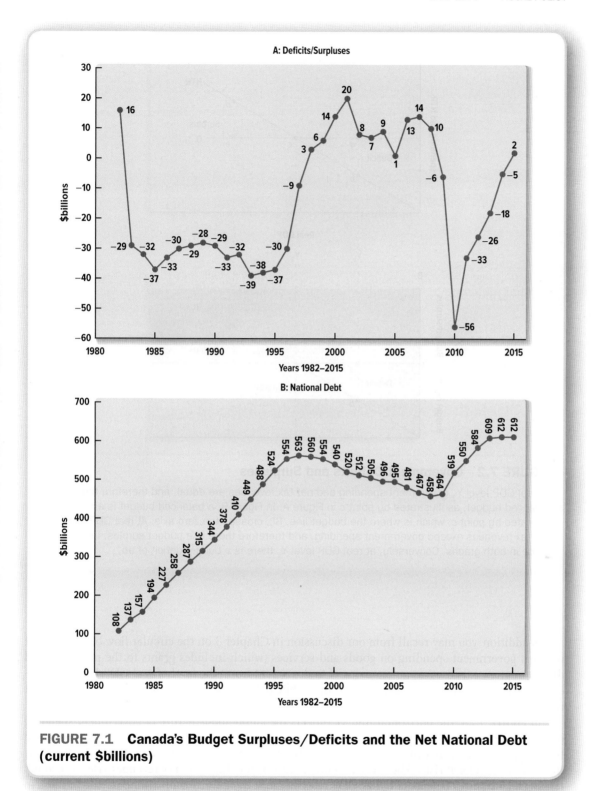

FIGURE 7.1 Canada's Budget Surpluses/Deficits and the Net National Debt (current $billions)

Source: Department of Finance Canada, *Fiscal Reference Tables*, September 2015. Reproduced with the permission of the Department of Finance, 2016.

years, the size of the budget deficit dropped from $30 billion to $9 billion. As we mentioned, while transfer payments did decrease, the reduction in the deficit was greatly helped by the continued growth in the economy, which raised government revenues. This illustrates an important generalization in the model we are building:

NTR and GDP are directly related.

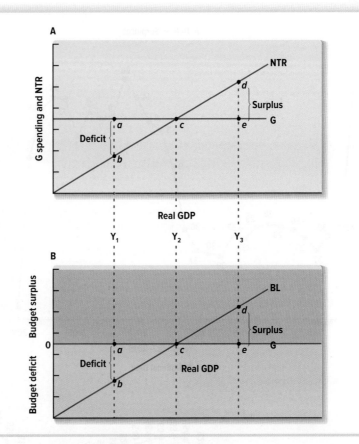

FIGURE 7.2   Government Deficits and Surpluses

At real GDP level Y$_2$ government spending and net tax revenues are equal, and therefore there is a balanced budget, as illustrated by point c in Figure A. In Figure B, a balanced budget is also indicated by point c, which is where the budget line, BL, crosses the zero axis. At real GDP level Y$_3$ net tax revenues exceed government spending, and therefore there is a budget surplus, indicated by de in both graphs. Conversely, at real GDP level Y$_1$ there is a budget deficit of ab.

In addition, you may recall from our discussion in Chapter 3 on the circular flow of income that we treat government spending on goods and services (which includes grants to the provinces and direct program expenses) as autonomous of (independent from) the level of real GDP. However, government transfer payments to persons and the public debt charges are deducted from NTR. We put revenue and spending together in **Figure 7.2**.

In **Figure 7.2A**, the horizontal line, G, reflects the autonomous nature of government spending on goods and services. We also have assumed that when GDP is zero, so too are tax revenues and transfer payments so that the net tax revenues (NTR) line begins at the origin. Note that the NTR line rises as real GDP rises. There are two main reasons for this: first, tax revenues rise as incomes rise; second, transfer payments fall as GDP rises, because the government will be paying out less in terms of EI and welfare payments. At a GDP level of Y$_1$, NTR is less than the level of government spending, and there would be a budget deficit equal to ab. At a GDP level of Y$_3$, NTR exceeds G, and there would be a budget surplus equal to de. When GDP is at a level indicated by Y$_2$, there would be neither a budget surplus nor a deficit, as illustrated by point c. The effect of different levels of GDP on the budget itself is shown explicitly in the budget line in **Figure 7.2B**. You will recall from Chapter 6 that the budget line shows the budget balance (NTR minus G) explicitly at all levels of GDP: the same deficit, ab, at GDP level Y$_1$ and the same surplus, de, at GDP level Y$_3$. Point c on both figures represents a **balanced budget**.

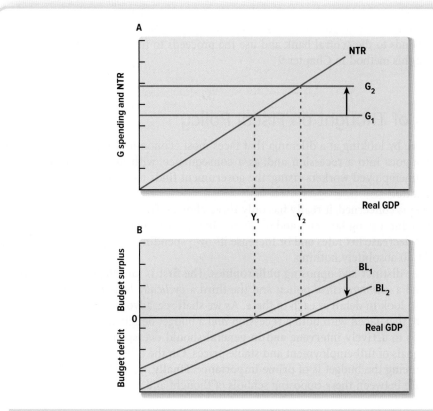

FIGURE 7.3   The Effect of an Increase in Government Spending

An increase in government spending shifts the G line up from G$_1$ to G$_2$ in Figure A, and as a result shifts down the budget line from BL$_1$ to BL$_2$ in Figure B.

Figure 7.2 shows that there are two things besides the level of GDP that will affect a government's budget and therefore the position of the budget line: a change in either the amount of government spending or net tax revenues. An increase in government spending, for instance, will increase the amount of the budget deficit (or reduce the surplus) at every level of GDP and result in the budget line shifting down. This is shown in **Figure 7.3**. Here we see that an increase in government spending will shift the G curve up from G$_1$ to G$_2$. With the government increasing its level of spending, the budget deficit is higher (or the budget surplus lower) at each level of income. This means that the budget line shifts down from BL$_1$ to BL$_2$. (Note that shifts in the G line and the BL line are in the opposite direction.) The result is that the government is now able to achieve a balanced budget only at a higher level of income, at Y$_2$ instead of at Y$_1$.

You can perhaps work out for yourself that an increase in autonomous taxes would cause a smaller deficit (or increased surplus) at every level of income and is shown as a parallel shift upward in *both* the NTR line and the budget line. In contrast, an increase in the tax rate would also see a shift upward in both the NTR and budget lines; however, the shift would be greater at higher levels of GDP than at lower levels. We could call this an upward pivot in both lines. The essential point is that:

> The state of government's budget depends on the level of GDP in the economy as well as on tax rates and its own spending.

A question that often springs to people's minds at this point is: How is a government's budget deficit financed? There is no mystery. It is financed by borrowing. For example, when private institutions or individuals buy a government bond (such as a Canada Savings Bond or a treasury bill), they are, in effect, lending some of their savings to government so it can finance a deficit. A second way government can borrow is to sell bonds to the central bank and use the proceeds to finance spending. We will return to a discussion of this method in Chapter 9.

Three Schools of Thought on Fiscal Policy

Let us set the scene here by looking at a dilemma that faces most economies from time to time. Suppose that the country goes into a recession and, as a consequence, with tax revenues falling and transfer payments to unemployed workers rising, the government finds itself facing a serious budget deficit. What should it do?

As far as its budget is concerned, it really has only three choices. First, it might take aim directly at the budget deficit by increasing tax rates and/or decreasing its own spending. Second, it might do the exact opposite and decrease tax rates and/or increase its own spending. Third, as far as the budget is concerned, it might do absolutely nothing.

We have here three distinct and opposing philosophies. The first is known as a *balanced budget* fiscal policy, the second a *countercyclical* policy, and the third a *cyclically balanced* budget policy. In the next section we will look in detail at each of these. As we shall see, advocates of the countercyclical fiscal policy believe that, faced with both a recession *and* a budget deficit, the government's paramount responsibility is to actively intervene and in general should overspend in order to help the economy achieve the goals of full employment and stable prices. On the other hand, balanced budget advocates believe balancing the budget is of prime importance. Finally, we look at the views of those who offer a compromise between these opposing schools of thought and advocate a policy of a cyclically-balanced budget.

Let us begin by looking at countercyclical fiscal policy.

IT'S NEWS TO ME ...

In anticipation of the upcoming election (Nov. 2015) the Liberal party outlined the details of a $145.5 billion increased-spending plan as well some tax cuts aimed at middle income earners.

The bulk of the additional spending would be on numerous infrastructure projects ranging from highway and bridge building to new hospitals and education facilities.

The plan anticipates budget deficits in its first three years but a budget surplus by the end of the fourth year. To pay for increased spending a Liberal government would replace the Universal Child Care Benefit with a new program that would be based on family income and a tax increase on the wealthiest Canadians.

Source: *Star Power Reporting.* Fall 2015.

I. Which of the following accurately describes the planned increase in government spending on infrastructure projects?

a) It is expansionary fiscal policy that will raise the level of GDP.
b) It is contractionary fiscal policy that will lower the level of GDP.
c) It is expansionary fiscal policy that will lower the level of GDP.
d) It is contractionary fiscal policy that will raise the level of GDP.

II. Which of the following best describes the effect of replacing a universal child care benefit with one based on income?

a) It would hurt lower- and middle-income Canadians.
b) It would hurt all Canadians.
c) It would hurt higher-income Canadians.
d) It would help all Canadians

TEST YOUR UNDERSTANDING

Find answers on the McGraw-Hill online resource.

1. Draw a graph similar to **Figure 7.3**, showing the effect of a decrease in autonomous taxation.

2. Assume that current net tax revenues are $200 billion, government spending on goods and services is $180 billion, and the national debt at the beginning of the period was half the size of current net tax revenues. What is the size of the national debt at the end of the period?

3. Suppose that government spending is an autonomous $50 and net tax revenues are as shown in the table.

Real GDP	0	40	80	120	160
Net tax revenues	20	30	40	50	60
Budget balance	___	___	___	___	___

Complete the table, and plot the corresponding budget line.

SECTION SUMMARY

The state of the government's budget depends on

- its net tax revenues, which in turn depend on both the rate of taxation and the size of the GDP
- its own spending

7.2   Countercyclical Fiscal Policy

> **LO2**   Explain the pros and cons of a budget policy aimed at achieving full-employment equilibrium.

Interventionist philosophy is rooted in a very particular period of our history—the lost decade of the 1930s that we call the Great Depression. Prior to this devastating experience, the prevailing view was that government should play a minimal and "neutral" role in the economy—spend little and tax just enough to cover this minimal spending. But the Great Depression was a calamity. Millions of people were forced to the very edge of existence with unemployment rates as high as 25 percent and no social welfare net in place to buffer the fall in incomes. This rate is particularly ominous given that most families were dependent on a single wage earner. Prices were falling, yet producers' sales were dropping—manufacturers could not sell their cars, new house construction all but disappeared (despite record low interest rates), even farmers could not sell their food—and net investment in the economy became negative. Furthermore, this condition lasted the entire decade.

The result was that many people began to question the viability of capitalism as an economic system—and this was in the wake of "the ten days that shook the world"—the communist revolution in Russia. The fear that gripped society was not helped by the fact that economists as a group were frozen into silence, apparently unable to suggest what might be done to turn things around.

But there one economist was able to see through the fog. Using the analysis of the circular flow of income that you learned in Chapter 3, John Maynard Keynes built a model of the economy based on the level of aggregate expenditures: the familiar $AE = C + I + G + X_n$ equation. Keynes argued that the depression was caused by a series of events that dramatically reduced the level of AE in the economy and that only an increase in spending—an increase in aggregate demand—would pull the world's economies out of depression. He further reasoned that consumption (C) was not suddenly going to rise because unemployed people had little income to spend and that those who were still

Unemployed men line up waiting for a free meal in the 1930s.
© 2016 The Yonge Street Mission. All rights reserved.

employed were so frightened by the future that they held their spending to a minimum. Similarly, investment spending was not going to increase because no one would build new factories or buy new machinery when so many of the existing factories were idle. Nor were net exports (X_n) likely to increase because world trade had virtually collapsed. There really was only one sector of the economy that could come to the rescue: the government. As a result, Keynes called for a dramatic increase in government spending on goods and services (G), financed by borrowing, as the only way to get incomes up and unemployment down, and thus save the economic system itself.

This was radical stuff, and the reaction of most people, unacquainted with the idea that an increase in spending means an increase in income, was predictable: they screamed that the idea of "spending ourselves to prosperity" was totally insane! But, as history has shown before, it is in times of great strife that radical thinking rises to the surface. Keynes's groundbreaking idea, and the mostly negative reaction to it, were given a few years to stew before something even more dramatic occurred—the outbreak of World War II. As France, England, Canada, and later the United States entered the war, each nation dramatically increased government spending on armaments and "hired" hundreds of thousands of soldiers.

The economy returned to full employment almost overnight and the total output quickly exceeded even the most optimistic hopes of the war planners. This was exactly what Keynes had predicted. The Keynesian revolution in macroeconomics was complete when, following the end of the war, government after government passed various forms of full-employment acts, hoping to prevent another great depression from ever happening again. The idea that the government had a role in guiding the economy to a state of relatively full employment became cemented in peoples' consciousness and in law. This philosophy is what we today call **countercyclical fiscal policy**.

Very much in the spirit of the Keynesian revolution, today's interventionists advocate countercyclical fiscal policy to close recessionary and inflationary gaps. That is, figuratively speaking, government policy should always lean against the prevailing winds. If, for example, aggregate demand is weak and a recessionary gap exists, expansionary policy should be used to deliberately stimulate demand with higher government spending or lower taxes (or both). However, if aggregate demand is so strong that an inflationary gap exists, contractionary policy should be used to dampen demand through cuts in government spending or increases in taxes. The recessionary gap situation is illustrated in **Figure 7.4**.

Given the aggregate supply curve AS_1 and the aggregate demand curve AD_1, equilibrium GDP is Y_1. Since this level of GDP is below potential GDP (LAS) of Y_{FE}, we have a recessionary gap of $Y_{FE} - Y_1$. Countercyclical fiscal policy would call for either increased government spending or decreased taxes. This would have a multiplied impact on aggregate demand, as indicated by the shift from AD_1 to AD_2. If such a policy were well crafted, aggregate demand would increase just enough to eliminate the recessionary gap by moving the economy to Y_{FE}.

Suppose, on the other hand, the economy is experiencing an inflationary gap. Here, the appropriate countercyclical fiscal policy would be to decrease government spending or increase taxes in order to reduce the level of aggregate demand. This is illustrated in **Figure 7.5**.

An inflationary gap is present because the equilibrium level of GDP, Y_1, is above the full-employment level, Y_{FE}. Closing the gap requires a lower level of aggregate demand, as illustrated by the shift from AD_1 to AD_2. This could be accomplished by government reducing its spending or increasing taxes.

It is important to note here that the goal of countercyclical fiscal policy is to achieve full employment with minimal inflation. This means that the government's budget would sometimes be in deficit (stimulating demand) and sometimes in surplus (dampening demand). The goal here is to balance the economy, not the budget.

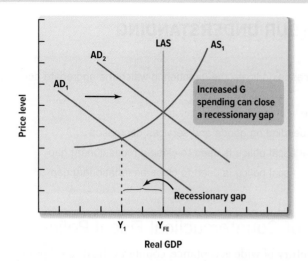

FIGURE 7.4 **Countercyclical Fiscal Policy with a Recessionary Gap**

A recessionary gap exists if the current level of GDP is below the full-employment level as illustrated by $Y_{FE} - Y_1$. Countercyclical fiscal policy is aimed at increasing the level of aggregate demand by either increasing government spending or decreasing taxes. It shifts the aggregate demand curve to the right from AD_1 to AD_2 and closes the recessionary gap.

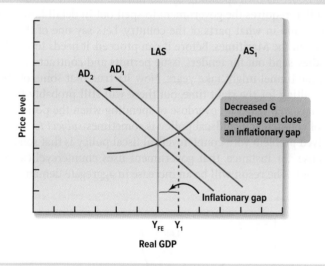

FIGURE 7.5 **Countercyclical Fiscal Policy with an Inflationary Gap**

If the economy is experiencing an inflationary gap, such as $Y_1 - Y_{FE}$, then the appropriate countercyclical fiscal policy aimed at closing the gap is to lower the level of aggregate demand by either reducing government spending or increasing taxes. This is illustrated by a leftward shift in the aggregate demand from AD_1 to AD_2.

In summary, countercyclical fiscal policy means that

- when aggregate demand is low and the economy is experiencing a recessionary gap, governments should spend and tax in a way that *increases* aggregate demand
- when aggregate demand is high and an inflationary gap is present, governments should spend and tax in a way that *reduces* the level of aggregate demand

Thus, government policy helps stabilize the economy and take some of the sting out of fluctuations in the business cycle.

TEST YOUR UNDERSTANDING

4. In the following cases, indicate the direction in which the aggregate demand curve will shift (right or left).

a) taxes increase

b) government spending on goods and services decreases

c) countercyclical fiscal policy is used to close a recessionary gap

d) countercyclical fiscal policy is used to close an inflationary gap

Shortcomings of Countercyclical Fiscal Policy

After a quarter of a century of wide acceptance, countercyclical fiscal policy began to receive a good deal of criticism in the early 1970s. To better understand why, we look at four potential problems associated with the use of countercyclical fiscal policy.

The first involves the fact that interventionists believe that the goal of countercyclical fiscal policy is to fine-tune the economy. This is done by adjusting government spending or taxation by just the right amounts to achieve a level of aggregate demand sufficient to bring about full-employment GDP with stable prices. Critics, however, argue that, in practice, the use of countercyclical fiscal policy lacks precision and its timing is problematic. Even if just the right amount of adjustment can be determined, countercyclical fiscal policy takes time to implement and is slow to take effect. Suppose for example, that the government intends to boost its own spending by $20 billion. Before it can do so, it first needs parliamentary approval, and that requires the government to spell out in detail how it proposes to spend the money: on what projects and in what parts of the country. Let's say one of these projects involves the building of a new tunnel in the Maritimes. Before it can proceed, it needs to get the permission of various environmental bodies, send out for tenders, issue permits and contracts, and so on. And, of course, the actual building of the tunnel might take years. Now, it's true that some of this can be preplanned and "put on the shelf" waiting for the right time, but there will still probably be considerable delay. As a result, the economy may well suffer an overdose of spending when the policy does take full effect. In short, the application of countercyclical fiscal policy is sometimes *subject to serious delays*.

The second perceived problem with countercyclical fiscal policy is that some believe *it has a built-in inflationary bias*. Suppose, for instance, that government uses countercyclical fiscal policy to get an economy out of a recession. The result will be an increase in aggregate demand, as shown in **Figure 7.6**.

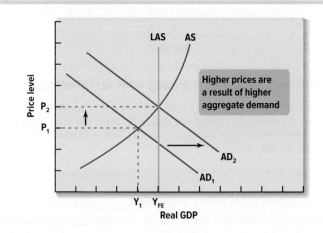

FIGURE 7.6   The Effect of Countercyclical Fiscal Policy on the Price Level

If the economy is experiencing a recessionary gap, countercyclical fiscal policy will increase the level of aggregate demand. This is illustrated by the shift from AD_1 to AD_2. The recessionary gap closes as real GDP increases from Y_1 to Y_{FE}. However, the price level will also increase from P_1 to P_2.

An increase in government spending (or a reduction in taxes) would shift the aggregate demand curve to the right, from AD_1 to AD_2. Clearly, the level of GDP increases from Y_1 to Y_{FE}. Unfortunately, the price level also rises, in this case from P_1 to P_2. It is argued then that countercyclical fiscal policy is subject to an inflationary bias. Just how serious this bias might be depends on the steepness of the aggregate supply curve. As you may recall from Chapter 5, as we approach the full-employment level of GDP, the rise in prices accelerates. While this inflationary bias is certainly possible, how serious this is does not depend on Canada's inflation rate alone but more on its rate of inflation compared with that in the countries that buy Canadian goods.

The third possible problem with countercyclical fiscal policy is what is termed the **crowding out effect**. This is the idea that using government stimulus to increase aggregate demand and close a recessionary gap means more government borrowing. The argument continues that this increased demand for loan money will mean that the interest rate—the price of money—will be pushed up and that this higher interest rate will mean less private investment business. As a result, the higher government spending is offset by lower investment spending. Thus the attempt to increase aggregate demand will be stunted—maybe even to the point of becoming ineffective. We will examine this argument in more detail in in Chapter 12.

The fourth, and some believe the most serious, problem with countercyclical fiscal policy is that *it completely ignores the effect it has on government's budget.* Over the past half-century, Canada's countercyclical fiscal policy has been aimed mainly at attempting to close recessionary gaps. Such policy involves either higher levels of government spending or lower levels of taxation. Either of these will mean that an existing budget deficit will rise, or there will be a decrease in the size of an existing budget surplus. This is illustrated in **Figure 7.7**.

Suppose that the current level of GDP in **Figure 7.7A** is Y_1. This means that the economy is experiencing a recessionary gap equal to the distance between the full-employment level of GDP, Y_{FE}, and the current level, Y_1. We can also see, in **Figure 7.7B**, that at GDP level Y_1 government has a

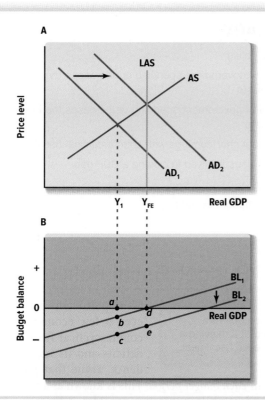

FIGURE 7.7   Effect of Countercyclical Fiscal Policy on Budget Deficits

Suppose the economy is originally at GDP level Y_1 with a budget deficit of *ab*. Countercyclical fiscal policy aimed at increasing aggregate demand from AD_1 to AD_2 will also shift the budget line down from BL_1 to BL_2. The result is a larger budget deficit, *de*, at the new equilibrium income of Y_{FE}.

budget deficit of *ab*. The recessionary gap can be closed by the use of countercyclical fiscal policy. This would imply an increase in government spending or a decrease in taxation. The effect, graphically, would be to shift aggregate demand from AD_1 to AD_2. However, the greater government spending (or lower tax rates) would also increase the size of government's budget deficit. This is illustrated in the downward shift in the budget line from BL_1 to BL_2, where the deficit immediately increases to *ac*. In time, though, the economy will recover and move to full-employment equilibrium at Y_{FE}. Here, we can see that the size of the deficit has been reduced from *ac* to *de* (a movement up the BL_2 curve) as a result of an increase in net tax revenues. However, this will still leave the economy with a larger overall deficit (*de*) than it began with (*ab*).

If the deficit-inducing effects occur often enough and are allowed to accumulate over a period of time, the size of government's national debt will grow substantially. Increased deficits mean increased borrowing, and this further requires government to use a larger percentage of its total spending to service its debt, leaving a smaller percentage for spending on such things as health care and education.

In summary, the four criticisms of countercyclical fiscal policy are that

- it is subject to serious time lags
- it results in the crowding out effect
- it has an inflationary bias
- it can cause serious budget deficits

 TEST YOUR UNDERSTANDING

5. What effect will countercyclical fiscal policy aimed at closing an inflationary gap have on the level of national income and prices?

SECTION SUMMARY

a) Countercyclical fiscal policy

- increases the level of government spending or decreases the level of taxation when a recessionary gap exists
- decreases the level of government spending or increases the level of taxation when an inflationary gap exists

b) There are three potential shortcomings with countercyclical fiscal policy:

- There can be time delays involved in closing a GDP gap.
- It may be inflationary.
- It can cause serious budget deficits.

7.3   Balanced-Budget Fiscal Policy

> **LO3**   Explain the pros and cons of a budget policy aimed at achieving a balanced budget in each fiscal year.

Some politicians and political commentators, and even a few economists, alarmed at the effect of countercyclical fiscal policy on the size of budget deficits and its negative effect on business confidence, argue that government should balance its spending and tax revenues in *each budget period*. This is known as a **balanced-budget fiscal policy** and is the second of the budget philosophies we consider. Advocates of a balanced-budget fiscal policy use three observations to support their position.

First, they consider the four shortcomings of countercyclical fiscal policy that we just discussed as a serious indictment of that approach and see the balanced-budget approach as the only alternative.

Second, advocates of a balanced-budget fiscal policy approach believe that because of **automatic stabilizers**, the modern economy has enough built-in safeguards to ensure that it avoids extremes of high inflation or unemployment. Automatic stabilizers are government programs that ensure that spending remains relatively stable even in times of rapid economic change. For instance, as we have seen, when an economy enters a recession, because of the progressive nature of taxes, disposable incomes do not fall as much as GDP does. In addition, the amount paid out in unemployment benefits and welfare assistance increases, and this buoys up disposable income and therefore consumption spending.

Automatic stabilizers also come into force when the economy is booming and in danger of "overheating." In this case, the higher levels of GDP generate proportionately higher taxes, and at the same time, the amounts paid out for unemployment benefits and welfare are also reduced. These both have the effect of dampening down expenditures.

The third point used in support of a balanced-budget fiscal policy is by far the most significant. As mentioned earlier, noninterventionists believe that if either a recessionary or an inflationary gap exists, the economy is capable of returning to full-employment equilibrium by itself through a *self-adjustment process*, unaided by interventionist polices of any kind. Let us review the argument that was presented in Chapter 5.

The key to understanding this position, which we termed the "modern view" in Chapter 5, is the belief that any temporary excesses of aggregate demand (inflationary gap) or a lack of aggregate demand (recessionary gap) would disappear through changes in prices and wage rates. If the economy were to experience a drop in aggregate demand leading to a recession, wage rates will eventually be forced down, which implies an increase in aggregate supply. This would lead to an increase in profits and production at the same time that prices start dropping. Prices and wages will fall until the economy has recovered and is back at full-employment equilibrium. This is illustrated in **Figure 7.8**.

Similarly, suppose the economy is initially in equilibrium and experiences an increase in demand. This will lead to higher prices and an inflationary gap. However, this above-full-employment equilibrium will eventually lead to higher wages, decreasing aggregate supply until the economy is back at full-employment equilibrium.

The essence of the argument by advocates of a balanced budget, then, is that government intervention is unnecessary, since the economy is quite capable of returning the economy to full employment unaided. Even Keynes admitted that this might happen in the long run. However, he felt that the adjustment process might take too long and in the meantime unnecessary suffering would prevail. To emphasize this point he pronounced: "In the long run, we are all dead!"

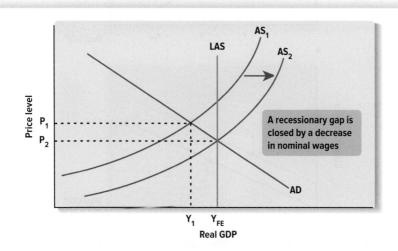

FIGURE 7.8   Adjustment from a Recessionary Gap

If the economy is in a recession at income Y_1, eventually wages will be forced down, thus increasing aggregate supply. The AS curve will continue to shift right until the economy is returned to full-employment GDP, Y_{FE}. This will also decrease the price level from P_1 to P_2.

In summary, the arguments in support of a balanced-budget fiscal policy are as follows:

- Countercyclical policy does not work well.
- The economy has effective automatic stabilizers.
- The economy is capable of returning to full-employment equilibrium through a self-adjustment process.

Shortcomings of Balanced-Budget Fiscal Policy

We now need to examine the economic effects when a government actually follows a balanced-budget fiscal policy. In doing so, we will find that the effects are significant and the policy is not at all neutral, as its proponents argue.

Suppose that, as in **Figure 7.9A**, the economy is at income level Y_1. Since income is below potential GDP (LAS), the economy finds itself in a recession. As is often the case in a recession, because of falling tax revenues, government suffers a budget deficit, as shown by the distance *ab* in **Figure 7.9B**. If government is intent on balancing the budget regardless of the condition of the economy, it will have no choice but to reduce government spending and/or increase taxation. The result, graphically, will be an upward shift in the budget line from BL_1 to BL_2 in **Figure 7.9B** so that at income level Y_1 the budget is initially balanced. However, the effect of cutting government spending or increasing taxes will have an impact on the economy as well as on the government budget. The result will be a reduction in aggregate demand. This is shown graphically in **Figure 7.9A** as a leftward shift in the aggregate demand curve from AD_1 to AD_2.

The drop in aggregate demand will cause GDP to drop by a multiple of the decrease in aggregate expenditures. At the lower equilibrium level of Y_2, NTR will be smaller, with the result that the budget deficit (*cd*) will persist (although it is now smaller than it was at *ab*).

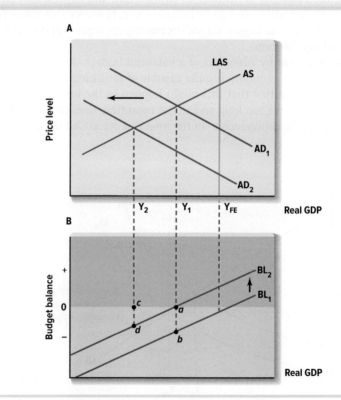

FIGURE 7.9   **Reduced Government Spending and the Deficit**

An attempt to eliminate the budget deficit that exists at Y_1 would call for a reduction in government spending or an increase in taxes. Thus, the budget line shifts up from BL_1 to BL_2, and the budget deficit appears to be eliminated (point *a*). However, this action reduces aggregate demand from AD_1 to AD_2, which causes the level of equilibrium GDP to decrease to Y_2, and at this lower level of GDP there is still a budget deficit of *cd*.

What we have just seen is that if the economy is experiencing a recessionary gap and a budget deficit, the pursuit of a balanced-budget fiscal policy will be **procyclical**. To understand this, note that a recession implies there is unemployment in the economy. If government takes action to try to eliminate the budget deficit rather than the unemployment, the level of unemployment will rise, since the level of GDP falls. In short, the recessionary phase of the business cycle creates a given level of unemployment, and government's fiscal policy aimed at reducing the deficit results in even *higher* unemployment.

Would a balanced-budget fiscal policy result in the same procyclical tendencies if the economy were experiencing an inflationary gap? The answer depends on the state of the budget associated with the gap. Recall that an inflationary gap is a result of high aggregate demand, which generates a level of income temporarily higher than the full-employment level of GDP.

Let us assume that this high GDP level generates sufficient tax revenue to create a government budget surplus. Strict adherence to a balanced-budget fiscal policy would then necessitate that either taxes be lowered or spending be increased to eliminate the budget surplus. Such fiscal policy action would *raise* aggregate demand and thus the level of GDP. This would increase the size of the inflationary gap, and we again see the procyclical effect of a balanced-budget fiscal policy in this situation.

To review, a balanced-budget fiscal policy will likely be procyclical when the economy is experiencing a recessionary gap, since the low levels of income will generate low levels of tax revenue, which create budget deficits. Similarly, such a policy will also be procyclical when the economy is experiencing an inflationary gap if the gap comes with a budget surplus.

There are times, however, when a balanced budget policy is effective in both reducing a budget deficit *and* helping the economy to move toward full employment. This would occur if the economy were in a recession and experiencing a budget surplus. In this case, an increase in government spending (or a decrease in taxes) would reduce the budget surplus but would also stimulate the economy. Similarly, a balanced-budget policy would be effective if the economy were experiencing an inflationary boom but running a budget deficit. In this case, contractionary fiscal policy would cure both problems. However, neither scenario is likely, since an economy suffering a recession is probably running a budget deficit and one experiencing an inflationary boom usually experiences a budget surplus.

Table 7.2 summarizes these various possibilities:

TABLE 7.2
Effectiveness of a Balanced Budget Policy

State of Economy	State of Budget	Policy Effectiveness
Recession	Deficit	Ineffective (procyclical)
Recession	Surplus	Effective (countercyclical)
Inflationary boom	Deficit	Effective (countercyclical)
Inflationary boom	Surplus	Ineffective (procyclical)

The Arithmetic of a Balanced Budget

Let us now examine another aspect of the procyclical nature of the balanced-budget philosophy in more detail. We will again assume that the budget is balanced and that the economy is at full-employment equilibrium. Now assume that a new government, which promised lower government spending, is elected. This new government is intent on carrying out its promise of cuts in spending. However, in consideration of the already-balanced budget and given the fact that the economy is at full employment, it also announces that taxes will be reduced by a similar amount. Since government spending and taxes are to be cut by the same amount, won't both the government's budget balance and the level of GDP be unaffected? That is to say, isn't it true that what government takes out of the economy in the form of reduced spending is exactly offset by what it puts back into the economy in the form of reduced taxes and is therefore neutral? It comes as a surprise to most people that the answer to this question is no.

Suppose that the economy is at a full-employment equilibrium of $1000, government spending is $200, and taxes—which, for simplicity, we assume are entirely autonomous—are also $200. Furthermore, suppose that the value of the multiplier is 2 and that the portion of disposable income (Y_d) that consumers spend is 0.8. As we know, a reduction in government spending will definitely reduce aggregate demand and therefore the level of GDP. Suppose government spending is cut by $40. With a multiplier of 2, this will reduce GDP by $80. Next, we know that the corresponding cut in taxes will increase aggregate demand and the level of the GDP. But how much will GDP increase? Will it increase by the same $80?

Well, a cut in taxes of $40 will immediately raise disposable income by the same $40. Does this mean that consumers will spend all of this additional disposable income? The answer is no, since we know that with an MPC of 0.80, the increase in spending will only be 0.8 × $40, or $32 (the other $8 will be saved). This additional $32 in spending, not the whole $40 cut in taxes, is the amount that gets multiplied.

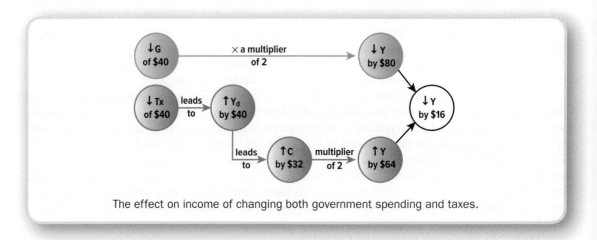

The effect on income of changing both government spending and taxes.

The cut in government spending reduces the level of GDP by $80, but the cut in taxes increases it by only $64. The net result is a drop in GDP of $16. In short:

> A policy that decreases both government spending and taxes by the same amount results in a lower real GDP and higher unemployment.

This means that a balanced budget does not have a neutral effect on the economy, as some have suggested. Instead, any change in the size of the government's budget—even if the budget remained balanced—will result in the level of GDP either rising or falling; it will not remain unchanged.

We want to emphasize that the two contrasting approaches to fiscal policy have dramatically different results. The essence of a countercyclical fiscal policy, which is aimed at the level of GDP and unemployment, is to use fiscal policy to address recessionary and inflationary gaps that might exist in the *economy*. In simple terms, it attempts to balance the economy, not the government's budget. By contrast, the essence of the balanced budget fiscal policy, which is aimed at the government's budget, is to use fiscal policy to balance that *budget*, not the economy.

It is now clear that the issues regarding the use of fiscal policy to address recessionary and inflationary gaps, and the question of the budget deficit are more complex than one would first imagine. It is true that some people object to countercyclical fiscal policy because such an approach ignores the issue of budget deficits and the associated level of the national debt. However, the balanced-budget fiscal policy has the potential to exacerbate the economy's situation because of its procyclical tendencies. Might another approach be used? In fact, the answer is yes. We now turn to a discussion of what could be described as a blend of the two philosophies just discussed.

TEST YOUR UNDERSTANDING

6. Assume that the economy is in a recession and that government is experiencing a budget deficit. If fiscal policy is used to try to eliminate the deficit, what will happen to

a) unemployment?

b) GDP?

c) NTR?

d) the deficit?

Next, assume the same conditions, but this time, fiscal policy is used to try to reduce unemployment. How will your four answers to the above change?

7. Suppose that the government increases both its own spending and autonomous taxes by $100 and the economy's multiplier equals 3. If consumers spend 75 percent of their disposable (after-tax) income, by how much will GDP change?

SECTION SUMMARY

a) Balanced-budget fiscal policy balances the government's revenues and overall spending each budget year and

- highlights the effect of automatic stabilizers

- argues that the economy is capable of achieving full-employment equilibrium through a self-adjustment process

b) The problem with a balanced-budget policy is that it is almost always procyclical and can make an existing economic condition, such as unemployment, more serious.

7.4 Cyclically Balanced Budget Fiscal Policy

LO4 Explain the pros and cons of a budget policy aimed at achieving both full employment and a balanced budget over the life of the business cycle.

Without overstating the obvious, one might ask what is so sacred about a year as far as budgets are concerned. Why not balance the budget every month, every week, or for that matter every day?

Well, a week or a month would simply not be practical from a data-gathering point of view; but more importantly, a government's flow of income and expenditures is not regular. Some weeks or months would have high deficits, whereas others would have high surpluses.

The same is true during any one year. Given this, and the fact that a government's budget also depends on the level of GDP in the economy, some economists—including Keynes himself—suggest that governments should instead try to balance the budget, not on an annual basis, but *over the life of the business cycle*. A typical business cycle can last for several years, so the use of fiscal policy to smooth out the business cycle would be viewed from a longer perspective than just each budget period. In these circumstances, deficits might be big in some years, as the economy enters a recession, which causes lower tax revenues and higher transfer payments. Conversely, when the business cycle moves into an expansionary phase, the result should be budget surpluses. This longer-view approach would to an extent continue to use countercyclical fiscal policy to lean against the prevailing winds while addressing the concerns of many people about budget deficits and the size of the national debt.

We should also point out that budget deficits can have two components. The first, the cyclical deficit, is the portion of the overall budget deficit that is caused by the cyclical conditions of the economy. This means that the larger the recessionary gap the higher the deficit. On the other hand,

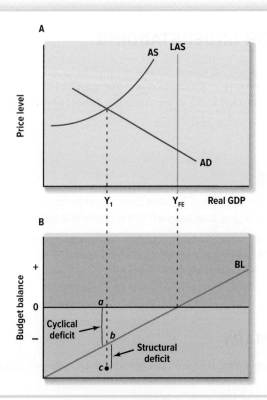

FIGURE 7.10   Cyclical and Structural Deficits

The distance *a–b* is the amount of deficit expected as a result of the economy being in a recession at Y_1, This is the *cyclical deficit*. If the actual deficit is greater than this, the excess deficit *b–c* is known as the *structural deficit*.

the cyclical deficit is zero when the economy is at full employment. Suppose for example that the economy is in a recession and given the low level of GDP (and the high unemployment) a **cyclical deficit** of, say, $35 billion is entirely understandable and expected. Thus, if the actual deficit turns out to be $35 billion there's no cause for alarm, as the budget will balance on its own when the economy picks up. If, on the other hand, the actual budget deficit is $50 billion there is a **structural deficit** of $15 billion and the budget balance will stay negative (although it will be smaller) even after the economy recovers from a cyclical downturn and moves to full employment. The fact that the federal government imposed austerity measures entailing serious cuts in government spending in their budget of 2012 and 2013 indicates that they believed that at least some its budget deficit was structural. The idea behind the cyclically balanced budget philosophy is that the structural deficit should be zero.

The difference between the two types of budget deficits is illustrated in **Figure 7.10**. The budget line is drawn on the basis that, given the budgeted amount of government spending and given its tax structure, the budget would be balanced if the economy were at full employment GDP, Y_{FE}. However, the economy is presently in a recession at Y_1 (in Figure A) and experiencing a budget deficit equal to *a–b* (in Figure B). This is the amount of its cyclical deficit, and it is considered an acceptable deficit given the present condition of the economy. However, if the government's present budget deficit is, in fact, the amount *a–c*. This extra—and unacceptable—deficit, *b–c*, is considered a structural deficit.

In this example, the government has not adhered to its own spending and taxation plan, so that even if the economy returns to full employment it will still be faced with a (structural) deficit.

The idea behind a **cyclically balanced budget fiscal policy** is that, as long as there is no structural deficit, governments should accept the presence of a cyclical deficit and refrain from any action to balance the budget. Furthermore, the government should not increase the size of the deficit anymore, as advocated by the countercyclical adherents. In other words, this policy is a compromise between the two approaches we have discussed. Advocates of a cyclically balanced budget, then, aim to balance the budget not on an annual basis but over the life of the business cycle. Such a policy would require governments to sometimes spend more (or tax less) and sometimes spend less (or tax more). It also implies, then, that cyclical budget deficits and surpluses should be tolerated, but that structural budget deficits and surpluses should be avoided so that over the long run the government's budget is balanced.

Although it does seem like a sound idea, there are three potential problems with this cyclically balanced budget fiscal policy.

The first is that there is no guarantee that, when government is running a budget deficit, the size and length of the recessionary gap will be exactly offset by the size and length of the inflationary gap when government is running a budget surplus. As a result, the end of the business cycle may still show a net budget deficit.

The second and perhaps the most difficult problem is that most governments find it easier to increase spending in bad times than to decrease it in good times. Can you imagine a government cutting its spending on some needed social project because the economic times are so good? In short, pursuing a cyclically balanced budget fiscal policy would take a remarkable amount of discipline on the part of government and understanding on the part of the electorate.

Third—and this is probably the major reason why few governments have adopted the cyclically balanced budget fiscal policy—is the fact that most business cycles are longer than the term of office of any particular government. This invites the existing government to leave the problem of balancing the budget to its successor.

Fiscal policy is a powerful tool, and getting it right is sometimes difficult. What we have established in this chapter is that when the economy takes a nosedive—as it did in the early 1930s and in 2008—there are three fundamentally different ways a government can react: to stimulate the economy with additional spending or tax reductions, to address the resulting budget deficits caused by the economic downturn and cut spending or raise taxes, or to do nothing.

We can briefly mention here that the Canadian government used countercyclical fiscal policy to counteract the effects of the 2008–10 recession that followed the global financial crisis. We will examine this action more closely, and contrast it with the actions of other governments, in Chapter 13.

IN A NUTSHELL ...

It can be really quite simple:

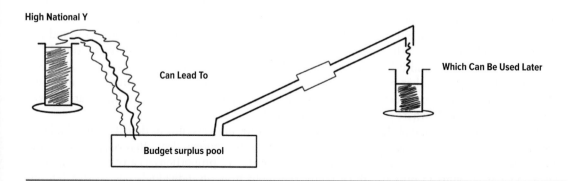

TEST YOUR UNDERSTANDING

8. Suppose an economy has a budget given by the equation Budget balance = −600 + 0.25Y. If the economy has GDP of $2000 and is experiencing a budget deficit of $120, what is the amount of its cyclical deficit, and how much is its structural deficit?

SECTION SUMMARY

a) A cyclically balanced budget policy attempts to meld the countercyclical and balanced-budget fiscal policies into a single policy in which the budget is balanced, but over the life of the business cycle and not in every budget year.

b) A cyclical budget deficit is one caused solely as a result of the economy going into a recession, whereas a structural budget deficit means that the economy would still be running up a deficit even at full employment.

7.5   Fiscal Policy and the National Debt

LO5   Discuss the cause, size, and problems of the national debt.

The size of the national debt is a topic that has received a great deal of attention lately. The use of countercyclical fiscal policy usually leads to growth in the debt, so its use has created a lot of debate. Let us examine all this more closely by asking: Just what is so bad about budget deficits and therefore a growing national debt?

First, let us establish to whom this debt is owed. Any Canadian individual, corporation, or bank that buys a Canada Savings Bond, a treasury bill, or other type of government bond is lending money to government. The payment of interest and the redemption of the bond is the responsibility of government. In this sense, it can be regarded as a debt that we Canadians owe to ourselves. However, one of the major problems with the debt is that the "we" and "ourselves" in the previous sentence do not refer to the same groups of people. We, the taxpayers, are responsible for paying off the interest and principal to ourselves, the bondholders. But while most bondholders are also taxpayers, not all taxpayers are bondholders. And therein lies one of the problems. As the size of the debt increases, and with it the interest payments, increasing amounts must be raised in taxes, and those amounts are then transferred to bondholders. Since it is normally the comparatively wealthy who hold the majority of bonds, while taxes are paid by rich and poor alike, the payment of interest on the national debt could represent a major *redistribution of income*.

For another angle on this redistributional aspect, let us assume that the debt is entirely internal and that in response to public pressure, it was decided to repay the entire debt of approximately $612 billion (as of 2015). How could this be done? The most straightforward answer is for the government to raise $612 billion additional dollars through increased taxes, of which all Canadians would pay some (relatively) small part. What then would Ottawa do with this incredible rush of additional revenue? Turn around and send it back to those Canadians who hold Canada Savings Bonds and those institutions holding the other bonds. The net effect: all Canadians pay $612 billion in additional taxes, and some Canadians receive $612 billion in bond repayments. As many might argue, why bother? Why not leave it where it was in the first place?

Before considering some of the problems associated with big government deficits and debt, let us look at the facts. It is unfortunate that public discussion of the national debt often runs to hyperbole, and we used to hear mention of a "staggering" debt of "enormous" proportions as a result of "crippling" deficits. Dollar amounts in billions are certainly enormous from an individual's perspective, but one seldom hears the size of Canada's GDP described as staggering. We therefore need to put things in perspective. Just how big is our national debt? It might help if we look at it over a period. Table 7.3 shows some figures for selected years.

TABLE 7.3
Net National Debt (nominal $billions)

1926	1940	1946	1967	1991	2015
2.4	3.3	13.4	17.7	377.7	612.3

Source: Adapted from Department of Finance Canada, Fiscal Reference Tables, 1926–2015. Reproduced with the permission of the Minister of Public Works and Government Services, 2016.

It certainly seems like a "staggering" increase. But since the population of Canada has increased appreciably during the past hundred years, it might be better to show the figures in terms of per capita debt, as in Table 7.4.

TABLE 7.4
Per Capita Net National Debt (nominal $)

1926	1940	1946	1967	1991	2015
254	287	1090	868	13 475	17 080

Source: Adapted by the authors from the Statistics Canada CANSIM database, http://cansim2.statcan.ca, Table 051-0001, September 1, 2016, and Department of Finance Canada, Fiscal Reference Tables, 1926–2015. Reproduced with the permission of the Minister of Public Works and Government Services, 2016.

So the average debt per person has increased from a mere $254 in 1926 to over $17 000 nearly ninety years later. It certainly looks like a fairly staggering increase. But we need to make one further adjustment to allow for the effects of inflation over the years. So let us show the total debt, but this time in constant 2007 dollars, as in Table 7.5.

TABLE 7.5
Net National Debt in Real Terms ($2007, billions)

1926	1940	1946	1967	1991	2015
34.1	51.8	165.7	107.0	520.2	545.2

Source: Adapted by the authors from the Statistics Canada CANSIM database, http://cansim2.statcan.ca, Table 380-0102, September 1, 2016, and Department of Finance Canada, Fiscal Reference Tables, 1926–2015. Reproduced with the permission of the Minister of Public Works and Government Services, 2016.

Finally, let us combine both factors in Table 7.6 to give us figures in terms of constant dollars per capita.

TABLE 7.6
Per Capita Net National Debt in Real Terms ($2007)

1926	1940	1946	1967	1991	2015
3613	4498	13 473	5248	18 846	15 200

Source: Adapted by the authors from the Statistics Canada CANSIM database, http://cansim2.statcan.ca, Table 380-0102 and 051-0001, September 1, 2016, and Department of Finance Canada, Fiscal Reference Tables, 1926–2015. Reproduced with the permission of the Minister of Public Works and Government Services, 2016.

This puts things in perspective. In real terms, the per capita debt increased 32 percent in the fourteen years leading up to World War II; it more than tripled during the war, declined to less than half by 1967, but has almost tripled again in the last 50 years.

Although Table 7.6 is helpful, it still does not tell us whether Canada's national debt is too big. The best measure of the size of any debt is relative to the ability to repay, and this is relative to income. Table 7.7 shows the size of Canada's debt relative to the country's income, that is, as a percentage of GDP (of GNP until 1967).

TABLE 7.7
Percentage of Net National Debt/GD(N)P

1926	1940	1946	1967	1991	2015
47%	49%	113%	23%	56%	31%

Source: Adapted from Department of Finance Canada, Fiscal Reference Tables, 1926–2015. Reproduced with the permission of the Minister of Public Works and Government Services, 2016.

In recent years, the percentage has steadily declined. In fact, since 1995, Canada's debt burden has fallen from being the second highest to the lowest of the G8 countries. (The United States sits at 79 percent, Italy at over 107 percent, and Japan at 122 percent, and Greece tops the list at 172 percent.)

These figures show clearly that one of the major causes of the growth of Canada's debt was the financing of World War II. During a major war, few nations are able to finance their military expenditures through taxation alone. They are often left with little choice but to borrow, and the majority of this borrowing is from the nation's own citizens. Most would feel this is a legitimate reason to increase the debt and might also agree that there are other legitimate reasons for the increased debt—for example, deficit financing to prevent or escape from a recession, or the financing of necessary infrastructure such as bridges and airports. The third explanation for the increased Canadian debt, especially since the early 1970s, has been the increase in the size of income-support programs. Here, controversy about whether this is a good reason for the debt to increase heats up; some have suggested that these programs are too generous in comparison with those of some other countries.

Finally, it should be noted that the very high interest rates between the mid-1970s and the 1990s compounded the size of the debt. (As we saw, some economists suggest that the reason that interest rates were so high in the first place was the result of borrowing by governments. Complicated world, isn't it?) Leaving the statistics behind, let us examine some of the problems associated with the debt.

 ADDED DIMENSION

Provincial Debt In Canada

The focus of this chapter is on the federal government, simply because it is by far the largest government entity in the country—over 30 times the size of Nova Scotia's government for example. In addition, it is the federal government that has nearly unlimited power to borrow—including its ability to use the central bank as a loan source—and tax.

Nonetheless, the provinces do also tax, spend, and borrow and also run deficits and surpluses. How large a debt do the provinces carry? As representative examples, the following shows the debt/GDP ratios for four provinces:

British Columbia	17%	Quebec	50%
Ontario	38%	Newfoundland	26%

Problems of the National Debt: Fact or Fantasy?

The first perceived problem involves the size of the foreign portion of the debt. Private financial agencies give ratings for government bonds sold around the world, to help their clients who wish to invest. The lower the rating for a particular government's bonds, the higher the perceived risk and therefore the higher the interest payments that must be paid by the borrower. In early 1995, there was a *perception* that Canada's national debt was too large. The result was a lower bond rating, and the outflow of interest payments on the foreign-held debt increased. (It should be noted, however, that in Canada's case 74 percent of the debt is owed to Canadians and 26 percent owed to foreign individuals, corporations, and financial institutions.)

Second, we noted that payment of interest on the debt represents a redistribution of income from lower-income to higher-income Canadians. This is because only higher-income Canadians receive interest payments that come out of the taxes of all Canadians, including middle- and low-income Canadians.

As a third point, large interest payments also mean that each year government must earmark 27 to 32 billion dollars in interest payments (the amount depends on the prevailing interest rates) before it can even start to consider other spending claims. This obviously curtails its ability to satisfy the desires by citizens for other items like health, education, or the nation's infrastructure. However, there is some good news on this front. In 2015 total interest payments were about 10 percent of tax revenue, down considerably from the peaks of the mid-1990s when it went as high as 38 percent. This is a reflection of low interest rates of recent years. Nonetheless, there is a conundrum working here. If government did not have to pay these interest charges, it would be much easier to balance the budget. But because it did not balance the budget in the past, it has to pay these interest charges.

A final criticism comes from the fact that a federal government has almost unlimited power to spend. Theoretically (and legally), there is no upper limit to how big a deficit can be. That does not mean that big deficits are not harmful to an economy; it simply means that a national government has supreme power to tax, to borrow, and to print money. This means that without checks on its spending, a government can become power-hungry and wasteful in its fiscal affairs. And for this we would all suffer.

In summary, these are the problems with high deficits and debt:

- the interest payments that must be paid on foreign-held debt
- the income redistribution effects of large interest payments
- the reduced ability of government to meet the needs of its citizens
- the possible increased power grabbing and wastefulness of government

Let us now take a brief look at what are sometimes seen as problems of the debt, but really are not.

One of the bogus arguments about the national debt seeks to draw an analogy between a household or a business and the operations of the federal government. It suggests that just like an individual or a business, if revenue falls short of expenses for a long enough period, bankruptcy will follow. This is just not a legitimate concern when applied to a federal government, which, as we just mentioned, has unlimited powers of taxation and borrowing, and has direct control over the nation's supply of money. Therefore, it is highly unlikely that the federal government of a large economy such as Canada will "go broke" as a result of *internal* borrowing. It is true that the German government went broke following World War I, but this was a result of external debt imposed on it by France and the United Kingdom. If urban decay and high taxes drive many higher-income taxpayers and businesses out of a city, that city might go broke in that it could default on interest payments on the bonds it sold to borrow money. The same might be said, although this would be stretching it, of a particular province or state, but not of a country as large and as desirable to live in as Canada.

Another argument suggests that a big national debt means that we are encumbering future generations, who will eventually have to pay it. It is true that our children and grandchildren will inherit a larger debt and the interest charges associated with it. However, it is also true that future generations will inherit the Canadian-held portion of the assets (bonds) represented by that debt. That is, if our descendants have to pay extra taxes to service a larger debt, they also, as a generation, will get those same taxes back as the interest payments are made to whoever holds those bonds.

While it is true that the federal government is in debt to the tune of hundreds of billions of dollars, it is also true that the government owns assets—airports, military hardware, land, buildings, and so on—that also total a great deal. Is the debt too large relative to the assets owned?

Most observers suggest that a debt/GDP ratio of less than 50 percent is not particularly worrisome. Canada's debt in the early 1990s was cause for some concern, but as we saw in Table 7.7, the national debt in 2015 has been reduced to a manageable 31 percent, one of the lowest in the world.

 ADDED DIMENSION

What Are Austerity Policies and Do They Work?

Austerity measures are reductions in government spending and increases in tax revenues in order to lower a government's budget deficit and avoid a perceived "debt crisis."

Such a perception is rooted in the idea that when a country's debt-to-GDP rises above a certain percentage—90 percent is often mentioned—its ability to continue to roll over such debt by new borrowing will be called into question by creditors.

Other measures, often advocated, include the privatization of state-owned industries (to encourage greater efficiency through foreign expertise) and the introduction of a VAT (value added tax) to discourage exports and thereby increase domestic competition. Supporters of these austerity packages argue that confidence in the way a government manages its budget will be enhanced, which will cause the debt crisis to fade away.

In 2010, Greece became the first country to initiate austerity policies, but the idea spread to include most other European countries from Italy to the United Kingdom. In 2011, the U.S. Congress, embracing the same idea, threatened that it would not increase the debt ceiling.

There is little evidence that any of this worked and, in fact, the International Monetary Fund (IMF) released a report (2012) that stated the Eurozone austerity measures had slowed economic growth and worsened the debt crisis and that growth in the United States was sluggish at best.

Critics of austerity policies argue that the only time—if ever—they should be used is when the economy is in the expansionary phase of the business cycle when putting the brakes on economic growth will not result in larger budget deficits.

In Canada, no such drama occurred for (at least) two reasons. One is that the deficit/debt issue here was not so pressing and the second is that neither the Harper nor the Trudeau government ever steered fiscal policy clearly to either side of the debate.

A Wrap-up and a Plea for Common Sense

When discussing policy, it is important to focus on the economic issues that are important to the well-being of the citizenship of a country as a whole. This means that in a recession unemployment is a serious concern for all of us, not just those without work. In this situation, the appropriate action should be expansionary fiscal policy implying a deficit in the government budget. However, it should also be recognized that government must keep the size of the national debt—as a percentage of GDP—under control. In the long run, these goals can be achieved if government policy is adjusted to fit the inevitable changes in the immediate economic circumstances. This means government budget surpluses in good times as well as budget deficits in times of recession. This long-run approach implies balancing the budget over the life of the business cycle and will serve the economy far better than getting caught up in any kind of single-minded ideology about how to manage fiscal policy in any particular year. By and large, Canadian governments of the past have done rather well in achieving all of this.

TEST YOUR UNDERSTANDING

9. Under what circumstances is it inappropriate for government to run up a budget deficit?

SECTION SUMMARY

a) The size of the national debt should be viewed in terms of
- per capita debt in constant dollars
- a percentage of real GDP

b) Canada's national debt has grown because of
- deficit financing to prevent or escape from a recession
- borrowing to finance World War II
- an increase in the size of income-support programs
- high interest rate costs in the last twenty-five years of the twentieth century

c) The potential problems with the national debt are
- the interest that must be paid on foreign-held debt, which does not go to Canadians
- the income distribution effects of large interest payments
- the reduced ability of government to meet the needs of its citizens
- the possible increased greed and wastefulness of government

Study Guide

Review

WHAT'S THE BIG IDEA?

Fiscal policy brings into sharp relief the possible conflict between economic goals that we looked at in Chapter 1, in this case the one between achieving a viable government budget balance and promoting economic growth and national prosperity. The problem is that the state of the budget and the state of the economy are intertwined. For example, an increase in GDP (more people working, more profits being made) will increase the government's tax revenue and thus decrease its budget deficit. But it is also true than an increase in the government's tax rates will also increase tax revenue and, at the same time reduce GDP since higher rates mean less consumption and investment spending.

The budget line is very useful here because it explicitly shows the relationship between the economy and the government's budget: at a glance we can see the amount of the budget deficit or surplus at every level of GDP—given the present level of government spending and the overall tax rate. However, if there is an increase in government spending or a decrease in taxes, the budget line will shift down indicating a higher deficit or lower surplus at each level of GDP.

In the chapter, we look at three very contrasting views on fiscal policy. The differences between them shows up markedly when an economy goes into a recession. The resulting drop in GDP will inevitably cause tax revenues to drop and government transfer payments—EI and welfare—to increase. This will usually result in the government facing a budget deficit. In these circumstances, advocates of a *balanced-budget philosophy* will regard the budget deficit as a more immediate problem than the recession and therefore recommend that the government increase taxes or reduce its own spending. Advocates of a *countercyclical philosophy*, on the other hand, would suggest exactly the opposite: government spending should be increased and/or taxes reduced in order to increase spending and thus national income, despite the fact that this will lead to an even bigger budget deficit. The *cyclically balanced budget philosophy* would suggest that the government do nothing as far as the deficit is concerned, but rather take a long-term view and wait for the inevitable recovery which will lead to budget surpluses.

NEW GLOSSARY TERMS AND KEY EQUATIONS

automatic stabilizers
balanced budget
balanced-budget fiscal policy
budget deficit
budget surplus
countercyclical fiscal policy
crowding out effect

cyclical deficit
cyclically balanced budget fiscal policy
fiscal policy
national debt
procyclical
structural deficit

Equations:

[7.1]   NTR = tax revenue − transfer payments

[7.2]   Budget balance = NTR − G

Comprehensive Problem

(LO 2, 3)   **Figure 7.11** shows the aggregate demand/supply and the government budget line for the economy of Mahdi. The economy is presently at equilibrium. For every $1 change in government spending, aggregate demand changes by $3.

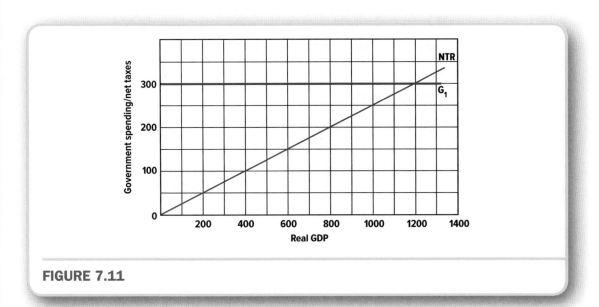

FIGURE 7.11

Questions

a) What is the present level of GDP and the price level in Mahdi?
b) Is there a recessionary or an inflationary gap? How much?
c) Does government have a budget deficit or a surplus? How much?

Answers

a) GDP = 1200; price level = 120
b) Recessionary gap of 400 (since the intersection of the AS and AD curves occurs to the left of the potential GDP curve, there is a recessionary gap)
c) Deficit of 200 (at a GDP of 1200, the BL line is below zero at −200)

Questions

d) By how much must aggregate demand increase or decrease in order to move the economy to full-employment equilibrium?
e) Draw in the new aggregate demand curve, labelled AD$_2$.
f) What change in government spending is necessary in order to move the economy to full-employment equilibrium?
g) What effect will this have on the level of GDP and price level?
h) If government makes the change in (f), draw in the new budget line, labelled BL$_2$.
i) What will be the new value of government's budget at this new GDP?

Answers

d) AD must increase by 600 which is 6 squares to the right.
e) See **Figure 7.11 (Completed)**.

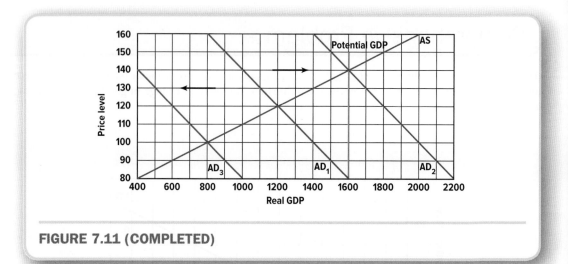

FIGURE 7.11 (COMPLETED)

f) Increase in government spending of 200 (200 times the multiplier of 3 equals the gap of 600)
g) The new GDP would be 1600 and the price level would be 140. (This where AD$_2$ intersects AS.)
h) See **Figure 7.11 (Completed)**.
i) Deficit of 200. (The increase in government spending of 200 will shift the BL down by 200 or 4 squares.)

Questions

Returning to the original equilibrium, suppose that government is committed to a balanced budget.

j) What change in government spending is necessary in order to balance the budget at the present income level?
k) Draw in the new budget line labelled BL$_3$.
l) What effect will the change in (k) have on aggregate demand?
m) Draw in the new curve, labelled AD$_3$.
n) As a result of this change in aggregate demand, what will happen to the value of GDP and price level?
o) What will be the new value of government's budget at this new GDP?

Answers

j) G needs to be reduced by 200. (Since at equilibrium of 1200 that is the amount of the government's deficit.)
k) See **Figure 7.11 (Completed)**. The BL shifts up by 200 (4 squares).
l) AD would decrease by 600 (3 × 200).
m) See **Figure 7.11 (Completed)**; the AD curve would shift back by 6 squares.
n) GDP would be 800 and the new price level 100.
o) Since the decrease in government spending would shift the BL up by 4 squares, at a GDP of 800 the budget would have a deficit of 200.

Study Problems

Find answers on the McGraw-Hill online resource.

Basic (Problems 1–3)

1. **(LO 1)** Table 7.8 shows the revenue and spending of the Canadian government. For simplicity, assume that all of the *spending grants to other levels of government* were spent in Canada on goods and services.

> ### TABLE 7.8
> #### Federal Government's Budget Plan for Fiscal Year
>
> | Revenues ($) | | Outlays ($) | |
> |---|---|---|---|
> | Personal income taxes | 103.7 | Transfers to persons | 52.6 |
> | Corporate income taxes | 31.7 | Spending grants to other levels of government | 42.8 |
> | Other income taxes | 4.5 | Public debt charges | 33.8 |
> | GST and excise taxes | 46.2 | Direct program spending | 81.8 |
> | EI premiums | 16.5 | **Total Outlays** | **209.0** |
> | Other revenues | 19.6 | **Projected Budget Plan Surplus** | **13.2** |
> | **Total Revenues** | **222.2** | | |

a) What are the projected NTRs in this budget plan? _____

b) What is the value of NTR less government spending on goods and services (G)? _____
What percentage of total revenue is

c) personal income taxes? _____

d) corporate income taxes? _____
What percentage of total outlays is

e) transfer payments to persons? _____

f) public debt charges? _____

2. **(LO 1)** Government spending in Robok is $140 billion, and its only tax is an income tax with a marginal tax rate of 0.35.

   a) What is the balance on the government's budget at a GDP level of $360 billion? _____

   b) What is the balance on the government's budget at a GDP level of $500 billion? _____

   c) At what level of GDP will the economy of Robok have a balanced budget? _____

3. **(LO 1, 2)** The economy of Morin is shown in **Figure** 7.12.

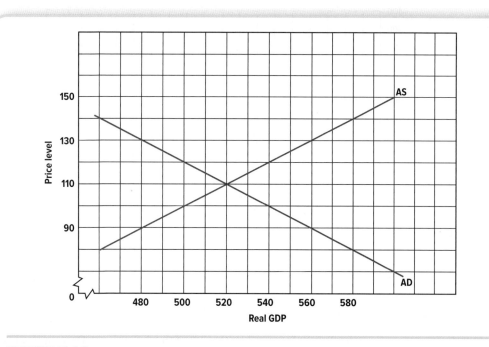

FIGURE 7.12

a) If potential GDP (LAS) is $540, and the economy is presently in equilibrium, is there an inflationary or a recessionary gap? How much of a gap? _____
b) By how much must aggregate demand increase in order to close this gap? _____
c) If every $1 change in government spending leads to a $4 change in aggregate demand, what is the amount by which government spending must increase? _____
d) Suppose that initially government has a balanced budget. If government increases its spending as in (c) and tax revenues are 0.25 of real GDP, what will be government's real budget surplus/deficit at the new full-employment equilibrium? (Deficit/surplus) of _____

Intermediate (Problems 4–8)

4. **(LO 2)** Answer the questions below for the economy of Motak, using the graph in Figure 7.13.

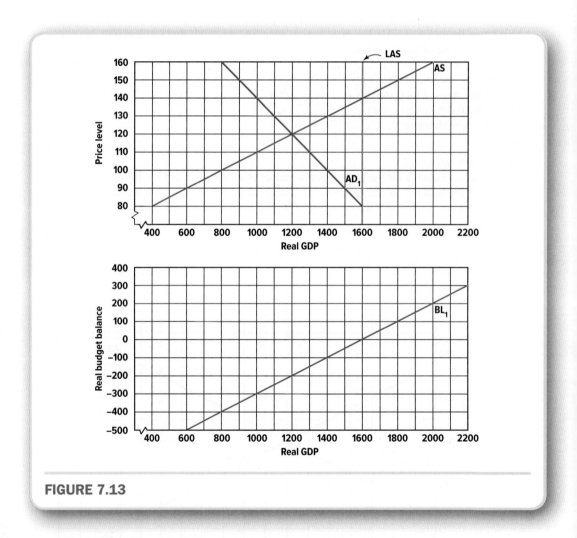

FIGURE 7.13

a) If GDP is $800 and government spending is G_1, what is the size of Motak's budget deficit? _____
b) Suppose government spending is decreased by the size of the deficit in (a). Draw in the new curve, labelled G_2 in Figure 7.13.

c) Suppose the multiplier has a value of 2. What is the new level of equilibrium
   GDP? _____
d) What is the size of Motak's deficit at this new level of equilibrium
   GDP? _____

5. **(LO 1, 2, 3)** The aggregate demand and supply for Cancum are shown in Table 7.9. Potential GDP
   (LAS) is \$1500 billion.

TABLE 7.9

Price Index	Aggregate Quantity Demanded	Aggregate Quantity Supplied
105	1600	400
110	1500	800
115	1400	1100
120	1300	1300
125	1200	1400
130	1100	1500
135	1000	1600
140	900	1650

a) If the economy is in equilibrium, is the economy experiencing an inflationary or a recessionary
   gap? _____ How much? _____
b) Suppose government uses countercyclical fiscal policy to close the gap. By how
   much and in what direction would AD have to change in order to achieve full
   employment? _____
c) As a result of this change, what would be the inflation rate? _____

6. **(LO 3)** The following are data for the economy of Moksha.

$$C = 25 + 0.6Y \qquad G = 160$$
$$I = 60 \qquad X_N = 55 - 0.1Y$$

a) Calculate equilibrium GDP. _____
b) Calculate the multiplier. _____
c) If the tax function is $T = 20 + 0.2Y$, calculate the size of the budget deficit or
   surplus. _____ of _____
d) Now, change government spending by the amount of the surplus or deficit in an attempt to
   balance the budget. What will be the new equilibrium income? _____
e) What is the budget surplus or deficit at the new equilibrium? _____ of _____

7. **(LO 2)** Examine the graph of government spending and net tax revenues in Figure 7.14A.

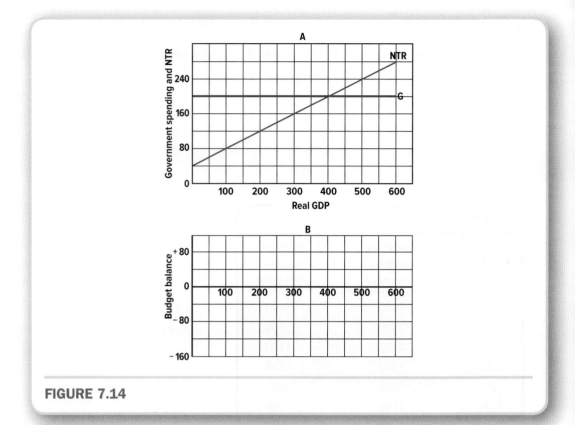

FIGURE 7.14

a) Draw the corresponding budget line in **Figure 7.14B**.
b) Suppose government spending were to decrease by 40, and draw in the new government spending and budget lines.
c) After the change in government spending, what is the budget balance at a GDP level of 500? _____ of _____

8. **(LO 4)** Suppose the equation for Loksha's budget is given as:

$$\text{Budget balance} = -300 + 0.2Y$$

If its level of income is presently $1200, and it has a budget deficit $90, how much is its cyclical deficit and how much is its structural deficit?
Cyclical deficit: $_____
Structural deficit: $_____

Advanced (Problems 9–11)

9. **(LO 2, 3)** The following is information for the economy of Tandor, where taxes are wholly autonomous.

$$C = 40 + 0.8Y_D \quad \text{where} \quad Y_D = (Y - T) \text{ and } G = T = 340$$
$$I = 100 \qquad\qquad\qquad X_N = 107 - 0.1Y$$

a) What is the value of equilibrium income? _____
b) At equilibrium, is there a budget surplus/deficit? How much? (Surplus/deficit) _____ of $_____
c) If government increased both its spending and taxes by $60, what would be the new equilibrium income? _____

10. **(LO 2, 3, 4)** The government of Osiris believes in balancing its budget over a seven-year cycle. Over the first six years, it has maintained its spending at $150 billion and its MTR at 0.25. (There are no autonomous taxes in Osiris.) Column 2 of **Table 7.10** shows the level of GDP in each of the first six years in the cycle.

TABLE 7.10

(1) Year	(2) GDP ($billion)	(3) Government Spending	(4) Tax Revenue	(5) Deficit/Surplus
1	600	____	____	____
2	580	____	____	____
3	560	____	____	____
4	612	____	____	____
5	620	____	____	____
6	608	____	____	____

   a) Complete Table 7.10. Suppose that the estimated level of GDP in year 7 is projected to be $600.
   b) What level of government spending (assuming no change in the tax rate) is necessary for the government of Osiris to end the seven-year cycle with its budgetary goal on target? _____
   c) Alternatively, what change in the tax rate (assuming no change in government spending) is necessary for the government of Osiris to end the seven-year cycle with its budgetary goal on target? _____

11. **(LO 2, 3)** Suppose that the government of Malud increases both its own spending and autonomous taxes by $100 and the economy's multiplier equals 2.5. If consumers spend 80 percent of their disposable (after-tax) income, by how much will GDP change? (Increase/decrease) _____ of $_____

Problems for Further Study

Basic (Problems 1–4)

 1. **(LO 2)** Figure 7.15 shows the economy of Tagara. Its aggregate demand is currently AD$_1$ and the budget line is BL$_1$.

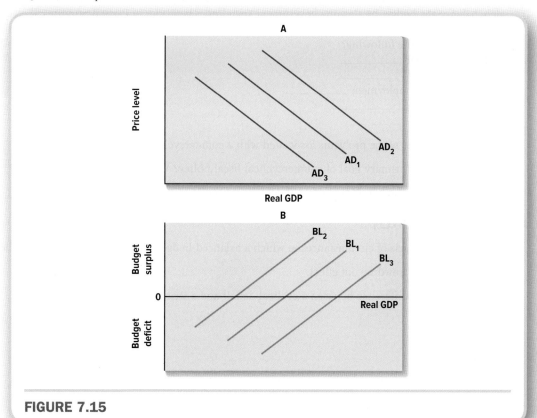

FIGURE 7.15

    a) What effect would an increase in government spending have on each of the graphs?
       In graph A the aggregate demand curve would shift from _____ to _____.
       In graph B the budget line would shift from _____ to _____.
    b) What effect would an increase in taxes have on each of the graphs?
       In graph A the aggregate demand curve would shift from _____ to _____.
       In graph B the budget line would shift from _____ to _____.

2. **(LO 5)** Complete Table 7.11 for the economy of Smetana.

TABLE 7.11

Year	Budget Surplus	Budget Deficit	National Debt	GDP	Debt/GDP %
2012	/	/	280	700	___
2013	/	14	___	725	___
2014	___	___	323	730	___
2015	8	/	___	___	45.0
2016	___	___	310	720	___
2017	/	6	___	750	___

3. **(LO 1)** Define *fiscal policy*.

4. **(LO 5)** To whom does the federal government owe most of its debt?

Intermediate (Problems 5–8)

5. **(LO 2, 3)** Suppose that a federal election is called at a time when the economy is experiencing a recessionary gap and there is a budget deficit. The leader of Party A promises, if elected, to immediately balance the budget by slashing government spending. The leader of Party B promises, if elected, to stimulate the economy with a tax decrease. What would be the effect of each party's proposed policy on each of the following?
    a) The level of GDP _____
    b) The level of NTR _____
    c) The level of unemployment _____
    d) The budget deficit _____
    e) The price level _____

6. **(LO 2)** Explain some of the problems associated with a countercyclical fiscal policy.

7. **(LO 2)** What is the primary goal of countercyclical fiscal policy? What are three criticisms of it?

8. **(LO 5)** Explain how paying off the national debt would redistribute income.

Advanced (Problems 9–11)

9. **(LO 3)** Explain two sets of circumstances in which a balanced-budget fiscal policy would be procyclical.

10. **(LO 3)** Explain the crowding out effect.

11. **(LO 4)** Explain the difference between a cyclical deficit and a structural deficit.

CHAPTER 8
Money and Banking

LEARNING OBJECTIVES

At the end of this chapter, you should be able to:

LO1 Describe the functions, characteristics, and history of money.

LO2 Explain what is and is not money, and describe the main function of modern banks as moneylenders.

LO3 Explain how a small amount of cash can support many loans and create more money.

 WHAT'S AHEAD ...

This is the first of two chapters on the money market and monetary policy. In this chapter, we look at the origins of money, its current definition, and the role that money plays in modern economies. We examine the role of our current banking system, the ability of that system to create new money, and how this helps the economy grow.

A QUESTION OF RELEVANCE ...

You and four friends decide to go out for a fancy meal to celebrate another successful year at university. When the bill arrives, you split it into five shares. Frederick pays by cheque. Sian pays by credit card. Althea digs deep into her pocket and comes up with 20 loonies. Bosie gives an IOU to the manager (a friend of his). You cannot use any of these payment methods, so you have to pay by washing dishes (for yourself and 200 others).

You all paid in different ways. But who used money? Some of you? All of you? So what does constitute money in our modern economy?

Money has been called humanity's greatest invention and its greatest curse. People fret over and sweat for it. For some it is the root of all evil and for others of all joy. Economists, being less fanciful and poetic, refer to it merely as a medium of exchange. The reason they do not wax quite so lyrical is that they regard it as merely one way to hold wealth. After all, it is possible to be extremely wealthy but literally have no money. In fact, there is a problem with holding wealth in the form of money, because money generally does not accumulate. That is, you cannot earn a return from money alone. This is not the case with other forms of wealth, such as stocks and bonds, real estate, or a term deposit in a bank. The other reason economists remain subdued on the topic of money is because they are concerned less with the effect of money on the individual (in that respect, most economists revere it as much as the next person) but rather more on its role in the whole economy.

A group of young students in Toronto take turns playing the game My Money. The former stockbroker who designed the game for the Bank of Montreal hopes it will help children learn to invest wisely once they get some money of their own.

CP/Toronto Star/Bernard Weil

On this subject, economists over the centuries have held differing views. Adam Smith suggested that money is a veil that often conceals the phenomenon of real production that lies behind it. He compared money to a river that helps bring goods to the market but does not in any way affect the actual volume of goods. However, today, we realize that money can, in fact, have a determining influence over "real" variables, such as production and employment. For example, we mentioned in Chapter 5 how an increase in the money supply can result in an increase in real GDP. It is these and other aspects of money that we will examine in this chapter and the next—including the obvious one of its importance in determining prices.

As the market economy was emerging in the sixteenth and seventeenth centuries, many people had personal experience of how the amount of money (and, more specifically, changes in the amount of money) in a society could affect prices. The huge influx of gold from the new American colonies into Europe produced a persistent and dramatic increase in prices in most European countries. In those days, gold meant money, and if the amount of money quickly increases while the volume of production changes slowly, you get the makings of what we previously called *demand-pull inflation*, sometimes characterized as "too much money chasing too few goods."

In the same vein, consider an apocryphal story that came out of World War II about a devious scheme by the Germans to disrupt the Allied war effort. This plan involved the dispatch of bombers over Britain, equipped not with bombs but with millions of counterfeit pound notes. These were to be rained down on the major British towns and cities. The effects would have been obvious. The British people, as heirs to this sudden windfall, would do the predictable: they would spend it, the demand for the limited quantity of consumer goods would rise dramatically, and since production could not increase immediately, the effect would be the bidding up of prices. Britain would have been faced with the same devastating phenomenon that the Germans themselves had experienced in the early 1920s: galloping inflation or hyperinflation. This story is used to illustrate the very strong link between changes in the supply of money and the level of prices. More on this later.

 TEST YOUR UNDERSTANDING

Find answers on the McGraw-Hill online resource.

1. What do you think Adam Smith might have meant when he said "Money is a veil."

8.1   Money: Functions, Characteristics, and History

LO1   Describe the functions, characteristics, and history of money.

So far, we have discussed some aspects of money without actually defining it. Let us continue to skirt around a formal definition for now with a question: What is money good for? The answer is, of course, to spend. In fact, it has been suggested that money imparts value only when we part with it. Thus, the first, and prime, function of money is that it acts as a **medium of exchange**. Without money, people would be forced to barter goods and services directly.

But barter requires what is called the *double coincidence of wants*. If I am to trade with you, you must have what I want and I must have what you want. If this is not the case, we must try to find a third, fourth, or fifth party to engage in multiple exchanges. So, to obtain a bare minimum of goods and services, a person would have to spend far more time and effort arranging exchanges than actually producing goods and services.

This is why economists describe the barter system as having very high *transactions costs*. The use of money, in short, reduces the wasted effort associated with barter.

Money can take almost any form, but its most important characteristic is that it should be *widely acceptable*. As long as members of a community all agree that they will accept a particular commodity or token as money, then it is money. But to make money acceptable, it also needs to be *easily recognizable* by those who are going to use it and *in a standardized form* (each unit of currency should be like all others) and of a form *that cannot be easily copied*. In addition, if we are going to carry it around with us, it should be reasonably *portable*. Finally, if we are going to make both large and small purchases, money should also be *divisible* and available in different denominations.

But money is not used just for exchange. Some of us like to keep it. In other words, money can be used as a **store of wealth**. This is its second function. As mentioned, wealth can be stored in other forms—from stocks and bonds to real estate, from savings accounts to art collections—but these other forms are not as convenient as money and often involve more risk. Compared with all other forms of wealth, money is the most liquid; that is, it can be used directly as a means of payment. If it is to act as a store of wealth, money should obviously possess other desirable characteristics. Besides the other characteristics we have mentioned, it should also be reasonably *durable* and of such a nature that people are willing to hold it.

Finally, money is used as a **unit of account** (or measure of value). Think of the problems in trying to value a commodity in a moneyless community. Assume, for instance, that a suit of clothes is worth ten litres of beer, that a litre of beer is worth two loaves of bread, and that you need a hundred loaves of bread to buy a table—how many suits of clothes does it take to buy a table? The answer is five suits, but the answer does not come quickly. By providing a single uniform measure of values, money simplifies comparisons of prices, wages, and incomes.

In summary, the functions of money are as

- a medium of exchange
- a store of value
- a unit of account

In a money-using society, every product and service can be valued in terms of a single commodity, money. If we measure everything in money terms, that is, in dollars and cents, we might ask what money itself is worth. The answer must be in relative terms—it is worth what we can get in exchange for it. And what we can get is determined by prices of the products we buy; lower prices means we can buy more and thus the value of money would be higher. The value of money is, therefore, inversely related to the price level. If prices were to increase, then the value of a unit of money would decrease. In other words,

$$\text{Value of money} = \frac{1}{\text{price level}}$$

ADDED DIMENSION

Money Increases Economic Well-Being

A society possessing no money would be very simple and materially very poor. This is because exchange would be difficult and time consuming. Imagine a person possessing a pound of honey but wanting a package of medium-sized, flathead screws. How long might it take to find someone with the right screws who just happened to want some honey? In short, almost everybody would be forced to produce most of the necessities of survival for themselves. Few could earn a livelihood by specializing in producing just one product and then trading it for other products. Such lack of specialization, along with the high cost of exchange, would result in an existence in which a minimal quantity of goods and services was exchanged. This is how the use of money increases a nation's potential to produce goods and services and thus increases its economic well-being.

Although anything can be (and many things have been) used as money, some things are definitely better than others. For instance, let us imagine a (particularly silly) society that hit upon the idea of using stones as a form of money. Well, certainly stones are durable, portable, divisible (big stones and little stones), and easily recognized by the general public, which are characteristics that all money needs. The problem is that without very much trouble at all, everybody would spend time collecting piles of stones and think they had become fabulously rich. The result would, of course, be rampant inflation. This would happen because although the amount of money has increased the amount of goods and services available has not. As a result, the prices of all products would rise significantly as demand far exceeds supply. To avoid this outcome, the supply of money in an economy needs to be sufficient to facilitate trade and economic growth, but it also needs to be controlled by a central authority so that the supply does not become too large relative to the real wealth of the country.

- acceptable
- durable
- portable
- divisible
- standardized, and easily recognized but not easily copied
- controlled by a central authority

TEST YOUR UNDERSTANDING

2. Given the clothes/table example above, how many suits of clothes would it cost to buy a table if a litre of beer is worth only one loaf of bread?

The History and Different Kinds of Money

The long-held view that money was invented to replace barter is currently being revised. It is now realized that ceremonial exchange, or what anthropologists call *gift economies*—think of the history of the potlatch among indigenous peoples on Canada's west coast, for example—were common before the emergence of the first agrarian societies in Mesopotamia. This new view argues that these ceremonies were, among other things, elementary credit systems. One group invited another group to a ceremonial feast where gifts were lavished upon the guests. The expectation was that this act would be returned—there was an implied reciprocity. It follows that as this practice expanded to include more and more groups who had a growing diversity of surplus goods to give away, the purpose of money as a unit of account was invented. This occurred once the unquantifiable obligation "I owe you one" transformed into the quantifiable notion of "I owe you one unit of something." In short, it is now believed that money emerged first as credit and only later acquired its functions as a medium of exchange and a store of value.

Furthermore, there is little evidence of a society or economy that relied solely on barter. Instead, nonmonetary societies used gift-giving to create productive reciprocal obligations and debt on the part of those who received the gift. Occasional incidents of barter did occur, but these were either between strangers or involved long-distance trade and transport of goods. The reason for this limited use of barter is obvious: barter means that goods are directly exchanged without the use of money, and for this to work, as we previously mentioned, a double coincidence of wants is an essential feature and this is something that simply doesn't happen often.

Though barter can involve the exchange of many different types of goods, in all past societies certain goods have always been traded more often than others, and these became valuable in their own right because they were so widely accepted. We need to recognize that when such things as beads, salt, or shells are used as money, they have intrinsic value in themselves as well as having value as money. This type of money is called **commodity money**. Even today, in jails and prisoner-of-war camps, for example, where people have no access to the outside community, such things as cigarettes or playing cards act as forms of commodity money.

It has long been assumed that metals, where available, were used primarily as proto-money because they have the characteristics of being durable, portable, and easily divisible. Nonetheless, such commodities as cattle, cowry shells (rounded, shiny porcelain-like shells of the sea snail), salt, or wampum (strings of beads made from clam shells) were also used when metals were not immediately available. Interestingly, the *shekel* (a term used to this day for money) was an ancient unit used in Mesopotamia around 3000 BCE to define a specific weight of barley. The use of gold as proto-money has been traced back to the fourth millennium BCE when the Egyptians used gold bars of a set weight as a medium of exchange, as had been done earlier in Mesopotamia with silver bars.

The first gold coins probably appeared in Greece about 700 BCE. The first manufactured coins seem to have been produced separately in India, China, and cities around the Aegean sea between 700 and 500 BCE. While the Aegean coins were stamped (heated and hammered with insignia), the Indian coins (from the Ganges river valley) were punched metal disks, and Chinese coins were cast bronze with holes in the centre to be strung together.

Gold has many of the desirable characteristics of money. It does, however, have one serious drawback: it does not come in standardized units. It needs to be weighed out every time a transaction is made. This was the obvious reason standardized metal *coins* of specific sizes and weights were introduced.

Another drawback is that gold coins are open to abuse. Since gold is a particularly soft metal, it is possible to "sweat" the coins—shake them up in a bag to produce a residue of gold dust that remained after removing the coins. Another example is shaving a thin sliver from the outside of unmilled coins and keeping it. Perhaps the worst practitioners of this type of theft were those with political power (the sovereigns) whose portraits on the coins were supposedly a mark of trust and integrity. An important event, such as a coronation or royal wedding, was an occasion for the sovereign to call in the old coins and replace them with newly minted coins. However, in the process of melting down the coins, a base metal, such as lead, was often added to the vat. Over time, the currency was more and more debased and inflation would invariably follow, since the quantity of coins grew faster than the output of real goods and services.

Gold has one more serious defect as a form of money: in large quantities it is very heavy. This is why people in Europe in the Middle Ages started to deposit their money in goldsmiths' (jewellers') vaults. When a deposit was made (for a fee), a *certificate of deposit* was issued by the goldsmith acknowledging the fact.

How much does this weigh and what is it worth?

© Pterwort | Dreamstime.com

The end of the fifteenth century saw a growing expansion of trade in parts of Europe. In an example of another form of money, a flourishing Italian wholesale trader in cloth who became dependent on credit for the rapid expansion of his business might sell goods to a buyer who would "pay" with a **bill of exchange**, which constituted the buyer's promise to make payment at some specified future date. Provided the buyer was reputable, the holder of the bill could then present it to a goldsmith-banker for redemption (at a discounted value) before it actually fell due.

Notice that both certificates of deposit and bills of exchange are a form of *paper money* and their creation was an important step in the evolution of modern commercial banks.

By the seventeenth century (and about a hundred years later in North America) these early goldsmith–merchant banks evolved into commercial banks that were issuing paper money as we know it today. However, this practice was gradually replaced by the issuance of currency authorized and controlled only by national governments. Since 1935, the Bank of Canada is the only bank in the country with the power to issue currency—sometimes called **fiat money** because it is declared legal tender by law. As we shall see later, Canada's central bank no longer acts as a commercial bank, as it once did, but now acts solely as an agent of government.

With the maturing of the modern banking system in the nineteenth and twentieth centuries, the use of *chequebook money* became commonplace. This means that, in return for depositing money with a bank, the depositor receives a chequebook from the bank. A cheque is nothing more than a standardized form of instruction by a customer to the bank, telling it to transfer a sum of money from the customer's account to the person specified on the cheque. As such, a cheque is not money but merely a method of accessing it. It is the deposit in your bank account that constitutes money. Let us now summarize the different kinds of money.

- commodity money (including gold and other precious metals)
- coins
- paper money
- chequebook money (bank deposits)

To complete our story of the history of money we need to recognize that modern banks do not act simply as big safety deposit boxes, guarding depositors' money until they require it. The implication of this point is rather interesting. If all the customers of a bank were to descend *en masse* demanding a return of their deposits, in what is called a *run on the bank*, that bank (and any in the modern banking world) would find itself acutely embarrassed. It simply would not have that amount of cash on hand. So what happened to the cash you and all the others deposited? The answer is that the bank loaned it out. Banks only keep a small fraction of the amounts deposited, so they may be vulnerable to a run.

Many transfers that were once carried out using cheques are now completed using electronic banking machines.

Ryan McVay/Getty Images

How did such a state of affairs come about? Let's begin our answer by returning to the certificates of deposits of the goldsmith-bankers discussed above. It did not take long for these early merchant banks to discover that they need not keep all the gold they held for others. Unless all of the customers arrived on the doorstep at the same time—a very remote possibility—there would be no harm in lending out some of it. So lend they did. In fact, the banks also learned that when they started offering loans, most people did not particularly want to receive gold but actually preferred one of the certificates of deposit. The bank could simply make loans by giving customers a piece of paper. The fact that these early merchant banks would make loans far in excess of the gold they held as deposits is one of history's first example of **leverage**. If, for example, they had deposits valued at 100, they would make loans valued at 400, 500, or more and thus leverage their deposits and collect much higher interest revenue on the loans.

Thus was born the final plank of our modern banking system: the **fractional reserve system**. With the rise of commercial banking, bankers discovered that they, like the goldsmiths, only needed to keep a small fraction of their customers' deposits in the form of cash reserves. Today, banks in Canada keep only a very small percentage of their customers' deposits in the form of cash. The fact that modern banks operate on this basis has important implications for the monetary system and for monetary policy, as we shall see.

Shells	Gold and Silver	Coins	Paper Money	Digital Money

The next evolutionary step in the history of money will almost certainly involve the use of private electronic money such as the bitcoin.

ADDED DIMENSION

Electronic Money

Traditional currency (coins and notes) has a number of advantages, including the fact that the transaction costs of using it are low. If I want to buy something, I just hand over the cash. I do not need to register the transfer, and the seller need not record that she received the cash from me. Also, mere possession of cash implies ownership. But this is also its great disadvantage. Cash is easy to steal and difficult to recover. For this reason, many people are embracing alternatives to cash.

For example, small plastic cards (smart cards) embedded with computer chips are becoming more common. You can buy, say, a $50 card that enables you to spend up to that amount using only your card to pay for such items as transit fares, parking meters, a quick coffee, and so on. Also, the debit card, which is an electronic form of cheque-writing, is now well established.

It is interesting to note that some observers see the smart card and the debit card becoming the customary circulating medium along with privately supplied digital cash, which is stored in computer hard drives. E-cash fits Internet commerce like a glove, but will it move beyond this?

It might. We now have the introduction of the bitcoin, a currency that can be transferred from person to person through computers or smart phones without passing through a bank or clearing house. No central authority manages it. There is a 21 million limit on the number of bitcoins, but each coin can be subdivided into 100 million smaller units called satoshis.

The bitcoin is very attractive to some people. Consider the case of high-tech worker who lives in a country where politics, inflation, fluctuating exchange rates, and difficulty moving money creates uncertainty about the future value of and access to personal savings. By changing the local currency into bitcoins, an individual can move savings across international borders where they may be safer or decide to keep them within the bitcoin system itself. Unfortunately, the bitcoin is also being used in the international drug trade as an easy way of moving money obtained through corruption and bribery.

TEST YOUR UNDERSTANDING

3. Explain the difference between commodity money and fiat money.

SECTION SUMMARY

a) Money functions as

- a medium of exchange
- store of value
- unit of account

b) Money must be

- acceptable
- durable
- portable
- divisible
- standardized and easily recognized but not easily copied
- controlled by a central authority

c) The origin of money is rooted in ceremonies of ancient gift economies.

d) Commodity money includes

- cattle and seashells
- salt and beads
- metals—particularly gold

e) The origin of paper money lies in both certificates of deposit and bills of exchange issued by the early goldsmiths in Europe.

f) The early goldsmiths evolved into merchant banks through the use of leverage.

g) The practice by merchant banks of issuing certificates of deposit in excess of the amount of cash reserves gave birth to the fractional reserve system.

h) The four types of money are

- commodity money
- coins
- paper money
- chequebook money

8.2 What Constitutes Money?

> **LO2** Explain what is and is not money, and describe the main functions of banks as moneylenders.

Recall from Chapter 3 that money is any item that is widely accepted as a medium of exchange, gives direct and immediate access to goods and services, and can be used to settle debts.

In the next chapter, we will see that the Bank of Canada needs to control the supply of money to the economy. Therefore, the nation's central bank needs to be able to clearly define and measure the amount of money circulating in the economy. However, what may come as a surprise to many is the fact that there really is not one single accepted measure of the money supply. Let us start with the simplest, most basic definition, called the **M1** definition, which includes currency in circulation (coins and paper bank notes) plus **demand deposits** in the chequing accounts of all commercial banks. The word *demand* in demand deposits refers to the fact that depositors can demand their deposits in cash at any time.

The money supply (in billions of dollars) in Canada in June 2016 was

$$M1 = \text{currency} + \text{demand deposits}$$
$$337 = \underset{(23\%)}{76} + \underset{(77\%)}{261}$$

You might well ask: If chequing accounts (demand deposits) are included as part of the money supply, why not also include savings accounts and other types of **notice deposits**? Notice deposits, as the name suggests, require the depositor to give notice to the bank before making a withdrawal.

Surely these accounts, in practice, are no different from chequing accounts, since banks seldom enforce the requirement of giving notice before withdrawal. So we have a wider definition of money, called **M2**, which includes all of M1 plus all notice deposits (savings accounts on deposit for an undefined length of time) and what are called *personal term deposits*, which are on deposit for a specific term such as six months. The amounts in June 2016 were

$$
\begin{array}{lll}
\text{M2} & = & \text{M1} & + \text{notice deposits and personal term deposits} \\
1426 & = & 337 & + \qquad\qquad 1089 \\
 & & (24\%) & \qquad\qquad (76\%)
\end{array}
$$

Finally, an even broader measurement, **M3**, includes M2 but adds to it term deposits of businesses (known as *certificates of deposit*), which are easily convertible into chequable deposits. The M3 measurement, then, includes all of M2 plus certificates of deposits. Again, for June 2016, the amounts were

$$
\begin{array}{lll}
\text{M3} & = & \text{M2} & + \text{certificates of deposit} \\
2158 & = & 1426 & + \qquad 732 \\
 & & (66\%) & \qquad (34\%)
\end{array}
$$

You can see from this that the various measures are ranked in order of liquidity, that is, the closeness to cash, M1 being the most liquid and M3 the least. The visual that follows illustrates the relative sizes of these three measures.

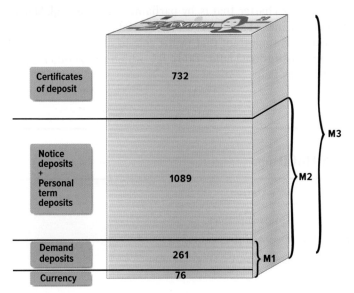

Now you might well ask: What is the point of multiple measures of the money supply—in short, who cares about the differences between M1 and M2 or M3? In Chapter 9, we will examine the role of monetary policy in stabilizing the economy and avoiding inflation. Since this kind of policy making involves controlling the money supply, just how we define the money supply becomes very important.

For expediency, we will confine our discussion and analysis of money to M1—currency in circulation plus demand deposits (chequing accounts). This keeps things simple while recognizing the essential characteristic of money: the direct and immediate control over goods and services.

What Is Not Money?

Not all currency issued by the Bank of Canada is included as money, only the portion in circulation. In other words, the currency in the vaults or tills of banks is not included in any definition of money.

This is because when you deposit currency in a bank, the balance of your bank account increases, and since the amount of deposits in your accounts is part of the money supply, it would be double counting to count both the increase in your accounts and the increase in the bank's tills. In other words, when people deposit currency in a bank, the amount of currency *in circulation* goes down and the amount in deposit accounts goes up. This means that:

A new deposit of currency into a bank changes the composition of the money supply but does not change its total.

Other exclusions from the money supply are gold (try paying for your designer jeans with an ingot); such financial securities as stocks and bonds; and the credit on credit cards.

Credit cards, and the more recent debit cards, are merely a means of accessing money. You might argue that in many instances, credit cards are more acceptable than personal cheques. That is true, but they merely represent a loan negotiated with a finance company. More importantly, you cannot pay off a debt with a credit card. Certainly, you can obtain cash, but that is the clue that it is not itself money. Similarly, cheques are not money but simply give you access to the money in your chequing account.

The final exclusion from the modern definition of money is chequable deposits at **near-banks**. Near-banks include credit unions, trust companies, and mortgage and loan associations. In other words, all of our three alternative definitions of money—M1, M2, M3—refer to accounts only at commercial banks. Canada's central bank, the Bank of Canada, exercises a degree of control over the commercial banks but has a lesser degree of power over near-banks (also termed *nonbank financial intermediaries*). The Bank of Canada prefers to count as money only the currency it can control directly, hence the exclusion of accounts at near-banks. Nonetheless, the Bank also measures what it calls M2+, which includes demand and notice deposits at near-banks, and M2AA, which further includes Canada Savings Bonds and other non–money market funds.

Chartered banks include the six major commercial banks in Canada (all of which received a charter under the *Bank Act*) and a few dozen much smaller banks. Their name derives from the fact that each was set up by federal charter, that is, by parliamentary approval. Starting a bank is not the same as starting your own business; banking is a very special business.

As we have now seen, it is important that we be able to clearly distinguish money from other types of assets people (and institutions) hold. Table 8.1, which shows other types of wealth holdings listed in order of liquidity, may help.

TABLE 8.1
Forms of Wealth Holdings

Money	Description
Currency	Coins and notes
Chequable deposits	Deposits in chequing accounts
Notice deposits	Deposits in savings accounts
Financial Assets	
Term deposits	Funds deposited for a fixed period (generally short-term) at a fixed interest rate
Treasury bills	Short-term security (usually for three months) in specific denominations issued by the federal government
Bonds	Securities (IOUs) issued by the governments and corporations, at a fixed rate of interest at a fixed term (often from one to ten years)
Certificates of deposit	A savings certificate, issued in many denominations, with a fixed maturity date and a specified fixed interest rate
Stocks (shares)	A part-ownership of a corporation that entitles the owner to a claim on its assets and profits (in the form of dividends)
Mutual funds	A part-ownership of a fund that has invested its clients' money in various assets, including shares in corporations
GICs	Guaranteed investment certificates; securities issued by financial institutions such as investment and insurance companies
Real Assets	
Personal assets	Ownership of things like cars, boats, jewellery
Real estate	Ownership of houses, commercial buildings and land

ADDED DIMENSION

Canada's Big Banks

The five largest banks in Canada in order of size are: Royal Bank, TD Canada Trust, Scotiabank, Bank of Montreal, and Canadian Imperial Bank of Commerce (CIBC). Credit unions, which are regulated provincially, are major players in British Columbia and in Quebec, where they are called *caisses populaires*. In the last twenty years, the world has seen a trend to big-bank mergers. However, in 1998, the attempted mergers between the Bank of Montreal and Royal Bank of Canada, and between CIBC and TD Canada Trust, were blocked by the federal government, indicating resistance to this trend in Canada.

And just how big are our banks? It might be instructive to compare them with the world's biggest banks (in April 2016):

World Rank	Bank	Assets ($billions CAN)
1.	ICBC (China)	3 420
2.	China Construction Bank (China)	2 826
3.	Agricultural Bank of China (China)	2 740
4.	Bank of China Ltd. (China)	2 590
5.	Misubishi,UFJ (Japan)	2 459
6.	HSBC (U.K.) BNP Paribus (France)	2 410
31.	Royal Bank (Canada)	853
33.	TD Canada Trust (Canada)	834
46.	Scotiabank (Canada)	654
51.	Bank of Montreal (Canada)	497
68.	CIBC (Canada)	341

Source: *S & P Global Market Intelligence*, April 2016.

TEST YOUR UNDERSTANDING

4. a) If David deposits $240 cash into his chequing account at a commercial bank, has the money supply changed?

b) If, later on, David transfers this $240 from his chequing account to a saving account in the same bank, has M1 changed? Has M2?

5. Given the following data (all in billions of dollars) what are the values of M1, M2, and M3?

Coins	13
Certificates of deposit	137
Demand deposits	72
Notice and personal term deposits	215
Notes	27

The Canadian Banking System

Banks, like other corporations, are in business to make profits. Most of these profits come from lending out excess deposits they might have. Their profit comes from the **spread**, the difference between the interest rate a bank charges to borrowers and the interest rate it pays to depositors. There is not much difference in the spread among Canada's major banks. The total profits of a bank come more from the total volume of its transactions rather than from a difference in the spread. Like any other business, banks do not like to carry excess inventories. In the case of banks, their inventory is money. They do not earn a return on idle money balances; therefore, they will always try to ensure that the amount of reserves they retain is kept to a minimum, consistent with security.

Until recently, the *Bank Act* specified exactly how much commercial banks had to keep in reserve. Although this is no longer required, banks still hold reserves and maintain what is referred to as a **target reserve ratio**, which is the proportion of demand deposits a bank wants to hold in the form of cash in its vaults or with the Bank of Canada. These reserves provide some degree of security for the bank's customers. However, the main security for depositors comes from insurance. All banks are required by law to take out insurance on customers' deposits. The deposits are insured with the Canada Deposit Insurance Corporation up to a maximum of $100 000 per depositor per bank.

Chances are your bank does not look like this. Canada's six major banks have several hundred branches across the country.

PhotoDisk

The Canadian banking system is remarkably secure. (There have been only three bank failures in all of the twentieth century, although two occurred within the last thirty years.) What economists call a branch banking system accounts for this stability. It is a system dominated by a few large banks, each of which has many branches operating across the country. For example, Canada's six big banks each have several hundred branches coast to coast. The sheer size and geographical diversity of this type of structure spreads the risk and therefore minimizes the possibility of bank failure.

Contrast this with a unit banking system, which, though it is currently in transition, is still the basic system in the United States. This system is made up of thousands of relatively small banks that have either only one branch or multiple branches that are confined to a single state. Such a system is less secure. For example, the First National Bank of Dalton (Nebraska) is small compared with the average branch of any one of Canada's big six banks. Furthermore, most of the loans by First National would be to local wheat farmers for equipment, seed, and so on. If a bad hailstorm wipes out the local wheat crop and most of the farmers go bankrupt, the bank could face the same fate.

Does this mean the Canadian banking system is superior? In a security sense, yes. But the source of this security is a system dominated by only six big banks, and this means that competition within the system is weak. This has several consequences. First, the merely irritating: long lineups for routine transactions, short operating hours—though this has certainly been changing in recent years—and the inability of customers to deal face to face with the decision makers.

More significantly, the size of the spread in the Canadian banking system is historically wider than that in the American system. Finally, there is the issue of the banks' loan policies. From time to time throughout history, one can find references to a recurring complaint by small businesses in Canada: large banks do not recognize the unique circumstances of a small business, and they do not make loans to unproven companies or ideas. Although one can understand the position of the large banks on this issue, it is also obvious that the whole economy does, from time to time, fail to benefit from the potential success of a new business or product because of the lack of loans needed to get started. In summary, the Canadian branch banking system is very secure and stable, but it is also very conservative.

Some of this may be changing. Foreign banks have recently been allowed to operate in Canada, although there are constraints on size. This should, at least to some extent, increase competition in this industry.

Balanced against all this is the fact that, compared with most banking systems around the world, Canada's is one of the safest. The financial and economic meltdown experienced by most economies (especially the American and European economies) around the world in 2008 left our banking system pretty much unaffected, largely because the banking regulations did not allow the extreme risk taking that was commonplace elsewhere—particularly in the United States. We will have more to say about this in Chapter 13.

ADDED DIMENSION

Financial Institutions

The financial market consists of different types of financial institutions. All of these have one thing in common: they are intermediaries and act as agents among households, businesses, and governments that have funds available for lending and others who want to borrow those funds. Canadian banks are the biggest borrowers as well as lenders.

Other institutions came into existence because banks were originally forbidden to provide certain types of loans. Mortgage companies specialized in long-term loans (mortgages) for people wishing to purchase real estate, such as houses or condos. Trust companies looked after the pensions and trust accounts of both firms and individuals. Credit unions (*caisses populaires* in Quebec) sprang up because many small firms were unable to obtain loans from the banks.

As the following table makes clear, in Canada the banks are, by far, the biggest source of credit.

	Debt Outstanding 2015 ($billions)	% of Total Debt
Domestic banks	415	56
Other banks (including trust companies)	100	14
Finance (including mortgage) companies	70	10
Credit unions	72	10
Other lending institutions	70	10
Total	727	100

Source: Adapted from Statistics Canada, Table 190-0003, http://www40.statcan.ca/l01/cst01/busi04-eng.htm, September 14, 2016.

SECTION SUMMARY

a) The modern definition of money includes

- M1, which is currency plus demand deposits

- M2, which is M1 plus notice deposits and personal term deposits

- M3, which is M2 plus certificates of deposit

b) Money is only one type of financial asset; others are bonds, stocks, mutual funds, and so forth. In addition, people also own real assets, such as personal assets and real estate.

8.3   The Creation of Money by the Banking System

> **LO3**   Explain how a small amount of cash can support many loans and create more money.

As we have mentioned, the Bank of Canada is solely responsible for determining the amount of currency in the economy. The public decides what fraction of this currency it wants to hold and what fraction it wants to deposit with banks and other financial institutions. The banks will then, decide how much of these deposits they wish to keep as reserves and how much they want to lend.

To understand how just a small amount of reserves can support many loans and deposits, we need first to understand a few very basic accounting terms.

Assets, Liabilities, and Balance Sheets

A balance sheet presents the financial condition of an institution at a particular moment in time. (The profit and loss statement is of no concern here.) On one side are listed all the assets and on the other side the liabilities. **Assets** comprise what a company owns or what others owe it. **Liabilities** comprise what a company owes to others. The difference between the two is the **net worth** of the company, otherwise known as *equity*. Equity is the book value of the company to its shareholders. (The company's market value may be more or less than its book value.) The following is a simplified balance sheet of the Saymor Bank Limited.

<table>
<tr><td colspan="4" align="center">**BALANCE SHEET OF SAYMOR BANK LTD.**
As of December 31, 2016</td></tr>
<tr><td>**Assets**</td><td></td><td>**Liabilities and Equity**</td><td></td></tr>
<tr><td>Reserves</td><td>$ 10 000</td><td>Demand deposits</td><td>$100 000</td></tr>
<tr><td>Loans to customers</td><td>60 000</td><td>Shareholders' equity</td><td>20 000</td></tr>
<tr><td>Securities</td><td>30 000</td><td></td><td></td></tr>
<tr><td>Fixed assets</td><td>20 000</td><td></td><td></td></tr>
<tr><td></td><td>$120 000</td><td></td><td>$120 000</td></tr>
</table>

The assets are all listed in terms of liquidity (closeness to cash), with the most liquid at the top. Reserves are the currency held, in part, by the bank as cash on hand (vault cash) and, in part, on deposit with the Bank of Canada. Loans to customers represent one of the income-earning assets of the bank and are their most important and most lucrative assets. Securities are shares (gilt-edged—that is, very secure, "as good as gold") or bonds (usually government bonds and treasury bills). Fixed assets include the buildings, equipment, and furniture of the bank. The major liability, and the only one shown here, is demand deposits, which represents the total amount of depositors' accounts owed by the bank to its customers. (We will ignore notice or savings deposits.) The equity figure shows that the book value of this bank is $20 000 (in millions of dollars).

Let us practise a few simple transactions to familiarize ourselves with bookkeeping entries. Standard accounting procedures require that every transaction involve two entries. After making any entries, the balance sheet should remain in balance. (The totals may change, but the assets should still equal liabilities plus equity.)

Transaction 1: Fred, a customer of the bank, deposits $200 cash in the bank. The reserves of the bank would, therefore, increase by $200. The other entry? Fred's bank balance will increase by $200. (An asset for Fred, of course, but a liability for the bank, since it now owes Fred $200 more.) So demand deposits increase by $200. In other words, both assets and liabilities have increased.

Transaction 2: Penny withdraws $500 cash from her account. This is straightforward, since it is just the reverse of Transaction 1. The bank's reserves are reduced by $500, and the demand deposits go down by $500; both assets and liabilities are reduced.

Transaction 3: The bank buys some securities for $200 cash. In this case, reserves decrease by $200, and securities increase by $200; one asset decreases and another increases. The net effect on total assets is zero.

The next transaction is of more significance, since it is the foundation for the commercial banks' ability to create money.

Transaction 4: Suppose the bank grants you a loan. What exactly does this imply? Generally speaking, it does not mean the bank gives you cash. Instead, in exchange for your written acceptance of the terms and conditions for repayment of the loan, the bank will give you immediate credit in your chequing account for the amount of the loan. Now, whether you actually draw out cash or write a cheque for all or part of the amount is up to you. But what the bank has given you is *direct and immediate access to goods and services* and the ability to settle a debt. It has, in other words, by a single bookkeeping entry, created money for you.

The two accounts affected are an increase in loans (an asset) and an increase in demand deposits (a liability). Cash reserves are unaffected.

> Every time a bank issues a loan, it creates money.

Now, having been granted the loan you might do one of three things:

Transaction 4a: You decide that you are going to withdraw some or all of the loan in cash. This means the bank's reserves decrease by the amount of the withdrawal, and the demand deposits are decreased by the same amount.

Transaction 4b: You write a cheque to buy an airline ticket. Suppose that the airline uses the same bank. In that case, your demand deposit balance is reduced by the amount of the cheque, and that of the airline company is increased by the same amount. Here, the total amount of demand deposits remains unchanged. In addition, note that the bank's reserves were unaffected.

Transaction 4c: You write a cheque to buy a new sofa from the Sogood Sofa Company. Sogood Sofa deposits your cheque at its bank, which is a different bank from yours. At the end of the day, its bank will come to yours for payment of the cheque. The cheque is then cleared against your bank, whose reserves will drop as a result. Therefore, your bank's reserves and demand deposits will be reduced, while the other bank's reserves and demand deposits will increase.

TEST YOUR UNDERSTANDING

6. Give the necessary bank bookkeeping entries for each set of circumstances below.

   a) The bank makes a $2000 loan to Fadia.

   b) Fadia writes a $2000 cheque to Middle East Travel, which has its account at a different bank.

The Money Multiplier

That is enough bookkeeping for the present. Now what we want to figure out are the implications for a bank and for the banking system when a bank holds more than its targeted reserves. Let us start off the analysis by assuming that the Saymor Bank and all other banks are just meeting their target reserves of 10 percent. Remember that this means each bank wants to hold a minimum of 10 percent of its demand deposits in the form of cash reserves.

$$\text{Target reserves} = \text{target reserve ratio} \times \text{demand deposits} \qquad [8.1]$$

For instance, assume that Saymor starts from the position indicated in this balance sheet.

BALANCE SHEET OF SAYMOR BANK LTD. As of December 31, 2016			
Assets		**Liabilities and Equity**	
Reserves	$ 10 000	Demand deposits	$100 000
Loans to customers	60 000	Shareholders' equity	20 000
Securities	30 000		
Fixed assets	20 000		
	$120 000		$120 000

Now, assume that Tom, rummaging under his bed one morning, comes across $1000 in currency. Not knowing what to do with it, he decides to deposit it in the bank. The bank credits the $1000 to his account. Its reserves now equal $11 000, and its demand deposits equal $101 000. The bank now finds that it has excess reserves, since it wants to hold only 10% × $101 000, or $10 100. It is over-reserved to the tune of $900; that is,

$$\text{Excess reserves} = \text{actual reserves} - \text{target reserves} \qquad [8.2]$$
$$900 = 11\ 000 - 10\ 100(10\% \times 101\ 000)$$

Or to look at it in another way, of the $1000 that Tom deposited, the bank aims to keep only 10 percent in the form of cash reserves and therefore has $900 more than it considers necessary to hold. As we mentioned before, banks do not like to have such idle cash; they want to earn some return on it. They will be very happy to lend it out.

Now, let us assume Wing Kee happens to come into the bank the next day in need of a $900 loan. The loan is happily granted, and he walks out with $900 more in his chequing account. Within a few hours, Wing Kee purchases a used Volkswagen from the New Star Car Company. A New Star employee deposits his cheque in another bank called the J.M.K. Bank. Recall our assumption that J.M.K., prior to the deposit by New Star, had no reserves in excess of its targeted amount. After J.M.K. clears Wing Kee's cheque against the Saymor Bank, the following accounts at J.M.K. will be affected:

Reserves + $900　　Demand deposits + $900

We assume that the J.M.K., like all other banks, also wants to keep 10 percent of the increased demand deposits, that is, 10% × $900, or $90. It therefore has $810 in **excess reserves**. It, too, is anxious to lend these reserves out. Now, let us assume that Sue is in need of $810 to pay off a debt to her friend Sarbjit and manages to negotiate an $810 loan from J.M.K., in the form of an increased credit balance to her chequing account. She immediately pays Sarbjit by cheque. Sarbjit deposits the cheque at his bank, which we will call the M.P.C. Bank. After he makes this deposit and Sue's cheque clears, the balance sheet of the M.P.C. Bank changes:

Reserves + $810　　Demand deposits + $810

The M.P.C. Bank now finds itself with excess reserves (over its targeted amount). It wants to keep back only 10 percent of the $810, or $81, as cash reserves. Therefore, it has $810 minus $81, or $729, in excess reserves. Let us assume that this amount is loaned out. Regardless of whom it is loaned to, and regardless of how the loan is spent (assuming that recipients of the cheque deposit it back into a bank), sooner or later one of the banks in the banking system will find itself again with excess reserves and be ready and able to lend. Although the cash moves from bank to bank, the banking *system* seems unable to get rid of this additional cash. A bank lends it out, but each time it is spent and returns to some other bank. However, each time it returns, the receiving bank retains 10 percent of that new deposit in additional reserves. Let us follow the trail resulting from Tom's initial deposit of $1000.

Reserves	Loans	Deposits
+1000		+1000 (Tom)
	+900 (to Wing Kee)	+900 (New Star)
	+810 (to Sue)	+810 (Sarbjit)
	+729	+729
	...	...
	...	...
	...	...

You can see that both the loans and the deposits column above follow a geometric pattern. What we are interested in finding out is the total of the deposits column. Why? Because *it is money.* Think back to the definition of money (M1): currency in circulation plus demand deposits. The banks' cash reserves are not part of the money supply, but the total amount in peoples' chequing accounts certainly is.

So what will be the total of all demand deposits that result from Tom's initial deposit of $1000? They will be 1000 + 900 + 810 + 729 + ...

It is reasonably easy to solve if you remember the formula for summing a geometric progression. But let us tackle the problem from a different perspective by looking at part of the balance sheet of the *whole banking system*. Assume it was as follows prior to Tom's deposit.

Reserves	$100 000	Demand deposits	$1 000 000
Loans	$900 000		

Staying with our assumption that banks want to keep a 10 percent reserve ratio, the banking system illustrated above is neither over- nor under-reserved. If the target reserves must equal 10 percent of deposits, it means that demand deposits will equal 10 times the amount of reserves. Now, Tom deposits $1000 in one of the banks so that reserves equal $101 000. Demand deposits can potentially rise to a maximum of 10 × $101 000, or $1 010 000. As a result of the lending process we described, the new combined balance sheet would look like this:

Reserves	$101 000	Demand deposits	$1 010 000
Loans	$909 000		

In other words, if the target reserve ratio is 10 percent, a new deposit of $X will lead to an increase in total deposits throughout the *whole* banking system of ten times $X. As you probably recognize, what we have here is another multiplier—this time, the **money multiplier**.

$$\text{Money multiplier} = \frac{\Delta \text{ deposits}}{\Delta \text{ reserves}} \qquad [8.3]$$

$$\text{Money multiplier} = \frac{1}{\text{target reserve ratio}} \qquad [8.4]$$

In our example, the target reserve ratio is 10 percent, or 0.1, and so the money multiplier is 1/0.1, or 10. If the target reserve ratio was 5 percent, or 0.05, it would mean that banks want to keep a smaller amount of reserves and therefore would have more to lend out. In this case, the money multiplier would be 1/0.05, or 20.

The principle of the money multiplier is based on the fact that banks only keep a small fraction of deposits in the form of cash reserves. Excess reserves allow banks to increase loans and, therefore, increase deposits by a multiple of the excess reserves. The money multiplier shows what will happen in the whole banking system over a period. Furthermore, banks are always interested in making more loans since the interest they earn on loans is their primary source of profits.

It is important to recognize that since banks only keep a fraction of the money that has been deposited with them, a small amount of cash reserves can support many more times the amount of demand deposits. Suppose for example that the banking system has demand deposits totalling $160 billion with $18 billion in cash reserves. If its target reserve ratio is 10 percent, the banking system is over-reserved by $2 billion (it requires 10% × $160 billion = $16 billion; but actually it has $18 billion). But look at it another way: it could increase its loans (and deposits) until the $18 billion in reserves are equal to 10 percent of those loans, and this would happen when the deposits have increased to $180 billion—an increase of $20 billion. A target reserve ratio of 10 percent (0.1) then means that deposits can be 10 times (1/0.1) as much as its reserves. A ratio of 5 percent (0.05) means that deposits can be 20 times (1/0.05) as much as its reserves. A bigger ratio such as 20 percent, however, means that its money multiplier would only be 5 (1/0.2), and it could only have deposits 5 times as much as its reserves. In short:

> The bigger the target reserve ratio, the smaller the money multiplier; the smaller the target reserve ratio, the bigger the money multiplier

Be careful not to confuse the effect of the money multiplier working through the whole banking system with the circumstances facing a single bank. Simply because a single bank happens to find itself with excess reserves does not mean that it could increase loans by a multiple of those excess reserves. For instance, look at the following circumstances for the Saymor Bank.

Reserves	$100	Demand deposits	$1000

The target reserve ratio is ten percent. Someone now deposits cash of $50. Excess reserves would then equal $45 (90 percent of $50), and this is all Saymor wants to lend. It could not lend out $450, since the bank would be in a very embarrassing situation if the borrower immediately asked for cash. In short:

A single bank has to tread carefully and limit its loans to the amount of its excess reserves.

IN A NUTSHELL ...

A small monetary base supports a large amount of deposits

TEST YOUR UNDERSTANDING

7. Assume that the nation's banking system is over-reserved by $20 million. What is the value of the money multiplier, and what is the maximum possible expansion in the money supply if the target reserve ratio is

a) 10 percent?

b) 2 percent?

c) 5 percent?

8. Suppose that the nation's banking system has a target reserve ratio of 4 percent, actual reserves of $9 billion, and deposits of $215 billion.

a) By how much could it increase the amount of deposits?

b) If instead the target reserve ratio was 3 percent, by how much could it increase the amount of deposits?

Can Banks Ever Be Short of Reserves?

It can certainly happen that, at the end of a day's business, a bank finds it has less reserves than it targeted. In that case, what can it do? It would need to borrow. The Bank of Canada will lend money to a commercial bank, but the bank must pay interest equal to the **bank rate** to the Bank of Canada. However, since this is regarded by the banks as a penalty rate (they can borrow from the public or from other banks at a much lower rate), commercial banks will try to ensure they pay off any loans from the Bank of Canada as quickly as possible. As a result, such loans tend to be very short-term.

IT'S NEWS TO ME ...

The share price of Deutsche Bank AG (Germany) dropped over 10% in early trading today when the Department of Justice in the US announced that it would seek $14B in its court action against the bank as a result of a probe that comes out of the 2008 financial crisis.

The probe began with an investigation into the banks action around the sale of residential mortgage-backed securities in the years leading up to the crisis. The probe was further expanded to include charges of currency exchange manipulation, gold and metals trading irregularities and illegal transfers of money coming out of Russia.

Deutsche Bank had set aside $6B for this litigation but this falls well short of the $14B that is now being sought in the US court action. Fraucine Lacque of Bloomberg TV observed that: "the bank may be forced to sell assets that it does not want to sell or find a new source of investors."

All of this calls into question whether the bank might well find itself short of reserves in the near future.

Source: *Star Power Reporting*, Fall 2016.

I. What would be the effect for the bank if it sold some of its assets?

a) It would increase its reserves and encourage potential new investors.

b) It would increase its reserves but discourage potential new investors.

c) It would decrease its reserves and encourage potential new investors.

d) It would decrease its reserves but discourage potential new investors.

II. All of the following, except one, are possible outcomes in this court action. Which is least likely?

a) The bank will fail.

b) The bank will survive but will be smaller.

c) New investors will be found and the bank will retain its current size.

d) The bank will win the lawsuit and pay no fine.

The Money Multiplier Also Works in Reverse

Are there other consequences if a single bank—Saymor, for instance—finds itself under-reserved? Well, after receiving a loan from the Bank of Canada, Saymor will have to increase its reserves in some more permanent way. Although it is not difficult for a single bank to increase its reserves, doing so will be at the expense of some other bank's reserves.

To explain, let us assume that Saymor calls in an outstanding loan that was made earlier to the New Star Car Company. New Star will be forced to quickly sell off some of its inventory. The car buyers involved in this selloff will be reducing their deposits in other banks as they pay for their purchases. This will result in other banks finding themselves under-reserved and thus forced to call in some of their loans. Soon, we will find the total loans in the whole banking system decreasing and, as a result, deposits also reduced by an amount determined by the money multiplier. As an example, look at the following combined balance sheet of a banking system:

| Reserves | $ 95 | Demand deposits | $1000 |
| Loans | $905 | | |

If the target reserve ratio is 10 percent, the banking system is under-reserved in the amount of $5. How can the whole banking system produce another $5 worth of reserves? It cannot, as only the Bank of Canada and not the commercial banks has the power to increase the amount of currency in the economy. What will happen, in fact, is that over a period the banking system will be forced to call in outstanding loans. In this case, the money multiplier is 10, and so the banks in total will have to call in 10 × $5, or $50, to get their reserves back in line with the deposits. After this contraction, the balance sheet will look like this:

| Reserves | $ 95 | Demand deposits | $950 |
| Loans | $855 | | |

We emphasize that banks can neither create nor destroy *currency*. What they can do is create or destroy loans and demand deposits, and this is what they do whenever they are over- or under-reserved. It is in this sense that we say that banks can create and destroy *money* (demand deposits). However, as we will see in the next chapter, it is the Bank of Canada that ultimately controls the money supply by determining the amount of currency held by the commercial banks.

A Smaller Money Multiplier?

Occasionally, the size of the money multiplier will be diminished. As we have already seen, if a bank increases its target reserves it lends less, and the money multiplier is reduced. But in a modern banking system, banks keep their targets as low as is safely possible, since they earn no return on idle cash. Something else that could reduce the money multiplier is if people decide to keep a larger portion of their assets in the form of cash. This increase in cash holdings will mean fewer deposits into the banking system and would reduce the size of the multiplier. (This is referred to as *currency drain*.) Further, simply because a bank has excess reserves does not mean that it will make more loans. It is possible that the banks may determine that there are not enough creditworthy applicants for loans and that their excess reserves should persist. Finally, it should be noted that in a recession banks often find it difficult to make loans, because many people simply do not want to accumulate more debt. Here again, the banks' excess reserves would persist and reduce the size of the multiplier. In summary, any of four factors may reduce the money multiplier:

- an increase in the banks' target reserves
- an increase in the amount of cash that people hold
- an insufficient number of creditworthy applicants for loans
- a reduced demand for loans by people in times of recession

TEST YOUR UNDERSTANDING

9. The following is the balance sheet for the Islanders' Bank.

Reserves	5 000	Demand deposits	60 000
Loans	41 000	Shareholders' equity	10 000
Securities	18 000		
Fixed assets	6 000		
	70 000		70 000

a) If the target reserve ratio is 8 percent, what is the amount of the bank's target reserves?

b) If the target reserve ratio is 5 percent, what is the amount of its target reserves?

10. a) Given the Islanders' Bank balance sheet in question 9, how much does it have in excess reserves if the target reserve ratio is 8 percent?

b) How much does it have in excess reserves if the target reserve ratio is 5 percent?

11. What will be the increase in total deposits in the whole banking system following a new deposit of $2000 into the XYZ bank in each of the following circumstances?

a) a target reserve ratio of 20 percent

b) a target reserve ratio of 5 percent

12. The J.M.K. Bank has demand deposits of $60 000 and reserves of $6000.

a) By how much can it increase its loans if the target reserve ratio is 8 percent?

b) By how much can it increase it loans if the target reserve ratio is 5 percent?

c) Assume the same $60 000 and $6000 applied to the entire banking system. What are your new answers to (a) and (b)?

SECTION SUMMARY

a) Modern banks keep only a small fraction of their deposits on reserve and loan out the balance. This fact allows the whole banking system to create money, since the new demand deposits of any one bank are spent and redeposited into other banks, and then loaned out again. This is the important money multiplier process.

b) The money multiplier varies inversely with the target reserve ratio; that is, the smaller the reserve ratio, the bigger the multiplier.

c) The money multiplier will be smaller if

• banks increase their target reserve ratios

• people hold more cash

• there are insufficient creditworthy applicants for loans

• people do not wish to take loans, for example in a recession

Study Guide

Review

WHAT'S THE BIG IDEA?

The concept of fractional reserve banking is the most important idea in this chapter. Simply put, the idea is that banks only need to keep a small fraction of the currency (notes and coins) deposited by their customers. That's because it is highly unlikely that on any single day the customers of a bank will all suddenly ask for their cash back. If they did, they would be sorely disappointed, because the banks have lent those funds to other customers—in the form of mortgages, car loans, student loans, and so on. And in many cases, those borrowers are not required to pay back for years. Thus, banks have learned that they need only keep a small portion of customers' deposits in the form of (cash) reserves. Of course, the major reason banks lend out customers' funds is to get interest revenue— idle cash earns nothing!

Since the banks only keep a small fraction of customers' deposits in cash (in Canada, less than 1 percent), whenever they find themselves with more than these (target) reserves, they will lend out the excess to other customers. This is where the money multiplier comes into play. People, like banks, generally prefer not to hold onto large amounts of cash. So the recipient of a loan will spend it—on a car, a vacation, new furniture—and the seller, not wanting to keep excess cash on the premises, will deposit it in some bank. Now this bank, in receipt of new cash, will find it has excess reserves and in turn lend out most of it. That borrower will then proceed to spend it—it gets deposited, perhaps at another bank, which then lends out most of it—the process being repeated many times. At the end of the day, the banking system will have increased loans and deposits by a multiple of the excess cash reserves it initially had.

Two words of caution. First, this process can only occur if the banking system gets access to "new" cash, say cash deposited by a new immigrant or from someone who decides not to keep cash locked up in a box under the bed, considering it safer to deposit it in the bank. Or, as we shall see in Chapter 4, it is initiated by the central bank (the Bank of Canada) indirectly increasing the commercial banks' reserves.

Second, the money multiplier process is something that happens to the whole banking system, not to a single bank. A single bank cannot lend out multiples of its excess reserves; it is limited to lending just that excess, nothing more.

NEW GLOSSARY TERMS AND KEY EQUATIONS

assets	leverage	net worth
bank rate	liabilities	notice deposits
bill of exchange	M1	spread
commodity money	M2	store of wealth
demand deposits	M3	target reserve ratio
excess reserves	medium of exchange	unit of account
fiat money	money multiplier	
fractional reserve system	near-banks	

Equations:

[8.1]   Target reserves = target reserve ratio × demand deposits

[8.2]   Excess reserves = actual reserves − target reserves

[8.3] $$\text{Money multiplier} = \frac{\Delta \text{ deposits}}{\Delta \text{ reserves}}$$

[8.4] $$\text{Money multiplier} = \frac{1}{\text{target reserve ratio}}$$

Comprehensive Problem

(LO 3) Table 8.2 is the current balance sheet for the Maple Leafs Bank. Answer the following questions, assuming that the bank's target reserve ratio is 5 percent.

TABLE 8.2
Maple Leafs Bank Balance Sheet as of the Current Date

Assets		1	2	Liabilities/Equity		1	2
Reserves	$ 100 000	_____	_____	Demand deposits	$1 000 000	_____	_____
Loans	650 000	_____	_____	Shareholders' equity	250 000	_____	_____
Securities	300 000	_____	_____				
Fixed assets	200 000	_____	_____				
Totals	$1 250 000	_____	_____		$1 250 000	_____	_____

Questions

a) Is this bank over- or under-reserved, and by what amount?
b) Suppose that a loan, in the amount of the excess reserves found in (a), is made to Kant Skate. Show the resulting balance sheet in column 1 in Table 8.2.
c) Suppose that Kant immediately spends all of his loan by writing a cheque to his psychologist, Freda Freud. She deposits it in her bank account, which happens to also be at the Maple Leafs Bank. By how much is the bank now over- or under-reserved?
d) Suppose, instead, that the bank makes a loan for the amount of your answer in (a), which then clears against the Maple Leafs Bank. Show the resulting balance sheet in column 2 in Table 8.2.
e) How much excess reserves does the bank have now?

Answers

a) Over-reserved by $50 000. A target reserve ratio of 5 percent means that the bank must have 0.05 times $1 000 000 or $50 000 in reserves. Since it has $100 000, the bank has $50 000 in excess reserves.
b) See Table 8.2 (Completed).

TABLE 8.2 (COMPLETED)
Maple Leafs Bank Balance Sheet as of the Current Date

Assets		1	2	Liabilities/Equity		1	2
Reserves	$ 100 000	$ 100 000	$ 50 000	Demand deposits	$1 000 000	$1 050 000	$1 000 000
Loans	650 000	700 000	700 000	Shareholders' equity	250 000	250 000	250 000
Securities	300 000	300 000	300 000				
Fixed assets	200 000	200 000	200 000				
Totals	$1 250 000	$1 300 000	$1 250 000			$1 250 000	$1 300 000	$1 250 000

Demand deposits and loans both increase by $50 000.
c) There would be no effect on the bank's accounts, since all that has happened is that one customer's bank balance has gone down by the exact amount that another's has gone up. However the bank is now over-reserved by $47 500. The bank's demand deposits are $1 050 000, so its target reserves need to be $52 500 (or 0.05 times 1 050 000). Actual reserves are still $100 000. Thus, the bank is now over-reserved by $47 500.

d) See Table 8.2 (Completed). Reserves and demand deposits are reduced by $50 000.
e) No excess reserves. The bank now has exactly the required reserves (5% × $1 000 000 = $50 000).

Questions

Now suppose that there are nine other banks in the economy and that the balance sheet for the whole banking system is presented in Table 8.3. You can assume that each of the other banks also has a target reserve ratio of 5 percent.

TABLE 8.3
Whole Banking System Balance Sheet

Assets			Liabilities/Equity		
Reserves	$ 1 000 000	_____	Demand deposits	$10 000 000	_____
Loans	6 500 000	_____	Shareholders' equity	2 500 000	_____
Securities	3 000 000	_____			
Fixed assets	2 000 000	_____			
Totals	$12 500 000	_____		$12 500 000	_____

f) In Table 8.3, show the balance sheet of the banking system when it is fully loaned up.
g) What is the increase in the money supply as a result of all the banks becoming fully loaned up?
h) Finally, returning to the balance sheet in Table 8.3, what would be the consequence of the economy's central bank imposing a 12.5 percent required reserve ratio on all banks? What amount of loans would have to be called in?

Answers

f) See Table 8.3 (Completed).

TABLE 8.3 (COMPLETED)
Whole Banking System Balance Sheet

Assets			Liabilities/Equity		
Reserves	$ 1 000 000	$ 1 000 000	Demand deposits	$10 000 000	$20 000 000
Loans	6 500 000	16 500 000	Shareholders' equity	2 500 000	2 500 000
Securities	3 000 000	3 000 000			
Fixed assets	2 000 000	2 000 000			
Totals	$12 500 000	$22 500 000		$12 500 000	$22 500 000

g) $10 000 000 increase in the money supply. The money multiplier is relevant here, since we are dealing with the whole banking system and not just a single bank. Its value is 1 divided by the targeted reserve ratio of 0.05 (5 percent) which equals 20. The excess reserves are equal to the actual reserves of $1 000 000 less the target reserves of $500 000 (0.05 of the demand deposits of $10 000 000). This comes to $500 000. Loans and demand deposits can therefore be increased by 20 times 500 000 or $10 000 000.

h) $2 000 000 in loans would have to be called in. The required reserves would now be 0.125 times $10 000 000 or $1 250 000. Actual reserves are only $1 000 000 so the banking system would be under-reserved by $250 000. Banks would therefore be forced to call in loans by 8 times (1 divided by 12.5 percent) $250 000 or $2 000 000. This would reduce demand deposits to $8 000 000 This is a decrease in demand deposits of $2 000 000.

Study Problems

Find answers on the McGraw-Hill online resource.

Basic (Problems 1–4)

1. **(LO 3)** Table 8.4 shows the balance sheet of the Bruins Bank.

TABLE 8.4
Bruins Bank Balance Sheet

Assets		Liabilities/Equity	
Reserves	$ 24	Demand deposits	$400
Loans	280	Shareholders' equity	20
Securities	80		
Fixed assets	36		
Totals	$420		$420

By how much is the Bruins Bank over- or under-reserved, if the target reserve ratio is
a) 2 percent? _____
b) 5 percent? _____
c) 8 percent? _____
d) 12 percent? _____

2. **(LO 3)** What is the value of the money multiplier if the target reserve ratios of all banks in the banking system are as follows?
a) 2 percent _____
b) 5 percent _____
c) 8 percent _____
d) 12 percent _____

3. **(LO 3)** Table 8.5 is the balance sheet for the Oilers Bank, which has a target reserve ratio of 5 percent.

TABLE 8.5
Oilers Bank Balance Sheet as of the Current Date

Assets		Liabilities/Equity	
Reserves	$ 6 000	Demand deposits	$ 80 000
Loans	68 000	Shareholders' equity	20 000
Securities	17 000		
Fixed assets	9 000		
Totals	$100 000		$100 000

a) By how much is the Oilers Bank over- or under-reserved?
b) If the bank makes a loan equal to the excess reserves and the borrower writes a cheque (for the full amount of the loan) to another customer of the bank, who then deposits it, what will be the new amount of excess reserves? _____
c) If, instead, the cheque written by the borrower is cleared against the Oilers Bank (the cheque was written to a customer of another bank), what will be the amount of excess reserves held by Oilers Bank? _____

4. **(LO 3)** Table 8.6 is the balance sheet for all banks combined in the banking system. All banks have a target reserve ratio of 8 percent.

TABLE 8.6
Whole Banking System Balance Sheet

Assets			Liabilities/Equity		
Reserves	$ 78 000	_____	Demand deposits	$ 900 000	_____
Loans	720 000	_____	Shareholders' equity	100 000	_____
Securities	100 000	_____			
Fixed assets	102 000	_____			_____
Totals	$1 000 000	_____		$1 000 000	_____

a) What is the amount of excess reserves? _____.
b) What is the maximum amount that loans and deposits can be increased? _____
c) Assuming that the system becomes fully loaned up, show the new balance sheet in Table 8.6.
d) By how much has the money supply increased now that the system is fully loaned up? _____

Intermediate (Problems 5–7)

5. **(LO 2)** Answer the questions below from the data in Table 8.7. (All figures are in billions of dollars.)

TABLE 8.7

Total currency issued by the Bank of Canada	$ 20
Total personal savings deposits	192
Total demand deposits	23
Deposits of the federal government at the Bank of Canada	2
Currency held by commercial banks	2
Government bonds owned by public	100
Nonpersonal fixed-term deposits (certificates of deposit)	46

a) What is the total currency in circulation? _____
b) How much larger is M1 than the total currency in circulation? _____
c) How much larger is M2 than M1? _____
d) How much larger is M3 than M2? _____

6. **(LO 3)** Fill in the blanks in the balance sheet of the Flames Bank in Table 8.8, assuming that the value of fixed assets is the same as shareholders' equity and that the bank is fully loaned up. The target reserve ratio is 5 percent.

TABLE 8.8
Flames Bank Balance Sheet

Assets		Liabilities/Equity	
Reserves	$_____	Demand deposits	$100 000
Loans	_____	Shareholders' equity	20 000
Securities	10 000		
Fixed assets	_____		_____
Totals			$120 000

7. **(LO 3)** Table 8.9 is the balance sheet for the Senators Bank. The target reserve ratio is 10 percent.

TABLE 8.9
Senators Bank Balance Sheet

Assets		1	2	Liabilities/Equity		1	2
Reserves	$ 60 000	_____	_____	Deposits	$400 000	_____	_____
Loans	260 000	_____	_____	Shareholders' equity	60 000	_____	_____
Securities	80 000	_____	_____				
Fixed assets	60 000	_____	_____				
Totals	$460 000	_____	_____		$460 000	_____	_____

a) What is the size of the bank's excess reserves? _____
b) Change the balance sheet in column 1 to show the effect of the bank loaning out an amount equal to its excess reserves.
c) Now change the balance sheet in column 2 to show the effect of a cheque for the amount of the loan in (b) clearing against the bank.
d) Suppose, instead, that the target reserve ratio is 20 percent. What is the bank's reserve situation, and what action will it take? _____

Advanced (Problems 8–12)

8. **(LO 3)** The central bank of Muldovia has issued $100 000 in Muldovian dollars. What is the size of the Muldovian money supply under the following circumstances?
a) Muldovians have deposited none of the currency in Muldovia's banks. _____
b) Muldovians have deposited all of the currency in Muldovia's banks, and the banks have a 100 percent target reserve ratio. _____
c) Muldovians have deposited 50 percent of the currency in Muldovia's banks, and the banks have a 100 percent target reserve ratio. _____
d) Muldovians have deposited 50 percent of the currency in Muldovia's banks, and the banks have a 10 percent target reserve ratio and are fully loaned up. _____

9. **(LO 3)** Table 8.10 is the balance sheet for all the banks combined in the banking system.

TABLE 8.10
Whole Banking System Balance Sheet

Assets		Liabilities/Equity	
Reserves	$ 50 000	Demand deposits	$500 000
Loans	450 000	Shareholders' equity	50 000
Securities	30 000		
Fixed assets	20 000		_____
Totals	$550 000		$550 000

a) Which one of the figures is part of the money supply? _____
b) If all banks maintain 100 percent reserves, what happens to the money supply eventually if $500 cash is deposited into one of the banks in the system? _____
c) If none of the banks maintains reserves, what happens to the money supply if $500 cash is deposited into one of the banks in the system? _____

10. **(LO 3)** Table 8.11 is the combined balance sheet for all the banks in a banking system. Each bank has a target reserve ratio of 4 percent.

TABLE 8.11
Whole Banking System Balance Sheet

Assets		1	2	Liabilities/Equity		1	2
Reserves	$ 200	_____	_____	Deposits	$3000	_____	_____
Loans	1800	_____	_____	Shareholders' equity	600	_____	_____
Securities	1300	_____	_____			_____	_____
Fixed assets	300	_____	_____		____	_____	_____
Totals	$3600	_____	_____		$3600	_____	_____

a) Fill in the blanks in column 1 reflecting the complete effect of all excess reserves being loaned out.

b) What is the maximum possible increase in the money supply? _____

c) If the target reserve ratio changes to 10 percent, what quantity of loans will the system be forced to call in? Write the figures in column 2 that show this process completed.

11. **(LO 3)** Rearrange the items in the balance sheet shown in Table 8.12 so each is in the correct position. Change one figure only to reflect the bank achieving a 5 percent target reserve ratio.

TABLE 8.12
Balance Sheet of Senators Bank Ltd.

Assets		Liabilities/Equity	
Reserves	$ 50	Demand deposits	$500
Loans	630	Securities	220
Shareholders' equity	80	Fixed assets	180

12. **(LO 3)** Given the target reserve ratios, amounts of reserves and deposits shown in Table 8.13, complete column 4 showing the amounts by which the deposits could increase (all dollar figures in billions).

TABLE 8.13

	(1) Target Reserve Ratio	(2) Reserves ($)	(3) Deposits ($)	(4) Maximum Increase in Deposits ($)
a)	5%	30	520	_____
b)	2%	80	3800	_____
c)	8%	20	240	

Problems for Further Study

Basic (Problems 1–5)

1. **(LO 3)** Name the necessary bookkeeping entries in the accounts of the Friedman Bank to record the following transactions.
   a) The Friedman Bank sells some of its old computers for $20 000 in cash. _____
   b) The bank buys $50 000 worth of government bonds from one of its customers and pays by cheque. _____
   c) The Friedman Bank calls in the $5000 loan of Kim's, who pays in cash. _____
   d) The bank grants a loan of $10 000 to Radim. _____
   e) Radim, a customer of the Friedman Bank, writes a cheque for $10 000 payable to his father, who deposits it in his own account at the same bank. _____

2. **(LO 3)** In which of the following circumstances has the money supply changed?
   a) Mario deposits $1000 at his bank.
   b) Mario withdraws $1000 from his bank.
   c) Mario lends Luigi $1000.
   d) The bank lends Mario $1000.
   e) Mario lends the bank $1000.

3. **(LO 1)** What are the three functions of money?
4. **(LO 2)** What is meant by the term *the spread*?
5. **(LO 1)** What is the earliest origin of money?

Intermediate (Problems 6–8)

6. **(LO 1)** What two key factors resulted in the early merchant banks becoming modern commercial banks?
7. **(LO 2)** Many students think that government (or the Bank of Canada) still has a pile of gold somewhere that backs our money. Since this is not true, what does back Canadian money?
8. **(LO 3)** What is included in a list of a bank's assets?

Advanced (Problems 9–10)

9. **(LO 3)** What does it mean for a bank to be over-reserved?
10. **(LO 2)** Many people believe that the ability to buy goods with credit cards makes such cards money. Explain why a credit card is not money. Do you think debit cards are money?

CHAPTER 9
The Money Market and Monetary Policy

LEARNING OBJECTIVES

At the end of this chapter, you should be able to:

LO1 Describe the determinants of money demand and supply, and explain how equilibrium in the money market is achieved.

LO2 Explain how the Keynesian transmission process works by targeting the money supply.

LO3 Explain why monetarists believe that controlling the money supply is vital.

LO4 Explain why many economists are critical of attempts to target the money supply.

LO5 Explain why most central banks around the world believe targeting the interest rate is the most effective monetary tool.

LO6 Explain why anti-inflationary policy emphasizes targeting the interest rate.

LO7 List some of the recent criticisms of anti-inflationary monetary policy.

WHAT'S AHEAD...

In Chapter 7, we saw how government is able to have a strong impact on the economy through the use of fiscal policy. In this chapter, we look at the other time-honoured method of bringing about economic growth and stability: the use of monetary policy. We begin by looking at the money market and see how it relates to the product market. We emphasize the importance of the interest rate that connects these two markets. The rest of the chapter then examines three different approaches to policy making. The first is the Keynesian, which proposes that the central bank should target the money supply as the major tool to achieve both full employment and stable prices. The second is that of the monetarist school, which believes that the central bank should not be given such power over the money supply and that its role should, in effect, be replaced by a simple monetary rule. The third approach, presently used by the Bank of Canada, seeks to exercise control only over inflation by targeting the interest rate.

A QUESTION OF RELEVANCE ...

Have you ever watched one of the many money shows on TV? Did you notice the emphasis analysts put on interest rates? "I expect the stock market to remain strong, as long as interest rates stay low" is a sentiment often expressed. Low interest rates are certainly good for the stock market, but are they also good for the economy and for you and me? Generally, the answer is yes.

But if low interest rates are so important, why aren't they always kept low? Is it because they have to be kept in line with those in the United States? Or are there sometimes good reasons for high interest rates? This chapter will help answer these questions.

9.1 The Money Market

> **LO1** Describe the determinants of money demand and supply, and explain how equilibrium in the money market is achieved.

Few people would dispute the usefulness of money to both individuals and society. In fact, most economists consider it one of the fundamental elements of a wealthy society, even though they do not consider money itself to be a form of wealth for a nation. However, as we shall see, economists most definitely disagree on the role of money in producing real change in the economy. In order to see just how money can affect things like production and employment, we need to understand the workings of the money market. The idea of a market for money might sound a little strange, if by this we mean a place where people come to buy and sell money. (What do you use to buy money?) But, as we shall see, money is a commodity, and like any commodity there is a demand for it and a supply of it; consequently, there is certainly a price for money. To begin with, let us look at the supply side of the money market.

The Supply of Money

For simplicity's sake, we will use the narrow definition of the money supply, M1, in our discussion. Thus, the supply of money, if you remember, is composed of currency in circulation and the total of all demand deposits at chartered banks. The Bank of Canada determines exactly how much currency is issued, but it is the public that decides what portion of this it wishes to keep in circulation (in our pockets, in the tills of shops, in office safes, and so on) and what portion is deposited with banks. The

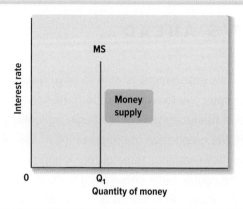

FIGURE 9.1   The Money Supply

Since the Bank of Canada can set money supply (MS) independently of the rate of interest, it plots as a perfectly inelastic (vertical) supply curve at the present quantity, Q_1.

portion deposited constitutes the banks' reserves, which in turn determine the amount of loans and demand deposits they are able to support. Recall from the last chapter that banks can leverage their excess reserves to make loans. That is, they can typically lend out ten to twenty times as much as they hold in reserves. We will see later how the Bank of Canada is able to affect the amount of money in the economy by influencing the level of bank reserves. The important point we wish to make at this stage is that, for all intents and purposes:

The supply of money is determined by the Bank of Canada, which can change the supply as it sees fit.

In economics, *supply* refers to "the quantities supplied at various prices." And what exactly is the price of money? In terms of opportunity costs, it is what is sacrificed as a result of holding money rather than holding some other financial instrument on which income could have been earned. In other words, the cost of holding money is equal to the interest that is forgone. For now, we will assume that the Bank of Canada does not automatically increase or decrease the quantity of money as a result of a change in its price level (the interest rate). In the short run, we can say that the money supply is autonomous with respect to its price—and the price of money, as we shall see, is the same thing as the **interest rate**. Graphically, then, the money supply plots as a straight vertical line, as shown in **Figure** 9.1. If the money supply were to increase, the curve would shift right; a decrease would move it left.

Since it is the Bank of Canada, and not government, that controls the supply of money and is responsible for enacting monetary policy, we need to understand exactly what its role is.

Functions of the Bank of Canada

The Bank of Canada building in Ottawa.

Sml/Dreamstime.com

In general, the Bank of Canada operates much like other central banks throughout the world. Some central banks are state-owned—the Bank of Canada and the Bank of England—whereas others are owned privately, such as the Federal Reserve in the United States. However, for all intents and purposes, ownership is unimportant. What is important is how they are alike, and the following functions are common to most central banks.

The first traditional function of the Bank of Canada is to be the *sole issuer of currency*. It acts as a reservoir in that it will issue more currency to the commercial banks when needed (just before Christmas, for instance), and at other times it will take back any surplus above the banks' and the public's requirements. You may recall that only the portion of the outstanding currency that is in the hands of the public is considered part of the money supply; the portion in bank vaults is excluded.

A second traditional function is that the Bank of Canada acts as the *government's bank*. It is the institution that looks after government's banking needs. More recently, individual government ministries have been given authority to deal with whichever commercial bank they choose, making this function of the Bank of Canada less important. In addition, the Bank of Canada *manages reserves of foreign currencies* (and gold) on behalf of government. This includes the buying and selling of Canadian dollars and other currencies in consultation with government and consistent with its policies.

Another important function of the Bank of Canada is to act as the *bankers' bank*. This means that each of the commercial banks has an account with the Bank of Canada to facilitate the borrowing and lending of funds between the two. The central bank stands prepared to make extraordinary loans to a commercial bank that is experiencing a liquidity problem to avert a loss of depositor confidence. In this respect, it is often known as the "lender of the last resort."

The *Bank Act* also stipulates that the Bank of Canada is to act as *auditor and inspector of the commercial banks*. The latter are required to submit periodic reports to the Bank of Canada and to open their books and accounts for inspection and audit.

A visitor to the currency museum in the Bank of Canada building in Ottawa looks at the half-burnt Canadian dollar. The display illustrates how old currency is disposed of.

The Canadian Press (Tom Hanson)

The final function of the Bank of Canada is the most important, and that is to *regulate the money supply*. It is interesting to note in this regard that although the federal government, through Parliament, has the power and the responsibility to effect fiscal policy, it does not itself directly control monetary policy: this is the prime function of the governor and the board of directors of the Bank of Canada. It is possible, therefore, for government and the Bank of Canada to be in conflict regarding the direction in which they want to move the economy. In fact, there was such a conflict between the two in the late 1950s. This does not happen often, however—not because the two always agree, but because a conflict in policy would be regarded as a political failure and thus something that policy makers wish to avoid.

ADDED DIMENSION

The Governor of the Bank of Canada

Economist Stephen Poloz became the new governor of the Bank of Canada in the spring of 2013. His appointment came as a surprise to most pundits, as he was not high-profile. Moreover, there were a number of colourful anecdotes about his past. For one thing, he had argued that Canada was suffering from the Dutch Disease—the whittling away of a country's manufacturing base due to an overly high Canadian dollar that was the result of its growing oil exports.

Poloz had made other arguments that raised eyebrows. As the financial crisis unfolded in 2008, he wrote an article positing a very interesting theory for what caused the crash: Blame 9/11. He wrote: "We

Stephen Poloz, Governor of the Bank of Canada.

The Canadian Press/Ryan Remiorz

now know that 9/11 spawned a 'live for the moment' boom in U.S. consumer spending and borrowing, the likes of which have never been seen before." The borrowing and spending boom was indeed unprecedented, but the theory that it was spawned by 9/11, rather than by years of cheap mortgage rates and unregulated lending, was novel.

Yet, four years later, there seems to be a growing feeling that Poloz is doing fine in his role and projects an air of steady competence.

In summary, the functions of a central bank, such as the Bank of Canada, are to act as

- the issuer of currency
- government's bank and manager of foreign currency reserves
- the bankers' bank and lender of last resort
- the auditor and inspector of commercial banks
- the regulator of the money supply

Let us now look at the other side of the equation: the demand for money.

The Demand for Money

Before you start thinking that the average person's demand for money is unlimited, remember that we are not talking about income. The average person's demand for *income* might well be unlimited, but we are speaking about (the stock of) money. As we noted in Chapter 8, money is a stock and is only one of many possible forms of wealth that people might hold.

Like any other form of wealth-holding, money has certain advantages and disadvantages. Except in times of high inflation, money maintains a reasonably stable value, unlike such things as land or stocks and bonds, whose value can vary greatly, both up and down. From this point of view, holding money involves less risk. The other advantage is that money is highly liquid. In contrast, real estate is not liquid in that it may take weeks or even months to convert it to money. Balanced against that is the fact that holding money does not produce a return, whereas most other forms of wealth can offer at least the prospect of some return in the form of interest, dividends or an increase in asset value. In general, the safer the investment, the lower the potential return; the greater the risk, the higher the potential return.

So why bother holding money at all? Why not, on receipt of income, immediately transfer it into some sort of financial investment? The reason is obvious: we need to keep a portion of our wealth in a chequing account or as currency simply because other forms of wealth are unacceptable as a means of payment. It is certainly true that over the years, the introduction of credit cards, debit cards, and Internet banking has meant that we need to keep only a smaller proportion of our wealth in the form of cash and chequing accounts since many of our transactions still require that we pay for them with money.

One reason to hold money, therefore, is what economists call the **transactions demand for money**. Simply put, we need money in order to transact many of our regular daily purchases. What determines this transactions demand? The value of transactions we make. And what determines the value of our transactions? The level of our income. The higher the income level of individuals, the more they will spend and the higher will be the transactions demand for money. This is similarly true for the whole economy. The higher the level of the gross domestic product (GDP), the higher the transactions demand for money.

Note here that we are speaking of nominal GDP. This means that a higher demand for money can come about either because real GDP increases or because prices increase. The major determinants of the transactions demand for money, then, are the level of real income and the level of prices; a change in either can cause a change in the transactions demand for money. (It should also be added that institutional factors, such as the increased use of credit cards, the regularity with which people get paid, the efficiency of the banking system in clearing cheques, and so on, can also affect the transactions demand in the long run.)

Exactly what does this mean in terms of the average consumer? Well, forty years ago, one of the authors could easily get through the week by taking out $50 in cash from the bank. This was more than enough to pay his immediate expenses for lunches, bus fares, and the occasional drink. These days, there is no way that $50 will last out the week; he finds that he needs over double this amount. Why is that so? Well, the first reason is simple: prices have gone up considerably over the last forty years. He needs more money just to make the same purchases that he did thirty years ago. But on top of this, he has found that his real income is a lot higher these days and he tends to buy more than he ever could afford in his younger days. So a higher price level and a higher real income will both increase the transactions demand for money.

Figure 9.2 shows the transactions demand for money graphically. Since the transactions demand for money does not depend on the prevailing interest rate, it plots as a straight vertical line. An increase in either the price level or in real GDP means that the value of transactions will

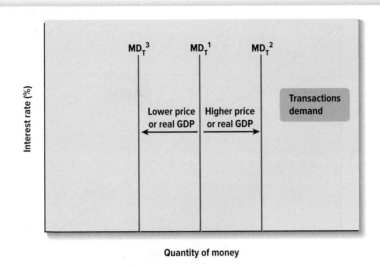

FIGURE 9.2   Transactions Demand for Money

The transactions demand is independent of the interest rate and plots as a vertical line. An increase in the price level or in real GDP will shift the curve to the right; a decrease in either will shift it to the left.

increase—simply put, people will need more money to buy the goods and services. This will be reflected in a rightward shift in the transactions demand curve. A decrease in either the price level or in real GDP will have the opposite effect, causing the curve to shift left. Another way of looking at the transactions demand is that it is related to the way money functions as a medium of exchange.

However, there is another reason why people might want to hold money: because it also acts as a store of wealth. This is termed the **asset demand for money**. There are two reasons people might wish to hold money in excess of the amount they need to make transactions. The first reason is for precautions—people like to be able to hold at least some money "for a rainy day." If the household water heater stops working there is really nothing else to do but lay out the money for a new one. If a close relative living across the country takes ill, an expensive airline ticket will not prevent most people from taking the trip. Unexpected things like this happen, and people like to keep a bit of precautionary money to meet such challenges of life.

It's also true that some people might temporarily hold money in excess of their normal amounts because they anticipate buying a big-ticket item, like a new computer, in the near future. People might also hold what could be called "idle cash" as a form of speculation. For instance, if interest rates are very low, people will be more inclined to keep their savings in the form of money rather than buying, say, a one-year term deposit. This is because they prefer to wait for a higher rate that they feel will occur soon. Similarly, when both stock and real estate prices are in decline and inflation is low, most people tend to regard money as a very secure "investment." When people are not sure what to do with their asset money, they hold on to it—at least for a while. So, when the return on other assets is low, people's demand for money tends to be high. Thus we can see that there is an inverse relationship between rates of interest and the asset demand for money. This idea is illustrated in **Figure 9.3**.

We can now bring together the transactions and asset demands for money to derive the total demand for money curve.

Figure 9.4A illustrates the fact that the transactions demand for money is unrelated to the rate of interest. We need a certain amount of money—in this example, $30 billion—regardless of how high or low the rate of interest is. As we said earlier, this demand would increase with a rise in real incomes or prices and decrease with a fall in either.

Figure 9.4B shows the inverse relationship between the asset money demand for money and the rate of interest. At an interest rate of 8 percent, the quantity of asset money demanded will be relatively low at $20 billion. At this high rate of interest, people will economize as much as possible in their holdings of money simply because holding money as an asset yields a zero percent rate of

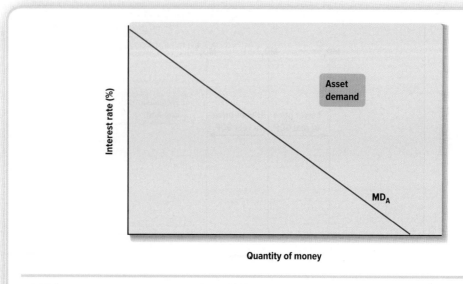

FIGURE 9.3   Asset Demand for Money

When the rate of interest is high, people will economize on the amount of asset money they hold. At a lower interest rate people will be willing to hold a bigger quantity of asset money. There is, therefore, an inverse relationship between the rate of interest and the quantity of asset money.

return. Thus, they will try to put any excess cash into some form of income-earning asset. At an interest rate of 2 percent, however, the asset demand at $50 billion is high. At this low rate of interest, many people are fairly indifferent about holding other financial investments and would just as soon hold onto money, especially if they believe that the interest rate is likely to rise.

Figure 9.4C shows the total demand for money, which is simply the addition of the transactions and asset demands. (The two curves are just summed together horizontally.) It shows that when the rate of interest is at 8 percent, the total demand for money is $50 billion. This total is composed of $30 billion transactions demand plus $20 billion, the amount of idle money or asset demand. When the rate of interest is 2 percent, the total demand for money is $80 billion: transactions demand of $30 billion and asset demand of $50 billion.

What we see, then, is that people will hold enough money to finance their daily transactions but will often possess an additional amount of "idle balances," which is what we have called the *asset*

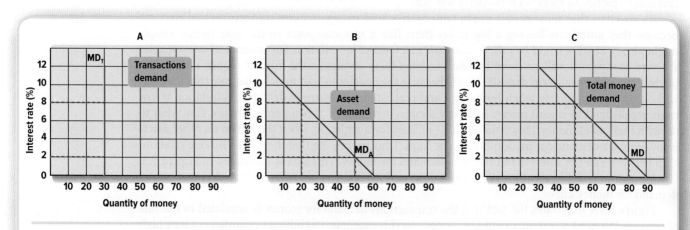

FIGURE 9.4   Transactions, Asset, and Total Demand for Money

Graph A shows the transactions demand for money, which is equal to $30. Graph B shows the asset demand for money. When the rate of interest is 8 percent, the quantity of money demanded for asset purposes is $20, and at an interest rate of 2 percent, it is $50. The final graph, C, shows the total demand for money, which is obtained by summing the first two graphs horizontally.

demand. There is controversy among economists regarding such idle balances. Keynes, for example, gave other explanations for why people might want to hold such additional balances of money. He suggested it is perfectly rational to hold idle balances in situations where purchasing bonds is risky. This might happen if the interest rate is low (and bond prices are high) and people expect the interest rate to rise. In this case, they will hold onto money. If the interest rate does go up, they will be able to purchase bonds more cheaply (as we will see later). Keynes called this the *speculative motive* for holding money.

Besides offering this explanation, Keynes felt that many people might hold cash as a form of security, or insurance, for the future (what he termed the *precautionary motive*). Even allowing for the fact that the value of money erodes through inflation, many people may still want to hold on to money because of its immediate accessibility in an emergency.

In summary, the demand for money in the economy is determined by

- the level of transactions (real GDP)
- the average value of transactions (the price level)
- the rate of interest

TEST YOUR UNDERSTANDING

Find answers on the McGraw-Hill online resource.

1. Assume you are given the following asset demand for an economy:

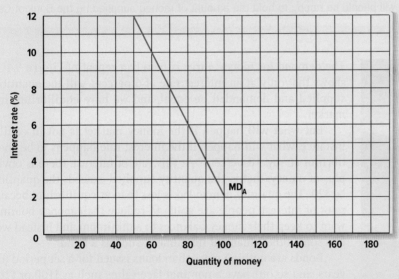

a) Assume that the nominal GDP in this economy is $800 and that the transaction demand for money is equal to 10 percent of nominal GDP. Draw the total demand for money curve.

b) If the money supply is $150 billion, draw in the money supply curve.

c) What is the equilibrium interest rate and the quantity of money?

d) If the interest rate is 10 percent, is there a surplus or shortage of money? How much?

Equilibrium in the Money Market

We have now looked at both the supply of money and the demand for money in an economy. Do you know what is coming next? To find out under what circumstances the public will be happy to hold the amount of money that the Bank of Canada has supplied, we need to put the two together. Figure 9.5 does this.

The supply of money, as mentioned before, is determined by the Bank of Canada, and we regard it as independent of the rate of interest. It is simply a fixed autonomous amount equal to $60 (billion).

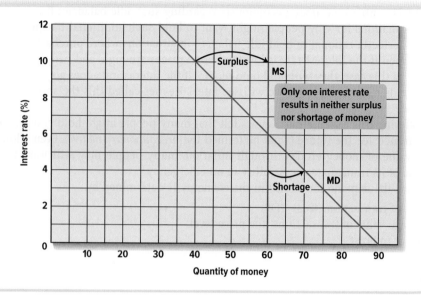

FIGURE 9.5   Surplus and Shortage of Money

At an interest rate above equilibrium (such as at 10 percent) there is a surplus of $20 of money. This will lead to a drop in interest rates until people are content to hold the supply of money issued by the central bank. Conversely, at interest rates below equilibrium (such as at 4 percent) there will be a shortage of $10 of money, causing the rate of interest to rise. Only at equilibrium interest rate of 6 percent will people be happy to hold the amount of money supplied by the Bank of Canada.

A pressman stacks some of the new Canada Premium Bonds as they come off the presses at the Canada Bank Note Company in Ottawa.

The Canadian Press (Tom Hanson)

The demand for money curve is merely a repeat of **Figure 9.4C**. The graph shows that only at an interest rate of 6 percent will the quantities of money supplied and demanded be equal, and we have equilibrium in the money market.

But what will happen if the money market is not in equilibrium? For instance, what will happen if the interest rate happens to be above the equilibrium at, say, 10 percent? At this rate of interest, there is obviously a surplus of money; that is, the quantity supplied exceeds the quantity demanded by $20. The quantity demanded is less than at equilibrium because at higher rates of interest, people are going to reduce their money holdings; they will want to keep their money balances to a minimum and instead would want to buy some other financial instrument, such as a bond.

Bonds are nothing more than loans issued for a set period (one year, five years, and so on), have a nominal face value, such as $100 or $1000, and pay a fixed rate of interest (the coupon rate) to the holder of the bond. They are issued by corporations, by banks, and by various levels of government: municipal, provincial, and federal. An essential feature of a bond is that it can easily be bought and sold in the market. This means that the return you earn on a bond depends not just on the coupon rate but also on the profit (or loss) from its resale. Suppose for instance that you bought a two-year $100 bond which pays an annual coupon rate of 5 percent ($5). Say you bought this bond exactly one year after it was issued for the now-lower price of $96. How much will you earn on this purchase? Well, during the next year you will receive interest of $5, but, in addition, at the end of the year the bond will be redeemed at its face value of $100, giving you a profit of $4. So in total you will have earned $9 on your initial investment of $96. Your annual return as a percentage could be stated as follows:

$$\text{Rate of return (rate of interest)} = \frac{\text{coupon interest} +/- \text{ change in the bond price}}{\text{price paid for bond}} \times 100 \qquad [9.1]$$

In our example, the rate of return is

$$\frac{\$5 + \$4}{\$96} \times 100 = \frac{\$9}{\$96} \times 100 = 9.5\%$$

(*Note:* If there were only nine months left until redemption, the annual rate would be only $\frac{9}{12}$ of the rate of return calculated here.)

Now what if, instead of paying $96 for it, the bond was in such great demand that you had had to pay $102? What would your return be in this case? Well, you would get the coupon rate of $5 per annum irrespective of the market value of the bond, but in this instance you will have lost $2 when you redeemed it at the end of the year. Your rate of return therefore would be

$$\frac{\$5 - \$2}{\$102} \times 100 = \frac{\$3}{\$102} = 2.9\%$$

We can conclude therefore that the higher the price of a bond, the lower the rate of return (interest) earned on it.

To cement this idea, suppose a $5000 bond with a coupon rate of 4 percent (= $200) with one year left until redemption is sold at the following prices; in each case, let us work out the rate of return (interest):

$$\$4700: \text{Rate of return} = \frac{(\$200 + \$300)}{4700} \times 100 = 10.64\%$$

$$\$4900: \text{Rate of return} = \frac{(\$200 + \$100)}{4900} \times 100 = 6.12\%$$

$$\$5100: \text{Rate of return} = \frac{(\$200 - \$100)}{5100} \times 100 = 1.96\%$$

In other words:

> The lower the price of bonds, the higher the return (the rate of interest); the higher the price of bonds, the lower the yield (rate of return).

 ADDED DIMENSION

Gold and Wealth

One of the reasons Adam Smith's *The Wealth of Nations* (1776) became the seminal work in economics is that it attempted to look beyond the economic fears and aspirations of the individual and shift the focus to a study of the whole economy. The title of Smith's opus is, after all, "The Wealth of Nations," not "The Wealth of People." It would have been very simple for Smith to have defined what constitutes wealth as far as the individual is concerned. It is far less obvious and far more interesting to figure out what constitutes the wealth of nations.

At first glance, it would seem it is made up of the total wealth of all individuals plus any assets held in common. However, there was major disagreement at the time on whether money should be included. Although gold could certainly be used as an international medium of exchange, did this mean that the more gold a country had, the richer it was? What if a country's stock of gold were to increase appreciably—would the country be any richer? Well, by and large, people in possession of gold are able to buy more foreign goods, and they probably want to buy more domestic goods, too. However, an increase in the amount of gold possessed by a nation does not mean the amount of goods produced will change. Therefore all that is likely to happen is an increase in prices, which eventually will be in line with the greater amount of gold. The net result is that people are no better off than before.

What Smith tried to do in his book was redirect people's views regarding wealth. Being wealthy for Smith meant that a nation was producing an abundance of goods and services—not that it merely owned a stock of glittering metal. Gold is not wealth in the same way labour and capital goods are. The latter are regenerative in that they can recreate themselves; gold, in contrast, is totally sterile.

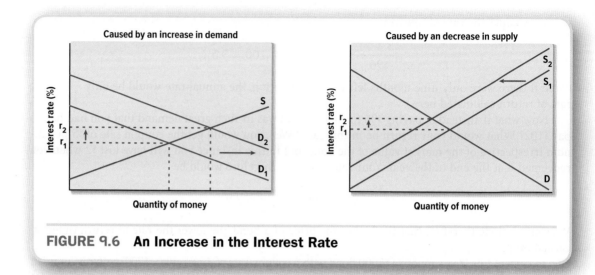

FIGURE 9.6   An Increase in the Interest Rate

Returning to Figure 9.5, we note that when there is a surplus of money, people will be inclined to put that excess into buying bonds (or some similar financial instrument). This will increase the demand for bonds and increase their price and this in turns means that the return (the interest) on those bonds will fall. The bond prices will continue to rise and the rate of return fall until people will no longer want to get rid of any surplus money, that is, when the rate of return is at the equilibrium of 6 percent.

Let us now look at the effect of an interest rate lower than equilibrium, say 4 percent.

At this lower interest rate, people will be more than willing to hold the quantity of money of $70, since the return on bonds and other financial securities is low. However, since the quantity of money supplied, $60, is less than the amount people wish to hold, there is a money shortage of $10. To obtain more money, people will want to sell off bonds or other financial instruments. The effect of this action will be to increase the supply of these types of instruments as people cash them in. This causes their price to fall and the rate of interest to rise until the money market is back in equilibrium at an interest rate of 6 percent.

It is clear from our analysis so far that the interest rate is determined by *both* the demand for and supply of money, and a change in either will cause the interest rate to be affected. This means that the interest rate will increase if there is either an increase in the demand for money or a drop in the supply of money. This idea is illustrated in Figure 9.6. Similarly, a decrease in the interest rate is caused by either a drop in the demand for money or an increase in the supply of money.

When we say there is an increase in the demand for money, we mean that people are willing to hold more money at all the various rates of interest. In effect, an increase in the demand for money could be caused by either an increase in the transactions demand for money, and this, in return, must be the result of an increase in either the price level or real GDP. (Additionally it might be caused by a change in institutional factors—how often people get paid and so on.) A higher demand for money will cause the interest rate to increase; a fall in the demand will cause the interest rate to also fall.

> An increase in the interest rate is caused by either a rise in the demand for money or a fall in the supply of money.

> A decrease in the interest rate is caused by either a fall in the demand for money or a rise in the supply of money.

So far, this whole discussion (in fact, this whole book) has spoken of "the" interest rate as if there were one single rate. In fact, what we have in any economy is an interest-rate *structure* made up of the rate paid by banks on savings accounts, the rate charged by banks for loans of different types (mortgages, personal loans, or credit card charges), and the bank rate, which we will look at shortly. For convenience, however, we will continue to speak of "the interest rate," and students can use the context of the discussion to determine whether it would be for saving or for borrowing.

Now that we have examined the mechanics of the money market, it is time to look at how the Bank of Canada and other central banks bring about changes in the money market and how this affects the product market. We will be looking at three different philosophies. The first two, those of Keynes and the monetarists, emphasize controlling the money supply; the third and more recent is that of those who advocate anti-inflationary **monetary policy**, which seeks instead to control interest rates.

TEST YOUR UNDERSTANDING

2. Suppose Jan buys a 3-year $500 bond with a coupon rate of 2 percent for $480. The bond has 1 year left before its redemption. What is the rate of return on this final year?

3. Assume that the money demand for a particular economy is as follows (all figures in billions of dollars):

Rate of Interest (%)	Asset Demand ($)	Transactions Demand ($)	Total Demand ($)
12	50	80	_____
11	55	80	_____
10	60	80	_____
9	65	80	_____
8	70	80	_____
7	75	80	_____
6	80	80	_____

Complete the table, and answer these questions:

a) If the money supply equals $150, what must be the equilibrium interest rate?

b) If the money supply equals $140, what must be the equilibrium interest rate?

c) If the rate of interest is 11 percent and the money supply is $150, what are the implications?

SECTION SUMMARY

a) The Bank of Canada is able to control the amount of money in the economy because it controls the amount of currency (reserves). It also acts as

- government's bank
- the bankers' bank
- auditor and inspector of the commercial banks
- regulator of the money supply

b) Money demand can be subdivided into

- the transactions demand, which depends on the level of nominal GDP
- the asset demand, which varies inversely with the rate of interest

c) The interest rate is the price of money and, like other prices, it is determined by the interaction of supply and demand.

- A higher interest rate is caused either by an increase in the demand for, or a decrease in the supply of, money.
- A lower interest rate is caused either by a decrease in the demand for, or an increase in the supply of, money.

9.2   Targeting the Money Supply: Keynesian Monetary Policy

> **LO2** Explain how the Keynesian transmission process works by targeting the money supply.

The essence of Keynesian monetary policy is that the various macroeconomic markets, the money market, the product market (which we looked at in Chapters 5 and 6), and the international market (which we will investigate in Chapter 11) are all intrinsically linked. Changes in one market will bring about changes in the other(s). In his *General Theory*, Keynes was especially interested in the product market (since production, economic growth, and employment are directly related to it) and sought to understand and explain what caused change in this market. We saw in Chapter 7 how fiscal policy can directly influence this market. We will now look at Keynes's belief that changes in the money market could also indirectly impact the product market. The agent of change here is the central bank, which has a degree of control over the supply of money and can thus affect interest rates. Before we take a look at that process, let us first examine the two tools that are at the disposal of the Bank of Canada when it wishes to change the supply of money.

Monetary Tools

Let us assume that the Bank of Canada wishes to adopt an **expansionary monetary policy** (also called an *easy money policy*). This involves increasing the money supply. How could this be done? Well, we know from Chapter 8 that if the Bank could increase the amount of cash reserves held by the commercial banks, any reserves that banks consider in excess of their target reserves would be loaned out and, through the money multiplier process, would lead to an increase in loans and demand deposits (the main portion of money supply). A **contractionary monetary policy** (or a *tight money policy*) implies the opposite.

One simple way the Bank of Canada might increase the commercial banks' cash reserves would be to give them additional amounts of reserves. However, some of us might complain about a free gift of cash to the banks! The Bank of Canada therefore has to use a more subtle and businesslike process known as **open-market operations**, so called because it involves the Bank of Canada (or at least its agent) buying or selling treasury bills (short-term bonds) in a market that is open to anyone.

In other words, the Bank of Canada buys and sells government bonds in the same way that any individual or corporation might. It should be noted that these are second-hand bonds—bonds previously issued and sold to the public.

To better understand just how this market works, we need to understand the role of treasury bills. A treasury bill is a type of short-term bond, or fixed-term debt, issued by the Bank of Canada, acting as the agent of government. Next, we need to recognize that corporations, commercial banks, and life insurance and pension fund companies, as well as other organizations, find themselves with excess cash from time to time. Usually, this cash will be needed by these organizations in the near future, so the question of what to do with, say, $2 million for 60 days can arise. One of the most popular revenue-earning assets is treasury bills (or T-bills), which can be bought in various denominations for either a three- or a six-month term. They differ from longer-term government and corporate bonds in that they are short-term and do not pay interest. Instead, return is earned on them because they are sold at a discount (at a price below the face value) and then redeemed at the end of the fixed term at face value.

If it wished to increase the amount of cash reserves of the commercial banks, the Bank of Canada would buy outstanding T-bills on the open market. The seller of the T-bills would receive a cheque from the Bank of Canada, which would then be deposited in the seller's bank account. At the end of the day, the commercial bank involved would look to the Bank of Canada for reimbursement. The Bank of Canada could transfer the required amount of reserves to the commercial bank in question. Rather than doing this, however, the Bank of Canada just credits the account that the commercial bank has with the Bank of Canada. It in effect tells the commercial bank that the amount of credit it has "on reserve" at the Bank of Canada has been increased. The commercial banks' reserves have therefore increased, and this recently acquired surplus will be loaned out, leading to a multiple expansion of money in the economy, as we discussed in Chapter 8.

It should be noted that some of the world's central banks—the U.S. and the U.K. in particular—have recently extended the use of open market operations with the introduction of what has come to be called **quantitative easing**. Whereas open-market operations involve the central bank buying and selling short-term government bills, quantitative easing applies to its purchase of both long-term bonds (both public and privately issued) and of shares. The result is the increased liquidity of the commercial banks leading, it is hoped, to an increase in loans to those who will make direct investment in the economy.

To reduce the money supply, the Bank of Canada would, of course, do the opposite and sell T-bills to whomever wished to purchase them. These people would have to make payments to the Bank of Canada. Their bank account balances would be thus reduced and so would the reserves of the commercial banks. As a result, banks would be forced to restrict the creation of new loans or even call in outstanding loans, and this would reduce the amount of money in the economy.

Open-market operations are not the only tool of monetary policy; but they are important and frequently used, as they can be initiated on short notice, take effect quickly, and can be undertaken in any amount.

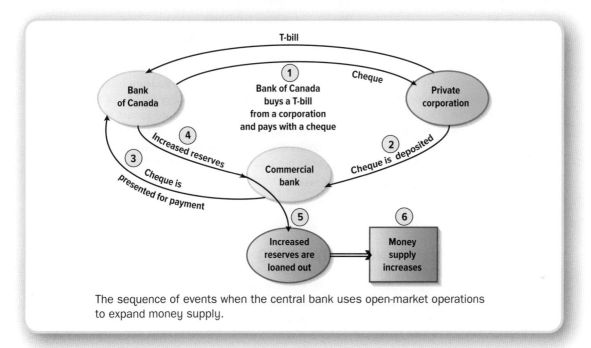

The sequence of events when the central bank uses open-market operations to expand money supply.

 TEST YOUR UNDERSTANDING

4. In terms of the banking system's ability to create money, what difference, if any, does it make if the Bank of Canada buys bonds from a commercial bank rather than from a member of the public?

A second way that the Bank of Canada can affect the money supply is by *switching government deposits*. For instance, if the Bank of Canada wants to contract the money supply it can, with the approval of the finance ministry, transfer some of government's deposits from a commercial bank to the Bank of Canada. It does this, in effect, by writing a cheque on government's account at the commercial bank made payable to the Bank of Canada. Conversely, if it wished to increase the money supply, it would switch government deposits from the Bank of Canada to the commercial banks. The effect of switching deposits is similar to open-market operations. In both cases demand deposits and reserves are affected. Switching deposits has become an increasingly popular monetary tool for the Bank of Canada.

ADDED DIMENSION

The Bank of Canada's Balance Sheet

The operations of the Bank of Canada affect the economy, but they also affect the balance sheet of the bank itself. The following table shows the Bank of Canada's balance sheet in simplified form as of December 31, 2015. All figures are in millions.

Assets		Liabilities	
Cash and foreign deposits	11	Notes in circulation	75 497
Short-term loans to banks	6 089	Government of Canada deposits	22 617
Treasury bills of Canada	18 220	Deposits of banks	500
Government bonds	75 764	Other deposits	1 475
Other assets	1 063	Other liabilities	560
		Shareholders' equity	498
Total	101 147	Total	101 147

The biggest asset of the bank is its holdings of government bonds and treasury bills, and it is the sale and purchase of these that we term *open-market operations*. The major liability of the bank, as you can see, is the amount of notes in circulation. Although these notes are assets to members of the public who own them, they represent a liability to the issuing bank, the Bank of Canada. Another liability is the reserves that the commercial banks deposit with the Bank of Canada. Such reserves are, of course, an asset to the commercial banks but a liability to the Bank of Canada.

Source: Adapted from the *Bank of Canada Annual Report, 2015*.

TEST YOUR UNDERSTANDING

5. The following table presents balance sheets for the commercial banking system and for the Bank of Canada (all figures are in billions). Show the effects on the balance sheets of both the Bank of Canada and the commercial banks when the Bank of Canada buys $2 billion worth of securities directly from the commercial banks.

ALL COMMERCIAL BANKS

Assets		Liabilities	
Reserves:		Deposits	$800
In vaults	$ 70		
On deposit with the Bank of Canada	10		
Securities	120		
Loans	600		—
Totals	$800		$800

BANK OF CANADA

Assets		Liabilities	
T-bills and bonds	$ 80	Notes in circulation	$ 65
		Deposits of banks	10
		Other liabilities	5
Totals	$ 80		$ 80

6. Suppose that the banking system's target reserve ratio is 10 percent and the Bank of Canada switches $100 million of government funds from government's account with the Bank of Canada to an account at a commercial bank. Since neither government's accounts with commercial banks nor the commercial banks' reserves are considered to be part of the money supply, how might such a switching of funds have any effect on money supply?

Source: Adapted from the *Bank of Canada Annual Report*, 2010.

As we shall see when we look at the policy of targeting interest rates rather than the money supply, the Bank of Canada has two additional monetary tools available to it: targeting the overnight rate and moral suasion. More about these later.

Now that we have looked at the mechanics of how the Bank of Canada is able to affect the money supply, let us see how Keynes believed such changes affect the whole economy.

Expansionary Monetary Policy and the Transmission Process

Keynesian monetary policy envisions an active process of setting macroeconomic goals and then adjusting policy to achieve those goals. As an example, the Bank of Canada used Keynesian monetary policy for some time after the bank was established in 1935. The Bank's mandate then was:

To regulate credit and currency in the best interests of the nation . . . and to mitigate by its influence fluctuations in the general level of production, trade, prices, and employment.

ADDED DIMENSION

Bills and Bonds

Bonds and bills are nothing more than types of IOUs, but whereas bonds are issued by all types of institutions, including corporations and governments (at all levels), treasury bills (T-bills) are issued only by the federal government. Both bills and bonds are freely negotiable financial instruments, which means that they can be easily bought and sold at any time at their current market value (which may well be different from their nominal, or face, value). Although bonds and T-bills are offered in any number of denominations, $500, $1000, and so forth, the major difference between the two is that bonds are long-term IOUs, whereas bills are usually of short duration, with the typical T-bill issued for a 91-day period. Another difference is that a bond pays a fixed annual interest rate (the coupon rate), whereas a T-bill does not pay any interest at all. Consider, for instance, the issuance of a T-bill at a face value of $1000 that will be redeemable in 91 days. Since no one would pay $1000 for a bill that will give them $1000 in three months' time, T-bills are sold at a discount.

Now, suppose this bill is sold at a discounted price of $975. This means that anyone buying it will expect to earn a return of $25 in just three months. As a percentage of the investment outlay, this represents a return of $\frac{25}{975} \times 100$ or 2.564 percent. To find the annual return, we multiply this rate by $\frac{365}{91}$, which gives us a rate of return (interest rate) of 10.28 percent. The formula is

$$r = \frac{F - P}{P} \times \frac{365}{\# \text{ days to maturity}} \qquad [9.2]$$

where r = annual interest rate, F is the face value, and P is the price paid for the T-bill. So, to confirm our calculation,

$$r = \frac{25}{975} \times \frac{365}{91} = 0.1028 \text{ or } 10.28\%$$

As you can see, implied in that mandate is the use of monetary policy to assist in achieving four separate goals:

- steady growth in real GDP
- an exchange rate that ensures a viable balance of trade
- stable prices
- full employment

Keynesian theory also suggests, as we mentioned earlier, that the money market and the product market are intrinsically linked: changes in one will bring about changes in the other. Not only that, but for the economy to achieve a stable equilibrium, *both* the product and the money markets need to be in equilibrium. How exactly does this work out? Well, suppose that the Bank of Canada wishes to effect expansionary monetary policy in order to stimulate an economy that is suffering a recession. Let us work through how a change in the money supply affects the product market. In doing this, we will see that what is called the **transmission process** puts the emphasis on the interest rate, which provides the link between the two markets.

We start our analysis with **Figure 9.7A**, which shows the money market initially in equilibrium. Now let us see what happens when the Bank of Canada increases the money supply from MS_1 to MS_2. This will immediately cause a surplus of money, which will lead individuals and institutions to rid themselves of this surplus by buying bonds. This increased demand for bonds will push up their prices, lowering the interest rate. You will recall from Chapter 5 that a lower interest rate will increase the quantity of investment spending, because firms will be willing to borrow more and invest the proceeds in new capital goods, as depicted in **Figure 9.7B**. This increase in investment spending from I_1 to I_2 will increase aggregate expenditures and shift up the aggregate expenditures curve from AE_1 to AE_2, as shown in **Figure 9.7C**. We also know from Chapter 5 that anything (apart from a change in the price level) that increases aggregate expenditures will increase aggregate demand. Thus, the aggregate demand curve in **Figure 9.7D** will shift to the right from AD_1 to AD_2. For clarity's sake we have not drawn in the AS or potential GDP curves. However, you can surmise that the increase in AD will also increase both the level of real GDP and the price level.

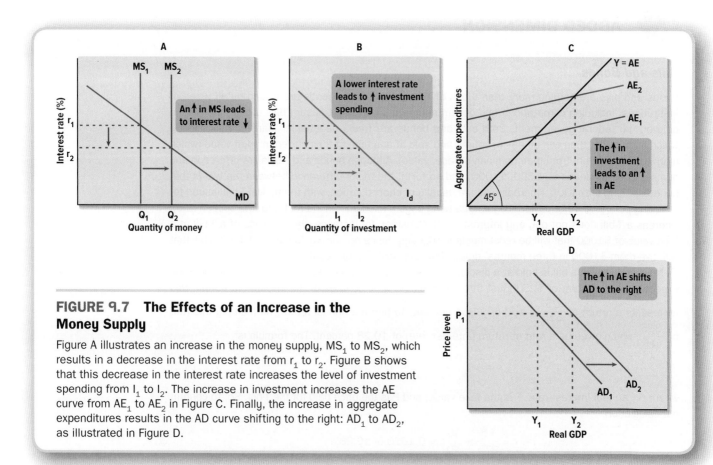

FIGURE 9.7   The Effects of an Increase in the Money Supply

Figure A illustrates an increase in the money supply, MS_1 to MS_2, which results in a decrease in the interest rate from r_1 to r_2. Figure B shows that this decrease in the interest rate increases the level of investment spending from I_1 to I_2. The increase in investment increases the AE curve from AE_1 to AE_2 in Figure C. Finally, the increase in aggregate expenditures results in the AD curve shifting to the right: AD_1 to AD_2, as illustrated in Figure D.

It is important for you to realize that the shift from AD_1 to AD_2 is larger than the increase in investment spending from I_1 to I_2. The existence of the multiplier is the reason for this. As we saw in earlier chapters, an increase in investment spending will trigger a series of increases in income and spending. The multiplier ensures that the increase in aggregate demand from AD_1 to AD_2 will be greater than the investment increase from I_1 to I_2.

The following graphic shows the chain of events that results from an increase in money supply.

Money Market Changes			Transmit into	Product Market Changes
$M_s\uparrow \Rightarrow$ Surplus of Money $\Rightarrow$	Purchase of Bonds $\Rightarrow$	Bond Prices $\uparrow$	$\Rightarrow r\downarrow \Rightarrow$	$I\uparrow \rightarrow Y\uparrow$ (Shift in AD Curve)

IN A NUTSHELL ...

The Keynesian Transmission Process

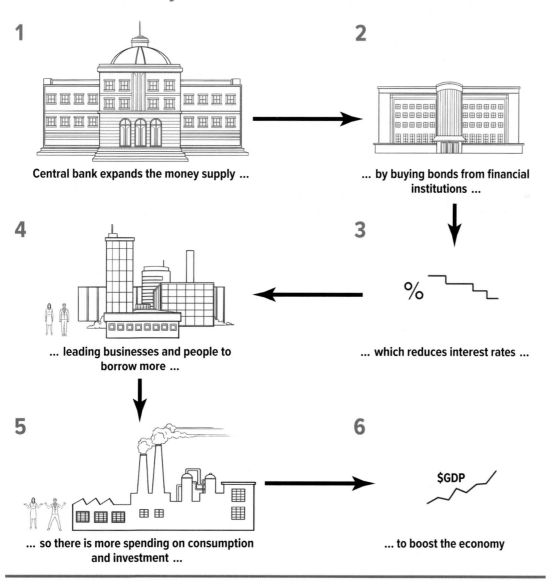

1 Central bank expands the money supply ...

2 ... by buying bonds from financial institutions ...

3 ... which reduces interest rates ...

4 ... leading businesses and people to borrow more ...

5 ... so there is more spending on consumption and investment ...

6 ... to boost the economy

Contractionary Monetary Policy to Fight Inflation

Now let us see how monetary policy can be used to fight an inflationary boom. Suppose that initially the economy is suffering from inflation. In this situation, Keynesian monetary policy would call for contractionary monetary policy. The Bank of Canada would therefore reduce the money supply from MS_1 to MS_2, as shown in Figure 9.8A. This will cause a shortage of money that, in turn, will cause people to sell bonds to increase their money holdings. The result will be a drop in bond prices, causing the interest rate to rise from r_1 to r_2. Figure 9.8B shows that the increase in the interest rate reduces investment spending from I_1 to I_2, which will then decrease the level of aggregate expenditures in Figure 9.8C from AE_1 to AE_2. Finally, the lower level of aggregate expenditures will reduce aggregate demand from AD_1 to AD_2 in Figure 9.8D. Again, for simplicity's sake we have omitted the AS and Potential GDP curves. However, we know that a decrease in AD will decrease real GDP, and, more importantly in this case, will also reduce the price level. In summary, inflation is reduced by contracting the money supply, thereby increasing interest rates and reducing overall spending in the economy.

TEST YOUR UNDERSTANDING

7. Which of the four former goals of the Bank of Canada are in conflict with each other, and which are compatible?

8. If the Bank of Canada wanted to decrease the money supply, should it buy or sell government bonds?

In summary, Keynesian monetary policy aims to stabilize the level of spending in the economy. If the economy is underspending and a recessionary gap exists, expansionary monetary policy would

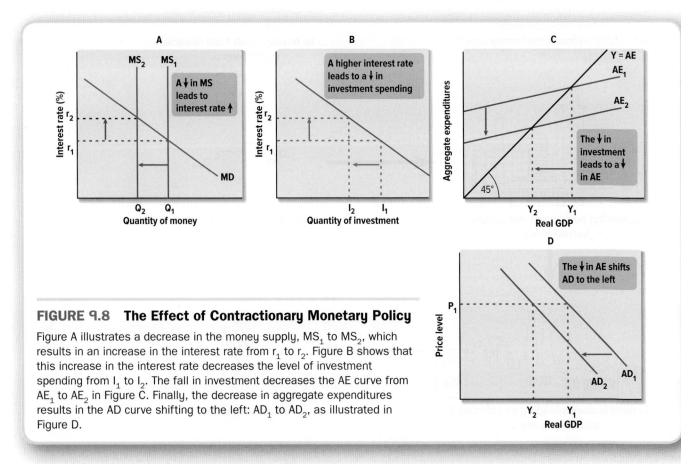

FIGURE 9.8   The Effect of Contractionary Monetary Policy

Figure A illustrates a decrease in the money supply, MS_1 to MS_2, which results in an increase in the interest rate from r_1 to r_2. Figure B shows that this increase in the interest rate decreases the level of investment spending from I_1 to I_2. The fall in investment decreases the AE curve from AE_1 to AE_2 in Figure C. Finally, the decrease in aggregate expenditures results in the AD curve shifting to the left: AD_1 to AD_2, as illustrated in Figure D.

be used to raise spending. Similarly, if an expansionary gap exists as a result of overspending in the economy, contractionary monetary policy would be used to reduce that spending.

You can appreciate from the analysis that this transmission process involves several steps of cause and effect. As we will see in the next section, Keynesians believe that the effect on the economy of a change in the money supply may not always be powerful enough to achieve the desired results. In contrast, monetarists believe that the effects of changes in the money market are much simpler, far more direct, and certainly more potent than Keynesians believe. Let us take a look at this view.

SECTION SUMMARY

a) Keynesian monetary policy puts emphasis on the power of the central bank to control the money supply. It does this using one of two tools: open-market operations (and lately also through quantitative easing) and the switching of government deposits.

b) The aim of the policy is to produce steady economic growth, an exchange rate that ensures a viable balance of trade, stable prices, and full employment.

c) Expansionary monetary policy, according to Keynes, operates through the transmission process: an increase in the money supply reduces the interest rate, which increases investment spending and therefore aggregate expenditures and demand. The result is higher real GDP and a higher price level. Contractionary policy implies a reduction in the money supply, an increase in the interest rate, and lower investment, aggregate expenditure, and demand. The result is lower prices (and therefore inflation) and a lower real GDP.

9.3   Targeting the Money Supply: Monetarist Policy

LO3 Explain why monetarists believe that controlling the money supply is vital.

Monetarism refers to a school of thought popularized by Nobel Prize–winning economist Milton Friedman. From the monetarist perspective, GDP determination can be summarized in what is referred to as the **equation of exchange**:

$$MV = PQ \tag{9.3}$$

M is the supply of money that we have been discussing in this chapter. V refers to the velocity of money (also called *velocity of circulation*), which we began to discuss in Chapter 3 and which now needs further explanation. If, for example, the GDP in a given year was $800 billion and the supply of money was $80 billion, the velocity would be 10. What this means is that every loonie, every $5 bill, every $10 bill, and so on changes hands, from person to person, an average of ten times during the year. The velocity of money is therefore the rate at which the money supply turns over in generating income.

Q refers to the quantity of goods and services sold (real GDP), whereas P is a composite (or index) of their prices.

Remember the very simple economy that we briefly looked at in Chapter 3. In this economy, Bill, the baker, suddenly discovers he is short of soap and so rushes over to the shop of Ani, the soap maker, who has just produced bars of soap and is selling them for $1 each. Bill pays with a $10 bill. With this $10 income, Ani decides to buy a new pair of jeans produced by Tammy, the tailor, and pays for them with the $10 bill. Feeling a little hungry after working on the jeans, Tammy decides to indulge herself by spending the $10 bill on five loaves of fresh bread, at $2 a loaf, from Bill, the baker. (All right, so she is more than a little hungry!) Now, in summarizing this economic activity, we could use the method that Statistics Canada uses, as described in Chapter 3, by adding the market value of each product—that is, by multiplying the quantity of each product (Q) by its price (P) and then aggregating the totals.

$$
\begin{aligned}
\text{10 bars of soap @ \$1} &= \$10 \\
\text{1 pair of jeans @ \$10} &= \$10 \\
\text{5 loaves @ \$2} &= \$10 \\
(Q \times P) &\quad \$30
\end{aligned}
$$

However, we could have worked out the value of market sales by simply noting that these sales were financed by a single \$10, which was used (spent) three times:

$$\$10 \times 3 = \$30$$
$$(M \times V)$$

In other words,

$$\text{Nominal GDP} = Q \times P \qquad [9.4]$$

ADDED DIMENSION

The Velocity of Money

The velocity of money can also be used to describe the number of times that money is actually used each year. In this case, we are looking at money used to finance all sorts of expenditures, including stock market transactions, second-hand sales, and all those other transactions not included in GDP. Defining V this way results in the following equation of exchange:

$$MV = PT$$

where V relates to the number of times money is used to finance all transactions and T is the number of transactions (not just those involving GDP items).

We are usually more interested in looking at the effect of money changes on GDP rather than its effects on all transactions in an economy during a year. However, it is only a short step from one formulation to the other, since the level of GDP is usually closely related to the total of all transactions that take place.

Determining the actual size of V in Canada very much depends on which definition of money is used. This is because the actual velocity cannot be directly measured but is obtained by dividing nominal GDP (P × Q) by the size of the money supply (M). If we use the narrow (M1) definition, empirical data show that the value of V increased steadily from approximately 7.5 in the early 1960s to over 17 in the early 1990s. Using the broader (M2) definition of money yields a value of V that has remained a fairly constant 3 over the last 30 years.

But this could also be measured as

$$\text{Nominal GDP} = M \times V \qquad [9.5]$$

It therefore follows that MV equals PQ, in that they both equal nominal GDP. In short, the two terms equal each other *by definition*.

Now that this basic equation has been established, we can explore some of its implications. A fundamental assumption of the monetarists is that one can treat V (the velocity of money) as a constant. Thus,

$$M\overline{V} \equiv PQ$$

(The line above V indicates that the term is a constant; the triple equality symbol means that this is an identity—it is true by definition—rather than just an equality.)

If velocity is indeed constant, then we immediately know that any change in M will have an impact on the right side of the equation: on prices or on the quantity of goods that, combined as we just saw, is the same thing as nominal GDP. That is, if M were to rise by 10 percent, then either the price level or quantity of goods and services produced, or a combination of the two, would also rise by 10 percent.

If we were to assume further that the economy is currently at full-employment output, Q would not be able to rise (at least not permanently), and any increase in M would have a direct and proportional impact on P—the price level. That is, if both V and Q are constant, increases in M translate into inflation—pure and simple. Thus the saying "Inflation is a monetary phenomenon."

Let's use some numbers to illustrate this situation. We could rewrite equation 9.4 as follows:

$$P = \frac{MV}{Q}$$

If V is constant and Q cannot rise because the economy is at full capacity, a 10 percent rise in M would translate into a 10 percent rise in the price level. As an example, assume that initially the money supply equals 100, the velocity of money is 8, and real GDP is 80. The price level therefore is

$$P = \frac{100 \times 8}{80} = 10$$

Now suppose that the money supply, M, increases by 10 percent to 110. The result is

$$P = \frac{110 \times 8}{80} = 11$$

which is a 10 percent rise in the price level. In other words, a change in the money supply leads to an equally proportionate change in the price level.

We should also point out that monetarists believe, in fact, that V is constant because they feel that individuals only demand money for transaction purposes—that is, that there is no asset demand for money. For monetarists, it is irrational for anybody to hold idle balances of money for any purpose. They suggest that there are a whole host of financial instruments (bonds, term deposits, and so on) that are as safe and convenient as money but also provide an income. Therefore, if people find themselves with excess cash balances—because of, for example, a recent increase in the supply of money—they will divest themselves of these by purchasing either financial instruments or goods and services, rather than hold them.

According to the monetarist position, an increase in the money supply would cause a big drop in interest rates and a significant increase in investment spending. But its impact is likely to be more direct than this. As we saw according to the Keynesian view, an increase in the money supply will lead to an increase in the purchase of bonds, but to monetarists it will in addition lead to an increase in the purchase of goods and services. It will *also* cause an increase in consumption of major consumer goods, such as cars, as people try to rid themselves of what they see as excess cash balances. If the economy is experiencing a recessionary gap, this additional demand will raise the *real* GDP. If the economy is already at full-employment equilibrium, the increase will directly raise only *nominal* GDP by pushing up prices.

 GREAT ECONOMISTS: MILTON FRIEDMAN

Milton Friedman, the 1976 Nobel Prize winner for economics, had an enormous influence on modern economic thinking. As a lifelong professor at the University of Chicago, he is most famous for his work in the field of monetary policy. However, he was also influential in many other areas, as illustrated by his seminal works on the consumption function, the role of expectations, the idea of a negative income tax, and the concept of the natural rate of unemployment. Also, he gained fame outside of economics as a journalist for *Newsweek*, in a television

© CSU Archives/Courtesy Everett Collection

documentary series, and as advisor to then–presidential candidates Barry Goldwater and Richard Nixon. His book *Capitalism and Freedom* is an elegant presentation of his laissez-faire views. He died in November 2006.

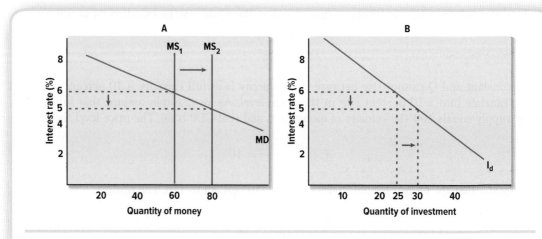

FIGURE 9.9   Keynesian View of an Increase in Money Supply

In Figure A, an increase of 20 in the money supply reduces the rate of interest from 6 to 5 percent. In Figure B, this decrease of 1 percentage point only increases investment spending by $5 (from $25 to $30).

Contrasting Keynesian and Monetarist Policies

We graphically illustrate the big difference between the two schools of thought in the diagrams that follow. The two graphs in **Figure 9.9** represent the view of Keynes, who believed that the asset demand for money was fairly sensitive to changes in the interest rate. Consequently, the money demand curve is quite flat; that is, the demand is elastic. But Keynes also believed that the investment demand by firms was inelastic (not very sensitive to interest rate changes), since there are many other factors that influence their decisions. Therefore, a small change in interest rates is unlikely to have much of an impact on firms. This implies a fairly steep investment demand curve. The combination of a flat (elastic) money demand curve and a steep (inelastic) investment demand curve means that a change in money supply has only a small impact on investment, and thus on real GDP.

Keynes believed that sometimes it is quite sensible for people to hold cash as an asset. If the money supply were to increase, it would not affect interest rates much. It is true that some people might get rid of the extra money and buy bonds, which would push up bond prices and thus reduce interest rates. However, only a small drop in interest rates would be required to make people feel comfortable holding increased amounts of money. In **Figure 9.9A**, then, an increase in the money supply of $20 billion has very little impact on the interest rate and it falls only from 6 to 5 percent. **Figure 9.9B** shows that this reduction in the interest rate does not seem to impress businesses greatly, since it encourages them to only increase their investment spending from $25 billion to $30 billion.

The monetarist school, in contrast, believes that people would be foolish to hold idle cash balances, because, as mentioned, many types of financial investments are as secure as cash but offer a return. Therefore, it believes an increase in the money supply would lead people to quickly get rid of the extra money by buying bonds, causing a big increase in bond price and a big drop in interest rates. In **Figure 9.10A**, an increase in the money supply from $60 to $80 causes interest rates to fall from 6 to 2 percent.

Also in contrast to Keynes, monetarists believe that firms are particularly sensitive to interest rate changes, implying a flat investment demand curve as shown in **Figure 9.10B**. A drop of 4 percentage points has a very big impact on investment spending, causing it to increase from $25 billion to $65 billion as firms take advantage of this low rate of interest.

In summary, then, the same $20 billion increase in the money supply would increase investment spending by a meagre $5 billion according to the Keynesians, but by a whopping $40 billion according to the monetarists.

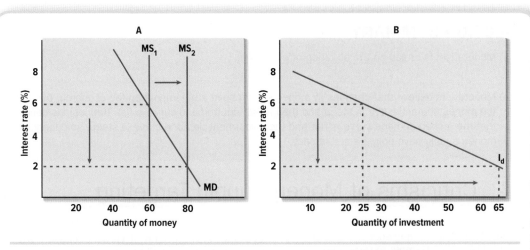

FIGURE 9.10   Monetarist View of an Increase in Money Supply

In Figure A, an increase in the money supply from $60 to $80 causes the interest rate to drop from 6 percent to 2 percent. In Figure B, this drop causes a big change in investment spending, increasing it from $25 to $65.

 TEST YOUR UNDERSTANDING

9. If the price level increases, what effect will this have on interest rates, investment, and the aggregate quantity demanded?

10. What would be the effect on the level of investment and real income if the money supply were reduced?

11. a) If M is $100, P is $2, and Q is 500, what is the value of the velocity of money?

   b) Given the same parameters as in (a), if the velocity of money stays constant, and assuming the economy is at full employment, what will be the level of P if M increases to $120?

Monetarist economists view the use of activist monetary policy as advocated by Keynesians with alarm. They believe that changes in the money supply can have such a powerful and unpredictable impact on the economy that they advocate restricting the central bank's role to the implementation of certain agreed-upon monetary rules. Their goal is to ensure that the money supply is increased only enough to accommodate the expected real growth in the economy. Emphasizing long-run stability, they suggest that the central bank's function is merely to ensure that the money supply is increased smoothly and predictably in line with estimates of the long-run economic growth rate. The result, they suggest, is the creation of a stable and predictable economic climate, which will be beneficial for all. In effect, this policy would replace the central bank by a simple monetary rule or at least with a computer capable of implementing such a rule.

In addition, monetarists are highly critical of the stated goals of Keynesian monetary policy as interpreted by central banks around the world. They feel that using such policy to stimulate economic growth, while also promoting full employment, ensuring an acceptable exchange rate, and fighting inflation, is hugely overambitious and thus doomed to fail. It would be better, they argue, to actually achieve a few goals rather than fail to achieve many. The only goal of monetary policy should be to preserve the internal and external value of the currency. In other words, the Bank of Canada should do what it does best: keep prices and the exchange rate stable. As we shall see, this is the present-day focus of many central banks around the world.

But it is not just Keynesian monetary policy that has been under attack in the last couple of decades. The monetarist view also came under severe criticism and this led to a whole new approach to monetary policy. Let us look at these new ideas.

SECTION SUMMARY

a) Monetarism is based on the equation of exchange:

$$MV = PQ$$

b) Monetarists believe that changes in money supply have a big impact on the economy, because the money demand curve is steep and the investment demand curve is flat. Keynesians believe that the money demand curve is flat and the investment demand curve is steep, so changes in money supply have only a small impact.

9.4   Criticisms of Money Supply Targeting

L04   Explain why many economists are critical of attempts to target the money supply.

A number of economists became critical of both the Keynesian and monetarist views, because both emphasized the importance of the central bank's ability to control the money supply, which they believed was difficult if not impossible. But why exactly do they think this?

Firstly—to focus on Canada—although the Bank of Canada may well be able to control the amount of cash reserves in the banking system through open-market operations, it cannot subsequently control the total money supply (cash plus deposits) because it cannot control the process of deposit expansion by the commercial banks. For instance, although a commercial bank may find itself with excess reserves as a result of open-market operations by the Bank of Canada, it may be unwilling or unable to increase customer loans, and so may not increase the amount of deposits. As we saw in Chapter 8, a commercial bank may decide not to increase loans even though it has excess reserves if it feels there are not enough creditworthy customers looking for loans. As well, in times of recession (which is when the Bank of Canada might well want to enact expansionary policy) most people the banks consider creditworthy may be fearful of getting further into debt.

A second reason the Bank of Canada should not target the money supply is that even if it had total control over the supply, it cannot control the demand and does not know for certain what the level of demand is. This means it cannot predict the extent of the reaction to holding any given size of surplus or shortage of money. We learned earlier that if people are holding more or less money than they wish to hold, they will buy or sell bonds, affecting bond prices and therefore interest rates. However, since the Bank of Canada does not know how sensitive the public may be to changes in money holdings that result from a change in the interest rate (in technical terms it cannot be certain of the slope of the money demand curve), it cannot be sure of the extent that interest rates will be affected by a change in the money supply. And the interest rate is the key variable in bringing about a change in aggregate demand. Besides all this, many institutional factors also affect the demand for money. For instance, the demand for money has changed a great deal in recent decades with the increased use of credit and debit cards, the rise of Internet banking, and the creation of new types of bank accounts.

The upshot is that many factors affect the demand for money and their impact is unpredictable. This makes it very difficult for the monetary authorities to achieve their desired aims.

In summary, the Bank of Canada no longer tries to target the money supply because

- the Bank cannot control the creation of loans by the commercial banks
- the Bank of Canada cannot know for certain what the demand for money is and so cannot predict with certainty what effect a change in the money supply will have

SECTION SUMMARY

Attempts to target the money supply have been criticized because

- the Bank of Canada cannot control the creation of loans by commercial banks
- the slope of the money demand curve is uncertain
- the position of the money demand curve is uncertain

9.5   Targeting the Interest Rate

LO5   Explain why most central banks around the world believe targeting the interest rate is the most effective monetary tool.

By the late 1980s, the Bank of Canada (along with many other central banks) abandoned Keynesian monetary policy, believing it attempted to achieve too much with too little. In addition, it rejected both Keynesian and monetarist policies for emphasizing the money supply as the key variable. Instead, the Bank began to target interest rates directly as the main policy variable and, in addition, restricted its own role to that of controlling inflation rates. Let us see graphically what this entails by looking at **Figure 9.11**.

Suppose the Bank of Canada wishes to dampen spending in the economy by raising interest rates. The market rate is presently 3 percent and the quantity of money demanded is Q_1. If the Bank successfully targets a higher interest rate of 4 percent, the quantity of money demanded will fall to Q_2. What it must then do is *accommodate* this change in the money demanded by reducing the money supply. In other words, the Bank of Canada adjusts the money supply to whatever quantity the public wishes to hold at any given interest rate.

But why does the Bank of Canada target the interest rate in this way? The answer is that it has much more control over interest rates than it does over the money supply. In addition, it is easier for the Bank to communicate its policy to the general public if it targets interest rates. After all, most of us are aware of the impact on us personally of a rise in interest rates, but we are generally ignorant of, and oblivious to, changes in the money supply.

Now we need to look a little more closely at how the Bank of Canada goes about targeting interest rates. As we have already mentioned, there is no such thing as *the* interest rate—there are, in fact, many different interest rates. However, they are all related to the official interest rate, which sets the trend for all other rates. The key rate for the Bank of Canada is the **overnight interest rate**, which refers to the rate of interest commercial banks charge each other on short-term (often overnight) loans. As we saw in Chapter 8, one commercial bank might easily find itself with insufficient reserves after cheques have been cleared for the day, while another might have surplus reserves. The rate at which these loans are transacted, called the *overnight interest (or lending) rate*, can fluctuate daily as the cash requirements of the banks change. The Bank of Canada can exercise a huge influence on this overnight rate. It does this by setting a target for that rate (it does this eight times a year on

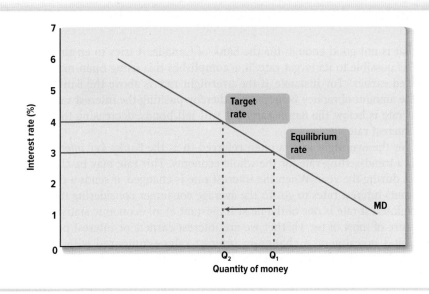

FIGURE 9.11

The present equilibrium rate is 3 percent and the quantity of money demanded is Q_1. When the bank targets a higher interest rate of 4 percent, it must reduce the money supply to Q_2 to accommodate the lower quantity demanded.

pre-announced dates) and this **target for the overnight rate** is the midpoint of the Bank's 50-basis-point (0.5 percent) operating band—the range of acceptable interest rates. For example, when the operating band extends from 2.25 percent to 2.75 percent, the target for the overnight rate is set at 2.5 percent. The bank rate is the upper limit (2.75 percent) of this band—recall from Chapter 8 that it is the rate at which the Bank will lend to commercial banks. The lower limit (known as the *bankers' deposit rate*) is the rate the Bank will pay on any deposits made by those same institutions.

The overnight interest rate will always be within the Bank of Canada's operating band. Why should that be? Well, suppose that the bank rate (the top of the operating band) happens to be 2.75 percent and the actual overnight rate is 3 percent. Why would a commercial bank short of cash reserves borrow from the other banks at 3 percent when it could easily borrow funds from the Bank of Canada at 2.75 percent? It wouldn't. Alternatively, suppose the overnight rate is 2 percent, which is below the bankers' deposit rate (the bottom of the range) of 2.25 percent. In this instance, why would a commercial bank with excess reserves lend money to another bank at 2 percent when it could earn 2.25 percent by depositing the money with the Bank of Canada? Again, it wouldn't. In short, the overnight interest rate must fall somewhere within the Bank of Canada's operating band.

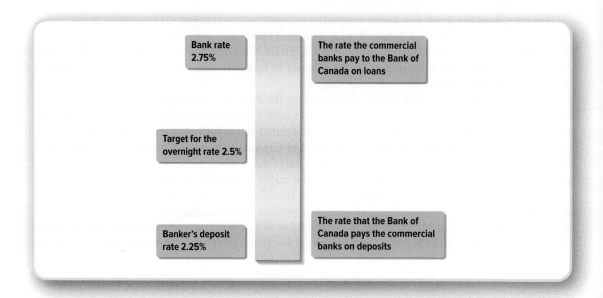

However, that is not good enough for the Bank of Canada; it tries to ensure that the overnight rate is as close as possible to its target rate. It accomplishes this using open-market operations (the ones we discussed earlier). For instance, if the overnight rate is above the Bank's target, it will buy bonds so that the amount of money is increased, thereby pushing the interest rate down. Conversely, if the overnight rate is below the Bank's target, it will sell bonds, decreasing the money supply and increasing the interest rate.

The target for the overnight rate is often referred to as the Bank's *key interest rate* or *key policy rate*, in that it is a trend-setting rate for the whole economy. This rate may be changed on any of the eight fixed dates during the year. When the interest rate is changed, it sends a clear signal about the way the Bank wants interest rates to go. To the average consumer considering the purchase of a new house or car, the interest rate is one of the most important of all economic statistics. It has the power to shape the future of most of us, whether we are interest earners or interest payers. To a company considering capital investment, a change in interest rates—compared with its expected rate of return—will often be the deciding factor when deciding whether to go ahead.

It is important to realize that the bank rate is just one of the many rates that make up the whole interest-rate structure. For example, the rate commercial banks charge their best customers, the *prime rate*, is just slightly higher than the bank rate. Moving up the scale, the mortgage rate would be next, and above that the personal loan rate. All the various rates on savings would be below the bank rate, with the highest interest rate paid on large sums of money committed for a long time and the lowest interest rate paid on small sums invested for short periods. When we speak of a change in the interest rate, we are referring to the whole interest-rate structure.

The following visual gives you some idea on interest rate structure with approximate rates at August 2016.

Credit card rate	**20%**
Personal loan rate (3-year)	**8.2%**
Mortgage rate (5-year)	**4.7%**
Prime rate	**2.7%**
Bank rate	**0.75%**
Basic savings rate	**0.5%**
Basic chequing rate	**0%**

Sources: Statistics Canada Table 176-0043 and www.ratesupermarketca.

Therefore, a drop in the bank rate signals expansionary policy, which we now know means that credit is more freely available and cheaper. A contractionary policy, which means credit is harder to obtain, is reflected in a higher bank rate.

IT'S NEWS TO ME ...

At a luncheon meeting today in Quebec City with a group of economists and financial planners, Bank of Canada governor Stephen Poloz said that he expects Canada's historically low interest rates to remain "for a long time."

As a result, he feels that individual Canadians need to adjust their retirement expectations by setting aside more savings each month, plan on working longer in life and changing their investment mix to include more stocks, fewer bonds and some real estate holdings. He also commented that we should all be watching as the full effects of the government's planned fiscal stimulus unfold.

Agreement with this outlook came from Brian DePratto of the TD bank who went on to say that he felt "the cruising speed of the Canadian economy will continue to tick lower in the coming years and that the central bank in unlikely to increase interest rates until early 2019."

Source: *Star Power Reporting*, Fall 2016.

I. Which of the following groups is adversely affected by historically low interest rates?

    a) real estate agents
    b) home buyers
    c) savers
    d) those involve in the construction industry

II. What action might the Bank of Canada take when it finally does decide it wants higher interest rates in the markets?

    a) transfer government deposits from the Bank of Canada to commercial banks
    b) sell more treasury bills on the open market
    c) encourage commercial banks to lower their target reserves
    d) none of the above would be appropriate

ADDED DIMENSION

Why Are Interest Rates So Low?

The *real* interest rate (nominal rate less the inflation rate) among the G7 nations (Italy excluded) has been in steady decline since the mid-1990s. Furthermore, the very low rates of inflation over the same period of time have resulted in low *nominal* rates as well. In short, interest rates have been at historic lows for some time, and are the result of the policies of the world's central banks of setting near zero *overnight rates* in combination with a massive injection of quantitative easing.

But some ask whether there isn't more beneath the surface. There might well be: there is a world-wide glut in savings, and many observers think this is also putting downward pressure on interest rates.

Why is there so much savings? First, in the rich world the population is aging and average lifespans are rising, while the average working-life term has not changed much. This means more people are having to save more to fund their retirement. Furthermore, with the integration of China into the world's economy, we see the effect of a billion people with traditional savings rates of 40 percent (the one-child policy in China depresses traditional reliance on children as old age security) coming into play. Add to all this the fact that the collapse of housing prices in some countries (particularly the U.S. and the U.K.) has forced people to save more to compensate for a decrease in their house equity.

In addition to this, investment spending on the part of business remains generally sluggish as a result of low business confidence caused by the austerity policies in Europe and the political stalemate in the United States. Thus, with low investment and a reluctance by many governments to use expansionary fiscal policy, the only thing left to counteract the sluggish growth experienced by most of the leading economies is expansionary monetary policy—and this means low interest rates.

SECTION SUMMARY

The Bank of Canada sets a target for the overnight interest rate at the mid-point of a 0.5 percent operating band. It then *accommodates* the supply of money to whatever the quantity demanded might be at that interest rate.

9.6   Targeting Interest Rates: Anti-Inflationary Monetary Policy

> **LO6** Explain why anti-inflationary policy emphasizes targeting the interest rate.

As we have mentioned, the Bank of Canada now targets the interest rate rather than the money supply as its main tool of policy. However, perhaps more significant than that is the change in its goal. Its present approach is to:

Contribute to solid economic performance and rising living standards for Canadians by keeping inflation low, stable, and predictable.

In other words, the Bank tries to preserve both the internal and the external value of currency. The Bank's current mission is to maintain low inflation rates and a stable exchange rate. Its recent target has been an inflation rate between 1 and 3 percent per year. In this, it has been markedly successful. Recent inflation rates are in stark contrast to the experience of most of the 1970s and 1980s. Following the OPEC-imposed oil price increases of the early 1970s, inflation rates around the world,

Canada included, were in the range of 8 to 12 percent per year. In addition to holding the rate of inflation down, the Bank is also concerned with the external value of the currency (the exchange rate), with an eye to maintaining its stability.

Those who support this new monetary policy argue that the underlying purpose of preserving the internal and external value of a country's currency is to create the right atmosphere for investment. Price stability is the key condition for stimulating investment and thus for maintaining the highest possible levels of productivity, real incomes, employment, and global competitiveness. As we saw in Chapter 4, the worst enemy of new investment is uncertainty. High rates of inflation, or even unpredictable changes in the inflation rate, create an atmosphere of uncertainty. Foreign investors, in particular, need the assurance that both the external value (the exchange rate) and the internal value (the price level) of a currency will not change dramatically in the near future. In short, uncertainty and the lower levels of investment spending that go with it reduce the rate of economic growth and the prosperity of the nation.

ADDED DIMENSION

The Correct Measure of Inflation?

When the Bank of Canada sets an inflationary-control target range, such as the 1 to 3 percent range mentioned in this chapter, it has always been an unstated assumption that this range referred to changes in Canada's CPI (consumer price index) as measured monthly by Statistics Canada. Other central banks around the world (but, interestingly, not the U.S. Federal Reserve) that have explicit inflation targets also target domestic consumer price indexes, such as the CPI.

However, some central bankers are now suggesting that the prices of such assets as houses and shares should also be taken into account. That is because surging house prices (for example) can occur, even when inflation (measured in the conventional sense) is tame. The result is distorted price signals that encourage too much investment in housing and, as a result, too little saving in the economy as a whole. This would result in too little investment in other industries in the economy.

It is easy to see how this idea has recently surfaced. Thanks to low inflation in most countries around the world in the last few years, interest rates have remained at near-record lows. To achieve these lows, more liquidity has been pumped into the economy, and this additional liquidity has in the past few years spilled over into rapidly rising house prices in Canada rather than an increase in the CPI. So where might this leave us? Perhaps the conventional idea that inflation can be described as "too much money chasing too few goods" should now be revised to say "too much money chasing too few assets."

In consideration of this effect of uncertainty, the federal government and the Bank of Canada made a joint statement in December 1993 announcing their objective of keeping inflation between 1 and 3 percent; they also made it clear that more target-range announcements would be forthcoming.

We have already seen that controlling inflation means preventing aggregate demand from becoming too strong, and this is done by keeping the pace of monetary expansion in line with economic growth, and occasionally by adopting a contractionary monetary policy.

Let us now turn to the other part of the Bank of Canada's new mandate—preserving the value of Canada's flexible exchange rate. Is this possible if the bank is focused primarily on an anti-inflationary monetary policy? Not only is it possible, but the two goals are quite compatible.

The most noticeable effect of a tight monetary policy is a higher interest rate. These same higher interest rates, which dampen spending and keep inflation low, will also encourage foreigners to buy Canadian securities, which as we shall see in more detail in Chapter 11, increases the demand for the Canadian dollar and strengthens its value on international money markets. The higher Canadian dollar will decrease Canadian exports and cause an increase in imports. Net exports, then, will decrease. Because of flexible exchange rates, monetary policy becomes a far more effective anti-inflation tool. We can show this schematically.

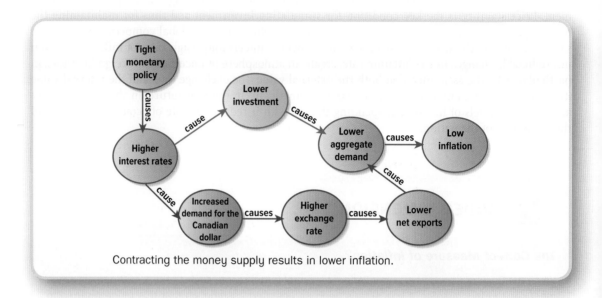

Contracting the money supply results in lower inflation.

SECTION SUMMARY

The present policy of the Bank of Canada is to keep inflation within the range of 1 to 3 percent. In doing so, it aims to preserve the internal and the external value of the currency. This can be done by keeping interest rates high, which reduces domestic spending and encourages foreign investment.

9.7   Criticisms of Interest Rate Targeting

LO7   List some of the recent criticisms of anti-inflationary monetary policy.

The most serious criticism of anti-inflationary monetary policy is that if the Bank of Canada is overly concerned about controlling inflation it will lose sight of other, equally valid goals, such as economic growth and low unemployment.

An example of this concern can be found in a study done by Professor Pierre Fortin of the University of Quebec. Fortin points out that between 1981 and 1989, real short-term interest rates were about 1 percent higher in Canada than in the United States, but between 1990 and 1996, the gap rose to 3.6 percent. He attributes this to the zeal with which the Bank of Canada pursued an anti-inflationary monetary policy. Further, Fortin and others argue that these high interest rates cost the Canadian economy dearly in the form of lost GDP and higher unemployment. Along the same lines, a recent American study argues that a modest amount of inflation, say 2 to 3 percent, is a necessary lubricant for economic growth.

The second criticism of anti-inflationary policy is that by using high interest rates to control inflation, the central bank has helped increase the cost of servicing the national debt. Just a 1 percentage point difference in interest rates translates into a $5 billion difference in the annual interest payments that government has to make. Many observers have suggested that, especially in the early 1990s, the Bank of Canada could have reduced interest rates significantly without triggering inflation. The benefit of doing so would have been not only higher growth and employment as previously mentioned, but also lower budget deficits and debt.

ADDED DIMENSION

A Return to Gold as Money?

The aftermath of the financial crisis of 2008–10 saw the re-emergence of a simple idea. If governments are prevented from printing and then spending too much money, prices will be stable. It is a simple idea but also one that is just plain wrong. In both Canada and the United States, from the end of World War I to early 1933, the money supply of each of the economies was fixed to the quantity of gold held by the respective central banks. This means that the money supply could not increase without the stock of gold first increasing. This, it was felt, would ensure that governments could not arbitrarily increase the supply of money on a whim. It also meant, for some, that the money supply was supported and underpinned by something of "real value," that is, gold. However, despite this supposed constraint, during this period prices were anything but stable with periods of both inflation and deflation.

Changes in a nation's balance of international trade and swings in the physical stock of gold held by the government are the primary causes of price instability under this kind of system. In contrast, consider the past twenty years or so, when both the Canadian and the U.S. central bank have pursued the inflation-targeting system of monetary policy: prices have been quite stable with no deflation and with inflation rates stable and below 2 percent.

Most economists see the idea of fixing the money supply to gold as a solution in search of a problem. Prices would have to fall a great deal if we adopted such a system in today's economic environment. In other words, it would turn the imagined problem of price stability into a real problem of price stability. And, of course, this ensuing deflation would send the economy into a death spiral due to still-high levels of household debt.

It simply doesn't make any sense to crucify our economy on a cross of gold.

SECTION SUMMARY

The Bank of Canada's current anti-inflationary policy has come under fire for keeping interest rates higher than they need be. The result has been lower growth, higher unemployment, and big government budget deficits because of the high interest costs.

Study Guide

Review

WHAT'S THE BIG IDEA?

The three contrasting monetary policies described in this chapter are reasonably easy to understand. Keynesian monetary policy tends to put the emphasis on controlling the money supply in pursuit of stable inflation, full employment, and stable growth. Anti-inflationary monetary policy, on the other hand, directs its attention to controlling interest rates, and has a narrower focus: keeping inflation low and the exchange rate stable.

In contrast to these two, the policy of monetarists is to limit the role of the central bank to that of merely increasing the money supply by a predetermined amount in line with anticipated economic growth. They feel that efforts by the central bank to improve the economy might, in fact, make matters worse, because changes in the money supply and interest rates can be both too powerful and unpredictable.

Perhaps the most difficult part of the chapter is the idea of the transmission process: how changes in the money supply impact other aspects of the economy such as real GDP, economic growth, and exchange rates. Working the process back, if the central bank wishes to expand the economy, it needs to increase spending. This can be done by getting the commercial banks to increase the loans given to their customers. This will happen if the banks get their hands on more cash reserves, and the central bank has the power to make that happen by buying government treasury bills, thereby putting cash in the hands of the banks' customers. Alternatively, the central bank might switch funds from the government's account held by the central bank itself to one of the commercial banks. In either case, the resulting increase in loans and deposits will also reduce interest rates, making it cheaper for customers to borrow—particularly firms who want to invest. On the other hand, if the central bank wants to contract the economy and slow down inflation, it does the opposite and reduces the reserves of the commercial banks so that they are forced to call in loans. This reduction in the money supply will also lead to higher interest rates which in turn will reduce investment spending.

NEW GLOSSARY TERMS AND KEY EQUATIONS

asset demand for money
contractionary monetary policy
equation of exchange
expansionary monetary policy
interest rate

monetarism
monetary policy
open-market operations
overnight interest rate
quantitative easing

target for the overnight rate
transactions demand for money
transmission process

Equations:

[9.1]   Rate of return (rate of interest) $= \dfrac{\text{coupon interest } +/- \text{ change in the bond price}}{\text{price paid for bond}} \times 100$

[9.2] $r = \dfrac{F - P}{P} \times \dfrac{365}{\text{\# days to maturity}}$

[9.3] $MV = PQ$

[9.4]   Nominal GDP $= Q \times P$

[9.5]   Nominal GDP $= M \times V$

Comprehensive Problem

(LO 1, 2, 6) The money market in the country of Everton is depicted in **Figure 9.12** (all figures are in billions of dollars). The investment demand curve is shown in **Figure 9.13** and the product market in **Figure 9.14**. Both the money market and the product market are in equilibrium.

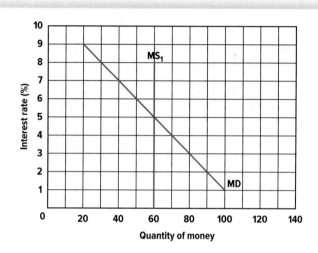

FIGURE 9.12

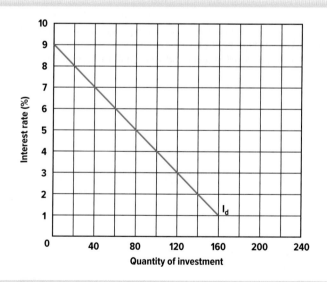

FIGURE 9.13

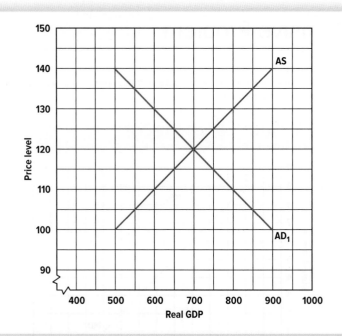

FIGURE 9.14

Questions

Suppose that the central bank of Everton wishes to implement an expansionary monetary policy and increases the money supply by $10 billion.

a) Draw the new money supply curve, labelled MS₂, in **Figure 9.12**.
b) What is the new equilibrium interest rate in Everton?
c) By how much will investment spending in Everton change as a result of the increase in the money supply?
d) Suppose that for every $1 change in investment spending, aggregate demand changes by $5. Draw the new AD curve, labelled AD₂, in **Figure 9.14**.
e) What will be the new equilibrium price level and real GDP in Everton?

Answers

a) See the following figure:

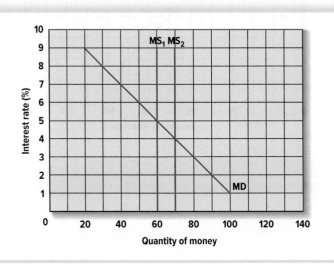

FIGURE 9.12 (COMPLETED)

b) 4 percent. This is where the new MS_2 curve intersects the MD curve.
c) Increase of $20 billion. Figure 9.17 shows that at the previous interest rate of 5 percent, the quantity of investment was $80. At the new interest rate of 4 percent, the quantity of investment is $100. The difference is $20 billion higher.
d) See the following figure:

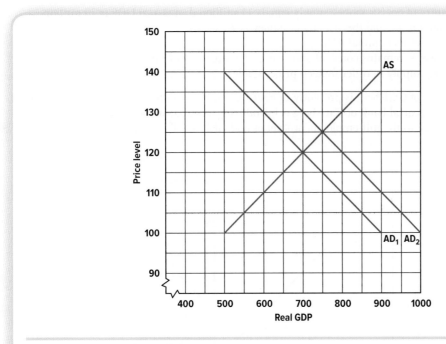

FIGURE 9.14 (COMPLETED)

e) Price level = 125; real GDP = $750 billion. (Where AD_2 intersects AS.)

Questions

Starting from the initial equilibrium, suppose *instead* that the central bank of Everton is concerned about the high inflation rate and wishes to reduce the price level to 110.

f) By how much must aggregate demand be decreased?
g) Again supposing that aggregate demand changes by $5 for every $1 change in investment, how much must investment be decreased?
h) In order to decrease investment by the amount in (g), what must be the bank's target interest rate?
i) At this new interest rate, by how much must the money supply be decreased in order to accommodate the new quantity of money demanded?

Answers

f) AD must be decreased by $200 billion. (The AD curve must be shifted 4 squares to the left so that it intersects the AS curve at a price level of 110 and a GDP level of $600.)

g) Decrease of $40. (The change of investment is $\frac{1}{5}$ of the change in AD.)

h) Target interest rate = 7 percent. (For investment to fall by $40 [2 squares], the interest rate must increase from 5 to 7 percent.)

i) Decrease of $20 billion. (The money supply must drop by 2 squares in order to increase the interest rate from 5 to 7 percent.)

CHAPTER 9 THE MONEY MARKET AND MONETARY POLICY

Study Problems

Find answers on the McGraw-Hill online resource.

Basic (Problems 1–6)

1. **(LO 3)** In the country of Sparta, money supply equals 11 million drams, real GDP is 70 million drams, the price level is 1.1, and the velocity of money is 7.
   a) What is the value of its nominal GDP? _____
   b) If, in the next year, V remains constant and real GDP increases to 77 million drams, what must happen to money supply in order to keep prices stable? _____

2. **(LO 2)** The economy of Carlsberg is presently in equilibrium but is suffering a recession as depicted in Figure 9.15. The central bank of Carlsberg is introducing an expansionary monetary policy to get the economy back to the full-employment level of real GDP.

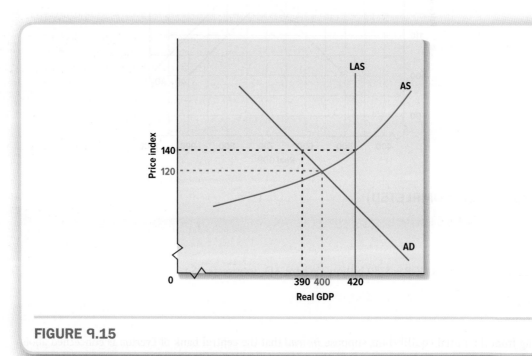

FIGURE 9.15

   a) What increase in aggregate demand is necessary to achieve this? _____
   b) If the policy is successful, what will be the growth rate? _____
   c) If the policy is successful, what will be the inflation rate? _____

3. **(LO 3)** In the country of Juventus, the money supply is equal to $40 (billion), the velocity of circulation is 5, and real GDP is $100 (billion).
   a) What is the price level in Juventus, and what is the value of its nominal GDP?
      Price level: _____ Nominal GDP: _____
   b) If money supply increases by 20 percent, what will be the new values of the price level and nominal GDP, assuming that V and real GDP remain constant?
      Price level: _____ Nominal GDP: _____
   c) What does this suggest about the connection between money supply and price level?

4. **(LO 1)** Andra has just been given a $5000 one-year bond with a coupon rate of 7 percent per year. However, she needs the money now and is surprised to find that the market value of the bond has increased to $5200. What rate of return (interest) would a prospective buyer earn on this bond? _____

5. **(LO 2)** Figure 9.16 illustrates the money demand and investment demand for the economies of Pabst and Kokanee.

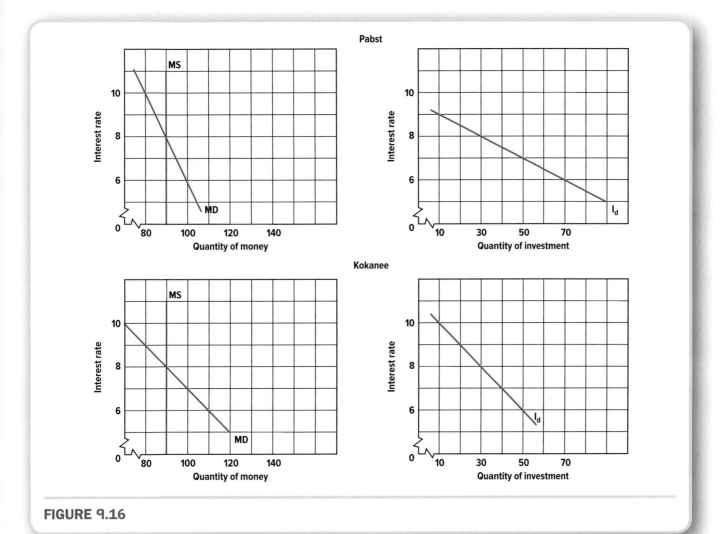

FIGURE 9.16

a) If money supply is increased by 10, what will be the new interest rate?
   Pabst: _____ Kokanee: _____
b) What will be the increase in investment spending as a result of this new interest rate?
   Pabst: _____ Kokanee: _____
c) If the multiplier is 2 in each economy, what will be the increase in GDP?
   Pabst: _____ Kokanee: _____
d) In which economy would monetary policy be more effective in closing a recessionary gap?

6. **(LO 2)** Figure 9.17 shows information for the economy of Tantalus.

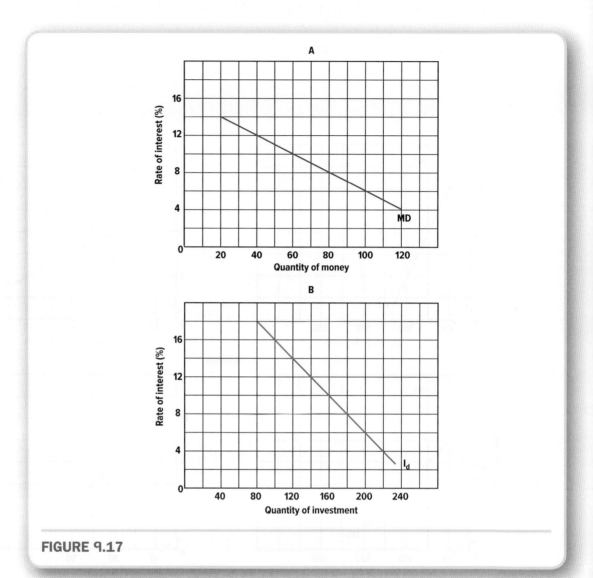

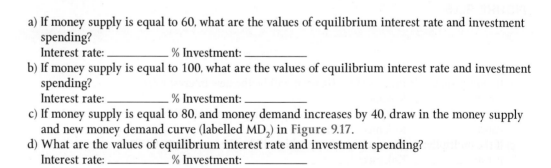

FIGURE 9.17

a) If money supply is equal to 60, what are the values of equilibrium interest rate and investment spending?

Interest rate: _____ % Investment: _____

b) If money supply is equal to 100, what are the values of equilibrium interest rate and investment spending?

Interest rate: _____ % Investment: _____

c) If money supply is equal to 80, and money demand increases by 40, draw in the money supply and new money demand curve (labelled MD$_2$) in Figure 9.17.

d) What are the values of equilibrium interest rate and investment spending?

Interest rate: _____ % Investment: _____

Intermediate (Problems 7–9)

7. **(LO 2)** Figure 9.18 shows information for the economy of Heart.

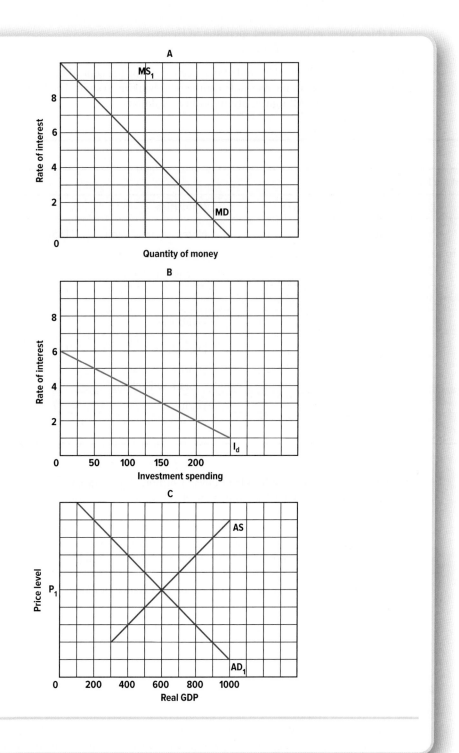

FIGURE 9.18

a) In Figure A illustrate the effect of an increase in money supply, which reduces the interest rate to 4 percent, and in Figure B illustrate the effect of the lower interest rate on the level of investment spending.

b) What is the new level of investment spending? _____

c) Suppose that for each $1 change in investment, aggregate demand changes by $4. Show the effect of this change in investment spending in Figure C.

d) What is the new level of real GDP? _____

8. **(LO 1)** Table 9.1A shows abbreviated balance sheets for the central bank in the country of Beckland. Table 9.1B shows tables for its whole commercial banking system. The target reserve ratio for the banks is 10 percent. (All figures are in billions of dollars.)

TABLE 9.1

A) Central Bank of Beckland

Assets		(1)	Liabilities		(1)
Treasury bills	190	_____	Notes in circulation	185	_____
Short-term loans to banks	5	_____	Government deposits	6	_____
			Deposits of banks	4	_____

B) Beckland's Banking System

Assets		(1)	(2)	Liabilities		(1)	(2)
Reserves:				Deposits	120	_____	_____
In vaults	8	_____	_____	Short-term loans from			
In Bank of Beckland	4	_____	_____	Bank of Beckland	5	_____	_____
Securities	30	_____	_____	Equity	7	_____	_____
Loans to customers	90	_____	_____				

a) Suppose that the Bank of Beckland buys $1 billion of government securities (T-bills) from the commercial banks. Show the immediate effects of this transaction on the balance sheets in column (1) of Tables 9.1A and B.

b) What effect does this transaction have on the money supply of Beckland? _____

c) What effect does the transaction have on the banking system's excess reserves? _____

d) If the banks were to fully loan-up, show the result in column (2) of the banking system's balance sheet.

e) By how much has money supply now changed? Change in money supply: +/−_____ of $_____

9. **(LO 1)** Assume that the original price of a 3-month treasury bill with a redeemable value of $100 was $96, and one month later it was sold for $96. What is the change in the rate of return on this bill? _____

Advanced (Problems 10–13)

10. **(LO 1)** Adriana's cousin has sent her a $20 000 bond, which pays annual interest of $1600. The bond has 2 years left until redemption. Adriana wants to cash in the bond to buy a truck. The current interest rate is 5 percent. Ignoring brokerage and other costs, approximately how much will Adriana get for the bond? _____

11. **(LO 3)** Use **Figure 9.19** to answer the following questions.

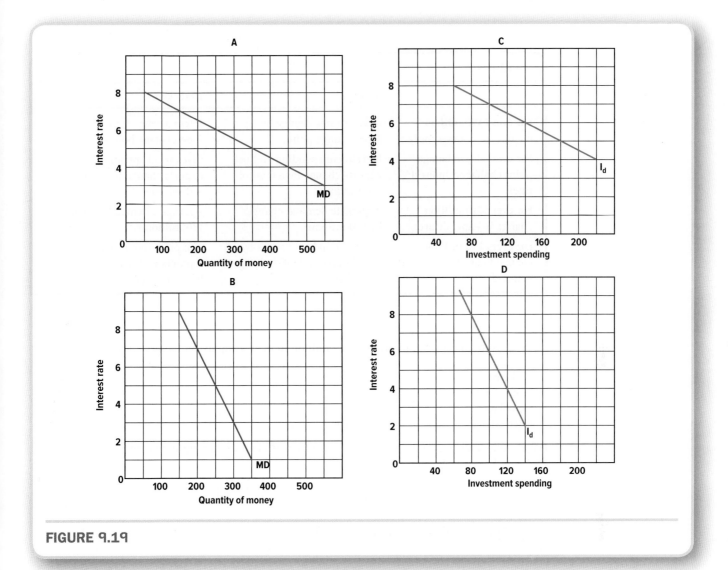

FIGURE 9.19

a) Which graph in **Figure 9.19A** or **B** depicts the Keynesian view of the money market? Which is the monetarist view?

b) Which graph in **Figure 9.19C** or **D** depicts the Keynesian view of investment demand? Which is the monetarist view?

c) According to the Keynesians, how much would investment spending change if the money supply were to increase by $100? (Increase/decrease) _____ by $_____

d) According to the monetarists, how much would investment spending change if money supply were to increase by $100. (Increase/decrease) _____ by $_____

12. **(LO 2)** Table 9.2 shows the effect of changes in various economic variables in the countries of Beckland and Heineken.

TABLE 9.2

	Beckland	Heineken
For every $10 million change in money supply	Interest rates change by 1 percentage point.	Interest rates change by 2 percentage points.
For every 1 percentage point change in interest rates	Investment spending and net exports change by a total of $20 million.	Investment spending and net exports change by a total of $10 million.
For every $10 million change in expenditures	Aggregate demand changes by $20 million.	Aggregate demand changes by $30 million.
For every $10 million change in aggregate demand	The price index changes by 1 point and real GDP changes by $5 million.	The price index changes by 2 points and real GDP changes by $3 million

---

a) What is the effect of an increase of $10 million in money supply on the price level and the level of real GDP in each country?
Beckland
Price change: _____ GDP change: _____
Heineken
Price change: _____ GDP change: _____

13. **(LO 2)** Akio bought a $5000 3-month treasury that still had 73 days until maturity. If he paid $4900 for the bill, what is its annual rate of return?

Problems for Further Study

Basic (Problems 1–3)

1. **(LO 1)** Explain why (or why not) each of the following will cause an increase in the transactions demand for money.
   a) an increase in price level
   b) an increase in real income
   c) an increase in nominal income
   d) an increase in both price level and nominal income by same percentage

2. **(LO 1)** What are the two determinants of the transactions demand for money?

3. **(LO 1)** What do we mean when we say a treasury bill is sold at a discount?

Intermediate (Problems 4–8)

4. **(LO 3)** Table 9.3 shows actual data for the Canadian economy for the period 2011–15 (all money figures in billions of dollars). For each year, calculate the velocity of money. (*Hint:* You may need to rearrange the equation of exchange and divide by 100.)

TABLE 9.3

Year	M1	Price Level (2007 = 100)	Real GDP (GDP at 2007 prices)
2011	283	107.9	1634
2012	296	109.2	1662
2013	281	110.9	1690
2014	298	112.9	1734
2015	337	112.3	1752

What is the value of the velocity of money in each of the five years?

2011 _____ 2012 _____ 2013 _____ 2014 _____ 2015 _____

5. **(LO 1)** Justin's grandfather left him a $10 000 bond with exactly 1 year left until redemption. Its coupon rate is 8 percent per annum. The current rate of interest on similar bonds is 5 percent. Unfortunately, Justin has to sell this bond to raise money for tuition next semester. Ignoring brokerage fees and other transaction costs, approximately how much will Justin get for his bond? _____

6. **(LO 1)** How does a surplus of money disappear?

7. **(LO 2)** Why does contractionary monetary policy imply a leftward shift in the aggregate demand curve?

8. **(LO 2, 3)** Explain how an increase in money supply affects the interest rate, investment, and income. How do the Keynesians and the monetarists differ in their views of this?

Advanced (Problems 9–10)

9. **(LO 2)** Would Keynesian monetary policy be more effective in dealing with a recessionary gap or an inflationary gap? Why?

10. **(LO 3)** What do monetarists say about the asset demand for money? Why do they believe this?

CHAPTER 10
International Trade

LEARNING OBJECTIVES

At the end of this chapter, you should be able to:

LO1 Explain the importance of international trade and why nations trade with each other.

LO2 Explain why nations import certain goods, even though they can be made more cheaply at home.

LO3 Explain how the gains from trade are divided between trading partners.

LO4 Describe why some groups win and others lose as a result of freer trade.

LO5 Identify various restrictions to, and some arguments against, free trade.

WHAT'S AHEAD ...

We start this look at international trade by asking why people trade with each other, and in answering that question we discover that all nations trade for exactly the same reason. We explain Ricardo's theory of comparative advantage, which (approximately 200 years ago) helped to sort all this out. We then look at the terms of trade and show how this determines who gets what share of the increased production that results from trade. Finally, we examine some of the reasons nations have restricted trade in the past and what methods they use to do this.

A QUESTION OF RELEVANCE ...

Have you looked at the little tag on your jeans lately? Were they made in Canada? What about your camera? Your fishing rod? Your tennis racket? Your smart phone? Does it concern you that they all might well have been made abroad? It will probably not come as a surprise to you that Canada imports over a third of all its products. Is this good for the country? Surely it would be in Canada's interests to produce its own goods. Or would it? This chapter looks at the question of whether Canada is better or worse off as a result of international trade.

People have traded in one form or another since the dawn of time, and most of the great powers in history have also been famous traders: the Phoenicians and the Greeks, medieval Venice and Elizabethan England, and the early American colonies and modern Japan. It seems obvious that great benefits are obtained from trading, but there has always been the underlying suspicion that someone also loses as a result. For many, a great trading nation is one that consistently, and through shrewd practice, always manages to come out on top during trade negotiations. This "beggar thy neighbour" attitude was no great concern for writers immediately preceding Adam Smith, who thought it was part of the natural state of affairs that there are always winners and losers in trade. It was the job of policy makers, they felt, to ensure that their own country was always on the winning side.

It took the mind of Adam Smith to see that whenever two people enter into a voluntary agreement to trade, both parties must gain as a result. If you trade a textbook with a friend in exchange for a ticket to a Maple Leafs hockey game, you obviously want that ticket more than the textbook, and your friend must want the textbook more than the ticket. Trade is to the advantage of both of you, or it would not take place. When we look at international trade, we are simply looking at this single transaction multiplied a billionfold. It is not really nations that trade, but individuals and firms buying from foreign individuals and firms. In many ways, you trade with a friend for the same reason for which you buy products from a Toronto brewery, a Winnipeg car dealer, or a Tokyo fishing rod manufacturer: you hope to gain something as a result, and what you give up in return (usually money) is of less value to you than what you obtain in return.

All of which raises the question of why you personally (or a whole nation, for that matter) would want to buy something rather than make it at home. In other words, why are people not self-sufficient? Why do they not produce everything they personally consume? Well, Adam Smith had an answer for this (as for many things):

> It is the maxim of every prudent master of a family, never to make at home what will cost him more to make than to buy.[1]

There, in essence, is the main argument for trade: Why make something yourself if you can buy it cheaper elsewhere? If it takes Akio three hours to make a certain product, but he can buy it elsewhere from the income he gets from one hour's work in his regular job, why would he bother to make it? In fact, it would pay him to do his own job for three hours; he could afford to buy three units of the product. An additional consideration is the fact that Akio cannot make most of the things he wants—or could make them only after extensive training and with the help of very expensive equipment.

---

[1] Adam Smith, *The Wealth of Nations* (Edwin Cannan edition, 1877), p. 354.

10.1   Specialization and Trade

> **LO1**   Explain the importance of international trade and why nations trade with each other.

Before we start looking at the theory behind international trade, let's look at some data that highlight what can only be called an explosion in international trade over the last thirty years or so.

Current Trends in World Trade

In 1983, the total value of world trade was just over $1800 billion. By 2015, that figure had increased to just under $16 000 billion. Furthermore, for most countries, trade as a percentage of GDP has also risen appreciably. There are a number of reasons behind this. First, there have been significant improvements in transport (think of container ships and ports) and communications technology (think of the Internet) that have both opened up world markets and reduced the cost of moving goods internationally. Second, there has been a movement internationally to reduce, and in some cases remove, trade barriers such as tariffs and quotas between nations. Allied to this, the last thirty years or so have seen the formation or expansion of common trade associations such as the European Union (EU) and the North American Free Trade Agreement (NAFTA). Finally, we should mention the fall of the Soviet Union and the trade-liberalizing policies that followed in China, as well as the fifteen newly independent nations that were previously part of the closed Soviet system.

Figure 10.1 shows just how much international trade has increased since 1970. While world GDP has risen 290 percent over this period, world trade (despite an appreciable downturn due to the 2008–10 recession) has increased a whopping 52 times.

While all regions on the planet have experienced big growth in international trade, the leading areas have been Europe and Asia as Figure 10.2 shows. Note that although the world experienced a big decline due to the 2008–2010 recession, by 2011 international trade had bounced back to continue its upward trend.

It should be noted that a good part of this massive increase in international trade in these three geographical areas has been the result of trade *within* the areas following the introduction of free trade agreements. However, trade *between* these regions is also significant, as Figure 10.3 shows. (The percentages show the portion of total trade.)

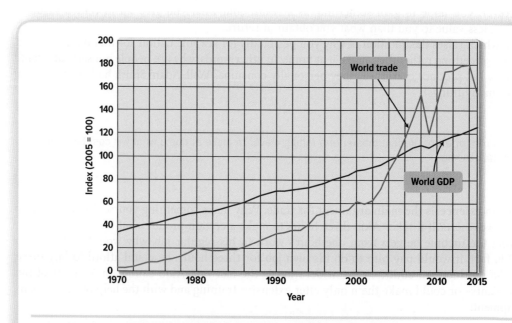

FIGURE 10.1   Trends in World Trade and GDP, 1970–2015

Source: World Trade Organization, *Statistical Review 2016.*

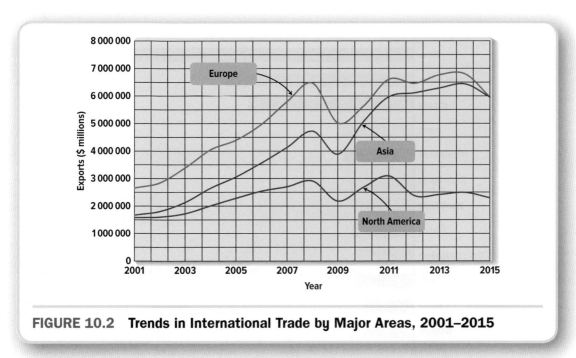

FIGURE 10.2 **Trends in International Trade by Major Areas, 2001–2015**

Source: World Trade Organization, *Statistical Review 2016*.

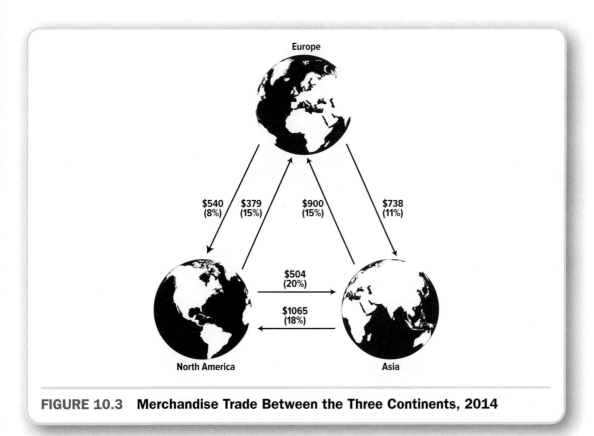

FIGURE 10.3 **Merchandise Trade Between the Three Continents, 2014**

Source: World Trade Organization, *International Trade Statistics 2015*.

And just who are the leading trading nations these days? Well, perhaps it comes as no great sur-prise to learn that in the past few years, China has overtaken the United States in the world league, as we can see in **Figure 10.4**. Although down in eleventh place, Canada is still one of the world's great trading nations in terms of the percentage of its GDP traded internationally.

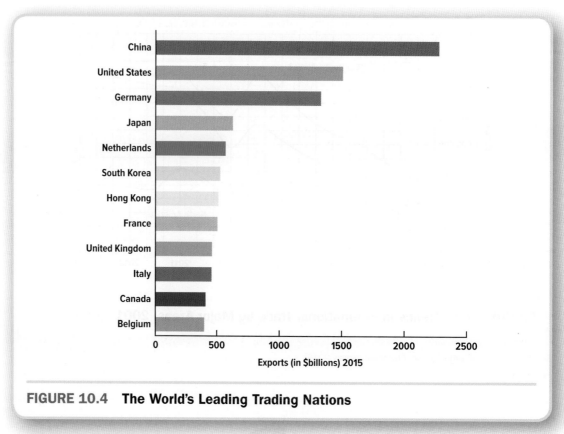

FIGURE 10.4   The World's Leading Trading Nations

Source: World Trade Organization, Statistical Review 2016.

Specialization

Specialization is the cornerstone of trade. We pointed out in Chapter 1 that there are big advantages to be gained from specialization. From an individual point of view, each of us is better suited to doing certain things than doing others. Rather than trying to grow all our own food, make our own clothes, brew our own beer, and so on, it makes more sense to specialize in our chosen occupation and, with the proceeds, obtain things other people can make better and more cheaply. Similarly, firms will be far more productive if they specialize in the production process, that is, make use of the division of labour. As we shall see in this chapter, there are also great benefits to be enjoyed by countries by specializing.

Specialization and trade go hand in hand, so it follows that more specialization means more trading. Modern nations, firms, and individuals have become increasingly specialized, and with this has come a huge increase in the volume of trade, domestically and internationally. But is there a limit? From a technical point of view, Smith thought not. But he did believe specialization would be limited by the size of the market: the smaller the market, the smaller the output, and therefore the less opportunity or need for extensive specialization. The larger the market, the greater the opportunity for specialization, which would then lower the cost of producing goods. The prime driving force behind the expansion of markets is that it enables firms to produce in higher volumes at a lower cost. All things being equal (including demand), it is the cost of production, and therefore the price of the product, that induces trade. If you can produce a product more cheaply than I, it makes no sense for me to try to produce it myself. And why are you able to produce certain products more cheaply? The answer, presumably, is that you have certain advantages over me. Let us look at some pf these possible advantages.

Factor Endowment

One person has an advantage in production over others if he or she is endowed with certain natural or acquired skills, or has more or better equipment or other resources. Just as there are many reasons some people are better gardeners or truck drivers or hockey players than others, so it is with countries. A country will have a great advantage in producing and trading pineapples, for instance, if it possesses the right type of soil and climate. But the same country might well be at a disadvantage in growing coniferous trees. Another country has an advantage in producing electronic equipment if it has the right capital, the technical expertise, and a well-educated labour force. It might not, however, be able to compete with other countries in raising sheep. Just as with people, countries are well endowed in certain areas and impoverished in others. Japan has a well-educated and motivated work force, possesses great technical expertise, and is highly capitalized, yet it is very poorly provided with arable land and mineral resources.

An expensive way to grow most produce?
© Fgcanada | Dreamstime.com

It is often suggested that countries trade primarily to buy resources they do not naturally possess. Although there is some truth in this, it often obscures the main motivation. Canada, for instance, though not naturally endowed with a warm and sunny climate throughout the year, *could* produce bananas commercially using geodesic domes with artificial light and heating. But the cost would be enormous. It is far cheaper to buy bananas from countries that grow them more easily. Most countries can overcome a resource deficiency by using different methods or other resources, but it does not make sense if this production method results in products more expensive than those obtainable abroad.

In summary, there are four areas of difference between countries that lead to their specialization in certain products. First are the obvious differences in *climate*. Second are major differences in the quantity and quality of *natural resources* a country possesses. Third are the appreciable differences in *human capital* whereby a country might well have a big advantage in traditional skills, educational attainment, or the motivation or entrepreneurial spirit of its people. Finally, the *role of government* is vital and can have enormous impact in overcoming whatever inherent disadvantages a country might have. It can do this by, for example, providing incentives to certain industries or investing in education and training in particular trades or professions.

ADDED DIMENSION

Canada, the Great Trader

Canada is certainly one of the world's great trading nations, at least in relative terms. In 2015, for example, it exported $625 billion worth of goods and services and imported $671 billion. Each of these figures represents approximately 30 percent of Canada's GDP. Only a few developed countries, such as Austria and the Netherlands, trade a larger fraction. The United States and Japan, in comparison, trade only about 12 percent of their GDPs (though, of course, in actual dollars, this represents a lot more). The United States is Canada's predominant trading partner, purchasing more than all other countries combined (buying approximately 72 percent of our exports). In fact, Canada sells over twice as much to the United States as it does to all other countries combined and buys approximately 64 percent of all of its imports from that country.

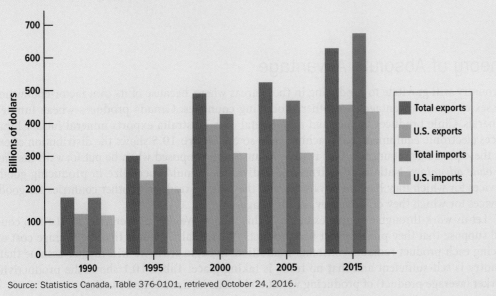
Source: Statistics Canada, Table 376-0101, retrieved October 24, 2016.

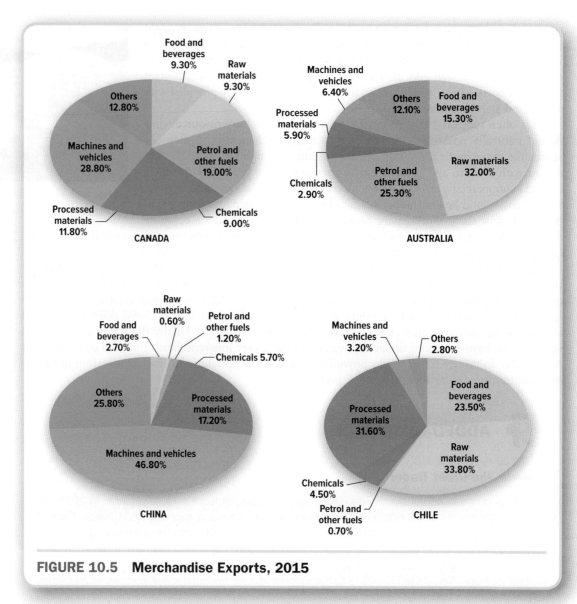

FIGURE 10.5   Merchandise Exports, 2015

Source: Adapted from *Commodity Trade Statistics Database*, United Nations, 2016. The United Nations is the author of the original material.

Theory of Absolute Advantage

A country will gravitate to producing in those areas where, because of its own factor endowments, it possesses a cost advantage over other producing countries: Canada produces wheat, lumber, and minerals, Chile produces copper and other metal ores, Australia exports mineral fuels, China produces electronic equipment and machines, and so on. **Figure 10.5** shows the distribution of exports for these particular countries. This is what Adam Smith proposed when he put forward his *theory of absolute advantage*. Nations, like firms and individuals, should specialize in producing goods and services for which they have an advantage, and they should trade with other countries for goods and services for which they do not enjoy an advantage.

Let us work through a simple example of this theory. We will concentrate on just two countries and suppose that they produce just two products. We will also assume that the average cost of producing each product remains constant. In addition, to begin with, we will further assume that each country is self-sufficient and that no trade is taking place. **Table 10.1** shows the productivity per worker (average product) of producing wheat and beans in Canada and Mexico.

TABLE 10.1
Output per Worker by Country and Industry

	NUMBER OF BUSHELS PER DAY		
	Wheat		Beans
Canada	3	or	2
Mexico	1	or	4

We can see at a glance that Canada produces more wheat than Mexico, whereas Mexico produces more wheat than Canada.

Let us suppose that initially the two countries do not trade with each other and that the working population in each country is 16 million, divided equally between the two industries. Table 10.2 shows what the two countries produce.

TABLE 10.2
Total Outputs Before Trade

	TOTAL NUMBER OF BUSHELS PER DAY (in millions)	
	Wheat	Beans
Canada	24	16
Mexico	8	32
Total	32	48

In this case, half the working population of Canada—8 million workers—is producing wheat. Since each person is capable of producing 3 bushels, the total production is 8 million times 3, or 24 million bushels. The other figures are similarly derived.

Now, suppose the two countries decide to enter into a free trade agreement, each country totally specializing in what it does best: Canada producing wheat and Mexico producing beans. With the whole of the working population of 16 million in Canada producing wheat and all 16 million people producing beans in Mexico, the totals can be seen in Table 10.3.

TABLE 10.3
Total Outputs After Trade

	TOTAL NUMBER OF BUSHELS PER DAY (in millions)	
	Wheat	Beans
Canada	48	0
Mexico	0	64
Total	48	64

With specialization, the two countries combined could produce an additional 16 million bushels of wheat (48 minus the previous 32) and an additional 16 million bushels of beans (64 minus the previous 48). These are referred to as the *gains from trade*. Strictly speaking, the increased total production is really the result of increased specialization. But if a country is going to specialize, it will need to trade in order to obtain those products it is not producing. Specialization, then, implies trade, and it would be impossible to have one without the other.

TEST YOUR UNDERSTANDING

Find answers on the McGraw-Hill online resource.

1. The following table shows the productivity per worker in the beer and wine industries of Freedonia and Libraland:

	OUTPUT IN HUNDREDS OF LITRES		
	Beer		Wine
Freedonia	4	or	1
Libraland	3	or	4

a) Which country should specialize in which product?

b) Suppose that initially the working population of each country is 20 million, with 10 million working in each industry. What is the total output of the two countries?

c) Now suppose that each country decides to specialize in the product in which it has an advantage. What will be the total output of each product, and what are the gains from trade?

SECTION SUMMARY

a) Since 1980, international trade has increased tenfold, and China is now the world's biggest exporter. If trade is voluntary, both parties to the trade must benefit.

b) Differences in factor endowments between nations and the theory of absolute advantage explain why, for example, Canada exports lumber and imports bananas.

c) Differences in trade patterns are the result of
- differences in climate
- differences in natural resources
- differences in human capital
- government policies

10.2 Theory of Comparative Advantage

LO2 Explain why nations import certain goods, even though they can be made more cheaply at home.

The eminent economist David Ricardo, following in the footsteps of Adam Smith, agreed in principle with Smith, adding a subtle but important refinement to Smith's theory of trade. To see the effect of his modification, let us change our example to that of theoretical trade between the United States and the Philippines, keeping the same two products, wheat and beans. The output per worker in each country is shown in Table 10.4.

TABLE 10.4
Output per Worker by Country and Industry

	NUMBER OF BUSHELS PER DAY		
	Wheat		Beans
United States	4	or	4
Philippines	1	or	3

Unlike in our last example of Canada and Mexico, here we see that one country, the United States, can outproduce the other, the Philippines, in *both* products. In fact, you can see from the table that U.S. wheat production is four times that of the Philippines; similarly, the U.S. is one and one-third times as productive as the Philippines in beans. If we were to follow Smith's dictum, presumably the U.S. should produce both products itself. After all, how can it possibly be of any advantage to trade with the Philippines, since it could produce both products more cheaply? The heart of Ricardo's idea is that it is not *absolute advantage* but **comparative advantage** that provides the mutual gains from trade. Let us see exactly what this means, through an example.

Suppose you happen to be absolutely the best lawyer in town. Not only that, but you are also its greatest secretary. Given this, why would you bother to hire a secretary to do your clerical work, since you are faster and, by all measurements, more efficient than anyone you could possibly hire? The answer is that the opportunity cost of doing secretarial work is far greater than that of doing legal work. Your opportunity cost of being a lawyer is the lost salary of not being a secretary. Your opportunity cost of being a secretary is your lost earnings as a lawyer. But because you can earn *comparatively* more as a lawyer than as a secretary, you are well advised to concentrate on that career and hire someone (admittedly less productive than you) to act as your secretary.

GREAT ECONOMISTS: DAVID RICARDO

Ricardo (1772–1823) was a self-made English businessman who turned to economics and politics at a relatively young age. His *Principles of Political Economy and Taxation* in 1817 made him the acknowledged leader of classical economics and the intellectual heir to Adam Smith. By building a model of the economic world, Ricardo gave the powerful tool of abstraction to economics, and the gift of enabling it to be considered a science.

Granger Historical Picture Archive/Alamy Stock Photo

Ricardo's idea of comparative advantage directs attention away from comparisons between countries and toward comparisons between products. In **Table 10.4**, for instance, we might ask: How much does it cost the United States to produce wheat? One might express the cost in dollars and cents. However, knowing that the value of money varies over time and that it is often misleading to translate one currency into another, Ricardo was at pains to express costs in more fundamental terms.

One way would be to use the number of hours it takes to produce something. For instance, if the average worker in the United States can produce four bushels of beans in an average eight-hour day, the cost of one bushel of beans would be 8/4, or 2.0 hours. In contrast, the cost of one bushel of beans in the Philippines would be 8/3, or about 2.66 hours. So beans are more expensive to produce in the Philippines.

However, it is more illuminating to measure costs in terms of *opportunity costs*. This was the method chosen by Ricardo. Recall that the opportunity cost of producing one thing can be measured in terms of another thing that has to be sacrificed in order to get it. As far as the United States and the Philippines are concerned, the cost of producing more wheat is the sacrifice of beans, and the cost of increased bean production is the loss of wheat. Let us work out these costs for each country. The cost of employing a worker in the wheat industry is what that worker could have produced in the bean industry, assuming that the country is fully employed. In other words, for every 4 bushels of wheat an American worker produces, the country sacrifices 4 bushels of beans. In per-unit terms, in the United States 4 bushels of wheat costs 4 bushels of beans, so 1 bushel of wheat costs 1 bushel of beans, and 1 bushel of beans costs 1 bushel of wheat.

In the Philippines the cost of 1 bushel of wheat is 3 bushels of beans, and the cost of 1 bushel of beans is 1/3 bushel of wheat. We summarize these figures in Table 10.5.

TABLE 10.5
Opportunity Costs of Production

| | COST OF PRODUCING ONE UNIT | |
	Wheat	Beans
United States	1 beans	1 wheat
Philippines	3 beans	1/3 wheat

Now you can understand the significance of comparative costs. If you measure the costs in absolute terms, using hours as we did in our example above, then beans are cheaper to produce in the United States. But in comparative terms, they are very *expensive*. Why is that? Because to produce beans, the United States has to make a big sacrifice in the product in which it is even more productive: wheat. Similarly, although beans, in absolute terms, are very expensive in the Philippines, they are cheap in comparative terms; to produce them the Philippines sacrifices little in wheat production because productivity in the wheat industry is low.

In this example, then, the United States should specialize in producing wheat, since the opportunity cost is only one unit of beans compared with three units of beans in the Philippines. Conversely, the Philippines can produce beans comparatively cheaply, at the cost of 1/3 unit wheat, while in the United States the cost is one unit of wheat. Although the United States has an absolute advantage in both products, it has a comparative advantage only in wheat production and the Philippines has a comparative advantage in bean production.

Let us extract further insights by showing the production possibilities of the two countries on the assumption that the size of the labour force in both the United States and the Philippines is 100 million, and that unit costs are constant. (We are assuming constant unit costs to keep the analysis simple. If you remember from Chapter 1, in reality the law of increasing costs applies, which means that the slope of the production possibilities curve is concave. Assuming constant costs means that the production possibilities curves in this chapter plot as straight lines.)

The respective production possibilities for the United States and the Philippines are shown in Table 10.6. The 400 bushels of wheat, under option A in the United States, is the maximum output of wheat if all of the 100 (million) workers were producing 4 bushels of wheat each. Similarly, if the

TABLE 10.6
Production Possibilities

| UNITED STATES: OUTPUT (millions of bushels per day) | | | | | | |
	A	B	C	D	E	F
Wheat	400	320	240	160	80	0
Beans	0	80	160	240	320	400
PHILIPPINES: OUTPUT (millions of bushels per day)						
	A	B	C	D	E	F
Wheat	100	80	60	40	20	0
Beans	0	60	120	180	240	300

100 million American workers produced only beans and no wheat, they would also produce 400 bushels of beans as seen under option F. The figures for B, C, D, and E are derived by calculating the output if 80, 60, 40, and 20 million workers are employed in wheat production, while 20, 40, 60, and 80 million workers are employed in bean production. The figures for the Philippines are similarly obtained.

Suppose that initially the countries do not trade with each other, with the United States producing combination C and the Philippines producing combination B. Before specialization and trade, therefore, their joint totals are as shown in Table 10.7.

TABLE 10.7
Output of Both Countries Before Specialization and Trade

	TOTAL OUTPUT (millions of bushels per day)	
	Wheat	Beans
United States	240	160
Philippines	80	60
Total	320	220

If the two countries now specialize, the United States producing wheat and the Philippines producing beans, their output levels would be as shown in Table 10.8.

TABLE 10.8
Output of Both Countries After Specialization and Trade

	TOTAL OUTPUT (millions of bushels per day)	
	Wheat	Beans
United States	400	0
Philippines	0	300
Total	400	300

You can see by comparing the before and after specialization positions of the two countries that production of both products is now higher. Table 10.9 outlines the gains from trade.

TABLE 10.9
Gains from Specialization and Trade

TOTAL OUTPUT (millions of bushels per day)	
Wheat	Beans
+80	+80

Thus, we can conclude that:

As long as there are differences in comparative costs between countries, regardless of the differences in absolute costs there is a basis for mutually beneficial trade.

What this example shows is that it is possible for both countries to gain from trade, but several questions remain. Will they? How will the increased production be shared? Will it be shared equally, or will one country receive more than the other? Discussion of the terms of trade will help answer these questions.

TEST YOUR UNDERSTANDING

2. Suppose that the labour force in Freedonia is 10 million. Six million people are producing apples, and the rest are producing pears. Libraland's labour force is 16 million, divided equally between the production of apples and the production of pears. The labour productivity in the two countries is given in the following table:

	OUTPUT PER WORKER (bushels per day)		
	Apples		**Pears**
Freedonia	5	or	2
Libraland	1	or	3

Make a production possibilities table for Fredonia (A to F) and for Libraland (A to E).

a) Which is Fredonia's present combination (A–F)?

b) Which is Libraland's present combination (A–E)?

3. a) Given the data in question 2, what is the total output of the two countries for both products?

b) If each country were to specialize in the product in which it has a comparative advantage, what will be the total output of the two countries for both products?

c) What will be the gains from trade?

SECTION SUMMARY

a) The theory of comparative advantage explains why one nation is willing to trade with another nation, even though it may be more efficient in producing both (all) the products involved.

b) The trade in any two products between any two nations will result in gains from trade unless the opportunity costs of production happen to be exactly the same in each country.

10.3 Terms of Trade

LO3 Explain how the gains from trade are divided between trading partners.

The expression **terms of trade** refers to the price at which a country sells its exports compared with the price at which it buys its imports. Statistics Canada regularly measures Canada's terms of trade using the following formula:

$$\text{Terms of trade} = \frac{\text{average price of exports}}{\text{average price of imports}} \times 100 \qquad [10.1]$$

If the worldwide demand for Canadian softwood lumber were to increase, for example, it would increase the average price of Canadian exports, with the result that the terms of trade would be said to have moved in Canada's favour. The result would be the same if Canadian prices remained the same but the price of imports dropped. In either case, the sale of our exports would enable us to purchase more imports. Conversely, the terms of trade would shift against Canada if Canadian export prices dropped and/or the price of imported goods rose. This is illustrated in **Figure 10.6**.

Changes in the terms of trade can have a significant effect on Canada's economic performance. This ratio of our exports to import prices directly affects our nominal trade balance and indirectly affects the level of real GDP in Canada. A higher ratio reflects a situation in which most Canadians are better off since our exports would be high—which means more jobs—and the price of imports

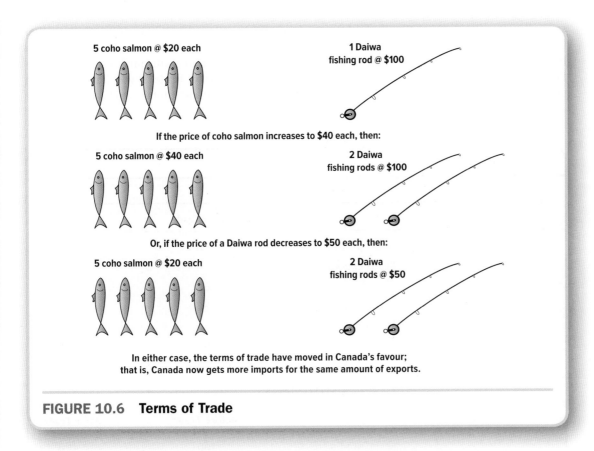

5 coho salmon @ $20 each

1 Daiwa
fishing rod @ $100

If the price of coho salmon increases to $40 each, then:

5 coho salmon @ $40 each

2 Daiwa
fishing rods @ $100

Or, if the price of a Daiwa rod decreases to $50 each, then:

5 coho salmon @ $20 each

2 Daiwa
fishing rods @ $50

In either case, the terms of trade have moved in Canada's favour;
that is, Canada now gets more imports for the same amount of exports.

FIGURE 10.6   Terms of Trade

that Canadians buy would be lower. Canada's terms of trade peaked at a ratio of approximately 112 in 1973 when world commodity prices were very high, then declined to 82 in 1998. By 2008 the ratio had risen to 104 but has fallen in recent years. It sat at 93 in 2015 as Canada's oil exports continued to drop and the price of oil remained low.

Given our U.S./Philippines example, what would be acceptable prices from the two countries' points of view? Remember that the United States is the wheat producer and exporter. A glance back at Table 10.4 shows that in the United States, 1 bushel of wheat costs 1 bushel of beans. Given this, what price would it be willing to sell its wheat for? Presumably for as high a price as it can get, but certainly not for less than 1 bushel of beans. What about the Philippines? How much would it be willing to pay for wheat? Remember, Table 10.4 tells us that in the Philippines, 1 bushel of wheat costs 3 bushels of beans. Therefore, we can conclude that the Philippines would certainly not pay any higher than this price and would be happy to pay less. As long as the price is above the American minimum and below the Philippines' maximum, both countries would be willing to trade. In other words, feasible terms of trade between the two countries would be anywhere between 1 and 3 units of beans for 1 unit of wheat.

If the price of 1 unit of wheat is less than 1 unit of beans, the U.S. would not sell its wheat, as it is below its costs and less than what sellers can receive at home. Similarly, if the price of 1 wheat was above 3 beans, the Phillippines would refuse to buy wheat, as it could make it domestically at a lower cost.

We could have just as easily expressed things in terms of beans, and a glance back at Table 10.5 shows that feasible terms of trade would be anywhere between 1/3 and 1 bushel of wheat for 1 bushel of beans. In other words, the feasible terms of trade will be between the costs of each product in the two countries. The final terms of trade will depend on the strength of demand in the two countries for these products.

Let us choose one particular rate among the many possible terms of trade and work out the consequences. Suppose, for instance, that the terms end up at 1 bushel of wheat = 2 bushels of beans (or 1 bushel of beans = 1/2 bushel of wheat). Let us now assume, since we need some point to start from, that the Philippines is quite happy consuming the 60 million bushels of beans it was producing before it decided to specialize, as was shown in Table 10.6. However, because of specialization, it is now producing only beans and will therefore have $300 - 60 = 240$ million bushels available for export, which it sells to the United States at a rate of one bushel for half a bushel of wheat. It will receive back 120 million bushels of wheat and will finish up with 60 million bushels of beans and 120 million bushels of wheat. Because of trade, it will have gained an additional 40 million bushels of wheat compared with its self-sufficient totals shown in the Before Trade column in Table 10.10.

TABLE 10.10

PHILIPPINES		Before Trade	After Trade
	Beans produced	60	300
	Beans exported	0	−240
Beans consumed		60	60
	Wheat produced	80	0
	Wheat imported	0	+120
Wheat consumed		80	120
		Gain = 40 Wheat	

UNITED STATES		Before Trade	After Trade
	Beans produced	160	0
	Beans imported	0	+240
Beans consumed		160	240
	Wheat produced	240	400
	Wheat exported	0	−120
Wheat consumed		240	280
		Gain = 80 Beans and 40 Wheat	

The United States will also gain. It was the sole producer of wheat, and of the total of 400 million bushels produced, it has sold 120 million bushels to the Philippines in exchange for 240 million bushels of beans. It will end up with 280 million bushels of wheat and 240 million bushels of beans, which is 40 million bushels of wheat and 80 million bushels of beans more than when it was producing both products as shown by comparing the Before Trade and After Trade columns for the United States. In reviewing Table 10.10 recall that we are assuming the Philippines consumes the same 60 million bushels of beans before and after trade.

Terms of Trade and Gains from Trade, Graphically

Let us now look at each country's trading picture separately. Using a graphical approach, Figure 10.7 shows the production possibilities curve for the United States. Before it decided to trade, this was also its consumption possibilities curve, since it could obviously not consume more than it produced. The slope of the curve is 1, which is the cost of 1 bushel of beans (that is, it equals 1 bushel of wheat). The curve to the right is its trading possibilities curve, which shows how much the United States could obtain through a combination of specializing its production and trading. Note that the slope of the trading possibilities curve is equal to 0.5. This is the terms of trade established between the two countries: 1 bushel of wheat for 2 bushels of beans.

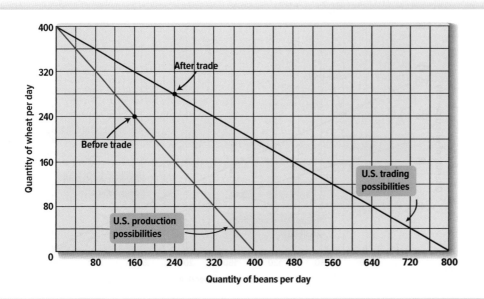

FIGURE 10.7   U.S. Production and Trading Possibilities Curves

The slope of the production possibilities curve shows the cost of producing beans in the United States is 1 bushel of wheat = 1 bushel of beans. The slope of the trading possibilities curve shows the terms of trade: 1 bushel of wheat = 2 bushels of beans. The previous maximum obtainable quantity of beans was 400 million bushels when the United States was self-sufficient. Its new maximum, as a result of trading, is now 800 million bushels.

 ADDED DIMENSION

North American Free Trade Agreement (NAFTA)

In 1993, Canada, the United States, and Mexico formalized the North American Free Trade Agreement (NAFTA) despite considerable political opposition in both Canada and the United States. This agreement was an expansion of the earlier Canada–U.S. Free Trade Agreement of 1988. Unlike the European Union, NAFTA does not create a set of supranational governmental bodies, and it does not create a body of law that supersedes national law.

Since NAFTA, trade has increased dramatically among the three nations. For instance, from 1993 to 2015, total trade between Canada and the United States increased by over 200 percent. In 2015, 78 percent of Canada's merchandised trade was destined for our NAFTA partners.

There is no question that the NAFTA trade agreement had a dramatic impact on trade between the three nations, and many would argue it has benefited all three economies.

You can see from this graph that the United States, at one extreme, could produce the maximum quantity of 400 million bushels of wheat and keep all of it. However, before trade, the maximum amount of beans available was 400 million bushels. Now, if it wished, the U.S. could produce 400 million bushels of wheat, trade *all* of it, and receive in exchange 800 million bushels of beans. (We presume it is able to buy these beans from other countries as well as from the Philippines, given that the latter can only produce 300 million bushels of beans.) More likely, of course, it will opt to have a combination of both products, such as 280 million bushels of wheat and 240 million bushels of beans, as in our numerical example above.

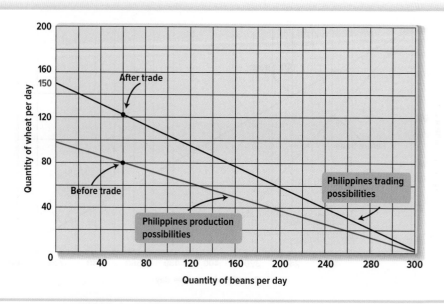

FIGURE 10.8   Philippines Production and Trading Possibilities Curves

The Philippines specializes in the production of beans, and its trading possibilities curve lies to the right of the production possibilities curve. In other words, whether it trades or not, the cost of beans remains the same; the cost of wheat, however, is now lower as a result of trade, since the Philippines can now obtain wheat at a cost of 2 bushels of beans per 1 bushel of wheat, whereas producing its own wheat costs 3 bushels of beans per 1 bushel of wheat.

Figure 10.8 shows the situation from the point of view of the Philippines. The inside curve is its production (and therefore its consumption) possibilities curve, representing the maximum of both products that can be produced when the country is self-sufficient. The slope of the curve represents the cost of 1 bushel of beans and is equal to 1/3 bushel of wheat. The outer curve is the trading possibilities curve if the terms of trade are 1 bushel of beans = 1/2 bushel of wheat. You can see that trading allows the Philippines to enjoy increased consumption as well. After specialization, the maximum amount of beans remains unchanged at 300 million bushels. However, the maximum amount of wheat has increased from 100 (if produced in the Philippines) to 150 (by trading all of its 100 million bushels of beans for this quantity of wheat).

The Benefits of Free Trade

Ricardo's theory of comparative advantage, which we have been looking at, is very important because it clearly highlights the major benefits of trade. Free and unrestricted trade gives nations and individuals the opportunity to sell in world markets, and this enables them to specialize production in areas wherein they enjoy a cost advantage over others. The effect will be lower costs of production generally, which translates into *lower prices* for consumers. This in turn will reduce the cost of living and enable people to enjoy a higher standard of living. In addition, free trade increases the levels of output worldwide and means *higher levels of income*, which in turn will lead to improved standards of living.

It all boils down to the fact that specialization increases productivity, so people as a group are better off as the result of lower production costs and higher incomes. But in addition, consumers in countries that do not specialize and do not trade will generally have to make do with a limited choice of domestically produced products that are of lower quality. With global markets, the variety and quality of products are much greater.

IT'S NEWS TO ME ...

The German Federal Constitutional Court today rejected the call for an injunction against its government from finalizing the Canada–European Union trade deal known as CETA.

In response, Germany's Economy Minister, Sigmar Gabriel, said "I am very satisfied with the outcome of the hearing."

Canada's International Trade Minister Chrystia Freeland—who has been actively promoting Canada's interests in several EU countries—has called CETA a gold-plated deal that will give Canada access to a market of 400 million people.

The thrust of the opposition to CETA among some Europeans is that they see it as a blueprint for the Trans-Atlantic Trade and Investment Partnership (TIPP) between the EU and the US which is in an earlier stage of negotiations. They fear that TIIP will undermine the consumer and labour rights of Europeans and weaken environmental protection.

Canada and the EU has committed to signing the deal this year and to seek ratification in their respective parliaments in 2017.

Source: *Star Power Reporting.* October 2016.

I. Which one of the following is most likely false?

   a) CETA will reduce Canada's heavy dependence on the United States as the primary market for her exports.
   b) CETA will achieve more gains from trade for the Canadian economy.
   c) CETA will lower the prices paid by Canadians for many European goods.
   d) CETA will lower Canada's GDP.

II. The opposition to CETA among some Europeans is an example of which one of the following?

   a) the strategic industry argument
   b) the infant industry argument
   c) the cultural identity argument
   d) none of the above

A final benefit of free trade is that it exposes companies to international competition. This means that they cannot sit complacently behind protective barriers but are forced to compete for business with firms around the world. This also tends to discourage the formation of monopolies, since it is much more difficult to be a monopolist in the world market than it is to be a monopolist in the home market. In summary, free trade has the following advantages:

- lower prices as the result of lower costs of production
- higher incomes
- a greater variety and quality of products
- increased competition

The 1988 Free Trade Agreement with the United States caused a dramatic increase in the volume of trade that Canada has done with that country, as **Figure 10.9** demonstrates.

Some Important Qualifications

These are, indeed, powerful arguments in favour of free trade, but before we leave the topic, let us look at some of the qualifications that must be introduced. First, free trade is never free; transport, insurance, and other freight charges will always need to be added to the cost of production, and that will usually reduce the trading advantage of foreign sellers. (However, in a country as large as Canada, it is often cheaper to transport products to the bordering American states than to transport them from one end of Canada to the other.)

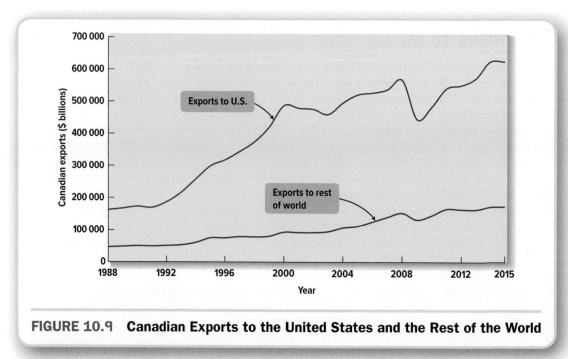

FIGURE 10.9   Canadian Exports to the United States and the Rest of the World

Source: Statistics Canada, Table 376-0101. Accessed January 22, 2014.

In addition, selling in a foreign country is always going to be more difficult (and often more expensive) than selling in the domestic market because of the differences in language, culture, taxation, regulations, and so on.

Besides cost differences, the analysis we have presented so far has assumed constant costs. This leads to the result in our examples that countries should specialize in, perhaps, a single product and produce that product to a maximum. However, as we learned in Chapter 1, if any country tries to concentrate on a single product, its production is subject to the law of increasing costs. This means that one country only enjoys a cost advantage over others *up to a point*. As it tries to push production levels higher, its cost will start to increase so that it no longer enjoys a competitive advantage. This is the reason why few countries specialize entirely and why many countries both produce *and* import the same product. The presence of increasing costs will also lessen the advantages that one country enjoys over another in trade.

 ADDED DIMENSION

Organizations and Treaties of Major Importance for Trade

WTO: The World Trade Organization (WTO), created in 1995 and with 153 member nations, is the only international organization that deals with the rules of trade among nations. Its purpose is to promote free trade and to attempt to resolve trade disputes between member countries.

IMF: The International Monetary Fund (IMF) was created at the Bretton Woods Conference in 1944 in response to the experience of the interwar period (1918–39) when world trade collapsed. Headquartered in Geneva, Switzerland, the IMF has 184 member countries and is dedicated to the promotion of international monetary cooperation, exchange stability, economic growth, and international trade. It makes loans to national governments—at the request of governments themselves—and provides a very sophisticated level of technical assistance.

OECD: The Organisation for Economic Co-operation and Development (OECD), based in Paris, includes thirty developed-nation members and has working relationships with some seventy less-developed countries. The mission of the OECD is to promote policies that achieve sustainable economic growth and development of the world economy, help countries realize sound economic expansion and development, and help world trade grow on a multilateral, nondiscriminatory basis.

EU: The European Union (EU) currently has twenty-eight members (however, the U.K. is negotiating an exit) and grew out of the six-member former European Economic Community, which was established in 1957. The EU, whose capital is in Brussels, is the largest economic/social experiment ever attempted among nations. Over time, the EU has established a common market for goods, services, capital, and labour. Given the size of its population (495 million people) and huge contribution to the world's GDP, its decisions on competition, labour and safety standards, and environmental policies have profound effects on the behaviour of other nations.

G8: This group of eight nations consists of Canada, the United Kingdom, France, Germany, Italy, Japan, the United States, and, recently, Russia. It represents (along with China and Spain) the ten largest economies in the world. The heads of state of these eight countries hold summits in various locations around the globe in which the world's pressing economic, political, and social issues are discussed.

G20: This is an expanded version of the G8. In this case, the ministers of finance and heads of the central banks of the twenty member nations meet to promote financial stability in the world's markets.

NAFTA: The North American Free Trade Agreement (NAFTA) was established with the signing of the 1994 agreement that formed the world's largest free trade area made up of Canada, the United States, and Mexico.

TEST YOUR UNDERSTANDING

4. The following table shows the average productivity in Freedonia and Libraland:

	OUTPUT PER WORKER (bushels per day)		
	Apples		**Pears**
Freedonia	6	or	3
Libraland	3	or	2

Assuming the two countries wish to trade, would terms of trade of 1 bushel of pears = 2.5 bushels of apples be feasible? What about 1 bushel of pears = 1 bushel of apples? 1 bushel of pears = 1.75 bushels of apples?

5. From the data contained in **Figure 10.7** or **Table 10.6**, how many beans can the United States obtain if it is self-sufficient and producing 240 million bushels of wheat? If, instead, it specializes in wheat production and can trade at terms of 1 bushel of wheat = 2 bushels of beans, how many bushels of beans could it have to accompany its 240 million bushels of wheat? What if the terms were 1 bushel of wheat = 3 bushels of beans?

SECTION SUMMARY

a) How the gains from trade are divided between the trading partners is determined by the terms of trade, calculated as the average price of exports divided by the average price of imports times 100.

b) The major benefits of free trade are
- lower prices
- higher incomes
- a greater variety and quality of products
- increased competition

10.4   The Effect of Free Trade

> **LO4**   Describe why some groups win and others lose as a result of freer trade.

Despite the cautions mentioned in the last section, it is still true that there are a number of benefits to be obtained from trade. This leads us to ask: Why does free trade tend to be the exception rather than the rule throughout history? Why does the question of free trade still divide countries and lead to such acrimonious debate? To understand part of the reason, we need to acknowledge that not everyone within a country will benefit from free trade. Let us look at a detailed example.

Suppose that initially we have two self-sufficient countries, France and Germany, each producing wine. The demand and supply conditions in the two countries are different, of course, with both the demand and supply being greater in France than in Germany, as is shown in Table 10.11.

TABLE 10.11
The Market for Wine in France and Germany (millions of litres per month)

FRANCE			GERMANY		
Price ($ per litre)	Quantity Demanded	Quantity Supplied	Price ($ per litre)	Quantity Demanded	Quantity Supplied
3	19	7	3	17	2
4	17	11	4	15	3
5	15	15	5	13	4
6	13	19	6	11	5
7	11	23	7	9	6
8	9	27	8	7	7

The equilibrium price in France is $5 per litre and the equilibrium quantity is 15. In Germany, the equilibrium price and quantity are $8 and 7, respectively. These are shown graphically in Figure 10.10.

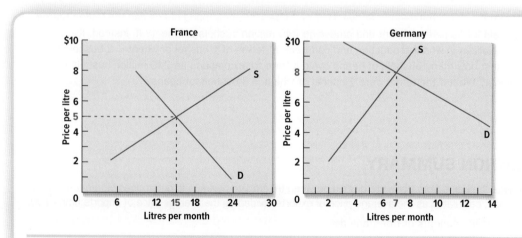

FIGURE 10.10   Demand and Supply of Wine in France and Germany

In France the demand and supply of wine are both higher than in Germany. The consequence is a greater quantity of wine traded in France: 15 million litres compared with 7 million in Germany. The price of wine, however, is lower in France than in Germany.

Now suppose that the two countries decide to engage in free trade. To keep things simple, let us assume there are no transport costs. If free trade is now introduced, what will be the price of wine in the two countries? Since we have assumed there are no transport costs, the price in the two countries should be the same. To find this price, all we need do is look at the combined market of France and Germany. In other words, we simply add the demands and supplies of the two countries, as shown in **Table 10.12.**

TABLE 10.12
Deriving the Total Market Demand and Supply of Wine for France and Germany (in millions of litres per month)

	FRANCE		GERMANY		TOTAL MARKET	
Price ($ per litre)	Demand	Supply	Demand	Supply	Demand	Supply
3	19	7	17	2	36	9
4	17	11	15	3	32	14
5	15	15	13	4	28	19
6	13	19	11	5	24	24
7	11	23	9	6	20	29
8	9	27	7	7	16	34

The total market demand is obtained by adding together the French demand and the German demand at each price. For instance, at $3 per litre, the quantity demanded in France is 19 and in Germany 17, giving a total for the two countries of 36. Similarly, the quantity supplied at $3 is 7 in France and 2 in Germany, giving a total market supply of 9. This is done for all prices. The new market price (let us call it the "world price"), then, will be $6 per litre, and at that price a total of 24 million litres will be produced and sold.

Now let us look at the effect in each market. French winemakers are delighted at the situation, because the world price for wine is higher and their volume of business

Bottled wine aging in storage.
Corel

is higher. They are now producing 19 million litres, up from the 15 million produced before trade, and the price they receive is $6, up from $5. Note also that in France, the quantity produced (19) exceeds the demand from French consumers (13). What happens to the surplus of 6 million litres? It is being exported to Germany. And what is the situation in that country? Well, certainly German consumers are delighted, because the new world price of $6 is lower than the previous domestic price of $8. But we can imagine that the German winemakers are far from happy. The new lower world price has caused a number of producers to cut back production, and presumably some producers are forced out of business and some employees have lost their jobs. Therefore, although the populations of both France and Germany as a whole benefit, not everyone in those countries gains. At the world price of $6, German producers are only producing 5 million litres, down from the previous 7 million and which is below the German demand of 11 million. How is

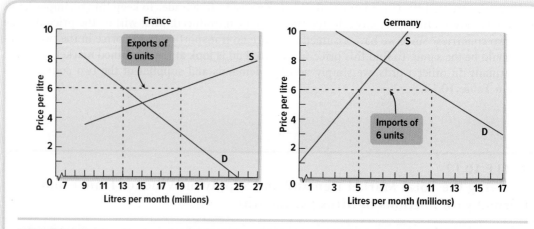

FIGURE 10.11   Demand and Supply of Wine in France and Germany with Free Trade

The new world price of wine is above the previous French price but below the previous German price. The result is a surplus of wine in France of 6 million litres but a shortage in Germany of 6 million litres.

this shortage going to be made up? From the import of French wine. This simply means that the French export of 6 million litres equals the German import of 6 million litres. These points are illustrated graphically in Figure 10.11.

So who loses and who gains as a result of markets being opened up? The answer in our example is that both German wine consumers and French wine producers gain, and French wine consumers and German wine producers lose. Free trade has cost French consumers $1 a litre, and it has cost German winemakers $2 per litre. Previously, German winemakers were selling 7 million litres at $8 per litre, for a total revenue of $56 million. Now, they are selling only 5 million litres for $6 per litre, for a total revenue of $30 million. In total, then, these producers, of whom there may be fewer than 100, have collectively lost $26 million in revenue. It is easy to see why these producers may not be in favour of free trade! In fact, it would pay them to lobby their own parliament and to launch publicity campaigns in an attempt to keep out "cheap" French wines. If they are successful and efforts do not cost more than $26 million, they will be ahead of the game. Table 10.13 illustrates the winners and losers from the introduction of free trade.

TABLE 10.13

Winners	Losers
Domestic (German) consumers who have a greater choice of products at lower prices	**Foreign (French) consumers** who have to pay higher prices
Foreign (French) producers who have a bigger market and can get higher prices	**Domestic (German) producers** who get lower prices as a result of greater competition

This example demonstrates why powerful lobbies and special interest groups have been very vocal throughout history in trying to persuade governments and the public that it is in the country's interests to ban or curtail foreign imports. They will ask their governments to protect them from foreign competition. Such **protectionism** can take many forms, which we will now examine.

ADDED DIMENSION

Trade, Politics, and the Future

We all wonder about what the future holds for humankind. For clues, some of us like to read science fiction books and even more of us are enthralled by futuristic movies such as the *Star Wars* series.

And what do we learn from such fascination?

Well, trade between planets pops up surprisingly often in the *Star Wars* series. Episode I opened with the details of a trade dispute and moved on to the invasion of the peaceful planet of Naboo by the Trade Federation. Yet we also see ample evidence of the idea that the freer the trade between planets the better: the desert Planet Tatooine and the ice planet Hoth would be uninhabited if not for trade, while Coruscant is completely urbanized (one thinks of Dubai here) and other planets have turned their entire surfaces over to agriculture (the young Luke Skywalker harvested atmospheric moisture on a very poor planet).

Operating within the Republic's political system of many planetary members is the Trade Federation with its focus on trade franchises that stunt the possible gains from trade by rent-seeking monopolies. This leads to attempts by some of the heroes in the series to circumvent the legal monopolies, as seen in the smuggling of the narcotic spice (think of the movie *Dune*) by Han Solo in cohort with the gangster Jabba the Hutt.

In short, there is a view of the future as including the familiar pull between the benefits of freer trade and the often uneven distribution of the resulting increased wealth. Furthermore, we see the depiction of the incentive to gain advantages using trade-subverting franchises (at one point Naboo's senator says, "the Republic's bureaucrats are on the payroll of the Trade Federation") which will lead to political challenges that twist and turn in unexpected ways.

Today's world has its counterpart in the 2016 U.S. election's exposing the fact that a vast number of white, working class voters in that country have lost their $35-per-hour manufacturing jobs to free trade and have been left with a sense that the political establishment is strongly pro–free trade and does not represent them anymore. This same sense of disentitlement was also seen in the U.K. referendum being won by the Brexit side, which called for the United Kingdom to leave the European Union.

SECTION SUMMARY

Although the population of a country as a whole gains from free trade, not everyone within that population wins:

- the importing country's producers lose and its consumers gain
- the exporting country's producers gain and its consumers lose

10.5   Trade Restrictions and Protectionism

LO5 Identify various restrictions to, and some arguments against, free trade.

Despite nearly four decades of trade liberalization, there remain many examples of trade restrictions in the world today. We now look at five ways in which this occurs.

The Imposition of Import Quotas

The most obvious way to restrict imports is to ban them entirely or partially, and this can be done with an import **quota**, which is simply a maximum limit placed on each individual foreign exporter. It can also take the form of a requirement that each foreign exporter reduce its exports by a percentage of the previous year's sales.

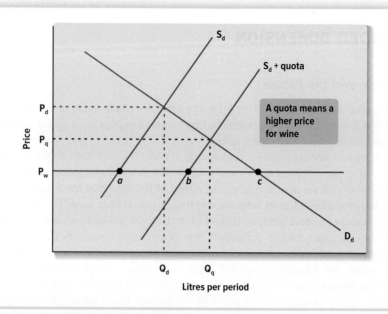

FIGURE 10.12   The Effects of a Quota

Initially, the Canadian domestic demand and supply are D_d and S_d, and the world price is P_w. The quantity demanded in Canada at the world price P_w equals c, of which Canadian producers would produce a and foreign producers would export ac to Canada. A quota of ab would raise the price to P_q. As a result, domestic production will increase, and imports would drop to the amount of the quota.

What will the effect of a quota be? To revisit our wine example, suppose that German winemakers were successful in their efforts to keep out French wines, and the German government imposed a total ban on French wines. At the current price of $6 per litre, there will be an immediate shortage in Germany, whose result will be to push up the price. The rise will continue, encouraging increased German production until the price returns to the pre-free-trade price of $8. In France, the immediate effect of the quota will be a surplus of French wine, which will depress the price of French wine until it, too, is back at the pre-free-trade price of $5 per litre.

Let us move on from our European example and look at trade from the Canadian perspective. Unlike in our example, where the market price was determined by the total demand and supply in just two countries, in reality the prices of wine—and of most products traded internationally—are determined by the world's demand and supply. That is to say, for any one small country, such as Canada, the world price is a given; that country's action will have little impact on the world price. This situation is illustrated in **Figure 10.12**, which shows the domestic demand (D_d) and supply (S_d) of wine in Canada. P_d would be the domestic price and Q_d the domestic production if Canada were totally closed to foreign trade. Suppose that the world price is P_w and that Canada now freely allows imports into the country. This means that if the world price of P_w prevails within Canada, the amount produced by domestic Canadian producers is a, and the amount demanded is c. Since Canadian consumers want to purchase more than Canadian producers are willing to produce, the difference of ac represents the amount of imports.

Now suppose that the Canadian government yields to pressure from Canadian wine producers and imposes a quota of ab on imported wine. In effect, the total supply is equal to the domestic supply plus the amount of the quota. This is represented by the new supply curve, S_d + quota. Since the total available has now been reduced, the price will increase to P_q, and the quantity will fall to Q_q.

From this, it can be seen that the losers will be Canadian consumers (who are paying a higher price for less quantity and variety of wines) and foreign winemakers whose exports are being restricted. The winners will be Canadian winemakers, who are producing more wine and receiving a higher price.

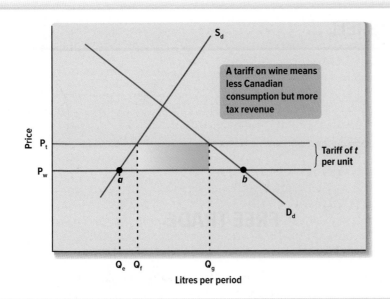

A tariff on wine means less Canadian consumption but more tax revenue

FIGURE 10.13 The Effects of the Imposition of a Tariff

The imposition of a tariff, *t*, will increase the price of wine in Canada to P_t from P_w. As a result, Canadian production will increase from Q_e to Q_f and imports will drop to $Q_g - Q_f$. The tax revenue to government is equal to *t* times the quantity of imports, $Q_g - Q_f$, the shaded area.

The Imposition of Tariffs

A second way of restricting imports is by the use of a **tariff**, which is a tax on imports. Tariffs are implemented more often than import quotas, because governments can derive considerable revenue from them.

The effects of a tariff are much the same as those of a quota; in both cases the price of the product will increase. With a quota, however, the domestic producers get the whole benefit of the higher price, whereas with a tariff the benefit is shared between the domestic producers and government. An additional benefit of a tariff over a quota is that a quota tends not to discriminate between foreign producers—each and every producer is treated the same way. With a tariff, only the more efficient producers will continue to export, since only they will be able to continue to make a profit. A tariff discriminates against the less efficient producers, and therefore, from an efficiency point of view, it is superior to a quota.

In **Figure 10.13**, suppose, again, that we are describing the Canadian wine market. At the world price of P_w, Canadian producers are supplying *a*, and Canadian consumers are buying *b*. The difference, *ab*, is the amount of imported wine. Suppose that the Canadian government imposes a tariff of *t* per unit. The price in Canada will rise to P_t. Note that at the higher price, Canadian producers (who do not pay the tariff) will receive the whole price P_t, and will increase production to Q_f. Canadian consumers will reduce consumption to Q_g. In addition, imports will fall to a level represented by the distance $Q_f - Q_g$. The result is very similar to what we saw in the analysis of quotas. Again, it is Canadian consumers and foreign producers who lose out and Canadian producers who gain.

The other winner in this scenario is the Canadian government, which will receive tax revenue equal to the shaded rectangle in **Figure 10.13**.

Other Trade Restrictions

Besides the two most popular protectionist measures—tariffs and quotas—a number of other available methods deserve mention. **Currency-exchange controls** are similar to quotas, but instead of

IN A NUTSHELL ...

FREE TRADE

Many Winners   **Few Losers**

each of whom gain a little   **each of whom lose a lot**

a restricting the importation of goods, currency-exchange controls limit the availability of foreign currencies (that is, foreign exchange). The effect is the same because foreigners wish to be paid in their own currencies, and importers unable to get their hands on the appropriate currency will not be able to buy the foreign goods.

The controls might be across-the-board restrictions or restrictions on particular currencies, products, or industries. The effect in all cases will be to increase the domestic price of the products affected, which will be to the benefit of the domestic producer at the expense of the domestic consumer. Another, more subtle but often equally effective way to cut imports is by *bureaucratic regulations*, though not all regulations have that intent. A government might make trade so difficult or time-consuming for the importer that the amount of trade is significantly reduced. For instance, the customs department of a country might tie the importer up with red tape by requiring that all imports be accompanied by ten different forms (all in triplicate) obtainable from ten different government departments. Or the product might have to meet very unrealistic standards of safety, packaging, or hygiene not required for domestically produced items.

A more recent type of trade restriction is known as a **voluntary export restriction** (VER). Rather than imposing tariffs and import quotas, the importing country requests that the exporting country itself voluntarily restrict the amount being exported. In this way, the exporting country is given the power to administer the quotas, which will also prevent the importing country from receiving tariff revenue on the imports. Since the restrictions are voluntary, the exporting country does not have to comply. However, since the importing country has other weapons at its disposal, these restrictions are usually adhered to. One of the first VERs was entered into between the United States and Japan in the early 1980s. At the time, the American economy was suffering a recession, the American auto industry being particularly hard hit. Then–U.S. President Ronald Reagan was able to get the Japanese car manufacturers to limit the number of cars entering the United States to 1.68 million (which was increased in later years). Another example took place in the late 1990s when Canadian exporters of softwood lumber agreed to restrict their exports to the U.S. (under threat of painful tariffs).

In summary, trade can be restricted in five ways:

- import quotas
- tariffs
- currency-exchange controls
- bureaucratic regulations
- voluntary export restrictions

 TEST YOUR UNDERSTANDING

6. In **Table 10.12**, if the demand for wine in Germany increased by 9 (million litres) at every price, how much wine would now be produced in Germany and how much would be imported from France?

Protectionism

In this chapter, while we have avoided an outright declaration of support for free trade, we have alluded to the many benefits of trade; and the majority of economists feel that the freer the trade, the better. Nevertheless, even the notable free-trader Adam Smith recognized that some degree of protectionism in ways we have just discussed might be called for at times.

He suggested, for instance, that a country's strategic industries should be offered protection so that, for instance, the country does not become dependent on foreign manufacturers for the production of military hardware and related technology. The problem with this *strategic industry argument*, however, is that most industries would claim to be of strategic importance and therefore deserving of similar protection. The classic example of such thinking occurred in 1845 with the release of an open letter to the French parliament that called on the government to take protective action against unfair competition from the sun. This appeal called for requirements that windows, dormers, skylights, shutters and curtains in all French buildings be permanently closed. The reasoning for this rather exotic appeal was that industries in the lighting industry would have an increase in sales and everyone would be better off.

However, Smith was prescient enough to realize that if a country has had a long history of protectionism, the sudden arrival of free trade is likely to cause dramatic shifts of labour and capital away from industries that can no longer compete to those industries that are growing. This may cause a great deal of suffering in the short term, so Smith felt that a wise government would introduce free trade gradually, to mitigate any suffering. This caveat was of particular importance at the time when Canada, the United States, and Mexico were negotiating the North American Free Trade Agreement. Although many felt that there would be great long-term benefits for all the participating countries, it is equally certain that in the short term a great deal of suffering would be experienced by those industries, firms, and individuals who, through no fault of their own, found themselves unable to compete. This is why tariffs were reduced in stages over a ten-year period.

It should also be mentioned that some economists believe certain infant industries should be given a helping hand by government until they are sufficiently mature to take on foreign competition. This *infant industry argument* is strongest when government feels that undue reliance on the exportation of a few staple products would leave the country in a vulnerable position if a future change in demand or technology were to occur. In order to diversify the economy and develop other industries, many feel that infants should be sheltered from competition. The trouble is, these infant industries often never grow up! In addition, even if there are persuasive arguments in favour of protecting or assisting certain industries, it may be better for government to give this aid in the form of direct subsidies rather than by interfering with normal trading patterns through the imposition of tariffs and quotas.

A third argument against free trade is the *cultural identity argument*. This one is difficult to dismiss solely on economic grounds. Many commentators feel that free trade brings with it mass production and standardization, which may harm the importing country's sense of individuality and cultural identity. As a result, some are totally against free trade, whereas others feel that it should not extend into such areas as communications, health, and education. They firmly believe that a country's radio and television stations, its newspapers and magazines, and its educational institutions and hospitals should not be owned or controlled from abroad. (In some ways, this might also be regarded as a "strategic industry" argument.)

A fourth argument is the belief that the environmental and labour standards of developed nations may be eroded as they try to compete with countries whose standards may be considerably lower and who may have a cost advantage as a result. This could trigger a race to the bottom as standards are lowered in all countries.

Finally, and importantly, it should be stressed that most of this chapter has been about the free trade in *goods and services*. However, the concept of open markets also implies the free movement of both capital and labour. This generally is what is meant by the term *globalization*. And it is this idea of unfettered mobility that has alarmed many who are greatly concerned that their country's resources and its major companies might all become foreign-owned. Further upsetting for many—and one of the major reasons why the majority of Britons voted to leave the European Union (EU)—is the idea of uncontrolled immigration implicit in the idea of labour mobility.

In summary, there are five arguments against free trade:

- the strategic industry argument
- the infant industry argument
- the cultural identity argument
- the lower environmental and labour standards argument
- the argument of lack of control over movements of capital and labour

 TEST YOUR UNDERSTANDING

7. Which industry in Canada do you feel deserves protection because it falls into the category of

   a) strategically important?

   b) infant industry?

   c) culturally important?

   d) environmentally important?

ADDED DIMENSION

Free Trade Versus Fair Trade and the Race to the Bottom

Many supporters of free trade in developed countries are nonetheless afraid that entering into a trade agreement with a less-developed country means that they will be competing for jobs with low-wage workers in those countries. The result, they suggest, is that they will either lose their jobs to these other countries or be forced to take lower wages themselves. The idea behind this is that low wages translate to lower prices for goods, which means that production and trade will inevitably shift to low-wage countries. However, there is a logical fallacy to this argument. If low-wage countries had an advantage in trade over high-wage countries, countries like Botswana, Peru, and Cambodia would be the world's great traders. Instead, countries like the United States and others lead the world in trade, despite the fact that they pay some of the highest wages in the world. The reason is that, although they might pay higher wages, they also have much greater productivity rates than other countries, and it is this that largely determines the price of goods. In fact, high-wage countries tend to be high-productivity ones, and low-wage countries low-productivity ones.

However, a recent, and for some alarming, trend is the realization by many multinational corporations that they can get the best of both worlds: the high productivity associated with richer nations and the low wages found in the poorer ones. They are able to do this because proponents of free trade in goods and services have also been successful in advocating the free movement of capital and labour between countries. The result of increased globalization is that multinational corporations now have the freedom to search out those countries with lower wages as well as weaker labour and environmental regulations. In order to attract these multinationals, governments may compete with one another by relaxing standards and eliminating regulations that protect labour, health, and environmental standards. This, it is suggested, will lead to a race to the bottom.

But there is a counterargument: the important thing in trade is the cost per unit of a product and that, as we have suggested, is determined by both the cost of resources and productivity. Now, productivity increases can come from many things, including increased education, a health work force, and improved infrastructure. It is quite possible, then, that freer trade might result in a race to the top through attempts to raise productivity rather than a race to the bottom by reducing costs.

SECTION SUMMARY

a) The two most common forms of trade restrictions are tariffs and quotas, both of which
  - increase the domestic price of a product that is imported
  - reduce the quantities traded of that product

  The other two types of restrictions are
  - exchange controls
  - voluntary exports restrictions

b) Five arguments against free trade are
  - the strategic industry argument
  - the infant industry argument
  - the cultural identity argument
  - the lower environmental and labour standards argument
  - the uncontrolled movement of capital and labour argument

Study Guide

Review

WHAT'S THE BIG IDEA?

The idea of a country buying products from abroad which could be just as easily made at home is, to many, one of the more difficult aspects in this chapter. But as the man said, "Just cos we coulda, doesn't mean we shoulda." It's true that even a tiny country like Iceland, for instance, is capable of making cars and computers and growing coniferous trees and wheat. It could even grow pineapples, if it wanted to. But should it? Most definitely not. It is better for that country to concentrate on what it does best—catch fish and mine aluminum and leave it to other countries to produce those other products.

Another principle difficult for many to grasp is that of comparative advantage. Most would agree that if another country can produce a product cheaper than us, perhaps it might be a good idea to buy from them. However, Ricardo would suggest that rather than "How much do beans cost to produce in the U.S. as compared to the cost in, say, the Philippines?" the more important question might be "How much do beans cost to produce in the U.S. as compared to the cost of producing wheat?" It might well be that, in absolute terms, the United States can easily produce beans cheaper than the Philippines; but in fact beans are very expensive to produce in the U.S., because that country is so much better at producing wheat. In other words, producing beans would mean a big sacrifice in producing wheat, whereas producing wheat is a lot cheaper because it does not have to sacrifice many beans.

The other difficult concept is that of the terms of trade. Although it is better to measure costs—as we do throughout this chapter—in terms of units of a product sacrificed, let's use actual dollars in this example. Suppose wheat costs $5 to produce in the United States, whereas the cost is $8 in the Philippines, and suppose the U.S. is the exporter. Now, how much would the U.S. accept for its wheat? Well, certainly as much as possible, but it would accept anything above $5. How about the Philippines? Since it could itself produce wheat for $8, it wouldn't pay more than that; but it would certainly be happy to pay anything less than $8. In other words, anything above $5 but less than $8 would be acceptable to both countries. The terms of trade then would fall somewhere between $5 and $8. (Closer to $5 and the Philippines would be happy; closer to $8 and the U.S. would be.) In other words, the terms of trade range between the cost in the cheaper country to the cost in the more expensive one.

NEW GLOSSARY TERMS AND KEY EQUATION

comparative advantage
currency-exchange
   controls

protectionism
quota
tariff

terms of trade
voluntary export restriction

Equations:

[10.1]   Terms of trade $= \dfrac{\text{average price of exports}}{\text{average price of imports}} \times 100$

Comprehensive Problem

(LO 2, 3)   Suppose that Richland and Prosperity have the output figures shown in Table 10.14.

TABLE 10.14

	AVERAGE PRODUCT PER WORKER		
	Wheat		Wine
Richland	4 bushels	or	2 barrels
Prosperity	2 bushels	or	6 barrels

Assume that cost and productivity remain constant.

Questions

a) What is the opportunity cost of producing one bushel of wheat in Richland?
b) What is the opportunity cost of producing one barrel of wine in Richland?
c) What is the opportunity cost of producing one bushel of wheat in Prosperity?
d) What is the opportunity cost of producing one barrel of wine in Prosperity?
e) In what product does Richland have a comparative advantage?
f) In what product does Prosperity have a comparative advantage?

Answers

a) 1 bushel of wheat = ½ barrels of wine. (A worker in Richland can produce either 4 bushels of wheat or 2 barrels of wine. The opportunity cost of 4 wheat is therefore 2 wine. The cost of 1 unit of wheat = 2/4 or ½ wine.)
b) 1 barrel of wine = 2 wheat. (To find the cost of 1 unit of wine, simply take the reciprocal of the wheat cost (that is, invert the number). This gives a cost of 1 wine = 2 wheat.)
c) 1 bushel of wheat = 3 barrels of wine. (In Prosperity, a worker can produce either 2 wheat or 6 wine. The opportunity cost of 2 wheat is therefore 6 wine. The cost of 1 unit of wheat = 3 wine.)
d) 1 barrel of wine = ⅓ (= 0.333) bushels of wheat. (To find the cost of 1 unit of wine take the reciprocal of the wheat cost. This gives a cost of 1 wine = ⅓ wheat.)
e) Richland: wheat. (It can produce wheat cheaper than Prosperity.)
f) Prosperity: wine (It can produce wine cheaper than Richland.)

Questions

Suppose that the labour force in each country is 10 million.

g) Fill in the missing production possibilities data for both countries in Table 10.15

TABLE 10.15

	RICHLAND'S PRODUCTION POSSIBILITIES (millions of units)				
	A	B	C	D	E
Wheat	40	30	20	10	0
Wine	——	——	——	——	——

	PROSPERITY'S PRODUCTION POSSIBILITIES (millions of units)				
	A	B	C	D	E
Wheat	——	——	——	——	——
Wine	0	15	30	45	60

Suppose that both countries are presently producing combination C.

h) Fill in the blanks in Table 10.16.

TABLE 10.16

	TOTAL OUTPUT IN MILLIONS OF UNITS	
	Wheat	Wine
Richland	_____	_____
Prosperity	_____	_____
Total: Both countries	_____	_____

Answers

g) To figure out the production possibilities data for Richland, start at combination E where no wheat is produced. All the labour (10 million) must be employed producing wine, and since each worker can produce 2 barrels of wine, total output = 20 million barrels. Moving to combination D, which represents an additional 10 units of wheat, you know that each unit of wheat costs 1/2 wine. Therefore an additional 10 units of wheat will cost 10 × 1/2 or 5 wine, so that production of wine drops to 15. In general, moving from right to left on the production possibilities table implies that each extra 10 wheat costs 5 wine.

Now do a similar exercise with Prosperity's production possibilities data and note that since 1 wine costs 1/3 wheat, each additional 15 wine costs 15 × 1/3 or 5 wheat.

This gives us the following table:

TABLE 10.15 (COMPLETED)

RICHLAND'S PRODUCTION POSSIBILITIES (millions of units)					
	A	B	C	D	E
Wheat	40	30	20	10	0
Wine	0	5	10	15	20

PROSPERITY'S PRODUCTION POSSIBILITIES (millions of units)					
	A	B	C	D	E
Wheat	20	15	10	5	0
Wine	0	15	30	45	60

h) This requires that you copy combinations C from the two production possibilities tables above and total them:

TABLE 10.16 (COMPLETED)

	TOTAL OUTPUT IN MILLIONS OF UNITS	
	Wheat	Wine
Richland	20	10
Prosperity	10	30
Total: Both countries	30	40

Questions

Now suppose that each country specializes in the product in which it has a comparative advantage.

i) Show the results in Table 10.17.

TABLE 10.17

	Wheat	Wine
Richland	——————	——————
Prosperity	——————	——————
Total: Both countries	——————	——————

j) What is the joint gain from trade? Suppose that the two countries establish the terms of trade at 1 wine = 1.5 wheat, and Prosperity decides to export 12 wine to Richland.

k) In Table 10.18, show how the two countries will share the gains from trade.

TABLE 10.18

	GAINS FOR EACH COUNTRY IN MILLIONS OF UNITS	
	Wheat	Wine
Richland	——————	——————
Prosperity	——————	——————
Total: Both countries	——————	——————

Answers

i) Since you've already decided that Richland will specialize in the production of wheat, the production possibilities table above shows the country's maximum wheat production (combination A). Similarly, Prosperity will specialize in wine production and its maximum is shown as combination E in its PP table. This gives us:

TABLE 10.17 (COMPLETED)

	Wheat	Wine
Richland	40	0
Prosperity	0	60
Total: Both countries	40	60

j) 10 wheat and 20 wine. This requires you to simply subtract the pre-trade totals, shown in (h), from these new totals resulting from specialization.

k) As a result of specialization, Prosperity is producing 60 wine. If it trades away 12, it will be left with 48 wine, and in exchange for those 12 wine will receive 12 × 1.5 wheat = 18 wheat. Richland in return will receive these 12 wine and pay 18 wheat. Since it produced 40 wheat, it will be left with 40 − 18 or 22 wheat. The gains for each country, therefore, are (in millions of units):

TABLE 10.18 (COMPLETED)

	GAINS FOR EACH COUNTRY IN MILLIONS OF UNITS	
	Wheat	Wine
Richland	2	2
Prosperity	8	18
Total: Both countries	10	20

Study Problems

Find answers on the McGraw-Hill online resource.

Basic (Problems 1–5)

1. **(LO 3)** If the terms of trade for the country of Onara equals 0.9 and the average price of its imports is 1.4, what is the average price of its exports? _____

2. **(LO 2)** In Onara, the average worker can produce either five bags of pummies or three kilos of clings, whereas in Traf the average worker can produce either four bags of pummies or six kilos of clings. Which country can produce pummies more cheaply and which can produce clings more cheaply? Show the cost in each country.
   Pummies: _____ Cost: _____
   Clings: _____ Cost: _____

3. **(LO 2, 3)** Table 10.19 below shows the maximum output levels for Here and There.

   TABLE 10.19

	Cloth		Computers
Here	100	or	50
There	60	or	120

   a) What is the cost of 1 unit of cloth and a computer in Here?
      1 unit of cloth: _____ 1 computer: _____
   b) What is the cost of 1 unit of cloth and a computer in There?
      1 unit of cloth: _____ 1 computer: _____
   c) In what product does each country have a comparative advantage?
      Here: _____ There: _____
   d) What is the range of feasible terms of trade between the two countries?
      1 unit of cloth: _____ 1 computer: _____

4. **(LO 2)** Table 10.20 below shows the productivity for the countries of Yin and Yang.

   TABLE 10.20

	Machines		Bread
Yin	2	or	10
Yang	3	or	2

   a) If the working populations of Yin and Yang are both 40 million, divided equally between the two industries in each country, show in Table 10.21 how many machines and bread are currently being produced in Yin and Yang.

   TABLE 10.21

	Machines	Bread
Yin	_____	_____
Yang	_____	_____
Total	_____	_____

b) If the two countries decide to specialize, in which product does each country have a comparative advantage?

Yin: _____ Yang: _____

c) If the two countries were to totally specialize, show the totals in the Table 10.22.

TABLE 10.22

	Machines	Bread
Yin	_____	_____
Yang	_____	_____
Total	_____	_____

d) Show the gains from trade in Table 10.23.

TABLE 10.23

Machines	Bread
_____	_____

5. **(LO 2, 3)** Table 10.24 shows the production possibilities for Concordia and Harmonia.

TABLE 10.24

	CONCORDIA'S PRODUCTION				
Product	A	B	C	D	E
Pork	4	3	2	1	0
Beans	0	5	10	15	20
	HARMONIA'S PRODUCTION				
Product	A	B	C	D	E
Pork	8	6	4	2	0
Beans	0	6	12	18	24

a) What are the costs of the two products in each country?

Concordia: 1 unit of pork costs _____

1 unit of beans costs _____

Harmonia: 1 unit of pork costs _____

1 unit of beans costs _____

b) What products should each country specialize in and export?

Concordia: _____

Harmonia: _____

c) If, prior to specialization and trade, Concordia produced combination C and Harmonia produced combination B, what would be the total gains from trade?

Pork: _____

Beans: _____

d) What would be the range of feasible terms of trade between the two countries? _____

Intermediate (Problems 6–10)

6. **(LO 2)** The graph in Figure 10.14 shows the domestic supply of and demand for mangos in India.

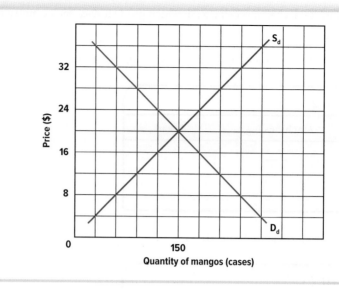

FIGURE 10.14

The world price is $16 a case, and India is open to free trade.
a) Will India export or import mangos? _____
b) What quantity will domestic producers supply? _____
c) What quantity will India export or import? _____
d) If the world price is $28, will India export or import mangos? How much?
   (Exports/import): _____ Quantity: _____

7. **(LO 1, 5)** Table 10.25 shows the market for wool in Canada, which is closed to trade.

TABLE 10.25

Price per Tonne ($)	Quantity Demanded Domestically	Quantity Supplied Domestically
1700	145	45
1800	140	60
1900	135	75
2000	130	90
2100	125	105
2200	120	120
2300	115	135
2400	110	150

a) What is the present equilibrium price and domestic production?
   Price: _____ Domestic production: _____
b) Suppose that Canada now opens to free trade and the world price of wool is $2000 per tonne. How much wool will Canada produce domestically, and how much will it import?
   Domestic production: _____ Imports: _____
c) Assume that the Canadian government, under pressure from the Canadian wool industry, decides to impose an import quota of 20 tonnes. What will be the new price, and how much will the Canadian industry produce? Price: _____ Domestic production: _____
d) Now suppose that the Canadian government decides to replace the import quota with a tariff. If it wishes to maintain domestic production at the same level as with a quota, what should be the amount of the tariff, and how much revenue will government receive?
   Tariff: $_____ Tariff revenue: $_____

8. **(LO 4)** Table 10.26 shows the production possibilities for Canada and Japan. Suppose that, prior to specialization and trade, both Canada and Japan are producing combination C.

TABLE 10.26

	CANADA'S PRODUCTION POSSIBILITIES				
Product	A	B	C	D	E
DVD players	30	22.5	15	7.5	0
Wheat	0	10	20	30	40
	JAPAN'S PRODUCTION POSSIBILITIES				
Product	A	B	C	D	E
DVD players	40	30	20	10	0
Wheat	0	5	10	15	20

a) In **Figure 10.15**, draw the production possibilities curve for each country, and indicate their present output positions.

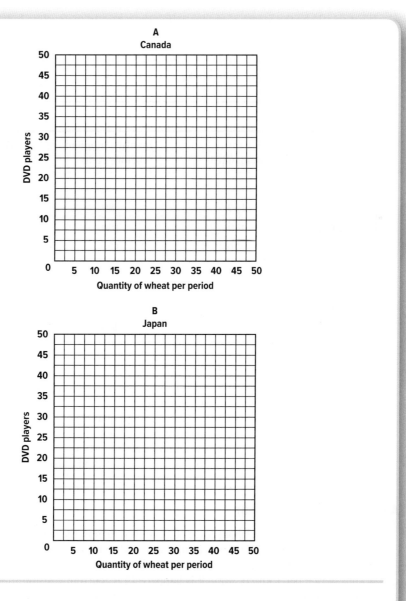

FIGURE 10.15

b) Suppose that the two countries specialize and trade on the basis of 1 DVD player = 1 wheat. Draw the corresponding trading possibilities curves.

c) If Canada still wishes to have 20 wheat, how many more DVDs could it have? _____

d) Show the new combination in **Figure 10.15**.

e) If Japan still wishes to have 20 DVDs, how much more wheat could it have? _____

f) Show the new combination in **Figure 10.15**.

9. **(LO 2)** The incomplete Table 10.27 shows the productivity levels of producing beer and sardines in Canada and Mexico.

TABLE 10.27

	PRODUCTION PER WORKER (average product)	
	Beer	Sardines
Canada	6	4
Mexico	3	_____

What should be the Mexican productivity per worker in the sardine industry for no advantage to be gained from trade? _____

10. **(LO 5)** Suppose the Canadian demand for and the Japanese supply of cars to Canada is shown in Table 10.28 (quantities in thousands).

TABLE 10.28

Price ($)	Quantity Demanded	Quantity Supplied (before tariff)	Quantity Supplied (after tariff)
12 000	180	60	_____
13 000	160	80	_____
14 000	140	100	_____
15 000	120	120	_____
16 000	100	140	_____
17 000	80	160	_____
18 000	60	180	_____
19 000	40	200	_____

a) The present equilibrium price is $_____ and quantity is _____ (thousand).

b) Suppose that the Canadian government imposes a $2000 per car tariff on imported Japanese cars. Show the new supply in the last column above.

c) The new equilibrium price is $_____ and quantity is _____ (thousand).

d) The total revenue received by government will be $_____.

e) Assume, instead, that government imposes an import quota of 100 000 cars. The new equilibrium price is $_____ and quantity is _____ (thousand).

f) Does government now receive any revenue? _____

Advanced (Problems 11–13)

11. **(LO 2, 3, 4)** Latalia has a labour force of 12 million, half in the wool industry and half in rice farming. The labour productivity in the wool industry is 40 kilos per worker per year, and in rice farming it is 100 kilos per worker per year. Latalia has discovered that the international terms of trade are 2 kilos of rice per 1 kilo of wool. It is happy with its current consumption of rice but would like to obtain more wool.

a) Assuming constant per-unit costs, on the graph in **Figure 10.16** draw the production and trading possibilities curves for Latalia.

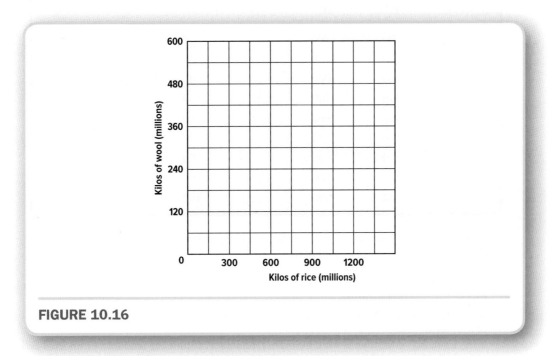

FIGURE 10.16

b) If Latalia were to specialize and trade, what product should it produce? _____
c) What would be Latalia's gain from trade? _____
d) On the graph, indicate the consumption levels before and after trade.

12. **(LO 2, 3)** Suppose three countries have productivity data as shown in **Table 10.29**.

TABLE 10.29

	PRODUCTIVITY PER WORKER	
	Wheat	Beans
Alpha	1	2
Beta	4	2
Gamma	2	2

a) What is the cost of wheat in each country?
   In Alpha, 1 unit of wheat costs _____.
   In Beta, 1 unit of wheat costs _____.
   In Gamma, 1 unit of wheat costs _____.
b) Which country can produce wheat the most cheaply (comparatively)? _____
c) Which country can produce beans the most cheaply (comparatively)? _____
d) Suppose that the international terms of trade were 1 wheat = 3/4 beans.
   Which countries would export wheat? _____
   Which countries would import wheat? _____
e) Suppose, instead, that the international terms of trade were 1 wheat = 1½ beans.
   Which countries would export wheat? _____
   Which countries would import wheat? _____

13. **(LO 2, 3)** Table 10.30 shows the annual demand and supply of cell phones in Canada (in tens of thousands), where D_C is the domestic demand, D_W is the demand in the rest of the world, S_C is the Canadian supply, and S_W is the quantity supplied by manufacturers in the rest of the world.

TABLE 10.30

Price ($)	D_C	D_W	D_T	S_C	S_W	S_T
25	200	1200	_____	20	1200	_____
50	180	1100	_____	30	1250	_____
75	160	1000	_____	40	1300	_____
100	140	900	_____	50	1350	_____
125	120	800	_____	60	1400	_____
150	100	700	_____	70	1450	_____
175	80	600	_____	80	1500	_____
200	60	500	_____	90	1550	_____
225	40	400	_____	100	1600	_____

a) Complete the total demand (D_T) and total supply (S_T) columns.
b) What are the world price and quantity?
   Price: _____ Quantity: _____
c) If Canada was closed to international trade, what would be the price and quantity in Canada?
   Price: _____ Quantity: _____
d) If Canada were open to international trade, how much would Canada import from the rest of the world? _____
e) If the Canadian government were to impose a quota and limit the amount of imported cell phones to 90 (tens of thousands), what would be the new price and quantity in Canada?
   Price: _____ Quantity: _____

14. **(LO 2, 3)** The average productivity per worker in the kumquat industry in Bolita is 8 kilos; productivity in the daikon industry is 5 kilos. In Neru, the corresponding figures are 6 kilos and 2 kilos.
   a) According to the theory of comparative advantage, Bolita should specialize in and export what product? What product should Nertu specialize in and export?
      Bolita should specialize in _____ and Neru should specialize in _____.
   b) What are the possible terms of trade for daikons between the two countries?
      Between _____ and _____ kumquats per daikon.

Problems for Further Study

Basic (Problems 1–4)

1. **(LO 3)** What is meant by *terms of trade*?
2. **(LO 1)** What is meant by *factor endowment*?
3. **(LO 4)** Who gains and who loses when a country enters into a free trade agreement?
4. **(LO 3)** What are the full names and functions of the following: WTO, EU, NAFTA, OECD?

Intermediate (Problems 5–8)

5. **(LO 1)** How are trade and specialization related?
6. **(LO 3)** List three arguments against free trade.
7. **(LO 1)** Which country, the United States or Canada, exports more as a percentage of its GDP? Why?
8. **(LO 2)** If Japan can produce kumquats cheaper than the Philippines, why would it import them from the Philippines?

Advanced (Problems 9–10)

9. **(LO 2, 5)** If comparative cost is the basis for trade, why are the developing countries (which have very low wage rates) not the world's greatest trading nations?
10. **(LO 1, 2)** Explain the theory of comparative advantage. How does it differ from the theory of absolute advantage?
11. **(LO 1)** What are the four major reasons for differences in trade patterns between countries?

CHAPTER 11
Exchange Rates and the Balance of Payments

LEARNING OBJECTIVES

At the end of this chapter, you should be able to:

LO1 Calculate the value of the Canadian dollar in terms of other currencies and explain the purchasing power parity theory.

LO2 Identify who wants to buy and sell Canadian dollars in foreign exchange markets.

LO3 Explain why the value of the Canadian dollar fluctuates.

LO4 Compare flexible and fixed exchange rate systems.

LO5 Explain the meaning of a balance of payments surplus and deficit.

 WHAT'S AHEAD ...

We now turn our focus to exchange rates and international finance. This is the last step on our way to revisiting economic policy making which will come in Chapter 12.

We begin by discussing a nation's exchange rate and then examine why it might appreciate or depreciate. We then look at the consequences of such changes under a flexible exchange rate system. This sets up our discussion of fixed exchange rate systems. Finally, we explain how international transactions of trade and finance are recorded in a nation's balance of payments statement.

A QUESTION OF RELEVANCE ...

The value of the CAN/US dollar exhibited some rather dramatic swings in the first two decades of the twenty-first century. In the first three years, the average annual exchange rate was in the $0.60s but rose to the $0.80s in the next four years. This was largely tied to the higher world-commodity prices of gold, copper, and grains. Then in the years 2007–13 it was in the $0.90s, and even over par ($1.00) at times, as the price of oil rose dramatically and some began to call the Canadian dollar a "petro-currency." When the price of oil collapsed, the Canadian dollar dropped back to the mid-$0.70s.

Are there other reasons for these swings in the exchange rate? Is a rising exchange rate necessarily a good thing for Canada? And is a falling dollar necessarily bad? These are important questions and this chapter will speak to them.

S uppose a resident of Alberta buys a product made in Quebec. This involves an economic exchange we can all understand. The product is moved west, the money payment flows east, and that is that. But now, suppose the same Alberta resident buys a product made in Japan. How is this exchange any different? In one sense there is no difference, in that the product goes one way and the payment the other. But in another sense it is different: two currencies are involved. The Alberta resident will want to pay in Canadian dollars, and the Japanese seller will want to be paid in yen. This means that an exchange between the two currencies will have to occur as the one currency is converted to the other. This exchange will involve at least one bank. Import and export regulations and procedures are also involved. Thus, international trade is more complicated than domestic trade, and the most obvious complication is the exchange rate itself. Let us now discuss exchange rates.

11.1   Exchange Rates

> **LO1**   Calculate the value of the Canadian dollar in terms of other currencies and explain the purchasing power parity theory.

For most people, an exchange rate is an enigma, and yet it is nothing more than the value of one currency compared to another. It is, if you like, the relative price of a currency. A few decades ago, it was possible to state the value of a currency in terms of an international medium of exchange: gold. When countries were on the gold standard, each currency could be valued in terms of a comparative amount of gold. Today, however, if you want to know how much a Canadian dollar is worth, the answer can be expressed only in terms of how many American dollars, British pounds, Swiss francs, or some other currency it can buy.

Before we look at the determinants of exchange rates, let us make sure you are able to easily convert one currency into another. For instance, if the Canadian dollar is worth $0.80 American, how much is an American dollar worth in Canada? The answer is $1.25 (not $1.20). If you are not sure why, ask yourself: What is the value of an American dollar if a Canadian dollar is worth $0.50 American? $1.50? $2? The answer is $2 Canadian.

Both the $0.50 and the $2 are **exchange rates**: the Canadian $ for the American $, and the American $ for the Canadian $. In general, to convert one currency into another, we simply take the reciprocal.

$$\frac{\text{1 Canadian dollar}}{\text{(in units of foreign currency)}} = \frac{1}{\text{foreign currency (in Canadian dollars)}} \qquad [11.1]$$

$$\frac{\text{1 unit of foreign currency}}{\text{(in Canadian dollars)}} = \frac{1}{\text{Canadian dollars (in foreign currency)}} \qquad [11.2]$$

If a Canadian dollar is worth 5 Mexican pesos, then one Mexican peso is worth 1/5, or $0.20 Canadian. If a Canadian dollar is worth 0.50 British pounds, then a British pound would be worth 1/0.50, or $2 Canadian. And if the Canadian dollar is worth 0.80 American dollars, then an American dollar is worth 1/0.80, or 1.25 Canadian dollars.

Exchange rates fluctuate, sometimes rising and sometimes falling. Such an increase or decrease is always in terms of another currency. For example, assume that instead of one British pound equalling $2 Canadian, it now equals $4 Canadian. How much is the Canadian dollar worth now? The answer is 0.25 pounds. In other words, when one **currency appreciates** in terms of another, the other **currency depreciates** automatically. This is not a case of cause and effect; it is simply true by definition.

Another point worth making is the fact that just because the Canadian dollar might be depreciating against the American dollar, it does not necessarily mean it is also depreciating against other currencies. In fact, it might well be *appreciating* against the Japanese yen or the euro.

We need to answer two questions in this chapter. What determines the value of any given currency? And what are the causes of changes in this value? The exchange rate is simply the relative price of a currency, and that price may be determined by either demand and supply in the marketplace or government decree. In the first case, we are looking at **flexible** (or floating) **exchange rates** and in the second, at **fixed** (or pegged) **exchange rates**. We will look at each in turn.

Before we get into a detailed analysis of currency value determination, we should mention a well-established economic theory known as the **purchasing power parity theory** of exchange rates. This theory suggests that, in the long run, exchange rates will adjust so as to equate the purchasing power of each country's currency. This means, for instance, that a pint of beer should have the same real price in every country. (You will have to use a different currency in each, of course.) It also means that a thousand Canadian dollars should have the same spending power in Canada as the equivalent number of euros in France or pesos in Mexico.

On the surface, this seems difficult to accept. Most international jetsetters (and anybody who shops south of the Canadian

Currencies	Per	We Buy	We Sell
AUSTRALIA	1	5.76510	6.70840
CANADA	1	6.82840	7.79440
CHINA	1	1.06130	1.19880
EURO	1	10.0154	11.3947
JAPAN	1	0.06840	0.07780
KOREA	1	0.00640	0.00790
PHILIPPINES	1	0.14800	0.19130
NEW ZEALAND	1	4.80760	5.49830
SINGAPORE	1	5.10260	5.83300
SWITZERLAND	1	6.38630	7.22410
TAIWAN	1	0.22530	0.27530
THAILAND	1	0.21090	0.26380
UNITED KINGDOM	1	12.8576	14.6689
U.S.A.	1	7.14730	8.09110

Most banks and exchange bureaus post the exchange rates on display boards so that they are readily accessible to travellers.
Bedo/Dreamstime.com

border) realize that commodities in some countries are relatively cheap for Canadians and one can have a reasonably good time for very little (in parts of Africa and Asia, and in most Latin American countries, for example), whereas commodities in other countries are prohibitively expensive for the average Canadian (such as Japan, the Scandinavian countries, and Switzerland). So why would anyone suggest that the cost of living in various countries should become comparable over time?

In answering this question, we will work through a model in which we assume that transport costs are negligible and that each country produces products that are identical to those from other countries. For instance, suppose Sweden produces and sells coal at 1000 kronor a tonne, and Canada also produces and sells coal for $200 a tonne. Further, suppose that the exchange rate is $1 Canadian = 5 kronor (*kronor* is the plural of *krona*, the Swedish unit of currency). The price of coal, therefore, is the same in both countries. Now, what would happen if the price of coal in Canada were to rise to $250 a tonne? If the exchange rate remained the same, everybody would buy their coal in Sweden. But, of course, the exchange rate would not remain the same. People would be demanding kronor in order to buy Swedish coal. The krona would appreciate (as would, in all likelihood, the price of Swedish coal). But by how much? Well, as long as there was a difference in prices, it would pay some enterprising company to buy coal in Sweden, where it is cheap, and sell it in Canada, where it is expensive.

Assuming that the price of coal in Sweden remains at 1000 kronor a tonne, the krona will appreciate until the prices in Canada and Sweden are the same—that is, until $250 is equal to 1000 kronor. In other words, the krona will appreciate until one Canadian dollar is worth only four kronor instead of five.

Once again, purchasing power parity theory says that if the same product is sold at different prices in different countries, it would be worthwhile buying it where it is cheap and selling it where it is expensive. This is referred to as **arbitrage**. But this action, by itself, will cause the exchange rates to adjust until there is no longer any difference in the relative prices.

Yet prices are not the same worldwide. Why? First, if the price of a haircut in Edmonton is only half the price of a haircut in New Orleans, we would not really expect a mass exodus of Edmontonians heading down to Louisiana to get their locks shorn. In other words, certain goods and services are not transportable, and therefore differences in the prices of these things may well persist over time between countries. Second, if transport and other shipping costs are taken into account, price differences might continue. Third, tariffs and import quotas limit the quantity traded and increase the costs of trade and lead to price differences between countries. Fourth, products are not identical. Some people do prefer, say, Japanese cars over North American cars. Fifth, and finally, exchange rates do not equate the purchasing power among countries because they are also greatly affected by the international sale and purchase of financial assets. Sometimes, there is a strong demand by foreigners for Canadian shares and bonds. At other times, Canadians may have a strong demand for foreign shares and bonds.

Before we leave this section we should point out that, unfortunately, some people regard the international value of the Canadian dollar as an indicator of our nation's economic strength and prestige on the international stage. Thus, when the Canadian dollar appreciates we hear and read the phrase "stronger dollar" in the news. But exchange rates merely appreciate and depreciate; they do not get stronger or weaker, any more than the price of cigarettes is now very strong.

 ADDED DIMENSION

The Big Mac Purchasing Power Parity Theory

Since 1986, the magazine *The Economist* has published a "Big Mac Index" comparing the relative prices of a Big Mac around the world and, with it, the relative value of currencies. Since countries no longer use gold as an international currency of exchange (and therefore of comparison), the *Economist* decided to use the Big Mac instead. So if a Big Mac costs $6 in Canada and 18.60 yuan in China (as of July 2016), 18.6 yuan should be worth $6, or one Canadian dollar should be equal to 18.6/6 or 3.1 yuan. The actual exchange rate was in fact 5.11 yuan per dollar. Most commentators would therefore suggest that the yuan is mightily undervalued against the Canadian dollar.

However, this comparison might be stated differently. For instance, if purchasing power were equal on all products between Canada and China, the price of a Big Mac in China should be the same as it is in Canada (converted at the actual exchange rate of 5.11 yuan per $1 Canadian). It should cost, therefore, 6 × 5.11 = 30.66 yuan. The actual price is in fact only 18.6 yuan, which means that you could almost buy two Big Macs in China for the price of a Big Mac in Canada. Pretty cheap! Contrast this with the price of a Big Mac in Norway, which should cost you 38.94 kronor ($6 times the exchange rate of 6.49), but in fact will set you back 47 kronor! This would suggest that the krone is greatly overvalued. (However, it is possible that the high price of a Big Mac in Norway is simply a reflection of the higher wage rates for workers in the fast-food industry in Norway, compared with the wage rates in Canada.) Here are some prices in other countries:

Country	Actual ER (cost of $1 Canadian)	$6 Big Mac Converted at Actual ER	Actual Cost of a Big Mac	Over-/ Undervalued
Switzerland	0.76 franc	4.56 francs	6.50 francs	+43%
Sweden	6.58 kronor	39.5 kronor	44.9 kronor	+14%
United States	0.77 $ U.S.	4.62 $ U.S.	5.04 $ U.S.	+9%
Brazil	2.50 real	15 real	15.40 real	+3%
United Kingdom	0.58 £ British	3.48 £ British	2.99 £ British	−14%
Japan	81.17 yen	487 yen	370 yen	−24%
Mexico	14.26 peso	85.6 pesos	44 pesos	−49%
Russia	49.14 ruble	295 rubles	130 rubles	−56%

Source: Adapted from *The Economist*, July 21, 2016, and Bank of Canada.

TEST YOUR UNDERSTANDING

Find answers on the McGraw-Hill online resource.

1. a) Assume that a Swedish krona is worth $0.20 Canadian. How much is a Canadian dollar worth in kronor?

  b) Assume that one Canadian dollar equals 70 Japanese yen. How much is a yen worth in Canadian dollars?

Five factors explain differences in purchasing power between countries:

- the fact that many services, such as haircuts, are not traded internationally
- the existence of transportation and insurance costs
- the existence of tariffs and other trade restrictions
- the expression of particular preferences by consumers
- the effect on the value of currencies of trade in financial assets

Despite all these reservations, many economists still hold that, with globalization and the freer movement of products and factors, in the long run there is a tendency for exchange rates to move toward equalizing the purchasing power of currencies. Whether or not this is true, we still need to explain day-to-day and year-to-year fluctuations in exchange rates.

SECTION SUMMARY

a) The exchange rate of any currency is calculated by dividing one by the unit value of the other currency.

b) The purchasing power parity theory suggests that the purchasing powers of different currencies will tend to become equal over time.

c) Several factors prevent purchasing power parity from becoming a reality:

- the impossibility of international trade in many services

- transportation and insurance costs

- tariffs and other trade restrictions

- consumer preference for the products of one particular country over another

- the effect on currency value of trade in financial assets

11.2 Flexible Exchange Rates

LO2 Identify who wants to buy and sell Canadian dollars in foreign exchange markets.

In the absence of government involvement, exchange rates are determined by the interplay of demand and supply in a free market. Canada has officially had a flexible exchange rate since the early 1970s, during which time the value of the Canadian dollar has fluctuated from a high of approximately US$1.04 in 1973 to a low of US$0.63 in 2001, then back up again to trade above par in the spring of 2011.

Even when governments do not actually *fix* exchange rates, the central bank may still think it necessary to intervene in international exchange markets to *influence* the value of currency, and so it becomes an active player. For the time being, however, we will ignore this factor and concentrate on the determination of exchange rates entirely by market forces.

Demand for the Canadian Dollar

Apart from Canadians, who wants to obtain Canadian dollars? The first and most obvious group is foreigners who want Canadian dollars in order to purchase Canadian goods and services. The demand for Canadian exports, such as forest products and automobiles, therefore creates a demand for the Canadian dollar. It is general knowledge that Canada is rich in natural resources such as gold, silver, copper, zinc, potash, coal, and, of course, oil. The prices of these commodities are world prices and can fluctuate considerably. Thus a boom in the prices of and demand for commodities has a double effect on the demand for the Canadian dollar—more exports physically and higher prices for this greater quantity. China's very rapid growth in the early years of this century is an example of this effect. Note, however, that some services can only be enjoyed in Canada. We are thinking here of restaurant, hotel, and other tourist services required by foreigners travelling in Canada. This means that tourism in Canada represents a (significant) Canadian export. (Conversely, spending by Canadians on imported goods or by travel abroad represents a Canadian import and thus increases the supply of Canadian dollars on foreign markets.)

A second demand for the Canadian dollar involves foreigners who want to purchase Canadian investments. These investments might include the purchase of Canadian real estate or real assets—such as a small software company—which are called **direct investment**, or they might include the purchase by foreigners of Canadian shares or bonds, known as **portfolio investment**. In either case, a demand is created for the Canadian dollar with which to purchase these investments. The level of portfolio investment in Canada by foreigners is partly driven by the interest rate paid on savings in Canada relative to that paid elsewhere. If Canadian bonds are paying an average of 4 percent, while similar bonds in the United States are paying only 2.5 percent, portfolio investment in Canada and the demand for Canadian dollars will be high.

This brings us to the third group who demand Canadian dollars: Canadians who receive income, gifts, or transfers from abroad. This includes, for instance, those who have previously bought foreign investments. These people will be earning returns, which will be paid to them in foreign currencies. As Canadians, of course, they do not have much use for foreign currencies, and they will want to convert into Canadian dollars.

A fourth group that wants to buy Canadian dollars is speculators. Speculators who deal in foreign exchange are no different from other types of speculators. They hope to buy when the price is low and sell when the price is high. Speculators buying Canadian dollars are therefore hoping for an appreciation of the Canadian dollar relative to foreign currencies sometime in the future, at which point they will sell. The level of currency speculation depends a great deal on the expectations that people have regarding the currency. If people expect the Canadian exchange rate to fall, speculators will sell Canadian dollars in exchange for other currencies. This action will have the effect of pushing the actual value of the dollar down and thus fulfilling people's expectations.

There is another group of currency dealers who also buy and sell Canadian dollars, but for a different reason. They buy Canadian dollars (or any other currency) whenever they see a difference in quoted exchange rates on different international exchanges. For instance, let us say that the Canadian dollar is quoted at $0.765 American on the Zurich exchange but at $0.768 on the Tokyo exchange. Someone will find it profitable to buy Canadian dollars in Switzerland (where they are cheap) and sell them in Japan (where they are relatively more expensive). As we mentioned earlier, this is known as *arbitrage*. Note that, unlike speculators, those engaged in arbitrage are not concerned with the future value of the Canadian dollar and are not holding them to sell at some later date; they are selling immediately.

To sum up, five groups have a demand for the Canadian dollar:

- foreigners who want to buy Canadian exports or who travel in Canada
- foreigners who want to purchase Canadian investments
- Canadians who receive income or gifts or transfers from abroad
- currency speculators
- arbitragers

Railway trains carrying grain for export are constantly on the move at the United Grain Growers elevator in Vancouver.

The Canadian Press (Chuck Stoody)

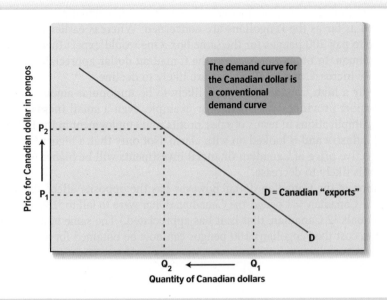

FIGURE 11.1 The Demand for the Canadian Dollar

The demand curve for the Canadian dollar is downward sloping, reflecting the inverse relationship between the price of the currency and the quantity demanded. At P_1 the quantity demanded is Q_1.

Finally, as noted above, central banks also sometimes buy and sell currencies, but more on this later.

Now, remember what we mean by the demand for a currency. It is no different from the demand for any other product or service; that is, it is defined as the quantities that people are willing and able to buy at various prices in the foreign exchange market. As you might expect, the demand curve for the Canadian dollar is downward sloping, as shown in Figure 11.1.

Note that on the vertical axis, we need to express the price of the Canadian dollar in terms of another currency. After all, it would be a bit silly to express the price of the Canadian dollar in Canadian dollars because it would always equal one. The currency you choose to express it in, other than the Canadian dollar, is of no importance. On our graph, we have used the pengo, the currency of the mythical and fascinating country of Pengoland. We do this to emphasize that the value of any given currency can be expressed in any other currency.

The demand curve is, of course, downward sloping, which implies that at a higher exchange rate the quantity of Canadian dollars demanded will be low; at a low exchange rate, the quantity demanded will be high. Now, let us figure out why that should be so. Remember that the demand for the Canadian dollar comes, by and large, from foreigners buying our goods, services, and investments, that is, from Canadian exports in the broad sense. To help you remember this, we have added the label Canadian "exports" to the demand curve. However, remember that the demand for the Canadian dollar comes not just from people who want to buy our products, but also from those who want to buy our assets as well as those speculators and arbitragers who just want the dollars themselves.

Let us start off by assuming that the Canadian dollar is worth 1 pengo and that one of our major exports to Pengoland is smoked salmon, which is priced at $100 a box in Canada and therefore sells for 100 pengos in Pengoland. Now, what would happen if the value of the Canadian dollar were to appreciate so that $1 Canadian is now equal to 2 pengos? (Note that as the Canadian dollar appreciates, the pengo depreciates; it is now worth only 50 cents.) The effect of such an appreciation is summarized in Table 11.1.

TABLE 11.1

Price of $1 Canadian	Price in Canada of a Box of Salmon	Price in Pengoland of a Box of Salmon
1 pengo	$100	100 pengos
2 pengos	$100	200 pengos

Despite the fact that the price of smoked salmon in Canada remains unchanged, its effective price has increased as far as the Pengolians are concerned. Whereas earlier they paid 100 pengos, now they will have to pay 200 pengos for the same box. One would expect therefore that they would buy less smoked salmon. In other words, when the Canadian dollar appreciates, the effective prices of Canadian exports increase, and total exports are likely to decline.

You can see why a high Canadian dollar is likely to be unpopular among Canadian exporters and in the high-export provinces of Canada. For example, even a small increase in the Canadian dollar can have big implications in terms of sales, profits, and employment in the B.C. lumber industry or the Alberta oil industry and is looked on with alarm. Not only that, a higher Canadian dollar also means that the effective price of Canadian financial investments will be higher for foreigners so that foreign investment is likely to decrease.

The depreciation of the Canadian dollar, however, has the opposite effect. Assume, for instance, that starting from $1 Canadian = 1 pengo, the Canadian dollar were to fall to $1 Canadian = 0.5 pengos. (The pengo now equals $2 Canadian; that is, it has appreciated.) The same box of Canadian smoked salmon that used to cost the Pengolians 100 pengos can now be obtained for a mere 50 pengos. This

ADDED DIMENSION

The Effective Exchange Rate

There is no single commodity whose value remains constant and against which all currencies can be measured. This means the Canadian dollar might well be *depreciating* against one currency, such as the American dollar, but at the same time appreciating against all other currencies. It is possible, however, to work out an average of what is happening to the Canadian dollar. This is what is referred to as the *effective exchange rate*.

The effective exchange rate compares the value of the Canadian dollar in terms of the average value of the currencies of all the countries with which Canada trades. It is a weighted average, which means that the value of the American dollar, for instance, would carry more weight than, say, the Swiss franc in calculating its value, since Canada does much more trade with the United States than it does with Switzerland. The effective exchange rate is also based on an index value of 100, assigned in the base year, which was 1992. The graph here shows how Canada has performed against the effective exchange rate and against major currencies this past decade.

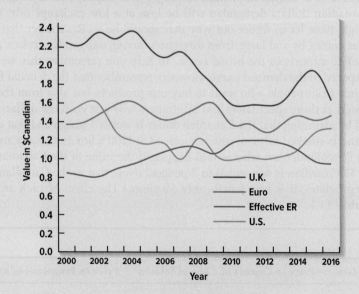

Source: Bank of Canada, *Banking and Financial Statistics*, October 2016, Table I1.

will then cause exports of smoked salmon to increase. In general, therefore, when the Canadian dollar depreciates, the effective prices of Canadian exports decrease, and total exports are likely to increase. Exporters will prefer a low Canadian dollar to a high Canadian dollar, since this makes Canadian products more competitive abroad.

We can summarize these results as follows:

> When the Canadian dollar depreciates, the effective prices of Canadian exports decrease, and total exports are likely to rise.

> When the Canadian dollar appreciates, the effective prices of Canadian exports increase, and total exports are likely to fall.

It should be pointed out, as this example makes clear, that a drop in the value of the Canadian dollar is not—as many people think—by itself a bad thing. Although there are undesirable aspects that we will look at later, for such a big exporting country as ours a lower dollar may be very good news: it stimulates export spending, which in turn will boost employment and incomes.

IN A NUTSHELL ...

It's Just Common Sense

| **Depreciating Canadian dollar** | **Decreases the effective price of Canadian products** | **And causes more Americans to visit Canada** |

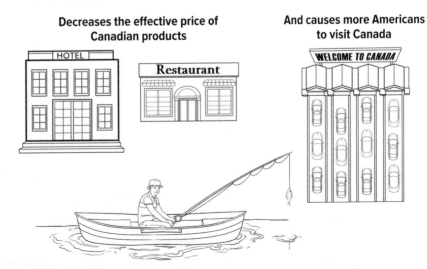

TEST YOUR UNDERSTANDING

2. Given the events described below, indicate whether the demand for the Canadian dollar would appreciate, depreciate, or not change.

a) Canadian exports rise.

b) Canada co-hosts the Soccer World Cup in 2026.

c) IBM, ITT, and the provincial government announce the construction of a $2 billion data processing and informational transfer complex in Halifax.

d) Migration from the Maritime provinces to Ontario increases appreciably.

Supply of Canadian Dollars

Let us now look at the other side of the coin, the supply of Canadian dollars on the foreign exchange market, and examine who exactly provides this supply. Most people probably think it is government or the Bank of Canada. That may be true under certain circumstances, as we shall see later. However, in a free market system, it is not really necessary for these institutions to supply Canadian dollars to foreigners, since dollars will be made available automatically on the world's money (foreign exchange) market through normal international trade. How does this come about? The simple fact is that if Canadians wish to purchase foreign currencies, we will use Canadian dollars to make these purchases. Thus, in obtaining foreign currencies, we must automatically supply Canadian dollars. In other words, if we send Canadian dollars to France to buy euros so that we can buy, say, French wine, France will now have Canadian dollars that it can use to buy Canadian products. In general, the supply of Canadian dollars comes from our demand for foreign currencies. This relationship between the supply of and demand for currencies is important enough to emphasize:

Demand for foreign currencies = Supply of Canadian dollars
Demand for Canadian dollars = Supply of foreign currencies

The supply of Canadian dollars is graphed in **Figure 11.2**. Why is the supply curve upward sloping? It is for the usual reason—an increase in the price (of a currency) will lead to an increase

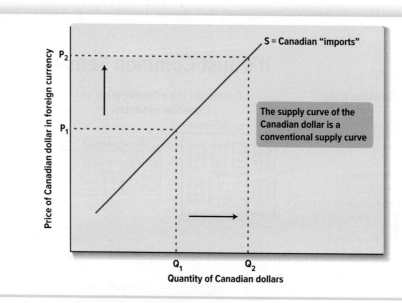

FIGURE 11.2   The Supply of the Canadian Dollar

The supply of the Canadian dollar is upward sloping, reflecting the direct relationship between the price of the currency and the quantity supplied. At price P_1, the quantity supplied is Q_1.

in the quantity supplied. Or, put another way, an appreciation of the Canadian dollar will lead to an increase in imports because we will be able to afford to buy more foreign goods with our dollars.

Let us make sure we understand this. Suppose Pengoland is famous for its production and export of wonderful smoked hams, which presently sell for 100 pengos each. At an exchange rate of $1 Canadian for 1 pengo, the hams cost Canadians $100 each. Now let us see the effect of the Canadian dollar appreciating, so that, for instance, the Canadian dollar is now worth 2 pengos. (The pengo has depreciated to $0.50 Canadian.) This is good news for Canadians, since they will now have to pay only $50 for a ham because the $50 will now give them the 100 pengos necessary to purchase the ham. Since a lower pengo is the same thing to Canadians as lower-priced ham, the sale of ham to Canada will increase, and so, too, will the quantity of Canadian dollars exchanged. The effect of the appreciation of the Canadian dollar is summarized in Table 11.2.

TABLE 11.2

Price of $1 Canadian	Price in Pengoland of Ham	Price in Canada of Ham
1 pengo	100 pengos	$100
2 pengos	100 pengos	$50

Just as we added an extra label to the demand curve, we have added the label Canadian "imports" to the supply curve to remind you that the supply comes from Canadians wishing to buy foreign currencies so that they can import foreign products. Again, we should add the caution that the supply also comes from purchases of assets as well as from speculators and arbitragers, who do not want to import any products but wish to just buy foreign currencies. Thus we have the following:

When the Canadian dollar depreciates, the effective prices of Canadian imports increase, and total imports are likely to fall.

Conversely:

When the Canadian dollar appreciates, the effective prices of Canadian imports decrease, and total imports are likely to rise.

This brings us back to one basic question. Is a higher Canadian dollar a good or a bad thing? In terms of Canadian jobs and income levels a lower Canadian dollar is preferable, since it will increase Canadian exports and boost production at home. However, from Canadian consumers' point of view, a lower Canadian dollar makes imported goods and travel abroad more expensive. Conversely, a higher Canadian dollar will tend to discourage exports but make cross-border shopping more attractive. This is summarized in Table 11.3.

TABLE 11.3

	Exports	Imports
Canadian dollar appreciates.	FALL Canadian commodity producers are hurt; tourism is down; foreigners invest less in Canada.	RISE Canadians shop more in the United States; more foreign cars are sold in Canada; Canadians invest more abroad.
Canadian dollar depreciates.	RISE Canadian commodity producers are helped; tourism booms; foreign investment in Canada is up.	FALL U.S. shoppers start showing up in Canada; more domestic cars are sold; Canadians invest less abroad.

ADDED DIMENSION

Canada and the Dutch Disease

The term "Dutch Disease" refers to an apparent relationship between an increase in the level of exports of natural resources (through either greater volume or higher resource prices) and a decline in a nation's manufacturing sector.

The thesis is that high levels of natural resource exports—oil, gas, copper, potash, and gold in Canada's case—drive up the value of the Canadian dollar and thus make Canadian manufactured goods less competitive in the world markets.

The term was coined by *The Economist* in 1977 to describe the decline of the manufacturing sector in the Netherlands after the discovery of a large natural gas field in 1959.

Does Canada suffer from Dutch Disease? The relative stagnation of the economies of Quebec and Ontario and the boom in the three Western provinces over the past two decades indicate that this might well be the case.

So now we need to think about what causes the dollar to appreciate and depreciate.

Equilibrium in Foreign-Exchange Markets

To obtain an equilibrium exchange rate, we put together the supply and demand curves, as is done in **Figure 11.3**.

Note that at the equilibrium exchange rate, the quantity demanded for the Canadian dollar is equal to the quantity supplied. The demand comes from foreigners (Canadian exports) and the supply comes from Canadians (Canadian imports). Can foreigners always get their hands on sufficient Canadian dollars to purchase Canadian goods? Certainly. It does not require any assistance from the Canadian government or from the Bank of Canada. With truly flexible exchange rates, sufficient Canadian dollars are made available by Canadians themselves, who automatically supply dollars when purchasing foreign currencies. Note also that at equilibrium not only are the quantity supplied and the quantity demanded

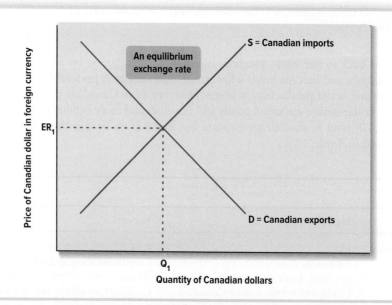

FIGURE 11.3   The Demand for and Supply of the Canadian Dollar

The intersection of the demand and supply curves yields the equilibrium exchange rate: ER_1. At ER_1 the quantity of dollars demanded and the quantity supplied are equal.

of Canadian dollars equal but the quantity demanded and the quantity supplied of foreign currencies in Canada will also be equal. Remember that foreign currencies are made available to Canadians whenever a foreigner purchases Canadian products or investments; at equilibrium, such foreign currencies will be just sufficient to satisfy the demand from Canadians for these currencies.

A further point worth mentioning about foreign exchange markets is that they provide "textbook" approximations of the perfectly competitive market. All the ingredients are present—large numbers of buyers and sellers, homogeneous product, easy entry and exit, and so on—plus arbitrage and speculation, both of which are unique to competitive markets.

TEST YOUR UNDERSTANDING

3. Imagine that the Canadian dollar appreciates.

    a) What would happen to Canadian imports?

    b) What would happen to Canadian exports?

SECTION SUMMARY

a) The demand for the Canadian dollar on the international market comes from
  - foreigners who want to buy Canadian exports or who travel in Canada
  - foreigners who want to buy Canadian assets
  - Canadians who receive factor income from abroad
  - currency speculators
  - arbitragers

b) The supply of Canadian dollars on the international market comes from
  - Canadians who want to buy foreign goods or who travel abroad
  - Canadians who want to buy more foreign assets
  - foreigners who receive Canadian factor income
  - currency speculators
  - arbitragers

c) Appreciation of the Canadian dollar will increase the effective price of exports and cause exports to fall and imports to rise. Depreciation of the Canadian dollar will decrease the effective price of exports and cause exports to rise and imports to fall.

11.3   Changes in Demand and Supply

LO3 Explain why the value of the Canadian dollar fluctuates.

Since the value of a currency is determined by the interplay of supply and demand, it follows that any change in supply or demand will change its value. We now focus on what could cause a change in demand or supply and how such a change will affect a currency's value. Let us start on the demand side. What could cause people to demand more Canadian dollars, even though there has been no change in the currency's value? Well, the first and most straightforward reason would be a rise in incomes in the countries that buy Canadian goods. It seems reasonable to suggest that if *foreign incomes* increase, then the demand for all available products, including Canadian ones, will increase. Let us trace the effects using **Figure 11.4**.

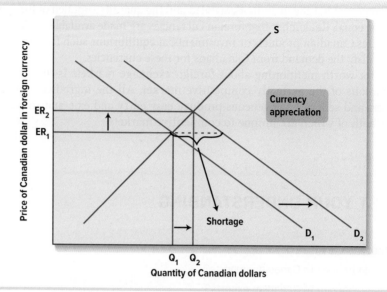

FIGURE 11.4   An Increase in the Demand for a Currency

A rightward shift in the demand for the Canadian dollar will cause the equilibrium exchange rate to rise from ER_1 to ER_2 and the equilibrium quantity to increase from Q_1 to Q_2.

 ADDED DIMENSION

Real Exchange Rates

How would you feel about emigrating to the fictitious country of Albioni, where the average monthly salary is 20 000 albions? Before making a decision, you would probably want to know, among many other things, what 20 000 albions are worth. Suppose that you learned that 1 albion equaled $1 Canadian, would that help you decide? If you still cannot make up your mind, perhaps some more data would be helpful. An average meal in Albioni will cost you 200 albions per person, a pair of socks 20 albions, and a new car 200 000 albions. It is now easier to make a rational decision.

In other words, in order to compare the values of currencies, we need to know not only the exchange rate but *also* the average price level in each country. This is what the real exchange rate measures. Its formula is

$$\text{Real exchange rate} = \frac{\text{price level in Canada}}{\text{price level in other country}} \times \text{nominal exchange rate} \qquad \textbf{[11.3]}$$

The nominal exchange rate is simply the value of the Canadian dollar, measured in terms of the foreign currency ($0.75 American, 80 yen, and so on). As an example, suppose that a brand new Toyota costs 1 600 000 yen in Japan and that an equivalent Ford car in Canada costs $20 000. If the exchange rate was equal to 80 yen per Canadian dollar, you can see that the two cars have equivalent value.

$$\text{Real exchange rate} = \frac{20\,000}{1\,600\,000} \times 80 = 1$$

The real exchange rate measures the comparative purchasing power of a currency. The formula tells you, for instance, that the value of Canada's real exchange rate will increase if either the nominal exchange rate or the Canadian price level increases, or if the Japanese price level falls. Now suppose instead that the price of a new Toyota was only 1 200 000 yen. The value of the real exchange rate would change.

$$\text{Real exchange rate} = \frac{20\,000}{1\,200\,000} \times 80 = 1.33$$

If this is the case, a Canadian would find living in Japan considerably cheaper than living in Canada. For example, you might sell your Ford in Canada for $20 000 and exchange the dollars for 1 600 000 yen. This would mean that you could easily afford a new Toyota in Japan and still have plenty of money left over.

The initial demand curve is D_1. The increase in foreign income and the resulting increase in the demand for Canadian exports will increase the demand for Canadian dollars. This is illustrated by the shift in the demand curve to D_2. The increase in demand creates a shortage of Canadian dollars, which results in the exchange rate rising from ER_1 to ER_2. At this higher exchange rate, we obtain a new equilibrium. This higher exchange rate means that the attractiveness of Canadian exports is reduced, because they are effectively more expensive. However, the volume of trade has still increased *despite* the higher Canadian dollar.

Note that imports and exports have increased. Why have imports increased? Remember that the higher exchange rate, ER_2, makes imports cheaper, and therefore more are bought. In other words, an increase in the demand for Canadian goods and services will increase Canadian exports, even though it has caused the Canadian dollar to appreciate. The amount of Canadian imports has also increased, but this is *because of* the appreciation.

Perhaps a small reminder is in order. The level of Canadian exports is independent of Canadian income; it is determined by the level of foreign income. Conversely, the level of Canadian imports definitely does depend on the level of our income: the greater our income, the more we import.

Other things will also cause a change in the demand for Canadian dollars. For example, the *price of Canadian products that are traded abroad* will have an impact on demand. A decrease in the price of these goods will cause the worldwide demand for such products to increase. We do need to be careful here and point out that we are speaking of Canadian products whose prices are determined domestically and not a product such as oil, which has a world price and is beyond the control of domestic producers. However, it must be added that it is not the absolute level of prices of traded goods that is important, but rather the relative level compared with that of other countries. An increase in the prices of foreign goods that compete with Canadian exports will have the same effect on the demand for Canadian exports as a decrease in Canadian prices.

Canada has no control over oil prices.
© Nerthuz | Dreamstime.com

Another factor affecting the demand for a currency is the view foreigners have of Canadian goods—in short, *foreigners' tastes.* For example, if tastes shift from wood-frame to metal-frame houses, this might well decrease Canada's lumber exports.

A final factor affecting the demand for Canadian dollars is *interest rates.* When foreigners are deciding whether to put money into Canada, they look at a number of factors, but the rate of interest they can get is certainly one of the most important. Traditionally, rates of interest in Canada have been kept above those in the United States expressly to encourage an inflow of American money and to discourage the outflow of Canadian dollars to the United States. Obviously, the higher the rate, the higher the level of foreign currency flow into Canada. This will mean a higher demand for Canadian dollars. As with prices, it is not the absolute level of interest rates that is important but the difference between Canadian rates and those in other countries. The demand for the Canadian dollar would therefore increase with a drop in interest rates abroad.

Perhaps we should add a note of caution here. As we mentioned in Chapter 10, high interest rates in Canada will tend to discourage investment by Canadian firms. They will be disinclined to borrow from Canadian financial institutions, as this would represent a high cost to them. However, high interest rates in Canada will certainly be attractive to an American investor who has borrowed funds from an American financial institution at lower rates.

In summary, the demand for the Canadian dollar is determined by four important factors:

- the level of foreign incomes
- the price of Canadian products relative to the price of foreign products
- foreigners' tastes
- comparative interest rates

We now need to recognize that any change in the demand for the Canadian dollar will have effects on the domestic economy. If the demand for the Canadian dollar has increased because Canadian exports have increased, aggregate demand will also have increased. Whether this increase in exports is because of higher foreign incomes, lower Canadian prices, or a change in tastes in favour of Canadian goods does not matter. The higher exports mean greater aggregate demand. This is illustrated in **Figure 11.5.**

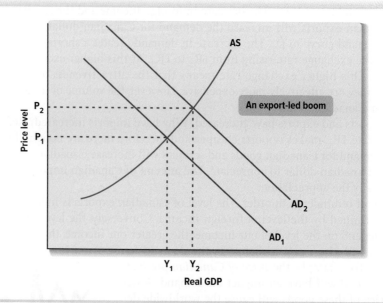

FIGURE 11.5   The Effect of an Increase in Exports on Aggregate Demand

An increase in Canadian exports increases aggregate demand, as illustrated by the shift from AD$_1$ to AD$_2$. This results in a rise in both the price level and GDP.

  ADDED DIMENSION

Foreign Financial Investment and Interest-Rate Parity

The amount of international money looking for a good (profitable) home is enormous. International investors are constantly seeking opportunities to earn the highest returns on their funds. Hundreds of billions of dollars are traded every day in foreign-exchange markets. (In contrast, the demand for Canadian dollars to buy Canadian products is less than $1 billion per day.)

An investor buying foreign financial assets can earn a return from both the return on that investment and an appreciation in the value of the currency in which it is denominated. For instance, suppose I buy a South African bond that has a value of 5000 rand and pays annual interest of 8 percent. If the exchange rate is 5 rand to the dollar, it will cost me $1000 to buy the bond. At the end of the year, I receive 5400 rand. Now, suppose that, during the year, the rand has appreciated to 4.5 rand to the dollar. Converting my rand back into dollars gives me $1200. I have therefore earned $200, or 20 percent, on my original $1000. I earned 8 percent in interest and 12 percent from the appreciation of the rand.

This also means that if the currency I hold drops in value, the interest earned is wiped out by the loss on the exchange rate. Foreign investors are therefore concerned not only with the return on investment but also with what might happen to the value of the foreign currency. This is the reason there are often big differences in interest rates around the world.

Ask yourself: If Canadians can earn only 5 percent interest in Canada but 20 percent in Mexico, why wouldn't all the funds flow out of Canada and into Mexico? The answer is that in order to earn that 20 percent, you have to convert your dollars into pesos and leave them in pesos for a whole year. But many are fearful that during the year the value of the peso will fall against the dollar. How much does the average investor think it will fall? Presumably 15 percent. Why this amount? Because they will earn a certain 20 percent in interest on their funds but expect to lose 15 percent on the depreciation of the peso, netting them 5 percent—the same amount they can earn in Canada. In other words, if you take into consideration both the interest earned and the gain or loss on the foreign currency, the rate of return you can earn is more or less equal around the world. This is often referred to as *interest-rate parity*, though perhaps it would be better to refer to it as *rate-of-return parity*.

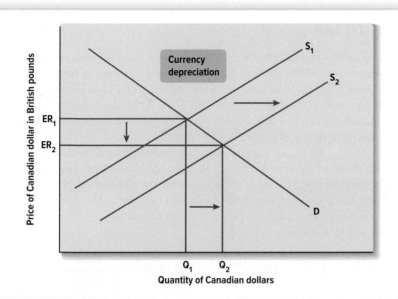

FIGURE 11.6   An Increase in the Supply of Canadian Dollars

An increase in the supply of Canadian dollars is represented by the shift from S_1 to S_2. As a result of this increase, the value of the Canadian dollar decreases and the quantity of Canadian dollars bought and sold increases.

An increase in Canadian exports does indeed raise the value of the dollar (and also imports), but it also raises Canadian GDP (assuming the increase in exports is greater than the increase in imports, which is almost always the case). This process is often called an *export-led boom*. Foreigners buy more Canadian goods, and this raises the value of the Canadian dollar; but it also increases aggregate demand within Canada, creating new jobs, raising GDP, and finally raising the price level.

You should also note that this export-led boom may reduce the size of the Canadian multiplier. This is because the boom will, as we just mentioned, likely increase the prices of Canadian products and raise the value of the Canadian exchange rate. Both of these effects will tend to dampen the effect of the initial rise in exports.

A very important point in all this discussion is that the exchange rate does not move in isolation from the domestic economy. What happens on the international market very much affects what happens internally. This has always been true, but it is becoming increasingly pertinent as the world's economies become more integrated, as we saw in Chapter 10.

Let us now work through a situation that affects Canadians' demand for imported goods. Assume that we were to remove the tariffs on British products coming into Canada. To the Canadian consumer, this lowers the price of British products, and we would expect the quantity demanded of such goods by Canadians to increase. This means that the Canadian demand for the British pound increases, and this implies that Canadians will be supplying more Canadian dollars on the world market. The last point is illustrated in **Figure 11.6**.

As Canadians demand more imports from the United Kingdom and thus more pounds, the supply curve of Canadian dollars shifts outward from S_1 to S_2. This will cause the exchange rate to drop to a lower level at ER_2. The removal of tariffs on British imports will tend to lead to a depreciation of the Canadian dollar and an appreciation of the pound.

In other words, British exports to Canada will increase *despite* the higher pound. In addition, British imports of Canadian products will increase *because* of the higher pound. The total value of trade will increase.

The intellectual appeal of market-determined flexible exchange rates is strong among most economists today. If the supply of or demand for a currency changes for any one of a variety of reasons, the exchange rate itself changes, and the economy adjusts automatically without any need for government policy and with a minimum of disruption to the domestic economy.

As we shall soon see, a fixed exchange regime also has some very appealing aspects, yet advocates of flexible exchange rates feel that the costs of a fixed exchange rate are far greater. Let us move to a discussion of fixed exchange rates and then compare the two systems.

IT'S NEWS TO ME …

The Bank of Montreal released a study today that concluded that the previously very tight relationship between price of oil and the value of the Canadian dollar seems to have been broken. In this study, economist Robert Kavcic points out that while the price of oil has gone up 17% in the last two months the Canadian dollar has dropped from US$0.767 to 0.757 (and today was 0.746).

In addition, Bloomberg markets has recently stated that the decoupling started in August when the link was weaker than in any of the previous 18 months.

The Bank report goes on to say that the more traditional determinants of Canada's exchange rate—interest rate differentials between the US and Canada; the relative prices of Canadian goods compared to foreign prices; and Canada's Balance of payments status—are coming to the forefront.

It went on to say that a lower exchange rate could well turn out to be a good thing since it should result in higher exports flowing from Canadian (non-oil) industries.

Source: *Star Power Reporting,* November 2016.

I. Which of the following is a determinant of Canadian exports not mentioned in the article?

   a) the level of Canadian GDP
   b) the level of government spending in Canada
   c) the level of foreign incomes
   d) the level of the stock prices of Canadian oil producers

II. Which of the following is most likely to result in the Canadian dollar reversing its fall and appreciating?

   a) a dramatic rise in the world price of oil
   b) the U.S. raising its interest rate while Canada does not
   c) Canadian imports increasing
   d) Canadian lumber and potash exports to Asia declining

 TEST YOUR UNDERSTANDING

4. Which of the following factors would cause the Canadian dollar to appreciate?

   a) a big increase in the popularity of wood-frame homes in China

   b) a drop in Canadian interest rates

   c) a big increase in Canadian incomes

   d) significantly higher inflation rates in the United States than in Canada

   e) a big economic growth in Japan

5. Assume that the demand for Canadian exports decreases. What would be the effect on

   a) the value of the Canadian dollar?   **c)** the level of GDP?

   b) the level of aggregate demand?   **d)** the price level?

SECTION SUMMARY

Changes in the demand for the Canadian dollar come from

- changes in the level of foreign incomes
- changes in the price of Canadian goods
- changes in foreigners' preferences
- changes in comparative interest rates

11.4 Fixed Exchange Rates

LO4 Compare flexible and fixed exchange rate systems.

Fixed exchange rates have been the rule rather than the exception over the centuries. Until the 1970s, most governments throughout the world were convinced that they needed to control the value of their currencies by fixing their exchange rate at a predetermined value—expressed in gold historically, and in American dollars after World War II. However, Canada's experience was different, since we had a flexible rate system for most of the 1950s, while other countries remained on fixed rates. During this time the value of the Canadian dollar rose above par with the American dollar and peaked at 1 Canadian dollar equal to 1.08 American dollars. In 1962, Canada adopted a fixed rate of US$0.925 at the urging of the IMF, but returned to a flexible exchange rate in 1970.

It is suggested that, by its very nature, international trading is fraught with problems and uncertainties. If, as a Canadian company, you want to trade with a firm in Japan, Germany, or any other country, you need to understand the different commercial laws and government regulations, the language and culture, the customs and history, and a host of other factors. What you do not need is the addition of another problem: fluctuating exchange rates. After all, if you have spent a good deal of time and money negotiating a contract with some foreign firm, you do not want to risk seeing all your profit wiped out by an unforeseen shift in exchange rates.

Fixed exchange rates can add a degree of certainty to international trade. Without this security, many feel that the volume of international trade would be considerably less. In addition, if flexible exchange rates change, both exports and imports are immediately affected. This means that employment and profits in the firms within these sectors can take rather abrupt swings up or down. An appreciation of the exchange rate, for instance, as we have seen will lead to a decline in exports and an expansion of imports. This will be good news for those firms that do the importing, but it will involve layoffs, cancellation of contracts, and postponement of investment plans for export industries.

The import industries, conversely, will be gearing up for the higher volumes by hiring additional staff, buying new equipment, and expanding capacity. What happens if the exchange rate now starts to depreciate? Everything will be thrown into reverse, with the export industries now booming, but the import industries suffering. Thus, it is argued, flexible exchange rates can lead to a great deal of domestic disruption and make long-term planning very difficult.

As a corollary, flexible exchange rates can be affected by the actions of a small group of speculators. Why, it is asked, should the fortunes of many firms and the livelihoods of millions of people be in the hands of a few speculators who are out for private gain and cannot be held accountable for their actions? It is true that fixed exchange rates are also open to currency speculation. However, this generally happens only occasionally, when pressure to devalue or revalue starts to mount. With flexible exchange rates, speculation occurs continuously.

Finally, it should be mentioned that, in some people's minds, there is a great deal of national prestige tied up in exchange rates. These people feel that their nation should have a "strong" currency. When the Canadian dollar was trading well below the value of the U.S. dollar, many Canadians felt that our dollar was "weaker" than theirs—but we are dealing with two different countries and two separate currencies. There is no reason that, except through coincidence, they should be at par. Hardly anyone would suggest that the Canadian dollar should be at par with the pound sterling, the euro, or the Japanese yen, and yet the comparison of the Canadian dollar with the American dollar persists.

In summary, there are four basic arguments in favour of fixed exchange rates:

- They add a degree of certainty to international trade.
- They prevent instability in the export and import industries.
- They discourage currency speculation.
- They appeal to people who tend to equate the exchange rate with national prestige.

These are the arguments for a fixed exchange rate. Let us now delve into how such a system would function.

Fixed Exchange Rates and an Increase in Demand

Assume that the government of Canada fixed the exchange rate. This means that anyone buying or selling Canadian dollars could only do so at the official rate decreed by government. Let us begin

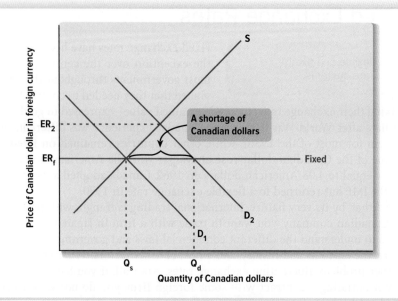

FIGURE 11.7   An Increase in Currency Demand Under Fixed Exchange Rates

An increase in the demand for the Canadian dollar does not lead to an appreciation of the Canadian dollar under a fixed exchange rate system. The result is therefore a shortage of Canadian dollars on the world market and an undervalued dollar.

with the rate fixed at the equilibrium market rate. Suppose that later, however, an increase in the demand for Canadian exports and thus the Canadian dollar occurs. This situation is illustrated in **Figure 11.7**.

Given a fixed exchange rate, an increase in demand for the Canadian dollar results in the dollar being undervalued compared with what its free-market value would be (the market rate ER_2 is above the fixed rate, ER_f in this case). Foreigners see Canadian goods as very attractive buys. At the fixed rate of ER_f the quantity demanded (Q_d) of Canadian dollars exceeds the quantity supplied (Q_s). Since government has fixed the exchange rate, it must ensure, for normal trading to continue, that enough Canadian dollars are made available to meet world demand. In other words, the Bank of Canada will have to supply this shortage by expanding the money supply. This strong demand for Canadian exports and the continual increase in money supply by the Bank of Canada will eventually be inflationary. If this inflation goes on long enough, the price of Canadian goods will rise, causing the export of these goods to fall. Eventually this will reduce the demand for Canadian dollars to equilibrium on curve D_1. However, during this period of adjustment, the economy will experience inflation.

Another implication for an undervalued currency is its effect on other countries. For instance, many observers considered that the Chinese yuan, which from 1995 to 2005 was fixed to the American dollar at a rate of 8.28 yuan per U.S. dollar, that is, 1 yuan is worth 12 cents American, was seriously undervalued and its market rate was likely much higher. Of course, this undervalued rate meant that Chinese exports were considerably cheaper than they would otherwise have been. More significantly, it also meant that exports to China were very much more expensive. The result was big trade deficits with China for the United States and other countries. This was the cause of a great deal of friction between them. In 2005, under pressure, the Chinese authorities allowed the value of the yuan a degree of flexibility and consequently it rose to 12.3 cents U.S. By October 2016, it had appreciated further, to 19.6 cents U.S., an appreciation of 63 percent from its previous fixed value.

Let us now look now at a different scenario. Many people view this next situation as more serious for an economy, so we will examine it in some detail.

Fixed Exchange Rates and a Decrease in Demand

Again, suppose that the Canadian government fixes the value of the Canadian dollar at ER_f. This time, however, the demand for the dollar drops, as shown in **Figure 11.8**.

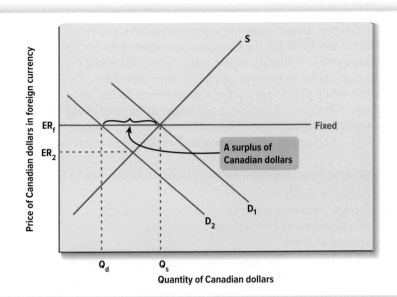

FIGURE 11.8 A Decrease in Currency Demand Under Fixed Exchange Rates

A decrease in the demand for the Canadian dollar does not lead to a lower Canadian dollar under a fixed exchange rate system. The result is a surplus of Canadian dollars on the foreign exchange market and an overvalued dollar.

The fixed exchange rate ER_f is now above what would be the free-market equilibrium rate ER_2, so there is a surplus of Canadian dollars on the world market. Let us examine what is happening. Before the change in demand, the quantity of dollars foreigners wanted to buy was equal to the quantity supplied of dollars on the foreign exchange market. Then the demand for the dollar dropped. Since foreigners are now buying fewer Canadian goods and services and therefore buying fewer Canadian dollars, the amount of foreign currencies available for Canadians to buy is reduced. Thus, this situation can be seen as either a surplus of Canadian dollars on the foreign exchange market or a shortage of foreign currencies in Canada. Whichever way you look at it, the fixed exchange rate ER_f is overvalued. So what happens next?

In instituting fixed exchange rates, the central bank must take responsibility for any surplus or shortage of currencies. Faced with an insufficient supply of foreign currencies from normal trading, government (through the Bank of Canada) must make good on the deficiency. One of the major assets of the Bank of Canada, apart from government bonds, is reserves of gold and foreign currencies. (In October 2016, for instance, these stood at approximately US$83 billion, of which $52 billion was in American dollars.) These official international reserves, or at least as much as necessary, have to be made available to Canadians. So, along with an overvalued fixed exchange rate, as in Figure 11.8, comes the depletion of the central bank's foreign reserves. Canada, like all other countries, possesses only a limited amount of gold and foreign currencies. Because of this, the draining of foreign-currency reserves cannot continue indefinitely, and government will, as a result, be forced to take some kind of action. There are few options open, none of them attractive.

One possible tactic to stem the demand for foreign currencies would be to introduce quotas or tariffs to reduce Canadian imports. However, introducing such trade policies to try to reduce the amount of imports would violate international trade agreements and probably result in retaliation against Canadian exports. A direct **subsidy** to increase Canadian exports could, again, be in violation of trade agreements and expensive for government.

Foreign-exchange control policies have been used by some governments in the past. Here, instead of directly restricting imports, the Canadian government would restrict the amount of foreign currencies available to Canadians. It rations the relatively scarce foreign currencies, in effect saying: This is the amount of currency being made available by foreigners buying our goods and services, and this amount only can be obtained by Canadians. Such policies restrict the amount of imports.

These foreign-exchange controls can take many forms, including quotas on foreign currencies available for foreign travel, placing currency quotas on importing companies or industries, or giving preference to certain imports over others. The problem with foreign-exchange controls is that they distort trade and production, favour some importers over others, and restrict consumer choice.

Another alternative would be for the Canadian government to convince countries that are big exporters to Canada to agree to voluntary export restrictions. This would restrict imports into Canada. This is not often an easy option to exercise and has been achieved by only a few countries recently.

There is only one other policy option for a government facing an overvalued fixed exchange rate. Since imports are a function of income, a reduction in imports could be achieved by reducing income. This involves reducing aggregate demand through contractionary fiscal or monetary policy. In short, the adjustment mechanism for an overvalued exchange rate may be the deliberate creation of a recession.

In summary, a government can defend an overvalued exchange rate in four ways:

- introducing quotas or tariffs
- introducing foreign-exchange controls
- negotiating voluntary export restrictions
- creating a recession at home

A government that finds it politically impossible to impose any of the above policies, or for which those policies fail, will be forced to **devalue** its currency, that is, refix the exchange rate at a lower level.

Devaluation of a currency has serious political ramifications. It is often interpreted as a failure of a government to control its own destiny and, from that point of view, may lead to a loss of confidence generally in a government's economic policies. Furthermore, once even the possibility of a devaluation is recognized by the market, international currency dealers will ask only "when" and not "if." This lack of confidence by itself may make devaluation an inevitability, because dealers will not want to hold a currency when there is a possibility it may be devalued. Their actions, in selling off the currency that is under siege, then become a self-fulfilling prophecy.

In sum, the adjustment mechanism for an under- or overvalued fixed exchange rate is very painful and throws the economy into either an inflationary situation or a recession.

One final criticism of fixed exchange rates should be mentioned. If a country decides to fix the value of its currency to that of another, it is the fixing country's responsibility to ensure that the value is maintained by buying or selling its own currency. But, just as importantly, it must also ensure that its interest rate is maintained at the same level of the other country's. Even the smallest difference in interest rates would cause a huge amount of money to flow between the countries. This is because financial investors need not be concerned about fluctuations in the value of currency; the only deciding factor for them will be interest rate differentials. In effect, then, the fixing country has to peg both the value of its currency *and its interest rate* to that of the other country. As a result, it effectively abandons any idea of having an independent monetary policy.

For many countries, this might be too big a sacrifice. This is the reason most economists favour the flexible exchange rate system. It's the main reason that Canada led the world to a return to flexible exchange rates in 1970, with the result that fixed exchange rates have been rare in the past thirty years (one exception to this is China). However, truly flexible rates are almost as rare. Instead, most countries, including Canada, operate a system of managed exchange rates, or a **dirty float**. This means that the degree to which a currency is allowed to float (or fluctuate) is managed by the central bank in order to stabilize the exchange rate.

In Canada's case, the Bank of Canada buys and sells foreign currencies to keep the value of the dollar within what it perceives to be permissible limits. In order to prevent too rapid a depreciation of the dollar, the government sells foreign reserves and buys dollars to support demand for the dollar. Similarly, to keep the dollar from appreciating too quickly, government will sell dollars in exchange for foreign currency. This hybrid of the fixed and flexible exchange rate systems will probably be the choice of governments for the foreseeable future.

 TEST YOUR UNDERSTANDING

6. Assume that the demand for the Canadian dollar increases. Describe the adjustment mechanism of this change, given (a) flexible exchange rates and (b) fixed exchange rates.

SECTION SUMMARY

a) The arguments for a fixed exchange rate are:

- It adds a degree of certainty to international trade.
- It prevents instability in the export and import industries
- It discourages currency speculation.
- It appeals to people who tend to equate the value of the exchange rate with national prestige.

b) Many economists favour a flexible exchange rate system because

- it avoids the necessary adjustment of inflation, which results when a fixed exchange rate is undervalued
- it avoids the necessary adjustment of recession, which results when a fixed exchange rate is overvalued

11.5   The Balance of Payments

LO5 Explain the meaning of a balance of payments surplus and deficit.

The Canadian **balance of payments** (or, more correctly, the balance of international payments) is an accounting of the international buying and selling of the Canadian dollar. In a sense, the term is a misnomer, since the accounting is more like an income statement than a balance sheet. The balance of payments has three main sections: the **current account**, the **capital account**, and the **official settlements account**. What it shows are the various categories of international buying and selling that involve the Canadian dollar during a year. Table 11.4 is a simplified balance of payments for Canada for 2015.

TABLE 11.4
Canada's Balance of International Payments 2015 ($billions)

Demand for Canadian Dollars		Supply of Canadian Dollars		Balance
Current Account				
Exports of goods and services	625	Import of goods and services	671	
		Balance of trade		−46
Foreign factor income from abroad	91	Factor income paid abroad	105	
		Net foreign factor income		−14
Transfers received from abroad	11	Transfers paid abroad	14	
		Transfers (net)		−3
		Balance on Current Account		−63
Capital Account				
Foreign investment in Canada	258	Canadian investment abroad	190	
		Net foreign investment		+68
		Balance on Capital Account		+68
		Statistical discrepancy		+6
Overall Balance (current + capital + statistical discrepancy)				+11

Source: Adapted from the Statistics Canada CANSIM database, http://cansim2.statcan.ca, Tables 376-0101, 376-0102, November 1, 2016.

In a sense, the current account shows income and expenditures from international trading. The first line, exports and imports of goods and services, is self-explanatory. The difference between the two represents the balance of trade (recall from Chapter 6 that this is the value of a country's export of goods and services less the value of imports). Imports create a supply of Canadian dollars, and exports create a demand. However, when looking at the balance of payments, it is often more illuminating to look at the corresponding flows of foreign currencies: imports create a demand from Canadians for foreign currencies and exports produce a supply of foreign currencies. Traditionally, Canada has had, until recent years, a *positive* balance of trade. With the onset of a world recession, Canadian exports fell off considerably and in 2015, Canada achieved a record trade deficit of $46 billion (compared with a record surplus of $63 billion a decade earlier). However, generally the trade surplus has produced a net inflow of foreign currencies to Canada.

Gold has been a means of international payment for centuries.

© Digital Vision/Getty Images

The next line, **foreign factor income** from abroad, includes the total amount of interest, dividends, and wages that Canadians received in this particular year from their previous foreign investments. This income produces an inflow of foreign currency into Canada. Foreign factor income *paid* abroad represents an outflow of foreign currencies. Since, over the entire history of Canada, foreigners have invested more in Canada than Canadians have invested abroad, the income going offshore as a result of this investment almost always exceeds the income flowing into Canada. In 2015, there was a net outflow of $22 billion.

Transfers—the last line in the current account—includes gifts and other remittances (pensions, for example) as well as foreign aid. In 2015, the outflows exceeded the inflow by $3 billion.

The balance on the current account equals −63, which means that $63 billion more in foreign reserves left Canada than entered Canada. Again, until 2009, the current account had a positive balance every year since 1998. The years since 2009 have been challenging ones for Canada, as far as international trade is concerned.

In summary, the current account section of the balance sheets shows the movement of Canadian and foreign currencies as a result of the buying and selling of goods and services internationally as well as the flow of incomes between Canada and the rest of the world. In contrast, the capital account section of the balance sheet shows the movement of Canadian and foreign currencies as a result of the buying and selling of assets internationally—this type of spending represents a change in the ownership of assets. This could come about either as a result of purchasing shares or bonds (portfolio investment) or from the purchase of an asset, such as a piece of real estate or a whole company in another country (direct investment). Table 11.4 shows that foreigners purchased a lot more Canadian assets ($258 billion) than Canadians purchased foreign assets ($190 billion). This represented an inflow of over $68 billion into Canada. So we had an outflow of funds of $63 billion in the current account, but an inflow of $68 billion in the capital account, giving an overall surplus of $5 billion. Adding in the statistical discrepancy of $6 billion makes an overall surplus of $11. (There is a statistical discrepancy because we do not have a complete record of funds crossing borders, especially in the case of the underground economy.)

A balance of payments surplus means that, overall, foreigners were buying more Canadian currency than Canadians were buying foreign currencies. The result is that the country (by way of the Bank of Canada) acquired $11 billion in foreign reserves during the year. In return the Bank of Canada issued $11 billion in Canadian dollars to buy those reserves. (The Bank of Canada can always print more!) A balance of payments deficit, on the other hand, means that the Bank of Canada will lose foreign reserves and will acquire more of our own dollars. This can present a problem, because as we saw earlier, Canada (like all countries) only possesses a finite amount of foreign reserves, and these could eventually become totally depleted.

Let us now pose a new question. Since, with flexible exchange rates, the balance of payments is automatically achieved, can balance of payments problems ever arise? Yes, because it really does make a difference what a country is importing and what it is exporting. Canada can earn foreign currencies by exporting goods or services, or by selling assets. Exporting goods and services does not lead to any future obligations on the part of anyone in Canada. However, selling off Canadian assets obliges some Canadians to pay out future income to foreigners and represents a drain on our foreign reserves in the future.

It is important that we clear up one particular myth relating to these flows. It is often suggested that Canada needs to encourage the inflow of foreign investment because we need this inflow to pay off the deficit that Canada, until recently, has had on its current account. Perhaps you have figured out why this is a myth. The reason Canada generally has a deficit on the current account is because of the amount of investment income that has to be paid abroad. This is high because of high levels of foreign investment in the past.

If we express this in terms of the individual, it might make more sense. Picture a student who defends her excessive borrowing every year by pointing out that she needs to borrow because her expenditures always seem to exceed her income, so she is left with no choice. But a significant reason her expenses are so high is that she must make huge interest payments on her previous loans.

Similarly, many suggest that if Canada were to cut down its dependence on foreign investment, it would not have current account problems in the future. However, as Table 11.5 shows, because of Canada's good trading performance, at least until the last few years, the current account has shown some impressive surpluses.

TABLE 11.5
Canada's External Performance (balances in $billions)

Year	Balance of Trade—U.S.	Balance of Trade—All Countries	Current Account Balance	Balance of Payments Overall Balance	Value of C$ (in US$)
2003	+81	+45	+15	−5	0.71
2004	+92	+55	+29	−3	0.77
2005	+99	+50	+26	+2	0.83
2006	+86	+35	+20	+1	0.88
2007	+73	+29	+13	+5	0.93
2008	+78	+28	+2	+2	0.94
2009	+23	−23	−46	+12	0.88
2010	+21	−32	−58	+4	0.97
2011	+34	−22	−48	+8	0.98
2012	+26	−36	−66	+2	1.00
2013	+29	−30	−60	+5	0.97
2014	+34	−19	−45	+6	0.91
2015	+21	−46	−63	+11	0.78

Source: Adapted from the Statistics Canada CANSIM database, http://cansim2.statcan.ca, Tables 376–0101 and 376–0102, November 1, 2016.

TEST YOUR UNDERSTANDING

7. Fill in the blanks in this hypothetical balance of payments statement.

Demand for Canadian Dollars		Supply of Canadian Dollars		Balance
Current Account				
Exports of goods and services	164	Import of goods and services	_____	
		Balance of trade		+2
Foreign factor income from abroad	8	Factor income paid abroad	_____	
		Net foreign factor income		−15
Transfers received from abroad	26	Transfers paid abroad	_____	_____
		Transfers (net)		
		Balance on Current Account		−17
Capital Account				
Foreign investment in Canada	_____	Canadian investment abroad	186	
		Net foreign investment		+18
		Balance on Capital Account		_____
Overall Balance (current + capital)				_____

SECTION SUMMARY

The balance of payments is an accounting of a country's international transactions and is made up of

- the current account (which adds the balance of trade [export of goods and services minus imports], net investment income, and transfers)
- the capital account (the net flow of all changes in the ownership of international assets)
- the official settlements account (which shows the movement of foreign reserves in and out of the Bank of Canada)

 Study Guide

Review

WHAT'S THE BIG IDEA?

Although governments, like Canada's, are able to affect the exchange rate by buying or selling their own currencies, generally their involvement in the market is limited to ensuring that the value of their currency does not change too erratically. Thus the exchange rate is mostly determined by the market. This means that your knowledge of markets from Chapter 2 is applicable when looking at the value of the Canadian dollar. For instance, an increase in the demand for or decrease in the supply of the Canadian dollar will cause it to appreciate; a drop in demand or increase in supply will cause it to depreciate. If a government were to peg its exchange rate above market equilibrium, it would cause a surplus in the quantity of Canadians dollars on the world's markets; pegged below equilibrium, it would cause a shortage. Given this, there are still areas of possible confusion.

First, the export of Canadian goods is determined, not by how well we are doing in Canada, but by how well other countries are doing. Second, American tourists coming to Canada is a Canadian export, not an import (unless we are importing Americans!). These are important factors when we look at the advantages and disadvantages of an appreciating (or depreciating) Canadian dollar. Bear in mind that an exchange rate does not increase or decrease without cause. Suppose that the American economy is doing very well, so that Americans are travelling in large numbers including many of them coming to Canada. This will increase the demand by Americans for Canadian dollars, causing the Canadian dollar to appreciate. This does two things: it makes foreign products more attractive to Canadians, increasing our imports; but it also makes Canadian products more expensive for foreigners, reducing exports.

In other words, the booming American economy causes a large number of America tourists to travel to our country. However, the rising dollar deters some some of them, and perhaps causes those here to spend less. So the rising Canadian dollar means the tourist sector will get a boost, but not a very big one.

NEW GLOSSARY TERMS AND KEY EQUATIONS

arbitrage
balance of payments
capital account
currency appreciation
currency depreciation
current account

devaluation
direct investment
dirty float
exchange rate
fixed exchange rate
flexible exchange rate

foreign factor income
official settlements account
portfolio investment
purchasing power parity theory
subsidy

Equations:

[11.1] $\dfrac{\text{1 Canadian dollar}}{\text{(in units of foreign currency)}} = \dfrac{1}{\text{foreign currency (in Canadian dollars)}}$

[11.2] $\dfrac{\text{1 unit of foreign currency}}{\text{(in Canadian dollars)}} = \dfrac{1}{\text{Canadian dollars (in foreign currency)}}$

[11.3] $\text{Real exchange rate} = \dfrac{\text{price level in Canada}}{\text{price level in other country}} \times \text{nominal exchange rate}$

Comprehensive Problem

(LO 2, 3, 4, 5)   Suppose that the international demand and supply of Canadian dollars (in billions) is as shown in Table 11.6. This represents the total market for Canadian dollars (that is, no transfers, speculation, or arbitrage).

TABLE 11.6

Value of Canadian Dollars (in US$)	DEMAND FOR CANADIAN DOLLARS				SUPPLY OF CANADIAN DOLLARS			
	Export of Goods and Services	Foreign Factor Income Earned Abroad	Foreign Investment in Canada	Total	Import of Goods and Services	Foreign Factor Income Paid Abroad	Canadian Investment Abroad	Total
$0.70	120	70	180	_____	80	67	146	_____
0.72	119	70	175	_____	83	67	148	_____
0.74	118	70	170	_____	86	67	150	_____
0.76	117	70	165	_____	89	67	152	_____
0.78	116	70	160	_____	92	67	154	_____
0.80	115	70	155	_____	95	67	156	_____
0.82	114	70	150	_____	98	67	158	_____
0.84	113	70	145	_____	101	67	160	_____
0.86	112	70	140	_____	104	67	162	_____
0.88	111	70	135	_____	107	67	164	_____
0.90	110	70	130	_____	110	67	166	_____

Questions

a) Calculate and fill in the total demand and total supply columns of the table.

Suppose that Canada is operating with a flexible exchange rate system.

b) What is the equilibrium value of the Canadian dollar?
c) What is the value of its balance of trade?
d) What is its current account balance?
e) What is its capital account balance?
f) What is the overall balance of payments (current and capital accounts)?

Answers

a)

TABLE 11.6 (COMPLETED)

Value of Canadian Dollars (in US$)	DEMAND FOR CANADIAN DOLLARS				SUPPLY OF CANADIAN DOLLARS			
	Export of Goods and Services	Income Earned Abroad	Foreign Investment in Canada	Total	Import of Goods and Services	Foreign Factor Income Paid Abroad	Canadian Investment Abroad	Total
$0.70	$120	$70	$180	$370	$80	$67	$146	$293
0.72	119	70	175	364	83	67	148	298
0.74	118	70	170	358	86	67	150	303
0.76	117	70	165	352	89	67	152	308
0.78	116	70	160	346	92	67	154	313
0.80	115	70	155	340	95	67	156	318
0.82	114	70	150	334	98	67	158	323
0.84	113	70	145	328	101	67	160	328
0.86	112	70	140	322	104	67	162	333
0.88	111	70	135	316	107	67	164	338
0.90	110	70	130	310	110	67	166	343

b) Canadian dollar: US$0.84
c) Balance of trade: +$12 (= exports of $113 – imports of $101)
d) Current account balance: +$15 (= $183 – $168)
e) Capital account balance: –$15 (= $145 – $160)
f) Total balance of payments: zero (= $328 – $328)

Questions

Now suppose that Canada fixes its exchange rate against the U.S. dollar at a value of $1 Canadian equals $0.82 American.

g) What is the value of its balance of trade?
h) What is its current account balance?
i) What is its capital account balance?
j) What is the overall balance of payments (current and capital accounts)?
k) What is the balance on its official settlements account?

Answers

g) Balance of trade: +$16 (= $114 – $98)
h) Current account balance: +$19 (= $184 – $165)
i) Capital account balance: –$8 (= $150 – $158)
j) Overall balance of payments: +$11 (= $334 – $323)
k) Official settlements account: –$11 (The opposite of the overall balance. This is the amount of Canadian dollars that left the bank of Canada. In exchange, Canada received $11 in foreign reserves.)

Study Problems

Find answers on the McGraw-Hill online resource.

Basic (Problems 1–3)

1. **(LO 1)** If a Canadian hockey stick has a price of $42, how much does it cost in
   a) Europe, assuming an exchange rate of 1 euro = $1.40 Canadian? _____
   b) the United Kingdom, assuming an exchange rate of 1 pound = $2.10 Canadian? _____

2. **(LO 1)** Fill in the blanks.
   a) If one Canadian dollar equals $0.75 American, then one U.S. dollar equals _____ Canadian dollars.
   b) If one Canadian dollar equals 80 yen, then one yen equals _____ Canadian dollars.
   c) If one euro equals 1.6 Canadian dollars, then one Canadian dollar equals _____ euros.

3. **(LO 5)** See the data in Table 11.7 (all figures are in billions of dollars).

TABLE 11.7	
Foreign investment in Etruria	90
Transfers (net)	+4
Foreign factor income from abroad	11
Imports of goods and services	153
Exports of goods and services	157
Etruria investment abroad	68
Foreign factor income paid abroad	29

a) What is the value of the balance of trade? _____
b) What is the balance on the current account? _____
c) What is the balance on the capital account? _____
d) Is there a balance of payments surplus or deficit? How much? _____

Intermediate (Problems 4–7)

4. **(LO 1)** Karen operates a small foreign currency exchange business. She begins each day with three boxes of cash. Each box contains 10 000 units of Canadian currency and 10 000 units of another currency. Table 11.8 shows Karen's holdings of each currency at the end of a day's business.

TABLE 11.8				
Box 1	Euros	8000	and	$12 800 Canadian
Box 2	Japanese yen	6000	and	10 050 Canadian
Box 3	British pounds	7000	and	15 000 Canadian

What is the value of the Canadian dollar in terms of the three currencies?
Dollar in terms of the euro: _____
Dollar in terms of the yen: _____
Dollar in terms of the British pound: _____

5. **(LO 3)** The graph in Figure 11.9 illustrates hypothetical supply and demand curves for the Canadian dollar. Use it to answer the questions below.

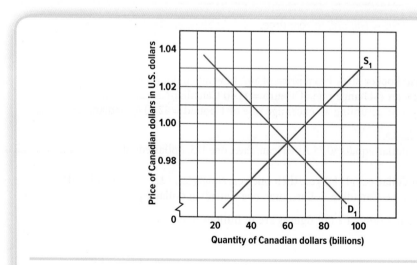

FIGURE 11.9

a) What is the quantity of dollars exchanged, given D_1 and S_1? _____
b) What is this quantity worth in U.S. dollars? _____
c) If the demand for the dollar increases by 20, draw in the new demand curve labelled D_2.
d) What is the quantity of Canadian dollars exchanged if the exchange rate is flexible? _____

Suppose instead that the dollar is fixed at the original value.

e) As a result of the change in (c), what is the quantity of Canadian dollars exchanged? _____
f) What is this quantity worth in U.S. dollars? _____

6. **(LO 3)** The hypothetical graph in Figure 11.10 is for the Canadian dollar with a fixed exchange rate of 1.2.

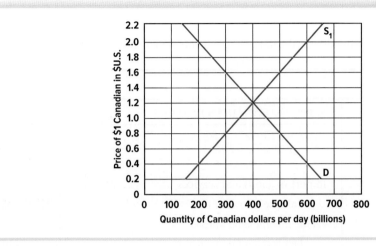

FIGURE 11.10

a) What is the equilibrium quantity of Canadian dollars traded? _____
b) If the supply of Canadian dollars increases by 200, draw in the new supply curve and label it S_2.
c) What is the new quantity demanded of Canadian dollars after the shift? _____
d) What is the new quantity supplied of Canadian dollars after the shift? _____
e) What would be the exchange rate after the shift if it were flexible? _____

7. **(LO 1)** Assume that you buy a 1-year, 200 000-peso Philippine bond that pays 9 percent when the exchange rate is 1 Canadian dollar for 40 pesos. If, after one year, the peso falls to 1 Canadian dollar equals 45 pesos, how much money in Canadian dollars will you have? _____

Advanced (Problems 8–10)

8. **(LO 3)** Suppose that a certain type of SUV costs $32 000 in Canada, but sells for 18 000 British pounds in the United Kingdom, and that the nominal exchange rate is 1 Canadian dollar = 0.45 British pounds.
a) What is the value of the real exchange rate? _____
b) In which country is the SUV cheaper? _____

9. **(LO 1)** Table 11.9 shows some actual data concerning exchange rates and the prices of Big Macs in the summer of 2012.

TABLE 11.9

Location	Big Mac Price		Actual Exchange Rate
Toronto	5.37	Canadian dollars	
Switzerland	6.50	Swiss francs	$1 Canadian = 0.90 Swiss francs
Singapore	4.60	Singapore dollars	$1 Canadian = 1.26 Singapore dollars
Hong Kong	15.41	Hong Kong dollars	$1 Canadian = 7.75 Hong Kong dollars

a) Assuming purchasing power parity, what should the price of Big Macs be in the three countries?
Switzerland = SF _____
Singapore = $_____ Singapore
Hong Kong = $_____ Hong Kong

b) Compared with the actual prices of Big Macs in the three countries, are the actual exchange rates overvalued or undervalued?
Swiss franc _____
Singapore dollar: _____
Hong Kong dollar: _____

10. Fill in the blanks in the hypothetical balance of payments statement in Table 11.10.

TABLE 11.10

DEMAND FOR CANADIAN DOLLARS		SUPPLY OF CANADIAN DOLLARS		Balance
Current Account				
Exports of goods and services	475	Import of goods and services	_____	
		Balance of trade		−32
Foreign factor income from abroad	61	Factor income paid abroad	_____	
		Net foreign factor income		−16
Transfers received from abroad	9	Transfers paid abroad	_____	
		Transfers (net)		_____
		Balance on Current Account		−50
Capital Account				
Foreign investment in Canada	_____	Canadian investment abroad	94	
		Net foreign investment		+60
		Balance on Capital Account		_____
Overall Balance (Current + Capital)				_____

Problems for Further Study

Basic (Problems 1–5)

1. **(LO 2)** Refer to the following list, and explain who will be buying Canadian dollars and who will be selling.
   a) a Canadian businesswoman visiting Japan _____
   b) a Russian tourist visiting Cape Breton _____
   c) an American corporation building a new plant in Saskatoon _____
   d) a Canadian bank expanding its operations in the United States _____

2. **(LO 2)** Refer to the following list, and identify who would be hurt or who would benefit from an appreciation of the Canadian dollar.
   a) an Italian father spending the summer with his daughter in Calgary _____
   b) a Canadian research scientist living in Washington, D.C., who is paid a monthly salary in Canadian dollars by his Ottawa employer _____
   c) a retired couple living in Ontario whose major source of income is from a British pension _____
   d) a nurse living in Windsor who works at a hospital in Detroit _____

3. **(LO 3)** What effect will the following events have on the value of the Canadian dollar versus the Mexican peso?
   a) Canadian interest rates rise significantly above Mexican rates. _____
   b) An especially bad winter causes tens of thousands of Canadians to escape to the Mexican Riviera for vacations. _____
   c) A Canadian telecommunications firm sells equipment to the Mexican government. _____
   d) The winter vegetable crop in Mexico is destroyed by unusually cold temperatures. _____

4. **(LO 2)** Where does the supply of Canadian dollars on foreign exchange markets come from?

5. **(LO 2)** What is arbitrage?

Intermediate (Problems 6–9)

6. **(LO 5)** A country that experiences a capital account surplus for many years will eventually experience many years of current account deficits. Explain.

7. **(LO 3)** Assume that the demand for the Canadian dollar increases because of a rising GDP level in the United States. What will happen to the value of the Canadian exchange rate, Canada's GDP, and the unemployment rate in Canada?
Exchange rate: _____
GDP: _____
Unemployment rate: _____

8. **(LO 2)** What happens to the effective price of Canadian products if the Canadian dollar appreciates? What happens to the volume of Canadian exports?

9. **(LO 4)** Contrast *flexible exchange rate* and *fixed exchange rate*.

Advanced (Problems 10–12)

10. **(LO 3)** An increase in the demand for Canadian products will cause the Canadian dollar to appreciate. Yet an appreciation of the dollar causes the demand for Canadian products to fall. How can you reconcile these two statements?

11. **(LO 4)** Explain why a country with a fixed exchange rate loses control over its money supply as an effective policy tool.

12. **(LO 1)** Explain purchasing power parity theory.

CHAPTER 12
Macroeconomic Policy Revisited

LEARNING OBJECTIVES

At the end of this chapter, you should be able to:

LO1 Describe the impact of a change in interest rates and exchange rates on the effectiveness of fiscal policy.

LO2 Explain how the effectiveness of monetary policy is enhanced under a flexible exchange rate.

LO3 Explain the trade-off between unemployment and inflation levels implied by the Phillips curve.

LO4 Describe what is meant by the term *supply-side economics*.

LO5 Show that Canada has been successful in maintaining the internal but not the external value of the Canadian dollar and why some people call for a fixed exchange rate.

LO6 Explain why economists are concerned about the possibility of deflation.

WHAT'S AHEAD ...

In this chapter, we return to the topics of fiscal and monetary policy, having opened up the economy to the effects of international trade and financial flows (Chapters 10 and 11). We shall see that changes in fiscal and monetary policy can affect both the interest rate and the exchange rate. In addition, we will see how changes in these two key economic variables will have a feedback effect on the level of GDP and employment. We will also look at supply-side economics and see how these ideas might fit into fiscal and monetary policy making. Finally, we will look at why some people call for a fixed Canadian dollar and briefly explore why economists fear deflation.

A QUESTION OF RELEVANCE ...

These are indeed confusing times that we live in. What will the world learn from the 2008–10 financial crisis, which led to the most severe economic disruption since the Great Depression of the 1930s? Could governments around the world have done more to help put economies back on the road to recovery? Is deflation a serious threat in today's economic environment? The significance of these questions cannot be overemphasized.

C anada is one of the most open economies in the world; our exports make up a high percentage of the national GDP, and imports from the rest of the world are a high percentage of our total consumption spending. Foreigners buy and sell stocks on the Toronto Stock Exchange and invest directly in Canada, while Canadians do the same in the rest of the world. Therefore, to truly understand all of the broad aspects of Canada's economy, we need to look at the effectiveness of economic policy in an open economy. To help us, we will revisit the discussions of fiscal policy from Chapter 7 and monetary policy from Chapter 9.

12.1   Fiscal Policy in an Open Economy

LO1 Describe the impact of a change in interest rates and exchange rates on the effectiveness of fiscal policy.

After investigating international finance in Chapter 11, we can move things forward with a more thorough examination of the effectiveness of fiscal policy in an open economy.

In Chapter 7, we learned that the use of fiscal policy can change the level of aggregate demand and thus the level of national income. An inflationary gap can be addressed by *contractionary* fiscal policy, which means either lower government spending or higher taxes. An increase in aggregate demand is called for in the case of a recessionary gap. This can be achieved using *expansionary* fiscal policy in one of two ways: through a cut in taxes or through an increase in government spending. We also learned that an increase in spending will be more effective than a decrease in taxes of the same magnitude simply because a portion of the higher disposable income resulting from lower taxes will be saved rather than spent on increased consumption, whereas *all* of the increase in government spending will translate into (a multiplied) increase in GDP. This is one of the reasons that expansionary fiscal policy usually takes the form of increased government spending. Another reason is simply that, for political reasons, most governments prefer to increase spending than reduce taxes.

Let us examine the effect of expansionary fiscal policy in more detail with the help of **Figure 12.1A**. Now, irrespective of whether this takes the form of higher government spending or lower taxes, the result will be an increase in aggregate demand and will lead to a rise in the level of income, from Y_1 to Y_3, and a rise in the price level, from P_1 to P_2. If prices had remained constant at P_1, real GDP would have risen to Y_2. However, since prices have risen to P_2, GDP only increases to Y_3. In other words, higher prices have dampened spending somewhat (there is a movement up the AD_2 curve). Let us review why this is the case.

There are three reasons a higher price level reduces the aggregate quantity demanded. First, recall the real-balance effect from Chapter 5—the value of people's savings has declined and this reduces consumer spending. Second is the foreign-trade effect mentioned in Chapter 5 and explained in Chapter 11: higher-priced domestic products become less competitive in world markets, so Canadian exports are reduced. Third is the interest rate effect, which lies behind Chapter 7's discussion of the crowding out effect. It is this last that we need to look at in more detail.

Recall from Chapter 9 that an increase in the price level will raise the transactions demand for money. Assuming no increase in the money supply, this increase in the demand for money will tend to push up interest rates as seen in **Figure 12.1B**. This in turn will reduce the level of private investment spending. That is to say, expansionary fiscal policy can lead to the crowding out of investment spending as illustrated in **Figure 12.1C**.

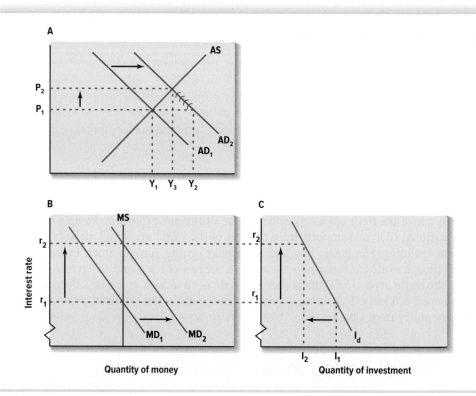

FIGURE 12.1   Effect of an Increase in Government Spending

Expansionary fiscal policy implies an increase in aggregate demand, shown as a shift from AD_1 to AD_2. If the price level remains constant at P_1, GDP would increase from Y_1 to Y_2. However, the price level increases to P_2, and as a result, money demand and interest rates increase as shown in Figure B. Then, the higher interest rate reduces the level of investment spending, as seen in Figure C. The lower investment spending in turn reduces the aggregate quantity demanded (a movement along AD_2) in Figure A and thereby reduces real GDP to Y_3.

 ADDED DIMENSION

Was the Crowding Out Effect Present in 2009–13?

It is interesting to note that the experience of the North American economies in response to fiscal-policy stimulus spending in 2009 does not fit the standard analysis of the crowding out effect. Despite the application of stimulus packages by both the Canadian and the U.S. government, interest rates showed no tendency to rise and, in fact, remained very low. Why was this? One high-profile economist, Paul Krugman, puts forward the following explanation.

The economic crisis of 2008–10 created a worldwide excess of savings; both businesses and consumers put spending plans on hold in the face of the uncertainty created by a near-collapse in the financial system. Given this, the standard analysis that more government borrowing would lead to a rise in the interest rate simply did not apply. Even in the face of very low interest rates, the excess of savings persisted because the demand for new loans was so weak. The result was that governments were able to fund expansionary spending through the creation of budget deficits (enabled with borrowed funds) without pushing up interest rates. It appears that the economy was in a state of persistent excess liquidity wherein the desire to hold cash was so strong that interest rates were held down. In other words, increased government spending did not lead to the crowding out of investment spending through higher interest rates.

We know from Chapters 5 and 6 that an increase in government spending—aimed at closing a recessionary gap—will increase the level of national income by an amount determined by the multiplier. However, we have just seen that the crowding out of investment spending offsets some of this increase in national income, resulting in a multiplier that is smaller than it appeared at first glance. Let us be clear: we are not saying fiscal policy is ineffective because of the crowding out effect or even that the crowding out effect is always present. What we are saying is that the crowding out effect might reduce the size of the expenditures multiplier when expansionary fiscal policy is applied.

So, in summary, a higher price level tends to dampen down both consumption and exports but also leads to a higher interest rate which will reduce investment spending. There is also a secondary effect of the higher interest rate, because it will attract foreign investment in Canada which will push up the Canadian dollar, further reducing exports (and increasing imports).

 ## TEST YOUR UNDERSTANDING

Find answers on the McGraw-Hill online resource.

1. a) Suppose that GDP in Newland is $800 billion and government increases spending by $25 billion. If the multiplier equals 4, what is the new level of GDP?

   b) Suppose that as a result of the increase in GDP the price level in Newland also rises, causing the demand for money to increase by $40 billion. Given the following graph of the money market and investment demand, by how much will investment fall?

   c) Given the same value of the multiplier, what will be the new level of GDP?

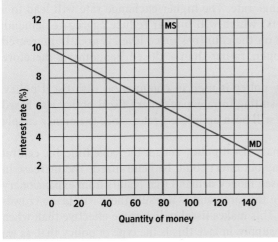

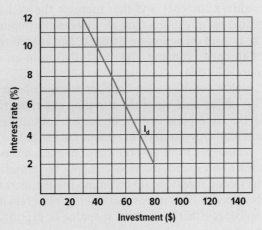

SECTION SUMMARY

a) Fiscal policy can influence the level of GDP through a decrease/increase in aggregate demand.

b) The strength of expansionary fiscal policy may be blunted by an increase in the prices level that will

   • reduce the value of people's real balances and thereby reduce consumption spending

   • reduce net exports

   • increase the transactions demand for money and thereby push interest rates up and investment spending down

c) Governments finance expansionary fiscal policy by borrowing, and this could also push up interest rates.

12.2 Monetary Policy in an Open Economy

LO2 Explain how the effectiveness of monetary policy is enhanced under a flexible exchange rate.

We learned in Chapter 9 that a central bank can expand or contract an economy's money supply and thereby push interest rates down or up. When, for example, the central bank buys T-bills from the public, whether from a corporation, bank, or individual, a swap takes place. A T-bill that was being held outside of the central bank (that is, was in circulation) moves to the central bank, and money that was held by the central bank moves to the general public and is then in circulation. This means the economy's money supply has expanded, and this additional money will push interest rates down. And, of course, the lower interest rates will stimulate additional investment spending which increases aggregate demand and the level of national income. This is expansionary monetary policy.

How does all this differ when looking at an open economy? Well, if the open economy has a flexible exchange rate, expansionary monetary policy will have an even larger effect on national income. This is because the lower interest rates will result in lower international demand for the Canadian dollar, and this will push the exchange rate lower. The lower exchange rate will stimulate exports and more exports means higher aggregate demand, and thus a larger increase in national income. This is why many economists consider the combination of monetary policy and flexible exchange rates a very potent policy weapon in the hands of the central bank.

Not only is expansionary monetary policy more effective in an open economy, but contractionary monetary policy also becomes more effective. Imagine a country that has been suffering high inflation rates and, as a result, its central bank decides to reduce the money supply in an attempt to combat it. The immediate effect will be to increase interest rates, which will in turn reduce investment spending and aggregate demand. But in addition to this, in an open economy the higher interest rate will attract foreign investment, which will increase the demand for the country's currency and thus increase the exchange rate. The higher exchange rate will lead to a reduction in exports (and an increase in imports), which will further reduce aggregate demand: the impact on aggregate demand, and therefore on the country's price level, is greatly increased in an open economy. Fighting inflation in an open, rather than a closed, economy is therefore more effective.

Now consider what happens when monetary policy is used in conjunction with fiscal policy. Our earlier analysis of the crowding out effect resulting from expansionary fiscal policy was based on the assumption that the higher level of income will push up interest rates, since the money supply was implicitly assumed to remain unchanged.

However, if the government applies expansionary fiscal policy and, at the same time, the central bank also expands the money supply, the crowding out effect could be neutralized. The increase in the money supply would accommodate the increased money demand that results from expansionary fiscal policy. This means that interest rates remain the same, and as a result, there will be no crowding out of either investment spending or exports. This makes fiscal policy more effective than when it is not supported by an expansion in the money supply. In fact, this is the type of policy that, as we saw in Chapter 9, the Bank of Canada presently uses. By targeting interest rates it automatically accommodates changes in the money demand by adjusting the money supply.

There is another way the two policies can be used in tandem, but it is certainly much more controversial.

Generally, a government finances expansionary fiscal policy and the resulting budget deficit through borrowing. A government borrows money by issuing new government bonds that are bought by banks, insurance companies, corporations, and the general public; money moves from the lenders to government. What the public might have spent is instead being spent by government, so there is no change in the money supply.

But very occasionally those bonds might be bought by the central bank rather than by the general public. Here, government, in a sense, lends to itself. This means that the money paid by the central bank *does* result in an increase in the money supply. Further, since the central bank is not a "spending agent," it does not in any sense reduce its own spending to compensate for the resulting increase in spending by government. This method of borrowing is called **monetizing the debt** and makes macroeconomic policy very powerful. It can also be highly inflationary, and for this reason it is seldom implemented by responsible governments.

ADDED DIMENSION

A Bold Proposal on Both Monetary and Fiscal Policy

It is now quite evident that the economic recovery following the 2008 crisis has been feeble. Government fiscal policy around the world has been either too weak or, in all too many cases, mis-directed. At the same time, rising income inequality has kept consumer spending anemic. In short, aggregate demand remains weak and is barely growing. The term "secular stagnation," coined by Larry Summers of Harvard University, has come into popular usage.

Many now argue that weak demand will be around for quite a while. Furthermore, Martin Wolf, a leading economic commentator with London's *Financial Times*, argues that the banking systems of developed economies are still a powder keg with insufficient capital and are likely to wreak havoc when they blow up.

So what might be done?

Martin calls for the replacement of the fractional reserve banking system with a system of "nar-row banking" in which bank deposits must be backed by government bonds. Furthermore, to boost and then sustain demand without relying on asset bubbles, he proposes a permanent "helicopter money" system whereby governments run budget deficits financed by the central bank that can fly in quickly and without the need of the slow—and often difficult to obtain—political process of legisla-tive approval. This is nothing more than monetizing the debt and if such action was taken by a government one would want to keep a sharp eye on the possibility of increases in inflation.

It is a straightforward and, to say the least, unusual solution.

TEST YOUR UNDERSTANDING

2. Given the graphs in question 1 for Newland, should its central bank increase or decrease the money supply to avoid crowding out? By how much?

SECTION SUMMARY

Monetary policy's effectiveness is enhanced when we take into account international financial flows. An increase in money supply reduces interest rates and this lowers the exchange rate. The result is a rise in both investment spending and exports. As well, using monetary policy to fight inflation is more effective in an open economy than in a closed economy.

12.3   The Phillips Curve

LO3 Explain the trade-off between unemployment and inflation levels implied by the Phillips curve.

The use of Keynesian fiscal and monetary policy to regulate aggregate demand in the twenty-five years following World War II was very successful, and, as a result, many people came to believe that serious macroeconomic trouble—especially of the magni-tude of the great depression of the 1930s—was a thing of the past. Throughout the 1950s and 1960s, there were only minor and brief exceptions to modest inflation, benign unemployment, and robust growth.

One glitch was somewhat troubling, however. It seemed that the twin goals of full employment and stable prices remained elusive. In 1958, British economist A.W. Phillips confirmed this with a time-series analysis of unemployment and inflation rates (actually, yearly changes in wage rates) for the British economy for the previous 100 years. He discovered that there were very few years of *both* low unemployment and low inflation rates. In fact, apparently when unemployment was low, inflation was above what was considered normal, and at another time, when unemployment was high, inflation rates were low. In other words, there appeared to be a trade-off between low unemployment and low inflation. Table 12.1 presents hypothetical data that illustrate this idea.

TABLE 12.1
The Trade-off Between Unemployment and Inflation

Unemployment Rate (%)	Inflation Rate (%)
4	12
6	8
8	5
10	3
12	2

The data collected for many other countries using various time periods confirmed that not only are low unemployment rates associated with high inflation and high unemployment with low inflation, but also the opportunity cost of trying to fully achieve either of the two goals becomes greater and greater as the respective rates fall. In other words, as Table 12.1 illustrates, to reduce unemployment by 2 percentage points when the economy is suffering 12 percent unemployment costs society only a 1-percentage-point increase in inflation—from 2 to 3 percent. But to reduce unemployment by a similar 2 percentage points when the economy is close to full employment, say from 6 percent to 4 percent, costs the country 4 percentage points in inflation as illustrated in Figure 12.2.

The relationship between unemployment and inflation, the **Phillips curve**, plots as a downward-sloping curve that shows a certain relationship between inflation and unemployment. As inflation rates fall, unemployment rates rise. Note that it does not plot as a straight line but as a parabola; lower inflation rates are associated with increasingly higher unemployment rates.

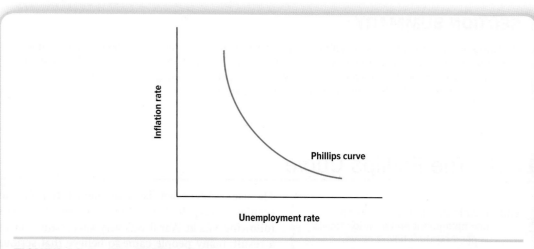

FIGURE 12.2   The Phillips Curve

The top of the curve illustrates the fact that high inflation rates are associated with low unemployment rates. As we move down the curve, lower inflation rates are matched with increasingly higher unemployment rates.

GREAT ECONOMISTS: A.W. PHILLIPS

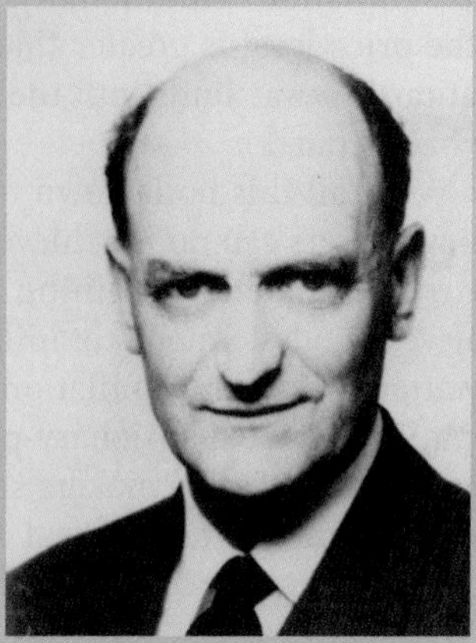

History collection 2016/ Alamy Stock Photo

A.W. (Bill) Phillips (1914–75) has been described as the "Indiana Jones" of economists. He grew up in an isolated part of New Zealand and became famous among his school friends as an inventor and tinkerer. Leaving secondary school during the height of the Great Depression, he went to Australia where he dabbled in gold mining and crocodile hunting and then on to China where he managed to survive on his own and learned the language. Japan's invasion of China caused him to flee across Russia to the London.

As war neared, Phillips joined the RAF where he was trained as a fighter pilot and sent to Singapore. Captured by the invading Japanese forces, he spent the next three and a half years as a prisoner of war during which time he engineered many ingenious devices—including a tiny water boiler so that he and his fellow prisoners could have their daily tea.

After the war, he returned to London and entered the London School of Economics. He secured a place on the faculty there (despite lacklustre academic performance as a graduate student) by building what amounted to a real-life model—using piping and hydraulic pumps—of the circular flow of income we saw in Chapter 3. Along the way he also built a computer that he used to analyze economic data and build simple economic models.

In 1958, he published his extensive, empirically based analysis of the relationship between inflation and unemployment, which came to be known as the *Phillips curve*. This etched his name in the history of economics. The curve was an idea based on data; thus, it opened the door to computer models, which drove the study of macroeconomics for the next seventy-plus years.

IN A NUTSHELL ...

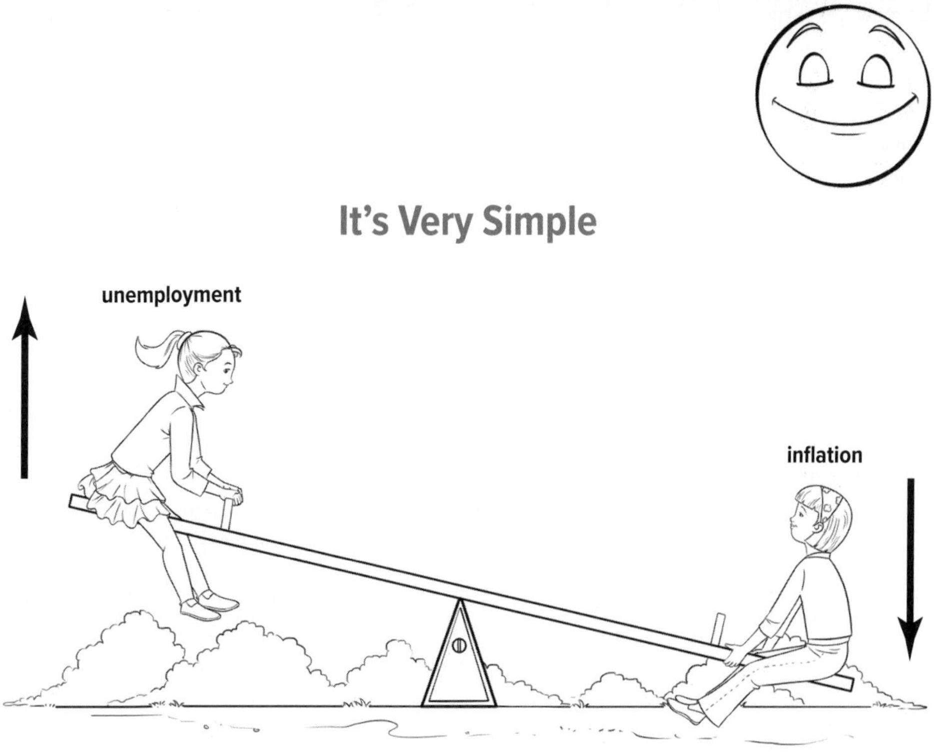

Although the idea looked like a breakthrough at the time, in hindsight the Phillips curve does nothing more than confirm the shape of the aggregate supply curve we introduced back in Chapter 5. You can validate this by picturing what would happen as aggregate demand increases and we move up on the AS curve. The result is, of course, higher GDP (lower unemployment) and higher prices (inflation). Additionally, as the economy moves closer to full-employment GDP, the increase in the price level is greater than the increase in GDP. Once people realized that the Phillips curve relationship was built into the aggregate supply curve, references to the Phillips curve faded into the background.

What all this boils down to, in terms of fiscal and monetary policy, is that apparently the best policy makers can do is achieve a delicate balance between full employment and stable prices without ever completely attaining both goals. For instance, they might be able to help the economy achieve a modest amount of inflation combined with a not-too-high level of unemployment. However, any attempt to reduce inflation further would likely provoke unacceptably high rates of unemployment. Similarly, expansionary policy designed to reduce unemployment would cause acceleration in inflation rates. Policy makers seem to be caught between a rock and a hard place. Nonetheless, this uneasy balance of using fiscal and monetary policy to maintain an acceptable level of employment and stable prices became standard doctrine for some time.

IT'S NEWS TO ME ...

Recently, the federal government announced plans to spend over $120 billion on new infrastructure projects over the next 12 years. To facilitate this massive effort the government will create a new infrastructure bank aimed at attracting private investment in major projects such as public transit, port facilities, airports and highways. The Prime Minister, and a cadre of cabinet ministers, met yesterday with major international and Canadian investment firms—including BlackRock and the Canadian Pension Plan Investment Board—in an effort to convince them to invest some of their billions in the country's infrastructure. Trudeau said that many of the large investors attending the meeting reported their eagerness to place some of their money in Canada which they see as an island of relative stability that is "looking very attractive" amid growing anti-globalisation sentiments around the world. The Liberals are hoping that the new infrastructure projects will stimulate economic growth across the country through increases in productivity and thereby generate higher levels of tax revenue in the future. The ultimate goal is to raise some $140 billion in private capital for the new investment bank which will be launched next year. Canadian firms, including the Canadian Pension Plan Investment Board, which manages CPP money for future retirees, have placed billions into airports, ports, hospitals, roads, railways and pipelines in Asia, Australia, Europe and the U.K. These investments are made in return for tolls and fees from users, something that would likely be replicated here in Canada if pension firms take the lead on building new projects. The Investment Board has produced impressive results over the years by growing the size of its fund to $280 billion in total investments, placing it among some of the largest such firms in the world.

Source: *Star Power Reporting*, November 2016.

I. Which of the following best describes the type of policy discussion in this article?

a) monetary policy
b) fiscal policy
c) exchange rate policy
d) trade policy

II. Which of the following best describes the effect of introducing user fees and tolls to pay for this private investment spending?

a) It has no financial effect on any Canadian consumer.
b) It has no financial effect on those Canadian consumers who do not use the newly built infrastructure.
c) It has the exact same financial effect as raising taxes to pay for the same level of investment made directly by governments.
d) None of the above.

TEST YOUR UNDERSTANDING

3. The following data are for the very volatile economy of Mobile. Given that the labour force remained a constant 320 million, calculate the unemployment and inflation rates for each of the years 2013–17. From the data collected, draw a Phillips curve.

Year	Price Index	Unemployment (in millions)
2012	120	—
2013	122.4	38.4
2014	126.1	25.6
2015	133.7	19.2
2016	147.1	14.4
2017	170.6	9.6

SECTION SUMMARY

Fiscal and monetary policy can push unemployment or inflation down by either increasing or decreasing aggregate demand. However, since it cannot push aggregate demand both ways at the same time, lower unemployment is usually associated with higher inflation and vice versa. This relationship between unemployment and inflation is illustrated by the Phillips curve.

12.4   The Argument of the Supply-Siders

LO4   Describe what is meant by the term *supply-side economics*.

In the fall of 1973, OPEC (Organization of the Petroleum Exporting Countries)—which at the time controlled a very large percentage of the world's oil exports—imposed dramatic increases in the price of oil on the world. Within two years, the results of this shock to the world's economic systems included rising levels of both unemployment and inflation, a state of affairs that came to be known as **stagflation**. The prevailing macroeconomic theory of the day was badly shaken, since the standard Keynesian analysis at the time indicated that an economy might suffer high unemployment rates *or* high inflation rates, but not both at the same time. The prolonged period of increases in both was a serious blow to the orthodox view and Phillips curve analysis seemed useless. This is because the Phillips curve showed that there were no occasions in which Britain had been able to attain the twin goals of full employment and low inflation. However, it also showed that there were no years in which Britain had experienced *both* high unemployment and high rates of inflation. Now countries around the world were, for the first time in their histories, suffering from the "twin evils." Economists began to scramble for explanations and this laid the groundwork for the rise of a new school of thought—supply-side economics.

It eventually became clear that the demand-orientated analysis of the Keynesian view was simply not able to explain the events that followed the dramatic price increase in the most important resource in our economy—oil. The Keynesian view implicitly assumed that aggregate supply always adjusted to changes in aggregate demand, and, furthermore, was not itself an active ingredient. They believed that the factors that could change aggregate supply, like changes in the growth of capital stock, an expansion in the labour force, and changes in technology, were slow to take effect. In this view there was only one aggregate supply curve, and it was horizontal until the full-employment level of income was reached, when it became vertical—aggregate supply played a passive role in orthodox Keynesian analysis. After all, firms would never produce unless there was a demand for their products. If demand increased, firms would meet the increased demand by producing more; if demand decreased, firms would react by producing less. What more needed to be said about supply?

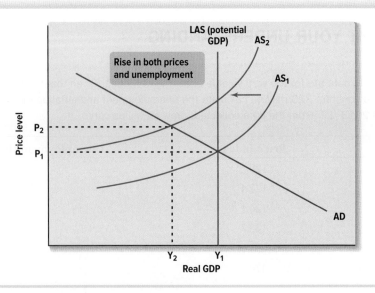

FIGURE 12.3   The Cause of Stagflation

An increase in the price of imported resources (such as oil in 1973) will decrease aggregate supply, causing it to shift left as seen by AS_1 to AS_2. The result will be a higher price level, P_1 to P_2, and a lower level of real GDP, Y_1 to Y_2.

The supply-side economists, however, took a contrary view. They believed that certain factors—and a change in the price of resources like oil was one—did have an immediate, short-run impact on the economy. In fact, as **Figure 12.3** illustrates, the only change that could cause both the price level to rise (from P_1 to P_2) and GDP to fall (from Y_1 to Y_2) was a decrease in aggregate supply. Furthermore, the only cure for stagflation would be a reversal of this change—that is, an increase in aggregate supply.

However, both governments and mainstream (Keynesian) economists clung to the idea that only changes in aggregate demand caused swings in GDP, inflation, and unemployment. This meant they were at first unable to correctly diagnose the problem of stagflation and, worse, offered the wrong sort of remedies. This can be seen in **Figure 12.4**.

Neither expansionary fiscal policy nor expansionary monetary policy is able to cure the simultaneous problems of high unemployment and inflation. Stimulation policies will increase aggregate demand, as shown by the rightward shift in the aggregate demand curve, from AD_1 to AD_2 in **Figure 12.4**. This will increase real GDP and reduce unemployment. Unfortunately, it will also push up prices, from P_1 to P_2.

Contractionary fiscal or monetary policy is no better. It will cause a decrease in aggregate demand, from AD_1 to AD_3, which will reduce prices from P_1 to P_3 thus curing inflation. However, it comes at the cost of an increase in unemployment, since GDP will fall.

In fact, the only way to boost production and employment, and reduce prices at the same time, is through policies designed to increase (short-run) aggregate supply. We learned in Chapter 5 that one of the fundamental ways to do this is through the economy achieving an increase in productivity.

The failure of aggregate-demand policies to cure stagflation meant the emerging supply-side economists called for a totally new direction in economic policy. This drive quickly became political when they started to argue that the large government budgets that were the legacy of active Keynesian management of aggregate demand had, in the long run, stifled business confidence, and thus private investment, and harmed international competitiveness.

It did not take long to see that these new supply-siders were reviving the early twentieth-century neoclassic view that aggregate supply was not simply a passive element responding to changes in aggregate demand, but was itself a prime mover of economic activity. The supply-siders' view of the stagflation of the 1970s was straightforward and transparent. While it had been triggered by the dramatic increases in the price of oil, it was rooted in sluggish rates of productivity growth over a period of decades. They believed that the cure was equally straightforward: increase aggregate supply. This is shown in **Figure 12.5**.

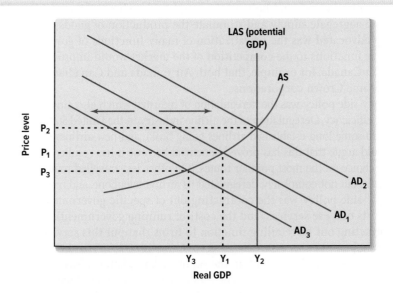

FIGURE 12.4   Aggregate Demand and Stagflation

The economy is in a stagflationary situation with a high price level, P_1 (inflation), and a low level of real GDP, Y_1 (high unemployment). Expansionary policy, either fiscal or monetary, will shift the aggregate demand curve from AD_1 to AD_2. The result will be a higher level of GDP, Y_2, but unfortunately this will cause even higher prices, P_2. Alternatively, government could use contractionary policy to curb inflation. This will result in a leftward shift in aggregate demand from the current AD_1 to AD_3. This will cut prices to P_3, but with the unfortunate result of reducing real GDP to Y_3, causing even higher unemployment.

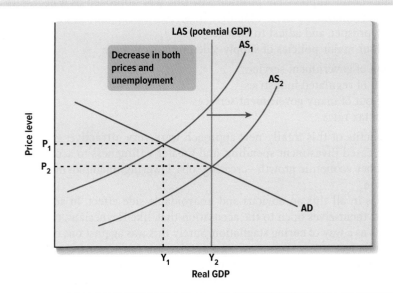

FIGURE 12.5   Increasing Aggregate Supply to Fight Stagflation

Assume that the economy is at a price level of P_1 and a GDP level of Y_1. An increase in aggregate supply will shift the aggregate supply curve from AS_1 to AS_2. The result will be a lower price level, P_2, as well as a higher level of GDP, Y_2, the latter implying a lower unemployment rate.

An increase in aggregate supply shifts the aggregate supply curve from AS_1 to AS_2. This results in a reduction in the price level, from P_1 to P_2, *and* an increase in GDP from Y_1 to Y_2. The result is lower inflation and reduced unemployment.

Let us now turn to the nuts and bolts of the supply-side school of thought by asking what policies might increase aggregate supply and stimulate the production of goods and services. One of the first policies they advocated was the privatization of many functions of government; it was thought that exposing these functions to the competition of the market would improve their efficiency. It was during this time, in Canada, for example, that both Air Canada and Canadian National Railway were privatized and became Crown corporations.

A second supply-side policy was the deregulation of industry, which also aimed to use the competitive market to increase efficiency. Deregulation of the airline industry in the United States is a dramatic example of this; it resulted in some long-established airlines going broke and new airlines successfully entering the industry. Most would argue that this has proved beneficial because it has resulted in lower airfares and increased consumer choice on the most popular routes. (On other, less-travelled routes, higher fares resulted.) Canada also partially, but not completely, deregulated its airline, telephone, and trucking industries.

A third supply-side policy was the contracting-out of specific government services in the name of reducing the costs of these services (and the costs of running government). An example of this was Canada Post contracting out its retailing function to firms that put this service into local drugstores and convenience shops.

The fourth and most significant plank in the supply-siders' platform was the cutting of tax rates on business profits and on individual incomes. The rationale was to increase incentives for people to work more, save more, and invest more. The result, it was believed, would lead to an increase in aggregate supply. If income tax rates were cut, many workers would work longer hours, since they believed that high marginal tax rates tend to deter people from working long hours. Additionally, many unemployed workers would seek employment with more enthusiasm, while some homemakers and retired people would be tempted to return to the labour force. The argument was made that these results would be enhanced if the social safety net of welfare payments, unemployment coverage, and lifetime disability income were restructured to aid only those in real need, ceasing to provide what was seen by some as an easy income for those who did not deserve it. Furthermore, total savings would increase, since a cut in personal taxes would increase disposable income. Likewise, a cut in corporate taxes would provide increased profits for firms that would then plough them back into the business in the form of new investment.

In short, advocates of the supply-side position saw this new approach as a necessary action to undo forty years of interventionist polices that, they believed, had sapped the economy of its vigour and its ability to grow, prosper, and adjust to change.

In summary, the four major policies of supply-side proponents were

- the privatization of government services
- the deregulation of regulated industries
- the contracting-out of many government services
- the reduction of tax rates

The promised benefits of this totally new approach were very attractive: greater competition, more work effort, increased investment spending, and greater willingness to accept risk. The result was believed to be higher economic growth—creating jobs, lowering unemployment, increasing output, and easing inflation.

However, there was in all this an obvious and unavoidable side effect. In advocating lower tax rates, supply-siders left themselves open to the accusation that, like Keynesians, they were proposing big government deficits as a way of curing stagflation. Surely this was against one of their fundamental principles: a balanced budget.

It was at this point (the late 1970s) that California economist Arthur Laffer came forward with the intriguing argument that a cut in tax rates in North America rather than decreasing government's tax revenues would, in fact, *increase* them.

The Laffer Curve

The essentials of Laffer's argument are contained in **Figure 12.6**. The curve, the **Laffer curve**, shows the amount of tax revenue received by government at various tax rates.

With a zero tax rate, tax revenue would, of course, be zero. At the other extreme, with a tax rate of 100 percent, presumably no one would work and tax revenue would again be zero. Between these extremes, there is a particular relationship between the tax rate and tax revenue. Supply-siders argued that, during the postwar years of Keynesian interventionism, tax rates had been pushed higher and higher so that

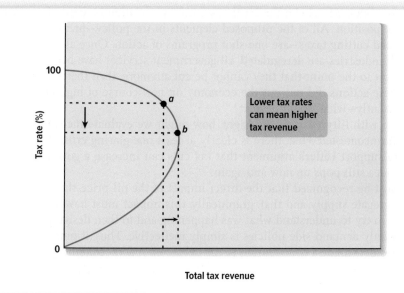

FIGURE 12.6   The Laffer Curve

If the economy is at point *a* on the Laffer curve, a drop in tax rates will cause an increase in tax revenues, pushing the economy to position *b*.

many countries found themselves at a point represented by *a* in **Figure 12.6**. What was needed, argued Laffer, was a massive cut in tax rates that would increase incentives so that production, and therefore income, would increase so much that tax revenues would actually go up. This result is indicated by a movement from point *a* to *b* on the Laffer curve. So, although tax rates are lower, tax revenues are higher.

If Laffer's argument was correct, a government could, figuratively speaking, have its cake and eat it, too. Appropriate tax cuts could increase work, savings, and investment, and slash both unemployment and inflation. On top of this, government's budget deficit would also be reduced. It sounded persuasive and the promised results were intoxicating. (Knowledge of this curve, legend has it, first bubbled up into social consciousness as a result of Laffer drawing it on a paper napkin in a Hollywood restaurant for President-elect Ronald Reagan.)

Unfortunately—but perhaps predictably—the debate that started out mostly about economic policy slopped over into a debate about social policy generally, as many advocates of the new supply-side argument also pushed vigorously for massive cuts to social programs (while leaving the military budget untouched) and for curtailing the power of trade unions (in the name of increased competition in the labour markets). Needless to say, this led to a backlash, both inside and outside of the economics profession. This backlash quickly became intensely political. Within the discipline of economics the dispute centred on two aspects of the supply-side philosophy.

First, the stimulative effect of tax cuts was questioned. A number of economists doubted that tax cuts would indeed increase the amount of work effort in the economy. Many of them criticized the supply-side argument on the grounds that a tax cut was likely to have a bigger impact on spending than on work effort and productivity. The average person in receipt of a higher disposable income is as likely to choose more leisure time as work more hours to obtain an even bigger income. In economic terms, this means that the substitution effect of a pay raise will likely exceed the income effect of such an increase. Similarly, firms with higher after-tax profits are just as likely to pay higher dividends to shareholders and reward corporate executives with big bonuses as they are to reinvest the increased earnings in their companies. In short, the criticism of many economists was not that tax cuts do not provide incentives to people, but that the effect on spending and aggregate demand will be greater than the effect on the supply side. If these criticisms were correct, the heart of the supply-side argument would be severely compromised. It would mean that aggregate demand would rise more than aggregate supply, and not only would GDP increase but so would the price level.

The second criticism was a head-on challenge of Laffer's argument that tax cuts would increase tax revenues. More and more economists rose to say that they simply rejected this proposition out of hand. They argued that Laffer had provided no empirical evidence of his contention because there was none.

Finally, there is one more obvious point that we need to mention here in reference to the thrust of the supply-side position. All of the proposed elements in the policy—privatization, deregulation, contracting out, and cutting taxes—are one-shot programs of action. Once all government functions are privatized, all industries are deregulated, all government services have been contracted out, and taxes have been cut to the point that they cannot be cut anymore, then there is no more powder in the cannon. If these actions did not put the economy on new course of high employment and low inflation—permanently—what would be next?

Looking back, with fifty years of hindsight, how might we evaluate the supply-side argument? Two points seem uncontested. First, there is clearly at least one glaring error. There is still no concrete evidence to support Laffer's argument that tax cuts can increase a government's tax revenue. Despite this, the idea still pops up now and again.

Second, it must be recognized that the direct impact of the oil price shocks of the 1970s must have been on aggregate supply and that, graphically, this impact must have been a shift of the AS curve to the left. To try to understand what was happening and to then design polices to counteract the effects using only demand-side policies is simply ineffective. Thus, it must be said that, on this point, the supply-siders made a contribution to the debate on macroeconomic policy.

 TEST YOUR UNDERSTANDING

4. Shown here are several different average tax rates (ATR) associated with various levels of GDP. Calculate the total tax revenue at each level of GDP, and indicate the tax rate that would maximize government's tax revenue.

ATR	GDP	Tax Revenue
0.30	$2000	
0.35	1900	
0.40	1700	
0.45	1500	
0.50	1300	
0.55	1100	

5. Supply-side economists say that a cut in tax rates will lead to an increase in real GDP. Keynesians agree with this, but for different reasons. In what ways do they differ?

SECTION SUMMARY

a) Traditional fiscal and monetary policy is aimed at the level of aggregate demand. The supply-side school of thought argues that the phenomenon of stagflation in the 1970s highlighted the need to consider policies aimed at aggregate supply, as well. These policies include

- privatization of government services
- deregulation of private industry
- contracting-out of government services
- the reduction of tax rates

b) A concern of supply-siders was that reducing tax rates by lowering government tax revenues would cause budget deficits. Economist Arthur Laffer suggested that a lowering of tax rates would actually increase tax revenues because that would increase incentives. His ideas are encompassed in the Laffer curve.

c) The ideas of supply-siders were challenged because critics suggested that

- the amount of work and investment would not increase; only spending would rise
- contrary to Laffer's views, tax cuts would not increase tax revenues
- supply-siders' policies can only be implemented once; if they fail, there are no alternatives

12.5   Fixed Versus Flexible Exchange Rates

LO5 Show that Canada has been successful in maintaining the internal but not the external value of the Canadian dollar and why some people call for a fixed exchange rate.

We saw in Chapter 9 that over the past thirty years or so the Bank of Canada has embarked on a new approach to monetary policy with its anti-inflationary program. Its stated goal is now to "preserve the internal and external value of the currency." Specifically, the Bank operates a target range for inflation of between 1 percent and 3 percent per year.

The success of the Bank in staying within this range over the decades has been remarkable. Inflation rates have stayed under 3 percent every year between 1992 and 2016. This is in stark contrast to the inflationary and turbulent decades that preceded the early 1990s. In addition, unemployment in Canada was relatively low and the growth of GDP was among the best in of the G8 nations until the financial crisis of 2008.

However, as we look back over this period, we note that the stated intent of the Bank of Canada's monetary policy was to preserve not just the internal value (stable prices) but also the *external* value of the Canadian currency (the exchange rate) as well as internal inflation. So what did happen to the Canadian–U.S. dollar exchange rate during this twenty-five-year period? In the first half of the period, the Canadian dollar dropped from US$0.85 to US$0.64. In the second half it rose from that all-time low to over par ($1.00). This can hardly be called "preserving the external value" of the Canadian currency. The fluctuations are illustrated in Figure 12.7.

It would seem that the experience of the past twenty-five years suggests Canada can enjoy low inflation and robust growth, and even low interest rates, but not in combination with steady, predictable exchange rates. In fact, the Canadian exchange rate has gone through rather dramatic swings.

There are advantages to a flexible exchange rate. Foremost is its tendency to stabilize fluctuations in trade. In other words, if the demand for Canadian products is falling, it will lead to a fall in the Canadian dollar, which in turn makes Canadian products cheaper for foreign buyers: the lower Canadian dollar cushions what otherwise might have been a more damaging fall in exports. However, as we saw in Chapter 11, there are a number of disadvantages associated with flexible exchange rates, especially a rate that, like Canada's, has fluctuated so wildly over the last two decades. This has led a number of economists to propose that a small country (economically speaking), such as Canada, would do better to adopt a fixed exchange system, with the Canadian dollar fixed to that of its largest trading partner, the United States.

Fixing Canada's exchange rate to the U.S. dollar would essentially let American monetary conditions set Canadian interest rates and would give Canada a long-term inflation rate equal to that in the United States. However, those who advocate a fixed exchange rate argue that since the American

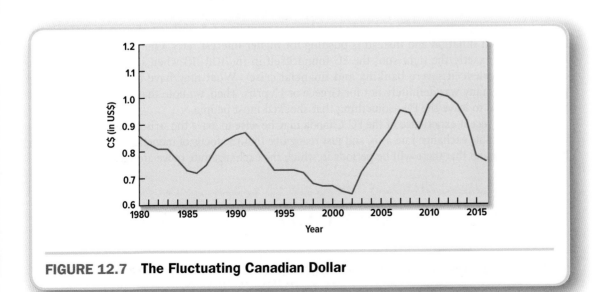

FIGURE 12.7   The Fluctuating Canadian Dollar

business cycle drives the Canadian business cycle anyway, Canadian monetary independence is in fact often overstated in importance and elusive.

And what would be the advantage of a fixed exchange rate? Again, as we saw in Chapter 11, it would increase certainty and thus boost trade between the nations. It would also lead to macroeconomic stability and encourage investment in plants and equipment, and in human capital. Such investment has been undermined by large swings in the Canada–U.S. exchange rate. For example, following the 12–14 percent fall in the exchange rate in 1998, many mostly young, highly skilled Canadians migrated to the United States, where wages, measured in U.S. dollars, were much higher. If these people do not return to Canada, it will prove a serious loss to the country over the next forty years.

There is a further advantage to a fixed exchange rate: it would make fiscal policy far more powerful. This is because with both interest rates and exchange rates fixed, there would be no crowding out of either investment or net exports, so expansionary fiscal policy would not be dampened down.

An alternative to a fixed exchange rate is to enter a common currency union. This means that instead of fixing the value of the Canadian dollar to that of the U.S. dollar (or indeed totally adopting the U.S. dollar as a few have suggested), Canada, the United States, and possibly some Latin American countries would adopt a common currency. This is what the majority of European countries did starting in 1999 with the introduction of the euro. Over a dozen local currencies were phased out when the euro was adopted. Today, 327 million Europeans in 17 countries use it daily, and a couple of dozen smaller countries have fixed their currency value to the euro. And what has changed over the fifteen-plus years of use in these countries? The list of benefits in terms of growth and employment was impressive—until the financial crisis of 2008.

The reasons for the initial impressive results are as follows. First, corporate and government bonds began selling at lower interest rates—even in the peripheral countries of south Europe—because of the credible claim that the European Central Bank would keep inflation low. (It is interesting to note that this bank has the preservation of the internal value of the currency as its sole goal and makes no attempt to establish a target range for the euro against other currencies.) Second, a common currency (or a fixed exchange rate) removes the uncertainty of doing business within the whole community and lowers the transactions cost of engaging in economic exchange or investment. Third, the areas within the European community that were depressed and lagging now have greater access to credit. As a result, the growth rate in these areas has increased. Fourth, the enlarged area of the common currency allows for greater specialization in banking that better fits the varied needs of business. Fifth, in the first few years of the Euro's experience, the value of trade within the community went up 5 to 10 percent, physical investment was up 5 percent, and foreign portfolio investment was up 20 percent.

Against that, it should be added that with a common currency union such as the European Union, interest rates, and indeed monetary policy, is determined by a central bank, the European Central Bank, and not by individual member countries. This means a lack of autonomy for those countries. It also has serious implications if one member country, such as Greece or Portugal or Spain, is suffering a serious recession and wants interest rates lowered while another, such as Germany, is worried about inflation and instead is pushing for higher interest rates. One size does not always fit all. This is exactly the tight spot the EU found itself in in 2011–13 when several of the smaller countries experienced severe banking and financial crises. What may have been good monetary policy for Germany was definitely not for Greece or Cyprus. Then, we note that, in 2016, the United Kingdom voted to leave the EU—something that shocked most people.

Given the recent experience of the EU, Canada may be wise to leave the structure of monetary policy and the flexible exchange rate as is, and just recognize that the focus of monetary policy will always be on inflation and that there will be periods in which the exchange rate move around quite a bit.

 TEST YOUR UNDERSTANDING

6. Name two major benefits of fixed exchange rates.

SECTION SUMMARY

a) In the years following stagflation, monetary policy makers shifted their goal to preserving the internal and external value of the currency, that is, maintaining internal price stability and a stable exchange rate. Canada was successful in curbing inflation; however, the exchange rate fluctuated greatly. Some suggested the introduction of a fixed exchange rate for Canada, which makes fiscal policy more effective because there is no crowding out of exports.

There are many benefits for countries entering a common currency union:

- Corporate and government bonds are sold at a lower interest rate.
- Uncertainty is reduced and transaction costs are lowered.
- Depressed areas have easier access to credit.
- It increases specialization in banking.
- It increases the volume of trade.

b) The argument against a common currency union is that member countries give up autonomy and an independent monetary policy.

12.6 The Fear of Deflation

> **LO6** Explain why economists are concerned about the possibility of deflation.

Stagflation was a new economic phenomenon when it struck most major economies in the mid-1970s. Another worrisome economic occurrence that some think North America could experience is **deflation**. Apart from a single year in the early 1950s, Canada has not suffered from falling prices since the early years of the Great Depression.

But why should deflation be regarded as a problem? After all, wouldn't everyone like lower prices? Part of the reason is the result of events in Japan in the 1990s. In that country, both the real estate market and the stock market were rocked by bubble bursts, and the Japanese policy stimulus proved inadequate. The result was twenty years of low growth that fluctuated between −4 and +2 percent along with persistent deflation. There is the worry that the United States (and by extension Canada) might experience the same fate.

Deflation and very sluggish growth go together. There are two primary reasons for this. The first is that deflation causes a reduction in both consumer and investment spending because when prices are falling, people sometimes put off purchases in order to take advantage of lower prices in the future, reducing aggregate demand and lowering economic growth. The second reason is the effects of deflation on the real interest rate. In a situation in which the inflation rate is 2 percent, a nominal rate of 6 percent is needed to ensure a real rate of 4 percent, which, we will assume, is needed to satisfy both lenders and borrowers. But what if prices instead are falling at a rate of 4 percent? Then those who have money to lend can gain a real rate of interest of 4 percent by doing nothing more than putting their money in a steel box under the bed. Therefore, they will not be willing to lend. Once this situation grips an economy, short-term interest rates will drop to zero, but they can go no lower. There is no such thing as a negative nominal interest rate in the credit market, and nothing can be done to correct this situation. Deflation freezes credit markets, and this has a depressing effect on real output.

Figure 12.8 shows Japan's experience since 1990. Deflation first hit the country in 1995. Over the next twenty years, Japan experienced an annual average drop in prices of just over 1 percent so that over the whole period 1995–2015 prices dropped by 20 percent. Along with this came a drop in its growth rate. After being one of the world's fastest-growing economies in the 1970s and 1980s, Japan saw its growth rate drop to 1.5 percent in the 1990s and to an even lower 0.5 percent in the 2000s.

So what causes deflation? Our understanding of basic markets tells us that the price level will fall if either aggregate demand falls or aggregate supply increases. In a modern, dynamic economy, both are likely to be changing at the same time; but if demand fails to keep pace with supply, the result is deflation. This is what happened in many economies, including the United States and Canada, at the beginning of the Great Depression of the 1930s. The major cause then was the sudden collapse

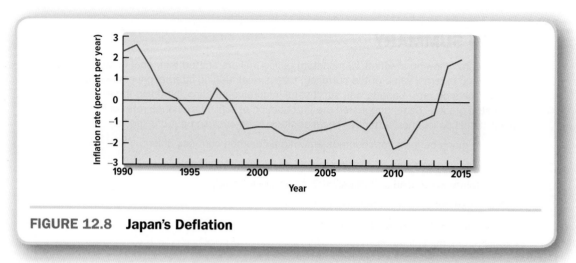

FIGURE 12.8   Japan's Deflation

of stock prices on Wall Street in 1929, bringing with it a major loss of consumer and business confidence. Similarly in the case of Japan, the major contributor initially was the bursting of the stock and land prices bubble that had been fuelled by easy bank loans. The problem was further exacerbated by the failure of its central bank to increase its money supply sufficiently to keep pace with the growth in productivity resulting from advances in technology. So demand was unable to keep pace with supply. The result: deflation.

However, some suggest that the problems of deflation—especially with rates below 5 percent—are often overstated. It is certainly likely that if deflation were 20 percent a year, many consumers and firms would delay their purchases. After all, a 20 percent saving is a significant amount. But are buyers really going to wait a year to buy products if the deflation rate is a mere 2 percent per year? More probably, at low rates of deflation (1 or 2 percent), especially if the rate is stable, businesses (including banks) and consumers will build these rates into their expectations. After all, buyers and sellers have no difficulty doing this with inflation rates of 1 or 2 percent.

Although most people have had less experience of deflation than they have of inflation and consequently have little understanding or fear of its consequences, it should be clear from the above that the problems it presents are both insidious and difficult to cure.

  TEST YOUR UNDERSTANDING

7. What is the difference between stagflation and deflation? What is similar under both of these circumstances?

SECTION SUMMARY

a) Some economists feared that the financial crisis of 2008–10 set the stage for the economy to slip into a period of prolonged deflation and that North America and Europe might suffer the same fate as Japan who suffered though two decades of deflation and the sluggish economic growth that is associated with deflation.

b) Deflation is caused when aggregate demand fails to keep pace with increases in aggregate supply. This often occurs when a drop in confidence follows the bursting of a "speculative bubble."

c) Deflation causes a drop in economic growth because

   • consumption and investment spending are reduced because people postpone spending decisions hoping for lower future prices

   • credit markets become less effective because a negative nominal interest rate is required to encourage savings and investment; a negative interest rate is impossible

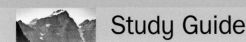

Study Guide

Review

WHAT'S THE BIG IDEA?

This chapter revisits fiscal and monetary policy, because when we initially looked at fiscal policy in Chapter 7 we ignored the impact on the money market and how the interest rate might affect things. Furthermore, in both that chapter and Chapter 9's look at monetary policy we ignored international markets and how the exchange rate might affect things. This chapter is designed to fill in these omissions.

First, fiscal policy is less effective when we consider how it impacts the money market. Expansionary policy, for example, which by increasing government spending or reducing taxes increases GDP, will also cause the price level to rise and in doing so increase the demand for money. This in turn will push up interest rates and cause a drop in investment spending. This is referred to as the *crowding out effect*. When we also take into consideration the fact that the higher interest rate also attracts foreign funds into the country, pushing up the exchange rate, this effect gets bigger—because the higher exchange rate will make exports more expensive and imports cheaper thus reducing net exports.

Things are different for monetary policy in an open economy. In fact, it becomes far more effective. This is because expansionary monetary policy pushes down interest rates, encouraging more investment. But those lower interest rates also tend to discourage foreign investment in the country. This will cause a drop in demand for the Canadian dollar, leading to a fall in the exchange rate. A lower Canadian dollar will make Canadian exports more attractive (and foreign products more expensive), causing an increase in net exports.

In summary: expansionary fiscal policy causes both the interest rate and the exchange rate to rise, which lowers both investment and net exports; expansionary monetary policy, on the other hand, lowers both the interest rate and the exchange rate, causing a rise in investment and net exports.

NEW GLOSSARY TERMS

deflation   monetizing the debt   stagflation
Laffer curve   Phillips curve

Comprehensive Problem

(LO 1, 2, 3)   Suppose that the economy of Basel, as shown below, was in equilibrium in 2015. (Calculate answers, where necessary, to one decimal place.)

Questions

In 2016, Basel's government uses expansionary policy and is able to increase AD by $400.
a) Draw AD_2 on **Figure** 12.9.

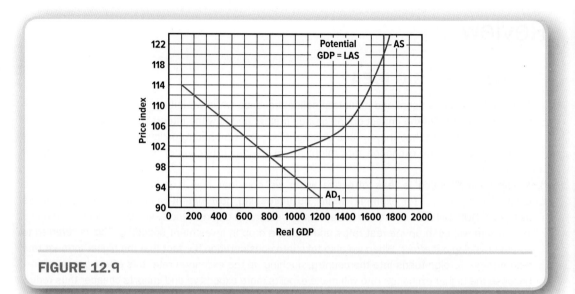

FIGURE 12.9

b) Suppose that the natural rate of unemployment in Basel is 6 percent and cyclical unemployment increases by 1 percentage point for each $100 of recessionary gap. Complete **Table** 12.2A.

TABLE 12.2A

Year	Price Index	Annual Inflation Rate (%)	Recessionary Gap ($)	Unemployment Rate (%)
2016	_____	_____	_____	_____

Answers

a) See the following figure:

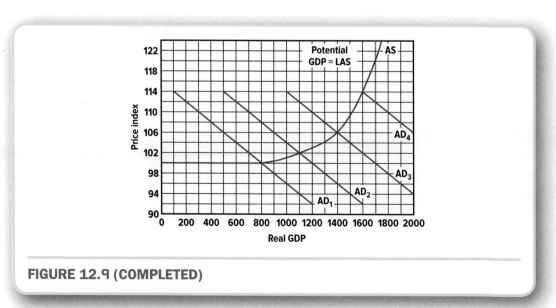

FIGURE 12.9 (COMPLETED)

b) See the following table:

TABLE 12.2A (COMPLETED)

Year	Price Index	Annual Inflation Rate (%)	Recessionary Gap ($)	Unemployment Rate (%)
2016	102	2%	$600	12%

The price index is where AD_2 intersects AS. Inflation = $(102 - 100)/100 \times 100$ = 2%. Cyclical unemployment = $600/100$ = 6%. Total unemployment = natural rate + cyclical unemployment = 6% + 6% = 12%.

Questions

In 2017, Basel's government uses more expansionary policy and is able to increase AD by a further $500.

c) Draw AD_3 on Figure 12.9.
d) Now complete Table 12.2B.

TABLE 12.2B

Year	Price Index	Annual Inflation Rate (%)	Recessionary Gap ($)	Unemployment Rate (%)
2017	_____	_____	_____	_____

Answers

c) See Figure 12.9 (Completed).
d) See the following table:

TABLE 12.2B (COMPLETED)

Year	Price Index	Annual Inflation Rate (%)	Recessionary Gap ($)	Unemployment Rate (%)
2017	106	3.9%	$300	9%

The price index is where AD_3 intersects AS. Inflation = $(106 - 102)/100 \times 100$ = 3.9%. Cyclical unemployment = $300/100$ = 3%. Total unemployment = natural rate + cyclical unemployment = 6% + 3% = 9%.

Questions

Finally, in 2018 Basel's government uses even more expansionary policy and is able to increase AD by a further $600.

e) Draw AD_4 on Figure 12.9.
f) Complete Table 12.2C.

TABLE 12.2C

Year	Price Index	Annual Inflation Rate (%)	Recessionary Gap ($)	Unemployment Rate (%)
2018	_____	_____	_____	_____

g) From the data you have now gathered for 2016, 2017, and 2018, draw a Phillips curve for Basel on
   Figure 12.10.

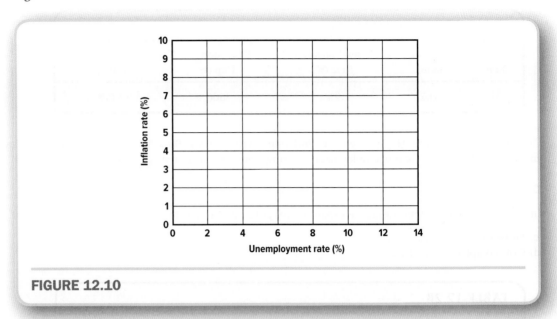

FIGURE 12.10

Answers

e) See **Figure 12.9 (Completed)**.

f) See the following table:

TABLE 12.2C (COMPLETED)

Year	Price Index	Annual Inflation Rate (%)	Recessionary Gap ($)	Unemployment Rate (%)
2018	114	7.5%	$100	1%

The price index is where AD_4 intersects AS. Inflation = $(114 - 106)/106 \times 100 = 7.5\%$. Cyclical unemployment = $100/100 = 1\%$. Total unemployment = natural rate + cyclical unemployment = $6\% + 1\% = 7\%$.

g) See the following figure:

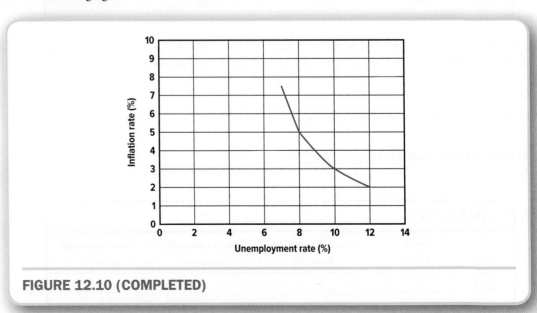

FIGURE 12.10 (COMPLETED)

Study Problems

Find answers on the McGraw-Hill online resource.

Basic (Problems 1–3)

1. **(LO 1)** In the queendom of Frankland, GDP is currently $500 million. Production in Frankland is un-affected by changes in tax rates until the rate hits 35 percent. Thereafter, for each 5 percent increase in the tax rate, GDP drops by $40 million.

   a) Complete Table 12.3 for the government of Frankland.

TABLE 12.3

%	GDP	Tax Revenue
0	$500	_____
5	_____	_____
10	_____	_____
15	_____	_____
20	_____	_____
25	_____	_____
30	_____	_____
35	_____	_____
40	_____	_____
45	_____	_____
50	_____	_____
55	_____	_____
60	_____	_____
65	_____	_____
70	_____	_____

   b) In Figure 12.11, graph Frankland's tax revenue curve.

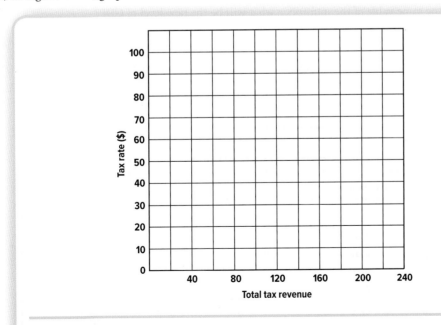

FIGURE 12.11

c) At what tax rate will the tax revenue be maximized? What will be the amount of tax revenue?
Percentage tax rate: _____ Tax revenue: $_____

2. **(LO 2)** The nominal GDP of Etruria is $1500 billion. Next year, the growth of nominal GDP is expected to be 2.4 percent. If the transactions demand in Etruria is 10 percent of nominal GDP, by how much must the money supply be increased in order to avoid crowding out? _____

3. **(LO 1, 2)** Suppose that GDP in Newland is $600 billion and government increases spending by $20 billion.
   a) If the multiplier equals 4, what is the new level of GDP? _____
   b) Suppose that as a result of the increase in GDP the price level in Newland also rises, causing the demand for money to increase by $60 billion. Show the new money demand, labelled MD_2, in Figure 12.12A.

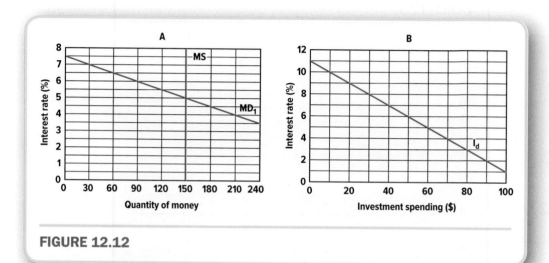

FIGURE 12.12

c) What will be the new interest rate? _____
d) Given Figure 12.12B showing the investment demand, by how much will investment spending change?

   (Increase/decrease) _____
   in investment of $_____
e) Given the same value of the multiplier, what will be the new level of GDP? _____

Intermediate (Problems 4–8)

4. **(LO 1, 3)** The data in Table 12.4 show Haydn's aggregate demand and aggregate supply. In this economy, the natural rate of unemployment is 6 percent, and for each $10 of recessionary gap, cyclical unemployment is 1 percent.

TABLE 12.4

Price Index	Aggregate Quantity Demanded	Aggregate Quantity Demanded 2	Aggregate Quantity Supplied
110	860	_____	740
115	840	_____	760
120	820	_____	780
125	800	_____	800
130	780	_____	820
135	760	_____	840
140	740	_____	860

Suppose the economy of Haydn is in equilibrium and experiencing a recessionary gap of $60 and inflation of 1 percent.
a) What are the price index, equilibrium GDP, potential GDP, and unemployment rate?
   Price index: _____
   Equilibrium GDP: _____
   Potential GDP: _____
   Unemployment rate: _____
b) In the following year, AD increases by 40. Complete the new demand column in Table 12.4.
c) What are the new unemployment and inflation rates?
   Unemployment rate: _____
   Inflation rate: _____
d) Sketch a Phillips curve from your answers to (a) and (b) in Figure 12.13.

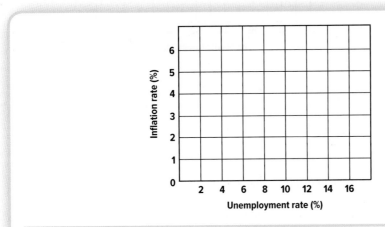

FIGURE 12.13

5. **(LO 2)**
   a) Suppose that GDP in Rutland is $400 billion and the government increases spending by $16 billion. If the multiplier equals 3, what is the new level of GDP? _____
   b) Suppose that, as a result of the increase in GDP, the price level in Newland also rises, causing the demand for money to increase by $10 billion. Given the graph of the money market, Figure 12.14, and investment demand, Figure 12.15, by how much will investment fall? _____

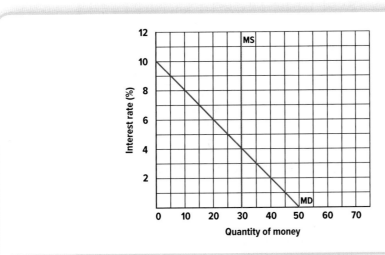

FIGURE 12.14

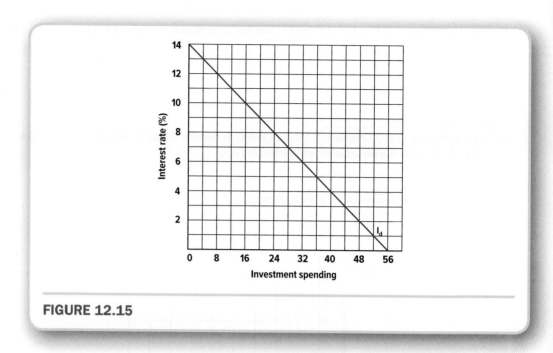

FIGURE 12.15

c) Given the same value of the multiplier, what will be the new level of GDP? _____

6. **(LO 1, 2)** Figure 12.16 shows the aggregate demand and supply for the economy of Etrusca.

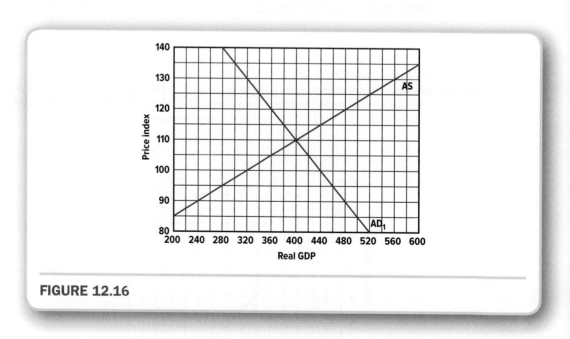

FIGURE 12.16

a) Draw AD$_2$ on **Figure** 12.16 assuming an increase in aggregate demand of 120.
b) What is the new level of equilibrium GDP? _____
c) What is the new equilibrium price level? _____
d) How much is the reduction in GDP due to the crowding out effect? _____

7. **(LO 1, 2)** Given **Figure** 12.17, suppose that aggregate demand increases by 60.

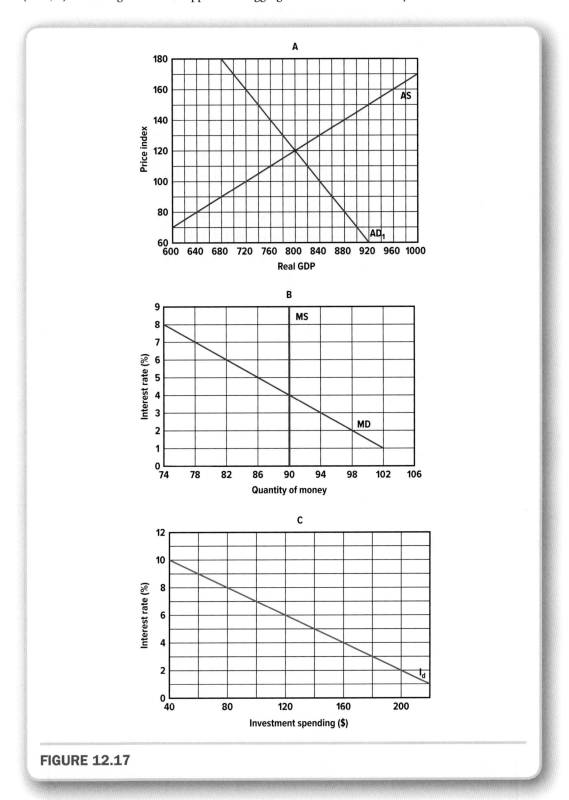

FIGURE 12.17

a) How much will GDP increase? _____
   Assume that the transactions demand for money in Etrusca increases by 10 percent of the
   increase in GDP.
b) Draw in the new MD_2 on **Figure** 12.17B.
c) What is the new equilibrium interest rate? _____
d) Given **Figure** 12.17C, what is the new level of investment spending? _____

8. **(LO 1, 4)** Figure 12.18 shows the economy of Parryland.
   a) Assume that a supply-side economist in Parryland advocates a big reduction in taxes to return the economy to full employment equilibrium GDP. What GDP and price levels does she expect if this policy is carried out?
      GDP: _____ Price index: _____

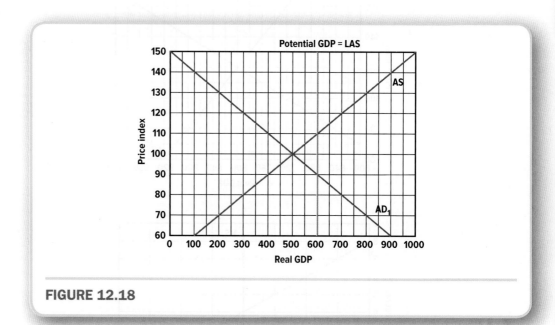

FIGURE 12.18

   b) Assume that a Keynesian economist in Parryland also advocates a big reduction in taxes to return the economy to full employment equilibrium GDP. What GDP and price levels does he expect if this policy is carried out?
      GDP: _____ Price index: _____

Advanced (Problems 9–10)

9. **(LO 3)** The data in Table 12.5 are for the economy of Hyaku.

	Price	Inflation	Unemployment	Unemployment
Year	Index	Rate (%)	(in millions)	Rate (%)
2012	100			
2013	102	_____	12.0	_____
2014	105.1	_____	9.6	_____
2015	110.4	_____	7.2	_____
2016	119.2	_____	6.0	_____
2017	133.5	_____	4.8	_____

TABLE 12.5

   a) Given that the labour force remained a constant 120 million, calculate the unemployment and inflation rates for each of the years 2013–17 in Table 12.5.

b) From the data collected, draw a Phillips curve in Figure 12.19.

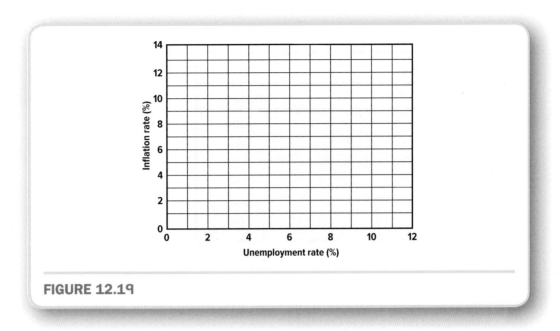

FIGURE 12.19

10. **(LO 5)** Tables 12.6A, B, and C relate to the economy of Grassland. Table 12.6A shows the money market.

TABLE 12.6A

Interest Rate	Asset Demand	Transactions Demand	Total Money Demand
6	50	80	————
5	60	80	————
4	70	80	————
3	80	80	————
2	90	80	————
1	100	80	————

a) Fill in the total demand for money.

Table 12.6B shows the relationship between interest rates and the exchange rate and investment spending in Grassland.

TABLE 12.6B

Interest Rate	Exchange Rate	Investment Spending
1	0.95	100
2	0.96	90
3	0.97	80
4	0.98	70
5	0.99	60
6	1.00	50

Table 12.6C shows the relationship between the exchange rate and net exports in Grassland.

TABLE 12.6C

Exchange Rate	Net Exports
0.95	+10
0.96	+6
0.97	+2
0.98	+2
0.99	−6
1.00	−10

b) If the money supply is 160, what are the values of the interest rate, the exchange rate, investment spending, and net exports in Grassland?
Interest rate: _____
Exchange rate: _____
Investment spending: $_____
Net exports: _____

c) If the level of government spending is 140, what is the value of total injections in the economy? _____

d) If government spending remains the same but the money supply increases to 170, what would be the new value of total injections? _____

Problems for Further Study

Basic (Problems 1–3)

1. **(LO 1, 2, 3, 4, 6)** Match each item in the left-hand column with a related idea or event in the right-hand column by writing a letter in each blank.

a) bubble bursts	1. Keynesians _____
b) demand management	2. OPEC-induced oil price increases _____
c) tax cuts as a stimulus to aggregate supply	3. Phillips curve _____
d) stagflation	4. deflation _____
e) trade-off	5. supply-siders _____

2. **(LO 2)** If the money supply increases, what effect will it have on the following variables?
Interest rate: _____ Investment: _____
Exchange rate: _____ Net exports: _____

3. **(LO 2)** Name two important benefits of fixed exchange rates.

Intermediate (Problems 4–7)

4. **(LO 5)** Assume that **Figure 12.20** refers to the Japanese economy in the 1990s. Describe in words what actually occurred during those years.

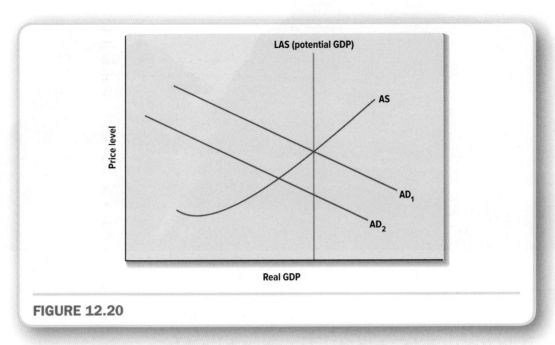

FIGURE 12.20

5. **(LO 1, 2)** Using AD/AS curves, in **Figure 12.21** illustrate a small (in A), a larger (in B), and a very large (in C) increase in the price level, resulting from expansionary fiscal (or monetary) policy.

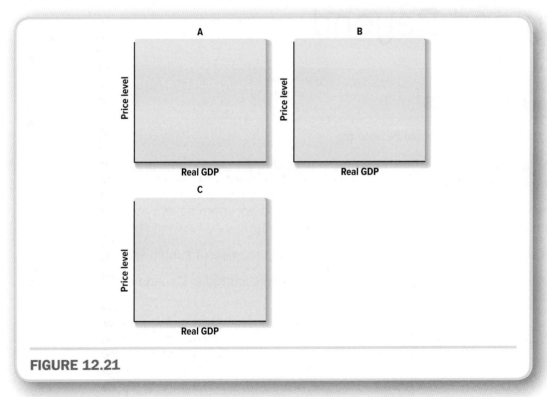

FIGURE 12.21

6. **(LO 3)** What is the Phillips curve?
7. **(LO 6)** Why will deflation lead to a drop in consumer spending and investment?

Advanced (Problems 8–10)

8. **(LO 4)** What are the causes of stagflation? How can it be cured?
9. **(LO 4)** According to supply-siders, a reduction in tax rates will increase work, saving, and investment. Explain why.
10. **(LO 5)** Are the prices of products in different countries that use a common currency (like Europe) the same or different? Explain your answer.
11. **(LO 1)** Give two reasons why an increase in the price level will lead to a drop in net exports.

CHAPTER 13
A Walk Through the Twentieth Century and Beyond

LEARNING OBJECTIVES

At the end of this chapter, you should be able to:

LO1 Explain why neoclassicists believe the economy will automatically achieve full-employment equilibrium.

LO2 Describe how Keynesian economics challenged accepted beliefs about curing economic depression and maintaining prosperity.

LO3 Describe the evolution of the welfare state and the rise of supply-side economics.

LO4 Recount the significant economic changes that occurred in Canada and around the world in the 1990–2008 period

LO5 Explain the cause of the 2008 financial crisis, its financial and economic consequences, and the political fallout.

WHAT'S AHEAD ...

This chapter examines the evolution of economic theory and the use of economic policy by looking at five specific periods of the twentieth and early twenty-first centuries. We begin with the classical world of Say's Law in the context of the first thirty years of the 1900s, which saw the evolution of neoclassical thought and the belief that economies are capable of self-correction. We then look at the Keynesian analysis and policies that emerged with the Great Depression. Next, we review the post–World War II wonder years that prevailed until the stagflation of the 1970s and the re-emergence of neoclassical thought. Next we examine Canada at the turn of the twenty-first century and the financial crisis of 2008. Finally, we look at the economic recession that followed the crisis as well as the return of Keynesianism in the face of the call for austerity policies in North America and their implementation in Europe. This final section also looks at the significant political events of the year 2016.

A QUESTION OF RELEVANCE ...

Imagine you are looking for an entry-level job as a graphic artist. After three months, you have gotten nowhere—not a single interview, let alone a job offer. What went wrong? Do you think the cause of your problem is personal? Or that you do not have the right qualifications? Or that you are asking for too high a wage? Is it the fault of businesses for their unwillingness to create enough jobs? Is it, instead, a problem to be laid at the doorstep of government for not pursuing policies that would ensure the economy created enough jobs?

I n the broadest sense there are two topics in this chapter. The first is the Canadian experience—with reference to events from other countries when appropriate—of the interaction of contemporary events, economic policy making, and the evolution of economic theory. Let us look at five significant periods within the last 120 years.

In the first thirty years of the twentieth century we see a wide acceptance of neoclassical thought that trumpeted the belief in the economy's ability to self-correct any deviation from full employment equilibrium. This ideology fitted nicely with the prevailing political mood of laissez-faire. In our second significant period we look at the Great Depression of the 1930s and how it forced both a political shift and a revolution in economic theory—the Keynesian revolution. In the third significant period following the end of World War II we see a period of relative calm before the stagflation of the 1970s gave birth to supply-side economics and a shift back toward neoclassical thought. In our fourth period—the twenty years straddling the turn of the twenty-first century—we witness profound changes sweeping across the world that set up the seismic changes to come. Finally, we arrive at the financial crisis of 2008, which marks the start of our fifth significant period and is where the debate between neoclassical and Keynesian thought becomes intense.

In moving through these five periods we try to show why economic theories should not be viewed as esoteric ideas dreamed up in the hallowed halls of academia, but rather as a response to real-world events, events that have often had a serious impact on peoples' lives. But just as theory is often a response to events in the "real" world, the reverse is also evident—our world is affected by economic ideas, which profoundly influence action by government, which in turn affect all our lives.

Our second main topic can be found lying just below the surface of all five of these periods. It is a most important question:

What is the appropriate role of government in ensuring a successful economy?

Two main topics, five significant periods—let us begin.

IN A NUTSHELL ...

A Tricky Juggling Act

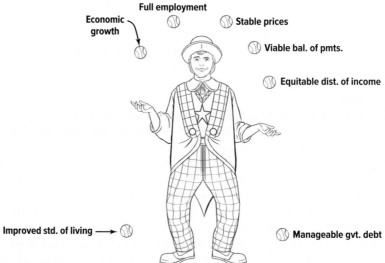

13.1   Canada and the First Thirty Years of the Twentieth Century

LO1   Explain why neoclassicists believe the economy will automatically achieve full-employment equilibrium.

At the beginning of the twentieth century, Canada stood on the cusp of a new era, one filled with the promise of growth and prosperity. The new Canadian Pacific Railway, and the resulting lower transportation costs, opened up the west in a way simply not possible before. European immigrants were pouring into the new provinces of Saskatchewan and Alberta at the same time that the world demand for Canadian products—especially wheat—was growing. This, combined with investment flowing in from the United States, helped create a period of fast-paced economic growth and led to Prime Minister Wilfrid Laurier declaring, "A new star has risen upon the horizon. And it is to that star that every immigrant . . . now turns his gaze." The Canadian miracle had begun. Perhaps the most significant statistic was that in the first twenty years of the twentieth century, Canada's population grew from just over five million to almost nine million—approximately 80 percent.

Classical Economics and Say's Law

As Canada was prospering, so too was the rest of the world. The new century was alive with promise, and this was echoed in the ideas of economists. Despite earlier gloomy predictions, capitalism was alive, well, and flourishing. Although there was a certain amount of government intervention for the purpose of nation building, this was a period in which the laissez-faire approach was dominant. Economists, policy makers, and indeed most of the public believed the government that governed least governed best.

By definition, a laissez-faire economy puts little emphasis on economic policy, and this was a source of disquiet for some who wondered if it was possible that an economy might produce more than people would be willing and able to consume. Isn't it likely, they suggested, that capitalism was prone to periodic bouts of overproduction? And wouldn't such overproduction, and the resulting increase in inventories, lead to firms reducing output and laying off workers? In short, isn't capitalism prone to recessions?

These questions were not new. Almost a century before, the loud and clear voice of David Ricardo, one of the giants of the classical school, had answered "no" to each of them. Ricardo's answers relied on what is known as **Say's Law**, which states that *supply creates its own demand*. What this means is that:

- The act of production (supply) requires the use of factors of production, which must be paid.
- Such payments are incomes to those who supply the factors, and these incomes are subsequently spent.
- This spending automatically creates enough demand to buy the supply.

This is actually a verbal description of the simple circular flow of income that we looked at in Chapter 3. Supply creates income, and this income creates enough demand to purchase the supply. If supply increases, income and (it was assumed) demand increase by an equal amount. Furthermore, if supply decreased, incomes and demand would also fall. That is, supply is active and demand is passive.

With Ricardo's endorsement of Say's Law, the prevailing view of the classical economists was that it ensured that all that was produced would be bought:

Equilibrium occurs automatically and is the normal state of affairs in a market economy.

This optimistic view was shared by most economists in the early years of the twentieth century. However, this sense of confidence was shaken by "the war to end all wars"—World War I.

At the end of the war, pent-up demand caused by shortages of consumer goods during the war acted as a stimulus to the economy. But this bubble soon burst and was followed by falling incomes, growing unemployment, and a stagnant economy. Then, slowly, the Canadian economy improved in tandem with a worldwide economic recovery. Fuelled by American investment (which surpassed that of Britain for the first time in 1921), Ontario in particular experienced a boom in industrial investment. Quebec saw a dramatic increase in the development of hydroelectric power, while the West enjoyed high world prices of grains and other resources. By the mid-1920s, the production of newsprint became the country's second-largest industry, next to agriculture. It seemed times of plenty had returned.

Neoclassical Economists and Aggregate Demand and Supply

Neoclassical economists of the time could rejoice in the recovery and remained as confident as Ricardo that market economies could recover from dislocations, even those caused by world wars. In short, they *believed that market economies were self-adjusting*. In fact, they went even further, and with

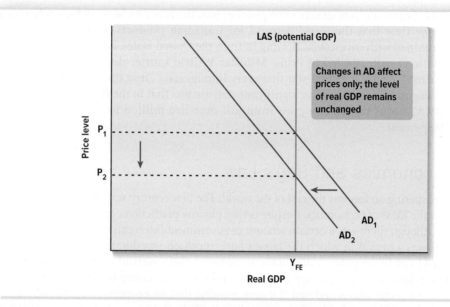

FIGURE 13.1   A Decrease in Demand in the Neoclassical Model

A decrease in aggregate demand will cause a leftward shift in the aggregate demand curve from AD_1 to AD_2. The effect will be a decrease in the price level from P_1 to P_2, but the level of real GDP will remain unchanged at Y_{FE}.

the addition of three specific propositions, they built an argument that concluded prolonged recessions were impossible in a market economy.

So, if economies are self-adjusting, what is it that adjusts? The answer is the price of economic variables: the price of goods and services, interest rates, and wage levels. Let us look at the first of these.

Suppose an economy is about to enter a recession and, fearful for the future, firms and households cut down on spending. The result will be a drop in aggregate demand. As we saw in Chapter 5, neoclassical economists believed aggregate supply is synonymous with potential GDP, since firms would always be willing and able to produce the maximum they are capable of. In other words, the natural state of the economy is full-employment equilibrium. Given this, a drop in aggregate demand would produce a surplus of goods and services as shown in **Figure 13.1**.

Firms, finding themselves with unsold inventory, would have little choice but to drop their prices; as prices started to fall, buyers would increase their purchases. This would continue until the economy was back at full-employment equilibrium. In other words:

In the neoclassical model, the level of real GDP is unaffected by changes in aggregate demand.

 TEST YOUR UNDERSTANDING

Find answers on the McGraw-Hill online resource.

1. Why did neoclassical economists feel that the aggregate supply curve is vertical at the full-employment level of GDP?

Theory of Loanable Funds

As we mentioned earlier, the basis for the belief of neoclassical economists that a long-term depression was impossible was Say's Law. Ricardo had clearly shown that production leads to an equal amount of income that in turn creates sufficient spending to buy that production. However, his close friend and colleague Thomas Malthus (famous for his work on population) was not convinced. "What would happen," he asked, "if all the money earned was not in fact spent, but saved?" Well, Ricardo countered, in that case any funds saved would automatically be invested. Since Ricardo wrote in the early nineteenth century, most savers were profit-earning business owners who were quite willing to turn their savings into investment with an eye toward even greater profits in the future. However, by the early twentieth century, the incomes of a large percentage of working people had risen sufficiently so that savers (householders) and investors (businesses) had become different groups with different motivations.

This led some to ask how we could be certain savings and investment would be equal in a modern market economy. Surely, their equality could come about only by coincidence! Not so, replied the neoclassical economists. After all, buyers and sellers of goods and services are different groups with different motivations, and yet they are still able to "come together." And what brings them together? The commonly agreed-upon price of a product. And what is the price of savings, or as they called them, loanable funds? The rate of interest.

Figure 13.2 shows the demand for loanable funds (from firms wishing to finance new investment spending) and the supply of such funds (from the savings of household and firms). The savings function is upward sloping, illustrating the fact that a higher rate of interest will encourage people to save more. Conversely, a higher rate of interest will discourage firms from borrowing in order to invest. Therefore, the investment curve is downward sloping. There can only be one interest rate, r_e, at which savings and investment are equal.

What would happen, though, if firms, worried about the future, decided to reduce their demand for investment (that is, the investment demand curve shifted to the left)? Would that likely cause a recession? No, according to neoclassical economists. This is because the ensuing surplus of loanable funds would cause a reduction in the interest rate, which in turn would induce firms to invest more. In conclusion:

Lower interest rates would induce more investment and would help prevent a recession.

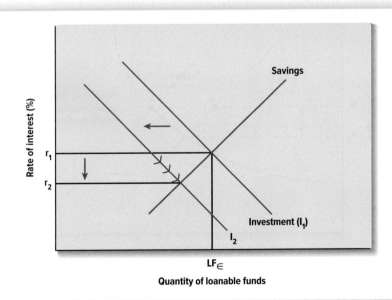

FIGURE 13.2   A Decrease in the Demand for Loanable Funds

A drop in investment demand causes the curve to shift from I_1 to I_2. The ensuing surplus of funds will cause a drop in the interest rate which will increase investment spending until it is again equal to savings.

TEST YOUR UNDERSTANDING

2. According to neoclassical economists, what two things could cause a decrease in interest rates?

The Supply of Labour and the Demand for Labour

The third and final proposition of neoclassical theory in support of the idea of a self-adjusting economy was the claim that any unemployment that might exist in the economy is temporary. This conclusion was arrived at by applying supply-and-demand analysis to the labour market. The demand for labour is inversely related to the wage rate, which means that a higher wage would cause firms to economize on their use of labour. In contrast, the supply is positively related, since a higher wage rate would induce more people to work or existing workers to work longer. Thus, there is only one equilibrium wage level at which the quantity supplied and the quantity demanded for labour are equal. Once this rate is achieved, there would be no surplus or shortage of labour, that is, no unemployment. How, then, can unemployment be explained? **Figure 13.3** illustrates what neoclassical economists believed would happen if firms became fearful of a future recession and started to lay off workers. Graphically this would imply a decrease in the demand for labour.

A drop in the demand for labour by firms would lead to a surplus of labour; the number of workers looking for a job now exceeds the number of jobs available. There is unemployment in the amount *a-b*. However, such unemployment cannot continue indefinitely. Competition for jobs among the employed and the unemployed will force wage rates down, and in doing so will induce firms to hire more. Flexible wage rates therefore ensure full employment. This means that if there are unemployed workers, they must be voluntarily unemployed, because if they were willing to offer their services at a lower wage, they would be able to obtain a job. If they are instead holding out for a better wage, they must be doing so voluntarily.

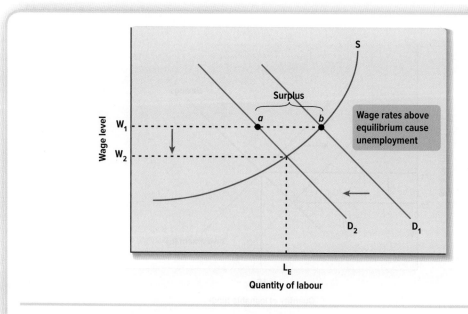

FIGURE 13.3   A Decrease in the Demand for Labour

A fall in the demand for labour would cause the demand curve to shift left from D_1 to D_2. This would result in a surplus of labour (unemployment) equal to the distance *a–b*. This in turn would cause the wage rate to drop from W_1 to W_2. At the new, lower wage rate, there is no surplus of labour.

In summary, neoclassicists built their view of how the macroeconomy works on four pillars:

- the validity of Say's Law
- the flexibility of prices
- the flexibility of interest rates
- the flexibility of wages

Given these four factors, neoclassical economists were convinced that serious or long-lasting recessions were an impossibility. Any recession would be short-lived since flexible prices, flexible wages, and flexible interest rates would all ensure that the macroeconomic market would quickly return to its normal equilibrium. If the economy was starting to fall into a recession, the resulting drop in the price level would encourage buyers to spend more, a drop in wages would induce firms to hire more people, and lower interest rates would entice firms to invest more. As a result, recession would be averted. This remained the prevailing view of most economists until the Great Depression of the 1930s.

 TEST YOUR UNDERSTANDING

3. The accompanying table shows the labour demand and supply in a hypothetical economy.

a) What is the equilibrium wage rate, and how many workers would be employed?

b) Suppose that the wage rate increases to $8.50. How many workers are employed? How many are unemployed?

c) How many of the unemployed are workers who have lost their jobs? Why is this figure less than the total number of unemployed?

Quantity of Labour Demanded (in millions)	Wage Rate ($)	Quantity of Labour Supplied (in millions)
12.8	6.00	11.0
12.4	6.50	11.5
12.0	7.00	12.0
11.6	7.50	12.5
11.2	8.00	13.0
10.8	8.50	13.5
10.4	9.00	14.0
10.0	9.50	14.5

SECTION SUMMARY

At the turn of the last century, Say's Law and the philosophy of laissez-faire prevailed. During this period, *neoclassicists* were convinced that full-employment equilibrium was automatic because of

- the flexibility of prices
- the flexibility of interest rates
- the flexibility of wages

13.2   The Great Depression and the Rise of Keynesianism

The Depression

> **LO2**   Describe how Keynesian economics challenged accepted beliefs about curing economic depression and maintaining prosperity.

In the fall of 1929, Wall Street's stock market crashed, and over the next three years the American economy experienced such a severe depression that many observers at the time felt it signalled the death throes of capitalism itself. Production in the United States dropped by 42 percent between 1929 and 1933, 85 000 businesses failed, 5000 banks closed their doors, and unemployment increased from 3 to 25 percent. The American experience spread quickly to Canada and was soon repeated in economies around the world. Clearly, something had gone wrong with the market economies.

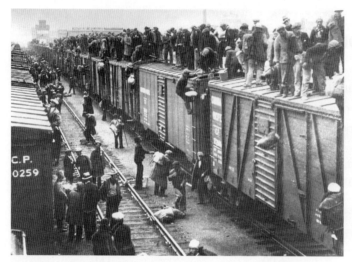

Thousands of unemployed men from British Columbia, Alberta, and Saskatchewan climbed aboard freight trains in an on-to-Ottawa protest against conditions in Depression-era job camps in 1935.

Toronto Star/The Canadian Press

Economic historians now recognize that the buoyant American economy of the 1920s was mainly built on hopes and dreams that lacked a solid foundation in reality. Firms and individuals overextended their credit limits in the hopes of making a fast fortune, not through hard work, improved productivity, and innovation, but by playing the stock market. When the stock market bubble burst in a dramatic way, people were left to wonder how the problem might be cured. To the neoclassical economists of the day the answer was clear and obvious: the economy should be left alone to cure itself. They felt that prices would soon drop, which would encourage people to buy more, and this would stimulate production; that interest rates would soon fall, stimulating investment; and that wage rates would soon drop, encouraging firms to increase hiring.

The Canadian experience in these early years of the Great Depression can be used to show just how right and how wrong neoclassicists were. Between 1929 and 1933, prices in Canada did drop by 23 percent. But production continued to fall. Wage rates also dropped by approximately 20 percent, but unemployment continued to hover around the 20 percent mark. Interest rates dropped to 2 percent, but gross investment remained low, and in 1933 net investment actually became negative.

It would be difficult to overstate the fear and pain experienced by Canadians during these dark years. The beginnings of a social safety net was in place, but this was hardly enough to cushion the fall into unemployment and poverty—no unemployment insurance, a very limited pension plan, very limited and localized welfare payments (with the exception of a national war-widows benefits plan), no baby bonus cheques, no subsidized medical care, and no subsidized housing. The freight trains that pulled into many Canadian towns and cities carried dozens of men riding the empty boxcars in search of a new place that might have some work. The problem was that the trains leaving that same city heading in the other direction had just as many unemployed souls hoping that the next stop might offer something better. And it was not just the unemployed who were suffering. Those still working often faced the prospect of pay cuts, which they were in no position to argue with because they might be laid off next. And those in business faced falling sales and meagre profits.

ADDED DIMENSION

Too Much or Too Little?

This extract from *Canada's Illustrated Heritage Series* neatly sums up the times: "The strange and ter-rifying thing about the depression was that there was too much of almost everything. Too much food. In Prince Edward Island, potatoes were left rotting in the ground, and on the prairies wheat was burned because it was not worth shipping. Too many houses. There were vacant houses on every street and you could rent a good-sized one for $10 a month. Too many automobiles. Factories could turn out 400 000 a year but only 40 000 were bought in 1932. Too many men for the jobs that needed doing. There was too much of everything, in fact, except jobs and money."

Through all this there was a nagging question that continued to go unanswered: Why wasn't the economy adjusting in the way neoclassicists thought it would? It took Keynes and his General Theory to finally provide some answers.

The Keynesian Response to Neoclassical Theory

In the previous chapters, we looked at many of Keynes's ideas on how the macroeconomy works. Nonetheless, let us do an overview. First, Keynes disagreed with neoclassical economists as to how the economy adjusts to the possibility and actuality of a recession. Whereas neoclassicists predicted that prices would fall, Keynes believed that prices were sticky and would fall only slowly, if at all. Neoclassicists and Keynes saw the flexibility of prices so differently because each built their models on different assumptions. Neoclassicists assumed that both the product and the labour markets were perfectly competitive. Keynes, however, argued that the product market was dominated by large oligopoly firms with the power to set their own prices, and this meant that the forces of competition were weaker than envisioned by the neoclassicists. Furthermore, there is a more simple, practical way to explain why prices are inflexible downward: for a firm to change prices is both time-consuming and expensive. This is because existing labels, catalogues, advertisements, inventory valuations, and billing codes all have to be changed in order to institute a price adjustment.

The reason for sticky wages, Keynes argued, was that trade unions had the power to resist wage cuts once labour contracts had been signed. In addition, even non-union workers would resist the idea of wages that fluctuate along with the employer's fortunes, since in the modern world most wages are fixed in the short run and reviewed only periodically (often once a year).

Given this, what was the economy's response to a decrease in demand? The Keynesian answer was that firms were more likely to cut back on production and lay people off than they were to cut the prices of what they sold. This increases the level of unemployment but does not lead to much downward pressure on wages because, as we said, they, too, are sticky downward.

Keynes saw the adjustment process in terms of a fall in production and employment, rather than a fall in prices and wages.

Keynes also disagreed with neoclassicists about the way in which the equality of savings and investment in the economy is brought about. To Keynes, this occurs as a result of a painful adjust-ment of production and income and not by changes in the interest rate, as suggested by neoclassi-cists. If savings are greater than investment, the value of total production must be greater than aggregate expenditures. This will lead to a cut in production, income, and savings until once more savings and investment are equal. In contrast, according to neoclassicists, a surplus of savings would simply lead to a fall in interest rates, which would increase investment until savings and investment were again equal. Keynes believed that changes in the interest rate have very little effect on the level of total savings, which are, instead, *determined by the level of income*. Finally, he believed, as we saw in Chapter 8, that interest rates are determined by the demand and supply of money and not by the interaction of total savings and investment demand in the economy.

If prices, wages, and interest rates do not adjust quickly, if they adjust at all, to a decrease in aggregate demand, an economy can fall into a recession and remain there indefinitely. In this situation, only active government intervention will get the economy on the road to recovery. This is illustrated in Figure 13.4.

Let us assume that initially the economy is at full-employment equilibrium, Y_{FE}, with a price level of P_1. As the recession takes effect, aggregate demand decreases from AD_1 to AD_2 causing the price level to fall to P_2 and GDP falling to Y_2. However, once in a recession the economy will find that prices and wages fall no farther and the economy is caught in a low-level trap with no automatic mechanism to help it escape. Furthermore, if the combination of fear, uncertainty, high unemployment, and excess plant capacity mean that neither households nor businesses are likely to increase their spending—and if exports do not go up—the only way to increase aggregate demand is through more government spending.

In a sense, Keynes turned Say's Law on its head by proposing that demand creates its own supply. The engine of change for Keynes was aggregate demand. If people are willing to spend, firms will be happy to produce. Therefore, anything that cuts spending will simply worsen a recession. In other words, instead of cutting back during a recession, people should spend more. Yet this seemed to go against common sense. It would mean, for instance, that households, many of whom were experiencing unemployment and facing government-mandated cuts in wages, would need to suddenly start spending more. Or perhaps firms working well below capacity and in danger of being forced out of business should start to spend more on investment. This obviously was not going to happen. The only alternative would be for the government to stimulate an increase in spending either by cutting tax rates or by increasing its own level of spending. But to expect them to do this at a time when governments were already facing big budget deficits as a result of falling tax revenues seemed ludicrous. You can see why Keynes was regarded as a heretic. He was suggesting that people should spend more when times are bad, and less when times are good. Of course, as we have seen in earlier chapters, there is a lot more to the basic expenditure theory than this, but:

Spending and aggregate demand lie at the heart of Keynesian analysis.

So how did governments initially react to Keynes's ideas? In most cases, the reaction was negative. It is true that the Canadian government did spend more to provide some limited relief for many of

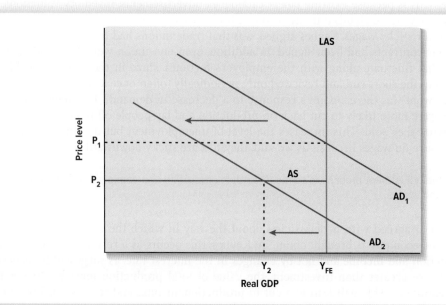

FIGURE 13.4   A Recessionary Gap with Sticky Prices

Originally, the economy is at full-employment equilibrium at Y_{FE} and the price level P_1. If aggregate demand decreases, we have a shift from AD_1 to AD_2 resulting in prices falling to P_2 and GDP dropping from Y_{FE} to Y_2.

its impoverished citizens. For example, in 1932 government established work camps that were run by military officers under the control of the Department of National Defence. However, this was as much to stem the possibility of violent protests as to aid the unemployed. Wearing army fatigues, those in the work camps, mostly young men, worked on roads, bridges, historic sites, and so on. They received food, clothing, lodging, and 20 cents a day. Needless to say, the camps were not too popular.

There was also direct relief in the form of money or vouchers, but the amounts were small. In rural Quebec, for instance, a family of five received a food allowance of $3.25 per week. Despite the small amounts, government was often criticized for its generosity. In a 1934 article, for instance, *Maclean's* magazine complained that total spending of all governments—municipal, provincial, and federal—had reached the incredible figure of $1 billion! Despite all this, the Canadian government did not spend a fraction of what would have been needed to pull the economy out of the depression. Furthermore, most governments of the time regarded Keynes as a radical who had dangerous ideas about the economy. This situation persisted through the 1930s and the validation of his theory had to await the arrival of an event even more traumatic than the Great Depression: World War II.

TEST YOUR UNDERSTANDING

4. Explain why Keynes felt that the level of savings is not affected greatly by changes in interest rates.

5. According to Keynesian theory, will an increase in aggregate demand cause an increase in real GDP, nominal GDP, or both?

SECTION SUMMARY

The Great Depression led to the development of Keynesian economics, which argued that

• the economy could get trapped in a long-term depression

• the solution was an increase in aggregate demand

13.3 After World War II: From the Welfare State to the Rise of Supply-Side Economics

> **LO3** Describe the evolution of the welfare state and the rise of supply-side economics.

Canadians entered World War II in a far more sombre mood than they had entered World War I. They had lived through a decade of despair, and the optimistic patriotism of the earlier age had given way to a grim realization that the task ahead, however necessary, might not yield a quick and easy victory.

War meant mobilization on all fronts. The Canadian government, like other governments around the world, suddenly opened the spout and out flowed massive government spending on military goods, all in the name of defending democracy. Economies responded very quickly to this dramatic increase in aggregate demand. In Canada, the war quickly converted a surplus of labour into a shortage. By 1941 the unemployment rate had fallen from the double-digit rates of the 1930s to 4.1 percent, and by 1944 it was down to 1.2 percent. Factories that had been standing idle for years were now humming, turning out Bren guns, military aircraft, tanks, and ships. GDP grew by double digits—14.1 percent in 1940 and a whopping 18.6 percent by 1942. In addition, as Keynesian theory would suggest, such increases were accompanied by inflation: from the deflation of 0.9 percent in 1939, prices rose by 4 percent in 1940 and 6.3 percent in 1941. This is illustrated in **Figure 13.5**.

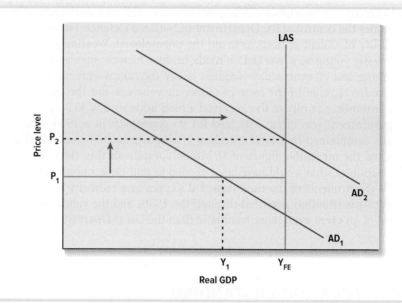

FIGURE 13.5   Return to Full Employment

The increased government spending on the war effort greatly increased aggregate demand, as illustrated by the shift of the aggregate demand curve from AD_1 to AD_2. As a result, the price level increased from P_1 to P_2.

The increased aggregate demand resulting from massive military spending is illustrated as a rightward shift in the aggregate demand curve from AD_1 to AD_2. This led to an increase in real GDP from Y_1 to Y_{FE} as well as an increase in the price level from P_1 to P_2.

The depression was over, and massive increases in government spending had ended it. This fact resulted in a growing recognition that Keynes was probably right about how the macroeconomy works.

Keynesian Economics in the Postwar Years

Following World War II, there was a widespread sentiment among politicians, a growing number of economists, and a majority of the population that the experience of the Great Depression should never be allowed to happen again. Prime Minister Mackenzie King, who had led Canada in wartime, was re-elected in 1945, partly on the strength of his New Social Order, which promised social and economic policies designed to prevent a recurrence of the economic woes of the 1930s. The cautious beginnings of Keynesian countercyclical policies, which had started in 1940 with the introduction of an unemployment scheme, were augmented by a system of family allowances that, combined with the Old Age Pension Plan, laid the foundation of the welfare state. In addition, measures were introduced to promote home building, to provide work for demobilized war veterans, and to increase aid to health care.

Such measures were not unique to Canada. In fact, governments around the world passed legislation that could be described as full-employment acts. It was becoming accepted ideology that governments had a responsibility to actively ensure that the economic goals of full employment and stable prices were maintained. The doctrine of laissez-faire was replaced by the ideology of interventionism, dressed in the clothes of Keynesian economics. This represents a fundamental shift in the perception of *government's role in the economy.*

For the twenty-five years following World War II, the ideas of Keynes reigned supreme almost everywhere in Europe and North America. Economies were now "managed" by governments using countercyclical fiscal and monetary policy to "fine-tune" them. This sentiment was greatly enhanced by another brilliant and influential economist, Paul Samuelson, who authored an introductory textbook that dominated the market for a quarter of a century.

During this time, the Canadian economy entered a period of remarkable stability. Between 1945 and 1970, except for four years, the unemployment rate was never above 6 percent and inflation was consistently held below 5 percent. The trick, it seemed, was to steer the ship of state at a steady pace while not getting too close to the banks of inflation or to the reefs of unemployment. If the economy was a little sluggish and in danger of falling into a recession, then a dose of expansionary fiscal and/ or monetary injection was called for. If, however, it looked like the economy was overheating and a period of inflation threatened, the solution was a measure of contractionary fiscal and/or monetary policy.

It became apparent that economic stabilization might be even more effective if the two policies—fiscal and monetary—operated in tandem. After all, one of the drawbacks of expansionary fiscal policy is that it crowds out both private investment and net exports by pushing up interest rates. This makes fiscal policy less effective. But what if interest rates could be held down in the face of the increased demand for money? Then the crowding out effect would be eliminated. And how could this be achieved? Simply by increasing the money supply. This combination of fiscal and monetary policies produced a very powerful mixture and was used often in Canada. Occasionally, however, a conflict of policies occurred, as in the late 1950s when government wanted to pursue expansionary fiscal policy, while the Bank of Canada was intent on using contractionary monetary policy. Fortunately, such instances have been rare.

 ## GREAT ECONOMISTS: PAUL SAMUELSON

Paul Samuelson (1915–2009) grew up in Gary, Indiana, and earned an undergraduate degree the University of Chicago and a Ph.D. from Harvard. His entire academic career was spent at MIT and he won the very first Nobel Prize in Economics in 1970.

Among economists, he is perhaps most famous for his introduction of what was then called the *neoclassical synthesis*, which merged the neoclassic macroeconomic belief in the powers of the free market with Keynes's arguments for government intervention. The crux of this synthesis is that nations today can successfully control either recession or inflation by fiscal and monetary policies.

Hundreds of thousands of students cut their economics teeth on Samuelson's *Economics*, which was first published in 1948 and is now in its nineteenth edition. This introductory textbook has been translated into forty languages and has sold over four million copies.

He had a dry, cutting humour, as seen in a quote for one of his many *Newsweek* magazine columns:

Rick Friedman/Contributor

> To prove that Wall Street is an early omen of movements still to come in GNP, commentators quote economic studies alleging that market downturns predicted four out of the last five recessions. That is an understatement. Wall Street indexes predicted nine out of the last five recessions! And its mistakes were beauties.

Samuelson leaves an immense legacy, as a researcher and a teacher, as one of the giants on whose shoulders every contemporary economist stands.

In summary, the quarter-century following the end of World War II was a period of comparative prosperity for Canada, in which the size of the public sector grew significantly and people accepted the idea that government policy should be used to stabilize the economy. The growing income levels of this period caused the bad memories of the Great Depression to fade and gave rise to a new generation who were confident that all things could be accomplished.

The Rise of Supply-Side Economics

By the early 1970s, the certainties of the postwar era had started to fade. The United States devalued its currency by abandoning a fixed gold price around the same time that its defeat in Vietnam seemed inevitable. The countries that would later be called the Asian Tigers—Hong Kong, Taiwan, Singapore, and South Korea—were beginning to challenge established industries in both Canada and the United States. And in Canada, despite strong exports of prairie wheat to the Soviet Union and huge new contracts for sales of British Columbian and Albertan coal to Japan, total exports began to falter. This was also the time when three million baby boomers first began entering the labour market.

Then, in 1973, the Organization of Petroleum Exporting Countries (OPEC), dominated by the Arab states and angered by the falling value of the dollars that its members received for their oil and by the West's support of Israel during the Yom Kippur War, decided to reduce its exports of oil. The result was a quadrupling of prices in less than sixteen months. The shock was felt around the world. The Liberal government of Pierre Trudeau tried to insulate Canada from this shock by providing subsidies for Eastern Canadian oil imports, financed by a special tax on Western Canadian oil exports to the United States. This created intense antagonism in the West and seriously intensified regional tensions in Canada.

As we saw in Chapter 12, the main problem facing the Canadian government, as well as other governments around the world, was how to deal with the OPEC-induced stagflation. With the increase in both inflation rates and unemployment rates, Canadian policy makers faced a dilemma they had never experienced before. Unemployment rose from a low of 4.1 percent in 1967 to over 7 percent by the mid-1970s. Worse still, inflation reached double digits and stood at 12.6 percent in 1974. Feeling that the latter was the more serious of the two problems, the Trudeau government introduced wage and price controls in October 1975, whereby the newly created Anti-Inflation Board could roll back price and wage increases it felt were excessive. However, despite the best of intentions, this was a little like trying to control inflation by declaring it illegal!

In another attempt to protect Canadians from the ravages of inflation, government tied the wages it paid, government pension benefits, and welfare payments to a rising consumer price index. Furthermore, it also indexed tax exemptions to that same price index, which guaranteed that tax revenue would not rise as fast as government spending. These measures laid the groundwork for the huge budget deficits that followed in the late 1970s and 1980s.

We learned in Chapter 12 that to cure stagflation through traditional fiscal and monetary policies is impossible. In that same chapter, we looked at the rise of supply-side economics.

Let us quickly summarize that discussion. Supply-siders believe that the Keynesian approach to macroeconomic policy puts far too much emphasis on curing economic problems solely through manipulating aggregate demand, an approach that became known as *demand management*. They go on to argue that the only cure offered by the Keynesian interventionists was to throw more money at the problem, whatever the problem might be. In the period following the OPEC-induced stagflation, these economists felt that attention must be focused on what they considered the underlying malaise crippling North America's economies: falling rates of productivity. Supply-siders argued that it is only through increased productivity that a country can lay the foundation for dealing with both inflation and unemployment.

Like the neoclassicists earlier in the century, supply-side economists believed that the aggregate supply was not simply a passive element that responded to changes in aggregate demand but was itself a prime mover of economic activity. Their diagnosis of the stagflation of the 1970s was straightforward. It was caused by the high price of imported oil and further accentuated by declining productivity rates. Both these factors caused a decrease in aggregate supply. They felt that the cure was equally straightforward: an increase in aggregate supply.

At different times in the 1980s, this argument caught the attention of a number of governments around the world, including the Brian Mulroney government in Canada, the Ronald Reagan government in the United States, and the Margaret Thatcher government in the United Kingdom.

Thus, looking back, we see the years 1945–90 as a period in which, at first, Keynesian macroeconomic policy was embraced but then when the oil price shock hit neoclassical policies took hold in the form of supply-side policies.

ADDED DIMENSION

The Triumphant Three of the 1980s

It is interesting to note that the 1980s saw the rise of three political leaders with similar beliefs about economic policy. Ronald Reagan in the United States, Margaret Thatcher in the United Kingdom, and Brian Mulroney in Canada each had clear leanings toward supply-side economics.

First on the scene was Thatcher—the U.K.'s first female prime minister and the longest-serving prime minister of the twentieth century. She came to be known as the Iron Lady and served from 1979–93. Her policies included deregulation (especially in the financial sector), anti-union legislation in order to achieve more flexible labour markets, and the privatization of state-owned companies, of which the U.K. had many. Her first re-election in 1983 was fuelled by the Falklands War. She died in 2012 at the age of 87.

Within several months of Thatcher's election, Ronald Reagan was elected to the first of two terms as U.S. president (1980). His version of supply-side economics, dubbed "Reaganomics," included significant tax cuts (which he later partially reversed), deregulation of most regulated

The triumvirate: Reagan, Thatcher, and Mulroney.

Source: Hans Deryk/The Globe and Mail

industries, reduced government spending (more rhetoric than action), and pressure on the Federal Reserve to keep a tight control on the money supply as an anti-inflation strategy. He is credited with the renaissance of the American political right. He died in 2004 at the age of 93.

Brian Mulroney was Canada's prime minister from 1984 to 1993. He came to power by building a tenuous coalition of socially conservative populists from the West, Quebec nationalists, and fiscal conservatives from Ontario and Atlantic Canada. He, too, pushed privatization of Crown corporations such as Air Canada and Petro-Canada and argued for lower federal budget deficits—something he failed to achieve. He will perhaps be best remembered for marshalling the Free Trade Agreement with the United States, which later grew into NAFTA.

History will probably put all three of these leaders into the category of very good politicians. Just how it will rate their economic policies is an open question.

TEST YOUR UNDERSTANDING

6. Describe what will happen to real GDP, the unemployment rate, and the price level as a result of a massive increase in military spending.

7. If fiscal and monetary policy are used in tandem to address a recessionary gap, which of the two is made more effective? Why is this?

SECTION SUMMARY

Keynesian economic policies prevailed in the quarter-century following World War II, which proved the longest period of relative stability in the macroeconomy of the century. Then, by the early 1970s, stagflation led to the rise of supply-side economics.

13.4   Straddling the Twenty-First Century

LO4   Recount the significant economic changes that occurred in Canada and around the world in the 1990–2008 period.

The years 1990–2008 were very much a period with a very distinct flavour as another chapter in the incredible story of **globalization** was written. Let us explain.

Throughout the 1970s and 1980s, consistent decreases in the costs of the transportation of products and bulk commodities had led to dramatic increases in world trade. In addition, international flows of capital also increased. As a result of these two trends, multinational corporations began to establish production facilities outside of their traditional home-country-based locations, and the word "globalization" found its way into people's normal communication. Globalization called for a greater integration of economies through trade agreements and through the the free passage of capital and (to a lesser extent) labour.

Nonetheless, even though moving goods became cheaper and capital mobility became much more routine, the movement of ideas and information remained expensive. The authors, and perhaps your instructor, can easily remember international phone calls of $5 a minute and overnight document delivery of $50. This meant that the growing production was centred in hubs of urban areas in what we now call the G7 nations.

Then, in the mid-90s access to the World Wide Web changed all this. Rather suddenly, the cost of moving information and ideas was no longer tied to the physical location where production occurred. Within a few years we see a Canadian airplane maker directing a team of Japanese engineers and an American auto maker combining domestic design with Mexican assembly lines. Faster and safer supply chains, which ignored national borders, resulted in production becoming more specialized, and many individual products that contained parts from a half-dozen countries became commonplace.

The daily flow of products, physical capital (and the technology embedded within it) and information across national boundaries represented a convergence of ideas, places, and things that gave the impression of a world becoming smaller. Globalization came to be seen as a powerful, pervasive reality analogous to forces of nature like wind and water.

This same period saw the creation of the North American Free Trade Agreement (NAFTA) in 1992, which eliminated most tariffs and trade barriers on goods and services between Canada, the United States, and Mexico. Similarly, the European Union was adding more new member countries and, in 1999, nineteen of the EU's twenty-eight member nations adopted a common currency, the euro. These two events led to increased labour mobility across regions and later to serious political consequences. This issue did not receive much discussion at the time.

In addition, other significant political events accompanied the unfolding drama swirling around globalization. First was the collapse of the Soviet Union and the resulting re-emergence of seventeen nations stretching eastward from the Baltic Sea to the edges of southern Asia. At the same time, the communist leaders of China began to open up their markets to the world. Finally, let us note that the rate of economic growth around the globe was above average during the 1990s.

The result was that the years of 1990–2008 saw a combination of

- the spread of globalization
- the fall of the Soviet Union
- New trade treaties and common currency in the EU
- China's new direction
- high growth rates among many nations around the world

All this led many observers to declare that a liberal, market-oriented, democratic ideology had triumphed.

Let us now look at what was happening in Canada specifically. The decade of the 1990s began with a brief but sharp recession that some Canadian economists felt was induced by the very tight monetary policy of the Bank of Canada. The criticism focused on what was seen as the Bank's obsession with holding inflation rates below 2 percent regardless of the effects on both employment and economic growth. Despite this criticism, and despite four changes in the position of governor of the bank during this period, its anti-inflationary policy was maintained and the inflationary rate remained low.

On the fiscal side of policy, the big issue at the time was the federal government's annual budget deficits, which had occurred for nearly twenty years straight and were getting larger as the years went by. The reasons for these huge deficits were at least threefold. First was the government's own attempt to shield Canadians from the adverse effects left over from the turbulent economics times of the 1970s and 1980s. Second was unusually high interest rates in the early 1980s, which dramatically raised the (unavoidable) interest payments on the public debt. Third was the simple fact that government was significantly larger than it had ever been. All this led to a growing chorus of political commentators, joined by some economists, who called for reduced deficits, or even balanced budgets—regardless of the costs of achieving this. The government responded to this call when then–Finance Minister Paul Martin instituted massive cuts in federal government transfers to the provinces in the form of cuts to health and education spending. As can be seen in **Figure 13.6**, by fiscal year 1997–98 the federal government's budget showed a modest surplus, followed by larger surpluses in the ensuing years.

In the first half of this period and despite a high level of Canadian exports, the Canadian dollar declined in value against the U.S. dollar and fell to historic lows in the early twenty-first century. A long-term downward trend in commodity prices and an economic crisis in Asia certainly contributed to this. Perhaps more significant was the fact that long-term foreign investment into Canada slowed considerably

The Fall and Rise of the Loonie

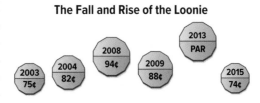

in the mid-1990s and continued to do so into the early 2000s. The reasons for this included political uncertainty about Quebec and a growing international perception that Canada had a restrictive

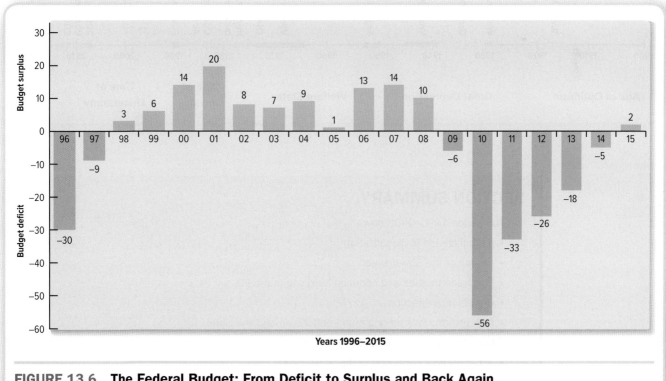

FIGURE 13.6   The Federal Budget: From Deficit to Surplus and Back Again

Source: Department of Finance Canada Fiscal Reference Tables, 2015. Licensed under the Open Government Licence—Canada.

business environment and high taxes. The external value of the loonie began a remarkable turn-around in the first half of 2003 and then underwent a gradual appreciation until it hit par with the American dollar in September 2007. This was at a time when China's incredible construction boom was at its peak and world commodity prices were high.

In closing this section, let us point that the one thing that the twentieth century as a whole so clearly highlighted is the fact that the economic goals Canadians are concerned with are a reflection of the times they live in and are very much subject to change. At the beginning of that century, the problems of nation building and economic growth took centre stage. By the 1920s, there was growing concern that the benefits of economic growth were not always shared equitably among people. The 1930s understandably put full employment at the top of everyone's list of economic goals. The postwar period saw the balancing of the twin goals of full employment and stable prices. In the 1970s, Canadian concerns went in two very different directions. Increasing anxiety about stagflation was followed by an increasing worry over resource depletion and environmental degradation. In the 1980s, bigger government deficits and debt became the major issue for many. This worry continued into the 1990s and then faded, to be replaced by alarm over the depreciating Canadian dollar. Then, a quiet kind of optimism settled in—only to be scattered by the financial crisis that we will discuss next.

There is a clear message in all this: *What is seen as the most important goal today is unlikely to be as important tomorrow.* Problems arise and then get dealt with, only to be replaced with some new problem that attracts concern and attention. That is why the study of economic principles must remain broad and flexible. Too much focus on any one problem or issue is myopic and might prove counterproductive.

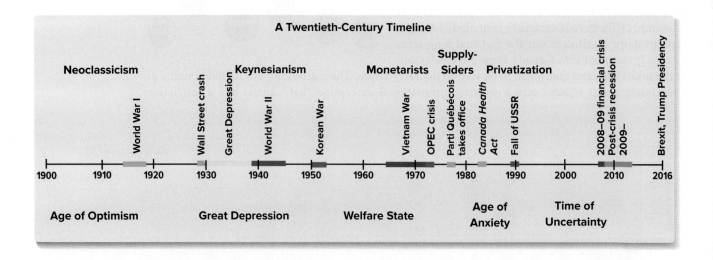

SECTION SUMMARY

a) The period 1990–2008 saw

- a big increase in globalization
- the fall of the Soviet Union
- new trade treaties and common currency in the EU
- China's new direction
- high growth rates among many nations around the world

b) From a Canadian perspective, the country

- experienced a recession in the early 1990s
- continued with low inflation and a fluctuating dollar
- turned budget deficits into surpluses as a result of cutting transfers to the provinces

13.5   The Financial and Economic Crisis of 2008 and Its Aftermath

> **LO5**   Explain the cause of the 2008 financial and economic crisis, its economic consequences, and the political fallout.

The trigger for the financial crisis of 2008 and the ensuing economic recession was a bursting of the real estate price bubble in the United States. Just how huge this bubble became before the crash can be seen from the fact that, between 1997 and 2006, the price of what was defined as a "typical American house" increased by more than 120 percent. So what caused the bubble, and why did it get so big?

A major underlying reason was that in the years during the escalation of house prices, interest rates were low and credit very easy to obtain. As the easy credit conditions began to fuel an increase in house prices, existing homeowners experienced an increase in their home equity and many of these homeowners refinanced their houses to take advantage of the very low mortgage rates and put some cash in their pockets. In addition it encouraged prospective new homeowners to enter the market feeling that prices would soon rise even further.

Furthermore, the rise in house prices led to a booming house construction industry that created jobs and steady growth rates in the economy generally. At the same time, the consumer price index reported low inflation (house prices are not part of the index), and the good times extended to a large percentage of the population.

Then, something phenomenal occurred—the idea that house prices could only go up and never would fall began to grip the nation. Easy credit, low interest rates, good growth, low inflation, rising incomes, and the intoxicating illusion of house prices continuing to rise all led to what *The Economist* came to call "the biggest bubble in history."

Along with all these changes came the introduction by investment banks of new types of financial securities known as **derivatives**. They were so named because their value was *derived* from the holding of house mortgages on which homeowners made monthly repayments as well as on the house prices themselves. In effect, Wall Street connected the giant pool of money that was floating around the world to the mortgage market in the United States. This created a supply chain of new mortgage money. The players in this new financial security game were the mortgage brokers offering mortgage loans to new home buyers, the small banks that funded the these brokers, and the giant **investment banks** and **hedge funds** that supported the small banks by buying the completed mortgages from the small banks.

The investment banks and hedge funds that promoted these new securities argued that the practice of spreading both the location and the degree of risk of each mortgage across a wide spectrum of thousands of securities reduced the overall risk of default. In the years leading up to the crash, security credit rating agencies gave these new securities high marks—what is called a *triple-A* rating. As a result, these new securities paid a higher rate of return than old-fashioned T-bills or bank savings accounts. Where money managers now put their clients' money thus came to be a "no-brainer."

What a wonderful world! Easy credit. Poorer people who had never owned a house were now in the market. Enormous commissions were being made at so many levels. The supply of riskless bonds that paid good interest seemed endless.

Common sense told sober minds that this was all a house of cards built on a totally faulty foundation—the most obvious of which was the fact that housing prices could not go up at incredible rates forever. However, the bright young math whizzes from prestigious business schools were confident that the ultimate power of the market was just being realized and that risk aversion had become a simple matter of finding the right formula for the mix of mortgages in the derivative.

The inevitable collapse began in 2007, but it was 2008 that was the really bad year for declines in house prices. Fifteen banks failed, including Washington Mutual, the biggest failure in U.S. history. Later, Congressional investigations revealed that fraud and grossly irresponsible policies were rampant at this bank—and, it appeared, at many other banks as well. And 2008 was also a bad year for the stock market. By March 6, 2009, the Dow Jones had dropped 54 percent to 6469 from its peak of 14 164 on October 9, 2007. This was the year mortgage foreclosures reached 2.3 million, with even higher numbers expected in the years to follow. In 2008, over 9 percent of all mortgages were in default or delinquent, and this would grow to over 14 percent in the next year. A number of "solid"

This became a common scene in many U.S. neighbourhoods.

Steve Debenport/Getty Images

investment banks soon started to go under. Lehman Brothers was liquidated; Bear Sterns went on the block at fire-sale prices; and Goldman Sachs and Morgan Stanley were forced to become traditional depository banks as the age of investment banking faded.

This also spread to Europe, where Iceland was the hardest hit—its entire banking system collapsed. The governments of Europe purchased $1.5 trillion worth of bank stocks to keep their banking system afloat. The idea of mortgage-backed derivatives was a blunder of classic proportions.

What about Canada? None of our banks failed, we did not experience a massive increase in mortgage foreclosures, and our housing prices did not plummet. In short, we escaped the biggest bubble-burst in history without serious injury. All of this was summed up by a leading economic commentator declaring that "Canada got it right."

How did we do it? The short answer is that we have good banking regulations and these regulations were not abandoned. Canada has good consumer-protection regulations that restricted the use of **sub-prime mortgages**. These types of mortgages, given by lenders in the United States at relatively low interest rates to high-risk borrowers, were one of the causes of the financial crisis in that country. The banking regulations in Canada also limited the use of financial derivatives. Canada kept its banking system safe by keeping it centred on the old-fashioned, boring model of the past.

 TEST YOUR UNDERSTANDING

8. What were the major causes of the 2008 financial crisis?

The Immediate Response to the Economic Recession

In Chapter 5 we saw that there is a very strong link between the confidence level of businesses and consumers and the spending plans of those two sectors. This elusive confidence, which Keynes termed "animal high spirits," rapidly faded as a result of the financial crisis. Consumption spending and business investment fell and what followed, not surprisingly, was that the industrial nations of Europe and North America fell into recession.

The immediate reaction by government was a series of policy pronouncements, all with a common theme: the desire to prevent a repeat of the depression of the 1930s. The prevention mechanism seemed obvious and straightforward: fiscal stimulus. It came as a surprise to many that the name John Maynard Keynes was once again being bandied about in the corridors of power, from Washington to Ottawa to Beijing. Although expansionary monetary policy was a possible option for some countries, for the majority this was out of the question, since their interest rates were already at historically low levels. By November 2008, economists at the International Monetary Fund (IMF) and the United Nations (UN), and political leaders, such as U.S. President Barack Obama and then–British Prime Minister Gordon Brown, were calling for a coordinated international approach to stimulating the world economy through expanded government spending. The UN, in fact, suggested that countries should spend at least 2 percent of their GDP on programs to kickstart their economies. Following their lead, in February 2009 the United States passed a stimulus bill amounting to almost $800 billion. The Chinese government followed suit with its own fiscal package amounting to $586 billion. Not to be left out, the European Union immediately announced plans to inject 30 billion euros and suggested that member countries should each add 1.2 percent of their GDPs (a total of 170 billion euros) into their own stimulus packages. Canada put together its own expansionary fiscal program (the Canada Action Plan) in early 2009, and by the end of that year what proved to be the largest (compared with the size of the GDP) increase in government spending among the G20 was funding hundreds of new labour-intensive projects across the country.

TEST YOUR UNDERSTANDING

9. Why were most of the stimulus efforts by governments in the 2008–10 recession focused on fiscal rather than monetary policy?

By June 2010, the OECD reported that as a result of these stimulus policies, there were clear signs that the majority of nations were coming out of recession and recording positive growth rates again. In fact, by the second quarter of 2010, only six out of the thirty-four member nations were still suffering negative growth. The United States and Canada, in fact, had only experienced three consecutive quarters of negative growth, and both were in positive territory by the fourth quarter of 2009. The IMF also credited these stimulus packages with helping nations to rapidly recover. However, they cautioned governments to avoid complacency and not to abandon their expansionary policies too quickly.

The Neoclassical Challenge to the Policy Response

Despite the obvious success of these stimulus packages, neoclassical economists and a number of government leaders became alarmed at the size of the resulting budget deficits that were being racked up. The result was a call to reduce the size of government deficits and debt, and institute "austerity" measures to restructure the economy. In other words, governments, particularly in Europe, were persuaded that high deficits and debts had somehow become the cause of the recession rather than the inevitable consequence. In fairness, it is certainly true that many governments, particularly in Europe, had become bloated and their people had, in some cases, become overly dependent on redundant government jobs and generous pension benefits. Consequently, it was suggested that this time of crisis had created conditions that were ripe for major structural reforms that would lay the foundation for much improved economic growth in the future.

In essence, the argument between those who wanted a continuation of stimulus packages (Keynesians) and those who instead advocated government austerity program (neoclassicists) was really an argument about timing. After all, very few economists (or government policy makers for that matter) believed that rising deficits and debt were a good thing for the economy. The dispute between the two camps was not so much over whether but *when* action should be taken. As mentioned, neoclassicists felt that the current crisis meant that people would be more accepting of radical reforms while Keynesians felt that trying to balance government budgets in the middle of a recession is a recipe for economic disaster.

A number of arguments were brought forward to support the idea that the stimulus packages should be abandoned in favour of policy aimed at reducing deficits. It was suggested that the idea of deliberately running up deficits to cure recessions may well have worked during the 1930s (a curious argument since such policies were never tried), but the current situation was vastly different.

A second argument used to reject Keynesian theory is that it tends to overemphasize government spending since it is focused entirely on aggregate demand. Implied here is the idea that expansionary fiscal policy will have little effect if the increased spending is entirely offset by a reduction in consumer and business spending—by crushing business and consumer confidence. In other words, it is suggested that, because of the crowding out effect, the value of the multiplier is far smaller than Keynesians claim.

Finally—and probably the pivotal point of the neoclassical criticism—is that although fiscal stimulus packages may work in the short term, they may well harm the economy in the long term. Behind

Visible protests against austerity polices were common in Greece.

© Diamantis Seitanidis | Dreamstime.com

this suggestion is the idea that the major target of policy should be to provide a stable framework for growth, and this growth depends on consumer and business confidence. The huge deficits and debts that governments are running, they said, threaten to destroy that confidence by allowing politicians to "recklessly overspend" with the result that citizens would begin to lose faith in the legitimacy of the political system.

As a result of these criticisms of the recovery programs, a number of European countries reversed course and began to introduce restraint programs—higher taxes and cuts to government services. In the summer of 2010, for instance, the newly formed conservative government in the United Kingdom introduced a series of austerity measures to cut their ballooning deficit. Needless to say, these announcements were greeted with protests and demonstrations. In France and Spain, the most vexatious point of the governments' restraint programs was their plan to raise the early retirement age from 60 to 62 years (and the regular retirement age from 65 to 67 years), which caused violent demonstrations on the streets of Paris and Madrid.

The result of these austerity measures particularly in France, Italy, Spain, Greece, and the United Kingdom, exacerbated the problem, rather than helped their economies. The scope of the economic pain was brought into sharper focus when data showed that nearly 20 million Europeans in the seventeen euro-area member countries—some 12.2 percent of the workforce—were without work. In addition, while countries like the United States and Canada had weathered the storm and were recording positive growth rates from 2010 onwards, Europe continued to suffer negative or at best very low growth for those years. **Figure 13.7** illustrates the point.

If the aim of these restraint programs was to restore the confidence of the people, it is difficult to see how the threat of higher taxes, reduced benefits, and a loss of government services and jobs would exactly do that. In the United States, once the stimulus package had burned out (after giving the economy an initial boost), the Obama administration could not get Congress to follow up with more stimulus spending and the business of policy making of any kind ground to a halt.

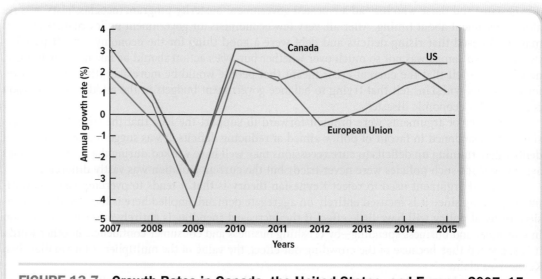

FIGURE 13.7   Growth Rates in Canada, the United States, and Europe, 2007–15

TEST YOUR UNDERSTANDING

10. What three arguments did neoclassicists present as to why austerity programs are better than stimulative programs?

By 2013, it was clear that Europe was growing weary of austerity—especially as higher taxes and government spending cuts plunged the continent deeper into recession, with sharp contractions in Greece and Spain. As economies shrink, they generate lower tax revenues, making spending gaps even more painful to close.

As a result, by the middle of 2013 a slowly turning tide for Keynesian theory became evident as many of the neoclassical advocates fell silent and some even admitted they were wrong. It is a sad comment on the state of how confused things got during this debate that some experts started denying what they had said, despite the public record to the contrary. Most significantly, the IMF issued a paper publicly acknowledging that they had misjudged the severe effects of austerity in Europe and therefore called for a re-examination of such polices. The ideas of Keynes seemed to have carried the day—again.

ADDED DIMENSION

The Flawed Structure of the European Union

When nineteen of the twenty-eight member countries of the European Union chose to adopt a common currency (the euro) in 1999, we were provided a real-life experiment that brings the interplay between fiscal, monetary, and exchange rate policies into clear focus.

Sixteen years later, led by Nobel laureate Joseph Stiglitz (Columbia University), we are now reading more and more discussion about how this move was fatally flawed from its birth—something that a very few economists had said at the time.

One of the major criticisms is focused on the fact that, within the member nations, the euro is fixed and there is a single interest rate. This means that individual member countries do not have the option of devaluing their currency or using expansionary monetary polices in times of economic recession.

A country that knows this all too well is Greece (along with Spain and Italy and other smaller member countries such as Portugal) whose GDP dropped 25 percent and unemployment rose to 25 percent in the seven years following the economic crisis in 2008.

The response to the recession, created by the financial crisis of 2008, on the part of the EU policy makers was to impose a program of austerity throughout the union that blocked any fiscal policy response to the growing economic crisis.

Thus we have a union of 340 000 000 people in twenty-eight widely diverse economic countries facing economic stagnation in several regional areas and having a common restrictive monetary policy, a fixed exchange rate, and a contractionary fiscal policy.

In the meantime, Germany's (and to a lesser extent France's) economy rode the union's low inflation rate and fixed internal exchange rate to increase its exports to other member countries and to the rest of the world. Germany was helped, not hurt, by all this.

Needless to say, tensions between the member nations are severe and the EU's flaws are now very evident.

Shock, Backlash, and Challenge

Looking back from the year 2016 we can more clearly see that what followed the crash of 2008 was a serious failure in economic policies. The expansionary fiscal policies, while initially promising, were simply too small to sustain a strong recovery. In the United States, the attempt to continue the government's stimulus policy was blocked by an intransigent Congress. In Europe, stimulus policies were reversed by the misguided experiment of austerity policies. Even Canada let up on expansionary policy too soon. Monetary policy was also greatly constrained by the fact that there was no way to push interest rates much lower.

From 2012 to 2016, growth rates among the G7 were positive but never robust. Unemployment rates remained high in Europe and fell very slowly in the United States. The feeling among most economists was that the recovery from the crash of 2008 was anemic and for most people in these countries "things were not going well." Then, in 2014 Canada's economy was badly hit by the collapse in oil prices and as a result its growth rate also started to fall.

It seems clear that the slow recovery contributed to a social phenomenon that had been heating up for a long time. For some twenty to thirty years the tide of increasing globalization had eliminated many jobs in the U.S. "rust belt" states, in the industrial areas of the United Kingdom midlands and north, and across much of Europe. The 2008 crisis intensified this trend and hundreds of thousands of workers and their families were thrown onto the street. This angered a significant percentage of the populations of the industrialized countries.

The extent of this anger is clearly expressed in various surveys done in 2016. As just one example, when asked if they believed that globalization was "a force for good," less than 50 percent of people in the U.S., the U.K., and France answered in the positive.

And it was not just slow growth and fewer jobs that people were reacting to. Statistics on income distribution across the G7 in general showed growing inequality. This is particularly so in the United States, where the percentage of income going to the top 1 percent of income households rose from 10 percent in 1980 to 23.5 percent in 2007. While this figure did slide back to just over 20 percent post-2008, the rise from 10 to 20 percent is still shocking in the light of the fact that between 1950 and 1980 the 10 percent figure had held relatively stable. This increase in income going to the top income earners clearly came at the expense of middle-income earners whose real wage rate did not increase at all between 1980 and 2015. Meanwhile the poor remained poor. In short, as globalization extended its reach, income inequality increased considerably; and while people may not have been aware of the actual statistics, they certainly felt and lived the effects.

By 2016 it had become clear that a deep and widespread anti-globalization feeling had spread across the United States and Europe. It was probably inevitable that this sentiment was wedded to a growing anti-immigration feeling, since it had become apparent that the free trade agreements of the 1990s had also dramatically increased labour mobility. News sources reported, and causal observation confirmed, the effects of this mobility—Polish workers in London, Balkan-states workers in Germany, Hungarian and Romanian workers in France, and Mexican workers across the United States. Just why the in-retrospect-predictable issue of labour mobility and the resulting immigration flows received such little attention in the planning and implementation of the many free trade agreements is indeed a surprise. At the same time, Muslim workers—in some cases so easily identified by customary dress—seemed to be overwhelming the labour markets in Europe. The Syrian migrant crisis certainly added fuel to this perception.

Whole populations were angry, fearful, and looking for answers. Then two political bombshells went off in 2016.

The first was the June Brexit plebiscite in the United Kingdom whereby 52 percent of the electorate voted to leave the EU. The second was the election of Donald Trump as President of the United States in November. The parallels between the "leave" campaign in the U.K. and the Trump campaign in the U.S. are remarkable. Both campaigns railed against "the elites"—political insiders, CEOs, union leaders, academics, central bank governors, Wall Street/City of London financial wizards—all of whom, it was suggested, had forgotten the ordinary middle-class workers. Both campaigns had two strong themes: a play on the feeling of many that immigration was not a good thing, and a sense that globalization had cost many their jobs and left their lives in shambles. In the United Kingdom "Take back control" and in the United States "Make America great again" resonated in a very similar way.

IT'S NEWS TO ME ...

Following the Brexit vote in late June several prestigious sources in the UK such as the "Business Insider" predicted negative GDP growth rates for the third and fourth quarters of 2016.

It came as a bit of a surprise then when the most recent statistics out of the UK were published today. The third quarter GDP growth rate is reported at 0.4%. While this is lower than the first two quarters, it was not negative.

On the other hand, the pre-vote predictions of a drop in the value of the Pound were bang on. It plummeted like a stone the day after the vote and continued in a downward trend well into the fourth quarter. Despite a bit of recovery in November, some predictions are for the Pound and the Euro to be at par sometime in the first quarter of 2017. If this happens it would represent a 30% fall since the vote.

Source: *Star Power Reporting.* December 2016.

I. Which of the following is not a plausible reason for a decrease in the rate of economic growth in the United Kingdom as a result of the Brexit vote?

a) the fear of future inflation
b) a decrease in consumption spending due to consumers feeling uncertain about what it all means
c) a decrease in investment spending as business wonders about the timely the formal exit
d) a decrease in U.K. exports to Europe

II. Which of the following is not a likely outcome of the fall in the value of the Pound?

a) a rise in the price of foreign products in the United Kingdom
b) an inflow of foreign investment into the United Kingdom
c) more foreign tourist visiting the United Kingdom
d) increased uncertainty among both consumers and investors

Add to this the prospect of (Muslim) Turkey joining the EU, over a million Syrian refugees stagnating in camps in Greece waiting for a place to settle, and the ISLM attacks in France, the U.K., and the U.S., we see the uneasiness about immigration taking on hues of Islamophobia. When the elites said that all was well—globalization was a net gain and that immigration was labour mobility benefiting the economy—the ordinary, middle-class workers simply did not agree. The elite's argument was lost and with that the trust that they had held for decades evaporated. The political winds had reversed and the world had changed.

Just where the U.K. exit from the EU and the Trump administration in the U.S. will take us is an open question as the fateful year 2016 draws to a close. It goes without saying that its repercussions will be significant and are likely to be felt for decades.

SECTION SUMMARY

The collapse of the housing market in the United States in 2008 was the result of unregulated and reckless actions by mortgage brokers, local banks, investment banks, insurance companies, and security rating agencies. The result was a serious recession that drove up unemployment rates in the United States, which persisted for several years. Canada's unemployment rate turned back down, after two years of increases, because of the federal government's expansionary policy. The recession hit even deeper and lasted far longer in Europe, where it resulted in a raging debate between neoclassical views, which favoured restraint and austerity, and Keynesianism, which favoured stimulative programs.

Study Guide

Review

WHAT'S THE BIG IDEA?

The big idea in this chapter—indeed the big idea in macroeconomics—is: How does the macroeconomy work? This question has been argued over for centuries. On one side of the debate, neoclassicists feel that an economy works best with limited government intervention. This belief is rooted in the conviction that the economy is quite capable of curing any problems it encounters. If that is true, for these advocates the most important goal is to limit the role of government by keeping its spending and taxation to a minimum. This provides a stable environment to attain other important economic goals such as growth, stable prices, and full employment. That is why the response of most conservative governments, at the beginning of the Great Depression in the early 1930s and during the financial crisis of 2008, was to preach the same lesson: Leave things alone ("laissez-faire"), as governments can only make matters worse, They advocated policies of restraint or austerity.

One the other side of the debate are those (Keynesians and others) who believe that, since free markets (particularity financial markets) are often the cause of economic problems, they can hardly be trusted to self-correct. Instead, these advocates believe that one of the prime functions of government is to manage the economy. In particular, government should take a leadership role, ensuring that aggregate spending is sufficient to ensure both full employment and stable prices. If, as usually happens in a recession, spending by both consumers and firms is cut back, the government must step in to stimulate the economy by either cutting taxes or increasing its own spending. They also believe that balancing a government budget, while important in the long run, is just one of the many economic goals a government should try to achieve. Finally, they suggest that a stable economic environment is provided better by full employment and a rising standard of living than by a balanced budget.

NEW GLOSSARY TERMS

derivative	hedge fund	Say's Law
globalization	investment bank	sub-prime mortgage

Comprehensive Problem

(LO 1, 2, 3)   The economy of Copland is in equilibrium, but suffering from a recessionary gap of $10 billion. Its aggregate demand and supply curves are shown in **Figure** 13.8.

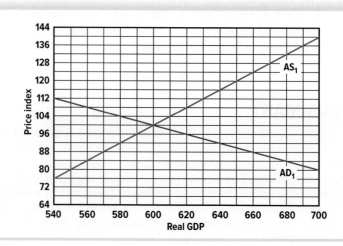

FIGURE 13.8

Questions

a) Draw the potential GDP (LAS) curve, and label it LAS. Both demand-side and supply-side economists in Copland have been advising government to reduce taxes in order to cure the recession. Independent economic research has determined that for every 1 percent change in taxes, aggregate demand changes by $20 billion.

b) Assuming that government decides to cut taxes by 6 percent, and that aggregate supply is unaffected, draw and label the new curve, AD_2, on **Figure 13.8**.

c) At the new equilibrium, by how much have real GDP and the price level changed?

Answers

a) See **Figure 13.8 (Completed)**.

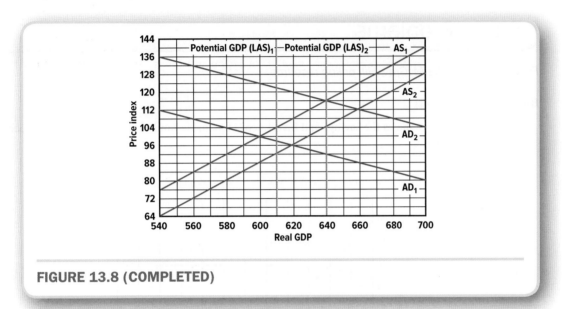

FIGURE 13.8 (COMPLETED)

b) The AD curve shifts to the right by 12 squares. (Since aggregate demand changes by $20 billion for every 1 percent change in taxes, a 6 percent decrease in taxes will cause a $120 billion increase in aggregate demand.)

c) Real GDP has increased by $40, and the price level has increased by 16 points. Reading the graph shows that the new equilibrium is at a real GDP level of $640 and a price level of 116.

Questions

d) Independent economic research has also determined that every 1 percent cut in tax rates in Copland will increase aggregate supply by $5 billion, because it stimulates productivity. For the same 6 percent cut in taxes, draw and label the new aggregate supply curve, AS_2 and the new potential GDP (LAS) curve LAS_2, on **Figure 13.8**.

e) Assuming that aggregate demand did not change, by how much would real GDP and the price level change?

Answers

d) The AS curve and the potential GDP (LAS) curve shift to the right by 3 squares as shown in **Figure 13.8 (Completed)**. Since aggregate supply changes by $5 billion for every 1 percent change in taxes, a 6 percent decrease in taxes will cause a $30 billion increase in both the AS and the potential GDP (LAS) curve.

e) Real GDP has increased by $20, and the price level has decreased by 4 points. Ignoring the new AD_2 curve, **Figure 13.8 (Completed)** shows that the increase in the aggregate supply curve to AS_2 which would bring about a new equilibrium at a real GDP level of $620 and a price level of 96.

Questions

f) Assuming that the change in tax rates affects both aggregate demand and aggregate supply, add together the changes in (b) and (d). What would be the total change in real GDP and the total change in the price level?

g) Is Copland's economy now at full employment? If there is a gap, what type is it, and how much?

Answers

f) The total increase is the sum of the aggregate demand increase of $40 and the aggregate supply increase of $20. The two together would therefore increase real GDP by $60. The increase in aggregate demand pushes up the price level by 16 points, whereas the increase in the aggregate supply pushes it down by 4 points. Overall, therefore, the price level has increased by 12 points.

g) Inflationary gap of $20. The potential GDP (LAS) initially was at the $610 level of real GDP. (Equilibrium was at $600, and the introduction to the question said there was a $10 recessionary gap.) The decrease in taxation shifted both the AS and the potential GDP (LAS) curve, since it increased the productivity of Copland. The new potential GDP (LAS) curve therefore increases by $30 and is located at the $640 level of GDP. Since equilibrium (the intersection of AD_2 and AS_2) is at $660, there is an inflationary gap.

Study Problems

Find answers on the McGraw-Hill online resource.

Basic (Problems 1–3)

1. **(LO 1)** **Figure 13.9** shows the savings and investment of loanable funds for the highly classical economy of Gluckland.

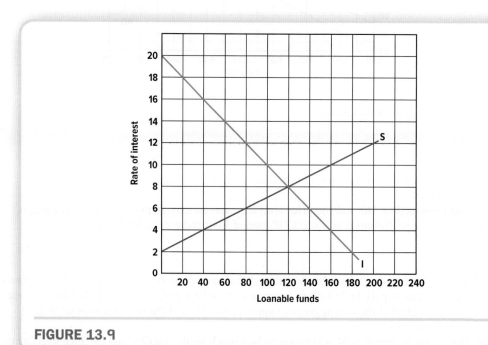

FIGURE 13.9

a) What is the equilibrium rate of interest in Gluckland? _____

b) According to the graph, what rate of interest would induce the people of Gluckland to save $100 billion? _____

c) According to the graph, what rate of interest would induce the firms of Gluckland to invest $100 billion? _____

d) What change in savings would reduce the interest rate to 6 percent from its present equilibrium, and how much would savings and investment be as a result?
   Change in savings: $_____ New level of savings/investment: $_____

e) Starting at the original equilibrium in **Figure 13.9**, what change in investment would reduce the interest rate to 6 percent, and how much would savings and investment be as a result?
   Change in investment: $_____ New level of savings/investment: $_____

2. **(LO 3)** Figure 13.10 illustrates the economy of Ukatria, which is in equilibrium.

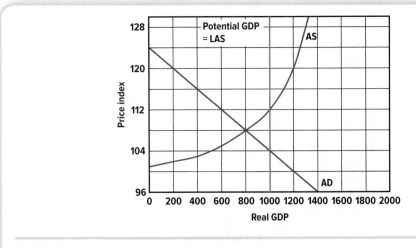

FIGURE 13.10

a) What are the present levels of real GDP and price?
   GDP: _____ Price level: _____
b) By how much must aggregate demand increase to return the economy to full employment?

_____

c) If aggregate demand is increased by the amount in (b), what will be the new levels of real GDP and price?
   GDP: _____ Price level: _____
d) Would using policies to increase aggregate demand be Keynesian or neoclassical?

3. **(LO 1)** Figure 13.11 shows the labour market for Lumberland.

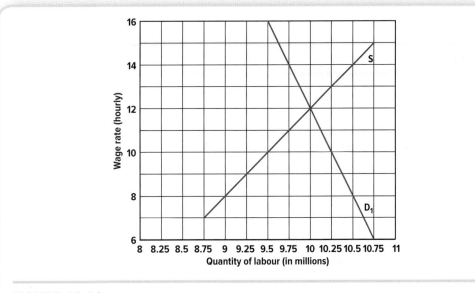

FIGURE 13.11

Suppose that, because of uncertainty in the economy, employers cut back on hirings with the result that the demand for labour falls by 0.75 (million) workers.
   a) Draw the new labour demand curve on **Figure 13.11**, labelled D_2.
   b) If the wage rate does not change, how much unemployment would there be in Lumberland? _____
   c) If the wage rate does adjust, what will be the new equilibrium wage and number of employed workers?
      Wage rate: $_____
      Quantity of labour: _____ (millions)

Intermediate (Problems 4–5)

4. **(LO 3)** Figure 13.12 shows the economy of Straussland is in equilibrium and suffering from stagflation.

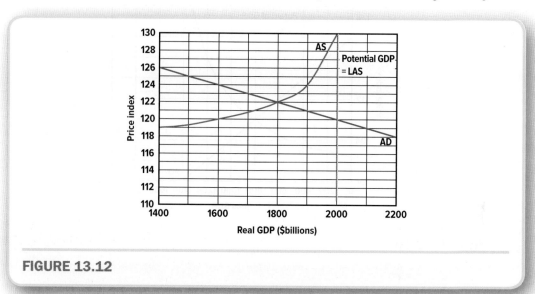

FIGURE 13.12

a) What are the present values of GDP and the price index?
   GDP: $_____ (billions)
   Price index: _____
b) By how much must aggregate supply change to get the economy to full-employment equilibrium?
   (Increase/decrease) _____ of $_____ (billions)
c) After the change in (b), what will be the new values of GDP and the price index?
   GDP: $_____ (billions)
   Price index: _____

5. **(LO 1)** Table 13.1 shows the savings and investment functions for the economy of Brittenia.

TABLE 13.1

(1) Rate of Interest (%)	(2) Investment Spending ($billions)	(3)	(4) Saving ($billions)	(5)
1	800	_____	200	_____
2	700	_____	250	_____
3	600	_____	300	_____
4	500	_____	350	_____
5	400	_____	400	_____
6	300	_____	450	_____
7	200	_____	500	_____
8	100	_____	550	_____

a) What is the equilibrium rate of interest and the amount of loanable funds?
   Rate of interest: _____
   Loanable funds: _____
b) Suppose that there is an increase of $150 billion in investment. Complete column 3 in Table 13.1.
c) According to the theory of loanable funds, what will be the effect? (Increase/decrease) _____ of $_____ (billions) in loanable funds, and an (increase/decrease) _____ of _____ percentage points in the rate of interest.

d) Suppose instead that there is an increase of $150 billion in saving. Complete column 5 in Table 13.1.

e) According to the theory of loanable funds, what will be the effect? (Increase/decrease) _____
of _____ $_____ (billions) in loanable funds, and an (increase/decrease) _____
of _____ percentage points in the rate of interest.

Advanced (Problem 6)

6. **(LO 1, 2)** Figure 13.13 shows the aggregate demand for the economy of Bachland. Its potential GDP (LAS) is $350.

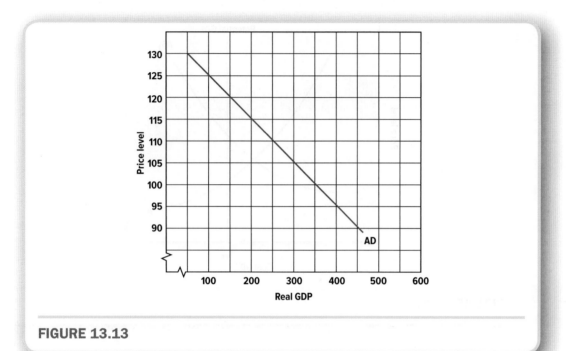

FIGURE 13.13

According to neoclassical theory:

a) If the price level is 110, is the economy of Bachland currently in equilibrium? If not, what might happen? _____

b) If, instead, the economy of Bachland were in equilibrium, what would happen to GDP and the price level if aggregate demand were to increase by $50? _____

c) According to Keynesian theory, if the present price level is 110 and the economy of Bachland is in equilibrium, what is the level of real GDP? _____

d) According to Keynesian theory, if the economy of Bachland were in equilibrium at a price of 110 and a GDP of 250, what would happen to GDP and the price level if aggregate demand were to increase by $50? _____

Problems for Further Study

Basic (Problems 1–3)

1. **(LO 1, 2, 3)** Match each item in the left-hand column with a related idea or event in the right-hand column by writing the appropriate letter in each blank.

a) laissez-faire	1. Keynesians	_____
b) demand management	2. OPEC-induced oil price increases	_____
c) tax cuts as a stimulus to aggregate supply	3. supply-siders	_____
d) stagflation	4. neoclassicists	_____

2. **(LO 1)** What is Say's Law?

3. **(LO 1, 4)** In what way were economic conditions in the first decade of the twenty-first century similar to those in the 1920s?

Intermediate (Problems 4–6)

4. **(LO 2)** Assume that Figure 13.14 refers to the 1930s. Describe in words what actually occurred that enabled the economy to return to full-employment equilibrium.

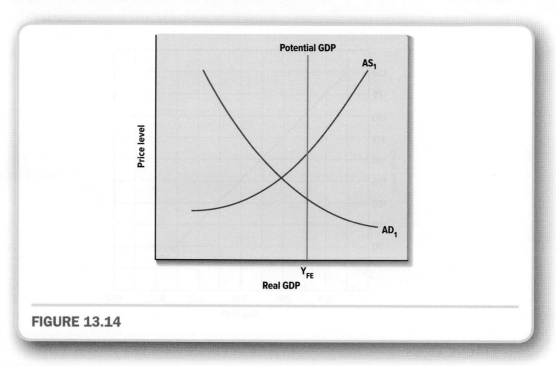

FIGURE 13.14

5. **(LO 5)** Why have many argued that the Canada Action Plan of fiscal stimulus in 2009–10 was a success?

6. **(LO 1)** Why is unemployment voluntary, according to neoclassical theory?

Advanced (Problems 7–11)

7. **(LO 2)** If you were a Keynesian, how would you explain the effect of an increase in savings on the economy? What if you were a neoclassicist?

8. **(LO 2)** Explain the circumstances in which economic policy might increase real GDP without affecting the price level.

9. **(LO 2)** How do Keynesians see the economy adjusting to a reduction in aggregate demand?

10. **(LO 5)** Why was Canada the first of the G20 nations to recover from the 2008 financial crisis?

11. **(LO 5)** What three arguments were brought forward to support the idea that the stimulus packages of 2009–10 should be abandoned in favour of policy aimed at reducing deficits?

STATISTICAL INFORMATION APPENDIX

World's Highest Unemployment Rates

Rank	Country	Unemployment Rate (%)
1	Namibia	29.7
2	Macedonia	28
3	Bosnia & Herzegovina	27.5
4	West Bank & Gaza	26.9
5	Greece	26.5
6	South Africa	24.9
7	Lesotho	24.4
8	Spain	24.4
9	St. Lucia	22.2
10	Serbia	22.1

Source: *World Bank: World Development Indicators 2016.*

World's Richest Countries

Rank	Country	GNI per capita (in US$)
1	Qatar	$140 720
2	Singapore	81 190
3	Kuwait	79 970
4	Luxembourg	70 750
5	United Arab Republic	70 570
6	Norway	64 590
7	Switzerland	61 930
8	Hong Kong	57 650
9	United States	56 430
10	Saudi Arabia	54 730

Source: *World Bank: World Development Indicators 2016.* Gross national income based on the purchasing power of each country's currency.

World's Poorest Countries

Rank	Country	GNI per Capita (in US$)
1	Central African Republic	$ 600
2	Congo, Democratic Republic of	720
3	Liberia	720
4	Burundi	730
5	Niger	950
6	Guinea	1120
7	Malawi	1140
8	Mozambique	1170
9	Togo	1320
10	Madagascar	1400

Source: *World Bank: World Development Indicators 2016.* Gross national income based on the purchasing power of each country's currency.

World's Highest Inflation Rates

Rank	Country	% Inflation Rate
1	Venezuela	122
2	South Sudan	50
3	Ukraine	49
4	Malawi	21
5	Ghana	17
6	Sudan	17
7	Russian Federation	16
8	Iran	14
9	Belarus	14
10	Myanmar	11

Source: *World Development Indicators 2016.*

World's Highest Life Expectancy

Rank	Country	Age
1	Monaco	89.5
2	Singapore	85.0
3	Japan	85.0
4	Macau	84.5
5	San Marino	83.3
6	Iceland	83.0
7	Hong Kong	82.9
8	Andorra	82.8
9	Switzerland	82.6
10	Israel	82.5
19	**Canada**	**81.9**

Source: *CIA—World Factbook 2016.*

World's Largest Countries by Population

Rank	Country	Millions
1	China	1374
2	India	1269
3	United States	324
4	Indonesia	258
5	Brazil	206
6	Pakistan	202
7	Nigeria	186
8	Bangladesh	156
9	Russia	142
10	Japan	127

Source: *CIA—World Factbook 2016.*

Best Global Brands

Rank	Brand	Brand Value (in $Millions)
1	Apple (U.S.)	178
2	Google (U.S.)	133
3	Coca-Cola (U.S.)	73
4	Microsoft (U.S.)	72.8
5	Toyota (Japan)	54
6	IBM (U.S.)	53
7	Samsung (South Korea)	52
8	Amazon (U.S)	50
9	Mercedes-Benz (Germany)	44
10	General Electric (U.S.)	43.5

Source: *Interbrand's Best Global Brands 2016.*

World's Most Expensive Cities

Rank	City	Country
1	Zurich	Switzerland
2	Grand Cayman	Cayman Islands
3	New York	U.S.A.
4	Geneva	Switzerland
5	San Francisco	U.S.A.
6	Washington, D.C.	U.S.A.
7	Hong Kong	Hong Kong/China
8	Reykjavik	Iceland
9	Lausanne	Switzerland
10	Oslo	Norway

Source: Expatistan.com, Cost of Living Index, 2016.

World's Cleanest Cities

Rank	City	Country
1	**Calgary**	**Canada**
2	Adelaide	Australia
3	Honolulu	U.S.A.
4	Minneapolis	U.S.A.
5	Kobe	Japan
6	Copenhagen	Denmark
7	Wellington	New Zealand
8	Helsinki	Finland
9	Oslo	Norway
10	Freiburg	Germany

Source: Based on data from http://www.huffingtonpost.ca/cody-battershill/calgary-one-accolade-after-another_b_3620825.
html, Mercer Global Financial and HR Consulting. Accessed at Miratel Solutions January 2017.

World's Most Prosperous Countries	
Rank	Country
1	New Zealand
2	Norway
3	Finland
4	Switzerland
5	**Canada**
6	Australia
7	Netherlands
8	Sweden
9	Denmark
10	United Kingdom

Source: Legatum Prosperity Index™ 2016, developed by the Legatum Institute, available at www.prosperity.com.

World's Most Livable Cities		
Rank	City	Country
1	Vienna	Austria
2	Zurich	Switzerland
3	Auckland	New Zealand
4	Munich	Germany
5	**Vancouver**	**Canada**
6	Dusseldorf	Germany
7	Frankfurt	Germany
8	Geneva	Switzerland
9	Copenhagen	Denmark
10	Sydney	Australia

Source: Mercer, *Quality of Living Survey 2016.*

World's Most Visited Countries		
Rank	Country	Annual Number of Arrivals (in millions per year)
1	France	84.5
2	United States	77.5
3	Spain	68.2
4	China	55.6
5	Italy	50.7
6	Turkey	39.5
7	Germany	35.0
8	United Kingdom	34.4
9	Mexico	32.1
10	Russia	31.3
17	**Canada**	16.5

Source: UN World Tourist Organization, 2015.

GLOSSARY

A

aggregate demand: the total quantity of goods and services that consumers, businesses, government, and those living outside the country would buy at various price levels.

aggregate expenditures: total spending in the economy, separated into the four components: C, I, G, and (X – IM).

aggregate supply: the total quantity of goods and services that sellers would be willing and able to produce at various price levels.

allocative efficiency: the production of the combination of products that best satisfies consumers' demands.

arbitrage: the process of buying a commodity in one market, where the price is low, and immediately selling it in a second market where the price is higher.

asset demand for money: the desire of people to use money as a store of wealth, that is, to hold money as an asset.

assets: the part of a company's balance sheet that represents what it owns and what is owed to it.

automatic stabilizers: provisions of tax laws and government spending programs that automatically take spending out of the economy when it is booming and put spending in when it is slowing down.

autonomous spending (expenditures): the portion of total spending that is independent of the level of income.

B

balance of payments: an accounting of a country's international transactions that involves the payment and receipt of foreign currencies.

balance of trade: the value of a country's export of goods and services less the value of imports.

balanced budget: net tax revenues equal government spending on goods and services.

balanced-budget fiscal policy: the fiscal policy whereby a government's budget is balanced in each budget period.

bank rate: the rate of interest that the Bank of Canada charges a commercial bank for a loan.

bill of exchange: paper that was a buyer's promise to pay in the future for goods received.

budget deficit: government spending on goods and services in excess of net tax revenues.

budget surplus: net tax revenue in excess of government spending on goods and services.

business cycles: the expansionary and contractionary phases in the growth rate of real GDP.

C

capital: the human-made resource that is used to produce other products.

capital account: a subcategory of the balance of payments that reflects changes in ownership of assets associated with foreign investment.

ceteris paribus: other things being equal, or other things remaining the same.

change in demand: a change in the quantities demanded at every price, caused by a change in the determinants of demand.

change in supply: a change in the quantities supplied at every price, caused by a change in the determinants of supply.

change in the quantity demanded: the change in quantity that results from a price change. It is illustrated by a movement along a demand curve.

change in the quantity supplied: the change in the amounts that will be produced as a result of a price change. This is shown as a movement along a supply curve.

commodity money: a type of money that can also usefully function as a commodity.

comparative advantage: the advantage that comes from producing something at a lower opportunity cost than others are able to do.

complementary products: products that tend to be purchased jointly and for which demand is therefore related.

consumer goods and services: products that are used by consumers to satisfy their wants and needs.

consumer price index (CPI): a measurement of the average level of prices of the goods and services that a typical Canadian family consumes.

consumption: the expenditure by households on goods and services.

consumption function: the relationship between income and consumption.

contractionary monetary policy: a policy in which the amount of money in the economy is decreased and credit becomes harder and more expensive to obtain.

cost-push inflation: inflation caused by an increase in the costs of production or in profit levels, affecting the supply side.

countercyclical fiscal policy: deliberate adjustments in the levels of government spending and taxation in order to close recessionary or inflationary gaps.

crowding out effect: the idea that when governments borrow to finance a budget deficit, it tends to crowd out private investment because it causes interest rates to rise.

currency appreciation: a rise in the exchange rate of one currency for another.

currency depreciation: a fall in the exchange rate of one currency for another.

currency-exchange controls: government restrictions limiting the amount of foreign currencies that can be obtained.

current account: a subcategory of the balance of payments that shows the income or expenditure related to exports and imports.

cyclical deficit: the budget deficit that results from a recession; the difference between the actual deficit and the structural deficit.

cyclical unemployment: a situation of the economy that occurs as a result of the recessionary phase of the business cycle.

cyclically balanced budget fiscal policy: the use of countercyclical fiscal policy to balance the budget over the life of the business cycle.

D

deflation: a decrease in the overall price level.

demand: the quantities that consumers are willing and able to buy per period of time at various prices.

demand deposit: money deposited in a chequing account that is available on demand.

demand schedule: a table showing the various quantities demanded per period of time at different prices.

demand-pull inflation: inflation that occurs when total demand for goods and services exceeds the economy's capacity to produce those goods.

derivative: a financial instrument whose value is derived from some other fixed-return asset.

devaluation: the refixing by government of an exchange rate at a lower level.

direct investment: the purchase of real assets.

dirty float: an exchange rate that is not officially fixed by government but is managed by the central bank's ongoing intervention in the market.

dis-saving: spending on consumption in excess of income.

discouraged worker: an individual who wants work but is no longer actively seeking it because of the belief that no opportunities exist.

disposable income: the personal after-tax income of households.

E

economic growth: an increase in an economy's real GDP per capita, or an increase in the economy's capacity to produce.

employed: describes those who are in the labour force and hold paid employment.

enterprise: the human resource that innovates and takes risks.

equation of exchange: a formula that states that the quantity of money times the velocity of money is equal to nominal GDP (price × real GDP).

equilibrium: a state of balance between equal forces.

equilibrium price: the price at which the quantity demanded equals the quantity supplied such that there is neither a surplus nor a shortage.

equilibrium quantity: the quantity that prevails at the equilibrium price.

excess reserves: reserves in excess of what the bank wants to hold as its target reserves.

exchange rate: the rate at which one currency is exchanged for another.

excise taxes: sales taxes imposed on a particular type of product.

expansionary monetary policy: a policy that aims to increase the amount of money in the economy and make credit cheaper and more easily available.

expenditure equilibrium: the income at which the values of production and aggregate expenditures are equal.

exports: goods and services that are sold to other countries and create an injection into the circular flow of income.

F

factor market: the market for the factors of production.

factors of production: physical or virtual entities that can be used to produce goods and services.

fiat money: anything declared as money by government order.

financial intermediaries: financial institutions, such as banks, that act as agents between borrowers and lenders.

fiscal policy: government's approach toward its own spending and taxation.

fixed exchange rate: a currency exchange rate pegged by government and therefore prevented from rising or falling.

flexible exchange rate: a currency exchange rate determined by the market forces of supply and demand and not interfered with by government action.

foreign factor income: income (such as wages, interest, or dividends) that nationals receive from providing their services to another country.

foreign-trade effect: the effect that a change in prices has on exports and imports.

fractional reserve system: a banking system in which banks keep only a small fraction of their total deposits on reserve in the form of cash.

frictional unemployment: the part of total unemployment that is caused by the fact that it takes time for people to find their first job or to move between jobs.

full employment: what exists when there is frictional and structural unemployment, but cyclical unemployment is zero.

G

GDP deflator: a measure of the price level of goods and services included in the GDP, calculated by dividing the nominal GDP by the real GDP and multiplying by 100.

GDP gap: the difference between potential GDP and actual GDP (real or nominal).

globalization: the development of an increasingly integrated global economy marked by free trade and the free flow of capital, and the tapping of cheaper foreign labour markets.

government spending: purchases of goods and services by government.

gross domestic income (Y): total earnings received by households, business, and government in a certain period.

gross domestic product (GDP): the value of all final goods and services produced in an economy in a certain period.

gross investment: the total value of all new capital goods, both replacement and additional capital.

H

hedge fund: an unregulated investment fund that is open only to a limited range of investors who pay a performance fee to the fund's managers.

human capital: the accumulated skills and knowledge of human beings.

I

imports: goods and services that are bought from other countries and constitute a leakage from the circular flow of income.

income: the earnings of factors of production expressed as an amount per period of time.

income effect: the effect that a price change has on real income and therefore on the quantity demanded of a product.

induced spending: the portion of spending that depends on the level of income.

inferior products: products for which demand will decrease as a result of an increase in income and increase as a result of a decrease in income.

inflation: a persistent rise in the general level of prices.

inflationary gap: the difference between actual real GDP and potential real GDP when the economy is temporarily producing an output above full employment.

injection: any spending flow that is not dependent on the current level of income.

inputs: physical or virtual entities that can be used to produce goods or services.

interest: the payment made and the income received for the use of capital.

interest rate: the annual rate at which payment is made for the use of money (or borrowed funds), a percentage of the borrowed amount.

interest-rate effect: the effect that a change in prices, and therefore interest rates, has on investment; for example, higher prices cause higher interest rates, which leads to lower investment.

investment: spending on new capital goods.

investment bank: a financial institution that assists corporations and governments in raising money by acting as their agent in selling new bonds to the public.

L

labour: human physical and mental effort that can be used to produce goods and services.

labour force: all members of the working-age population, both employed and unemployed.

labour productivity: a measure of the output produced per unit of labour input in a specific period.

Laffer curve: the graphical representation of the idea that, in terms of tax revenue, there is an optimal tax rate; above or below this rate, tax revenue would be lower.

land: any natural resource that can be used to produce goods and services.

law of increasing costs: as an economy's production level of any

particular item increases, its per-unit cost of production rises.

leakage: income received within the circular flow that does not flow directly back.

leverage: the use of an asset (such as bank reserves) to increase the amount of loans and therefore the potential return on the asset.

liabilities: the part of a company's balance sheet that represents what it owes.

long-run aggregate supply: the relationship between potential GDP and the price level; it is independent of the price level and graphically plots as a straight vertical line.

M

M1: currency in circulation plus demand deposits.

M2: M1 plus all notice and personal term deposits.

M3: M2 plus nonpersonal term deposits known as *certificates of deposit.*

macroeconomic equilibrium: a situation in which aggregate demand equals aggregate supply.

macroeconomics: the study of how the major components of an economy interact; it considers unemployment, inflation, interest rate policy, and the spending and taxation policies of government.

marginal leakage rate: the ratio of change in leakages that results from a change in income.

marginal propensity to consume: the ratio of the change in consumption to the corresponding change in income.

marginal propensity to expend: the ratio of change in expenditures that results from a change in income.

marginal propensity to import: the ratio of a change in imports to the change in income that causes it.

marginal propensity to save: the ratio of the change in savings to the corresponding change in income.

marginal tax rate: the ratio of the change in taxation as a result of a change in income.

market: a mechanism that brings buyers and sellers together and assists them in negotiating the exchange of products.

market demand: the total demand for a product by all consumers.

market supply: the total supply of a product offered by all producers.

medium of exchange: something accepted as payment for goods and services.

microeconomics: the study of the outcomes of decisions by people and firms; it focuses on the supply and demand of goods, the costs of production, and market structures.

monetarism: an economic school of thought that believes that cyclical fluctuations of GDP and inflation are usually caused by changes in the money supply.

monetary policy: policy designed to change the money supply, credit availability, and interest rates.

monetizing the debt: when government borrows from its central bank to finance increased spending.

money: anything that is widely accepted as a medium of exchange and therefore can be used to buy goods or to settle debts.

money multiplier: the increase in total deposits that occur in the whole banking system as a result of a new deposit in a single bank.

multiplier: the effect on income of a change in autonomous spending, such as I, G, X, or autonomous C.

N

national debt: the sum of the federal government's budget deficits less its surpluses.

national income: the total income earned by Canadians after deductions for depreciation and indirect taxes.

national income equilibrium: that level of income where total leakages from the circular flow equal total injections.

natural rate of unemployment: the unemployment rate at full employment.

near-banks: financial institutions, such as credit unions or trust companies, that share many of the functions of commercial banks but are not defined as banks under the *Bank Act* (they are also known as *nonbank financial intermediaries*).

net domestic income (NDI): incomes earned in Canada after deduction for taxes on production and depreciation.

net domestic product (NDP): the value of total production after deductions for depreciation and indirect taxes.

net exports: total exports minus total imports of goods and services, which can be written as (X − IM) or as X_N.

net investment: the addition to the capital stock during a year (equals gross investment less depreciation).

net national product: the value of goods and services produced by Canadians after depreciation and indirect taxes. Derived by subtracting net foreign factor income from NDP.

net tax revenue: total tax revenues minus government transfer payments.

net worth: the total assets less total liabilities of a company—also called *equity*.

nominal GDP: the value of GDP in terms of prices prevailing at the time of measurement.

nominal income: the present dollar value of a person's income.

nominal wage: the present-day value of a current wage.

normal products: products for which demand will increase as a result of an increase in income and decrease as a result of a decrease in income.

normative statement: a statement of opinion or belief that cannot be verified.

notice deposit: money deposited in a savings account that is available only after notice is given.

O

official settlements account: a subcategory of the balance of payments that shows the change in a country's official foreign exchange reserves.

Okun's law: the observation that for every 1 percent of cyclical unemployment an economy's GDP is 2.5 percent below its potential.

open-market operations: the buying and selling of securities by the Bank of Canada on the open (to the public) market.

opportunity cost: the value of the next-best alternative that is given up as a result of making a particular choice.

output costs: (of inflation) costs of loss of output resulting from inflation.

overnight interest rate: the interest rate commercial banks charge one another on overnight loans.

P

participation rate: the percentage of those in the working-age population who are actually in the labour force.

personal income: income paid to individuals before the deduction of personal income taxes.

Phillips curve: a plotting of the inverse relationship between unemployment and inflation rates.

portfolio investment: the purchase of shares or bonds representing less than 50 percent ownership.

positive statement: a statement of fact that can be verified.

potential GDP: the total amount that an economy is capable of producing when all of its resources are being fully utilized.

procyclical: describes government action that tends to push the economy in the same direction it is leaning in.

product market: the market for consumer goods and services.

production possibilities curve: a graphical representation of the various combinations of maximum output that can be produced from the available resources and technology.

productive efficiency: the production of an output at the lowest possible average cost.

profit: the income received from the activity of enterprise.

protectionism: the economic policy of protecting domestic producers by restricting the importation of foreign products.

purchasing power parity theory: a theory suggesting that exchange rates will change so as to equate the purchasing power of each currency.

Q

quantitative easing: central banks' purchase of financial assets of longer maturity, such as 10-year bonds rather than 90-day T-bills, in an attempt to stimulate the economy.

quota: a production limit imposed on a foreign producer of a product.

R

real-balances effect: the effect that a change in the value of real balances has on consumption spending.

real GDP: the value of GDP measured in terms of prices prevailing in a given base year.

real income: income measured in terms of the amount of goods and services that it will buy. Real income will increase if actual income increases or prices fall.

real interest rate: the rate of interest measured in constant dollars.

real wage: the amount of goods and services an employee can buy for a given amount of nominal wage.

recession: a period when the economy is producing below its potential and has had two consecutive quarters of negative growth.

recessionary gap: the difference between actual real GDP and potential real GDP when the economy is producing below its potential.

redistributive costs: (of inflation) costs that are shifted from one group in society to another group by inflation.

rent: the payment made and the income received for the use of land.

resources: physical or virtual entities that can be used to produce goods and services.

S

saving: the portion of income that is not spent on consumption.

saving function: the relationship between income and saving.

Say's Law: the proposition that "supply creates its own demand"; that is, production (supply) creates sufficient income, and thus spending (demand), to purchase the production (attributed to French economist Jean-Baptiste Say).

scientific method: a method of research in which a problem is identified, relevant data are gathered, a hypothesis is formulated from these data, and the hypothesis is empirically tested.

shortage: what exists when, at the prevailing price, the quantity supplied is smaller than the quantity demanded.

spread: the difference between the rate of interest a bank charges borrowers and the rate it pays to savers.

stagflation: the simultaneous occurrence of high inflation and unemployment.

store of wealth: the function of money that allows people to hold and accumulate wealth.

structural deficit: the budget deficit that would exist at full-employment (potential) GDP. It is the amount of a budget deficit in excess of the cyclical deficit.

structural unemployment: the part of total unemployment that results from a mismatch in the skills or location between jobs available and people looking for work.

sub-prime mortgage: a mortgage made to a borrower with a low credit rating that carries a higher interest rate than that charged to a conventional borrower.

subsidy: a payment by government for the purpose of increasing some particular activity or increasing the output of a particular good.

substitute products: any products for which demand varies directly in relation to a change in the price of a similar product.

substitution effect: the substitution of one product for another as a result of a change in their relative prices.

supply: the quantities that producers are willing and able to sell per period of time at various prices.

supply schedule: a table showing the various quantities supplied per period of time at different prices.

surplus: what exists when, at the prevailing price, the quantity demanded is smaller than the quantity supplied.

T

target for the overnight rate: the Bank of Canada's key policy interest rate; it is the midpoint of the Bank's 50-basis-point operating band.

target reserve ratio: the portion of deposits that a bank wants to hold in cash.

tariff: a tax (or duty) levied on imports.

technology: a method of production; how resources are combined to produce goods and services.

terms of trade: the average price of a country's exports compared with the price of its imports.

transactions demand for money: the desire of people to hold money as a medium of exchange, that is, to effect transactions.

transfer payments: one-way transactions in which payment is made by the government but no good or service flows back in return.

transmission process: the Keynesian view of how changes in money affect (transmit to) the real variables in the economy.

U

unemployed: describes those who are in the labour force and are actively seeking employment, but do not hold paid employment.

unemployment: the number of persons fifteen years old and over who are actively seeking work but are not employed.

unemployment rate: the percentage of those in the labour force who do not hold paid employment.

unit of account: the function of money that allows us to easily determine the relative value of goods.

unplanned investment: the amount of unintended investment by firms in the form of a buildup or rundown of inventories—that is, the difference between production (Y) and aggregate expenditures (AE).

V

value of production: the total receipts of all producers.

velocity of money: the number of times per year that a unit of currency is used buying final goods and services.

voluntary export restriction: an agreement by an exporting country to restrict the amount of its exports to another country.

W

wages: the payment made and the income received for the use of labour.

wealth effect: the direct effect of a change in wealth on consumption spending.

working-age population: in Canada, the total population, excluding those under fifteen years of age, those living on aboriginal reserves, full-time residents of mental and penal institutions or hospitals, and those in the armed forces.

INDEX